Fodor's
Greece

Fodor's Travel Publications, Inc.
New York • Toronto • London • Sydney • Auckland

Fodor's Greece

Editor: Conrad Little Paulus
Contributors: Bob Blake, Toula Bogdanos, Melissa Dailey, Daniel Gorney, Kerin Hope, Mark Rose, Linda K. Schmidt, B. Samantha Stenzel, Catherine Vanderpool
Creative Director: Fabrizio La Rocca
Cartographer: David Lindroth
Illustrator: Karl Tanner
Cover Photograph: Dubin/Wheeler Pictures

Design: Vignelli Associates

Special Sales

Contents

Maps and Diagrams

Foreword

We wish to express our gratitude to those who helped in the preparation of this guide: Maria Sarafoglou and C.M.S., Ltd., in Athens; the Greek National Tourist Office in Corfu; Jacky Keith of Esplanade Tours, Boston; and the Rowland Company, New York.

While every care has been taken to ensure the accuracy of the information in this guide, the passage of time will always bring change, and consequently, the publisher cannot accept responsibility for errors that may occur.

All prices and opening times quoted here are based on information supplied to us at press time. Hours and admission fees may change, however, and the prudent traveler will avoid inconvenience by calling ahead.

Fodor's wants to hear about your travel experiences, both pleasant and unpleasant. When a hotel or restaurant fails to live up to its billing, let us know and we will investigate the complaint and revise our entries where the facts warrant it.

Send your letters to the editors of Fodor's Travel Publications, 201 E. 50th Street, New York, NY 10022.

Highlights and Fodor's Choice

Highlights

Work has begun on two new **electric train lines** in **Athens**, scheduled to be completed in 1997, and the new landscaping in Syntagma Square will be dug up and reinstalled. The lines will lessen driving in the city center. Traffic there remains on an alternating system (cars with an even last number on the license plate can drive one day, those with an odd number, the next; taxis can drive every day). A recently spotted bumper sticker reads: "Fast cars don't kill; slow drivers do." So, beware.

Surface transport in Athens has been speeded by special black-and-yellow lanes for buses and trolleys only. The news in late 1992 is that public buses have been privatized by the government (which wants to sell the lines to individuals). The **Benaki Museum** in Athens will close in early 1993 for long-planned renovations that are expected to take as much as three years.

In 1992, 235 Greek **beaches** and five **marinas** qualified to fly the Blue Flag of Europe, the symbol of a clean environment. In 1992 Greece's beaches were 33% cleaner than in 1991. There are 35 approved beaches in Crete, 24 in the Dodecanese, 13 in Lesbos, and 15 in Argolida, Peloponnese.

In 1992 on **Spetses,** in the Saronic Gulf, the belle-époque **Hotel Posidonios** reopened in splendor after a five-year renovation.

The newly completed **Corinth–Tripolis highway** makes travel into the Peloponnese easier and faster. In the northern Peloponnese, the ancient site of **Tiryns** was closed in late 1992 for renovations and repairs.

On **Corfu,** the town is gearing up for the 1994 European Community (EC) conference to be held in the Palace of St. Michael and St. George; tourists may find parts of the palace closed because of construction.

On **Crete** there's continuing renovation at the Heraklion Archaeological Museum, which will close some galleries during 1993. At Knossos, cracks have appeared in some of Arthur Evans's restorations, which will necessitate restorative measures during the year, with some areas roped off.

The airport on **Naxos** was completed in 1992, making the island the fifth in the Cyclades accessible by air. The Apollo Theater on **Syros,** in Hermoupolis, is being renovated with EC funding and is scheduled to reopen in 1993. The trip from **Mykonos** to **Delos** has now been made faster and smoother by the addition of a larger boat, which can set sail in all weather, takes more people, and cuts about 20 minutes off the crossing. New luxury hotels opened in 1992 on **Paros** (the Yria) and **Santorini** (the Aressana).

Fodor's Choice

No two people will agree on what makes a perfect vacation, but it can be fun and helpful to find out what others think. Here are a few choice ideas to enhance your visit to Greece. For more details, refer to the appropriate chapter.

Hotels

Akti Myrina, Limnos (*Very Expensive*)

Doryssa Bay, Samos (*Very Expensive*)

Grande Bretagne, Athens (*Very Expensive*)

Case Delfino, Hania (*Expensive*)

Europa, Olympia (*Expensive*)

Golden Star, Mykonos (*Expensive*)

Malvasia, Monemvassia (*Expensive*)

Kavalari, Santorini (*Moderate*)

Restaurants

Bajazzo, Athens (*Very Expensive*)

Ta Kioupia, outside Rhodes Town (*Very Expensive*)

Chez Cat'rine, Mykonos (*Expensive*)

Greek Taverna at Rethymna Beach Hotel, Crete (*Expensive*)

Phanaria, Nauplion (*Inexpensive*)

Taverna Restaurant, Patras (*Inexpensive*)

Museums

Cycladic Museum, Athens

Museum of the Peloponnesian Folklore Foundation, Nauplion

Olympia Archaeological Museum

Theophilos Museum, Varia, Lesbos

Works of Art

Bronze charioteer, Delphi Museum

Hermes Holding Infant Dionysos, Olympia Museum

Heroic-size Kouros from the temple at Heraion, Samos Museum

Korai in Acropolis Museum, Athens

Minoan gold-and-ivory figurine from Palaio Kastro, Siteia Museum, Crete

Ancient Sites

Akrotiri, Santorini

Ancient Agora, Athens

Late-Minoan town of Gournia

Mystras

Temple of Aphaia, Aegina

Temple of Apollo, Bassae

Tower of the Winds Square, Athens

Picturesque Villages and Towns

Agiassos, Lesbos

Ano Vathi, Samos

Kalavrita

Lindos (in off-season)

Monemvassia

Pirgi, Chios

Venetian Quarter of Hania

Churches and Monasteries

Arkadi Monastery near Rethymnon, Crete

Ayia Lavra, Kalavrita

Little Metropolis, Athens

Mega Spileo, Zakhlorou

Panayia Ekatontapyliani, Paros

Taste Treats

Assorted *mezzes* and ouzo in an *ouzerie* in Athens

Bourekakia at Asklepios on Kos

A glass of *tsikouthia* with a plate of walnuts and honey in a Cretan village

Meatballs at Lilis in Ermoupolis, Siros

Rebithokeftedes (fried garbanzo-bean balls) at Gerania, Samos

Wild artichokes (in spring) at Semiramis, Sparta

Moments to Remember

Gazing at the view from Kanoni on Corfu

Improvising *mantinades* verses with a Cretan *lyra* player at a village wedding

A performance at Epidauros

Picnicking at Molyvos castle on Lesbos

Sipping ouzo at dusk overlooking the bay at Santorini

Sitting on the promenade wall west of Hydra Town at dusk

Walking through wildflowers in Gortyna's ruins on an April day

Watching the sunset from Philopappou Hill, Athens

Greece

BULGARIA

SKOPJE

Seres

Philippi

ALBANIA

Ka

Edessa

MACEDONIA

Thessaloniki

Kastoria

Thermi

CHALKIDIKI

Veria

Kozani

Katerini

Dafni

Mount Olympus

Gulf of Thermaikos

Mount Athos

Metsovo

Kalambaka

Agia

Corfu

Corfu

Igoumenitsa

Ioannina

Trikala

Larissa

THESSALY

Volos

SPORADE

IONIAN ISLANDS

Parga

EPIRUS

Arta

Karditsa

Skiathos

Preveza

Lefkas

Skopelos

Skyros

Lamia

CENTRAL GREECE

EVIA

Kymi

Kephalonia

Ithaki

Nafpaktos

Orhomenos

Delphi

Missolonghi

Gulf of Corinth

Patras

Diakofto

Thebes

Athens

Corinth

Piraeus

Killini Loutras

Egina

Sounion

Zakynthos

Pyrgos

Olympia

Argos

Poros

K

Tripolis

Nauplion

Kythnos

Andritsena

Hydra

Serifos

PELOPONNESE

Spetses

Messini

Sparta

Ionian Sea

Pylos

Kalamata

Mystras

Methoni

Gythion

Milos

Monemvassia

Kythira

N

Mediterranean Sea

Hania

0   50 miles
0   75 km

CRETE

Black Sea

T U R K E Y

Istanbul

Sea of
Marmara

Xanthi

THRACE

Makri

assos

Samothrace

Limnos

Aegean Sea

N
O
R
T
H
E
R
N

Lesbos

T U R K E Y

Chios

I
S
L
A
N
D
S

Izmir (Smyrna)

Andros

A E G E A N

I S L A N D S

Samos

Tinos

Ikaria

ros

Mikonos

Delos

Patmos

Paros

Leros

nos

Naxos

Kalimnos

Bodrum

Kos

YCLADES

Amorgos

Kos

Ios

Astypalea

Nissyros

Symi

Santorini

Anafi

DODECANESE

Tilos

Rhodes

Chalki

Rhodes

Sea of Crete

Karpathos

CRETE

Heraklion

Ay.
Nikolaos

Kassos

Ierapetra

Europe

Reykjavik

ICELAND

NORWAY

Bergen

SCOTLAND

NORTHERN
IRELAND

Edinburgh

*North
Sea*

Skager

Belfast

IRELAND

*Irish
Sea*

DENMARK

GREAT
BRITAIN

Dublin

WALES

ENGLAND

THE NETHERLANDS

Hambur

Cardiff

Amsterdam

London

The Hague

Rotterdam

GER

*ATLANTIC
OCEAN*

English Channel

Brussels

BELGIUM

Bonn

Frankfurt

Paris

LUXEMBOURG

FRANCE

Zürich

Mun

Bern

Salzb

SWITZERLAND

Lyon

LIECHTENS

Milan

Ve

Nice

PORTUGAL

ANDORRA

Marseille

Monaco

Florence

Lisbon

Madrid

Barcelona

Corsica

SPAIN

Seville

Granada

*Balearic
Islands*

Sardinia

Gibraltar

Mediterranean Sea

Tyrrhe

MOROCCO

ALGERIA

|0   400 miles|

|0   600 km|

TUNISIA

World Time Zones

Numbers below vertical bands relate each zone to Greenwich Mean Time (0 hrs.).
Local times frequently differ from these general indications,
as indicated by light-face numbers on map.

-1 0 +1 +2 +3 +4 +5 +6 +7 +8 +9 +10

Greenwich
Mean Time

Introduction

By Mark J. Rose

Mark Rose, a doctoral candidate in Classical Archaeology at Indiana University, is managing editor of Archaeology Magazine in New York and visits Greece regularly.

Mighty indeed are the marks and monuments of our empire which we have left. Future ages will wonder at us, as the present age wonders at us now. . . . For our adventurous spirit has forced an entry into every sea and into every land; and everywhere we have left behind us everlasting memorials of good done to our friends or suffering inflicted on our enemies.

—Thucydides, *The Peloponnesian War*, Pericles's funeral oration

Greece is a bleak, unsmiling desert, without agriculture, manufactures, or commerce apparently. What supports its poverty-stricken people or its government is a mystery. I suppose that ancient Greece and modern Greece compared furnish the most extravagant contrast to be found in history.

—Mark Twain, *The Innocents Abroad*

Welcome to Greece. And please forgive my trotting out a couple of quotations to begin this essay, but you have to keep in mind that the ancient civilization and the modern nation are two very different things. In the world of today the legacy of classical Greece must be at times a burden to this small country, and if you get off the airplane expecting to step into the Athens of Pericles, you will be disappointed. A yellow taxi, not a chariot, will drive you into the city by way of a traffic-choked road, past bright white buildings of stuccoed concrete instead of marble. Although there are ruins that evoke Homer, Sophocles, Plato, and the rest, and secluded beaches and traditional whitewashed houses, today's Greeks are not just the cut-rate descendants of a noble people living in the ruined halls of their ancestors—this is also modern Greece, a vital, living nation.

Officially called the Hellenic Republic, the country is inhabited by about 10 million people living in an area of about 133,000 square kilometers, or 51,000 square miles (a bit larger than Pennsylvania). The southernmost part of the Balkan Peninsula, Greece is bounded by the Adriatic Sea to the west, the Aegean to the east, and the Mediterranean to the south. The northern border, from west to east, is shared with Albania, the disintegrated remains of Yugoslavia, Bulgaria, and Turkey. Nearly 80% of the land is mountainous, with Olympus the highest peak, at 9,570 feet, and no spot in Greece is more than 115 kilometers (70 miles) from the coast. Many think this combination of rugged terrain and proximity to the sea gave rise to the independent nature of the people; others feel Greeks would be independent minded regardless of geography.

The Mediterranean climate brings hot, dry summers and cold, rainy winters. May counts as the first day of summer, and from June through September it doesn't rain—like *Camelot*, but the Greek beaches are better than those in England. Barometric lows over the Mediterranean in summer attract winds from the Sahara, notably the sirocco, which blows in hot and dry with reddish-yellow dust. More common is the *meltemi*, a cooling wind from northern Europe that picks up in summer.

The ancient forests that once covered Greece are long gone—for construction of ships and buildings, for fuel to heat public baths and pottery kilns, and to smelt ore for the likes of the silver mines at Lavrion. Today Greece has vegetation characteristic of the Mediterranean: beginning at sea level the lower mountain slopes are covered in evergreen Aleppo pines and live oaks, with plane trees and willows along streams. Where this forest has been removed the distinctive maquis—a dense collection of shrubs, largely such broad-leaved evergreens as holm and kermes oaks, junipers, laurel, myrtle, and rosemary—takes over. But even maquis can be killed off by browsing sheep and goats, and then an even tougher group of spiny, low-lying shrubs, known as *phrygana* (or "kindling," because it produces only small sticks), moves in. It consists of thyme, basil, garlic, hyssop, lavender, oregano, rosemary, rue, sage, and savory—as aromatic a plant community as one could hope for. If you walk into a Greek grocery store and ask for dried oregano you'll get a look that means "poor child, must be touched," because the landscape is covered by fresh oregano.

Especially in northern Greece, above the evergreen forest and its maquis and phrygana replacements, there's a belt of deciduous oak, elm, beech, chestnut, ash, and hornbeam. Still higher grows a coniferous forest of pines, silver fir, cedars, and junipers, and on the highest peaks, above the tree line, you even find an alpine tundra of dwarfed flowering plants and lichens.

Modern Greece was born during the Second World War and its aftermath, the civil war between communist (EAM–ALAS) and royalist (EDES) forces, which lasted until late 1949. After the civil war a constitutional monarchy was reestablished, and the country gradually rebuilt. In 1965 Constantine II succeeded to the throne. In 1967 rightist army officers, headed by George Papadopoulos, staged a successful coup; Constantine went into exile; and the junta abolished the monarchy in 1973. In a second coup general Phaedon Gizikis ousted Papadopoulos, in late 1973. After his failure to annex Cyprus and the subsequent Turkish invasion of the island in 1974 (when Greek Cypriots were dispossessed and the island divided), Gizikis stepped down voluntarily, and civilian government was restored. At the end of that year voters rejected a return of the monarchy and Constantine remained in exile.

Since then the government has been in the hands of either the conservative New Democracy (ND) party or the Panhellenic Socialists (Pasok), with the communist (KKE) party a distant third. Pasok, in power since 1981, began slipping in popularity in 1988, as Prime Minister Andreas Papandreou was caught up in sex and corruption scandals. Under this cloud Pasok lost ground in the election, but the conservative (ND) party failed to win enough seats to form a government. Demonstrating that politics do make strange bedfellows, ND made common cause with an alliance of leftist parties, including the KKE, to form a coalition government. The 1989 elections were inconclusive, but, in April 1990, ND won a slim majority and formed a government under Prime Minister Constantine Mitsotakis. Constantine Karamanlis, the 83-year-old founder of ND, was chosen as president.

Relations with Turkey have always been a chief concern among Greek politicians and the general populace. The two countries have long been antagonistic, and today the sore points are the eastern Aegean and Cyprus. In 1988 there was a brief détente as the prime ministers met, establishing business agreements and a crisis hot-line. In 1989, however, there was a confrontation between Greek and Turkish fighter planes over the eastern Aegean, and, in 1990, local politicians called for autonomy for northeastern Greece, which has a substantial Turkish minority. In an effort to dilute this minority, the Greek government has resettled ethnic Greeks from the former Soviet Union in the region. Cyprus remains a barrier to better relations: No other nation has recognized the separate government for northern Cyprus set up by the Turks, and United Nations–sponsored talks on the Cyprus question have been unproductive.

With the election of the conservative ND government under Mitsotakis, relations between the United States and Greece have improved noticeably. An agreement was quickly reached on U.S. military bases, and the two largest were closed; for many Greeks, this action was an important symbol of American respect for Greek sovereignty. President George Bush subsequently visited Greece, the first such visit since Dwight Eisenhower's, in 1959.

In an effort to maintain a spot on the international stage, Prime Minister Mitsotakis visited the former Soviet Union in 1991, promising aid after the unsuccessful coup. Similar aid missions to Poland and Hungary were undertaken by the foreign minister. Full diplomatic relations with Israel were established in 1990, and, although many Greeks sympathize with the plight of Palestinian refugees, terrorist attacks within Greece have led to strict antiterrorist laws. Security at Athens's airport is today much improved over what it was in the '80s. In 1991 Greece allowed the U.S. naval base at Suda Bay, Crete, to be used in transporting supplies for the Gulf War and contributed to the naval blockade of Iraq.

In the postcommunist era Greece sought to be the regional leader and intermediary between the EC and the Balkan countries. In 1988, in Belgrade, at the first high-level meeting of all Balkan states since World War II, Greece and Albania signed trade and travel agreements. But in 1990, as the situation deteriorated in Albania, refugees began crossing the border, and by August some 50,000 (50% ethnic Greeks) had arrived in Greece. (Thousands of Romanians, Bulgars, and Gypsies have also fled to Greece in recent years.) But the greatest challenge Greece faces in the Balkans concerns the former Yugoslav province of Skopje, which chose the name Macedonia in declaring independence, sparking fears in Greece that it would press claims to Greek Macedonia.

During the past five years inflation rates in the high teens have plagued Greece. In 1990 the EC and International Monetary Fund prompted the imposition of austerity measures—higher taxes on tobacco, alcohol, gasoline, and luxury goods—to help head off an economic crisis. In 1991 the EC withheld $3 billion in loans until fiscal improvements were made and a plan implemented to lower inflation to 7% by the end of 1993. More bad economic news for Greeks is that tourism has been way down for the past two years. In 1993 you can expect warm greetings and courteous service from hotel managers and restaurant owners.

A Once-Over

Athens, known as the Big Olive, is the cultural and transportation center of Greece, from which you can take day or overnight trips to sites such as Delphi and Sounion; to Corinth, Mycenae, and Epidauros, in the Peloponnese; and to the Saronic Gulf islands of Aegina, Poros, Spetses, and Hydra. Off the Adriatic Coast, ferry service leads to Corfu, the most popular destination of the Ionian islands.

Northern Greece (not covered in this guide) is less frequented than the south, although its popularity is growing.

The Peloponnese, the southern part of the Greek peninsula, offers a tour through history. En route from Athens you first pass ancient Corinth and Mycenae, the palace fortress of Agamemnon, on the way to Nauplion, Greece's first modern capital. Turning west you come to Patras, Greece's third largest city, and the sanctuary of Zeus at Olympia, home of the Olympic Games. Farther south are the temple of Apollo at Bassae; the ruined Byzantine city of Mystras, near Sparta; and the extraordinary Gibraltarlike fortress of Monemvassia overlooking the Aegean.

The **Cyclades,** in the Aegean, are the circular group of islands southeast of Athens, of which the most interesting
are Andros; Mykonos, a tourist sun-'n'-fun scene of the first
magnitude; Delos, once sacred to Apollo; Paros; Naxos; and
magical, tourist-ridden Santorini, the rim of an ancient volcano, with the haunting ruins of Akrotiri, buried by an
eruption three millennia ago. Farther southeast, off the
coast of Turkey, lie the **Dodecanese:** Karpathos; Rhodes,
home of the Knights of St. John, where the Colossus once
bestrode the harbor; Symi; Kos; and Patmos, with its huge
fortress-monastery of St. John. Stretched along the Turkish coast in the eastern Aegean are the large islands of
Lemnos, Lesbos, Chios, and Samos, which are greener,
less developed, and less overrun than the Cyclades. Farther south lies Crete, kingdom of the legendary Minos, rich
in spectacular scenery and ruins of the Minoan civilization—the palaces of Knossos, Phaistos, and Mallia.

1 Essential Information

Before You Go

Government Tourist Offices

By Mark J. Rose

Contact the Greek National Tourist Organization for information on all aspects of travel to and in Greece.

United States: Olympic Tower, 645 5th Ave., New York, NY 10022, tel. 212/421–5777, fax 212/826–6940; 168 N. Michigan Ave., Chicago, IL 60601, tel. 312/782–1084, fax 312/782–1091; 611 W. 6th St., Suite 2198, Los Angeles, CA 90017, tel. 213/626–6696, fax 213/489–9744.

Canada: Upper Level, 1300 Bay St., Toronto, Ont. M5R 3K8, tel. 416/968–2220, fax 416/968–6533; 1233 Rue De La Montagne, Suite 101, Montréal, Qué. H3G 1Z2, tel. 514/871–1535, fax 514/871–1498.

United Kingdom: 4 Conduit St., London W1R D0J, tel. 071/734–5997, fax 071/287–1369.

Group Tours

With one of the world's oldest cultures, scenic splendors, and more than 14,500 kilometers (9,000 miles) of coastland, the options offered by a trip to Greece are nearly limitless. How to enjoy them is up to you. If you're heading to Greece for the first time, consider an escorted tour, which usually packs in more sightseeing than you could manage on your own and can also save you money on airfare and hotels. If you prefer more independence, there are still plenty of creative alternatives available. You can enjoy a fly/drive package with an optional cruise, arrange your own itinerary, or select an independent package vacation, participating in optional planned activities as you choose. Before picking a tour, be sure to find out exactly what expenses are included (particularly tips, taxes, service charges, side trips, additional meals, and entertainment) and expect only what is specified. In addition, check the ratings of all hotels on the itinerary and their facilities, cancellation policies for you and the tour operator, and, if you are traveling alone, the cost of a single supplement.

Listed below is a sample of the tours and packages available. Most tour operators request that bookings be made through a travel agent—there is no additional charge for doing so. For additional resources, contact your travel agent or the tourist office of Greece.

General-Interest Tours
United States

American Express Vacations (300 Pinnacle Way, Norcross, GA 30093, tel. 800/241–1700 or in GA, 800/421–5785) offers three tours of Greece (12–16 days) that include Athens, Olympia, and Delphi, and a variety of cruises of the islands.

Caravan Tours (401 N. Michigan Ave., Chicago, IL 60611, tel. 312/321–9800 or 800/227–2826) has "The Best of Greece," in 19 days, including Athens, Corfu, Olympia, and a one-week cruise of the islands.

Globus-Gateway/Cosmos-Tourama (95–25 Queens Blvd., Rego Park, NY 11374, tel. 718/268–7000 or 800/221–0090) provides a number of eight- and nine-day tours of Greece and a 12-day tour and cruise to Mykonos, Rhodes, and Crete.

Maupintour (Box 807, Lawrence, KS 66044, tel. 913/843–1211 or 800/255–4266) offers 15- and 22-day tours of Greece, which both include three days in Athens and visits to such islands as Mykonos, Crete, and Rhodes. Another 15-day tour combines the Greek isles with Egypt.

Olson Travelworld (Box 10066, Manhattan Beach, CA 90226, tel. 310/546–8400 or 310/421–2255) traverses Greece in two weeks, including a four-day island cruise to Crete, Mykonos, and Rhodes, and to Ephesus on the Turkish coast.

Tourlite (1 E. 42nd St., New York, NY 10017, tel. 212/599–3355 or 800/272–7600) has eight and nine-day tours of Athens, Olympia, and Delphi, with extension options to the Greek islands.

Trafalgar Tours (11 E. 26th St., Suite 1300, New York, NY 10010, tel. 212/689–8977 or 800/854–0103) offers a two-week island-hopping excursion that visits eight islands plus Athens, and four other mainland-island tours of nine to 13 days.

Travcoa (Box 2630, Newport Beach, CA 92658, tel. 714/476–2800 or 800/992–2004) puts together a "Greek Odyssey" in 18 days that visits Athens, Corinth, and Olympia; and cruises to Hydra, Crete, Rhodes, and Ephesus on the Turkish coast.

United Kingdom **Airtours** (Wavelli House, Helmshore, Rossendale, Lancashire BB4 4NB, tel. 0706/260000) offers one- and two-week packages to Corfu, Crete, Cyprus, Kos, Rhodes, and other islands, with accommodations in pensions, tavernas, and self-service catering apartments and studios.

Cosmos (Ground Floor, Dale House, Tiviot Dale, Stockport, Cheshire SK1 1TB, tel. 061/480–5799) has one- or two-week package holidays throughout the Greek islands and on the mainland, and to resorts catering to singles, families, teens, and young adults.

Martyn Holidays (390 London Rd., Isleworth, Middlesex TW7 5AD, tel. 081/847–5031) has numerous packages to several Greek Islands, including Skiathos, Crete, and Kefalonia, some with self-catering apartments.

Thomson Holidays (Greater London House, Hampstead Rd., London NW1 7SD, tel. 081/200–8733) offers numerous packages from seven to 14 nights to the major Greek island resorts, with accommodation in hotels, self-catering apartments, and studios.

Special-Interest Greece's archaeological heritage and its claim to be the cradle
Tours of democracy have drawn romantics for nearly two centuries.
Archaeological Edgar Allan Poe wrote of "the glory that was Greece," and even Mark Twain forgot his cynicism when recounting his moonlight visit to the Parthenon in *Innocents Abroad*. Today many of Greece's ancient monuments are overrun with visitors, but some specialized tours go to more remote ruins, where Byron and Shelley's mythic Arkady still exists.

American School of Classical Studies at Athens (41 E. 72 St., New York, NY 10021, tel. 212/861–0302) offers the most comprehensive archaeological tours. Others that provide scholarly guides include **Archaeological Tours** (30 E. 42nd St., Suite 1202, New York, NY 10017, tel. 212/986–3054), **FreeGate Tourism** (1156 Ave. of the Americas, No. 720, New York, NY 10036, tel. 212/764–1818 or 800/223–0304), **Hellastours** (1100 Glendon

Ave., Los Angeles, CA 90024, tel. 310/208–8700 or 800/824–8535).

Cruises   Cruising is experiencing a resurgence in popularity. It can be a pleasant, leisurely way to travel without the complications of rental cars, trains, reservations, frequent packing and unpacking, and the rest. Many cruise companies offer Aegean voyages to the islands and longer trips, from Venice down the Adriatic, and through the Aegean to Athens and Istanbul. **Swan Hellenic Cruises** (581 Boylston St., Boston, MA 02116, tel. 617/266–7465 or 800/426–5492), for example, conducts a number of well-organized voyages, accompanied by classical scholars and expert guides. Other cruise lines include **Classical Cruises** (132 East 70th St., New York, NY 10021, tel. 212/794–3200 or 800/252–7745); **Club Voyages** (Box 7648, Shrewsbury, NJ 07702, tel. 201/842–4946), which offers small yacht cruises in the islands; **Epirotiki Line** (551 5th Ave., Suite 605, New York, NY 10176, tel. 212/599–1750 or 800/221–2470); **Sun Line Cruises** (1 Rockefeller Plaza, Suite 315, New York, NY 10020, tel. 212/397–6400 or 800/872–6400); and **Valef Yachts** (Box 391, 7254 Fir Rd., Ambler, PA 19002, tel. 215/641–1624), which offers cruises in small yachts to the Sporades and Cyclades. In addition, some museum programs offer Greek cruises. Check with the **Metropolitan Museum of Art** (contact Raymond & Whitcomb Co., 400 Madison Ave., New York, NY 10017, tel. 212/759–3960 or 800/245–9005) and the **Smithsonian National Associate Program** (1100 Jefferson Dr. SW, Washington, DC 20560, tel. 202/357–4700). *See also* Cruises in Arriving and Departing, *below.*

Package Deals for Independent Travelers

Astro Tours (216 4th Ave. S, Seattle, WA 98104, tel. 206/467–7777 or 800/543–7717) offers a broad selection of packages, including optional sightseeing tours and cruises.

Delta Dream Vacations (tel. 800/872–7786) offers six-night minimum stays in Athens, with breakfast, sightseeing, flights, and car rental or rail passes.

Extra Value Travel (683 S. Collier Blvd., Marco Island, FL 33937, tel. 813/398–4848 or 800/255–2847) offers self-drive tours of Greece, with a range of hotel choices and personalized itineraries.

Freelance Vacations from American Express Vacations (*see* Group Tours, *above*) combines the freedom of independent travel with optional planned activities on its 10- and 13-day tours of Athens with an island cruise.

GoGo Tours (69 Spring St., Ramsey, NJ 07446, tel. 800/821–3731) offers two eight-day packages to Greece, including cruises to selected islands.

SuperCities (7855 Haskell Ave., Suite 300, Van Nuys, CA 91406, tel. 818/988–6774 or 800/633–3000) offers a package with a two-day minimum stay in Athens, along with optional city tours and day trips. Car rental and airfare are available.

Trafalgar Tours (*see* Group Tours, *above*) offers four independent mainland-island tours of nine to 13 days.

Travel Bound (599 Broadway, Penthouse, New York, NY 10012, tel. 212/334–1350 or 800/456–8656) will help travelers to

Greece plan an itinerary based on à la carte selections of hotels, sightseeing, and transportation options.

Triaena (850 7th Ave., Suite 604, New York, NY 10019, tel. 212/ 245–3700 or 800/223–1273) offers a wide variety of packages for independent travelers to Greece, of from four to 14 days, as well as design-your-own "Freewheeler Holidays."

When to Go

Go to Greece between the middle of May and the middle of July. The days are warm, even hot, but dry, and the sea water has been warmed by the sun. The cool evenings of midsummer, which seem to last forever, are perfect for dining outside. For sightseeing, exploring the cities or countryside, or hitting the beach, this is the time. Greece is relatively tourist-free in the spring. If you don't like crowds, and the beach and swimming aren't high on your agenda, April and early May are a good time to tour the country. Carnavali, at the beginning of Lent, and Greek Easter, with its religious processions, lambs, and red eggs, are the highlights of the season.

September and October are a good alternative to spring and early summer. Things begin to shut down in November, however, and the winter chill and rains begin. Winter in Greece is deceptive. Any given day may not be very cold, may even be mild. Except in the mountains, snow is uncommon in Athens and to the south. But the cold is persistent, and the level of heating we're accustomed to in the United States is not usual in Greece. Over the course of a few days you will feel chilled to the bone. Transportation to the islands is limited in winter, and many hotels outside large cities are closed until the beginning of April. Unless you are going to Greece in pursuit of winter sports, try a different season.

Toward the end of July and through August the temperatures climb, pushing the 100°F (38°C) mark. In the south a dry, hot wind may blow across the Mediterranean from the coast of Africa. The air quality in Athens, which is surrounded on all sides by mountains (except in the direction of the harbor and oil refineries of Piraeus), is often unhealthy during August, and air-conditioning is far from ubiquitous. Coincident with these unfortunate climatic conditions is the peak of the tourist season. In August you should flee Athens as soon as possible and head off the beaten track.

Climate Greece enjoys a typical Mediterranean climate: hot, dry summers and cool, wet winters. The average high and low temperatures for Athens and Heraklion (Crete) are presented below. Note that although *average* temperatures in the north and the south may not be too dissimilar, the temperature on a given day can differ substantially.

Athens								
Jan.	5F	13C	**May**	77F	25C	**Sept.**	84F	29C
	43	6		61	16		66	19
Feb.	57F	14C	**June**	86F	30C	**Oct.**	75F	24C
	45	7		68	20		59	15
Mar.	61F	16C	**July**	91F	33C	**Nov.**	66F	19C
	46	8		73	23		54	12
Apr.	68F	20C	**Aug.**	91F	33C	**Dec.**	59F	15C
	52	11		73	23		46	8

Heraklion

Jan.	61F	16C	**May**	73F	23C	**Sept.**	81F	27C
	48	9		59	15		66	19
Feb.	61F	16C	**June**	81F	27C	**Oct.**	75F	24C
	48	9		66	19		63	17
Mar.	63F	17C	**July**	84F	29C	**Nov.**	70F	21C
	50	10		72	22		57	14
Apr.	68F	20C	**Aug.**	84F	29C	**Dec.**	64F	18C
	54	12		72	22		52	11

Call the Weather Channel Connection at 900/WEATHER (900/923–8347) from a touch-tone phone for current weather information for foreign cities, their local time, and helpful travel tips. The call costs 95¢ per minute.

Festivals and Seasonal Events

The Greek calendar is filled with religious celebrations, cultural festivals, and civic occasions. Those events with roots in Byzantine Greece are especially intriguing, as they combine religious belief and national pride in a way unfamiliar to most Americans. Shops may close early for local or national celebrations, and hotels may be booked during major events (like Carnavali at Patras). Verify the dates of events with the Greek National Tourist Organization (Festivals Box Office, 4 Stadiou St., Athens, tel. 01/322–1459 or 01/322–3111 ext. 240). Public holidays of 1993 are January 1 (New Year's Day), January 6 (Epiphany), March 1 (Clean Monday, first day of Lent), March 25 (Feast of the Annunciation and Independence Day), April 16, 17, 18 (Good Friday, Holy Saturday, and Easter), April 26 (Orthodox Easter), May 1 (Labor Day and Flower Festival), August 15 (Dormition of the Holy Virgin), October 28 (national holiday), December 25–26 (Christmas Day and Boxing Day).

January 1: The **Feast of Saint Basil** marks the beginning of the New Year. A special cake, the *Vassilopita*, is baked with a coin in it, which brings good luck to the finder.

January 6: Epiphany, the day for blessing the waters, is the occasion for an official ceremony at Athens's harbor, Piraeus. Elsewhere, crosses are immersed in seas, lakes, and rivers.

January 8: Gynaecocracy, in northeastern Greece, reverses the traditional roles of men and women: In the area around Serres, Kilkis, Xanthi, and Komotini, women spend the day at the cafés while the men do the housekeeping until evening.

February 7–28: Carnavali, like Mardi Gras, celebrates the period before the beginning of Lent. The evenings are marked by parades, music, and dancing, and costumes are required to participate. Towns and islands known to celebrate Carnavali in style are Patras, Naousa, Veria, Kozani, Zante, Skyros, Xanthi, Mesta and Olimbi on Chios, Galaxidi, Thebes, Poligiros, Thimiana, Lamia, Cefallonia, Messini, Soho, Serres, Agiassos on Lesbos, Karpathos, Heraklion and Rethymno on Crete, Amfissa, Efxinoupolis, and Ayia Anna on Evia.

March 25: Independence Day commemorates the call for independence in 1821 by Germanos, the Metropolitan of Patras, which began the uprising in the Peloponnese that eventually freed Greece from Ottoman rule. Today it is marked by parades of the armed forces, especially in Athens.

April 16–18: Good Friday, Holy Saturday, and **Easter Sunday** are the most sacred days on the Orthodox calendar. The traditional candlelight funeral processions staged throughout the country on Good Friday are very powerful to watch. Not only do they attest to the strength of the participants' faith, but they link modern Greece with its Byzantine roots, and the soldiers carrying the coffins illustrate the ties between church and government. Processions to churches on the night of Holy Saturday are a memorable sight. Following the midnight ceremony of the Resurrection, the congregations head homeward to feast, with the traditional red-dyed eggs and *mayiritsa* soup. More red-dyed eggs and roast lamb highlight the feasting on Easter Sunday. Seeing the rituals of Holy Week makes you understand the depth of meaning that the Easter greeting *Christos aneste*, "Christ is risen," has for most Greeks.

April 23: The **Feast of Saint George** is a day for horse racing at Kaliopi on Lemnos and at Pili on Kos. On Crete, a three-day-long feast begins at Arahova, near Delphi, while at Assi Gonia, near Hania, a sheep-shearing contest follows the religious fiesta.

May–September: Performances of **folk dancing** are given at the amphitheater on Philopappou Hill in Athens.

May 21–23: The **Anastenaria,** a traditional fire-walking ritual with pagan roots and a Byzantine overlay, is performed in Ayia Eleni near Ayia Serres, and in Langada near Thessaloniki, where villagers dance on live embers while clasping icons of Saint Constantine and Saint Helen.

June–September: The **Athens Festival** presents ancient dramas, operas, music, and ballet performed by nationally and internationally famous artists, in the 2nd-century Odeon of Herodes Atticus on the south slope of the Acropolis.

June–October: Folk-dancing performances are held in the theater in the old town of Rhodes on that island.

Mid-June–late August: Lycabettus Theater presents a variety of performances in the amphitheater on Lycabettus Hill overlooking Athens.

Late June–early July: Coastal towns honor the Greek navy with the celebrations of **Navy Week.** Fishermen at Plomari on Lesbos and Agria near Volos stage festivals, and at Volos the last day of Navy Week is marked by a reenactment of the mythical voyage of the ship *Argo*, with its crew led by Jason in search of the Golden Fleece.

July–September: The **Epidauros Festival,** world-renowned for the excellence of the performances, is held in the ancient theater, known for its superb acoustics. Watching a classical comedy or tragedy in this peaceful rural setting sends chills down your spine—twilight falls, the audience quiets, and a play first performed 2,500 years ago begins. The **Dodoni, Philippi,** and **Thassos festivals,** like the better-known one at Epidauros, stage classical dramas in ancient theaters.

August: The **Epirotika Festival** in Ioannina, Epirus, celebrates Epirotikan authors and artists with exhibitions, theatrical performances, and concerts. At the **Olympus Festival,** a series of cultural events is held at the village of Litohoro near Olympus, in the well-preserved Frankish castle of Platamona. The

Hippokrateia Festival on the island of Kos honors the father of medicine, a native son. Events include performances of ancient dramas and music, a flower show, and a costumed reenactment of the first swearing of the Hippocratic oath.

August–September: At the **Aeschilia** festival, ancient dramas are staged at the archaeological site of Eleusis near Athens.

September–October: Following Thessaloniki's International Trade Fair in September come the **Festival of Popular Song,** the **Film Festival,** and the **Demetria Festival,** with theater, concerts, ballet, and opera.

December 31: New Year's Eve is the occasion for carol singing by children and the exchange of gifts. On the island of Chios the day is marked by a contest for the best model boat.

What to Pack

Take what you *will* need, not what you *might* need. You can rent a cart at the airport, but from then on you'll have to carry your own luggage. Getting on and off the train, buses, and boats can be easy or a pain, depending on how much you're hauling around. Also, remember that you'll be carrying souvenirs on your way out. It's a good idea to itemize the contents of each bag and keep the list, in case you need to file an insurance claim. Be certain to put your home or business address on each piece of luggage, including carry-on bags.

Clothing Outside Athens, Greek dress tends to be middle of the road—you won't see patched jeans *or* expensive suits. In the summer bring lightweight, casual clothing and good walking shoes. A light sweater or jacket would be useful for cool evenings, especially in the mountains. There's no need for rain gear in high summer, but don't forget sunglasses and a sun hat. Be prepared for cooler weather and some rain in spring and fall, and in winter, add a warm coat.

Casual attire is acceptable everywhere except in the most expensive restaurants in large cities, but you should dress conservatively when visiting archaeological sites, museums, churches, or monasteries. It's not appropriate to show a lot of bare arm and leg. Armless, low-neck sun shirts or bathing suit tops, and very short shorts and short skirts are out; shirts with sleeves and slacks or longer skirts are in. Swimsuits are required on most beaches in Greece, but the number of beaches where topless and nude bathing are acceptable is slowly growing. Err on the conservative side.

Miscellaneous An extra pair of glasses, contact lenses, or prescription sunglasses is always a good idea; pack any prescription medicines you use regularly (and a copy of the prescription, written generically), and any allergy medicine you may need. The electric current in Greece is 220 volts, and the plugs take two round prongs. You'll need an adapter for hair dryers and other small appliances. A small flashlight comes in handy, as does a jacknife with a corkscrew and screwdriver. Zip-closing plastic bags, pocket packs of tissues and moist towelettes, a roll of transparent tape, a washcloth, and a pocket calculator are all sometimes indispensable.

Carry-on Luggage Airlines generally allow each passenger one piece of carry-on luggage on international flights from the United States. The bag cannot exceed 45 inches (length + width + height) and must fit under the seat or in the overhead compartment.

Checked Luggage Passengers are generally allowed to check two pieces of luggage, neither of which can exceed 62 inches (length + width + height) or weigh more than 70 pounds. Baggage allowances vary slightly among airlines, so check with the carrier or your travel agent before departure.

Taking Money Abroad

Before going, you may want to chart the U.S. dollar for a couple of weeks against the Greek drachma. If the dollar is weakening, consider buying traveler's checks in foreign currency and prepaying for hotel rooms and train or plane tickets. If the dollar is improving, buy traveler's checks in U.S. dollars, and use a credit card to pay for costly items after you arrive. (Overseas charges often don't appear on your bill for two or three months, and you pay the exchange rate of the day the vendor posts the charge). Always carry some cash with you in smaller cities and rural areas, where credit cards and traveler's checks might not be widely accepted. Regardless of how the dollar is faring abroad, it's wise to change a small amount of money before you go: Lines at airport currency-exchange booths can be very long. If your local bank can't change your currency, go to Thomas Cook Currency Services. To find the office nearest you, ask at 630 Fifth Avenue, New York, NY 10111 (tel. 212/757–6915).

The most recognized traveler's checks are American Express, Barclay's, Thomas Cook, and those issued through such major commercial banks as Citibank and Bank of America. American Express now issues **Travelers Cheques for Two**—a system that allows both you and your traveling companion to sign and use the same checks. Some banks will issue the checks free to established customers, but most charge a 1% commission. Buying part of the traveler's checks in small denominations to cash toward the end of your trip will save you from ending up with more foreign money than you need. (Hold on to your receipts after exchanging your traveler's checks; it's easier to convert foreign currency back into dollars if you have them.) Remember to take the addresses of offices where you can get refunds for lost or stolen traveler's checks.

Getting Money from Home

Cash Machines Where possible, use automated-teller machines (ATMs) to withdraw money from your checking account with a bank card or, though it's more expensive, advance cash with your credit card. Before leaving home ask your local bank for a personal identification number (PIN) for your bank and credit cards; find out its affiliated cash-machine networks (like **Cirrus** and **Plus**), the fees for withdrawals or cash advances made overseas, and limits on these transactions within given time periods. Also ask for a list of ATM locations in Greece, which are only in major cities. Not all overseas ATMs have prompts in English, so learn the Greek equivalent for key words like *withdraw, amount, cancel*, etc. Cash advances on a credit card can also be made through bank tellers, but either way you pay interest from the day of posting, and some banks tack on a service charge.

Bank Transfers Just have your bank send money to another bank overseas. It's easiest to transfer from one branch to another of the same bank; otherwise the process takes a couple of days longer and costs more.

American Express The company's **Express Cash** system links your U.S. checking account to your Amex card (apply for a PIN at least two–three weeks before departure). Overseas you can withdraw up to $1,000 in a 21-day period (more if your card is gold or platinum). For each transaction there's a 2% fee (minimum $2, maximum $10). Call 800/227–4669 for information. In Greece, you can get cash and/or traveler's checks from the Express Cash machine in the Banking Hall opposite the customs exit at the Athens airport east terminal, and cash only at all Creditbank branches.

If you are a cardholder, you can cash a personal check or a counter check at an American Express office for up to $1,000 ($5,000 for gold cardholders; $10,000 for platinum), of which up to $200 may be claimed in local currency ($500 with a gold or platinum card) and the balance in traveler's checks carrying a 1% commission.

Wiring Money Have a friend at home send you an **American Express MoneyGram** overseas, by filling out a form for up to $10,000 at an Amex MoneyGram agency (call 800/543–4080 for locations). Up to $1,000 may be paid for by credit card (AE, D, MC, or V); the balance must be in cash. Your friend then telephones you with a reference number, and the MoneyGram agent authorizes an immediate funds transfer to the participating office nearest you. Present proper ID and the reference number for payment. It costs roughly 5%–10%, depending on the amount and method of payment.

Greek Currency

The drachma (dr.) is the Greek unit of currency. Bills are in denominations of 10,000, 5,000, 1,000, and 500 drachmas (100- and 50-drachma bills are going to be taken out of circulation). Coins are 100, 50, 20, 10, 5, 2, and 1 drachma. At press time (fall 1992) the exchange rate was 189 drachmas to the U.S. dollar, 149 drachmas to the Canadian dollar, and 318 drachmas to the pound sterling.

What It Will Cost

Although prices have risen since Greece joined the EEC, the country will seem inexpensive to travelers from the United States and Great Britain. Popular tourist resorts (including some of the islands) and the larger cities are markedly more expensive than the countryside. Though the price of restaurant meals has increased over the past several years, it remains a bargain. Hotels are generally reasonably priced, and the extra cost of accommodations in a luxury hotel, compared to an average hotel, often seems unwarranted.

Transportation is a good deal in Greece. Bus and train tickets are inexpensive, though renting a car is a bit more costly; there are relatively cheap—and slow—ferries to the islands, and express boats and hydrofoils that cost more. If your time is limited, domestic flights are a fair trade-off in cost and time saved, against sea and land travel.

Taxes Value-added tax (or sales tax) of varying percentages is included in the cost of hotels, restaurant meals, car rentals, and many categories of consumer products, and it is very difficult to get a refund on departure. Unless the amount is substantial, most people feel it is not worth the trouble. A tax-reform movement is afoot, but nothing concrete has yet occurred.

Sample Prices Admission to archaeological sites: 400 dr.–1,000 dr.; authentic Greek sponge: 1,500 dr.; coffee: 120 dr.–200 dr.; beer (500 ml): 200 dr.–400 dr.; Coca-Cola: 200 dr.; spinach pie: 150 dr.; taxi ride: about 1,000 dr. from the airport to downtown Athens; local bus: 140 dr. in one zone; foreign newspaper: 200 dr.–400 dr.

Passports and Visas

Americans All U.S. citizens need a valid passport to enter Greece for stays of up to 90 days. First-time applicants should apply in person to one of the 13 U.S. Passport Agency offices at least five weeks before their departure date (renewals can be obtained by mail). In addition, local county courthouses, many state and probate courts, and some post offices have forms and accept passport applications. Bring with you (1) a completed application (Form DSP-11); (2) proof of citizenship (certified birth certificate issued by the Hall of Records of your state of birth, or naturalization papers); (3) proof of identity (valid driver's license or state, military, or student ID card with your photograph and signature); (4) two recent, identical, 2-inch-square photographs (black-and-white or color), with a white or off-white background; and (5) $65 application fee for a 10-year passport (those under 18 pay $40 for a five-year passport). You may pay with a check, money order, or exact cash amount; no change is given. Passports are mailed to you in about 10–15 working days. To renew your passport by mail, send a completed Form DSP-82, two recent, identical passport photos, your current passport (if less than 12 years old and issued after your 16th birthday), and a check or money order for $55.

For visits exceeding three months, authorization must be obtained by applying in person to the Aliens Bureau at least 20 days prior to the three-month expiration date (173 Alexandras Ave., Athens 11522, tel. 01/646–8103; 37 Iroon Politechniou St., Piraeus 18510, tel. 01/412–2501; 25 Tsimiski St., Thessaloniki, tel. 521067).

Canadians All Canadian citizens need a valid passport to enter Greece. To acquire a passport, send a completed application (available at any post office or passport office) to the Bureau of Passports, Suite 215, West Tower, Guy Favreau Complex, 200 René Levesque Blvd. W, Montréal, Québec H2Z 1X4. Include $25, two photographs, a guarantor, and proof of Canadian citizenship. Application can be made in person at the regional passport offices in Calgary, Edmonton, Halifax, Montréal, St. John's (Newfoundland), Toronto, Vancouver, Victoria, or Winnipeg. Passports are valid for five years and are nonrenewable. A visa is required for a tourist stay exceeding three months (*see above*).

Britons You need a valid 10-year passport to enter Greece (cost: £15 for a standard 32-page passport, £30 for a 94-page passport). Application forms are available from most travel agents and major post offices, or contact the **Passport Office** (Clive House, 70 Petty France, London SW1H 9HD, tel. 071/279–3434). A British

Visitor's Passport is also acceptable. It is valid for one year only and costs £7.50. Apply at your local post office. You'll need two passport photographs and identification.

Customs and Duties

On Arrival Passing through customs on your arrival in Greece can be a puzzling experience if you expect to be questioned or have your luggage examined as a matter of routine. If you have nothing to declare, you can simply walk through a green-marked lane. Red-marked lanes are for people with articles that must be declared and those who like having their baggage inspected. You may bring into Greece duty-free: food and beverages up to 22 pounds (10 kilos); 200 cigarettes, 100 cigarillos, or 50 cigars; 5 boxes of matches; two packs of playing cards; one liter of alcholic spirits or two liters of wine; and gift articles up to a total of 9,000 drachmas.

Only one per person of such expensive portable items as cameras, camcorders, typewriters, tape recorders, and the like, is permitted into Greece. Sports equipment, such as bicycles and skis, are also limited to one (pair) per person.

To bring in a dog or a cat, you need a health and rabies-inoculation certificate issued by a veterinary authority and dated (for dogs) not more than 12 months and not fewer than six days before arrival, and for cats not more than six months and not fewer than six days before arrival.

On Departure
Antiquities The export of antiquities from Greece is forbidden. If any such articles are found in a traveler's luggage, they will be confiscated and the individual will be liable for prosecution. Reproductions of ancient works of art, some of very high quality, can be purchased throughout Greece, and may be exported freely.

U.S. Customs If you take into Greece any foreign-made equipment from home, such as a camera, it's wise to keep the original receipt with you or register it with U.S. Customs before you leave (Form 4457), to avoid the possibility of having to pay duty on your return. Contact the **U.S. Customs Service** (1301 Constitution Ave., Washington, DC 20229) for a free copy of "Know Before You Go," its brochure outlining what you may and may not bring back home and at what cost, and containing a list of the local customs offices throughout the country.

You may bring home duty-free up to $400 worth of foreign goods, as long as you have been out of the country for at least 48 hours and you haven't made an international trip in the past 30 days. Each member of the family is entitled to the same exemption, regardless of age, and exemptions may be pooled. For the next $1,000 worth of goods, a flat 10% rate is assessed; over $1,400, duties vary with the merchandise. Included for travelers 21 and older are one liter of alcohol, 100 cigars (non-Cuban), and 200 cigarettes. Only one bottle of perfume trademarked in the United States may be imported. There is no duty on antiques or works of art more than 100 years old. Anything exceeding these limits will be taxed at the port of entry and may be taxed additionally in the traveler's home state. Gifts valued at under $50 may be mailed duty-free to friends or relatives at home (not more than one package per day to a single addressee), if they do not contain tobacco, liquor, or perfumes costing more than $5.

Canadian Customs Exemptions for returning Canadians range from $20 to $300, depending on length of stay out of the country. For the $300 exemption, you must have been out of the country for one week. In any given year, you are allowed one $300 exemption. You may bring in duty-free up to 50 cigars, 200 cigarettes, 2.2 pounds of tobacco, and 40 ounces of liquor, provided these are declared in writing to customs on arrival and accompany the traveler in hand or check-through baggage. Personal gifts should be mailed labeled "Unsolicited Gift—Value under $40." Obtain a copy of the Canadian Customs brochure *I Declare* for further details.

U.K. Customs Since Greece and Great Britain are both members of the EC, the following customs allowances apply upon entering Greece and returning home. Travelers age 17 and over have one allowance for goods bought in a duty-free shop and another for goods bought elsewhere (i.e., tax-paid) within the EC. Pooling the allowances is not permitted.

In the first category you may import duty-free: (1) 200 cigarettes or 100 cigarillos or 50 cigars or 250 grams of tobacco; (2) two liters of still table wine; and (3) one liter of spirits over 22% volume or two liters of spirits under 22% volume (fortified or sparkling wine) or two more liters of still table wine; (4) 60 milliliters of perfume and 250 milliliters of toilet water; and (5) other goods up to a value of £32, but not more than 50 liters of beer or 25 mechanical lighters.

In the second category you may import duty-free: (1) 300 cigarettes or 150 cigarillos or 75 cigars or 400 grams of tobacco; (2) five liters of table wine and (3) 1.5 liters of alcoholic drink over 22% volume or three liters of alcohol under 22% volume (fortified or sparkling wine) or three more liters of still table wine; (4) 90 ml of perfume and 375 ml of toilet water; and (5) other goods up to a value of £425, but not more than 50 liters of beer or 25 lighters.

Traveling with Film

If your camera is new, shoot and develop a few rolls of film before you leave home. Pack some lens tissue and an extra battery if you have a built-in light meter. Film doesn't like hot weather, so if you're driving in summer, don't store it in the glove compartment or on the shelf under the rear window. Put it behind the front seat on the floor, on the side opposite the exhaust.

On a plane trip, never pack unprocessed film in check-in luggage; if your bags get X-rayed, your film could be ruined. Always carry undeveloped film with you through security and ask to have it inspected by hand. It helps to keep your film in a plastic bag, ready for quick inspection. Inspectors at American airports are required by law to honor requests for hand inspection; abroad, you'll have to depend on the kindness of strangers. The newer airport scanning machines used in all U.S. airports are safe for anything from five to 500 scans, depending on the speed of your film.

Language

Greek is the native language not only of Greece but also of Cyprus, parts of Chicago, and Astoria, New York. Though it's a byword for incomprehensible ("it was all Greek to me," says

Casca in Shakespeare's *Julius Caesar*), much of the difficulty lies in its different alphabet. Not all the 24 Greek letters have precise English equivalents, and there is usually more than one way to spell a Greek word in English. For instance, the letter *delta* sounds like the English letters "dh," and the sound of the letter *gamma* may be transliterated as a "g," "gh," or "y." Because of this the Greek for Holy Trinity might appear in English as *Agia Triada*, *Aghia Triada*, *Ayia Triada*, or even (if the initial aspiration and the dh are used) *Hagia Triadha*. It seems complicated, but don't let it throw you. With a little time spent learning the alphabet and some basic phrases, you can acquire enough Greek to navigate—i.e. exchange greetings, find a hotel room, and get from one town to another. Many Greeks know some English, but will appreciate a two-way effort.

If you only have 15 minutes to learn Greek, memorize the following: *miláte angliká?* (do you speak English?); *den katalavéno* (I don't understand); *parakaló* (please); *me signómi* (excuse me), *efcharistó* (thank you); *pósso?* (how much?); *pou íne i trápeza?* (where is the bank?), *...i toaléta?* (...the toilet?), *...to tachidromío?* (...the post office?); *kaliméra* (good morning), *kalispéra* (good evening), *kaliníchta* (good night). Also see the Vocabulary section at the back of the book.

Staying Healthy

The Department of State **Citizens Emergency Center** (tel. 202/647–5225) provides information about health conditions in other countries. Greece's strong summer sun and low humidity can lead to sunburn or sunstroke if you're not careful. A hat, long-sleeve shirt, and long pants or a wrap are essential for a day at the beach or visiting archaeological sites. Sunglasses, a hat, and sun-block are necessities, and insect repellent may keep the occasional horsefly and mosquito at bay. Drink plenty of water.

Food is seldom a problem, but because refrigeration may not be up to par, you should avoid ice cream and dishes made with ground meat. The liberal amounts of olive oil used in Greek cooking may be indigestible for some. Tap water in Greece is fine, and bottled spring water is readily available. No special shots are required before visiting Greece. If you take any medication regularly, have your doctor write a prescription using the drug's generic name, as brand names vary from country to country. Newspapers carry a listing of pharmacies that are open late or, in large cities, all night. In and around Athens you can call a first aid center (tel. 166) or ambulance (tel. 150) in an emergency.

The **International Association for Medical Assistance to Travelers (IAMAT)** is a worldwide organization that publishes a list of approved English-speaking doctors whose training meets British and American standards. For a list of Greek physicians and clinics that belong to this network, contact IAMAT (417 Center St., Lewiston, NY 14092, tel. 716/754–4883; in **Canada**: 40 Regal Rd., Guelph, Ontario N1K 185; in **Europe**: 57 Voirets, 1212 Grand-Lancy, Geneva, Switzerland). Membership is free.

Insurance

Travelers may seek insurance coverage in four areas: health and accident, lost luggage, trip cancellation, and flight. Your first step is to review your existing health and home-owner policies; some health insurance plans cover health expenses incurred while traveling, some major medical plans cover emergency transportation, and some home-owner policies cover the theft of luggage.

Health and Accident Several companies offer coverage designed to supplement existing health insurance for travelers: **Carefree Travel Insurance** (Box 310, 120 Mineola Blvd., Mineola, NY 11501, tel. 516/294–0220 or 800/343–3149) provides coverage for emergency medical evacuation and accidental death and dismemberment. It also offers 24-hour phone medical advice.

International SOS Assistance (Box 11568, Philadelphia, PA 19116, tel. 215/244–1500 or 800/523–8930), a medical-assistance company, provides emergency evacuation services, worldwide medical referrals, and optional medical insurance.

Travel Assistance International (1133 15th St. NW, Suite 400, Washington, DC 20005, tel. 202/331–1609 or 800/821–2828) provides emergency evacuation services, 24-hour medical referrals, and medical insurance.

Travel Guard International, underwritten by Transamerica Occidental Life Companies (1145 Clark St., Stevens Point, WI 54481, tel. 715/345–0505 or 800/782–5151), offers emergency evacuation services and reimbursement for medical expenses with no deductibles or daily limits.

Wallach and Company, Inc. (Box 4800, Middleburg, VA 22117–0480, tel. 703/687–3166 or 800/237–6615) offers comprehensive medical coverage, including emergency evacuation services worldwide.

Lost Luggage On international flights, airlines are responsible for lost or damaged property to a value of $9.07 per pound (or $20 per kilo) for checked baggage and up to $400 per passenger for unchecked baggage. If you're carrying valuables, either take them with you on the plane or purchase additional insurance. Some airlines will issue extra luggage insurance when you check in, but many do not. If your luggage is lost or stolen and later recovered, the airline will deliver it to your home free of charge. Insurance for lost, damaged, or stolen luggage is available through travel agents or direct, usually as part of a comprehensive package that includes personal accident, trip cancellation, and sometimes default and bankruptcy insurance. Two companies that issue luggage insurance are **Tele-Trip** (Box 31685, 3201 Farnam St., Omaha, NE 68131–0618, tel. 800/228–9792), a subsidiary of Mutual of Omaha, and **The Traveler** (Ticket and Travel Dept., 1 Tower Sq., Hartford, CT 06183–5040, tel. 203/277–0111 or 800/243–3174). Other companies with comprehensive policies include **Access America Inc.,** a subsidiary of Blue Cross–Blue Shield (Box 11188, Richmond, VA 23230, tel. 800/334–7525 or 800/284–8300); **Near Services** (450 Prairie Ave., Suite 101, Calumet City, IL 60409, tel. 708/868–6700 or 800/654–6700); and **Travel Guard International** and **Carefree Travel Insurance** (*see above*).

Trip-Cancellation and Flight Consider purchasing trip-cancellation insurance if you are traveling on a promotional or discounted ticket that does not allow changes or cancellations. It is usually included in combination travel insurance packages available from most tour operators, travel agents, and insurance agents. Flight insurance, which covers passengers in the case of death or dismemberment, is often included in the price of a ticket when paid for with a major credit card.

For general advice in the United Kingdom on all aspects of holiday insurance, contact **The Association of British Insurers** (51 Gresham St., London BC2V 7HQ, tel. 071/600–3333) or **Europ Assistance** (252 High St., Croyden, Surrey CR0 1NF, tel. 081/680–1234).

Renting and Leasing Cars

All major car-rental companies are represented in Greece, and visitors are advised to make a reservation in advance. Usually, you must be over 21 to rent a car (some rental companies say 25) and some restrictions may apply to drivers over 60. Most companies will accept your current driver's license, but some may require an International Driver's Permit, available through your Automobile Club (AAA or CAA) office.

Fourteen-day advance booking plans offer lower rates than last-minute arrangements either at home or in Greece. Daily rates for Athens (including the 18% tax and daily collision damage waiver fee) vary from about $65 for a two-door with standard transmission to $80 for a midsize car with automatic shift and air conditioning. Weekly rates, with unlimited mileage, run between $235 and $355 (around $800 for minivans). Costs may be higher outside major cities. You must specify automatic or air conditioning if you want them. Minivans (and campers, motor homes, and four-wheel-drive vehicles, if available) must be booked well in advance. One-way rentals usually involve a drop-off charge. Special fly/drive packages offer discount rates. For trips of 21 days or more it will probably save money to lease a car. **Kemwell** (*see below*) makes leasing arrangements before you go; the plans range from $541 to $1,189 for three weeks. The company also rents cars.

Reservations can be made by calling: **Avis** (tel. 800/331–1084 or in Canada 800/879–2847); **Budget** (tel. 800/472–3325 in the U.S. and Canada); **Dollar** (tel. 800/800–4000 in the U.S. and Canada); **Europe by Car** (1 Rockefeller Plaza, New York, NY, 10020, tel. 212/245–1713, 800/223–1516, or in CA 800/253–9401); **Hertz** (tel. 800/654–3001; in AK and HI 800/654–3131; or in Canada 800/263–0600); and **Kemwell** (106 Calvert St., Harrison, NY 10528, tel. 800/678–0678). Rental agents can be found in most large towns and all cities in Greece, or you can reserve through the **Association of Car Rental Enterprises** (314 Syngrou Ave., Kallithea, Athens 10564, tel. 01/951–0921).

Rail Passes

The **EurailPass,** valid for unlimited first-class train travel through 20 countries, and the new **EurailDrive Pass,** good for combined train and rental-car travel in 16 countries, are useful *only* if you plan to travel around the Continent before or after going to Greece. If you are traveling by rail through Italy and want to cross over and see some of Greece, your rail pass can be used on ferries of Adriatica Lines and Hellenic Mediterranean Lines from Brindisi to Patras. Given the limited rail system in the country, a rail pass for use in Greece alone is no bargain, even if your destinations are on the railroad line. These passes are available only if you live outside Europe or North Africa and must be bought before you go. You can apply through an authorized travel agent or through **Rail Europe** (226–230 Westchester Ave., White Plains, NY 10604, tel. 914/682–5172 or 800/345–1990).

The ticket is available for periods of 15 days ($430), 21 days ($550), one month ($680), two months ($920), and three months ($1,150). For two or more people traveling together, a 15-day rail pass costs $340 each, but between April 1 and September 30, you need a minimum of three in your group to get this discount. The new EurailDrive Pass gives you, for example, four days on trains and three days in a Hertz economy car within a 21-day period for $269 per person for two people traveling together or $439 for a single person, including taxes and drop-off fees in selected cities. There is a new **Greek Rail 'N Drive** plan good for any eight days (five rail, three car) of travel within 15 days ($129 per person of a couple; $209 per single person; economy car) or for any 13 days (10 rail, 3 car) within one month ($179 per person of a couple; $259 per single person; economy car).

For those 25 years old and younger (on the first day of travel), there is the **Eurail Youthpass,** for one or two months' unlimited second-class train travel at $470 and $640. For travelers who like to spread out their train journeys, there is the **Eurail Flexipass.** With the 15-day pass ($280), travelers get five days of unlimited first-class train travel but can spread that travel out over 15 days. A 21-day pass ($450) gives you nine days of travel, and a one-month pass gives you 14 days of train travel ($610). The Eurail Youth Flexipass allows for 15 days of unlimited second-class travel within a two-month period ($420).

Student and Youth Travel

The **International Student Identity Card** (ISIC) entitles matriculated students to special fares on local transportation, rail passes, intra-European student charter flights, and discounts at museums, theaters, sports events, and many other attractions. If the ISIC card is bought in the United States, the $14 cost also includes $3,000 in emergency medical coverage, plus hospital coverage of $100 a day for up to 60 days. Apply to the **Council on International Educational Exchange** (CIEE) (205 E. 42nd St., New York, NY 10017, tel. 212/661–1414). In Canada, the ISIC is available for $13 (Canadian) from **Travel Cuts** (187 College St., Toronto, Ont. MST 1P7, tel. 416/979–2406). In the United Kingdom, students enrolled in university programs can purchase the ISIC at any student union or student travel company upon presentation of a valid university ID.

Travelers (students and nonstudents) under age 26 can apply for a **Youth International Educational Exchange Card** (YIEE) issued by the **Federation of International Youth Travel Organizations** (FIYTO, 81 Islands Brugge, DK-2300 Copenhagen S, Denmark). It provides similar services and benefits as the ISIC card, and is available in the United States from CIEE.

An **International Youth Hostel Federation** (IYHF) membership card is the key to inexpensive dormitory-style accommodations at more than 6,000 hostel locations in 70 countries around the world. Hostels provide separate sleeping quarters for men and women at rates ranging from $7 to $20 a night per person, and many have family accommodations. Youth Hostel memberships, which are valid for 12 months from the time of purchase, are available in the United States through **American Youth Hostels** (AYH, Box 37613, Washington, DC 20013–7613, tel. 202/783–6161), in Canada through the **Canadian Hostelling Association** (CHA, 1600 James Naismith Dr., Suite 608, Gloucester, Ontario K1B 5N4, tel. 613/748–5638), and in the United Kingdom through the **Youth Hostel Association of England and Wales** (Trevelyan House, 8 St. Stephen's Hill, St. Albans, Herts. AL1 2DY, tel. 0727/55215). By joining one of the national (American, Canadian, or British) Youth Hostel associations, members automatically become part of the International Youth Hostel Federation, and are entitled to special reductions on rail and bus travel around the world. Handbooks listing these special concessions are available from the associations. The cost for a first-year membership is $25 for adults 18–54. Renewal thereafter is $20. For youths (17 and under) the rate is $10, and for seniors (55 and older) the rate is $15. Family membership is available for $35.

Economical **bicycle tours** for small groups of adventurous, energetic students are a popular AYH student travel service. For information on these and other AYH activities and publications, contact the AYH.

Council Travel, a CIEE subsidiary, is the foremost U.S. student travel agency, specializing in low-cost charters and serving as the exclusive U.S. agent for many student airfare bargains and tours. CIEE's 72-page "Student Travel Catalog" and "Council Charter" brochures are available free from any Council Travel office in the United States (enclose $1 postage if ordering by mail). In addition to CIEE headquarters at 205 East 42nd Street (tel. 212/661–1450) and branch office at West 8th Street in New York City, there are Council Travel offices in Arizona (Tempe); California (Berkeley, La Jolla, Long Beach, Los Angeles, San Diego, San Francisco, and Sherman Oaks); Connecticut (New Haven); Washington, DC; Florida (Miami); Georgia (Atlanta); Illinois (Chicago, Evanston); Louisiana (New Orleans); Massachusetts (Amherst, Boston, Cambridge); Michigan (Ann Arbor); Minnesota (Minneapolis); North Carolina (Durham); Ohio (Columbus); Oregon (Portland); Rhode Island (Providence); Texas (Austin, Dallas); Washington (Seattle); and Wisconsin (Milwaukee).

CIEE's **Work Abroad Department** (206 E. 42nd St., New York, NY 10017, tel. 212/661–1414, ext. 1130) arranges paid and voluntary work experiences overseas for up to six months. CIEE also sponsors study programs in Europe, Latin America, Asia, and Australia, and produces several books of interest to the student traveler. These include *Work, Study, Travel Abroad: The Whole World Handbook* ($12.95 plus $1.50 book-rate postage or $3 first-class postage); *Volunteer! The Comprehensive Guide to Voluntary Service in the U.S. and Abroad* ($8.95 plus $1.50 book-rate postage or $3 first-class postage); and *The Teenager's Guide to Travel, Study and Adventure Abroad* ($11.95 plus $1.50 book-rate postage or $3 first-class postage).

The Information Center at the **Institute of International Education (IIE,** 809 UN Plaza, New York, NY 10017, tel. 212/984–5413) has reference books, foreign-university catalogs, study-abroad brochures, and other materials that may be consulted free. It is open weekdays 10–4 and closed on holidays.

In Greece Students receive reduced-price admission to most festivals, theaters, and artistic events in Greece. For information on discount travel, tours, and accommodations, contact **International Student and Youth Travel Service** (ISYTS Ltd., 11 Nikis St., 2nd floor, 10557 Athens, tel. 01/322–1267 or 01/323–3767; open weekdays 9–5, Sat. 9–1).

Traveling with Children

Greek parents, who dote on their children to the point of spoiling them, believe this is the natural order of things: You marry, have children, then shower them with attention. They will dote on your children, too, if you take them along. Couples traveling without children, on the other hand, are likely to be interrogated: How many do you have at home? When do you expect your first child? Despite this fondness for children, organized child-care services are scarce. You'll have to make arrangements for special activities and baby-sitting on an ad hoc basis.

Publications *Family Travel Times* is a newsletter published 10 times a year by **TWYCH** (Travel With Your Children, 45 W. 18th St., 7th Floor Tower, New York, NY 10011, tel. 212/206–0688). A one-year subscription costs $35 and includes access to back issues. The organization also offers a free phone-in service with advice and information on specific destinations.

Great Vacations with Your Kids, by Dorothy Jordan and Marjorie Cohen, offers complete advice on planning your trip with children, from toddlers to teens ($12.95, E.P. Dutton, 375 Hudson St., New York, NY 10014, tel. 212/366–2000).

Kids and Teens in Flight, a useful brochure about children flying alone, is available from the U.S. Department of Transportation. To order a free copy, call 202/366–2220.

Innocents Abroad: Traveling with Kids in Europe, by Valerie Wolf Deutsch and Laura Sutherland, is a new guide to child- and teen-friendly activities, food, and transportation in Britain and on the Continent, with individual sections on each country ($15.95 paperback, New American Library, Penguin USA, 375 Hudson St., New York, NY 10014, tel. 212/366–2000).

Traveling with Children—and Enjoying It: "Impossible!" you say? Maybe, but this book offers tips on how to cut costs, keep kids busy, eat out, reduce jet lag, and pack properly ($11.95, Globe Pequot Press, Box Q, Chester, CT 06412).

Getting There All children, including infants, must have a valid passport for foreign travel. Family passports are no longer issued. On international flights, children under two not occupying a seat pay 10% of the adult fare. Various discounts apply to children ages 2–12, so check with your airline.

Regulations about infant travel on airplanes are in the process of changing. Until they do, however, if you want to be sure your infant is secure, you must bring your own infant car seat and buy a separate ticket. Check with the airline in advance to be sure your seat meets the required standard. If possible, reserve a seat behind one of the plane's bulkheads, where there's usually more legroom and enough space to fit a bassinet (which is available from the airlines). The booklet *Child/Infant Safety Seats Acceptable for Use in Aircraft* is available from the Federal Aviation Administration (APA-200, Independence Ave. SW, Washington, DC 20591, tel. 202/267–3479). If you opt to hold your baby on your lap, do so with the infant outside the seat belt. When reserving tickets, also ask about special children's meals or snacks. The February 1990 and 1992 issues of *Family Travel Times* include TWYCH's *Airline Guide*, which contains a rundown of the children's services offered by 46 different airlines.

Home Exchange   Exchanging homes is a surprisingly inexpensive way to enjoy a vacation abroad, especially if you plan a lengthy visit. The largest home-exchange company, **Intervac U.S./International Home Exchange** (Box 590504, San Francisco, CA 94159, tel. 415/435–3497 or 800/756–4663), publishes three directories a year. The $45 membership entitles you to one listing and all three directories (there is an additional charge for postage). Photos of your property cost an additional $11, and listing a second home costs $10.

Loan-a-Home (2 Park La., Apt. 6E, Mount Vernon, NY 10552, tel. 914/664–7640), which publishes two worldwide directories and two supplements a year, is popular with academics on sabbatical, with businesspeople on temporary assignments, and retirees looking for a home base from which to explore. Although there's no membership fee or charge for listing your home, one directory and a supplement cost $35; both directories and supplements, $45.

Vacation Exchange Club (Box 820, Halweiwa, HI 96712, tel. 800/638–3841) specializes in both international and domestic home exchanges. The club publishes four directories a year, and updated late listings throughout the year. Annual membership, which includes your listing in one book, a newsletter, and copies of all publications (mailed first class), is $50.

Apartment/   **Villas International** (605 Market St., Suite 510, San Francisco,
Villa Rentals   CA 94105, tel. 415/281–0910 or 800/221–2260) has houses, apartments, villas, and cottages to rent in a variety of towns, cities, and resort areas.

Twelve Islands and Beyond (5431 MacArthur Blvd., Washington, DC 20016, tel. 202/537–3550) offers villa accommodations in many parts of Greece, from Athens to the islands and remote parts of the Peloponnese. Minimum stay is four or five nights.

Hotels   At the **Best Western** hotels (reservations tel. 800/528–1234) in Athens, Olympia, Tinos, Ayios Constantinos, Arahova, and Glyfada, one child under 12 may stay free when sharing a room with two paying adults. There is an extra charge if a rollaway bed is needed. The **Hilton** hotels (reservations tel. 800/445–8667) in Athens and Corfu allow one child of any age to stay free in his parents' room. They also maintain lists of baby-sitters. **Club Med** (reservations tel. 800/258–2633) operates recreational "mini clubs" for children (activities include swimming and other water sports, games, and arts and crafts) at its resorts in Kos, Gregolimano, and Olympia.

Check with concierges and tourist offices for information about baby-sitting. Many large hotels have services. You can also call the **Pan-Athenian Union of Baby-Sitters** (Glafkonos 5, Omonia, tel. 01/361–1685 or 01/363–5798), but you should give two to three days' notice. The basic charge is 1,000 dr. per hour.

Hints for Disabled Travelers

Handicapped visitors to Greece will probably find it easier to manage in the modern resorts and hotels than in villages and islands. Many cruise ships are equipped to accommodate disabled people, but access to archaeological sites can present some difficulty. Public transportation is generally crowded, and few special provisions are available. Traveling with an able-bodied companion or joining a group tour is advisable. For information on such tours contact **Lavinia Tours** (101 Egnatias St., Thessaloniki 54635), **Catholic Travel Office** (4701 Willard Ave., Suite 226, Chevy Chase, MD 20815, tel. 301/564–1904), and **Arista Travel and Yachting Corp.** (251–16 Northern Blvd., Little Neck, NY 11363, tel. 718/224–9691).

The **Information Center for Individuals with Disabilities** (Fort Point Pl., 1st floor, 27-43 Wormwood St., Boston, MA 02210, voice and TDD, tel. 617/727–5540) offers useful problem-solving assistance, including lists of travel agents who specialize in tours for the disabled. The center also publishes two fact sheets, "Tips on Planning a Vacation" and "Tour Operators and Travel Agencies." Enclose $5 (to cover postage) for each sheet.

Moss Rehabilitation Hospital Travel Information Service (1200 W. Tabor Rd., Philadelphia, PA 19141, tel. 215/456–9603; TDD 215/456–9602) provides information for a small fee on tourist sights, transportation, and accommodations in destinations around the world. They also provide toll-free telephone numbers for airlines with special lines for the hard of hearing.

Travel Industry and Disabled Exchange (TIDE, 5435 Donna Ave., Tarzana, CA 91356, tel. 818/368–5648) publishes a quarterly newsletter and a directory of travel agencies and tours catering specifically to the disabled. The annual fee is $15.

Mobility International USA (Box 3551, Eugene, OR 97403, voice and TDD tel. 503/343–1284) is an internationally affiliated organization with 500 members. For a $20 annual fee, it coordinates exchange programs for disabled people around the world and offers information on accommodations and organized study programs. The organization also publishes *A World of Options for the 90s*, a guide to international exchange and travel for people with disabilities ($16, including postage).

The **Society for the Advancement of Travel for the Handicapped** (SATH, 347 5th Ave., Suite 610, New York, NY 10016, tel. 212/447–7288, fax 212/725–8252) provides access information and lists of tour operators specializing in travel for the disabled. Annual membership costs $45 or $25 for students and seniors. Send $2 and a stamped, self-addressed envelope for information on a specific destination.

Publications The **Itinerary** (Box 2012, Bayonne, NJ 07002, tel. 201/858–3400) is a bimonthly travel magazine for the disabled. Call for a subscription ($10 for one year, $20 for two); it's not available in bookstores. **Twin Peaks Press** (Box 129, Vancouver, WA 98666, tel. 206/694–2462 or 800/637–2256 for orders only) specializes in books for the disabled. *Travel for the Disabled* offers helpful hints as well as a comprehensive list of guidebooks and facilities geared to the disabled. *The Directory of Travel Agencies for the Disabled* lists more than 350 agencies throughout the world. *Wheelchair Vagabound* and *The Directory of Accessible Van Rentals* provide information for the worldwide RV/camping traveler. Twin Peaks also offers a "Traveling Nurse's Network," which provides registered nurses to accompany and assist disabled travelers.

Hotels The **Intercontinental Hotel** (reservations tel. 800/327–0200) in Athens has a number of rooms specifically adapted for handicapped guests. The **Hilton** hotels (reservations tel. 800/445–8667) in Corfu and Canoni are equipped with wheelchair ramps, extra-wide doors, and accessible bathrooms. **Club Med** (reservations 800/258–2633) has facilities accessible to the disabled at its "Olympie" resort in Pyrgos Ilias, near Olympia.

Hints for Older Travelers

Special consideration and accommodation for the older visitor to Greece may be more forthcoming at higher-priced hotels and with tour groups. In general, remember that some of the archaeological sites are on steep or rugged terrain, and in summer a hat and plenty of water are mandatory. Those with respiratory problems should avoid Athens in August.

The **American Association of Retired Persons** (AARP, 601 E St. NW, Washington, DC 20049, tel. 202/434–2277) has two programs for independent travelers: the Purchase Privilege Program, which offers discounts on hotels, airfare, car rentals, RV rentals, and sightseeing; and the AARP Motoring Plan, provided by Amoco, which furnishes emergency road-service aid and trip-routing information for an annual fee of $39.95 per person or couple. AARP members must be 50 years or older; annual dues are $8 per person or couple. The AARP also arranges group tours, cruises, and apartment living in Europe through **American Express Vacations** (400 Pinnacle Way, Suite 450, Norcross, GA 30071, tel. 800/927-0111, for cruise information tel. 800/745–4567; TDD 800/659–5678) and through travel agents and American Express offices.

If you're allowed to use an AARP or other senior-citizen identification card to obtain a reduced hotel rate, mention it at the time you make your reservation rather than when you check out. At participating restaurants, show your card to the maître d' before you're seated, because discounts may be limited to certain menus, days, or hours. When renting a car, be sure to ask about special promotional rates which might offer greater savings than the available discount.

Elderhostel (75 Federal St., 3rd floor, Boston, MA 02110, tel. 617/426–7788) is an innovative, educational program for people 60 and older. Participants live in dorms on some 1,200 campuses around the world. Mornings are devoted to lectures and seminars; afternoons to sightseeing and field trips. Fees for two- to three-week trips—including room, board, tuition, and round-trip transportation—range from $1,800 to $4,500.

National Council of Senior Citizens (1331 F St. NW, Washington, DC 20004, tel. 202/347–8800) is a nonprofit advocacy group with some 5,000 local clubs across the United States. Annual membership is $12 per person or couple; people of any age can belong. Members receive a monthly newspaper and an ID card for reduced-rate hotels and car rentals.

Mature Outlook (6001 N. Clark St., Chicago, IL 60660, tel. 800/336–6330), a subsidiary of Sears Roebuck and Co., is a travel club for people over 50 that provides hotel and motel discounts and publishes a bimonthly newsletter. Annual membership is $9.95; there are 800,000 members. Instant membership is available at Sears stores and participating Holiday Inns.

Saga International Holidays (120 Boylston St., Boston, MA 02116, tel. 800/343–0273) specializes in group travel for people over 60. A selection of variously priced tours allows you to choose the package that meets your needs.

Publications · *The International Health Guide for Senior Citizen Travelers*, by W. Robert Lange, MD, is available for $4.95 plus $1.50 for shipping, from Pilot Books (103 Cooper St., Babylon, NY 11702, tel. 515/422–2225).

Further Reading

C. M. Woodhouse's *Modern Greece: A Short History* succinctly covers the development of modern Greece, from the fall of the Byzantine Empire, to the War of Independence and the monarchy, to the recent struggle between the socialist PASOK party and the conservative New Democracy party. The more recent *A Traveller's History of Greece* by Timothy Boatswain (Interlink Books) may be easier to find in the United States. *Flight of Ikaros* by Kevin Andrews is the suspenseful account of travel in the Greek countryside during the chaotic period of civil war that followed the Second World War. Another powerful story based on the tragic events that took place during this time is Nicholas Gage's *Eleni*.

The idyllic youth of naturalist Gerald Durrell on the island of Corfu is recalled in many of his books, such as *My Family and Other Animals*, which are written with an unpretentious, precise style in a slightly humorous vein and are underrated as works of literature. Henry Miller's *The Colossus of Maroussi*, an enjoyable seize-the-day-as-the-Greeks-do paean that veers from the profound to the superficial, sometimes verging on hysteria, is the product of a trip Miller took to Greece (during which he spent some time with Gerald Durrell's brother Lawrence) that caused in him something like a religious conversion. The wonderful *Zorba the Greek* by Nikos Kazantzakis, Greece's premier writer, captures the strengths and weaknesses and the color of traditional Greek culture. Other classics by Kazantzakis are *Christ Recrucified* and *The Odyssey*.

Some people like to go back to the classics while in Greece. Try either Robert Fitzgerald's or Richmond Lattimore's translations of the *Iliad* and *Odyssey* of Homer, done in verse, unlike the clumsy prose translations you probably read in school. Read the *Iliad* as a pacifist work exposing the uselessness of warfare; read the *Odyssey* keeping in mind the relationships between men and women as illustrated by Odysseus and Penelope, Circe, and Calypso. Lattimore also translated Greece's early lyric poets, Sappho and her lesser-known contemporaries, in a collection titled *Greek Lyric Poetry*. Aristophanes' play *The Wasps* is one of the funniest pieces of literature ever written. Although it isn't light reading, Thucydides' *Pelopon-*

nesian War details the long struggle of Athens and Sparta, fighting openly and through third parties, for and against democracy and autocracy. The events of the past 50 years and those of 2,500 years ago aren't so different.

Arriving and Departing

All transatlantic flights from the United States and Canada arrive in Athens, whose Ellinikon Airport has two terminals. The west terminal serves **Olympic** international and domestic flights only; the east terminal is used by all foreign carriers. There are also flights to Thessaloniki and Corfu from Europe.

From North America by Plane

There are three types of flights: nonstop—no plane changes, no stops; direct—no plane changes but one or more stops; and connecting—two or more planes and one or more stops. The nonstop flying time to Athens from New York is about nine hours; the return flight takes 10 hours 20 minutes.

Airports and Airlines
Olympic Airways (tel. 212/838–3600 or 800/223–1226) has eight nonstop flights to Athens from Kennedy airport in New York each week, two direct flights that serve Boston, two from Chicago via New York, and two flights per week each from Montréal and Toronto.

Delta (tel. 800/241–4141) flies via Frankfurt daily (except Tues. and Sun.) from Kennedy airport in New York. **United** (tel. 800/241–6522) has daily flights to Athens via Paris. **KLM** (tel. 800/777–5553) flies several times a week from Vancouver, Calgary, Toronto, Montréal, and Halifax to Amsterdam and from there to Athens.

Enjoying the Flight
Because the air on a plane is dry, it helps to drink a lot of nonalcoholic beverages in flight; alcohol contributes to jet lag, as does eating heavy meals on board. Feet swell at high altitudes, so it's a good idea to remove your shoes at the beginning of your flight. Sleepers usually prefer window seats to curl up against; those who like to move about the cabin ask for aisle seats. Bulkhead seats (located in the front row of each cabin) and some seats near the service pantries have more legroom, but seat trays are attached rather awkwardly to the arms of the seat rather than to the back of the seat ahead. Generally bulkhead seats are reserved for the disabled, the elderly, or people traveling with babies.

Discount Flights
The major airlines offer a range of tickets that can differ (for the price of any given seat) by more than 300%, depending on the day of purchase. As a rule, the farther in advance you buy the ticket, the less expensive it is and the greater the penalty (up to 100%) for canceling. Check with airlines for details.

APEX (advance purchase) tickets on the major airlines carry certain restrictions: They must be bought in advance (usually 21 days), they restrict your travel, usually with a minimum stay of seven days and a maximum of 90, and they also penalize you for changes—voluntary or not—in your travel plans. But if you can work around these drawbacks (and most travelers can), they are among the best-value fares available, although not necessarily the lowest.

Travelers willing to put up with some restrictions and inconveniences, in exchange for a substantially reduced airfare, may be interested in flying as air couriers. A person who agrees to be a courier must accompany shipments between designated points. There are several sources of information on courier deals: Send $5 and a self-addressed, stamped, business-size envelope to **Pacific Data Sales Publishing** (2554 Lincoln Blvd., Suite 275-F, Marina Del Rey, CA 90291) for a telephone directory listing courier companies by the cities to which they fly; send $15.95 (includes postage and handling) to **Guide**, Box 2394, Lake Oswego, OR 97035, for "A Simple Guide to Courier Travel," or call 800/755–4483 or 503/684–0778; contact **Now Voyager**, 74 Varick St., Suite 307, New York, NY 10013, tel. 212/431–1616; or **Courier Travel Service**, 530 Central Ave., Cedarhurst, NY 11516, tel. 516/374–2299 or 800/922–2359.

Charter flights offer the lowest fares but often depart only on certain days, and seldom on time. Though you may be able to arrive at one city and return from another, you may lose all or most of your money if you cancel your trip. Don't sign up for a charter flight unless you've checked with a travel agency about the reputation of the packager. It's particularly important to know the packager's policy concerning refunds should a flight be canceled; some travel agents recommend that travelers purchase trip-cancellation insurance if they plan to book charter flights. One of the most popular charter operators to Europe is **Council Charter** (205 E. 42nd St., New York, NY 10017, tel. 212/661–0311 or 800/800–8222), a division of the Council on International Educational Exchange (CIEE). **Homeric** (55 E. 59th St., 17th floor, New York, NY 10022, tel. 800/223–5570) specializes in low-cost New York–Athens fares. Other companies advertise in Sunday travel sections of newspapers.

Somewhat more expensive—but up to 50% below the cost of APEX fares—are tickets purchased through consolidators, companies that buy blocks of tickets on scheduled airlines and sell them at wholesale prices. Tickets are subject to availability, so passengers must generally have flexible travel schedules. Here again, you may lose all or most of your money if you change plans, but at least you will be on a regularly scheduled flight with less risk of cancellation than on a charter. As an added precaution, you may want to purchase trip-cancellation insurance. Once you've made your reservation, call the airline to confirm it. Among the best-known consolidators are **UniTravel** (Box 12485, St. Louis, MO 63132, tel. 314/569–2501 or 800/325–2222) and **Access International** (101 W. 31st St., Suite 1104, New York, NY 10001, tel. 212/465–0707 or 800/825–3633). Others advertise in newspaper Sunday travel sections.

Another option is to join a travel club that offers special discounts to its members. Several such organizations are **Discount Travel International** (114 Forrest Ave., Narberth, PA 19072, tel. 215/668–7184); **Moment's Notice** (425 Madison Ave., New York, NY 10017, tel. 212/486–0503); **Travelers Advantage** (CUC Travel Service, 49 Music Sq. W, Nashville, TN 37203, tel. 800/548–1116); and **Worldwide Discount Travel Club** (1674 Meridian Ave., Miami Beach, FL 33139, tel. 305/534–2082). Compare these cut-rate tickets with APEX tickets on the major airlines.

Smoking If cigarette smoke bothers you, ask for a seat far from the smoking section. It is best to request a nonsmoking seat at the time that you book your ticket. If a U.S. airline representative tells you there are no seats available in the nonsmoking section, insist on one: Department of Transportation regulations require U.S. flag carriers to find seats for all nonsmokers on the day of the flight, provided they meet check-in time restrictions.

From the United Kingdom by Plane, Car, Ferry, Train, and Bus

By Plane British Airways and Olympic Airways serve Athens with four flights daily from London's Heathrow Airport. The flying time is about 3 hours 45 minutes. There are also connecting flights from Aberdeen, Belfast, Birmingham, Bristol, Edinburgh, Glasgow, Leeds, Liverpool, Manchester, Newcastle, and Southampton (via Heathrow or Amsterdam), some stopping in Thessaloniki.

A large number of charter operators sell seats on flights from London Gatwick airport to a wide range of destinations in Greece including Athens, Thessaloniki, Corfu, Kefalonia, Zakynthos, Rhodes, Kos, Heraklion, Mykonos, Skiathos, Simos, Mytilini (Lesbos), and Kavala. These services only operate a couple of days a week, usually from May to October. It may be less expensive to book a flight and hotel package and then use the pre-booked accommodation for only part of the time.

By Car and Ferry Driving to Greece from Britain is not recommended. The shortest route (a mere 3,060 kilometers [1,900 miles]) is from Ostend via Frankfurt, Munich, Salzburg, Ljubljana, Beograd and Skopje to the Greek border station of Evzoni. The Balkan chaos makes this route and the more scenic Adriatic highway (which turns inland before Albania and connects with the Greek roads at Niki) equally dangerous. Though it is expensive, you can take a car to Greece (and at the same time greatly reduce your driving and save gasoline and hotel costs) by using the Paris–Milan and Milan–Brindisi car sleeper and then a car ferry to Corfu, Igoumenitsa, or Patras.

There are frequent sailings between Italy and Greece—at least seven a day in summer from Brindisi, two each from Bari and Ancona, one from Otranto, and two–three a week from Trieste; all go to Corfu and/or Igoumenitsa and Patras (three a week call at Kefalonia). There is also one sailing (sometimes more) a week from Venice to Piraeus. Some of the shipping lines are the **Adriatic Ferries, Adriatica, Anek, Fragline, Hellenic Mediterranean, Karageorgis, Marlines, Minoan, Strintzis,** and **Ventouris.**

British Ferries operate a weekly service from Venice to Athens on their luxury car ferry *Orient Express* from May to October. Details from **Orient Express** (Suite 200, Hudson's Place, Victoria Station, London SW1V 1JT, tel. 071/834–8122). Details of the **Adriatica Lines** services from Brindisi to Igoumenitsa and Patras and from Venice to Piraeus can be obtained from the **Sealink Travel Centre** (London SW1V 1JT, tel. 071/828–1940) opposite Platform 2 in Victoria Station. For information on the **Minoan Lines** car ferries between Ancona and Igoumenitsa and Patras contact **P&O European Ferries** (Channel House, Channel View Road, Dover CT17 9TJ, tel. 0304/203–388). Bookings for summer should be made well in advance and reconfirmed shortly before sailing.

By Train Of the two main routes to Greece by train from the United Kingdom, the overland route via Munich, Salzburg, Ljubljana, and Zagreb was essentially closed during 1992 because of the turmoil following the disintegration of Yugoslavia. It is more pleasant in any case to travel through Italy, then go by ferry from Brindisi to Patras in the Peloponnese. In high summer, catch the train from London's Victoria to Dover for the crossing to Calais and the connecting service to Paris Gare du Nord. From there, transfer to the Gare de Lyon for the train that runs via Switzerland to Milan. Switch there and travel through to Brindisi Maritime station, where you connect with the ferry to Patras (17 hrs.), and arrive the following day. From Patras there is bus and train service to Athens (total time London–Athens 2½ days). For planning your rail journey to Greece the Thomas Cook European Timetable is essential. It is available in the United Kingdom from Thomas Cook, Timetable Publishing Office (Box 36, Thorpe Wood, Peterborough, Cambridgeshire PE3 6SB); in the United States from Forsyth Travel Library (Box 2975, Shawnee Mission, KS, 66201–1375, tel. 800/307–7984). For train information, call RailEurope at 914/682–5172.

By Bus You can go from the United Kingdom through the Balkans or via Italy. Both routes are operated by **Eurolines** (52 Grosvenor Gardens, London SW1W OAU, tel. 071/730–0202) and take four days of essentially nonstop traveling. The overland route via Munich and through the Balkans to Thessaloniki and Athens was effectively cut off during 1992 (as was the Hellenic State Railways' bus service that ran from Paris and Dortmund, through the Balkans to Thessaloniki and Athens). The bus trip via Paris and Rome to Brindisi, then by ferry to Patras, and finally by coach to Athens begins at Victoria Coach Station (164 Buckingham Palace Rd.; adult round-trip fare: £206; luggage space is severely restricted).

Cruises

Many travelers with limited time find traveling by boat an ideal way to see Greece's mainland ports and islands. It spares you the planning headaches of solitary island-hopping, when you can be stranded en route, waiting several days for the next ferry. Cruise ships cover great distances at night, leaving days free for exploring, although there's time for only a superficial visit to the ports of call. This overview can be useful to planning a return trip to the more appealing stops. Trips range from a one-day, three-island cruise to 21-day odysseys. Cruises of a week or two can combine Greek ports of call with stops in Turkey, Israel, or Egypt. Passengers are often surprised to find that port taxes and land excursions are not included in the cost of the cruise. The optional land excursions are actually quite reasonable and provide a different perspective from the ports. Cabins usually have two beds, occasionally four, and the most expensive are on the outside. The rare single rooms carry a supplement of at least 50%.

Cruising is a popular way of seeing the Mediterranean countries, and new itineraries are developed each year. Prices vary widely, and it pays to compare. Consult with a reliable agent before choosing, and ask about such specialty cruises as **Epirotiki's** Festival of Music, from Venice to Turkey and Greece, on which classical musicians give concerts on board and at ancient sites; or **Swan Hellenic's** cruises accompanied by expert lecturers and guides. **Cycladic Cruises** (Patission 81 and

Heyden, Athens, tel. 01/883–2111, 01/883–2112, or 01/883–2113, fax 01/822–5132) focuses on shorter cruises, and **Sun Line** is noted for luxury. **Viking Travel** (Filellinon 3, Athens, tel. 01/322–9383) and **Zeus Tours** (Amalias 32, Athens, tel. 01/323–3391) offer packages on smaller boats (36–55 passengers). These agencies can book cruises, or you can apply directly to the lines listed below. The ships named (passenger capacity in parentheses) will cruise the Mediterranean in 1993.

Chandris Fantasy Cruises (tel. 800/423–2100; in Piraeus, 01/412–0932): *Britanis* (926 p), *Amerikanis* (609 p), *Victoria* (548 p), *Azur* (650 p). **Classical Cruises** (tel. 212/794–3200 or 800/252–7745): *Aurora I* (80 p). **Club Med Cruises** (tel. 800/258–2633): *Club Med I* (400 p). **Costa Cruise Lines** (tel. 800/662–6782): *Daphne, EnricoCosta, EugenioCosta, CostaClassica* (1,300 p each), *CostaMarina* (770 p), *CostaRiviera* (974 p). **Cunard Line** (tel. 800/221–4770 or 800/458–9000): *Cunard Princess* (750 p), *Vistafjord* (736 p), *Sea Goddess I* and *II* (116 p each). **Dolphin Hellas Cruises** (tel. 310/544–3551): *Aegean Dolphin* (558 p). **Epirotiki Cruise Lines** (tel. 212/599–1750 or 800/221–2470; in Piraeus, 01/452–6641): *Triton* (706 p), *Odysseus* (452 p), *Pallas Athena* (746 p), *Jason* (278 p), *Neptune* (186 p), *Argonaut* (166 p), *World Renaissance* (536 p). **P & O Cruises** (tel. 800/223–5799): *Ausonia* (600 p). **Princess Cruises** (tel. 800/568–3262): *Star Princess* (1,494 p), *Royal Princess* (1,200 p). **Renaissance Cruises** (tel. 800/525–2450): *Renaissance I–VIII*, eight identical ships (114 p each). **Royal Cruise Line** (tel. 800/792–2992; in CA, 800/227–4534): *Royal Odyssey* (765 p), *Crown Odyssey* (1,054 p). **Royal Viking Line** (tel. 800/422–8000): *Royal Viking Sun* (740 p). **Seabourn Cruise Line** (tel. 800/351–9595): *Seabourn Spirit* (204 p). **Special Expeditions** (tel. 800/527–6298): *Sea Cloud* (70 p). **Starlauro Cruises** (tel. 310/544–3551): *Achille* (788 p). **Sun Line Cruises** (tel. 212/397–6400 or 800/872–6400): *Stella Solaris* (620 p), *Stella Oceanis* (300 p), *Stella Maris* (180 p). **Swan Hellenic Cruises** (tel. 617/266–7465 or 800/426–5492): *Orpheus* (250 p). **Windstar Cruises** (tel. 800/258–7245): *Windspirit* (148 p).

Staying in Greece

Getting Around

By Plane Domestic air travel in Greece is provided only by **Olympic Airways** (tel. 01/926–9111 or 01/966–6666, fax 01/921–6087), which operates out of Athens's West Terminal. There is service to Alexandroupoli, Ioannina, Kastoria, Kavala, Kozani, Larissa, and Thessaloniki, all on the mainland; to Kalamata in the Peloponnese; to the Aegean islands: Karpathos, Kythira, Crete (Hania, Heraklion, and Sitia), Chios, Kos, Lesbos, Limnos, Leros, Milos, Mykonos, Naxos, Paros, Rhodes, Samos, Skiathos, Syros, and Santorini; Corfu, Kefalonia, and Zakynthos in the Ionian Sea.

The frequency of flights varies according to the time of year, and it is essential to book well in advance for summer or for festivals and holidays. Domestic flights are a good deal for many destinations. In early 1992 the one-way Athens–Rhodes fare was 15,300 dr.; to Corfu, 13,600 dr.; and to Heraklion, 12,200 dr. Unless the flight is part of an international journey the baggage allowance is only 15 kilos (33 lbs.) per passenger.

By Train The limited Greek rail system has a narrow-gauge line that covers the Peloponnese, in a circuit from Athens through Corinth, Patras, Pyrgos (Olympia), Kalamata, Megalopolis, Tripolis, and Argos (Nauplion). The fares are reasonable, and trains offer a good alternative to long drives or bus rides. The leisurely Peloponnesian train is a pleasant way to see southern Greece, but the Patras–Athens leg can be crowded during the high season because of tourists arriving in Patras from Italy. The assigned seating of first class may be a good idea at such times.

By Bus Organized bus tours can be booked together with hotel reservations by your travel agent. Many tour operators have offices in and around Syntagma in Athens, including American Express (Syntagma), CHAT (4 Stadiou St.), Helios Tours (4 Stadiou St.), and Key Tours (2 Ermou St.). Bus tours often depart from Syntagma or adjacent streets.

Greece has an extensive passenger bus service (KTEL) that consists of regional associations of bus operators. The characteristic green-and-yellow buses seem to travel to even the smallest villages. Frequencies vary, but once a day is the minimum, with hourly service to major cities. The fares are very low.

By Taxi "On our three-week vacation, we were faced with some form of overcharging *every other day*. Taxi drivers were the worst—about half tried or succeeded to charge more. We found that being firm with the price we thought appropriate, combined with a demand for them to call the police, usually worked." So wrote a Fodor's reader in 1991. In Greece, as everywhere, unscrupulous taxi drivers will try to take advantage of out-of-towners or foreigners. Rather than memorize all the allowable surcharges, you might ask your hotel concierge or owner before engaging a taxi what the fare to your destination ought to be. You are more likely to be overcharged in Athens and vicinity than elsewhere, especially when traveling to and from airport terminals. It should cost no more than 1,200 dr.–1,500 dr. from the airport to city center. If you feel you are being overcharged, check with someone at your destination before paying. Asking for a signed receipt, including the driver's number, may not be a bad idea if the fare seems excessive. As a last resort contact the tourist police (tel. 171 in Athens).

By Car Regular registration papers and an international third-party insurance certificate (green card) are required, in addition to a driver's license (American, EC, or international). An entry card, valid for four months, is issued free. The car may be kept in Greece for a further eight months without payment of import duty, provided a guarantee for payment is given by a Greek national and provided it can be proved (with receipts of foreign-currency transactions) that the car's driver is a tourist and not working in Greece. Monthly road tax must also then be paid. Full insurance, including coverage against collision with an uninsured motorist, is recommended. Accidents must be reported (something Greek motorists often fail to do) before the insurance companies consider claims.

Local car-rental agencies can be reached as follows:

Avis (Athens East and West Airport, tel. 01/322–4951 or 01/322–4955), **Budget** (Athens East and West Airport, tel. 01/961–3634 or 01/984–5538), **Hertz** (Athens East and West Airport, tel. 01/961–3625 or 01/981–3701), **Interrent-Europcar** (Athens

East and West Airport, tel. 01/961–3424 or 01/982–9565), and **Thrifty** (20 Hatzichristou and Syngrou, Athens, tel. 01/923–8842 or 01/902–8220). *See also* Renting and Leasing Cars, *above*.

Car Ferries On the west coast the local ferry between the island of Corfu and Igoumenitsa runs many times daily in each direction. The coastal highway leads directly to Preveza and the ferry across the strait to Actium. You go via Missolonghi to the Rion–Antirion ferry, which connects Epirus with the northwestern Peloponnese. Ferries go frequently from Piraeus (the port of Athens) to Methana and to the islands of Aegina and Poros in the Saronic Gulf. From Piraeus there's service to the Cyclades and to Hania and Heraklion on Crete. Shorter crossings to the Cyclades can be made from the other side of Attica, from Rafina and from Lavrio, to Kea and Kythnos. You can go Piraeus–Kos–Rhodes; Piraeus–Chios–Lesbos; Piraeus–Samos. There are crossings to Turkey from Lesbos to Dikeli, from Chios to Cesme, and from Samos to Kusadasi.

Road Conditions and Traffic The many motorcycles and scooters weaving through traffic and the aggressive attitude of fellow motorists can make driving in Greece's large cities less than enjoyable—and the life of a pedestrian actively dangerous (Greek drivers seem to regard pedestrians as expendable nuisances; people are regularly killed in crosswalks). In the countryside, off the toll roads, traffic is light, and driving is more pleasant but difficult; highway route numbers are largely nonexistent. The **Automobile Touring Club of Greece** (ELPA, Athens Tower, 2 Messogion St.) has a special telephone line for tourist information (tel. 174). To reduce traffic noise, congestion, and air pollution severe restrictions are placed on driving cars in central Athens. Cars with license plates ending in odd numbers are prohibited on one day, those with even numbers on the following day. This regulation applies to visiting motorists only after they have been in Greece for 40 days.

Rules of the Road International road signs are in use throughout Greece. You drive on the right, pass on the left, and yield right-of-way to all vehicles approaching from the right (except on posted main highways). Speed limits are posted: 30–50 kilometers per hour (18–31 miles per hour) in built-up areas; 110 kph (68 mph) maximum on the Patras–Corinth–Athens–Thessaloniki–Evzoni toll road; 100 kph (63 mph) on all other roads, unless lower limits are posted. In many streets, alternate-side-of-the-street parking rules are in effect. Although it's illegal, sidewalk parking is common. The ways of the police are unpredictable; they are empowered to impose on-the-spot fines but do so rarely. The use of seat belts is compulsory.

Breakdowns You must put out a triangular danger sign if you have a breakdown. Roving repair trucks, manned by skilled ELPA mechanics, patrol the major highways (tel. 104); the service is free, but a tip is expected. Road-service addresses and telephone numbers are: **Athens** (2–4 Messogion St., tel. 104, 01/779–1615, or for information 174; 6 Amerikis St., tel. 01/363–8632), **Heraklion** (Knossou Ave. and G. Papandreou St., tel. 081/289440), **Patras** (Astingos and 127 Korinthou Sts., tel. 061/425422 or 061/425141), and **Volos** (2 Eolidos St., tel. 0421/25001).

By Hydrofoil The Flying Dolphin hydrofoils carry passengers from Zea in Piraeus to the Saronic islands and eastern Peloponnesian ports, including Aegina, Hermioni, Hydra, Kyparissi, Kythira, Leonidion, Methana, Monemvassia, Nauplion, Neapolis, Poros, Porto Heli, and Spetses. In summer there is additional service. These boats are somewhat pricey, but fast and fun to ride on. Tickets can be purchased through authorized agents or at 8 Themistokleous St., Piraeus, tel. 01/452–7107.

Telephones

Local Calls The Greek telephone company, the OTE (pronounced "oh-tay"), has some pay phones on the streets of larger towns, but most are at the local OTE office. Pay phones at hotels and kiosks cost more to use than those of the OTE, but for local calls (about 10 dr.) their convenience may outweigh the cost.

In general, beware of doing business over the phone in Greece —the lines always seem to be busy, and English-speaking operators and clerks are few. You may also find they are too busy to address your problem—the independent-minded Greeks are not very service-conscious. It is far better to develop a relationship with someone, for example a travel agent, to get information about train schedules and the like.

International Calls To call Greece, the country code is 30; from Greece the U.S. country code is 1. For long distance calls from Greece it's best to avoid the kiosk and hotel phones and use the metered phones at the OTE offices, at which you can call collect, or use a calling card. Both AT&T and MCI have direct-calling programs overseas that put you in touch with English-speaking operators and have free customer-service numbers. For AT&T's **USA Direct** service from Greece, dial 00-800-1311; customer service 412/553–7458, ext. 314 collect. There's a $2.50 surcharge, $5.75 for collect calls, $2.17 for the first minute, and $1.22 each minute thereafter. For MCI's **Call USA,** dial 00–800–1211; customer service 00800/12–2007. There's a $2 surcharge, $5 if collect, $2.16 first minute, $1.21 each minute thereafter. For more information within the United States: for AT&T dial 800/874–4000, for MCI dial 800/444–3333.

Information and Emergency Numbers In large towns the OTE office may be open 24 hours a day and have a complete set of telephone books you can consult. In the greater Athens area the following numbers help with information 24 hours a day (English spoken): **police** 100, **ambulance** 150, **first aid** 166, **SOS support line** 644–2213, **emergency road service** 174. The **Tourist Police** (171 in Athens, 922–777 outside Athens) can provide general information, help in emergencies, and can mediate disputes.

Mail

Postal Rates Post offices in large cities are open Monday–Saturday 7:30 AM–8 PM, elsewhere they may close at 2:30 and be closed on Saturday. At press time airmail letters and postcards to the United States cost 100 drachmas (80 dr. to the United Kingdom).

Receiving Mail Mail service in Greece is not the fastest, but it is generally reliable. Mail marked "post restante" sent to post offices in Greece will be held until picked up by the addressee, who must show identification. Clients of American Express (i.e. card holders and those with Amex travel vouchers, tickets, or traveler's checks) can have mail (but not registered or certified mail or parcels) sent to them c/o American Express offices abroad. It can be collected in person with identification and will be returned after 30 days. A forwarding address can be left for a nominal charge. Amex offices in Greece providing this service are in Athens, Corfu, Heraklion, Mykonos, Patras, Rhodes, and Santorini.

Keeping in Touch

Many English-language newspapers are available in Greece and are sold at kiosks in major cities and at some tourist shops. Radio and television broadcasts in English include the Greek ERT 1 network (weather and news bulletin at 7:40 AM) and Armed Forces Radio, which broadcasts on AM 1484 and AM 1594 around the clock, with news and weather on the hour. Some luxury hotels have cable television.

Tipping

How much to tip in Greece, especially at restaurants, is confusing. By law a 15% service charge is figured into the price of a meal (menus sometimes list entrées with and without service, to let you know their net cost—not to imply you have a choice of how much to pay), so, technically, you don't have to leave any additional tip. If the service was poor or the waiter rude (very unlikely), you are not obligated to do so, but if the service was good, it's customary to reward it by leaving 5%–10% more. At cafés, after an ouzo or Greek coffee, you can just leave the change if it's around 10%; i.e. 20 dr.–30 dr. per drink. The same is true for taxis; if the fare was 270 dr., give 300.

The appropriate tip for maid service at your hotel will depend, of course, on the quality of the service and the quality of the hotel. A service charge is included in the price of the room, but you might consider leaving an additional 100 dr. per person per night, or more for an extended stay. Porters, found only at the more expensive hotels, will be very pleased if you give them 100 dr. per bag, and hatcheck persons would like the same amount. For restroom attendants 20 dr.–50 dr. is appropriate.

Opening and Closing Times

Banks Banks are normally open Monday–Thursday 8–2, Friday 8–1:30. The Credit Bank Exchange Center (Syntagma Square, tel. 01/322–0141 and Kifissia, tel. 01/671–2838), the Ionian Bank of Greece in the Hilton Hotel (tel. 01/722–1182), and the National Bank of Greece (tel. 01/323–6481) are open Friday until at least 7 PM, and the Credit Bank Syntagma and the National Bank have Saturday and Sunday hours. Most foreign banks stay open until 2. Hotels and tourist shops also will cash traveler's checks on weekends.

Museums and Sights The days and hours for museums and sights vary; they are usually open daily 8:30–1 except one weekday, although in summer important museums stay open until 7 weekdays and until 6 on weekends, and sights may stay open as late as 7. On major holidays, sights and museums are closed; on minor holidays they may have Sunday hours or close at 12:30. In Athens, for instance, the Byzantine Museum, National Archaeological Museum, and Agora Museum are closed Monday; the Benaki

Museum is closed Tuesday; and the Goulandris Museum of Cycladic Art is closed Tuesday and Sunday. Admission to most museums is free on Sunday.

Shops Nominally shops are open Monday and Wednesday 9–5; Tuesday, Thursday, and Friday 10–7; and Saturday 8:30–3:30. In smaller towns, however, shops are likely to stay closed after lunch on Monday and Wednesday. In the Plaka, Athens's popular tourist bazaar, shops are open until about 9 PM daily, or later in summer.

Shopping

Many of the goods tourists purchase in Greece are inspired by the country's ancient civilization. Reproductions of early bronzes, Cycladic figurines, and Geometric, Corinthian, and Athenian vase paintings are ubiquitous. Some are poorly made and some feature rude subjects, but others are charming and even of museum quality. Leather bags and sandals and heavy wool sweaters are popular; some may be good buys, but some may soon fall apart. Take your time and inspect the seams and stitches before buying.

Objects made of the fragrant olive wood—from worry beads to bowls and sculptures—can be very attractive. Lightweight sun dresses may look wonderful on the hanger in a store, but they're often made of flimsy fabrics—beware their transparency in the bright Greek sunlight. Also, tourist-trade T-shirts shrink considerably when washed.

Wooden bread stamps and hand guards used in harvesting grain are among the more easily found items of Greek folk culture. Old jewelry and textiles, which are getting rather expensive, can still be a good deal and an adventure to track down.

Sports and Outdoor Activities

Once content to put on weight and slide into middle age without a fight, Greeks are now on the fitness trail. Gymnasiums, aerobics studios, and martial arts schools can be found in cities and larger towns. Water sports, skiing, and mountaineering are gaining in popularity. Soccer is king of the spectator sports in Greece, and the World Cup brings the country to a standstill.

Bicycling is impossible on the crowded city streets, although some use bikes to go to and from work in smaller towns. For recreational biking programs contact the **Greek Cycling Federation** (28 Bouboulinas St., tel. 01/883–1414) in Athens.

For information on **sailing** and **boating** in Greece contact the **Hellenic Yachting Federation** (7 Akti Navarchou Koundourioti, Piraeus 18534, tel. 01/413–7351), the **Sailing Federation** (15A Xenofondos St., Athens, tel. 01/323–5560), and the **Rowing Federation** (34 Voukourestiou St., Athens, tel. 01/361–2109). The International Aegean Sailing Week, held in July, is the most important regatta in Greece—information and entry applications can be obtained from the **Hellenic Offshore Racing Club** (4 Papadiamanti St., Mikros Limin, Piraeus, tel. 01/412–3357).

Other **water sports** in Greece include sailboarding (**Hellenic Wind-Surfing Association,** 7 Filellinon St., Athens, tel. 01/323–0068), waterskiing (**Water Skiing Federation,** 32 Stournara St.,

Athens, tel. 01/523–1875), and fishing (**Amateur Anglers' and Maritime Sports Club**, Motsopoulou Quay [Akti], Piraeus, tel. 01/451–5731). Scuba diving is restricted, in an effort to protect Greece's underwater archaeological remains. Areas where limited diving is permitted include Corfu, Mykonos, and Rhodes (contact the Greek National Tourist Organization or the **Hellenic Federation of Submarine Activities**, Ayios Kosmas, Elliniko, tel. 01/981–9961).

Camping in Greece can be a family affair at a seaside National Tourist Organization campground, with amenities like showers, laundry facilities, playgrounds, snack bars, etc. The country offers plenty of rugged terrain for serious **hiking** and **mountaineering.** The **Greek Skiing and Alpine Federation** (7 Karageorgi Servias St., Athens, tel. 01/323–4555) operates more than 40 mountain refuge huts that are available to the public by prior arrangement. The **Greek Touring Club** (12 Politehniou St., Athens, tel. 01/524–8600) and **Federation of Excursion Clubs of Greece** (4 Dragastaniou St., Athens, tel. 01/323–4107) can provide additional information on mountain climbing.

Skiing has gained tremendously in popularity, and over the past decade slopes have been developed as far south as Crete. The longest season (as late as May) and best skiing are found in the north. Mt. Parnassus is the most developed ski resort, but there are others. Contact the Greek Skiing and Alpine Federation for details.

Tourists with troglodyte tendencies are welcome to subterranean Greece. Eight of the caves have some facilities for tourists, and four more are being developed. **Spelunkers** in search of wild caves should contact the **Hellenic Speleological Society** (8 Mantzarou St., Athens 10672, tel. 01/361–7824).

Golfing in Greece is possible, but there aren't many 18-hole courses. Those with complete facilities include the **Glyfada Golf Course and Club** (tel. 01/894–6875) near Athens, the **Afandou Golf Club** (tel. 0241/51255 or 0241/51256) on Rhodes, the **Corfu Golf Club** (tel. 0661/94220 or 0661/94221). There are **tennis** clubs in virtually every city and many in and around Athens. The hotel concierge or local tourist office can help you find one that admits nonmembers.

Equestrian tourists can go **riding** at the **Hellenic Riding Club** (tel. 01/682–6128 or 01/681–2506) or the **Athens Riding Club** (tel. 01/661–1088) in Attica and the **Corfu Riding Club** (tel. 0661/30776) on Corfu.

Beaches

More than 3,200 kilometers (2,000 miles) of Greece's coastline qualify as bathing beaches. Keep in mind, however, that many of these are in remote areas or are cobble beaches, fine for swimming but not so good for sunning. On the other hand, there are many beautiful beaches, like Kyllini Loutras on the western coast, the black volcanic sand beach at Perissa on Santorini, and Vai on the northeast coast of Crete. Most beaches are clean, except those adjacent to major urban centers—but you don't want to swim in the waters off Piraeus, anyway. At the vast majority of beaches in Greece you might, at worst, find yourself swimming with a plastic bag or, rarely, a globule of congealed oil.

Dining

Mealtimes   Slow down; the sites aren't going anywhere, the beaches will be there tomorrow, and the restaurants will be open late. Breakfast ends about 10, lunch is usually between 1:30 and 3:30, after which restaurants close for the afternoon. Dinner starts late; 8 is on the early side.

Cuisine   Breakfast in Greece is pretty light. Hotels will ply you with a Nescafé-and-bread Continental breakfast, but you might try a "toast," a sort of dry grilled-cheese sandwich (a "mixed toast" if it has a paper-thin ham slice added), or a sesame-coated bread ring sold by street vendors in the cities. Local bakeries may offer fresh doughnuts in the morning. Lunch can be fairly substantial. Heavyweight meat-and-potato dishes are available at the restaurants, but you might prefer a real Greek salad (no lettuce, a slice of feta with a pinch of oregano, and ripe tomatoes) or souvlaki or grilled chicken from a taverna.

The hour or so before restaurants open for dinner is a pleasant time to have an ouzo or glass of wine and try Greek hors d'oeuvres, called *mezedes*. As the sun sets over the Aegean, seek out a seaside ouzeria. It's the perfect setting for conversation or postcard writing. Dinner is the main meal of the day, and there's plenty of food. Starters include *taramasalata* (a dip or spread made from fish roe) and *melitsanasalata* (made from smoked eggplant), along with the well-known yogurt-cucumber-and-garlic *tzatziki*.

On menus all over Greece you'll run into three categories of staple entrée dishes: There's *mayirefta*, food that has been cooked in the oven in advance and left in the pan all day, usually served at room temperature—like moussaka, *pastitsio* (a baked dish of minced lamb and macaroni), or *gemista* (stuffed tomatoes or peppers, which usually has some ground lamb). Then there are *tisoras*, or grills, with a subcategory called *stakarvouna* (meaning "of the hour"), food that is cooked on the coals and served immediately—like chops or steak. And last, there is fish, of all kinds, which is outstanding (look for gilt-head bream, or *tsipoura*).

Liquor and Wine   Ouzo, a clear licorice-flavor drink, and brandy are the national aperitifs of Greece. Served in small glasses and diluted with water (which turns the liqueur milky white), ouzo is usually drunk on summer evenings and should be lingered over. Try a tiny sip undiluted first, and ask for *mezedes* (appetizers), which might include anything from tomato slices, olives, and cheese to shrimp or sausage. Give the stale crackers that accompany ouzo at outdoor cafés to the sparrows flitting around the café chairs. In winter, people usually ask for brandy: Botrys and the higher-grade Metaxa are both good, and you might also like the heavy dessert wine known as *mavrodaphne*.

Wine was a centerpiece of social life in ancient Greece, especially at *symposia*, banquets featuring drinking, discussion, and courtesans. The ancient Greeks usually diluted their wine with water; the Spartan king Cleomenes is said by Herodotus to have lost his mind from drinking too much unmixed wine, a habit he had learned from the Scythians. Wine was used by ancient physicians to wash and dress wounds. Modern testing shows that pigments in the grapes acquire antibacterial properties during fermentation (wine from Samos proved most effective, killing *E. coli* bacteria in three minutes flat).

Greek wine is relatively inexpensive. Restaurants and tavernas often sell locally produced *kokkino* (red) and *aspro* (white) table wine from the barrel; many of them, purchased by the half-kilogram or kilogram, are perfectly good wines. For bottled wine, look for *Hymettos* from Attica, *Boutari* or *Tsantalis* from Naousa in Macedonia, *Carras Estate* from Chalkidiki, and red wines from Nemea in the Peloponnese. There are many others. Enthusiasts should consult Miles Lambert-Gocs's comprehensive *The Wines of Greece* (Faber and Faber: London, 1990) for a history of modern winemaking in Greece and for descriptions of regional wines. For additional information on Greek wines and wineries contact the **Federation of Greek Wine and Spirits Industries** (15A Xenofonto, Athens, tel. 01/322–6053) or visit the **Central Union of Vine and Wine Cooperatives of Greece** store (L. Riancourt St. at Panormou, Athens, tel. 01/692–3102, open Wed.–Mon. 8–2:30, Tues. 5–8).

The origins of *retsina*, the piney, aromatic, resinated wine that is Greece's *vin du pays*, are uncertain. According to ancient authors, resin was one of many ingredients added to wine to prevent it from turning to vinegar, but the substance may initially have been used to seal wine containers. Whatever the original intent, the results can be splendid. Give retsina a chance; don't take one sip, make a face, then declare you don't like it. Perhaps you've read or been told that retsina is an acquired taste. This isn't true: most people like it immediately. Besides, wouldn't it be fun to drink retsina drawn from the barrel while eating a traditional meal on a late summer's evening in Greece? If retsina out of the barrel isn't available, or if you feel safer with the bottled version, try *Achaia Clauss*, *Thebes*, *Botrys*, *Cambas*, *Kourtakis*, *Marko*, or *Pikermi*. Have it unchilled with *pastitsio*, moussaka, or grilled chicken, lamb, or souvlaki.

Lodging

While lodging is less expensive in Greece than in the United States, the quality tends to be a little lower. Many Greeks rent rooms in their houses, which can be less expensive and more homelike than a hotel, but you might have to scout around a bit to find them. Accommodations may be hard to find in smaller resort towns during the winter and beginning of spring.

Hotels The government classifies hotels into six categories: L (luxury), and A–E, which govern the rates that can be charged. Ratings are based on room size, size of the lobby and other public areas, bathroom facilities, and other amenities. There is a great deal of variation from one town to the next, and the classifications can be misleading—a hotel rated C in one town might qualify as a B in another. For the categories L, A, and B you can expect something along the lines of a chain motel in the United States, although the room will probably be somewhat smaller. A room in a C hotel can be perfectly acceptable; with a D the bathroom may or may not be shared. Ask to see the room before signing. You can sometimes find a bargain if a hotel has just renovated but not yet been reclassified.

Prices are posted in each room, usually on the back of the door or inside the wardrobe. The room charge varies over the course of the year, peaking in the high season when half-board may also be obligatory. An 8% government tax, 4.5% local tax, and 1.2% stamp tax (total 13.7%) is added to the bill.

Traditional Settlements In an effort to provide tourist accommodations in traditional settings, the Greek National Tourist Organization has begun a restoration program, converting older buildings into guest houses. Some of the villages developed so far include Oia on Santorini; Makrinitsa on Mt. Pelion; Mesta on Chios; the island of Psara, near Chios; and Monemvassia in the southern Peloponnese. For reservations call the **Greek Hotel and Cruise Reservation Center** (tel. 714/641–3502 or 800/736–5717, or fax 714/641–0303).

Youth Hostels Addresses and phone numbers of Greek youth hostels are listed in the international YHA directory, or you can check at the **Greek Association of Youth Hostels** (4, Dragatsaniou St., Athens, tel. 01/323–4107). There are hostels in Athens and Delphi on the mainland; Mycenae, Nauplion, Olympia, and Patras in the Peloponnese; Corfu; Santorini; and Ayios Nikolaos, Hania, Heraklion, Myrthios, Mallia, Rethymnon, and Sitia on Crete. The YMCA and YWCA operate hostels in Athens.

Camping There are numerous campgrounds, most privately owned, throughout Greece. One or more can usually be found in close proximity to popular archaeological sites and beach resorts— they aren't intended for those who want to explore the wilds of Greece. Their amenities range from basic to elaborate and those operated by the tourist organization are cushier than most. They are found at Bourla, Boula, Patras, and Kyllini Loutras.

Credit Cards

The following credit card abbreviations have been used: AE, American Express; DC, Diners Club; MC, MasterCard; V, Visa.

Great Itineraries

Because Athens is Greece's cultural center as well as its transportation hub, our itineraries begin there. Although this book does not cover the north or northwest of Greece, two of our itineraries will give you an overview of those areas. The third goes south to the Peloponnese. It's best to be flexible concerning the activities you schedule for each day. Don't overbook yourself, seeing many things in a rush and enjoying none, and keep alternatives in mind in case a museum, church, or sight is unexpectedly closed.

Macedonia: Crossroads of Empires

Northern Greece, although still less frequented than the south, deserves its growing popularity; it is a region of myth and history, full of architectural treasures, and the storied monuments of state and of religion. Head north from Athens on the expressway overlooking the Gulf of Evia, breaking the journey at **Thermopylae,** where Leonidas and his 300 Spartans stood against Xerxes and the Persian army. Stop overnight at the harbor town of **Volos** at the base of Mt. Pelion. En route to Thessaloniki the road passes the **Vale of Tempi** (Tembi), through which the Peneios River flows into the Aegean, before reaching **Dion,** at the foot of Mt. Olympus. Here, at the chief religious center of ancient Macedonia, Alexander made sacrifice to the gods before setting out to conquer the world. It is famous for its well-preserved sculptures and mosaics.

At the heart of Macedonia is **Thessaloniki,** whose Byzantine architectural treasures range from the 4th-century Rotunda to the 14th-century church of the Holy Apostles, the Arch of Galerius, and the White Tower. Its archaeological museum houses spectacular finds from royal tombs and the gilded bronze Derveni krater. West of Thessaloniki are **Vergina** (ancient Aigai), the original capital and royal cemetery of the ancient Macedonian empire, and **Pella,** its successor. The finds from an unplundered Vergina tomb, possibly of Philip II, are in Thessaloniki. Pella, birthplace of Philip II and Alexander, is known for its splendid mosaics. East, beyond the **Chalkidiki** peninsula and the religious state of **Mount Athos** (to which access is restricted to males), is **Kavala,** on the coast, whose busy waterfront, Roman aqueduct, and old Turkish quarter give it a distinctive character. A few miles north of Kavala is **Philippi,** on the Roman Via Egnatia, where the forces under Octavius and Antony defeated Cassius and Brutus in 42 BC.

Length of Trip Six–seven days plus return (five–six days if you begin from Thessaloniki)

Getting Around There's an express train to and from Thessaloniki, and all points are served by buses, but the trip can more easily be made in a car.

The Main Route **One night: Volos.** Explore the site at Thermopylae en route. Stop off to see Dion and its sculptures and mosaics.

Five or six nights: Thessaloniki. Visit the Byzantine buildings and the museum. Make excursions to Vergina and Pella; see the mosaics. Go to Kavala by the inland road via Serres, then visit Philippi and return along the coast road. Or, alternatively, explore the Chalkidiki peninsula, with its sweeping vistas and fine beaches, maybe sailing around the holy Mount Athos.

Another alternative is to take the route west from Thessaloniki to Kastoria, either through Edessa to the north or Kozani to the south. Edessa, a summer resort on the ancient Via Egnatia, has numerous waterfalls and a spectacular view of Pindos and Olympus, which make the northern route preferable. Kastoria, on a peninsula jutting into a large lake, owes its prosperity to the fur industry. It is known for its 17th- and 18th-century houses and numerous diminutive churches, many of Byzantine and medieval date. (Return either to Thessaloniki or join the Northwestern Greece itinerary at Ioannina, Metsovo, or Kalambaka).

Northwestern Greece: The Road Less Traveled

Least traveled of all major regions, the northwest offers some of the most rugged and spectacular countryside in Greece. At holy **Delphi,** on the slopes of Mt. Parnassus, the steep valley and towering cliffs are the perfect setting for the sacred precinct and the museum, which contains the famous bronze charioteer and the Omphalos stone, thought to be the navel of the earth. From Delphi the road runs to the coast at the charming little port of **Nafpaktos,** defended by diminutive medieval towers and overlooked by a ruined Venetian fortress. Push on to historic **Missolonghi,** known for its heroic defense during the War of Independence, thence north to **Preveza** via the ferry from **Actium,** the cape off which Octavius and Agrippa defeated the fleets of Antony and Cleopatra. (Alternatively the inland route leads from Missolonghi through Agrinio and Arta.) Just north of Preveza are the extensive ruins of **Nikopolis** (Victory City), built by Octavius when he became the emperor Augustus.

About 200 kilometers (125 miles) north of Preveza by the inland road is **Ioannina,** the capital of the early 19th-century despot Ali Pasha, surrounded by mountains and set on the shore of a large lake. Of the despot's palace only the reconstructed seraglio remains, and the town is dominated by an 11th-century Norman citadel. South of town is the oracle of Zeus at **Dodona,** with its magnificent theater; to the north are the cave of **Perama** and the spectacular gorges of **Zagoria.** East of Ioannina is the village of **Metsovo,** with wooden houses perched on the sides of a steep valley. Beyond, at the base of a cliff, is **Kalambaka,** the gateway to the 14th-century monasteries at **Meteora,** built on the heights of rock pinnacles rising more than 1,800 feet. Beautiful frescoes await those who climb to the monasteries atop the pinnacles. From here the road goes back to Athens.

Length of Trip   Seven days

Getting Around   All points are accessible by bus.

The Main Route   **One night: Delphi.** Visit the stadium, temple of Apollo, treasuries, and the museum.

One night: Missolonghi. En route stop for lunch at Nafpaktos and tour the town. Visit Actium along the coast road; take the ferry to Preveza.

One night: Preveza. Tour the ruins at Nikopolis. Drive to Ioannina via Filipiada (or you can visit the coastal resort of Parga and turn inland at Igoumenitsa, where there's ferry service to Corfu).

One or two nights: Ioannina. Explore Ali Pasha's palace ruins and the Norman citadel. Visit Dodona's theater and the interesting geology at Perama and Zagoria.

One night: Kalambaka. En route, visit Metsovo and its perched wooden houses. Climb the peaks to the Meteora monasteries' frescoes.

One night: Volos. Stop at a café in Trikala on the banks of the Lethaios River before proceeding to Larissa and the expressway to Volos and Athens.

The Peloponnese: Heartland of Greece

On a circuit of the southern peninsula, the Peloponnese, visitors cross the Isthmus of Corinth and pass near ancient Corinth, whose acropolis dominates the skyline. Head southward through the wine country around Nemea to Nauplion, once Greece's capital. Protected by a massive Venetian fortress, old

Nauplion retains considerable 19th-century charm. From there you can visit the Bronze Age citadels of Mycenae and Tiryns (home to Homer's heroes); the ancient sanctuary and theater of Epidauros is only a short drive away. Going inland you come to Tripolis; to the south are Sparta, the marvelous Byzantine ruins of Mystras, and the Gibraltarlike fortress of Monemvassia, on a massive rock connected to the mainland by a narrow strip of land. Heading westward in an arc around the Lakonian Gulf brings you to Gythion, with its pastel architecture. After a brief circuit of the remote Mani peninsula, with its characteristic tower houses, the route proceeds west to the port of Kalamata and Pylos, on the southwest coast, then north to the palace of Nestor or inland (via Megalopolis) to the ancient site of Olympia, perhaps most important in all of Greece. The tour ends at Patras, Greece's third-largest city.

Length of Trip Eight days

Getting Around This itinerary is intended for a car, but bus service is available to all points, and there is rail service to much of the area.

The Main Route **Two nights: Nauplion.** On the way south from Corinth, stop at the sanctuary of Zeus at Nemea en route through Argos. The next day, visit Mycenae and Tiryns and explore Nauplion and its fortress in the afternoon, or go to the beach at the nearby resort of Tolo.

One night: Sparta. Head overland to Tripolis and thence to Athens's ancient rival (of which little remains) and the ruins of the city of Mystras, which was under Byzantine control from the mid-13th century and was burned to the ground in the War of Independence.

One night: Monemvassia. From Sparta, drive to Geraki, another ruined Byzantine city, on the way to the fortified town of Monemvassia. Explore the town and the cliffside 14th-century church of Ayia Sophia, a late-Byzantine masterpiece.

One night: Pylos. Drive to Gythion to see its tall Neoclassical houses on the small harbor and eat some octopus, then continue across or around the Mani Peninsula and on to Kalamata, looking at architecture along the way. Push on from Kalamata (devastated by an earthquake in 1986) past the ruins of ancient Messene, west to the picturesque harbor town of Pylos, its fortresses, and its island.

One night: Olympia. Drive north along the coast, stopping at the Bronze Age palace of Nestor, or go inland via ancient Megalopolis and the temple of Apollo at Bassae. The coastal and inland routes converge at Krestena, just south of Olympia. Visit the spacious new museum and the sacred sanctuary of Zeus.

One night: Patras. En route from Olympia to Patras along the coast, you can visit Chlemoutsi Castle or sample the beach at Kyllini Loutras. The next day, the tedium of the drive from Patras to Athens can be alleviated by leaving the expressway at Diakofto and riding the funicular railway to Kalavrita. For more information, *see* Off the Beaten Track in Chapter 6. Or you can take the Rio–Antirion ferry and return by way of Nafpaktos and Delphi.

2 Portraits of Greece

Greece at a Glance: A Chronology

c. 3000 BC   Earliest Bronze Age settlements on Crete. This non-Greek-speaking culture is called "Minoan" after its legendary monarch, Minos

c. 3000 BC–2000 BC   Non-Greek-speaking settlements on the Greek mainland; this Bronze Age culture is known as "Helladic"

c. 1900 BC   First of successive waves of Greek-speaking invaders; important settlement at Mycenae

1900 BC–1400 BC   Height of Minoan culture. On Crete the Palace of Minos at Knossos is built, which includes indoor plumbing. Its mazelike complexity gives rise to the legend of the labyrinth

1400 BC–1200 BC   Height of Mycenean power: Crete is taken, and the city of Troy in Asia Minor is sacked. At Mycenae and Pylos impressive tombs mark this warrior culture

1200 BC–1100 BC   Mycenean civilization collapses: possible causes include a massive earthquake on Thira (dated anywhere from 1450 BC to 1200 BC) and an invasion by Dorians from the north

1100 BC–750 BC   The "dark ages": writing disappears. The legendary poet Homer narrates a history of the Trojan War and describes an aristocratic society; this oral tradition is later written down as the *Iliad* and the *Odyssey*

c. 750 BC   Establishment of the *polis*, or city-state, as the characteristic form of political and civic organization in Greece

c. 725 BC   The poet Hesiod describes rural life in *Works and Days* and establishes the pantheon of Greek gods in *Theogony*. The Olympic Games are established as a Panhellenic event, during which peace prevailed

700 BC–500 BC   Colonization builds Greek city-states throughout the Mediterranean. Meanwhile, social pressures at home lead to the rule of tyrants

621 BC   Dracon publishes a notoriously severe legal code in Athens

c. 600 BC   The legendary ruler Lykourgos establishes the Spartan system of a highly controlled, militaristic society. Thales of Miletus, the first Greek philosopher, starts wondering about the world

594 BC   Solon is given extraordinary powers to reform the Athenian government and constitution

c. 550 BC   Establishment of the Peloponnesian League, a military alliance of city-states dominated by Sparta. The philosopher Pythagoras propounds a famous theorem and sets up a monastic colony in southern Italy; the poet Sappho of Lesbos describes a particular kind of love

c. 508 BC–501 BC   Clisthenes establishes Athenian democracy

The Classical Era

499 BC–479 BC Persian wars: Athens leads Greek states against Kings Darius and Xerxes. 490 BC: Battle of Marathon is a critical victory for Athens. 480 BC: Xerxes invades Greece; the Greek League, which includes Athens and Sparta, defeats him in a series of battles at Thermopylae, Salamis, and Plataea

478 BC–477 BC Founding of Delian League of city-states under Athenian hegemony; it will evolve into an empire

c. 475 BC–400 BC Golden Age of classical Greek culture, centered at Athens. Aeschylus (525 BC–456 BC), Sophocles (c. 496 BC–406 BC), and Euripides (c. 485 BC–402 BC) form the great triumvirate of classical drama; the comedies of Aristophanes (c. 450 BC–385 BC) satirize contemporary mores. Socrates (469 BC–399 BC) and his disciple Plato (c. 429 BC–347 BC) debate the fundamental questions of knowledge and meaning. Herodotus (c. 484 BC–420 BC) and Thucydides (471 BC–402 BC) invent historical writing. The Acropolis epitomizes the harmony and precision of Classical architecture and sculpture

462 BC Pericles (c. 495 BC–429 BC) rises to the leadership of Athens and leads the city to its cultural height

460 BC–445 BC First Peloponnesian War between Athens and Sparta ends with the "Thirty Years' Peace" and recognition of the Athenian Empire. At the height of his power, Pericles rebuilds Athens

432 BC The Second, or Great, Peloponnesian War begins when Sparta declares war on Athens

429 BC A disastrous plague kills more than one-third of the Athenian population, including Pericles

421 BC Fighting ceases with the Peace of Nicias (which proves to be temporary)

415 BC–413 BC Athens's disastrous invasion of Sicily reopens the war and sets the stage for its downfall

404 BC Athens falls to Sparta and its walls are dismantled, ending an era

398 BC–360 BC Rule of Agesilaus at Sparta, whose aggressive policies lead to its ruin

394 BC Spartan fleet destroyed by Persians

386 BC Plato founds the Academy in Athens, a school of philosophy that trains statesmen

384 BC Birth of Aristotle, the greatest ancient philosopher and scientist (died 322 BC)

378 BC Second Athenian Confederation marks the resurgence of Athens

371 BC Spartan hegemony ends with a defeat at Leuctra by the Theban army under Epaminondas

362 BC Death of Epaminondas at the battle of Mantinea ends Theban dominance, documented by Xenophon (c. 434 BC–355 BC)

355 BC Second Athenian Confederation collapses, leaving Greece in chaos

The Hellenistic Era

351 BC Demosthenes (384 BC–332 BC) delivers the First Philippic, warning Athens of the dangers of Macedonian power

342 BC Aristotle becomes tutor to a young Macedonian prince named Alexander (356 BC–323 BC)

338 BC Alexander's father, Philip of Macedon (359 BC–336 BC) defeats the Greek forces at Chaeronea and establishes Macedonian hegemony

336 BC Philip is assassinated, leaving his empire to his son Alexander, soon to be known as "the Great." Aristotle founds his school, the Lyceum, at Athens

323 BC Having conquered the known world and opened it to Greek culture, Alexander dies of a fever in Babylon

c. 330 BC–200 BC Hellenistic culture blends Greek and other influences in a cosmopolitan style. Epicureanism, Stoicism, and Cynicism enter philosophy; Hellenistic sculpture blends emotion and realism. At the new city of Alexandria in Egypt, Greek science and mathematics flourish with Euclid (300 BC) and Archimedes (c. 287 BC–212 BC); Aristarchus (c. 310 BC–230 BC) asserts that the earth revolves around the sun

The Roman Era

215 BC The outbreak of the First Macedonian War signals Rome's rise in the Mediterranean

146 BC Rome annexes Greece and Macedonia as provinces. Roman culture becomes increasingly Hellenized

49 BC–31 BC Greece is a battleground for control of Rome's empire: 48 BC: Julius Caesar defeats Pompey at Pharsalus; 42 BC: Caesar's heir Octavian defeats Brutus at Philippi; 31 BC: Octavian defeats Mark Antony at Actium and becomes, as Augustus, the first Roman Emperor

AD 125 The guidebook of Pausanias makes Greece a favored tourist stop; the Emperor Hadrian undertakes the renovation of ancient monuments

394 The Emperor Theodosius declares Christianity the official religion of the Roman Empire and bans pagan cults, suppressing the Olympic Games and closing the oracle at Delphi

The Medieval Era

476 The fall of Rome leaves Greece open to waves of invaders, though it remains nominally under the hegemony of the Byzantine emperors at Constantinople

529 The Byzantine Emperor Justinian closes Plato's Academy in Athens

1054 The Great Schism divides the Christian church into Greek and Roman orthodoxies

1204–1261 Greece briefly reenters the sphere of western influence with the Latin capture of Constantinople in the Fourth Crusade

1453 The fall of Constantinople to the Ottoman Turks leads to nearly four centuries of Turkish rule

The Modern Era

1770 The Russian prince Orloff attempts but fails to establish a Greek principality

1814 The *Philike Hetairia*, a "friendly society" established by Greek merchants at Odessa (Russia), is instrumental in the growth of Greek nationalism

1821–1829 The Greek War of Independence. 1821: The Greek Patriarch, Archbishop Germanos, declares Greek independence, and war with the Turks breaks out. Among those aiding Greece in her struggle is the English poet Lord Byron. 1826: a Greek defeat at Missolonghi stirs European sympathy. 1827: the Triple Alliance of Great Britain, France, and Russia intervene against the Turks and their Egyptian allies. 1829: the Turks are defeated and Greece is declared an independent state, guaranteed by the Triple Alliance

1832 Prince Otho of Bavaria is offered the Greek throne by the Triple Alliance

1834 King Otho chooses Athens as his capital

1844 Greece adopts a constitution that establishes a constitutional monarchy

1863 As a result of Otho's pro-Russian policies during the Crimean war, he is forced to abdicate and is replaced on the throne by Prince George of Denmark

1909–1910 The Military League, a group of young army officers, leads a peaceful revolt and installs as prime minister Eleutherios Venizelos, who enacts a series of reforms

1912–1913 Greece gains Macedonia, Epirus, and Crete as a result of the Balkan Wars

1917–1918 Greece fights on the Allied side in World War I

1924 Greece is declared a republic

1935 Monarchy is restored; in the next year, King George II allows General Joannes Metaxas to establish a military dictatorship

1940 Italy invades Greece, leading to four years of Axis occupation

1946 Greece becomes a charter member of the United Nations

1946–1949 Communist rebellion is defeated with U.S. help

1952 Women are given the right to vote

1963 George Seferis wins the Nobel Prize for Literature

1967 A military coup ousts King Constantine II

1974 In the wake of the Cyprus crisis, the military government collapses and the first elections in 10 years are held. Constantine Karamanlis is named prime minister. The republic is confirmed by popular vote

1980 Odysseus Elytis becomes the second Greek to win the Nobel Prize for Literature

1981 Greece joins the European Economic Community

Edith Hamilton on . . .

Mind and Spirit

By Edith Hamilton, *from* The Greek Way

Egypt is a fertile valley of rich river soil, low-lying, warm, monotonous, a slow-flowing river, and beyond, the limitless desert. Greece is a country of sparse fertility and keen, cold winters, all hills and mountains sharp cut in stone, where strong men must work hard to get their bread. And while Egypt submitted and suffered and turned her face toward death, Greece resisted and rejoiced and turned full-face to life. For somewhere among those steep stone mountains, in little sheltered valleys where the great hills were ramparts to defend and men could have security for peace and happy living, something quite new came into the world; the joy of life found expression. Perhaps it was born there, among the shepherds pasturing their flocks where the wild flowers made a glory on the hillside; among the sailors on a sapphire sea washing enchanted islands purple in a luminous air. At any rate it has left no trace anywhere else in the world of antiquity. In Greece nothing is more in evidence. The Greeks were the first people in the world to play, and they played on a great scale. All over Greece there were games, all sort of games; athletic contests of every description: races—horse-, boat-, foot-, torch-races; contests in music, where one side outsung the other; in dancing—on greased skins sometimes to display a nice skill of foot and balance of body; games where men leaped in and out of flying chariots; games so many one grows weary with the list of them. They are embodied in the statues familiar to all, the disc thrower, the charioteer, the wrestling boys, the dancing flute players. The great games—there were four that came at stated seasons—were so important, when one was held, a truce of God was proclaimed so that all Greece might come in safety without fear. There "glorious-limbed youth"—the phrase is Pindar's, the athlete's poet—strove for an honor so coveted as hardly anything else in Greece. An Olympic victor—triumphing generals would give place to him. His crown of wild olives was set beside the prize of the tragedian. Splendor attended him, processions, sacrifices, banquets, songs the greatest poets were glad to write. Thucydides, the brief, the severe, the historian of that bitter time, the fall of Athens, pauses, when one of his personages has conquered in the games, to give the fact full place of honor. If we had no other knowledge of what the Greeks were like, if nothing were left of Greek art and literature, the fact that they were in love with play and played magnificently would be proof enough of how they lived and how they looked at life. Wretched people, toiling people, do not play. Nothing like the Greek games is conceivable in Egypt or Mesopotamia. The life of the Egyptian lies spread out in the mural paintings down to the minutest detail. If fun and sport had played any real part they would be there in some form for us to see. But the Egyptian did not play. "Solon, Solon, you Greeks are all children," said the Egyptian priest to the great Athenian. At any rate, children or not, they enjoyed themselves. They had physical vigor and high spirits and time, too, for fun. The witness of the games is conclusive. And when Greece died and her reading of the great enigma was buried with her statues, play, too, died out of the world. The brutal, bloody Roman games had nothing to do with the spirit of play. They were fathered by the Orient, not by Greece. Play died when Greece died and many and many a century passed before it was resurrected.

To rejoice in life, to find the world beautiful and delightful to live in, was a mark of the Greek spirit which distinguished it from all that had gone before. It is a vital distinction. The joy of life is written upon everything the Greeks left behind and they who leave it out of account fail to reckon with something that is of first importance in understanding how the Greek achievement came to pass in the world of antiquity. It is not a fact that jumps to the eye for the reason that their literature is marked as strongly by sorrow. The Greeks knew to the full how bitter life is as well as how sweet. Joy and sorrow, exultation and tragedy, stand hand in hand in Greek literature, but there is no contradiction involved thereby. Those who do not know the one do not really know the other either. It is the depressed, the gray-minded people, who cannot rejoice just as they cannot agonize. The Greeks were not the victims of depression. Greek literature is not done in gray or with a low palette. It is all black and shining white or black and scarlet and gold. The Greeks were keenly aware, terribly aware, of life's uncertainty and the imminence of death. Over and over again they emphasize the brevity and the failure of all human endeavor, the swift passing of all that is beautiful and joyful. To Pindar, even as he glorifies the victor in the games, life is "a shadow's dream." But never, not in their darkest moments, do they lose their taste for life. It is always a wonder and a delight, the world a place of beauty, and they themselves rejoicing to be alive in it.

Quotations to illustrate this attitude are so numerous, it is hard to make a choice. One might quote all the Greek poems there are, even when they are tragedies. Every one of them shows the fire of life burning high. Never a Greek poet that did not warm both hands at that flame. Often in the midst of a tragedy a choral song of joy breaks forth. So Sophocles, of the three tragedians the soberest, the most severe, sings in the *Antigone* of the wine-god, "with whom the stars rejoice as they move, the stars whose breath is fire." Or in the *Ajax* where "thrilling with rapture, soaring on wings of sudden joy," he calls to "Pan, O Pan, come, sea-rover, down from the snow-beaten mountain crag. Lord of the dance the gods delight in, come, for now I, too, would dance. O joy!" Or in the *Œdipus Coloneus*, where tragedy is suddenly put aside by the poet's love of the out-of-door world, of the nightingale's clear thrilling note and the stainless tide of pure waters and the glory of the narcissus and the bright-shining crocus, "which the quire of the muses love and Aphrodite of the golden rein." Passages like these come again and again, lifting the black curtain of tragedy to the full joy of life. They are no artifice or trick to heighten by contrast. They are the natural expression of men who were tragedians indeed but Greeks first, and so thrillingly aware of the wonder and beauty of life, they could not but give it place.

The little pleasures, too, that daily living holds, were felt as such keen enjoyment: "Dear to us ever," says Homer, "is the banquet and the harp and the dance and changes of raiment and the warm bath and love and sleep." Eating and drinking have never again seemed so delightful as in the early Greek lyrics, nor a meeting with friends, nor a warm fire of a winter's night—"the stormy season of winter, a soft couch after dinner by the fire, honey-sweet wine in your glass and nuts and beans at your elbow"—nor a run in the springtime "amid a fragrance of woodbine and leisure and white poplar, when the plane-tree and the elm whisper together," nor a banqueting hour, "moving among feasting and giving up the soul to be young, carrying a bright harp and touching it in peace among the wise of the citizens." It is a matter of course that comedy should be their invention, the mad, rollicking, irresponsible fun of the Old Comedy, its verve and vitality and exuberant, overflowing energy of life. A tomb in Egypt and a theatre in Greece. The one comes to the mind as naturally as the other. So was the world changing by the time the 5th century before Christ began in Athens.

"The exercise of vital powers along lines of excellence in a life affording them scope" is an old Greek definition of happiness. It is a conception permeated with energy of life. Through all Greek history that spirit of life abounding moves. It led along many an untried way. Authoritarianism and submissiveness were not the direction it pointed to. A high-spirited people full of physical vigor do not obey easily, and indeed the strong air of the mountains has never been wholesome for despots. The absolute monarch-submissive slave theory of life flourishes best where there are no hills to give a rebel refuge and no mountain heights to summon a man to live dangerously. When history begins in Greece there is no trace of the ancient state. The awful, unapproachable sacred potentate, Pharaoh of Egypt, priest-king of Mesopotamia, whose absolute power none had questioned for thousands of years, is nowhere in the scene. There is nothing that remotely resembles him in Greece. Something we know of the Age of the Tyrants in Greek history but what we know most clearly is that it was put a stop to. Abject submission to the power on the throne which had been the rule of life in the ancient world since kings began, and was to be the rule of life in Asia for centuries to come, was cast off by the Greeks so easily, so lightly, hardly more than an echo of the contest has come down to us.

In the *Persians* of Æschylus, a play written to celebrate the defeat of the Persians at Salamis, there is many an allusion to the difference between the Greek way and the Oriental way. The Greeks, the Persian queen is told, fight as free men to defend what is precious to them. Have they no master? she asks. No, she is told. No man calls Greeks slaves or vassals. Herodotus in his account adds, "They obey only the law." Something completely new is here. The idea of freedom has been born. The conception of the entire unimportance of the individual to the state, which had persisted down from earliest tribal days and was universally accepted in all the ancient world, has given place in Greece to the conception of the liberty of the individual in a state which he defends of his own free will. That is a change not worked by high spirit and abounding vigor alone. Something more was at work in Greece. Men were thinking for themselves.

The Greek Way of Writing

The art of the Greek sculptors of the great age is known to us by long familiarity. None of the Greek statues upon first sight appear strange in any respect. There is no need to look long, to orient mind and eye, before we can understand them. We feel ourselves immediately at home. Our own sculptors learned their art from them, filled our galleries with reminiscences of them. Plaster casts more or less like them are our commonest form of inappropriate decoration. Our idea of a statue is a composite of Greek statues, and nothing speaks more for the vitality of the originals than their survival in spite of all we have done to them.

The same is true of the Greek temple. No architecture is more familiar to us. That pointed pediment supported by fluted columns—we are satiated with it. Endless replicas of it decorate the public buildings of all our cities and the sight of it anywhere is an assurance of something official within. Greece has been copied by sculptors and builders from the days of Rome on.

The art of the literature of Greece stands in singular contrast to these, isolated, apart. The thought of the Greeks has penetrated everywhere; their style, the way they write, has remained peculiar to them alone. In that one respect they have had no copyists and no followers. The fact is hardly surprising. One must know a foreign language very well to have one's way of writing actually altered by it; one must, in truth, have entered into the genius of that language to such a degree as is hardly possible to a foreigner. And Greek is a very subtle language, full of delicately modifying words, capable of the finest distinctions of meaning. Years of study are needed to read it even tolerably. Small

wonder that the writers of other countries left it alone and,
unlike their brother artists in stone, never imitated Greek
methods. English poetry has gone an altogether different
way from the Greek, as has all the art that is not copied but
is native to Europe.

This art, the art natural to us, has always been an art of rich
detail. In a Gothic cathedral not an inch is left unelaborated
in a thousand marvellous patterns of delicate tracery
worked in the stone. In a great Renaissance portrait minutest distinctions of form and color are dwelt upon with loving
care, frost-work of lace, patterned brocade, the finely
wrought links of a chain, a jewelled ring, wreathed pearls in
the hair, the sheen of silk and satin and furbordered velvet,
beauty of detail both sumptuous and exquisite. It is eminently probably that if the temples and the statues of
Greece had only just been discovered, we would look at
them dismayed at the lack of any of the elaboration of beauty we are used to. To turn from St. Mark's or Chartres to
the Parthenon for the first time, or from a Titian to the Venus of Milo never seen before, would undoubtedly be a chill-
ing experience. The statue in her straight, plain folds, her
hair caught back simply in a knot, no ornament of any description to set her off, placed beside the lady of the Renaissance or the European lady of any period, is a contrast so
great, only our long familiarity with her enables us not to
feel her too austere to enjoy. She shows us how unlike what
the Greeks wanted in beauty was from what the world after
them has wanted.

So the lover of great literature when he is confronted all unprepared with the Greek way of writing, feels chilled at
first, almost estranged. The Greeks wrote on the same
lines as they did everything else. Greek writing depends no
more on ornament than the Greek statue does. It is plain
writing, direct, matter-of-fact. It often seems, when translated with any degree of literalness, bare, so unlike what
we are used to as even to repel. All the scholars who have
essayed translation have felt this difficulty and have tried
to win an audience for what they loved and knew as so great
by rewriting, not translating, when the Greek way seemed
too different from the English. The most distinguished of
them, Professor Gilbert Murray, has expressly stated this
to be his method:

*I have often used a more elaborate diction than Euripides
did because I found that, Greek being a very simple and
austere language and English an ornate one, a direct
translation produced an effect of baldness which was quite
unlike the original.*

The difficulty is there, no doubt, and yet if we are unable to
get enjoyment from a direct translation, we shall never
know what Greek writing is like, for the Greek and the English ways are so different, when the Greek is dressed in
English fashion, it is no longer Greek. Familiarity has made

their statues and their temples beautiful to us as none are more. It is possible that even through the poor medium of translation we might acquire a taste for their writings as well, if, in addition to the easily perceived beauty of such translations as Professor Murray's Euripides, we were willing to accustom ourselves to translations as brief and little adorned as the original, and try to discover what the art that resulted in the Parthenon and the Venus has produced in literature. To be willing to learn from the Greeks in this matter also and to be enabled not only to feel the simple majesty of the Greek temple along with the splendor of St. Mark's and the soaring immensity of Bourges, but to love the truth stated with simplicity as well as the truth set off by every adornment the imagination can devise, to care for the Greek way of writing as well as the English way, is to be immensely the richer; it is to have our entire conception of poetry widened and purified.

The Athenians as Plato Saw Them

Once upon a time—the exact date cannot be given but it was not far from 450 BC—an Athenian fleet cast anchor near an island in the Ægean as the sun was setting. Athens was making herself mistress of the sea and the attack on the island was to be begun the next morning. That evening the commander-in-chief, no less a one, the story goes, than Pericles himself, sent an invitation to his second in command to sup with him on the flag-ship. So there you may see them sitting on the ship's high poop, a canopy over their heads to keep off the dew. One of the attendants is a beautiful boy and as he fills the cups Pericles bethinks him of the poets and quotes a line about the "purple light" upon a fair young cheek. The younger general is critical: it had never seemed to him that the color-adjective was well chosen. He preferred another poet's use of rosy to describe the bloom of youth. Pericles on his side objects: that very poet had elsewhere used purple in the same way when speaking of the radiance of young loveliness. So the conversation went on, each man capping the other's quotation with one as apt. The entire talk at the supper table turned on delicate and fanciful points of literary criticism. But, nonetheless, when the battle began the next morning, these same men, fighting fiercely and directing wisely, carried the attack on the island.

The literal truth of the charming anecdote I cannot vouch for, but it is to be noted that no such story has come down to us about the generals of any other country except Greece. No flight of fancy has ever conceived of a discussion on color-adjectives between Cæsar and the trusty Labienus on the eve of crossing the Rhine, nor, we may feel reasonably assured, will any soaring imagination in the future depict General Grant thus diverting himself with General Sherman. That higher truth which Aristotle claimed for poetry over history is here perfectly exemplified. The little story, however apocryphal, gives a picture true to life of what the Athenians of the great age of Athens were like. Two cultivated gentlemen are shown to us, of a great fastidiousness, the poets their familiar companions, able the evening before a battle to absorb themselves in the lesser niceties of literary criticism, but, with all this, mighty men of action, soldiers, sailors, generals, statesmen, any age would be hard put to it to excel. The combination is rarely found in the annals of history. It is to be completely civilized without having lost in the process anything of value.

A Word about Greek Architecture

By Guy Pentreath

Although today we are able to study the remains of a great variety of ancient Greek buildings, the mental picture formed at the sound of the words "Greek architecture" is likely to be that of a temple, and a Doric one at that.

Though no city in Classical times (500 BC–355 BC) was deemed complete without its agora (or city-center), its defensible acropolis (*acro* = high; *polis* = city), its theater, gymnasium, and stadium, it was the temple of the city's patron god or goddess that was commonly given the dominant position and the greatest honor. The chief temple often stood at the highest point of the acropolis, the nucleus around which the city grew in safety, itself enclosed by fortification.

In Mycenaean Greece, 1,000 years before the Classical period, the chief building of a citadel was the king's palace, as seen at Mycenae, Tiryns, and Pylos. In these palace complexes the central feature is the *megaron*—a large rectangular room with the long walls extended to form the sides of an open porch, the roof of which was supported by columns. A single large doorway gives access to the megaron. In the center is a large hearth, the focus of the room: Around it, in a square plan, are four columns supporting the roof; in the right a raised platform for the royal throne. There are forecourts to these megara, and pillared gateways—copied from the Minoan palaces of Crete and replicated throughout Greek history. The Propylaea of the Acropolis at Athens (and of 20 other sites) derives from the Minoan gateway.

Clustered around the megaron and its forecourt are archive rooms, offices, oil-press rooms, workshops, potteries, shrines, corridors, armories, and storerooms for wine and oil and wheat—the whole forming an irregular complex of buildings quite unlike the precise, clear-cut arrangement that is later the hallmark of building in the Classical period. This irregularity, characteristic of the Minoan palaces at Knossos, Mallia, and Phaistos on Crete, was one of the influences of that earlier and foreign culture on the Mycenaeans of the mainland.

But the megaron is Greek. The king's megaron, indeed a "great room," was essentially only the ordinary man's house built large; in some ordinary houses, as at Priene, the same megaron is found. And when the shrine ceased to be a mere house-chapel in a corner of the palace complex, as at Knossos, and the god was given a house of his own, his tem-

Greek Architecture

The Megaron

Showing the development from the "House of the People" to the "House of the God"

A. TROY II

B. TIRYNS

C. OLYMPIA — Temple of Zeus

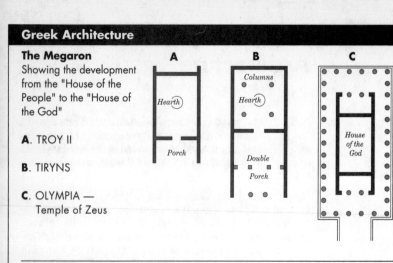

A

Hearth

Porch

B

Columns

Hearth

Double Porch

C

House of the God

The Orders of Greek Architecture

Doric

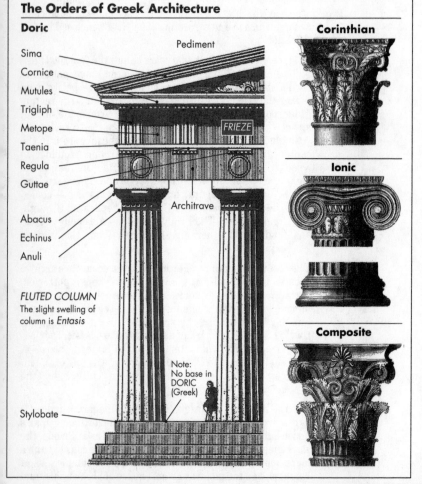

Pediment

Sima
Cornice
Mutules
Trigliph
Metope
Taenia
Regula
Guttae

FRIEZE

Abacus
Echinus
Anuli

Architrave

FLUTED COLUMN
The slight swelling of column is *Entasis*

Note:
No base in DORIC (Greek)

Stylobate

Corinthian

Ionic

Composite

ple had the ground plan of that porched megaron. In its full development there is a porch, or maybe a room, also at the rear, and around it all runs a peristyle of columns. Thus the Greek temple is literally the god's house, intended not for the assembly of worshipers, but as a great room to contain the statue of the god (*see* Figures A, B, and C).

The early temple builders found that sun-baked brick strengthened by horizontal and vertical timbers, if set on a stone footing, was a suitable material even for large buildings. This construction is seen at Knossos (circa 1900 BC) and at the Temple of Hera at Olympia 1,000 years later. The columns of the early temples were made of wood, and, later, when marble began to be used, constructional features appropriate to the use of timber were copied as decoration in the new material. It seems likely that the triglyph, the three-part stone slab set above the column and also above the space between columns in the Doric order, originates from a decorative wood slab that protected the beam ends of the ceiling from rain and rot—particularly when one looks at the six stone *guttae* always fixed below it, which seem to represent the six wood tre-nails, or pegs, that kept the slab in position. And the fluting of the Doric column is reminiscent of the grooves that the long strokes of the adze would make as the woodworker cut away the bark and sapwood of a tree trunk before erecting it as the column.

If the origins of the Doric order are a matter of guesswork, this much is clear: that the Greeks used an elementary formula of vertical and horizontal lines of stone, so refined with skill and taste, with strict rules of proportion, that the total effect is one of balance, symmetry, and power. At the highest development, they added a series of optical corrections to ensure that the human eye, easily misled by the effect of light and shade in alternation, saw the whole as an apparent pattern of truly horizontal and vertical lines. In fact, with the application of these optical corrections, the entire building is made up of subtly curving or inclined surfaces. These refinements called for mathematical ability of a high order in the design and for extreme skill on the part of the masons.

In the Parthenon (5th century BC), the slight swell (*entasis*) and inward slant of the columns makes them seem straight-sided and vertical (which they are not); actual straightness would cause the eye to see them as waisted, and if vertical they would seem to be inclining outward. Also, without its slight upward curve, the steps of the platform (*stylobate*), would seem to sag under the line of standing columns. In short, the Greek mind took the simple idea of the upright and the crossbar, the child's building-block technique and, in developing it to its zenith in the Parthenon, produced a masterpiece that still informs us about those ingredients in a building that make for serenity combined with power, repose with majesty.

Marble was the perfect material for buildings in which sharp edges, clear-cut outline, precision, and the beauty of uncluttered wall surfaces were desired, so that each part, functional and decorative (the sculptured metopes and pediment) might do its work, and the horizontal members could lie without stress or mortar, upon the supporting verticals.

The Doric order continued in use in Hellenistic (350 BC–215 BC) and Roman times, but it is easy to distinguish Greek from Roman Doric. The later architects dared a wider space, enough for three triglyphs, between columns; they used a base for their columns, whereas a Greek Doric column rests directly on the stylobate; they economized often by omitting the fluting in the lower part of a column (where damage most often occurred); and they reduced the size of the capital most meanly. All these Hellenistic and Roman "improvements" are seen in Delos.

T he Ionic order came to mainland Greece almost certainly from Asia Minor and the islands, when the Doric order was well established both there and in the colonies of Magna Graecia (southern Italy). Ionic columns have bases; the flutes have no sharp edges to them but are separated by a substantial fillet; the columns are more tall and slender; the capitals with their beautiful spiral volutes decorative; the architrave has lost its alternating triglyphs and metopes and, in Greece proper, has a frieze of plain or sculptured stone, in Asia Minor a string of dentils to suggest the beam ends of the ceiling. If the feeling of the heavier, more austere Doric order can be described as masculine, then the Ionic is certainly feminine (and very lovely), especially suitable for such smaller buildings as the Erectheum and the Temple of Nike on the Acropolis of Athens.

The Corinthian order came later. Its first appearances were in the temple at Bassae (circa 430 BC) and in the circular building (*tholos*) at Epidauros (360 BC), where one of the perfectly preserved capitals can be seen in the museum. It is decorative and graceful, and one may contrast the simplicity of its sculptured acanthus leaves and their slender tendrils with the complications bestowed on the Corinthian capital by later Hellenistic and Roman architects, in their constant striving for splendor and magnificence.

The Classical Greeks rarely departed from the straight line and the rectangular plan; only a few circular buildings have survived; for instance, the Tholos at Delphi, the "folly" of the family of Philip of Macedon at Olympia, a temple at Samothrace built by Queen Arsinoe, and in the Agora at Athens the building where the executive of the day lived.

Entirely aside from earthquakes, two factors have worked against the survival of the best Greek buildings. The name Marmaria ("marble quarry") for part of the ruins of Delphi reveals one reason for their destruction. There for the taking was a source of cheap marble already cut and squared. Where the ancient stones were not too big and heavy to be easily moved, a vast quantity was reused in later centuries. As recently as the 17th century the stones of the Temple of Zeus at Agrigento (Sicily) were used for the city's harbor wall.

The second factor was the need for lime and the comparative ease with which marble—statues, carved cornices, capitals and drums of columns, anything—could be burnt in a kiln and turned into cash. At one period there was a lime kiln on most of the now-famous classical sites, a kiln that devoured the greater part and left posterity the odds and ends. Perhaps because the stones of theaters are inclined to be large and of a shape useless in ordinary building, many theaters—for example, the one at Epidauros—have survived in a tolerable condition.

A Short Glossary
of Technical Terms

By Guy Pentreath **Acropolis:** the hill-top, fortified with walls and giving protection to the temple of the patron deity and, in early times, to the king's palace, which was the nucleus of an early community living normally outside the walls.

Agora: the "marketplace" or "city-center"; here were sited the shopping and commercial facilities and the main public buildings: the accepted open space where the citizens would gather.

Ambo: the raised pulpit in a Byzantine or Orthodox Christian Church.

Apse: the semicircular recess usually in the short end wall of the long basilica or Roman law-court in which was the dais for the tribunal. When early Christians built churches on the basilica plan, the seats of the Elders were ranged around the apse to the east of the altar, as in the early Christian Church at Delos.

Archaic Period: from 700 BC to the end of the Persian Wars in the early 5th century BC.

Archon: strictly, "one who rules": one of the chief magistrates of Athens, and in certain other city-states.

Arris: the sharp edge formed, for instance, at the meeting point of two flutes in the Doric column, a vulnerable feature of the order, rectified in the Ionic by the substitution of a flat narrow fillet between the flutes.

Ashlar: applied to masonry, of squared hewn stone.

Atrium: literally, the "place made black by the smoke" in a Roman house: a small court open to the sky, colonnaded, four or more columns supporting the roof, and rooms opening on to the colonnade. There are many fine atria or courts in the houses of Pompeii with mosaic designs on the tank tops (*impluvia*) onto which fell rain through the openings above (*compluvia*).

Bas-relief: sculpture on the surface of a slab in low relief, e.g. the Parthenon frieze.

Bema: the rostrum of a public speaker, e.g. in the agora at Corinth.

Bouleuterion: a council chamber.

Boustrophedon: an archaic method of writing, found on some inscriptions, for instance in Gortyna in Crete, where the code of laws is written not in lines from left to right, but as an ox turns with the plough at the end of the furrow and having gone from left to right, returns from right to left.

Caique: the small trading vessel, wooden, brightly painted and rigged for sail but usually today propelled by an engine; it adds color and charm to every Greek waterfront and every passage in the Aegean Sea.

Capital: the top element of a column above the drums or monolithic shaft: the three Greek orders are the Doric, Ionic, and Corinthian.

Caryatid: the sculptured figure of a woman acting in place of a column and supporting an architrave, e.g. in the porch of the archaic Siphnian Treasury at Delphi, or the Erechtheum at Athens.

Cathedra: the throne of a bishop in the early Church in the apse behind the high altar, e.g. at Paros.

Cavea: the auditorium of a theater usually, in Greek practice, in the hollow of a hillside. The Romans, aided by their wealth and their development of the arch and vault, usually built up theaters on arches and vaults precisely where they wanted them.

Cella: the great hall of a temple in which stood the generally colossal cult-statue of the deity.

Chimaera: a fire-breathing monster with a lion's head and dragon's after-quarters with the midship section of a goat: allegedly once a visitant to Lycia in Asia Minor: often used as a decorative design on vases of Rhodes and of Corinth whose trading connections with the East gave them familiarity with Oriental decorative motifs.

Chryselephantine: of a statue built up on a wooden core and covered with plates of gold—for the clothing—and of ivory—for the uncovered parts of the body, e.g. the Zeus at Olympia, and the cult-statue of Athena in the Parthenon.

Classical Period: from the Persian Wars to the unification of Greece under Philip II and the world empire of Alexander the Great, i.e. the 5th and 4th centuries, BC.

Coffer: the marble ceilings of important Greek and Roman buildings were patterned and lightened by rows of sunk panels in their surface, e.g. the coffered ceilings of the Propylaea on the Acropolis at Athens.

Composite Order: of architecture, a combination of the Corinthian capital's rows of acanthus leaves with the volutes, slightly reduced in size, of the Ionic order: a late development, seen at Pergamum and Ephesus.

Corinthian Order: of architecture, differing from the Ionic only in the capital, elaborately decorated with two or three tiers of carved acanthus leaves below small volutes. The considerable advantage over the Ionic lies in the four concave sides of the abacus, which give it, in plan, a cushion shape. For supported at the sharply pointed four corners by pairs of small volutes, this abacus solves the problem involved in the form of the Ionic capital, where the front and side views are different. The new capital was first found in the excavation of the temple at Bassae (5th century BC) and was used at Epidaurus in the tholos (4th century BC).

Cult statue: the statue of a god or goddess, to house which in great dignity was the purpose of a temple. Often it was more than life-size, i.e. "heroic," or "colossal."

Cyclopean: applied to a wall constructed, not of ashlar masonry however big the blocks, but of large boulders of a size which called for giants to handle them, and with interstices filled up with small stones. Early Mycenaean walls, at Mycenae, Tiryns, and also here and there on the Acropolis at Athens, were Cyclopean.

Dentils: the line of teethlike blocks of stone, suggesting the rafter ends of a flat roof, under the cornice of a building of Ionic or Corinthian Order.

Diolchos: literally, the "drag(way) across," i.e. for the portage of ships across the Isthmus of Corinth: invented by Periander in the 7th century BC: ships were hauled on a carriage running in grooves cut on a stone track across the Isthmus, thus avoiding the danger of the long haul around the southern promontories of the Peloponnese.

Dromos: the long horizontal passage, bordered by stone walls, cut into a small hill and giving access to a tholos, or beehive tomb, in Mycenaean Greece.

Ecclesia: the assembly of the whole male citizen body, which gave its decisive vote on policies put before it by the Boule or Council at Athens and elsewhere: later, the Christian Church.

Engaged column: a half-column (divided longitudinally), standing out on the surface of a wall.

Entablature: a term to cover all the horizontal stonework resting on a row of columns including the architrave (the lowest member), the frieze, and the cornice at the top.

Exedra: the curved marble wall, often used as a base for one or more statues, and provided with a marble bench that offered dignified and sheltered casual seating in public places.

Fillet: a flat and narrow molding on the surface of a wall, or between the flutes of an Ionic or Corinthian column.

Flutes: the vertical hollows cut into the sides of a column, which emphasized its rotundity—a device necessary in the brilliant sunlight falling on white marble—and which took off glare from the marble by the easy graduations of light.

Frieze: a band of alternating triglyphs and metopes, the central element of a Doric entablature: also a continuous band of bas-relief sculpture on an Ionic entablature, e.g. the temple of Nike on the Acropolis at Athens. (Part of the Ionic frieze, incorporated in the Doric Parthenon, is still visible inside the colonnade on the west end.)

Geometric Period: of the post-Mycenaean period when, with the Dorian invasions, the Iron Age was fully established throughout Greece and the country had settled again after a grim period of turmoil and population movement. A sub-Mycenaean, followed by a proto-Geometric period, is transitional to the Geometric period proper, which in Athens runs from about 900 BC to 700 BC. The period is characterized by its well-shaped pottery, decorated with horizontal bands of geometric patterns, later incorporating animal and human figures.

Gymnasium: physical education loomed large in the Greek curriculum, and the gymnasia were provided with spacious courts for exercise and games and with good washing-rooms: there were stone benches for the sedentary school periods, e.g. at Delos and Priene.

Helladic Period: applied to the Bronze Age civilization of the Greek mainland: as Cycladic refers to that of the islands, Melos and others in the Cyclades. The period corresponds roughly with that of the Minoan civilization in Crete and, like it, is subdivided into Early, Middle, and Late periods. It was during the Late Helladic period that the Mycenaean civilization developed, first at Mycenae, then at other centers in Greece and spreading throughout the Aegean.

Hellenistic Period: conventionally, from Alexander the Great to the time of Augustus and the Roman Empire, i.e. 300 BC to 30 BC.

Herm: a square-section pillar, tapering out from ground-level, about 5 or 6 feet high and surmounted by the sculptured head of Hermes, bearded in the 5th century BC: they were set up in cities in large numbers as boundary marks, and also outside houses and temples, and were treated as sacred, e.g. in Delos, at the entrance to the Sanctuary of Apollo.

Hippodrome: the course for horse and chariot racing, which had to be much larger than the stadium for athletics: at Delphi, in the Pythian Games, the chariot race was held on the plain below the sanctuary.

Iconostasis: the tall continuous screen in an Orthodox church that cuts off the sanctuary with the altar from the nave and usually, from the sight of the people until the central door is opened at the crisis of the Eucharist: icons of Our Lord, the Holy Mother, the patron saint of the church and of others are set up on the iconostasis, as its name states, and are used as an avenue of worship.

Impluvium: the tank to receive the rain that fell through the open center of a Roman house-roof (the compluvium).

Ionic Order: of architecture: a development, perhaps originating in Aeolia in northwest Asia Minor: an Order more decorative and elaborate than the austere and earlier Doric: its columns have bases, ornamented with a variety of moldings, and are more slender, with deeper flutes and no sharp and vulnerable edges as in the Doric Order: the capital has a pair of spiral volutes extending out on either side, front and back, over a ring of egg-and-tongue molding round the top of the column: there are no triglyphs.

Kore, Korai, Kouros, Kouroi: conventionally applied to the clothed female and the nude male sculptured figures of the Archaic, pre–Persian War period: they stand erect with the weight distributed between the feet, of which the left is slightly forward, but no motion is suggested; on their faces often the "archaic smile." The best of these beautiful korai, or maidens, are in the Acropolis Museum at Athens, and of the male figures in the National Museum, where the steady progress of the sculptor's art from the purely static figure to the dynamic is readily seen and enjoyed.

Labrys: a double-axe, i.e. with two blades facing right and left: a religious symbol in the Minoan period, carved on pillars and found in great numbers in miniature as votives in sanctuaries, and in more than life-size form as religious furniture.

Labyrinth: double-axes (*see* Labrys, *above*) were numerous as religious symbols at Knossos in the Minoan palace: the palace was a most elaborate complex of rooms, passages, and staircases: hence the "place of the double-axes" gained its second and commoner meaning.

Megaron: the central feature of a Mycenaean house or palace: the great room containing a large central hearth.

Metope (méh-to-pi): the plain panel, alternating with the decorated cover-plate for the roof beam-ends (the triglyphs) in the Doric frieze. In Classical times a sculptured relief decorated the plain space, the series of metopes round the temple illustrating a single theme, e.g. Greeks versus Amazons, Lapiths versus Centaurs, or the Labors of Herakles (as seen in the Olympia Museum).

Minoan: referring to the Bronze Age civilization of Crete: Sir Arthur Evans adapted the name of the legendary King Minos of Crete to this civilization when he discovered and excavated the king's palace at Knossos.

Mycenaean: from Mycenae, the principal center of the earliest Greek-speaking people in the late Bronze Age. This civilization, at first limited to mainland sites, spread throughout Greece and across the Aegean after the fall of the Minoan empire. It collapsed only after the capture of Troy by the Mycenaeans; their return to Greece was soon followed by the destruction of their fortress centers at the hands of the Dorians, another Greek-speaking people who entered through Northern Greece, armed with iron weapons and tools.

Nike: goddess of victory, portrayed in Greek art as a winged figure descending to award victory. The earliest Nike statue was found in Delos. The most famous are the winged *Victory of Paeonius* (Olympia Museum) dated 425 BC; and the *Victory of Samothrace* (Louvre; about 320 BC).

(Early) Neolithic Period: Professor John Evans by his excavation to the rock, 23 feet below the Minoan levels of the Palace of Minos at Knossos, has put back the date of the earliest known human settlement in Greece to about 6100 BC, a date derived from the radiocarbon-14 test on burnt grain found on a primitive campsite.

(Middle) Neolithic Period: At the top of 15 feet of accumulated soil deposit, Professor Evans found another Cretan settlement belonging to a period 1,000 years later, whose people could spin and weave. A charcoal sample submitted to the same test gave a central date 5050 BC.

(Late) Neolithic Period: Three other groups of Neolithic settlers have left traces of their homes, habits, and craft in many parts of Greece and the Aegean: (1) The seafarers, probably from the coasts of Asia Minor, who settled in Cyprus, in Crete, and in the Cyclades about 3000 BC. The Minoans who arrived in Crete about 500 years later were probably akin to the earlier settlers; (2) a group who preferred cooler climates and settled in the plains of Thessaly and Boeotia; and (3) a group from the forest-covered North who were hunters.

Odeum: a small building in form and plan like a theater with semicircular seating. Some were roofed. Chiefly used for musical contests and concerts and other meetings. Pericles built an odeum at Athens, the roof of which was carried on many pillars, as Plutarch says. Herodes Atticus presented a large odeum to Athens that is used, with new seating, for Greek Drama festivals today.

Orchestra: the large circular space for the dancing of the chorus in a Greek theater, with an altar of Dionysus in the center: it is similar to the circular threshing-floor still seen commonly in rural Greece; for the threshing-floor, when the harvest was in and the grain stored, was the scene of the country dances and thanksgiving, the seed of Greek drama.

Ostracism: from "ostrakon"—a potsherd used as a voting paper in democratic ancient Athens. The institution of ostracism is said to have been introduced by Cleisthenes as a device to eliminate a likely-looking tyrant before he gained excessive power: first used in 487 BC. Voting was secret: each citizen scratched on a sherd the name of a citizen he wished to see banished (without loss of property and for 10 years). Hundreds of ostraka were found in the Agora excavations. In fact, none of the leading citizens who suffered ostracism look to the historian to have been embryo tyrants. Ostracism was one of the least noble or ennobling of Greek institutions.

Palaestra: a building smaller than a gymnasium, often built as a colonnade around a central court, for the training of boxers, wrestlers, and pancratiasts.

Pancration: an "all-out" contest in the athletic games in which no holds were barred: boxing and wrestling combined, whose only rule forbade biting or the gouging out of eyes.

Pantocrator: literally, "the Almighty," nearly always the subject of a mosaic or fresco dominating from its central position at the height of the dome (inside) every eye that looked upward—as is inevitable on entering a domed building where most of the light comes from the windows of the dome; e.g. the famous Pantocrator of Daphni.

Parian Marble: the marble quarries of the island of Paros produced a white, close-grained marble peculiarly suitable for sculpture: it was widely used by the leading sculptors.

Pediment: in the Greek temple, the triangular space at the vertical ends of the ridge roof, and formed by the horizontal cornice and the raking cornices of the roof: pedimental sculpture in the round was often fixed in this space.

Pendentive: the curving and overhanging triangles of stone or brickwork that transmit, to four piers below, that part of the weight of a dome that is not carried by the four arches springing from those piers: in other words, the method of carrying a circular dome on four piers, square-in-plan.

Pentelic Marble: named from its source on the mountain bordering the Attic plain on the northeast: eminently suitable for fine building both in ancient and modern times. All the finer Athenian buildings of Pericles are made of Pentelic marble: the particles of iron in it give it the famous golden tinge of color.

Peribolos: the wall of a sanctuary or *temenos*.

Peristyle: the row, or occasionally rows, of columns around a temple.

Pinakotheke: picture gallery, e.g. the north room of the Propylaea on the Acropolis at Athens.

Pithos: a large earthenware vessel, from 4 to 8 feet high, especially used in Minoan Crete to contain oil, grain, etc.

Podium: the masonry platform on which a building (e.g. a Roman temple) might be laid.

Polygonal: of a wall made of stones with many angles, each stone being shaped and laid to fit tightly with the corresponding angles of its neighbors: an expensive but effective device to reduce the effect of earthquake.

Prophylactic: literally, "intended to guard against [evil]": used, for example, of the eyes painted on either side of the handles of a wine cup.

Propylon, Propylaea: the dignified entrance between columns to a sanctuary or an agora or major building within an enclosure: an idea from Minoan architecture adapted by the Mycenaeans and retained in the Classical period.

Proskenion: the front of the low building that supported the stage in a developed Greek theater.

Sibyl: perhaps originally a single prophetess who wandered from center to center; but later we hear of a Sibyl at Delphi, Claros, Dodona, Cumae, etc. That an early Sibyl was important at Delphi is proved by the preservation of an outcrop of rock, left unworked in its natural state, in the midst of an area of fine building and statues, just because in early times the Sibyl had given her utterances from that improvised platform.

Stadium: a Greek running-track, providing for spectators by raised earth banks. The stadium was shaped like a hairpin, one end curved and the other—the starting point— either open as at Athens and Delphi or squared as at Olympia, where a tunnel entrance was added. In the Roman period, stone seating was normal. Occasionally, as at Nicopolis, a Roman stadium was rounded at both ends. The standard length was 600 feet, which gave a straight course for the sprint race of about 200 yards. In the 400-yard race, the runners had to round a post at the far end of the course. The two-grooved starting line is seen at Corinth (in the Agora), Delphi, and Olympia; post-holes indicate a separation of the runners at the start. It appears to have been a standing-start, at the drop of a horizontal signal arm at the top of the post.

Steatite: a stone with a soapy feel and look about it, from the Greek word for tallow; sometimes used in Minoan art for ornamental vases, and covered with gold foil.

Stele: a stone slab set up in a public place, with an inscription recording a victory, treaty, or a decree; also a gravestone. Many beautiful funeral stelai, sculptured in relief, are to be seen in the National Museum, Athens, and in the Kerameikos.

Talent: In Pericles' time at Athens, we know that the talent was equivalent in value to 6,000 drachmae, and that a normal wage for a week's work was 3½ drachmae.

Temenos: the enclosed area in which stood a temple.

Templum-in-Antis: the simplest form of temple in which "the house of the god" is the same in plan as the ordinary house: a rectangular room, with the long side walls extended to form the walls of a porch, and with two columns between the antae (or wall endings) to support the porch roof and make a fine entry to the temple; e.g. the so-called Treasury of the Athenians at Delphi.

Theater: an essential building in every city, to the Greek mind.

Thermae: the Spartans are believed to have invented the heated sweat room as a method of removing dirt from the skin, a strigil being used to scrape away the sweat, which carried the dust with it out of the pores of the skin. This process was followed by a cold plunge. Cicero refers to this kind of bath as "Laconicum." But the Greeks did not go so far as to provide great public buildings for this purpose, merely attaching limited bathing facilities to their gymnasia. The Thermae are a development of the Imperial Roman period, and very large, beautiful, and elaborate public bathing centers were built in Rome and in all the major cities of the Empire, and small ones even in some villages.

Tholos: a circular building, such as that at Epidaurus, where the circular mazelike foundations can be seen, or at Delphi, where a Doric tholos has had several fallen columns re-erected: also of the numerous underground beehive tombs of the Mycenaean period, of which the so-called "Treasury of Atreus" at Mycenae is the best preserved and finest.

Treasury: the word used for the well-built, often marble, small buildings, put up by leading city-states at such pan-Hellenic centers as Delphi or Olympia; an Athenian citizen, going to Delphi, for instance, would find an Athenian official on duty in his Treasury to advise him. Doubtless festival robes and sacred vessels, etc., for use by representatives would be stored there.

Trilogy: when Greeks went to the theater to see a tragedy played, they were prepared to sit all day, for the great themes were divided into three plays that were put on in succession—e.g. the drama of Orestes in the plays *Agamemnon*, *Choephoroi*, and *Eumenides*—and the trilogy was concluded, for the relief of tension, with a satyric play.

Tripod: Homer writes of bronze tripods—large, three-footed vessels like cauldrons—as prizes; Linear B tablets from Knossos show a careful count of these valued objects. In Classical times we hear of their use, beautifully decorated, sometimes even made of gold, as gifts devoted to a god. On the plaster or beaten earth floor of a Mycenaean room, a three-legged vessel (or stand for a large amphora) would readily find stability. But granted this advantage to a tripod, and the possible explanation of its use as a means of storing wealth in bronze or other metals in negotiable form, the attraction of it to the Greek mind remains a mystery.

Trireme: the standard warship of the 5th and 4th centuries BC that displaced the old penteconter with 25 oarsmen a side. The trireme was about 120 feet long overall, with a beam of perhaps 20 feet and a shallow draught. It was of light construction, liable to hog or sag at the extremities and so likely to leak in a seaway that permanent undergirding cables were fitted (if one can judge from the carved relief of the stern quarters of a trireme on the rock face at Lindos in Rhodes).

Volute: the spiral element in the capital of columns of the Ionic, Corinthian, and Composite orders: derived from the voluted ram's horns, or of Geometrical origin, or perhaps suggested by the perfect natural spiral of the seed box of one of the commonest Greek clovers.

Votive: the offering to a deity of a terracotta model, often of an animal, seems to have been a device in Mycenaean times to make the donor's prayer more likely to be remembered by the deity. Little plaques of silver embossed with a leg, eye, ear, heart, arm, etc., are today often attached to an icon on the iconastasis of a church, and are either thanksgivings or petitions for the recovery of the limb or organ so devoted.

Xoanon: a primitive wooden image, so unlike marble sculpture that it was supposed to have fallen from heaven and was accordingly deeply revered. Such an image (of Athena) was housed in the Erechtheum and dressed in a new robe (*peplos*) at her great Panathenaic festival every fourth year.

Greek Mythology

By W. B.
Stanford

Mythology in its widest sense includes legend, parable, allegory, and fable, and all fictional figures, situations, and scenes—in fact the whole nonfactual, non-scientific, non-mathematical, gravity-free, miscegenetic world of the imagination and of dreams. As such it pervades almost all creative Greek art and literature. Whether we are looking at pedimental sculptures in Olympia or vase-paintings in Athens, whether we are reading the epics of Homer or the tragedies of Euripides, we are in the presence of the Greek mythopoeic mind. Even the philosophers and scientists used myths. When Plato wanted to describe the deepest truths of earth and heaven, he embodied them in myths. When the Greek astronomers charted the stars, they grouped them in mythological figures—Orion, Perseus, Andromeda, and the rest. In our own time psychologists like Freud and Jung have found names and symbols to express their discoveries in the unconscious mind with Greek mythology.

To describe this infinitely varied and variable world (for a Greek myth changed every time it was sympathetically retold), peopled with emblems of hope, fear, yearning, dim memories, patched-up misunderstandings, personifications of melting beauty or of petrifying ugliness, would be impossible here. Only a few types can be briefly mentioned.

Some myths try to answer questions about nature. How did the world and mankind first come into being? Hesiod in his magnificent *Theogony* answers with stories about Chaos and the marriage of Earth with her son Heaven, and the subsequent generations of gods and giants and men. Why do plants wither? Because Pluto takes Persephone down to Hades (and hence the wonderful myth and ritual of Eleusis). How does the sun cross the sky? In his golden chariot. What causes earthquakes? Poseidon with his trident. Who invented fire? Prometheus brought it down from Olympos. Others explore problems of human destiny. How did pain and sickness come into the world? Through the curiosity of Pandora (that other Eve). What is the nature of love? Read the myths in Plato's *Symposium*. What happens to us after death? Homer described the geography of Hades in the *Odyssey*, and dozens of other poets followed him in that macabre exploration; and the mysteries of Demeter, Orpheus, and Dionysos, offered guidance across those awesome rivers and through those forlorn shades.

Quite different are the myths based on historical events supplemented, adapted, and enriched by free imagination and wishful thinking. How much is factual, how much fictional, in the legends of Troy, in the stories of the *Odyssey*, in the saga of the Golden Fleece, in the exploits of Hercules and Theseus? No one can say for certain, except when firm historical evidence gives independent proof. Archaeology has an authoritative voice in this. But the evidence of the Greek historians must be scrutinized with care: they were sometimes mythologists, too—even Thucydides.

Then there were ethical, or even frankly moralistic, myths. Is gold the best thing of all? Consider Midas. Freedom from death, then? Think on Tithonos, or the Sibyl at Cumae (shrunk with age to the size of a pea, kept in a bottle for fear of being lost, and always squeaking with her pin-point voice "I want to die. I want to die."). Would it be a good thing for men to be able to fly? Icarus and Bellerophon did not find it so. Would you like to be married to Helen of Troy, or to Jason, the winner of the Golden Fleece? Consult Menelaos and Medea. How wonderful to be the supremely powerful and supremely popular ruler of a fabulously great city! Not for Oedipus. Well, is all human life doomed to disaster and woe? No, there are two large jars in the hall where Zeus makes his decisions, one of good fortune and one (but some think two) of ill fortune; and to most people he distributes portions fairly equally. The wisest and safest thing—and the hardest thing for Greeks—is to avoid all excess, and pride, greed, envy, and small-mindedness. But the Greek myths rarely preach directly: they prefer just to tell the story, with compassion and understanding and without useless grief.

When a genius—a Sophocles or a Pheidias or a Polygnotos—adopted these myths, they became new works of art. In less-talented hands they remained smaller and simpler, but no less memorable. Aesop's fables about Greek-speaking and Greek-thinking animals are now read mostly by children. But judgments and phrases from them—like "sour grapes," "King Stork"—remain part of our adult vocabulary and ethics. Proverbs are often shrunken myths.

To the ancient Greeks mythology was much more than a matter of literature, art, philosophy, and ethics. The whole countryside teemed with spirits and powers, to us mythical (in the sense of imaginary: but a lecturer on a Swan Hellenic Cruise has stated in print that he saw a satyr and perhaps also Pan), to them mythic (in the sense of belonging to traditional belief). Besides the loftier Olympian gods there were spirits of mountain, sea, tree, and stream—oreads, nereids, dryads, and naiads—sometimes benign, sometimes malevolent. (The Greek countryman still dreads the capricious nereids.) Pan (who gave the Christians a shape for the Devil) and the satyrs were there; and in the sea old Triton still blew his wreathed horn. In the darkness of the night or of the mind lurked figures of terror, the hideous turn-you-to-stone Gorgons, the ferocious Furies, and snatching demons, and shrivelling ghosts (one of them would take out her eye and wave it at you). Did they believe, actually and acutely, in minotaurs and chimaeras and sphinxes and centaurs and winged horses, those strange surrealistic figments embodying ancestral fears, perverse desires, dreams, visions?

Some myths are too profoundly moving and poetical to fit into any classification—Orpheus and Eurydice, Cupid and Psyche.

Made in Man's Image: A Chronicle of Gods and Heroes

Ancient Greece was happily free from the religious fanaticism of later ages for the Greek attitude toward their gods was remarkably eclectic and never hidebound by rigid tradition. Gods from many parts of the Ancient world were assimilated into the Olympian family. This extremely tolerant and open attitude toward their gods accounts to a very large degree for the development of the great Greek philosophic systems side by side with popular religion.

Like most Mediterraneans the original inhabitants of Greece worshipped the Great Triple Goddess. Her celestial symbol was the moon, whose three phases recalled the change from the maiden into the woman and finally into a crone. Ever since, three has remained a sacred number, playing a mystical part in religion.

In the pre-Hellenic matriarchal organization the tribes were ruled by a queen, whose annual lover was sacrificed at the end of the year and his blood sprinkled on trees and crops. His flesh was devoured by the priestesses disguised as mares, sows, or bitches. The frenzied followers of Dionysos indulged in this cannibalistic practice down to the 6th century, with Orpheus as their most famous victim.

Successive invasions of Hellenic tribes undermined the authority of the terrible Great Goddess, and introduced male supremacy and succession toward the close of the 2nd millennium BC. Yet the goddesses were never completely stripped of all influence, thanks to the great poets, especially Homer, who had clearly defined their spheres of action.

Religion was an imaginative comment on natural phenomena, without any rigid creed. As the moral consciousness developed, the notion of reward and punishment based on ethical conduct gained strength, and by the 6th century BC hell, purgatory, and paradise had become established concepts. But the gods were not exempt from passions and faults—they simply acted on a grander scale. Even their immortality depended on the divine food and drink of ambrosia and nectar. They were conceived as an upper class of very superior nobles, above the humans, yet essentially human.

Feasts and ceremonies followed largely older local traditions, while rules were concerned with pleasing the gods, not with regulating the belief of the worshipper. Impiety was a crime only when it led to a neglect of ritual determining the daily life. This close connection makes some familiarity with mythology essential for the better understanding of the Greek mind.

Owing to the different poetical interpretations, the gods were endowed with a bewildering assortment of vices and virtues to satisfy everybody's taste. Greek sense of humor, moreover, was stronger than blind respect for the immortals. The Olympians' amorous misadventures or their far from harmonious family life were discussed with relish.

The Creation Myth

At the beginning was Chaos, from which Gaea (Earth) emerged—though how successfully has remained a point of dispute. All by herself she bore a son, Uranos (Heaven), who was ashamed of his naked mother. His tears of indignation must have been copious, as rivers and seas, flowers and trees, and even animals sprang up where they had fallen. The earth became divided into two equal parts by the Mediterranean and the Black Sea, with the river Okeanos encircling the disc. Greece occupied the central position, while far north, in the inaccessible British Isles, lived the blameless Hyperboreans in perpetual springtide. (It is pleasant to reflect that Britain once enjoyed such a reputation.) They were often visited by the gods, like their southern counterpart, the equally virtuous Ethiopians.

Incest was a practical necessity for the first gods and men alike, in both cases with singularly unprepossessing results. Heaven's union with Mother Earth produced three 100-handed giants, followed by three hardly more attractive one-eyed Cyclopes. It is not surprising that the exasperated father flung his hideous brood into Tartaros, the remotest and gloomiest part of the underworld. Yet Uranos must have been fond of children, as he proceeded to father the seven Titans, more pleasing in appearance, but far more dangerous to their luckless progenitor. Urged on by their mother, who pined for her exiled Cyclopes, the Titans attacked their sleeping father with a flint sickle and castrated him.

The Titans divided the world among themselves under the leadership of the youngest, Kronos (Time). Mother Earth, however, failed in her attempt to set the beloved Cyclopes free. After one look Kronos confined them and their 100-handed brothers again to Tartaros; and in revenge the frustrated mother prophesied that he too would be dethroned by one of his own sons.

Kronos married his sister Rhea but, mindful of the prophecy, swallowed the children his wife bore him, a parable of Time annihilating all creation. On Mother Earth's advice Rhea substituted for her sixth child a stone wrapped in swaddling clothes which Kronos promptly devoured. It says a lot for his excellent digestion that he never noticed the fraud.

The infant Zeus was hidden in the cave of Dicte in Crete, under the care of the goat Amalthea, whose milk he drank together with his foster-brother Goat-Pan. Zeus showed his gratitude to his nurse by setting her image among the stars as Capricorn. Around the infant's cradle Rhea's priests performed wild dances, clashing shields and uttering piercing screams to drown the noise of his wailing. He grew up among the shepherds of Mount Ida, and with his mother's assistance was made cupbearer to his unsuspecting father. Rhea provided Zeus with a mixture so potent that even Kronos could not stomach it. He vomited up first the stone—venerated throughout antiquity in Delphi—and then disgorged his elder children.

After deposing their father, Zeus, Poseidon, and Hades drew lots for the division of the world. Zeus won the heaven, Poseidon the sea, and Hades the underworld. The earth was left common to all the gods under the vague sovereignty of Zeus, who only succeeded in controlling his quarrelsome family by the threat of the thunderbolts he alone might wield. And it was the thunderbolts—forged by the Cyclopes at last released—that give the third generation victory over those Titans who refused to acknowledge Zeus as their master. For 10 years a terrible war raged in Thessaly, the rebels piling mountain upon mountain to reach the abode of the gods, before Kronos was defeated and banished to the British Isles. According to another version, he was allowed to withdraw to Italy, where he ruled a prosperous kingdom, until in his dotage he was compensated with the Elysian Fields. Atlas, his second-in-command, was set to hold up the sky, while the lesser Titans took the Cyclopes' place in Tartaros.

Having successfully disposed of his uncles, Zeus settled down to enjoy his unlawfully obtained power. But Mother Earth changed sides, and, never averse to bringing forth a monster, now created the worst abomination of all, called Typhon.

To a hundred dragon heads spouting flames were added arms reaching a hundred leagues in either direction, while instead of legs he featured the coils of a serpent. One glance at Gaea's youngest sent the gods in headlong flight to Egypt, a favorite refuge for divinity in distress. For greater safeguard Zeus assumed the form of a ram, Hera became a cow, Artemis a cat, each god choosing the animal shape of his Egyptian counterpart.

But Zeus soon grew ashamed of his cowardice and resuming his true form pursued Typhon with thunderbolts, finally hurling Mount Aetna at him. Buried beneath the Sicilian mountain the monster still belches forth fire and flame, and when he occasionally changes his position an earthquake ensues.

The Story of Man

Prometheus (Forethought), the wisest of the Titans, had foreseen the outcome of Kronos's rebellion and loyally fought on the Olympians' side. As a reward he was entrusted with the creation of man. From a lump of clay kneaded with water Prometheus fashioned a creature in the image of the gods, and bestowed on man the supreme gift of fire, lighting a torch at the sun itself.

During the Age of Gold men lived without care and without women. After Zeus had fathered the seasons life became harder for men, who had to seek refuge from wind and cold in caves. No more could they live on fruit, milk, and honey, but had to work for their food. Contrary to expectation, work and sin went hand in hand, and as punishment Zeus extinguished the fire. Prometheus once again came to the rescue and brought a torch to earth hidden in the pithy hollow of a giant fennel stalk. But the gods took a terrible vengeance on both Prometheus and mankind. The Titan was chained to a peak in the Caucasian mountains, where an eagle tore at his liver all day; and there was no end to his pain, because every night the liver grew whole again and the ghastly process was resumed the next morning.

To men was meted out a fate hardly less atrocious. Haephaestos fashioned a woman, Aphrodite taking care of the sex appeal. This gift of all the gods, Pandora, was sent to Epimetheus (Afterthought), who in spite of his brother Prometheus' warnings was enslaved by her charms. As dowry Pandora had received a jeweled box, which Zeus had exhorted her never to open, realizing full well that disobedience and curiosity would distinguish the female. Before long Pandora did indeed open the box, and out flew all the mental and bodily diseases that have plagued mankind ever since. But caught under the lid remained Hope, which alone makes men's lives bearable.

Mankind degenerated so intolerably that Zeus resolved to destroy it in a flood. But there was one righteous man, Deukalion, who with his wife Pyrrha had been warned to take refuge in an ark, which floated about for nine days, before at last coming to rest on Mount Parnossos. When the flood receded a divine voice ordered them to fling the bones of their mother behind. This they rightly interpreted as meaning the bones of Mother Earth, the rocks. Those thrown by Deukalion became men, and those by Pyrrha women. Thus humanity was renewed, though the couple also produced one son in the orthodox way. He was called Hellen, who gave his name to the Hellenic race, and his sons Aelos and Doros, and grandsons Ion and Achaius, became the ancestors of the tribes bearing their names.

The Olympians—Zeus and Hera

Having thus connected the tribes, Greek love of systematization likewise wrought the principal gods into one great family, regardless of their varied origins.

Zeus fixed the abode of the gods in Mount Olympos, whence he decreed laws and controlled the heavenly bodies. When his mother Rhea forbade him to marry, he violated her and proceeded to court his sister Hera—unsuccessfully, until he transformed himself into a bedraggled cuckoo, which the merciful goddess warmed against her bosom. Resuming his true shape, Zeus ravished her, shaming her into marriage.

Mother, now grandmother, Earth gave Hera a tree with golden apples as a wedding present. The newlyweds spent the wedding night, lasting 300 years, on Samos, but in spite of the birth of two sons and one daughter, Ares, Hephaestos, and Hebe, the marriage could hardly be called happy. There was constant bickering over Zeus' numerous infidelities, which Hera proved utterly incapable of preventing, though she occasionally took terrible revenge on her rivals or their children.

She only rarely succeeded in arousing her husband's passion, even though she sometimes borrowed Aphrodite's girdle; perhaps the wedding night had been too prolonged. Their family, however, increased to 12, partly by children born in wedlock, partly through extramarital affairs with nymphs or mortals, a yield of four supplemented by two miraculous births.

Zeus grew increasingly overbearing, and at last the Olympians revolted, binding him, as he lay asleep, with rawhide thongs tied in a hundred knots. While the gods were quarreling over his succession, the sea nymph Thetis, fearing a civil war, set one of the 100-handed uncles to untie the knots all at once. No sooner was Zeus free than he hung Hera, the ringleader, in golden chains from heaven, with heavy anvils weighing down her ankles. She was only released after her fellow conspirators had taken an oath of loyalty.

Poseidon

Poseidon too had taken a prominent part in the rebellion, and was condemned to serve King Laomedon for one year, for whom he built with Apollo's assistance the city of Troy. He equaled his brother Zeus in dignity, though not in power, which was all for the good considering his perpetual bad temper.

In the best family tradition he raped his sister Demeter, then had a son, a most objectionable giant, by his grandmother Earth, before he began courting the sea nymph Thetis, to have a spouse who would feel at home in the depth of the sea. Zeus was his rival for Thetis' hand, but both desisted when it was prophesied that her son would outshine his father. They forthwith encouraged her to wed an innocuous mortal, King Peleus, the future father of Achilles.

Another sea nymph, Amphitrite, became his consort and though rather insignificant herself, she could rise to fits of jealousy worthy of Hera. Needless to say she had plenty of provocation. Her children were singularly undistinguished, with the exception of Triton, the dangerous and touchy merman.

Not content with the seas, Poseidon was exceedingly greedy for earthly kingdoms, quarreling fiercely with Dionysos over Naxos, with Hera over Argos, and especially with Athena over Athens.

Hestia and Demeter

Though both unmarried, these two sisters of Zeus were unlike in character. Hestia, alone of all Olympians, was never connected with any scandal, and it was probably her very purity that made her lose her place to the orgiastic Dionysos. The ancient Greeks were too fond of love and intrigue to honor greatly so placid, mild, and charitable a goddess as this protectress of the hearth.

Demeter, on the other hand, shared fully the stormy life of the Olympians. She did not escape Zeus' amorous advances and bore him Persephone. After a passing affair with a Titan, she was raped by brother Poseidon.

But this dallying came to a sudden stop when Hades abducted young Persephone while she was picking flowers. The disconsolate mother searched in vain, until she reached Eleusis, where the king's elder son had news of the vanished Persephone. He had seen a chariot drawn by black horses racing down a bottomless chasm. And then the earth closed again over the driver who was clasping a struggling girl. There could be no doubt as to the charioteer's identity.

Demeter instantly forbade all trees to bear fruit and all grain to grow, until life on earth was threatened with extinction. She only relented after a compromise was reached thanks to mother Rhea's intervention. Persephone was to spend the three winter months with Hades, and the rest of the year with her mother. Demeter lifted the curse, instructed the king's son in her mysteries and rewarded him with seed corn and a wood plow to teach mankind the art of agriculture.

Aphrodite and Eros

The goddess of love rose naked from the sea. Though originally an orgiastic Oriental, her cult, if not her conduct, improved in comformity with the Greek moral code. Only in

Corinth, the trading center most exposed to foreign influences, did temple harlots serve her in the Syrian fashion.

Aphrodite was exceedingly fickle and capricious, but worst of all, she hardly ever lent her magic girdle, which made its wearer irresistible. As punishment she was married off to Hephaestos, physically the least attractive Olympian. Yet this match was harder on the husband than on the wife, who had fallen for the virility of Ares. Hephaestos surprised the lovers in bed, and throwing an unbreakable net over them summoned the gods to witness their shame. The immortals were merely amused, while Poseidon and Hermes greatly appreciated Aphrodite's provocative helplessness. As reward for Hermes' flattering remarks she spent a night with him and bore double-sexed Hermaphroditos. Then she could not but do likewise with Poseidon, and, after rounding off a hectic season with Dionysos, she retired to Cyprus renewing her virginity in the sea, to the pained envy of mortals and immortals.

Woe to anyone who offended the goddess of love. Her main instrument of vengeance was her son Eros, whose progenitor could never be ascertained owing to the mother's promiscuity. Eros wantonly kindled passions with his golden arrows shot at random, yet he himself did not escape the fate he had meted out to countless victims.

He had been instructed by his jealous mother to make Psyche (Soul) fall in love. For once handling the fateful arrows clumsily, he wounded himself, while Psyche remained untouched. Aphrodite was enraged that his own weapon had been turned against her son. She set the desperate maiden some seemingly impossible tasks, which Psyche nevertheless accomplished, sustained by Eros' invisible assistance. As supreme trial she was bidden to fetch some of Persephone's beauty from the underworld, as Aphrodite had lost some of hers tending her love-sick son. Psyche was on her way back with the priceless gift wrapped in a box, when she bethought herself that a touch of divine beauty might not come amiss to restore any possible ravages caused by her sorrow. Pandora's heritage of disobedience and curiosity undid Psyche for a second time. Yet thanks to the power of love and Eros' fervent pleading, Psyche was made immortal and married her lover. Spiritual and bodily love were united and blessed with a child called Delight.

Athena

Some cannibalistic tendencies still persisted among the gods, especially within the close family circle. After having got his aunt, the wise Titaness Metis, with child, Zeus swallowed her. Surprisingly enough this did not cause indigestion, but a raging headache. As a drastic, though unusual remedy Zeus ordered Hephaestos to cleave his skull open with an axe. The fruit of this heroic midwifery was Athena, who sprang full-grown and fully armed from her father's head.

Though excelling in the domestic arts, she was a formidable warrior, but only supported just causes and, unlike Ares, did not love war for its own sake. She inherited her luckless mother's wisdom, which kept her from the petty jealousies so common on Olympos. Only once did the boast of Princess Arachne (Spider) that she wove more skillfully than the goddess, drive Athena to cruel revenge. Defeated in a competition, Arachne hanged herself and was changed into a spider weaving for all eternity.

Apollo

Leto was vainly seeking for a place to bear Zeus' child, abandoned by her lover to his wife's vindictiveness. Hera forbade Mother Earth to grant Leto hospitality and sent a monstrous serpent, Python, in pursuit. At last Poseidon took pity, and on the floating island of Delos, Leto gave birth to a son and a daughter.

In the land of the Hyperboreans Apollo grew into a skillful archer, ready to avenge his mother on the Python, who had been rewarded with the guardianship of the sacred cave in Delphi. To commemorate his slaying of the monster, Apollo instituted the Pythian games, culminating in a race from Delphi to Thessaly—what a pleasant stroll the Marathon seems in comparison!

The victor returned crowned with laurels, which recalled one of Apollo's many misadventures. In spite of his great beauty he was singularly unlucky in love, as Eros was determined to prove the superiority of his own bow and arrow: Apollo chased Daphne, Peneus' daughter, through the forest. In answer to the terrified maiden's prayers, Peneus, a river god, changed her into a laurel tree on the banks of his stream. In his grief Apollo decreed that laurel wreaths should thenceforward be the reward of athletes and artists.

A flower, too, bears witness to the god's misfortune. He loved a handsome youth named Hyacinthos, who was also coveted by Zephiros, god of the west wind. Apollo and the boy were throwing the discus at Amyclae, near Sparta, when Zephiros blew Apollo's discuss so violently aside that it wounded Hyacinthos mortally. The drops of blood were changed into a cluster of hyacinths.

Apollo usurped the place of the sun god Helios whose statue, the famous Colossus, stood astride the harbor of Rhodes. Heralded by his attendant Eos (Dawn), Helios drove the sun chariot daily from his splendid palace in the east to the far western sea. After pasturing his horses in the Fortunate Isles, he sailed back on the ocean stream which encircles the world. Because of the similarity of attributes and youthful beauty, Helios became identified

with Phoebus Apollo, and the myt'
merged into one cycle.

Artemis

Like her twin brother Apollo, Artemis usurped
the older goddess Selene, mistress of the moon. .
was a great huntress, and, when she had finished dri
the moon chariot she spent the rest of the night in the woods
with her attendant nymphs. From a silver bow she shot her
unfailing arrows indiscriminately at beasts and those unlucky huntsmen who accidentally saw her bathing in the
nude. Her inordinate irritability and morbid insistence on
chastity make her an obvious case of acute frustration. Yet
there were ugly rumors in connection with a handsome
shepherd, Endymion, whom Zeus put to perpetual sleep for
the sake of his daughter's reputation. Even more serious
was her infatuation with Orion, a fellow-hunter. Apollo,
aware that amorous Eros had already fallen for Orion's
charms, thought it necessary to intervene. Playing on his
sister's prejudice, he tricked her into shooting the object of
her affection. That he was subsequently placed with his
faithful dog Sirius among the stars seemed but little consolation.

Ares, Hephaestos, and Hebe

The impetuous god of war was exceedingly unpopular on
Olympos, even with his own parents, though his mother
Hera often used him for her own ends. Always spoiling for a
fight he was not consistently victorious. Athena twice wor-
sted him in battle, and Heracles sent him running back to
Olympos. Ares was among the numerous claimants to pa-
ternity of Eros, but his ascertained progeny was hardly less
formidable: Eris (Discord), Phobos (Fear), and Pallor (Terror).

His brother Hephaestos presented a startling contrast to
the general run of Olympian good looks. He was such an
ugly baby that his disgusted mother dropped him from
Olympos and forgot all about him. Kind Thetis brought him
up, and the child became exceedingly clever with his hands.
It was only when Hera inquired where Thetis's lovely jewelry came from that she learned of her son's matchless skill
and promptly fetched him home. Hephaestos was of a for-
giving nature and became strongly attached to his mother.
He even dared to draw up the chains by which she was hanging in punishment for her abortive rebellion. It was now
Zeus' turn to hurl his son from heaven. Striking the earth at
the island of Lemnos he broke both his legs and was permanently lamed. Zeus became reconciled to Hera, but neither
thought of recalling Hephaestos.

Hebe, the third legitimate child and personification of
youth, was never admitted into the inner council of the big

twelve. She was her father's cup-bearer, until she was
ousted even from this minor position by Ganymede. Zeus
had taken a passionate fancy to the boy and abducted him in
the disguise of an eagle. Despite Hera's violent protests,
Ganymede was constantly at Zeus's side. Hebe was married off to Heracles.

Hermes

One of Zeus's innumerable extra-marital relations was with
Maia, Atlas's daughter. Luckier than Leto, she met with no
particular difficulty in bringing Hermes into the world in an
Arcadian cave. No sooner had the mother turned her back
than the child prodigy left his cradle, strangled a tortoise
and from its shell made the first lyre, with which he lulled
Maia to sleep. He then went in search of adventures to Macedonia, stole 50 cows belonging to Apollo and drove them
backwards to Pylos, so that their hoofmarks pointed in the
opposite direction. He made sacrifice to the 12 Olympians,
among whom he modestly included himself, and returned to
his cradle. When Apollo came looking for his cattle, Maia in-
dignantly pointed at the child still wrapped in swaddling
bands and feigning sleep. But Apollo was not deceived and
hauled the culprit before their father, who was rather
proud of his youngest's cunning and bade them be reconciled. This was effected by exchanging the lyre against the
cattle, and the two half-brothers became friends.

For his ingenuity Hermes was chosen the herald and mes-
senger of the gods. His duties included the making of trea-
ties, the promotion of commerce, and the protection of
travelers. But in memory of his promising beginnings he
was also the god of thieves, and it must have happened
many a time that a robber and his victim both invoked
Hermes's help for opposite ends.

Dionysos

Semele, daughter of King Cadmus of Thebes, was proud of
Zeus's love. Rumors reached Hera, who assumed the shape
of Semele's old nurse and pretended to doubt the lover's divine nature. So Semele pestered Zeus to reveal himself in
all his splendor, but when he finally consented she had a
miscarriage and died. The infant was sewn up in the father's thigh and delivered three months later. That is why
Dionysos was called twice-born and became immortal.
When he grew up he discovered how to make wine, and
went roaming about the world, accompanied by a wild army
of Satyrs and Maenads.

Dionysos propagated the cult of the vine, and the resistance
to this innovation is the clue to his bitter struggles from
Asia Minor to India. The new intoxicant met with particularly strong opposition in Thrace, where beer had long been
established as the national drink. Only after the Thracian

king had gone mad and believing his son to be a vine, started pruning the poor boy's nose, ears, and fingers, did Dionysos triumph.

No better fate awaited the king of Thebes, who wanted to arrest his cousin for disorderly conduct. The raving Maenads rent the king limb from limb, led by his own mother who wrenched off his head. The constant recurrence of the madness theme in these myths shows the devastating effect of wine at its first appearance.

When all Boetia had acknowledged Dionysos's divinity, he made a tour of the Aegean islands, during which he was kidnapped by pirates. But his bonds fell off, vine and ivy grew about the mast and rigging, and to the sound of flutes, lions and tigers played around the god's feet. The terrified pirates leaped overboard and were turned into dolphins. Dionysos steered the ship to Naxos, where he married Cretan Ariadne, abandoned by Theseus.

The Underworld

To Hades, Kronos's eldest son, had been allotted the underworld, a gloomy, though vague concept trying to reconcile conflicting views of the afterlife.

The souls of the dead were ferried across the river Styx by Charon, who demanded the coin laid under their tongue before the burial. Yet why they should be so anxious to enter the underworld, instead of dallying with the penniless souls on the near bank, is hard to understand. The three-headed dog Kerberos guarded the entrance to the Asphodel Fields, a kind of purgatory for minor transgressions. In front of Hades's palace lay the twin pools of Forgetfulness and Memory, from which the souls might drink at their choice.

Though Hades only rarely visited the upperworld, being less amorous than his brothers, he delegated the judgment of the souls to the wise kings Minos, Radamanthys, and Aeakos; the second was competent for Asiatics, the third for Europeans, while Minos held a court of appeal. The evildoers were sent to Tartaros to undergo eternal punishment, as for instance Sisyphos, who had to roll a heavy stone up a hill only to see it crash down again.

Virtuous souls were allowed to enter the Elysian Fields, over which Hades had no power, but which formed the domain of old Kronos. In that paradise there was constant feasting, games, music, and dancing. Yet one grade superior were the Fortunate Isles, reserved for the privileged though undeserving few, like Achilles and Helen of Troy, who just failed to make Olympos.

Minor Deities

But there were also several divinities who never attained Olympian status. Zeus's foster-brother, goat-footed Pan, was content to live in Arcadia. When he was not guarding his numerous flocks, he was busy seducing nymphs, and boasted of having possessed all the drunken Maenads. An unusually chaste nymph preferred turning into a reed to his embrace. Unable to distinguish her from all the rest, he cut several reeds at random and made them into a pan-pipe, which was afterwards copied by Hermes and claimed as his own invention.

The Thessalian Princess Koronis was with child by Apollo. The correct behavior for a mortal pregnant by a god was to remain faithful till the child was born. But Koronis did not comply with this reasonable rule of conduct. Artemis avenged this insult by killing her with an arrow, but as she lay on the funeral pyre Apollo rescued the unborn baby and entrusted it to Chiron, the wise Centaur.

Under his tuition young Asklepios grew marvelously proficient in medicine, so that he not only cured the sick, but even restored a dead man to life. Zeus was annoyed at this interference with the normal course of events and hurled a thunderbolt at the culprit. Yet later Zeus himself repeated Asklepios' transgression and resurrected him as god of healing. Asklepios became increasingly popular, and at his shrines, especially at Epidaurus, medical science came into being.

Aeolos ruled the seven islands in the Tyrrhenian sea, which bore his name. Hera had entrusted him with the guardianship over the Winds, which were confined in deep caverns. At his own discretion or at the request of some Olympian, Aeolos would thrust his spear into the cliff and the appropriate wind would stream out of the hole, until he sealed it again.

Halfway between the Aeolian islands and the underworld lay the kingdom of Hypnos (Sleep), surrounded by the waters of Lethe (Oblivion). Round the entrance to his palace grew poppies and other plants that induce dreams.

The relationship between Zeus and the Moirai (Fates) always remained uncertain. Some held that Zeus determined destiny, while others believed that Zeus himself was subject to the Fates. The three sisters assigned to each newborn child his lot by spinning, measuring, and cutting the thread of life.

Apollo as patron of the arts was assisted by the nine Muses, the daughters of Zeus and Mnemosyne, goddess of memory. Each presided over a separate artistic or scientific sector, but they met regularly in the divinely inspired academy on Mount Helicon, to discuss the latest intellectual movement.

The Heroic Legends

The great cycles of legends that originated in Mycenaean times were grouped principally around two families: the descendants of Tantalos, and those of Io.

King Tantalos of Phrygia was the progenitor of the most intolerably tragic family ever known, each generation adding new, hateful crimes and punishments to an unparalleled record. Tantalos had been favored by the Olympians and even been admitted to their banquets. Yet in return he set before the gods the roasted flesh of his own son Pelops, as a test of their omniscience. The immortals were not deceived; only Demeter, distraught with grief over the loss of Persephone, helped herself to a tender shoulder. Tantalos was thrown into the underworld, eternally thirsting for the water in which he stood up to his neck, while Pelops was restored to life, complete with a miraculous ivory shoulder that healed all disease at a touch.

Unlike his sister Niobe, Pelops prospered and became Poseidon's lover. He left his native country for that part of Greece which was named after him, the Peloponnese, and with the god's help won the daughter of Oenomaos, king of Pisa. Oenomaos, who was in control of the Olympic games, had been forewarned that his son-in-law would cause his death. Confident in his superb horses, he stipulated that every suitor should compete with him in a chariot race, and pay with his life if defeated. Thirteen princes had already suffered this fate when Pelops appeared in a golden chariot, drawn by Poseidon's own horses. Yet Pelops did not rely entirely on his divine protector, but to be on the safe side bribed the king's charioteer to replace the linch-pins of his master's chariot with wax. The wheels fell off, the king was killed, and so was the charioteer on claiming his reward.

But not before he had cursed Pelops and his sons, Atreus and Thyestes, who later led the Achaeans to the conquest of Mycenae. Atreus succeeded to the dynasty founded by Perseus, but the gruesome family habits did not improve. Thyestes seduced his brother's wife, and in revenge Atreus followed their grandfather's example by serving up Thyestes' children at a banquet. One son however escaped, Aegisthos, who was instrumental in fulfilling the old curses, while becoming the cause of new blood-guilt. Atreus' son Agamemnon extended his hegemony over the entire Peloponnese, and was thus the natural leader of the Greek expedition against Troy, to recover his brother Menelaus' wife, Helen.

An adverse wind kept the fleet at Aulis, and Artemis demanded the sacrifice of Iphigenia, Agamemnon's daughter. Iphigenia and her mother Clytemnestra were lured to Aulis under the pretext of the girl's betrothal to Achilles, the most attractive of the Greek heroes. Clytemnestra never forgave her husband, even though the goddess relented in the last moment and substituted a hind for the victim kneeling at the altar. The inconsolable mother withdrew to Mycenae, where Aegisthos became her lover. On Agamemnon's return from Troy 10 years later, she murdered her victorious husband in his bath.

Their daughter Electra, in her turn, nagged her brother Orestes into avenging the beloved father. For his matricide Orestes was pursued by the Furies, till he rescued Iphigenia from Artemis' sanctuary in savage Tauris. The ancient curses were at last lifted and a double marriage provided an unexpected happy end: Electra to Pylades, her brother's companion in the Taurian adventure, and Orestes to his cousin Hermione, daughter of Menelaos and Helen. Their descendants ruled over Mycenae till the coming of the Dorians in the 12th century BC.

Menelaos was king of Sparta, but his main claim to fame was his marriage with Helen. She and her brother Polydeuces (Pollux) were Leda's children by Zeus, disguised as a swan, while Castor and Clytemnestra were fathered by Tyndareus, the lawful husband.

Helen's incomparable beauty attracted numerous suitors. To avoid quarrels Tyndareus made them swear to respect Helen's choice and to champion the cause of her future husband. She chose Menelaos, and when she eloped with Paris the rejected suitors kept their oath and followed Agamemnon to the war against Troy.

The Loves of Zeus

A considerable share of Zeus's amorous intrigues fell to one mortal family, which not only produced a corresponding number of heroes, but was also singularly geographically minded, naming seas, continents, and countries.

It all started with Io, daughter of the river god Inarchos of Argos. Although Zeus changed her into a heifer at the approach of his jealous spouse, long and bitter experience had made Hera distrustful and she set 100-eyed Argos to watch over the suspect. Hermes lulled Argos to sleep and slew him. Thereupon Hera placed her faithful servant's eyes in the tail of the peacock, and sent a gadfly to sting poor Io, who, maddened by pain, plunged into the sea, later called in her honor the Ionian Sea. After what must have been a record swim for a cow, Io came ashore in Egypt where Zeus, by a touch, restored her to human form. She bore him a son, Epaphos (him of the touch), whose daughter Libya became by Poseidon the mother of Agenor and Belos, the biblical Baal.

Zeus now lusted for Agenor's daughter Europa and approached her in the form of a gentle white bull. The misguided maiden jumped upon his broad back, to be carried away to Crete, where she gave birth to Minos, Rhadamanthys, and Sarpedon. Minos founded the Cretan dynasty and after his death became, together with his second brother, judge in the underworld. The love for bulls was pathological in the family and Minos' queen, Pasiphae, followed in Europa's footsteps but with less satisfying results, as her offspring, the Minotaur, was a most unprepossessing monster.

Agenor sent his sons Phoenix, Cilix, and Cadmos in search of their sister. Far and wide did they travel, until Phoenix and Cilix, weary of the hopeless quest, settled in the fertile countries they had reached named Phoenicia and Cilicia respectively. Cadmos consulted the Delphic oracle, and following a cow as bidden, built the Theban Acropolis, the Cadmea, where the beast lay down. He married Harmonia, daughter of Ares and Aphrodite, and one of their children was Semele. Oedipos likewise traced his descent from Cadmos.

Neither did Belus lack in progeny. His eldest, Pygmalion, fell in love with the statue he had fashioned and prayed to Aphrodite to make the smooth marble come to life. The goddess gladly acquiesced as Pygmalion had hitherto not been among her devotees. Galatea proved even more enchanting as a woman than she had been as a work of art.

The younger twins Aegyptos and Danaus quarreled over their inheritance, and the latter fled with his 50 daughters to Argos, which accepted him as king. The 50 sons of Aegyptos followed their cousins, and Danaus feigned agreement to a mass marriage, but secretly advised the brides to kill their husbands on their wedding night. All obeyed except Hypermnestra, who helped her husband to escape. He later returned, slew Danaus, and became the ancestor of a line of famous Argive kings. The murderous 49 Danaids were condemned to eternal frustration in Tartaros, carrying water in sieves to fill a cask with a hole in the bottom.

Hypermnestra's grandson Acrisios had been warned that his own grandson was fated to kill him. To prevent this he imprisoned his only daughter Danaë in a tower of bronze, a vain precaution against Zeus, who came upon the maiden as a shower of gold. When the distraught king was told of the birth of a grandson, he locked Danaë and the infant Perseus into a chest, which was cast into the sea. Washed ashore at the island of Seriphos, they were kindly received by King Polydectes, who fell in love with the appealing outcast. Wanting to rid himself of the brawny youth, he cajoled Perseus into fetching the head of the Gorgon Medusa, whose glance turned every living creature to stone. Medusa was the only mortal of three wildly unattractive sisters, who featured snakes instead of hair, and had faces to match.

Never could Perseus hope to carry out his rash enterprise unaided, but the gods gave a helping hand. Hades lent his

helmet of invisibility, Hermes his winged sandals, and
Athena her brightly polished shield, so that Perseus might
cut off Medusa's head, looking at her reflection.

Triumphantly holding his hideous booty, Perseus on his return flight turned the inhospitable Titan Atlas into a mountain. Somewhat off his course, he saw the Ethiopian
Princess Andromeda chained to a rock, waiting to be devoured by a sea monster. A display of the head, and Perseus
was at leisure to cut Andromeda's chains and take her back
to Seriphos. There was more work for Medusa's head, as
Polydectes had been bothering Danaë. The king and his
courtiers were promptly turned to stone; the circle of boulders is still shown on the island.

Perseus returned the magic objects to their kind owners,
trimming Athena's shield with the fatal head. Soon afterwards he fulfilled the prophecy by accidentally killing his
grandfather with a discus. Ashamed to succeed his victim
at Argos, the hero founded Mycenae and a new royal line.

Untiring Heracles

It was now his granddaughter Alcmene's turn to be favored
by Zeus, who showed great constancy in his inconstancies.
Their son Heracles gave from his birth undeniable proof
that he was destined to grow into the greatest of all the heroes, but also the object of Hera's unrelenting hatred. Not
unnaturally the Queen of Heaven wanted at last to get
even with the family that had caused her so much matri-
monial unhappiness. She sent two huge serpents, but the
amazing child in the cradle strangled them. Brought up like
all the best people by the wise Centaur Chiron—tutor of
Asklepios, Jason, and Achilles, to name but three—Heracles married the Theban Princess Megara, whom he killed
together with their children in a fit of madness. To expiate
the crime, the Delphic oracle decreed that Heracles should
perform 12 labors for his uncle Euristheus, king of Mycenae.

These labors included some useful work, as for example the
killing of the Nemean lion and the Lernean Hydra, and
above all the cleansing of the Augean stables by diverting
the river Alpheus. But there were also some utterly futile
enterprises, like the abduction of the hellbound Kerberos.

On that visit to the underworld, Heracles had to compete
with the river god Achelous, who assumed the form of a
bull. One of his horns was broken off and was presented by
the victor to the goddess of plenty. Filled with fruits and
grain, it is known as Cornucopia, the fabled Horn of Abundance.

Zeus caught him up to Olympos, where he was received
among the immortals. Even Hera at last relented and gave

the hero her daughter Hebe in marriage and the couple lived happily ever after. . . .

Divine IDs

The 12 chief gods formed the elite of Olympos. Each represented one of the forces of nature and also a human characteristic, interpreted by sculptors in their statues of the gods. They also had attributes, by which they can often be identified. The Romans, influenced by the arts and letters of Greece, largely identified their own gods with those of Greece, with the result that Greek gods had Latin names as well, by which they are known today.

Greek Name	Latin Name	Attributes and Associations	Symbols
Aphrodite	Venus	love, beauty	dove
Apollo	Phoebus	sun, music, and poetry	bow, lyre
Ares	Mars	tumult, war	spear, helmet
Artemis	Diana	moon, chastity	stag
Athena	Minerva	wisdom	owl, olive
Demeter	Ceres	earth, fecundity	sheaf, sickle
Hephaestos	Vulcan	fire, industry	hammer, anvil
Hera	Juno	sky, queen, marriage	peacock
Hermes	Mercury	trade, eloquence	caduceus, wings
Hestia	Vesta	hearth, domestic virtues	eternal fire
Poseidon	Neptune	sea, earthquake	trident
Zeus	Jupiter	sky, supreme god	scepter, thunder

3 Athens

By B. Samantha Stenzel

Samantha Stenzel has lived in Athens for 12 years, writing about cinema, the arts, and travel.

"I would urge that you fix your eyes on the greatness of Athens as she really is and fall in love with her. . . ." These are the words (as reported by Thucydides) of Pericles, the mastermind of Greece's Golden Age, in his famous oration for the dead of the Peloponnesian war. In 1185, Michael Akominatos, archbishop of the city, wrote otherwise: "You cannot look upon Athens without tears. . . . She has lost the very form, appearance, and character of a city." Today, after another 800 years, the cleric's description is even more apt. Residents and visitors alike commonly recite the city's faults: the murky brown pollution cloud (known familiarly as the *nefos*), the overcrowding, the traffic jams with their stench and din, and the characterless cement apartment blocks that line many streets. The city's defects largely stem from periodic building booms necessitated by sudden influxes of population and usually undertaken with little overall planning. When Athens became the capital in 1834, it was a marshy village of about 6,000 people, and today it is home to 3.1 million (⅛ of Greece's population) and covers 689 square kilometers (165 square miles).

Life in this temperate climate is played out on street corners and balconies from early morning until very late at night. This high visibility combined with the basically nonviolent nature of the Greeks accounts for the low crime rate, which compares favorably with that of other European capitals. Although the look of the city's housing belies the substantial wealth of some of its inhabitants, slums do not exist here. If you exercise normal caution, as in any large city, carrying your money safely and avoiding lonely walks late at night, your chances of running into trouble are very slim. You are in more danger of being hit by a careless driver while crossing the street, than of being mugged.

Although Athens may seem like one huge city, it is really a series of small villages strung together. Most of the major historical sites are within the central area; it is possible to see them by foot. When you (inevitably) wander off your planned route into less touristy areas, take the opportunity to explore. You will often discover pockets of incomparable charm, in refreshing contrast to the dreary repetition of the modern facades.

From many quarters of the city one can glimpse "the glory that was Greece" in the form of the Acropolis looming above the horizon, but only by actually climbing that rocky precipice can you feel the essence of the ancient settlement. In the National Archaeological Museum is a vast array of artifacts illustrating the many millennia of Greek civilization; smaller museums such as the Cycladic, the Benaki, and the Byzantine illuminate the history of particular regions or periods. Strolling through Plaka, a delightful area of tranquil streets lined with renovated mansions, you will get the flavor of the 19th century's graceful lifestyle.

Take a break from gazing at the monuments of previous generations and settle into a shady café on one of the squares that adorn each neighborhood, to observe today's Athens and the Athenians in their element. They are lively and expressive, their hands fiddling with worry beads or gesturing excitedly; earthy and fun-loving, occasionally irritating, even overbearing—they are very rarely boring. While often expansively friendly, they are aggressive and stubborn when feeling threatened, and they're also insatiably curious. You'll probably be asked direct questions about your personal affairs that might be considered rude at home; keep your sense of humor and parry with your own queries if you wish.

Athens is an intriguing crossroads, with both the city and its inhabitants blending elements of Middle Eastern and Western cultures. But underneath the confusion and modern clutter lies a palpable Mediterranean warmth that with a little encouragement will envelop you.

Essential Information

Important Addresses and Numbers

Tourist Information The main office of the **Greek National Tourist Organization** (EOT, Amerikis 11, near Syntagma Sq., tel. 01/322–3111) is the place for detailed questions or specialized brochures. Other EOT branches are in the National Bank Building (Karageorgi Servias 2, tel. 01/322–2545), in the General Bank (Ermou 2, tel. 01/325–2267), at East Terminal at Ellinikon Airport (tel. 01/970–2395), and at Zea Marina Piraeus (EOT Building, 01/413–5716).

The **tourist police** (Ellinikon Airport and Stathmos Larissis Railway Station, tel. 171) can answer questions about transportation, steer you to an open pharmacy or doctor, and give you phone numbers of hotels and shops, usually in English.

Embassies **United States:** Vasilissis Sofias 91, tel. 01/721–2951. **Canada:** Gennadiou 4, tel. 01/723–9511. **United Kingdom:** Ploutarchou 1, tel. 01/723–6211 through 01/723–6219.

Emergencies **Police,** tel. 100; **traffic police,** tel. 01/523–0111; **tourist police,** tel. 071; **fire,** tel. 199; **ambulance,** tel. 166.

Doctors Large hotels may have a staff doctor or be able to refer you to one nearby. For a doctor on call 2 PM–7 AM on Sunday and holidays, tel. 105.

Dentists Check with your hotel, embassy, or the tourist police.

Hospitals **KAT Hospital,** Nikis St. 2, Kifissia, tel. 01/801–4411 through 01/801–4420; **Asklepion Hospital,** 1 Vas. Pavlou Ave., Voula, tel. 01/895–8301 through 01/895–8305; **Aglaia Kyriakou Hospital,** Livadias and Thivon, Goudi, tel. 01/777–5610 or 01/778–3212; children go to **Ayia Sofia Hospital,** Mikras Assias and Thivon, Goudi, tel. 01/777–1811 or 01/777–1613.

English-Language Bookstores **The Booknest** (Folia Tou Bibliou, Panepistimiou 29, tel. 01/323–1703 or 01/322–9560) has an ample selection of American authors. **Compendium** (Nikis 28, Syntagma Sq., tel. 01/322–1248) has travel books, books on Greece, Athens's only women's-studies selection, and used books. **Eleftheroudakis** (Nikis 4, Syntagma Sq., tel. 01/322–9388 or 01/323–1401; Athens Tower, Building A, Sinopis 2, tel. 01/770–8007). **Psychiko shopping center** (Kifisias 294, tel. 01/687–8350) has technical books, language guides, and coffee-table editions. There's also **Kauffman** (Stadiou 28, tel. 01/322–2160), **Pantelides** (Amerikis 11, Syntagma Sq., tel. 01/362–3673), **Reymondos** (Voukourestiou 18, tel. 01/364–8188), and **Samouchos** (Amerikis 24, Syntagma Sq., tel. 01/362–4151).

English-Language At the Hellenic-American Union (Massalias 22, near Athens
Libraries Univ., tel. 01/363–8114),the **American Library** is on the fourth
floor, and the **Greek Library,** on the seventh floor, has a section
of books in English on Greek subjects. Or try the **British Council Library** (17 Filikis Eterias Sq. [Kolonaki Sq.], tel. 01/3633–
215) or the **Gennadius Library, American School of Classical
Studies** (Soudias 61, tel. 01/721–0536).

Late-Night Tel. 107. Each pharmacy posts a list of pharmacies open during
Pharmacies the afternoon break or late at night. Conveniently located
pharmacies where English is spoken include **Marinopoulos**
(Patission 12, Omonia, tel. 01/362–4909; Kanaris 23, Kolonaki,
tel. 01/361–3051) and **Thomas** (Papadiamantopoulou 6, near
Hilton Hotel and Holiday Inn, Ilisia, tel. 01/721–6101).

Travel Agencies All are on or near Syntagma Square. They include **American
Express** (Ermou 2, tel. 01/324–4975), **Amphitrion** (Karageorgi
Servias 2, tel. 01/322–8884, 01/323–8816, 01/323–8818, or 01/
323–8819; Merachias 3, Piraeus, tel. 01/411–2045 through 01/
411–2049), **CHAT Tours** (Stadiou 4, tel. 01/322–2886), **Key
Tours** (Ermou 2, tel. 01/323–2520), **Magic Bus** (20 Filellinon,
tel. 01/323–7471), **Thomas Cook** (Stadiou 7, tel. 01/923–5358),
Viking Travel Bureau (Filellinon 3, tel. 01/322–9383), and **Wag-
on-Lits Tourism** (Karageorgi Servias 2, tel. 01/322–0351 or 01/
324–2281).

Arriving and Departing by Plane

Airports and Athens's **Ellinikon Airport** is between Kalamaki and Glyfada on
Airlines the southeast coast of Attica. Domestic and international
Olympic Airways flights depart from the West Terminal (tel.
01/936–9111) on the coast side, and other airlines use the East
Terminal on the other side. A **shuttle bus** goes between the two
terminals every half hour until about 8 PM (fare: 160 dr.).

Between the Yellow-and-blue double-decker express buses go from both ter-
Airport and minals to Syntagma Square and Omonia Square every 20 min-
Downtown utes 6 AM–9 PM and at least hourly at other times (fare: 160 dr. 6
By Bus AM–midnight, 200 dr. midnight–6 AM). Blue buses also go to the
center and to Zappion; express bus 19 goes to Karaiskaki Square
in Piraeus (fare: 160 dr.). In summer a blue Olympic Airlines bus
goes from the west terminal to Olympic Airways offices at
Syngrou 96 and then on to Syntagma Square every half hour 6
AM–8 PM (fare: 160 dr.).

By Taxi A taxi to the center of Athens costs about 1,200 dr. from the
West Terminal and 1,500 dr. from the East Terminal before
midnight. From midnight to 5 AM, the fare will be about double.
If you want to arrive at your hotel in style, **Yiannis
Yannakopoulos Limousines** (tel. 01/323–3957; evenings 01/959–
6143; 7,000 dr., 8,000 dr. for deluxe Cadillacs) will pick you up
at the airport and drop you at your hotel or vice versa.

Arriving and Departing by Train, Bus, Car, and Ship

By Train Greek trains have a well-earned reputation for being slow and
unreliable, but the twice-daily express service from the north
is fast and reliable (Thessaloniki–Athens in five hours). Express service has also begun on the Athens–Patras line. On any
train, it is best to travel first class, with a reserved seat, as the
difference between the first-class and tourist coaches can be
vast: Without a seat reservation you could end up standing or

crouched between baggage. Call 145 for a recorded timetable, in Greek, of trains within Greece; call 147 for information on trains to Europe and Russia.

The two railroad stations of the **Greek Railway Organization (OSE)** are northwest of Omonia Square off Deliyanni Street; both stations have left-luggage offices and snack bars. OSE tickets are sold near Omonia Square at Karolou Street 1 (tel. 01/522–2491), at Sina Street 6 near the university (tel. 01/362–4402), and at Filellinon Street 17 near Syntagma Square (tel. 01/323–6747). Trains for northern Greece and international trains stop at **Stathmos Larissis** (tel. 01/524–0601). Trains to the Peloponnese depart on a parallel line at the quaint **Stathmos Peleponnissou** (tel. 01/513–1636), whose café continues the station's striking art-nouveau motif, from its burgundy ceiling with ornate moldings and antique crystal teardrop chandelier to its original bronze gas lamps.

By Bus **Terminal A,** at Kifissou Street 100, one block from the Stathmos Larissis Station, serves bus lines to Epidaurus, Mycenae, Corinth, and other Peloponnese destinations, each of which has its own phone number. EOT offices have a list. **Terminal B** (tel. 01/831–7153), serving central and northern Greece, including Delphi, is near Liossion 260, in a remote area northwest of Omonia Square near Tries Yefiris (Three Bridges) district, Peristeri. Since tickets for these buses are sold only at this terminal, you should buy tickets and make seat reservations well in advance during high season or holidays.

KTEL orange buses have a small terminal at Egyptou Square at Mavromateon Street and Alexandras Avenue next to Pedion Areos Park. For information on buses to Sounion, call 01/821–3203; to Marathon, Rhamnous, Nea Makri, and Rafina, 01/821–0872.

By Car The main highways going north and south link up in Athens and both are called simply The National Road. When arriving via either of them, signs in English clearly mark the way to both Syntagma Square and Omonia Square in the center of town. On the road map distributed by the National Tourist Organization, the National Roads are yellow and are marked by European road numbers, although these are not used on the roads themselves. These highways are very slick when wet. Avoid driving in rain and on the days preceding or following major holidays, so as not to add to the body count. The accident rate, already the highest in the EC, escalates wildly during the mass migrations to and from the city.

By Ship Cruise ships and ferries to and from the islands dock in **Piraeus** (the main port, 10 kilometers [6 miles] southwest of Athens). The quickest way to get into the center, if you are traveling light, is to take the electric train, a trip of about 25 minutes. Taxis are legally allowed to charge a 100-dr. supplement for picking you up at a port, but often they will insist on a flat rate much higher than the approximately 1,200-dr. fare.

The other main port is **Rafina,** on the eastern coast of Attica, where boats to and from the Cyclades and Evia dock. Orange KTEL buses make the trip to Athens every half hour 5:50 AM–10:15 PM (fare: 300 dr.), from the station slightly up the hill from the port. The trip takes about one hour. A taxi into town will cost at least 5,000 dr.

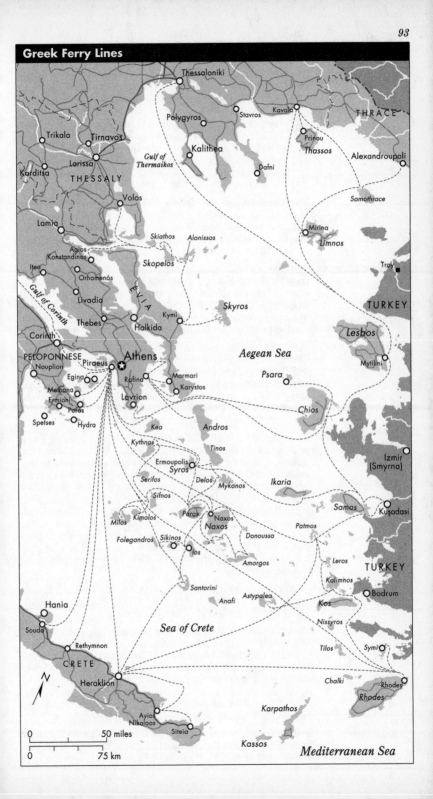

Greek Ferry Lines

Thessaloniki

Polygyros

Stavros

Kavala

THRACE

Trikala

Tirnavos

Prinou

Thassos

Alexandroupoli

Karditsa

Larissa

Kalithea

Dafni

THESSALY

Gulf of Thermaikos

Samothrace

Volos

Lamia

Skiathos

Alonissos

Mirina

Limnos

Troy

Agios Kohstandinos

Skopelos

TURKEY

Itea

Orhomenós

Gulf of Corinth

Livadia

EVIA

Skyros

Lesbos

Thebes

Halkida

Kymi

Corinth

PELOPONNESE

Athens

Aegean Sea

Nauplion

Piraeus

Rafina

Marmari

Mytilini

Egina

Psara

Melfiana

Lavrion

Karystos

Ermioni

Poros

Chios

Spetses

Hydra

Kea

Andros

Izmir
(Smyrna)

Kythnos

Tinos

Ermoupolis
Syros

Serifos

Delos

Mykonos

Ikaria

Samos

Kuşadasi

Sifnos

Paros

Naxos
Naxos

Patmos

Milos

Kimolos

Folegandros

Sikinos

Donoussa

Ios

Amorgos

Leros

TURKEY

Santorini

Astypalea

Kalimnos

Bodrum

Anafi

Kos

Hania

Nissyros

Souda

Sea of Crete

Tilos

Symi

Rethymnon

CRETE

Chalki

Rhodes

Heraklion

Rhodes

Ayios
Nikolaos

Siteia

Karpathos

Kassos

Mediterranean Sea

0 ____ 50 miles

0 ____ 75 km

Getting Around

The price of tickets on public transportation has risen steeply in the last couple of years, but it is still less than in other European capitals. Riding during rush hours is definitely not recommended. Keep your tickets until you reach your destination, as inspectors occasionally pop up to check that they have been canceled and validated. (The canceling machines, which stamp them with the route and time, are at the front and back of buses and trolleys and in the stations of the electric trains.) The fine for an unvalidated ticket is 1,500 dr., and the inspectors are strict about charging offenders, including tourists.

The **Organization for Urban Public Transportation** (OAS, Metsovou 15, tel. 185 or 01/883–6076), one block north of the National Archaeological Museum, answers questions about bus and train routes (usually only in Greek) and distributes clear maps with street names in Greek and all bus routes indicated.

By Electric Train
The one partially underground electric train line stretches from Piraeus to Kifissia, northeast of the city's center, with 20 stops in between. It was constructed in 1868, one of the earliest in Europe, and electrified in 1904. It is limited but functions well and is very safe, even late at night. The trains run 6 AM–midnight and the fare is 75 dr. (one zone) or 100 dr. (two zones).

By Bus and Trolley
Main bus stations are at Vasilissis Olgas Avenue next to Zappion, at Acadimias and Sina and at Kaningos Square. Bus and trolley tickets cost 75 dr., and no transfers are issued; monthly passes are available, but no daily or weekly ones. Tickets are sold in special booths at bus terminals and at selected *periptera* (street kiosks). Most bus lines run 5 AM–midnight, and major routes have infrequent owl service.

By Taxi
Taxi rates are still affordable compared to fares in other European capitals. It seems paradoxical that 17,000 taxis are on the streets of Athens, yet during peak hours it's impossible to find an empty one. A taxi driver may pass you up because it's not his day to enter the center of Athens. Taxis with passengers often operate unofficially (and illegally) on the jitney system, indicating willingness to pick up others by blinking their headlights. Would-be passengers shout their destination as the driver cruises past. Radio taxis can be booked by your hotel (a good idea when taking an early morning flight) with a surcharge of 200 dr. for immediate response and 300 dr. for an appointment to come later.

Some radio-taxi companies are: **Aris,** tel. 01/346–7137; **Ermis,** tel. 01/411–5220; **Omonia,** tel. 01/502–1131; **Parthenon,** tel. 01/581–4711; and **Proodos,** tel. 01/643–3400.

Most taxi drivers are honest and hardworking, but a few con artists infiltrate the ranks at the airports and near popular restaurants and clubs frequented by foreigners. Make sure the driver turns on the meter and that the rate listed in the lower corner is 1, the normal rate before midnight. Don't be alarmed if your driver picks up other passengers (although protocol indicates he should ask your permission first). Each passenger pays full fare for the distance he or she has traveled.

The fare begins at 200 dr. Note the fare on the meter if you get in an occupied taxi; the rate is 48 dr. per kilometer, 94 dr. outside the city limits and midnight–5 AM. Surcharges are made for fares from the airport (200 dr.); fares from ports, railway stations, and bus terminals (100 dr.); for each bag weighing more than 10 kilograms (40 dr.); fares 1 AM–6 AM; and waiting time (480 dr. per hour).

Taxi drivers know the major central hotels, but if your hotel is less well known, show the driver the address written in Greek and make note of the phone number and if possible a nearby landmark. If all else fails, the driver can call from a *periptero*. Athens has thousands of short side-streets, and few taxi drivers have maps. If your driver gets lost despite all precautions, use the time to practice answering personal questions gracefully.

Guided Tours

Orientation All the travel agencies mentioned above offer four-hour morning tours (5,000 dr.) by air-conditioned coach, which drive past the major central sites and museums and visit the Acropolis and the Cathedral. Reservations can be made at most hotels.

Special-Interest **Athens by Night** tours (offered by all agencies) are a convenient way to see some of the evening entertainment, especially for single travelers who may not want to venture out alone. One of the best buys is the **Theater Night** tour (5,000 dr.), which includes the Sound and Light spectacle and a performance of Dora Stratou folk dances on Philopappou Hill. **On the Town** tours (7,300 dr.) provide dinner at one of the tavernas and a Greek-dancing show; **Highlights of Athens** tours combine dinner with the Sound and Light Show.

The **Amphitrion** agency (*see* Important Addresses and Numbers, *above*) specializes in educational and offbeat tours in Athens and elsewhere, including island-hopping tours and treks in the Pindos mountains.

Excursions Most agencies offer excursions at about the same prices, but **CHAT** (*see* Important Addresses and Numbers, *above*) is reputed to have the edge in service and in the quality of its guides. Taking a half-day trip to the breathtaking **Temple of Poseidon** at Sounion avoids the hassle of dealing with the infrequent and crowded public buses or paying a great deal more for a taxi. The 3,700-dr. cost is well spent. A one-day tour to **Delphi** with lunch costs 11,400 dr. but the two-day tour (19,000 dr.) is far preferable. There's a two-day tour to ancient **Corinth, Mycenae,** and **Epidaurus,** including lodging and most meals (20,000 dr.), and a three-day tour that takes in both Delphi and the stunning monasteries of Meteora with accommodation in first-class hotels (50,000 dr.).

Personal Guides Major agencies can provide English-speaking guides and tailor-made tours, which are rather costly. The **Association of Guides** (Apollonas 9A, tel. 01/322–9705) provides licensed guides for individual or group tours at a rate of 15,000 dr. for four hours. It is advisable to arrange for a guide through a reliable agency rather than hiring one at random from those gathered near the foot of the Acropolis.

Exploring Athens

Although Athens covers a huge area, the major landmarks of the ancient Greek, Roman, and Byzantine periods are conveniently near the modern city center. You can easily stroll from the Acropolis to the other sites, taking time to browse in shops and relax in cafés and tavernas along the way.

The Acropolis and Philopappou, two craggy hills sitting side by side, form the core of Ancient Athens, and Lycabettus, the highest hill (909 feet), crowned by the little whitewashed chapel of Saint George, looms to the northeast. At the foot of Lycabettus is the Kolonaki area, the heart of which is a chic square surrounded by smart shops and exclusive bistros. Syntagma (Constitution) Square, the tourist hub, and Omonia (Concord) Square, the commercial heart of the city about a half-mile northwest, are connected by two wide parallel streets, Stadiou and Eleftheriou Venizelou (familiarly known as Panepistimiou). This area of the city is distinctly European, having been designed by the court architects of King Otho, a Bavarian. The Oriental character of Athens is evident as you go south from Omonia on Athinas Street, past the colorful produce and meat market, to Monastiraki, the flea market area nestled at the foot of the Acropolis.

Highlights for First-Time Visitors

Acropolis (*see* Tour 1)
Ancient Agora (*see* Tour 1)
Archaeological Museum, Piraeus (*see* Tour 6)
Benaki and **Byzantine Museums** (*see* Tour 5)
Little Metropolis (*see* Tour 3)
Lycabettus (*see* Tour 5)
Monastiraki Square (flea market) and **Tzistarakis Mosque Museum** (*see* Tour 4)
National Archaeological Museum (*see* Tour 3)
Plaka (*see* Tour 4)
Pnyx (*see* Tour 2)
Tower of the Winds (*see* Tour 2)

Tour 1: The Acropolis and Ancient Athens

Numbers in the margin correspond to points of interest on the Acropolis map.

Wear low-heel, rubber-sole shoes for this tour, as the marble on the Acropolis steps and near the other monuments is very slippery. The Parthenon and other monuments are roped off and cannot be entered. The earlier you start out the better, but a hat and protection against the sun are always necessary in summer. An alternative is to visit at about 4 PM in summer, when the light is best for taking photographs.

The **Acropolis,** or "High City," is a true testament to the Golden Age of Greece, from 461 to 429 BC, that magical period at the height of Pericles' influence when the intellectual and artistic life of Athens flowered. Archaeological evidence has shown that the flat-top limestone outcrop, 512 feet high, attracted settlers as early as Neolithic times, because of its defensible position and its natural springs. It is believed to have been continuously inhabited throughout the Bronze Age and since.

Foundations for the Acropolis, laid after the victory at Marathon in 490 BC, were destroyed by the Persians in 480–79 BC. After the peace treaty at Susa in 448 BC, Pericles undertook the ambitious project of reconstructing it on a monumental scale. This extraordinary Athenian general and statesman is an enigmatic figure in history, considered by some scholars to be the brilliant architect of the destiny of Greece at its height and by others, a megalomaniac who bankrupted the coffers of an empire and an elitist who catered to the privileged few at the expense of the masses.

The appearance of the buildings that comprised the major portion of the Acropolis in ancient times was largely unaltered until AD 52, when the Roman Claudius embellished the entrance with a typically flamboyant staircase. In the 2nd century Hadrian had his turn at decorating many shrines, and in 529 Justinian closed the philosophical schools in the city, emphasizing the defensive character of the citadel, and changing the temples into Christian churches.

Over the years the Acropolis buildings have been damaged by war and have endured many transformations: Florentine palace, a mosque, a Turkish harem, and a brothel. Despite all, the monument described by the French poet Lamartine as "the most perfect poem in stone" will not disappoint you. A visit to the Acropolis can evoke the presence of ancient heroes and the gods who were worshiped here. Look at the buildings first and save the museum for last; a grasp of the overall setting will give the statues and friezes more meaning.

Walk or take a taxi or bus No. 230 to Dionyssiou Areopagitou, the street that winds around the Acropolis. Approaching from the southwest, buy a ticket and enter through the **Beulé Gate,** a late Roman structure named for the French archaeologist Ernest Beulé, who discovered it in 1852. Made of marble fragments from destroyed monuments, it has an inscription above the lintel dated 320 BC, dedicated by "Nikias son of Nikodemos of Xypete," who had apparently won a musical competition. Before Roman times, the entrance to the Acropolis was a steep processional ramp below the Temple of Athena Nike. This Sacred Way was used every fourth year for the Panathenaia Procession, a spectacle that ended the festival celebrating Athena's remarkable birth (she sprang from the head of her father Zeus), which included chariot races, athletic and musical competitions, and poetry recitals. Toward the end of July, all strata of Athenian society gathered at the Dipylon Gate of Keramikos and followed a sacred ship wheeled up to the summit. The ship was anchored at the rocky outcrop below Areopagus (Hill of Ares), just northwest of the Acropolis.

The **Propylaea,** east of the Beulé Gate, is a typical ancient gate, an imposing structure designed to instill proper reverence in worshipers entering a sanctuary, for this was the main function of the Acropolis. Planned by Pericles, it was the masterwork of the architect Mnesicles. It was to have been the grandest secular building in Greece, the same size as the Parthenon. Construction was suspended because of the Peloponnesian War, and it was never finished. The Propylaea was used as a garrison during the Turkish period; in 1656, a powder magazine there was struck by lightning, causing much damage, and it was again damaged during the Venetian siege under Morosini in 1687.

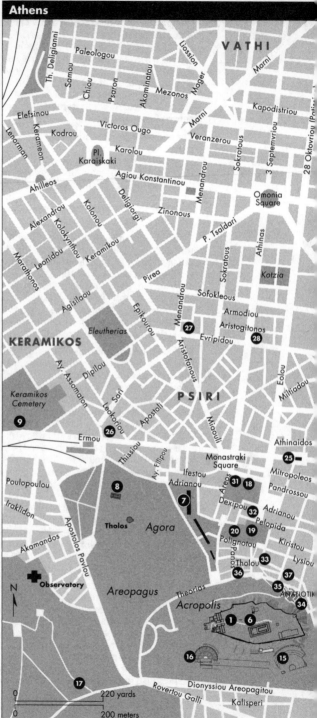

98

Athens

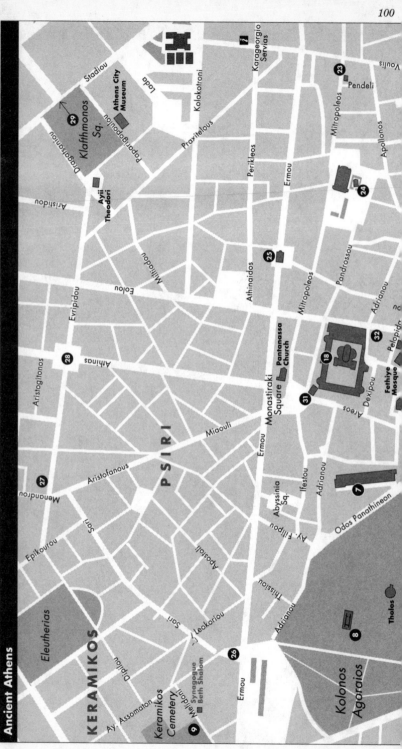

Ancient Athens

KERAMIKOS

Eleutherias

Keramikos
Cemetery

PSIRI

Monastiraki
Square

Klafthmonos
Sq.

Athens City
Museum

Ayii
Theodori

Pantanassa
Church

Fethiye
Mosque

Kolonos
Agoraios

Tholos

Pendeli

Stadiou
Lada
Kolokotroni
Karageorgio
Servias
Voulis
Mitropoleos
Apollonos
Praxitelous
Perikleos
Ermou
Pandrossou
Adrianou
Pelopida
Dexipou
Areos
Athinaidos
Mitropoleos
Eolou
Mitiadou
Evripidou
Aristidou
Dragatsaniou
Papariogopoulou
Athinas
Aristogitonos
Menandrou
Aristofanous
Miaouli
Sari
Epikourou
Aposroli
Sari
Leokoriou
Didlou
Melidoni
Ay. Assomaton
Ermou
Ermou
Ifestou
Adrianou
Abyssinia
Sq.
Ay. Filipou
Thissiou
Adrianou
Odos Panathineon

Synagogue
Beth Shalom

29
23
24
25
28
27
26
9
8
7
18
31
32

100

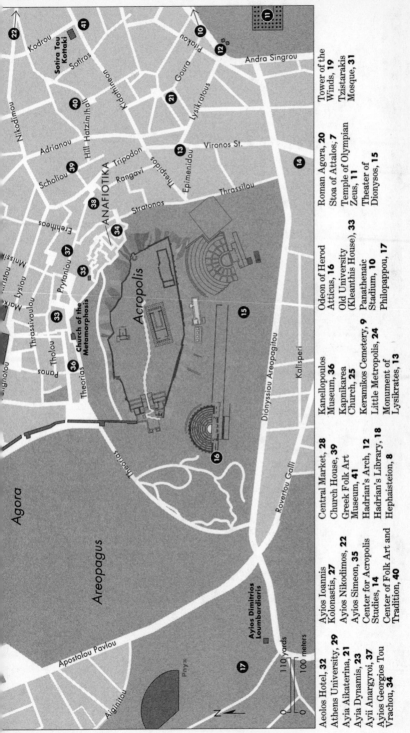

Aeolos Hotel, **32**
Athens University, **29**
Ayia Aikaterina, **21**
Ayia Dynamis, **23**
Ayii Anargyroi, **37**
Ayios Georgios Tou
Vrachou, **34**

Ayios Ioannis
Kolonastis, **27**
Ayios Nikodimos, **22**
Ayios Simeon, **35**
Center for Acropolis
Studies, **14**
Center of Folk Art and
Tradition, **40**

Central Market, **28**
Church House, **39**
Greek Folk Art
Museum, **41**
Hadrian's Arch, **12**
Hadrian's Library, **18**
Hephaisteion, **13**

Kanellopoulos
Museum, **36**
Kapnikarea
Church, **25**
Keramikos Cemetery, **9**
Little Metropolis, **24**
Monument of
Lysikrates, **13**

Odeon of Herod
Atticus, **16**
Old University
(Kleanthis House), **33**
Panathenaic
Stadium, **10**
Philopappou, **17**

Roman Agora, **20**
Stoa of Attalos, **11**
Temple of Olympian
Zeus, **11**
Theater of
Dionysos, **15**

Tower of the
Winds, **19**
Tzistarakis
Mosque, **31**

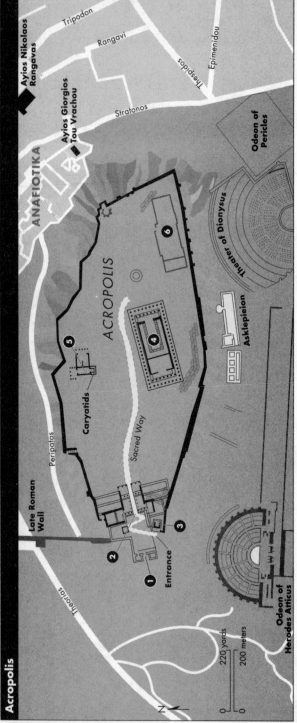

Acropolis

Ayios Nikolaos Rangavas

Tripodon

Rangavi

Stratonos

Epimenidou

Theorias

Iperidos

ANAFIOTIKA

Ayios Giorgios Tou Vrachou

Late Roman Wall

Peripatos

ACROPOLIS

Caryatids

Sacred Way

Entrance

Odeon of Herodes Atticus

Theater of Dionysus

Odeon of Pericles

Asklepieion

N

0   220 yards
0   200 meters

Acropolis Museum, **6**
Beulé Gate, **1**
Erectheion, **5**
Propylaea, **2**
Parthenon, **4**
Temple of Athena
Nike, **3**

The Propylaea shows the first use of both Doric and Ionic columns together, a style that can be called Attic. Six of the sturdier fluted Doric columns made from Pentelic marble correspond with the gateways of the portal. Processions with priests, chariots, and sacrificial animals entered via a marble ramp in the center, now protected by a wooden stairway; ordinary visitors on foot had to enter via the side doors.

The slender Ionic columns (⅖ the diameter of the Doric) had elegant capitals, some of which have been restored, along with a section of the famed paneled ceiling, originally decorated with gold eight-pointed stars on a blue background. The well-preserved north wing housed the Pinakotheke, or art gallery, specializing in paintings of scenes from Homer's epics and mythological tableaux on wooden plaques. Connected to it was a lounge with 17 couches arranged around the walls so that weary visitors could take a siesta. The south wing was a decorative portico (row of columns). The view from the inner porch of the Propylaea is stunning: The Parthenon is suddenly revealed in full glory, framed by the columns.

Walk south, to the edge of the fortifications, near a section of a Mycenaean tower. From here on a rare clear day, you can see Piraeus, the coastline toward Sounion and the Saronic Bay islands of Aegina and Salamina. It was from here that, according to Pausanias, the 2nd-century traveler and geographer, the distraught King Aegeus met his end. He leapt to his death when in the distance he saw the black sails on his son Theseus's boat returning from Crete and thought him dead. Theseus, succeeding his father, became a legendary national hero of Athens and united the different villages. Beginning in his time (12th–11th centuries BC), Athens was divided into two parts, the upper city with its temples and the lower city, or *asty*, with houses centered around the agora.

❸ The graceful all-marble **Temple of Athena Nike** on the bastion, built about 425–24 BC, has four Ionic columns on both a front and a rear porch. Pausanias called this the Temple of Nike Apteros, or Wingless Victory, for "in Athens they believe Victory will stay with them forever because she has no wings." The Nikes, wingless maidens attendant on Athena, can be seen on marble slabs from the parapet that are now in the Acropolis Museum. Only the badly weathered figures on the east frieze, all now headless including Athena, are originals. The other sections, depicting battle scenes with Greeks fighting the Boeotians and Persians, are cement copies of those in the British Museum.

❹ At the loftiest point of the Acropolis is the **Parthenon,** the architectural masterpiece conceived by Pericles and executed between 447 and 438 BC by the brilliant sculptor Pheidias, who supervised the architects Iktinos and Callicrates in its construction. Although dedicated to the goddess Athena (the name Parthenon comes from the Athena Parthenos, or the virgin Athena) and inaugurated at the Panathenaia Festival of 438 BC, the Parthenon was primarily the treasury of the Delian League. For the populace, the Erechtheion remained Athena's sanctified holy place.

As you walk along the south wall to enter the main area of the Acropolis, you are almost overwhelmed by the magnitude and power of the Parthenon. From here you see the side colonnade of 17 fluted Doric pillars, of white marble quarried from Mount Pentelikon (known as Pendelis today), now aged to a mellow honey color. Strangely enough, all 46 columns slope inward a slight fraction and are slightly swelled, optical tricks to create the illusion that they are straight.

Though the structure of the Parthenon is marble, the inner ceilings and doors were made of wood. The original building was ornate, covered with a tile roof, decorated with statuary and marble friezes, and so brightly painted that the people protested, "We are gilding and adorning our city like a wanton woman" (Plutarch). Pheidias himself may have sculpted some of the exquisite, brightly painted metopes, but most were done by other artists under his guidance. The only ones remaining in situ show scenes of battle: Athenians versus Amazons, and gods and goddesses against giants. One of the most evocative friezes, depicting the procession of the Panathenaia, was 524 feet long, an extraordinary parade of 400 people including maidens, magistrates, horsemen, musicians, and 200 animals. Showing ordinary mortals, at a time when almost all sculpture was of mythological or battle scenes, was lively and daring. About 50 of the best-preserved pieces, the "Elgin marbles," are in the British Museum, and a few others can be seen in the Acropolis Museum. In the first decade of the 19th century, during the time of the Ottoman Empire, Lord Elgin, British Ambassador in Constantinople, was given permission by the Sultan Selim III to remove most of the works of art from the Acropolis. It remains a highly controversial issue to this day: On one side, many argue that the marbles would have been destroyed if left on site; on the other side, a spirited campaign spearheaded by Melina Mercouri, the actress-turned-politician, aims to have them returned to Greece.

Pheidias's most awesome contribution to the Parthenon was the 39-foot-high statue of Athena that stood in the inner chamber of the sanctuary. It was made on a wooden frame, with ivory for the flesh and more than a ton of gold for the ankle-length tunic, helmet, spear, and shield. The alleged theft of some of this gold (some say the ivory) was the basis of charges against Pheidias, who is said to have cleared his name by removing it from the statue and having it weighed to prove it all was there. After the Christian emperor Thesodosius II closed all pagan sanctuaries in AD 435, the statue seems to have disappeared. The Parthenon was later converted into a church, but the basic structure was intact until the Venetian siege of Athens in the 17th century, when Morosini's artillery hit a powder magazine, causing a fire that burned for two days. Fourteen of the 46 columns were destroyed, along with the roof and most of the interior.

⑤ The **Erechtheion,** north of the Parthenon, is a distinctive structure built on uneven ground and incorporating two porticoes. Completed in 406 BC, it was divided into two Ionic sanctuaries, the eastern one containing an olive-wood statue of Athena Polias, protectress of the city, and the western one dedicated to Poseidon-Erechtheus.

In the contest between Athena and Poseidon for divine patronage of the city, the sea god dramatically plunged his trident into the rock next to the Erechtheion and produced a spring of water. Athena more prudently created an olive tree, the main staple of Greek society. The panel of judges declared her the winner, and the city was named Athena.

A gnarled olive tree outside the west wall was planted where Athena's once grew, and marks said to be from Poseidon's trident can be seen on a rock wedged in a hole near the north porch. His gift should not be slighted, for the continual springs of the Acropolis have made habitation possible from earliest times, as well as watering the olive trees.

The most endearing feature of the Erechtheion is the south portico facing the Parthenon, known as the **Caryatid Porch.** It is supported on the heads of six strapping but shapely maidens (Caryatids) wearing delicately draped Ionian garments, their folds perfectly aligned to resemble flutes on columns. What you look at today are copies. The originals were removed in 1977 to protect them from erosion caused by air pollution.

6 The **Acropolis Museum,** unobtrusively snuggled in the southeast corner of the plateau, has nine rooms filled with the sculptures found on the Acropolis plus the votive offerings to Athena. The displays are well executed, but the English labeling is sketchy.

In Room I, the anguished expression of a calf being devoured by a lioness in a poros-stone pediment of the 6th century BC brings to mind Picasso's *Guernica*. Room II contains the charismatic *Calf-Bearer*, an early Archaic work showing a man named Rhombos carrying on his shoulders a calf intended to be sacrificed. A poros-stone pediment of the Archaic temple of Athena shows Heracles fighting against the triton and on the right side the rather scholarly looking "three-headed demon," bearing traces of the original red and black embellishment.

The most notable displays of the museum are sculptures from the Archaic and Classical periods, pieces of unique appeal, including, in Room IV, the *Horseman* and the compelling *Hound*. Take a good look at the exquisite *korai*, in Rooms IV and V, young maidens dressed in Ionian garments, with fascinating details of hair, clothing, and jewelry of the Archaic period.

In Room VI is the 5th-century BC relief, *Mourning Athena*, a fine example of the severe style favored in the Classical period. In Room VIII, a superbly rendered slab from the eastern side of the Acropolis represents the seated Poseidon, Artemis, and Apollo (No. 856). Incomparably graceful movement is suggested in *Nike Unlacing Her Sandal* (No. 973) in Room VIII, taken from the parapet of the Temple of Athena Nike. In a dimly lit air-conditioned glass case in Room IX are four of the badly damaged original Caryatids (*see above*).

Numbers in the margin correspond to points of interest on the Athens and Ancient Athens maps.

After leaving the museum go back to the Beulé Gate and head down the slope, bearing to the right toward the Ancient Agora. Those wearing rubber-soled shoes might want to scramble up the limestone hill known as the **Areopagus** (Hill of Ares) to get a good view of the Propylaea and Ancient Agora below and the modern metropolis to the northwest. From this outcrop Saint Paul delivered such a moving sermon on the "Unknown God" that he converted the senator Dionysius who became the first bishop of Athens. Some of Saint Paul's words (Acts 17:22–34) are written in Greek on a bronze plaque at the foot of the hill.

Descend the slope from Areopagus, following the signs to the Ancient Agora, which lead to Vrisakiou and then left on Adrianou.

Time Out But first, turn right onto Kinetou before you reach the entrance, and take a break at the **Café Abyssinia,** in the center of the flea market on Abyssinia Square, with antique brass and china and a limited but unusual menu. The gregarious crowd spills out onto the square in warm weather, and an accordion plays spirited sing-alongs on weekends. George's Eggs, poached and served with sausage, are perfect for brunch.

After leaving Café Abyssinia, walk back on Ayiou Filippou to Adrianou and enter the **Ancient Agora,** a large site whose carefully landscaped grounds are scattered with Hellenistic and Roman fragments and ruins. In Ancient Athens the Agora was the center of all everyday activity. Besides the administrative buildings, it was surrounded by the schools, theaters, workshops, houses, stores, and market stalls of a thriving town.

7 Prominent on the grounds is the **Stoa of Attalos,** a two-story building, now a museum, designed as a retail complex and erected in the 2nd century BC by Attalos, a king of Pergamum. The reconstruction in 1953–56 (funded by private American donors) used Pentelic marble and creamy limestone from the original structure. The colonnade, designed for promenades, is protected from the blistering sun and cooled by breezes. The most notable sculptures, of historical and mythological figures from the 3rd and 4th centuries BC, are at ground level outside the museum. In the exhibition hall, chronological displays of pottery and objects from everyday life (note the child's terracotta pottery) demonstrate the continual settlement of the area from the Neolithic times to the Turkish. There are such toys as knucklebones and miniature theatrical masks carved from bone (case 50); bronze voting discs and a terracotta water clock (cases 26–28); and in case 38, bits of *ostraka* (pottery shards used in secret ballots to recommend banishment), from which the word "ostracism" comes. Among the famous candidates for a 10-year banishment, considered a fate worse than death, were Themistocles, Kimon, and even Pericles, who had his fair share of enemies. On the back wall are two segments of well-preserved Byzantine mosaics from the floors of the house.

Take a walk around the site and speculate on the location of Simon the Cobbler's house and shop, which was a meeting place for Socrates and his pupils. The carefully landscaped grounds display a number of plants known in antiquity, such as almond, myrtle, and pomegranate. Standing in the center, you have a glorious view up to the Acropolis, which on a clear day is given a mellow glow by the famous Attic light.

8 On a mound in the northwest corner of the grounds stands the best preserved extant Doric temple, the **Hephaisteion** (sometimes called the Theseion because of friezes showing the exploits of Theseus). Like the other monuments, it is roped off, but you can walk around it to admire its 34 columns. It was originally dedicated to Hephaistos, god of metalworkers; metal workshops still exist in this area near Ifestou Street. The temple was converted to Christian use in the 7th century, and the last service here was a Te Deum in 1834, held to celebrate King Otho's arrival.

Behind the temple, paths lead to the northwest slope of the **Kolonos Agoraios,** an area dotted with archaeological ruins half hidden in deep undergrowth, where you can sit on a bench and contemplate the scene that Englishman Edward Dodwell saw in the early 19th century, when he came to sketch antiquities. *Tel. 01/321–0185. Admission: 800 dr., students 400 dr., free Sun. and holidays. Open Tues.–Sun. 8:30–3.*

From the exit of the Agora, walk to Ayiou Filippou and north to Ermou; turn left and walk west to the entrance to **Keramikos Cemetery,** just outside the Themistoclean city wall. The name, taken from "Keramos," son of Ariadne and Dionysos, is associated with the modern word "ceramic." From the 12th century BC this was a district of potters, who used the abundant clay from the languid Eridanos River to make the funerary urns and grave decorations. To the left of the entrance is the **Oberlander Museum,** whose four rooms contain sculpture, terra-cotta figures, and some striking red-and-black-figured pottery. *Ermou 148, tel. 01/346–3552. Admission, including museum: 400 dr., free Sun. Open Tues.–Sun. 8:30–3.*

On the **Street of Tombs,** the thoroughfare leading away from the gates, a number of the distinctive stelae remain, including a replica of the marble relief of Dexilios, a knight who died in the war against Corinth, shown on horseback getting ready to spear a fallen foe. The extensive grounds are marshy in some spots, and in spring frogs exuberantly croak their mating songs near magnificent stands of lilies. Remains of the towers of the square **Dipylon** (Double Gate), the entrance to the ancient city, can still be seen.

Tour 2: Ancient Greek and Roman Athens

After 146 BC, when Greece was made a Roman province, the Pax Romana generally served the city well. Roman Athens reached its zenith during the reign of Hadrian (AD 177–AD 38), its greatest benefactor, who rebuilt the city and created many monuments. The most influential university town in the Roman Empire, Athens attracted such prominent students as Cicero and Horace and enjoyed a flowering of intellectual growth and architectural achievement before descending into the dark age after 330 AD, the beginning of the Byzantine period.

Begin your tour at the **Panathenaic Stadium,** on Vasileos Konstantinou Boulevard. Constructed by Lykourgus in 330 BC–29 BC and used intermittently for Roman spectacles, it was rebuilt by Herodus Atticus for the Panathenaic Games of AD 144. It later fell into ruin, and its marble was quarried for other buildings. By the mid-18th century, when it was painted by French artist Le Roy, it was little more than a wheat field with scant remains and was later the midnight site of the secret rites of the witches of Athens. It was rebuilt for the first modern Olympics, in April of 1896, and is now used mainly for concerts and the finish of the annual marathon.

From the stadium bear left on Vasilissis Olgas to the unobtrusive entrance to the site of the enormous **Temple of Olympian Zeus,** across from the Zappion. Begun in the 6th century BC, it was completed in AD 132 by Hadrian, who also built one huge gold-and-ivory statue of Zeus for the inner chamber and another, only slightly smaller, of himself. Only 15 of the original Corinthian columns remain, but standing next to them inspires a sense of awe at their bulk, which is softened by the graceful carving of the acanthus-leaf capitals. The clearly defined segments of a column blown down in 1852 give you an idea of the method used in its construction. The site is floodlighted in summer, a majestic scene when you round the bend from Syngrou Avenue. On the outskirts of the site to the north are remains of houses, the city walls, and a Roman bath. *Vasilissis Olgas Avenue, tel. 01/922–6330. Admission: 400 dr., free Sun. and for students. Open Tues.–Sun. 8:30–3.*

⑫ Proceeding west to Amalias Avenue you come to **Hadrian's Arch,** built in 131 BC. The marble gateway with Corinthian details was intended to honor Hadrian and separate the ancient and imperial sections of Athens. On the side facing the Acropolis an inscription reads THIS IS ATHENS, CITY OF THESEUS, but the side facing the Temple of Olympian Zeus proclaims, THIS IS THE CITY OF HADRIAN, NOT OF THESEUS.

Directly opposite Hadrian's Arch runs Lysikratous, a side street at the edge of Plaka. Walk northwest to an idyllic park and one of the least-known Athenian sights, the charming ⑬ **Monument of Lysikrates,** dating to 335 BC–334 BC. Six of the earliest Corinthian columns are arranged in a circle on a square base, topped by a marble dome designed like a branch of laurel leaves. In the 17th century the monument was incorporated into a Capuchin monastery (it was incorrectly known then as the Lantern of Demosthenes because it was believed to be where the famous orator practiced reciting his speeches with pebbles in his mouth to overcome his stutter).

Leave the square going south on Vironos Street; across Dionyssiou Areopagitou it becomes Makriyianni Street. Walk a short distance with a stone wall on your right, to an entrance ⑭ leading to the **Center for Acropolis Studies.** The spacious, sunny ground floor is devoted to casts of sculptures of lounging gods and friezes of heroes battling giants or centaurs that were once (or still are) on the Acropolis. The most notable are copies of the much-touted Elgin Marbles, presented as a consolation gift to Greece in 1846 (the British government kept the originals). On the second floor an exhibit of photos and drawings illustrates details of the painstaking restoration. Don't miss the display of terra-cotta antefixes, the decorations at the termination of the roofing tiles, invented by the classical Greeks. On one the elegant bright-on-dark abstract design is offset by a naughty gorgon with bulging black eyes sticking out his cherry-color tongue. *Makriyianni 2–4, tel. 01/9239–186. Admission free. Open Mon. and Fri. 9–2, Tues. and Thurs. 6–9, weekends 10–2.*

⑮ Go back to Dionyssiou Areopagitou, cross the street, and walk west to the **Theater of Dionysos,** which dates from about 330 BC. The theater's orchestra section was once made of dirt, trodden by actors during performances, and a large altar of Dionysos stood in the middle. Most of the upper rows have been destroyed, but the lower levels, with labeled chairs for priests and dignitaries, remain. The fantastic armchair in the center was reserved for the priest of Dionysos: It is adorned by regal lions' paws, and the back is carved with reliefs of satyrs and griffins. *Dionyssiou Areopagitou St., tel. 01/322–4625. Admission: 400 dr., free Sun. and to students. Open Mon.–Sat, 9–2:45, Sun. and holidays, 9–1:45.*

16 Continue along Dionyssiou Areopagitou to the **Odeon of Herod Atticus,** a hauntingly beautiful theater built Greek-style into the hillside but with typically Roman arches in its three-story stage building and barrel-vaulted entrances. It was dedicated by Roman citizen Herod Atticus of Marathon, a magistrate, senator, and wealthy patron of Athens. It is smaller than the Hellenistic theater of Dionysos just visited (holds slightly more than 5,000, versus 17,000), and the circular orchestra has become a semicircle. The long-vanished cedar roof probably covered only the stage and dressing rooms, not the 34 rows of seats. The theater was restored and reopened in 1955 for the Athens Festival and is now open only to ticket-holders a couple hours before summer performances.

Continuing west along Dionyssiou Areopagitou, take a path to the left, running past a large outdoor café (opposite the road **17** leading up to the Acropolis) and enter the area of **Philopappou.** A short distance ahead on the right is the delightful grove enclosing the church of **St. Dimitrios Loumbardiaris,** "the Bombardier." Here in 1656 on St. Dimitrios' Day, as is told in a text posted on the church, the congregation was gathered, while on the Acropolis a Turkish garrison commander had the cannons of the Propylaea ready to open fire during the final Te Deum. The moment it started, a bolt of lightening blew up the Propylaea, killing the commander and many of his men. The rustic stone church contains many icons and has an old-fashioned wood ceiling and roof.

Time Out The little **Tourist Pavilion** on natural terraces around St. Dimitrios is a blissful oasis far from the bustle of the archaeological sites and the streets. It is beautifully landscaped, shaded by overhanging pines, and the background music is provided by chirping birds. It serves drinks, snacks, and a few hot plates. *Open daily 10 AM–midnight.*

Continuing on a path south leads to the pine-clad **Mouseion** (Hill of the Muses), one of Philopappou's three summits, on which stands the strange **Monument of Philopappus,** a Syrian prince, who was a distinguished Athenian and a Roman consul. The marble monument is a tomb decorated by a frieze showing Philopappus driving his chariot. A path north from the Tourist Pavilion leads to the site of the **Pnyx** (meaning "crowded"), on which the general assembly met during the time of Pericles. Gathering the quorum of 5,000 citizens necessary to take a vote was not always easy. Slaves armed with red paint were sent out to dab it on vote-dodgers found on the streets; the offenders were then fined. North of the Pnyx, on the **Hill of the Nymphs,** stands an observatory, which is open to the public on the last Friday of each month.

Walk northeast down the hill to Aiginitou Street, turn right, then turn left on the main thoroughfare of Apostolos Pavlou, past the Ancient Agora, to Adrianou. Turn right on Adrianou to Areos Street, just below Monastiraki. To the right, behind **18** Tzistarakis Mosque, is the site of **Hadrian's Library,** built in AD 132. It is closed to the public, but you can easily see the remains from the street. The east wall is supported by six attached Corinthian columns, and Pausanias mentions "one hundred and twenty splendid columns of Phrygian marble," which apparently enclosed a cloistered court with a garden and pool. On the east side was the library itself, the intellectual center of its age, decorated with statues and murals. Other areas were used for lectures and classes. On the west wall are traces of a fresco showing the outline of the Byzantine Ayios Assomati, which stood next to it.

⑲ Continuing south on Areos, turn left onto Dexipou and then walk along Pelopida to the octagonal **Tower of the Winds (Horologion)**, the most appealing and well-preserved of the Roman monuments of Athens. It was originally a weather vane topped by a bronze Triton with a metal rod in his hand. Note the expressive relief showing the personifications of the eight winds, called *Ai Aerides* (the Windy Ones) by Athenians.

⑳ West of the Tower of the Winds is the **Roman Agora** (Market), which was the commercial center of the city at the time of Theseus, just as the Ancient Agora was the civic center. The large rectangular courtyard had a peristyle that provided shade for the arcades of shops. Its most notable feature is the **Gate of Athena Archegetis**, whose inscription records that it was erected with funds from Julius Caesar and Augustus and dedicated in 10 BC. Halfway up one solitary square pillar behind the north side of the gate is a price list for oil and salt that was carved in the time of Hadrian.

On the north side stands one of the few remains of the Turkish occupation, the hauntingly beautiful **Fethiye (Victory) Mosque**, dedicated by Mehmet II (the Conqueror) in 1456, two years after the Turks captured Athens. Built on the site of a Christian church, it was converted in the 17th century to a Roman Catholic church. Today it is used as a storehouse, closed to the public. Three steps in the right-hand corner of the porch lead to the base of the minaret, the rest of which has disappeared. *Pelopida and Eolou, tel. 01/324–5220. Admission: 400 dr., free on Sun. Open Tues.–Sun. 8:30–3.*

Tour 3: Byzantine Churches of Athens

The year 330 AD, when Constantine the Great changed his capital from Rome to Byzantium (and renamed it Constantinople), marked the beginning of the Byzantine Period. Athens declined into insignificance, its perimeter reduced to the line of the old Roman Wall. The few churches and monasteries built during the Byzantine Period are among the most attractive and characteristic Greek buildings of any era. Our tour begins in Plaka and takes in the National Archaeological Museum. Other notable Byzantine churches in Plaka will be included in Tour 4, which covers Plaka exclusively.

㉑ We first visit pretty **Ayia Aikaterina**, on Galanou and Goura, built in the late-11th–early 12th centuries and enlarged in 1927. Its name dates from 1769, when it was acquired by the Monastery of Saint Catherine in the Sinai. It is cruciform, with a dome resting on a drum supported by four interior columns; the large courtyard and garden make it popular for baptisms and weddings.

Take Farmaki north to Kidathineon and turn right, then left on Filellinon, and continue to Nikodimou; across Filellinon at the **㉒** corner of Souri is the 11th-century **Ayios Nikodimos**, once the chapel of a convent pulled down in 1780 by the notoriously brutal Hadji Ali Haseki, who used the stone for a defense wall around Athens. The church was sold to the Russian govern-

ment, who in 1852–56 modified it into a larger, cruciform building with a distinctive terra-cotta frieze; the separate tower was
built to hold a massive bell donated by Tsar Alexander II. Note
the displays of ornate Russian embroidery and the bright blues
of the Pantocrator overhead. The female chanters of this Russian Orthodox church are renowned.

Take a short detour over to Amalias 36 to visit the **Jewish Museum,** on the third floor of a handsome art deco building with a
Parisian-style lift enclosed in intricate wrought iron. The entrance to the building is on the left after you pass a huge
wrought-iron gate. The museum's collection of vivid memorabilia tells the story of the Jews in Greece, as far back as the 3rd
century BC in Thessaloniki. Eighty-seven percent of the Greek
Jews were killed during the Holocaust, and only 5,000 remain
in Greece today. Religious artifacts, costumes, embroideries,
and photos are well organized according to periods and themes.
One room contains an actual synagogue, moved from Patras
when part of the city was leveled by an earthquake in 1979. *Tel.
01/323-1577. Admission free. Open Sun.–Fri. 10–1.*

Walk back to Filellinon, turn right, then left on Mitropoleos,
and walk on the left side of the street. At Pendeli Street you'll
㉓ see a curious sight: tiny **Ayia Dynamis** (Divine Power) chapel,
topped by a dainty arch and bell, peeking out from the modern
building of the Ministry of Education built around it. Named
for the Virgin Mary's supposed power to help childless women
conceive, its romantic history makes it worth mentioning. A
Greek named Mastropavlis made cartridges here for the Turkish garrison, which had turned the church into a munitions
works. Unbeknownst to them, he also made ammunition for
Greek revolutionaries, which was smuggled out by a coura-
geous washerwoman. These were the first bullets fired at the
Turks on the Acropolis when the War of Independence broke
out.

Continue on Mitropoleos to Mitropolis Square, and walk across
㉔ it to the **Little Metropolis,** perhaps the most charming church in
Athens (next to the pompous **Metropolis,** the ornate Cathedral
of Athens). The Little Metropolis (Panayia Gorgoepikoos, the
Virgin Who Answers Prayers Quickly), dates to the 12th century, and its most interesting features are its frescoed outer
walls, covered with reliefs dating from the Classical to the Byzantine periods. Reliefs of figures and fanciful zodiac signs decorate slabs set above the entrance. Most of the paintings inside
were destroyed, but the famous 13th- to 14th-century Virgin,
said to perform miracles, remains. If you would like to follow
Greek custom and light an amber beeswax candle for yourself
and someone you love, drop the price of the candle in the slot.

Continue on Mitropoleos to Kapnikareas Street and turn right,
passing, at No. 49, a magnificently restored commercial building distinguished by elegant steel and bronze upper levels that
blend beautifully with the neoclassical facade below. Walk on to
Ermou. On an island right in the middle of the intersection is
㉕ the striking **Kapnikarea Church.** It is really two adjoining
chapels, one a cruciform structure of the 11th century, and the
other a handsome building of typical Byzantine raised brickwork, with a dome supported by four Roman columns. The latter was carefully restored by Athens University, of which it is
now the official church. A prominent modern mosaic of the Vir-

gin and Child adorns the west entrance, and inside are colorful frescoes.

Time Out At the end of Mitropoleos just before Monastiraki Square is a handful of no-frills restaurants featuring *souvlaki*, the best bargain in Athens. You have a choice of **Acropolis** (Mitropoleos 90), which has the most aggressive hawkers and the best spicy chicken souvlaki, or **Savvas** or **Mitropoli**, just up the street, which have tables spilling onto the narrow sidewalk. **Thanassis** (at Mitropoleos 69) is always crowded with Greeks. A more subdued atmosphere prevails at **Cafe Poseidon,** with tables under umbrellas on the square, and at **Platia Agoras** (Kapnikareas and Adrianou), shaded with mulberry and plane trees, where little traffic passes by.

Next we come to the **Panayia Pantanassa Church** (Great Monastery, in Monastiraki Square), which once flourished as an extensive convent, perhaps dating to the 10th century. The nuns took in poor people, who earned their keep weaving the thick textiles known as *abas*. The convent's basic basilica form, now recessed a few steps below street level, has been altered through a poor restoration in 1911, when the bell tower was added; it is now undergoing another restoration and is often closed.

Walk west along Ermou and enter the district of **Psiri,** which has many buildings older than those in Plaka, though it has always been less fashionable. Peek over the wrought-iron gates of the old houses on the narrow side streets between here and **Keramikou,** north of Keramikos Cemetery, to see the charming courtyards with long, low buildings whose many small rooms were rented out to different families. This was the setting of a number of popular Greek novels around the turn of the century and is now a mercantile area with small workshops supplying leather and glassware to retail shops. Signs of gentrification are evident in Psiri and Keramikou.

Cross to the left side of Ermou and turn left at an alley past Normanou to reach **Abyssinia Square** (Plateia Avissinias), lined with venerable antiques shops once renowned for great bargains. This area is especially lively on Sunday morning, when the *Yusurum*, or open-air bazaar, takes place as it has since 1910. Street merchants peddle an incredible array of goods, ranging from junk to genuine antiques.

Returning to Ermou, turn left and cross the street at the intersection with Ayion Assomaton, at the center of which stands **26** the church of **Ayii Assomati** (the Bodiless Angels). Dating to the 11th century, it was poorly rebuilt in 1880 and properly restored in 1959. It is in the form of a Greek cross, with a hexagonal dome and very impressive exterior stonework. Some fragments of frescoes inside are probably from the 17th century, but art historians dispute the claim that an oil painting to the left of the entrance is by El Greco.

This area was populated by Turkish gypsies before the War of Independence, giving the city gate here the name Gypsy Gate. It later became the heart of the Jewish community, and the neighborhood was called *Evraika*. The shops of the leading families, including the Cohens, Levis, and Camkhis, were along Ermou Street, and a couple of blocks north, on Melidoni Street, stands the new **Synagogue Beth Shalom,** with a classical marble facade. Across the street is the old synagogue, which once housed the Jewish Museum, now on Amalias Street.

Take Sari Street northeast to its end, where it joins Aristofanous and runs into Evripidou Street. To the right, across Evripidou, is **Ayios Ioannis Kolonastis** (Saint John of the Column), the most peculiar church in Athens. A Corinthian column protrudes from the tiled rooftop of the little one-sided basilica built around it in 565, and people with a high fever still come here to perform "curative" rituals that involve tying a colored thread to the column and saying a special prayer. Mosaic floors were unearthed here that were probably part of an ancient temple to Asklepeios.

Continue east on Evripidou, an intriguing street lined with aromatic shops selling herbs, nuts, olive-oil soap, and household items. You will end up at the **central market** on Athinas Street. On the left side are open-air stalls selling fruit and vegetables at the best prices in town, although wily merchants may slip overripe items into your bag. At the corner of Armodiou, shops sell live poultry and rabbits. Across the street, in the huge covered market built in 1870, the surrealistic composition of suspended carcasses and shimmering fish on marble counters emits a pungent odor that is overwhelming on hot days. At the north end of the market, to the right on Sofokleous Street, are the shops with the best cheese, olives, halvah, bread, and cold cuts (including *pastourma*, Mediterranean pastrami) in Athens.

Time Out   Stop for a drink or meal in one of the quaint tavernas or stand-up bars around the market and observe the action. At 100-year-old **Yiorgios** (Evripidou 40), where a cross-section of the local population comes to sample wine and liqueurs by the glass, you'll get the true flavor of unembellished Athens.

Turn east on Evripidou Street and walk toward **Klafthmonos Square** (Square of Wailing), so named because public servants loudly lamented here after being dismissed. At the corner of Evripidou and Aristidou you will pass **Ayii Theodori,** a lovely mid-11th-century cruciform church, probably the oldest in Athens. In a sub-basement at No. 6 Dragatsaniou, across from the square, you can see a segment of the ancient city walls. The **Athens City Museum** was the residence of teenage King Otho and his bride Amalia for seven years while they were waiting for the royal palace to be completed. A Throne Room still exists, and on the ground floor a model of Athens in 1842 shows how sparsely populated the new capital was. The first floor displays paintings by European artists who came to Athens, such as Edward Lear, Gasparini, and Dodwell. *Paparigopoulou 7, S.E. side of sq., tel. 01/323–0168. Admission: 100 dr. Open Mon., Wed., Fri., Sat. 9–1:30.*

Walk on the pedestrian mall at Korai to Panepistimiou (Venizelou) and cross over to the other side. You are facing a complex of three dramatic buildings belonging to **Athens University,** designed by the Hansen Brothers in the period after independence and built of white Pentelic marble, with tall columns and decorative friezes. In the center is the Senate House of the university; on the right is the Academy, flanked by two slim columns and topped by statues of Athena and Apollo; and on the left is the National Library, containing 500,000 books and 3,000 manuscripts. Along Panepistimiou just south of Amerikis stands the elegant **mansion of Heinrich Schliemann,** the German archaeologist and discoverer of ancient Troy, which was built in the style of a Venetian palace in 1879. The Numismatic Museum is scheduled to be moved here.

On Acadimias Street opposite the university is the **Municipal Cultural Center,** originally the city hospital and now used for lectures and exhibits. On the lower level is the cozy **Theater Museum.** It features dressing rooms and costumes of Greek stage and screen stars plus posters, playbills, and other memorabilia. In front of the center is the only known surviving statue of Pericles, a fine work in Parian marble by Heinrich Faltermeier, showing Pericles with sturdy legs and the helmet he always wore because his head was, it's said, slightly deformed—which explains his nickname, Onion Head. Almost directly across Acadimias, facing Pericles, is a much smaller and less skillful bust of Aspasia, the cultured courtesan who was his beloved companion and mother of his son. *Theater museum, tel. 01/362–9430. Admission: 300 dr., students free. Open weekdays 9–3, Sun. 10–1.*

You can take trolley no. 2, 4, 5, or 11 from Panepistimiou Street (or walk about 15 minutes) north to the wonderful **National Archaeological Museum.** If you walk, you will pass **Omonia (Concord) Square,** the oldest in Athens, which bustles with activity around the clock. It has been spruced up with a new fountain, palm trees, and a green glass abstract sculpture representing an Olympic runner.

The air-conditioned museum is a cool oasis to visit after lunch, when the ancient sites and shops are closed and the tour groups have mostly departed. Look at a floor plan to organize your plan of attack; the collection is too huge to cover comfortably in one day. Hang on to your admission ticket and take a break for a drink or a snack at the pleasant garden café in front of the museum.

The collection extends from Neolithic to Roman times; unfortunately, both the Greek and English labeling is woefully inadequate. Sculpture is on the ground floor, ceramics on the first floor, ceramics and frescoes from Santorini on the upper level of the first floor. These outstanding frescoes, delightful re-creations of daily life in Minoan Santorini should not be missed. They are scheduled to be sent back to Santorini on completion of the long-awaited museum there.

The most celebrated finds are in the Mycenaean Room, No. 4, the stunning gold treasure from Schliemann's excavations of Mycenae in 1876: the funeral mask of a bearded king believed to be the image of Agamemnon; a splendid silver bull's-head libation cup; and the 15th-century BC Vaphio Goblets, masterworks in embossed gold. Mycenaeans were famed for their miniature carving, and an exquisite example is the ivory statuette of two curvaceous mother goddesses with a child nestled on their laps.

Rooms 7–14 contain Geometric and Archaic art (10th–6th centuries BC), and Rooms 11–14 have funerary stelae and kouroi, among them the *Warrior of Marathon* by Aristokles and the unusual *Running Hoplite.*

Rooms 15–21 focus on Classical art (5th–3rd centuries BC). Be sure to see the bareback *Jockey of Artemision,* a 2nd-century

BC Hellenistic bronze salvaged from the sea; from the same find the bronze *Artemision Poseidon* (some say Zeus), poised and ready to fling a trident (or thunderbolt?); and the *Varvakion Athena*, a marble version of the goddess ½ the size of Pheidias's gigantic gold-and-ivory cult statue that stood in the Parthenon. Room 28 displays funerary architecture: the spirited 2nd-century relief of a rearing stallion held by a black groom, which exemplifies the transition from Classical to Hellenistic art. Room 30 holds the famous humorous marble group of a nude Aphrodite getting ready to slap an advancing Pan with a sandal, while Eros floats overhead and grasps one of his horns. *28 Oktovriou (Patission) 44, tel. 01/821–7717. Admission: 1,500 dr. adults, 800 dr. students; free Sun. Open summer, Mon. 12:30–7, Tues.–Fri. 8–7, weekends 8:30–3; winter, Mon. 11–5, Tues.–Fri. 8–5, weekends 8:30–3.*

Tour 4: Monastiraki, Plaka, and Anafiotika

Monastiraki is the core of the market area, the essence of Athenian grass-roots commercial activity. The adjacent **Plaka,** the main residential area, has been inhabited since prehistoric times. The section of Plaka called Anafiotika is built on winding lanes that climb up the slopes of the Acropolis, its upper reaches resembling a tranquil island village. Plaka is a splendid example of residents, architects, and academicians joining forces in the early 1980s to transform a decaying neighborhood. Noisy discos and tacky pensions were closed, streets were changed into walking malls, and old buildings were well restored. If you wander off the main streets you will be amazed at how tranquil the little lanes are even in the height of the summer. This tour is meant to impart the flavor of the traditional aspects of 19th-century Athens, with Byzantine accents provided by churches. Start at the newly opened **Museum of Greek Folk Art, Ceramic Collection** in the **Tzistarakis Mosque** of 1759, the focal point of Monastiraki Square. This collection is masterfully designed, with the exhibits properly lit and labeled. The mihrab niche facing Mecca is of delicate pastel stone.

Walk south along Areos, which is now lined with small shops; in Ottoman times it was a lovely street known as the Lower Bazaar, roofed and covered with vines. At Dexipou, turn left and pass the Army-Navy–style open stalls on the left and the wicker shops on the right. On the corner of Eolou is the former **Aeolos Hotel,** built in 1837 just after Athens was made capital of Greece. Advertisements boasted that it offered all European conveniences including beds, at a time when guests in public lodging usually brought their blankets and slept on the floor. The nicely restored Othonian building with blue shutters now has shops on its ground floor. This area was the edge of the Upper Bazaar.

Continue south on Eolou Street past the Tower of the Winds to Kiristou Street. On the right side opposite No. 7 is the boarded-up **Hamam of Abit Afenti,** a Turkish bath in use until about 1960 and scheduled for renovation. Note the metal crescent and star on its windows, symbol of the Ottoman Empire. Many buildings in the area have been skillfully restored, including some used by the municipality.

Continue to Mnissikleous Street and turn right. At night this street is crowded with merrymakers visiting the old tavernas, which feature traditional music and dancing, many with roof-tops facing the Acropolis. Continue to Tholou Street, only a narrow lane at this point passing between restaurants on one side and the **Boite Esperida** (a Plaka institution in operation since 1964) on the other. A little way up the hill is the **Old University,** or **Kleanthis House,** where King Otho's top architect, Kleanthis, lived, and which was used as the University of Athens for a few years. Private benefactors have restored the building and opened a museum of memorabilia. *Tholou 5. Admission 400 dr. Museum open weekdays 9–1.*

Head back east to Mnissikleous Street, turn right, then left on Prytaniou Street, and walk to Stratonas Street, a pretty lane with small cottages, charming murals painted on the stones, and a few little shops. Continue south and slightly uphill until you reach **Ayios Georgios Tou Vrachou** (Saint George of the Rock), one of the most beautiful churches of Athens, still in use today. Perched right on the bedrock of the Acropolis and white-washed a gleaming white, it marks the southeast edge of **Anafiotika,** an area unlike any ever seen in a major European capital. In Classical times it was abandoned because the Delphic Oracle claimed it as sacred ground. The buildings here were constructed by masons from Anafi, in the Cyclades, who came to find work in the rapidly expanding Athens of the 1830s and 1840s. They took over this area, whose rocky terrain was similar to Anafi's, building little landscaped dwellings illegally during the night. Ethiopians who had arrived during the Otto-man period and stayed on after independence lived higher up, in caves, on the northern slopes of the Acropolis.

Turn right (north) on the lane below the church, walk past the melon-colored building next door, and you will wind through an enchanting area of simple stone houses, nestled right into the bedrock, some changed little over the years, others stunningly restored. Cascades of bougainvillea and pots of geraniums enliven the balconies and rooftops, and the serenity is a blissful contrast to the cacophony of modern Athens. This is a true village, still populated by many descendants of the original islanders. As you reach the far end of the lane you walk slightly uphill to reach **Ayios Simeon,** a neoclassical church built in 1847 by the settlers from Anafi, which marks the western boundary of Anafiotika and contains a copy of a famous miracle-working icon from Anafi, Our Lady of the Reeds.

From the church you can walk up the lane and turn right to get to Theorias, which parallels the ancient *Peripatos*, or public roadway that ran around the Acropolis just below the cliffs. On the left is the **Church of the Metamorphosis** (Transfiguration), a high-domed stone chapel of the 14th century, which has a grotto carved into the Acropolis at the rear.

Just west of the church is the **Kanellopoulos Museum,** in the stately Michaleas Mansion built in 1884. The family collection spans Athens history from the 3rd century BC to the 19th century, with especially fine Byzantine icons, jewelry, and Myce-naean and Geometric vases and bronzes. *Theorias and Panos Sts., tel. 01/321–2313. Admission: 400 dr. Open Tue.–Sun. 8:30–3.*

Time Out Head north down the hill to 24 Panos Street to have a cool drink at the **Nefeli Café Restaurant,** a large complex with an idyllic outdoor café shaded by smart awnings and draped with grape vines. It's perched just below the Acropolis cliffs, looking down on Ayia Anna church.

---

37 Take Tholou east past Mnissikleous to Prytaniou and walk to the church of **Ayii Anargyroi.** According to legend, it was built in the late 8th century by the Empress Irene. The Church of the Holy Sepulchre at Jerusalem, needing a base in Athens, acquired it in the 1700s and continues to occupy it today. The picturesque church has a gingerbread exterior (being restored at press time), a delightful little garden containing fragments of ancient ruins, an antique gas lamp, and a well that was used as a hiding place in troubled times.

38 Back on Prytaniou, continue east to **Ayios Nikolaos Rangavas,** an 11th-century Byzantine parish church at the corner of Epicharmou. Walk to the southeast side of this pretty building to see fragments of ancient columns and capitals incorporated into its walls, an example of the pragmatic recycling of the time.

39 Continue on Epicharmou to the corner of Scholiou Street and the **Church House,** a striking abandoned tower house with tiny windows, thick stone walls, and a tall chimney, which bears traces of its former glory. Probably dating from the 18th century and then used as a Turkish police post, it later was the fortress of Richard Church, commander-in-chief of the Greek forces during the War of Independence. After the liberation, historian George Finlay, a veteran of the war, and his wife lived here for half a century, while he wrote his many volumes of Greek history, including what is considered the definitive work on the War of Independence.

40 Walk south on Scholiou to Hill Street, turn left and cross Adrianou to Hatzimichali Street. On your left you'll find the **Center of Folk Art and Tradition,** in the comfortable family mansion of Angeliki Hatzimichali, a folklorist. Exhibits include detailed costumes, ceramic plates from Skyros, handwoven fabrics and embroideries, and family portraits. *Hatzimichali St. 6, tel. 01/324–3987. Admission free; open Tues. and Thurs. 9–9; Wed., Fri., Sat. 9–1, 5–9; Sun. 9–1.*

Walk south on Geronda and turn left on Kidathineon. On the left on the next block you'll come to the 11th- to 12th-century church of **Sotira Tou Kottaki,** set in a tidy garden with a fountain that was the main source of water for the neighborhood until after Turkish times.

41 Across the street is the **Greek Folk Art Museum,** run by the Ministry of Culture, whose rich collection includes examples of folk arts from 1650 to the present, with especially interesting embroideries, stone and wood carvings, carnival costumes, and *Karaghiozis* (shadow player figures). Don't miss the room of uniquely fanciful landscapes and historical portraits by naive painter Theophilos Hatzimichael, from Mitilini, one of the most beloved Greek artists. *Kidathineon 17, tel. 01/321–3018. Admission: 200 dr. Open Tues.–Sun. 10–2.*

From this point you can walk in five minutes to **Syntagma Square** via Filellinon, which is two blocks east on Kidathineon, or you can walk two blocks west on Kidathineon to browse in the souvenir shops of Plaka or stop to have a coffee in one of the cafés in the neoclassical buildings on the main square, **Filomoussou Eterias,** a great hangout for people watchers.

Tour 5: Modern Athens—Lycabettus, Kolonaki, and Syntagma

Start your tour by taking a taxi or bus No. 23 to Ploutarchou and Kleomenous, the foot of **Lycabettus.** Walk up the footpath lined with souvenir shops to the **Teleferique** (fare 350 dr. round-trip, 200 dr. one-way; operates Fri.–Wed. 8:30 AM–12:15 AM, Thurs. 10:30 AM–12:15 AM), the steeply inclined electric train to the summit of Lycabettus, the highest hill in Athens. At the top is the picturesque whitewashed **Ayios Giorgios** chapel. The Café Dionysos here has drinks and a full menu but is pricey. You'll get a better deal at the café at the foot of the hill (Kleomenous and Ploutarchou), which serves coffee, fresh juice, and filling grilled sandwiches with any number of ingredients.

Continue on Ploutarchou south to Spefsipou and turn left. Continue east (Spefsipou becomes Souidias), passing on the right the spacious grounds of the British School of Archaeology and then the American School of Classical Studies. Just a little farther on the left is the **Gennadius Library,** completed in 1926, containing one of the world's greatest collections of books on Greek subjects. Besides the 24,000 volumes bequeathed by John Gennadius, the founder, there are many rare books and interesting paintings; for example, watercolors of Greece by Edward Lear. The library facade is imposing, a portico of Ionic columns in front of a brilliantly colored neoclassical facade.

Take Genadiou Street south from the front of the library, past the sweet little park at Iassou in front of the **Taxiarchi,** or **Church of Moni Petraki,** built in the 12th century and decorated with paintings by Yiorgios Markos in the 18th century. Continue to Vassileos Konstandinou and cross over to the corner of Vassileos Alexandreou, on which is the **Ethniki Pinakothiki,** or **National Gallery of Art.** Along with the permanent collections of Greek painting and sculpture of the 19th and 20th centuries, including a dozen paintings by naive artist Theophilos, are three El Grecos on the upper level. *Tel. 01/721–1010. Admission: 150 dr. Open Tues.–Sat. 9–3, Sun. 10–2.*

Walk west on Vasilissis Sofias, past Rizari, to the **Byzantine Museum,** in the mansion of the Duchess of Plaisance, built 1840–48 by Kleanthis. The beautiful grounds have a rose garden, a fountain, and fragments of statues. It's the only museum in Europe concentrating exclusively on Byzantine art, and the rooms are arranged to look like Greek churches of different eras. The outer wings contain mostly icons, many quite valuable, but some of the buildings are closed at this time for restoration. *Vasilissis Sofias 22, tel. 01/723–1570. Admission: 1,000 dr. adults, 500 dr. students, free Sun. Open Tues.–Sun. 9–3.*

Continue on Vasilissis Sofias and cross over at Irodotou to visit the new wing of the **Goulandris Cycladic Museum** in the gorgeous **Stathatos Mansion.** The main museum is on the next street, in a modern building of marble and glass. It has an outstanding collection dating from the Bronze Age, with especially notable marble idols, the primitive Cycladic form of the Great Earth Mother. *Neofitou Douka 4, tel. 01/ 724–9706; new*

wing, *01/723–4931. Admission: 200 dr. Open Mon. and Wed.–
Fri. 10–3:30, Sat. 10–2:30.*

46 Continue on Vasilissis Sofias to the corner of Koumbari, to the
Benaki Museum, a fascinating, eclectic display of Greek and
Oriental art in the Benaki family house. A number of rooms
will be closed for part of 1993, while a new wing is being built.
Outstanding exhibits include the costumes and folk crafts in
the basement, especially the handcarved wooden dowry chests,
and the Coptic artifacts and ceramics on the first floor. The
book-shop also sells ethnic records and fine copies of museum
pieces, and the café on the top floor has a good view.

Time Out   Walk north on Koumbari to **Filikis Eterias Square** (better
known as **Kolonaki Square**), crammed with chattering crowds
at outdoor cafés and surrounded by chic boutiques and galleries. **Le Quartier** on the west side is frequented by young
trendies, while the older establishment heads for **Lykovrissi** or
Kolonaki Tops, on the northeast end. If you prefer a quiet setting with no traffic, take Koumbari south and cross over
Vasilissis Sofias to Irodou Attikou (Herodes Atticus). Walk
along the National Gardens for two blocks; past the white gate
opposite Likiou Street is **Kipos,** a café in a lush setting under
flowering vines, with a cozy stone cottage for cool weather. The
menu is limited to a *poikilia,* or variety, of *mezze* (appetizers),
grilled "toast" (with ham and cheese), ice cream, apple pie, and
drinks.

Take a walk through the **National Gardens,** which have more
than 500 species of trees and plants, many labeled. A small bo-
tanical museum illustrates many of the plants found in the garden. Just south of the garden is the Zappion, a neoclassical hall
used for special events. At night, a café with cabaret acts attracts large crowds who pass the time gossiping and nibbling on
pastries and ice cream.

47 Leave the park at the large gate on Amalias and turn right,
ending your tour at the **Tomb of the Unknown Soldier** in front of
Parliament, formerly the Royal Palace. A bas relief of a dying
soldier is modeled after a sculpture on the Temple of Aphaia in
Aegina. The text is from the funeral oration said to have been
given by Pericles. The tomb is patrolled around the clock by the
Evzones, an honor guard of tall young men who on Sunday don
their dress wear, a short white *foustenella* (kilt) with 400 neat
little pleats and red shoes with pompons—and still manage to
look brawny rather than silly. On Sunday at 11 AM a band ac-
companies a large troop of them in a memorable ceremony. Every
morning, a group of the Evzones raise the Greek flag on the
Acropolis and return to take it down at closing time.

Tour 6: Piraeus

*Numbers in the margin correspond to points of interest on the
Piraeus map.*

The port of Athens, 11 kilometers (7 miles) from the center, is
a city in its own right (third-largest after Athens and
Thessaloniki), with a population including suburbs of about
500,000. To those who remember the film *Never On Sunday,*
the name Piraeus evokes earthy waterfront cafés frequented
by free-spirited sailors and hookers, though many Athenians

regard Piraeus (except for Microlimano or Kastella) as merely low class. Neither image is correct: the restoration of older buildings and the addition of smart shopping centers and cafés have brought about a rejuvenation of community pride. Piraeus caters more to Greek families and young singles than to the rough-and-tumble crowd, and living in some parts of it carries a certain cachet these days. Also, the air pollution, noise level, and temperatures are considerably lower than in inner Athens.

Piraeus, in ancient times an island surrounded by marshes, was settled by the Minyans, a warlike, seafaring people who built a temple to Artemis Munychia on the hill now known as Kastella. At first the Athenians docked their triremes at Phaleron (where Theseus set off on his journey to Crete), but around 493 BC Themistocles persuaded them to use Piraeus and built the *Makra Teixoi*, or Long Walls, from Kastella to Athens. Piraeus was razed by the Roman general Sulla in 86 BC and afterward remained virtually uninhabited.

In 1834, after independence, the government offered land on favorable terms in order to rebuild Piraeus (at that point a mere wilderness), and it was settled by immigrant groups from other parts of Greece. The first factory was founded by Hydriots in 1847, and by the turn of the century there were 76 steam powered factories. After the 1920s Piraeus developed as the economic center, while Athens maintained the cultural sphere. In the years following 1922, refugees from Asia Minor swelled the population, bringing with them *rembetika* music, a form of urban blues still popular today.

On a day trip to Piraeus you can see the main sights, explore the neighborhoods around its three harbors, and have a seafood meal before returning to Athens. And if you are taking an early morning ferry or seeing a performance at the Veakio Theater in Kastella, it makes good sense to stay in one of the seaside hotels. The fastest and cheapest way to get to Piraeus from central Athens is to take the electric train, a 25-minute trip from Omonia. The station is just off Akti Possidonos, running along the main harbor.

48 A short walk north is the area of Mavromichali and Dragatsoniou streets, where the Sunday-morning **flea market** is held. It consists of outdoor stalls overflowing with household items, electronic goods, and offbeat video cassettes, of more appeal to residents than tourists, although a few collectible white elephants emerge among the kitsch.

49 At the southern end of Akti Possidonos is the station for local buses and the shipping offices. On Navarinou Street, parallel to Possidonos is a **market** selling cheese, cold cuts, dried fruit, bread, and nuts. It's good to buy provisions before taking a ferry because the snack bars on board often have just a few items at high prices. Southeast of here near Korai Square, on **50** Ayiou Konstantinou is the splendid 800-seat **municipal theater**, modeled after the Opéra Comique in Paris and finished in 1895. In the same building are the **Municipal Art Gallery** and the **Panos Aravantinos Decor Museum**, displaying sketches and models of the artist's theatrical sets. *Tel. 01/412–2339. Admission free. Both open weekdays 9–2 and 4–8.*

Akti Possidonos runs into Akti Miaoulis if you continue south; at its end are the Customs House and Port Authority, through which one passes to board boats going to other countries. In

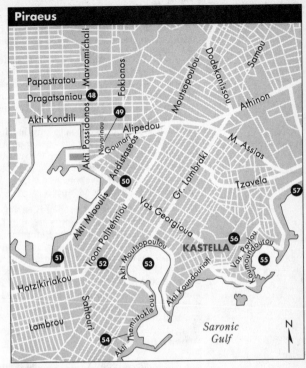

Piraeus

51 this area is a modern **exhibition center,** where the Poisidonia Shipping Exhibition is held in June in connection with a biannual Nautical Week.

52 Walk southwest (or take bus No. 904 or 905 from the station opposite the electric train) to the newly remodeled **Archaeological Museum,** which has an admirable collection of funerary stelae, urns, monuments, and korai. On the first floor, its prize exhibits, found in a sewage drain in 1959, include the masterfully crafted Piraeus Kouros (probably a cult statue of Apollo from the 6th century BC, and therefore the oldest known hollow-cast bronze statue); a 4th-century bronze of a pensive Athena, wearing a helmet decorated with griffins and owls; and two bronze versions of Artemis. *Harilaou Trikoupi 31 at Alkiviadou St., tel. 01/452–1598. Admission: 400 dr. adults, 300 dr. senior citizens, students free. Open Tues.–Sun. 9–1.*

53 **Zea Marina,** or **Pasalimani,** the small harbor on the other side of Piraeus, has a new marina, complete with shops and all yachting facilities, with berths for more than 400 boats. The surrounding area has been rejuvenated, with the addition of many enticing cafés and pubs. A GNTO Office with maps, brochures, and timetables is on the west side of the harbor close to the departure point for hydrofoils bound for the Saronic Gulf Islands.

54 A little farther west is the **Maritime Museum,** which has 13,000 items on display, including scale models and actual sections of triremes and famous boats, Byzantine flags, figureheads, documents, and uniforms. A section of the Long Walls is incorporated into the museum's foundation, and other well-preserved segments run along Akti Themistokleous, south of Zea Marina. The road across from the sea in this area has some reasonably priced seafood restaurants and pizza parlors.

55 The most touristy part of Piraeus is the lovely little crescent-shaped harbor of **Mikrolimano,** known to old-timers as **Turkolimano.** Sitting under awnings next to the sea and watching the water lap against the gaily painted fishing boats is the next best thing to going to an island. The hawkers in front of the restaurants are entertaining, but they can be aggressive. During high season, it is a good idea to have lunch here, as most of the 20 or so restaurants lining the harbor on Akti Koumoundourou are packed in the evening. Don't be afraid to ask to see the prices on the menu or go to look at the fish stored in iced compartments. Be sure to specify how large a portion you want, and find out its price in advance.

56 The **Veakio Theater** at the top of **Kastella,** the hill just behind the harbor, has an interesting festival in July and August featuring visiting dance troupes. Before or after the theater or dinner in Mikrolimano, make sure to take a walk in Kastella, an area that retains the charm of a bygone era, its neoclassical houses skillfully restored. A short walk to the north of **57** Mikrolimano brings you to the **Peace and Friendship Stadium,** nicknamed The Shoe because of its distinctive shape. Wrestling matches and other sporting events, concerts, and exhibitions are held here.

Athens for Free

For Athenians all the world's a stage. Watching the interplay between Greeks, complete with wildly gesturing hands and dramatic facial expressions, will provide hours of entertainment. The Sunday morning **flea market** in Monastiraki is a fitting setting in which to see lively haggling, and a fine destination in itself.

The sunset viewed from the Pnyx, with a full view of the Acropolis, is stirring. And one can walk up to the top of Lycabettus (although it is much easier to take the funicular) to watch the sunset and then turn in the other direction to see the moon rise over "violet-crowned" Hymettos, as the lights of Athens blink on all over the city.

The **Laiki,** the outdoor produce markets that rotate from one neighborhood to another, are fascinating to visit. Two of the best are the Friday markets on Xenokratous Street in Kolonaki and on Orminiou Street in Ilisia, just behind the Holiday Inn. Don't squeeze the fruit.

On Sunday many of the major sights and museums are free, including the Acropolis, the Roman and the Ancient agoras, Keramikos, and the National Archaeological Museum. Some interesting museums are free of charge, including the **Acropolis Study Center, Athens City Museum, Greek Popular Musical Instruments Museum, Jewish Museum, Pierides Gallery, Philatelic Museum,** and **Train Museum.**

What to See and Do with Children

Amusement Parks Small, movable amusement parks called **Luna Parks** are usually set up in the park next to the electric train station in Neo

Phaleron, near the beach at Alimos, and on Kifissias Avenue near Nea Psychiko and Marousi. They usually have merry-go-rounds, Ferris wheels, and bumper cars; some have roller coasters. For exact locations, ask at your hotel or ask a taxi driver to take you to the closest one.

Bowling, Billiards, and Roller Skating   **Blanos Bowling** has 18 lanes, billiards, and roller skating, at Colosseum Shopping Center (Vassileos Georgiou Ave. and Dousmani St., Glyfada, tel. 01/898–0159), and 12 lanes and billiards but no roller skating at Leoforos Vouliagmenis 239 (Platia Kalogyros, Dafni, tel. 01/971–4036 or 01/971–4660).

Karaghiozis Puppet Shows   This is a Punch and Judy–type shadow show starring Karaghiozis (the Black Eye), a character developed in Asia Minor and brought over to Greece. **Athanasiou Brothers** present free shows every Sunday at 11 AM, October–May at the **Moschato Theater** (Metamorphosis Sq., near Moschato Railway Station, tel. 01/293–2000). At a workshop in the same complex children can get a closer look at the painted-leather figures used in performances.

Thanasis Spyropoulos, one of the leading Karaghiozis players, puts on shows on Sunday at 11 and 5:30, October–May at the **Spyropoulos Theater** (Lambrinis and Ersis 9, Galatsi, tel. 01/293–2000 or 01/262–9046. Admission: 300 dr., good for two shows). In summer, the group travels all over Greece.

Libraries   **British Council Library** has many children's books and a table at which children can sit and read. *17 Kolonaki Sq., tel. 01/360–6011 or 01/363–3211. Open Mon., Wed., Fri. 9–1, Tues. and Thurs. 5 PM–8 PM.*

The **Children's Library,** for ages 5–15, is a rustic vine-covered stone cottage in a tranquil corner of the National Garden. Of its 4,000 books, 60 are in English and French. It also has games and puzzles (some in English), a chess set, dominoes, crayons, and coloring books. Albums, including a large selection of classical music, can be played on the turntable. *Tel. 01/323–6503. Open Tues.–Sat. 9–2:30.*

Museums   The **Athens Children's Museum** (tel. 01/729–0202) was in the planning stages at press time, but if you phone the office, Christiana Zotou can tell you how to get the pamphlet in English for children on the National Archaeological Museum (other pamphlets are being written).

Greek Folk Art Museum (tel. 01/321–3018). Children can tour the museum and then attend a workshop, where they learn to make traditional handicrafts. Special arrangements can be made for English- speaking groups.

Planetarium   The programs in the 250-seat auditorium at the **planetarium** are in Greek, but the stargazing projections in the dome are universally fascinating. *Syngrou 387, Paleo Phaleron, tel. 01/941–1181. Admission free. Shows hourly 10:30–4:30.*

Playgrounds   Playgrounds are at: the **national garden,** off Vasilissis Olgas Street near the bus station; in **Plaka** at Stratonos and Vironos; in **Kolonaki,** on Dinokratous and Irofilou, in a large, quiet pine forest; in **Ilisia,** behind Ayios Haralabos Church on Dragoumi Street; in **Alsos Syngrou,** a large wooded park not far from the Hilton and Holiday Inn Hotels; and in **Koukaki** at Koundourioti Square, a short walk northwest from the Athenaeum Inter-Continental and Ledra Marriott hotels.

Zoos The national garden's small zoo is fairly cramped and mainly has deer and smaller animals. Another small zoo in Nea Philadelphia is not worth the trip from the center of Athens.

Off the Beaten Track

The huge **First Cemetery,** off Marko Missourou behind the Panathenaic Stadium in Mets, is Athens's equivalent of Paris's Père-Lachaise, but it is whitewashed and cheerful rather than gloomy and Gothic. The graves are surrounded by well-tended gardens and decorated with small photographs of the departed, and doves coo perpetually from the stately cypress trees. The main entrance off Anapafseos Street leads to an open-air museum of mind-boggling funerary architecture. Stroll through here to see the Sleeping Maiden, a touching marble statue on the grave of Sophia Afendaki, while high up on a bluff stands the imposing temple of Heinrich Schliemann.

Shopping

One of the main hurdles is figuring out when shops in Athens are open. In 1990, the government changed shop hours to conform to those of other European countries, doing away with the traditional siesta period, in hopes of eliminating the pollution caused by the additional traffic. Hours fall–spring are Monday and Wednesday 9–4; Tuesday, Thursday, and Friday 10–8; and Saturday 9–3. In summer, because of the heat, shops are open Monday and Wednesday 9–4; Tuesday, Thursday, and Friday 9–1:30 and 5–8; and Saturday 9–3. Some shops, including dry cleaners and pharmacies (closed Sat.) and bakeries and hardware stores (closed evenings), follow their own drummer, so ask at your hotel before setting out. The souvenir shops in Plaka are usually open from early morning until the last tourist leaves. The unique Greek institution known as *periptera* (kiosks), set up by the government to provide employment for veterans, are a godsend; those in central squares are often open until very late, and occasionally around the clock. They sell newspapers, postcards, candy bars, cigarettes, batteries, pens, aspirin, playing cards, postage stamps, writing paper, toiletries, and an endless variety of other little items. Most of them have public phones, some metered for long-distance calls.

Fashion

Greece is known for well-made shoes, and many tourists bring back a pair of sandals from the legendary poet/sandal maker **Stavros Melissinos,** a gentle soul who runs a shop at Pandrossou 89, just before Monastiraki Square. He also makes handsome boots; for a larger selection, go to his brother-in-law's shop, **Tony's Sandals** (Adrianou 52), which specializes in made-to-order Western boots. A number of other shoe stores in this area offer real bargains. For more upmarket (and much more expensive) models, go to the shops on Kolonaki Square.

The best place to shop for furs is near Syntagma on Mitropoleos and Fillelinon streets. Among the smart ready-to-wear shops (starting at the lower range of prices) are **Tsantilis** (Ermou 23) and **Agenda** (Ermou 47). Then comes **Gucci** (Tsakalof in Kolonaki), especially for men's clothing. Some top Greek designers' menswear boutiques are **Aslanis** (Anagnastopoulou

24), **Loukia** (Kanari 24), and **Billy Bo** (Solonos 1), all in Kolonaki. **Simbolo** (Amerikis 18) has a great selection of trendy men's sportswear, and **Ascot** (Nikis 29) has well-made jackets and slacks.

Gifts

Athens has great gifts, particularly handmade crafts, traditional items old and new, and copies of these. Perennial favorites for presents are natural sponges, usually sold on the National Bank corner in Syntagma and in souvenir shops in this area and in Plaka. Look for those that are unbleached; the lovely lighter ones tend to fall apart quickly. Greek fishermen's caps, always a good present, have now surfaced at high prices across the United States. The natural wool undershirts also worn by fishermen are similarly sold—for four times the Athens price—in New York and Chicago. The main shopping districts are in the areas bounded by Syntagma, Monastiraki and Plaka, and Omonia and Kolonaki (Philikis Etairias) squares.

Handicrafts and Antiques

Some fine examples of folk crafts can be found at the **Hellenic Folk-Art Galleries** (Vasillis Sophias 135 in Ambelokipi, Ipatias 6 and Apollonas in Plaka, and 352 Syngrou in Kalithea). Stunning handwoven carpets, flat-weave kilims, and tapestries from original designs are on display, as well as hand embroidered tablecloths and wall decorations. Napkins and place mats, ceramics, and pillow cases make handsome presents, and the shaggy woolen *flokati* rugs can be found here too. Shops near Syntagma, like **Karamichos Flokati** (Voulis and Apollonos) and **Kokkinos** (Mitropoleos 3), have larger selections and will insure your purchases and mail them to your home. Along Skilitsi east of Platia Ipodamias in Piraeus are about half a dozen antiques shops. At one of them, **Ta Makra Teixoi** (Pilis 2), the back wall incorporates a section of the 5th-century Long Walls. Another outlet for quality handicrafts is the **Center of Hellenic Tradition** (upstairs at Mitropoleos 59, and at Pandrossou 36), where after shopping you can take a break in the wonderful café, in clear view of the Parthenon. An interesting shop is **Amorgos,** at Kodrou 3, which sells an eclectic mixture of crafts, from wood carvings to handmade lace.

A stroll through the Sunday-morning **flea market** may turn up weavings and parts of regional folk costumes. The rich cranberry and black designs from Metsovo are among the wares spread on the corner of Pandrossou and Kirikiou streets. Antiques and older wares are in vogue now, so these items have soared in price. Good buys in copper and brass can be found in **Sirapian Dikran**'s shop (Ifestou 13). Serious antiques collectors should head to **Martinos** (Pandrossou 50). **George Goutis** shops (Pandrossou 40 and 47) have a wide selection of jewelry, costumes, and Karaghiozi shadow puppets. **Konstantoglou**'s tiny shop (Athinas 17)—he also runs **Mati** (*see below*)—brims over with knitted socks, worry beads, *roka* (spindles in the shapes of figures), and Byzantine artifacts.

Handknit fisherman sweaters are good buys. Woolen and cotton sweaters with the Mykonos label are quite popular and can be found in many shops in Plaka. Colorful weavings can be found at the **Mykonos Tradition Shop** (G. Souri St. 3). The items here are no longer made and sold in Mykonos. The shop also has delicately carved roka, jewelry, and candlestick holders from Skyros.

The gaily colored Skyrian ceramics, including some delightful fish plates, are sold at a number of outlets: A good selection can be found at **Marina Shop** (Adrianou 87 in Plaka) and at **Ftoulis** (Nymphaiou 30 in Ano Ilisia). During the winter, potter **Yannis Komboyannis** sells items from his workshop (Dichiarhou 60–62, Pangrati, tel. 01/752–1539).

Jewelry

Prices are much lower for gold and silver than in many Western countries, and jewelry is of high quality. Little blue-and-white pendants and larger ceramic objects are designed as amulets to ward off the evil eye (*mati*). **Zodiaques Hellas,** the Pan-European Stones Center (Ermou 131, Monastiraki and Notara 79, Piraeus), is a tiny shop with a wide selection of these amulets and semiprecious stones. **Mati** (Voukourestiou 20) has finely designed amulets and an unusual collection of monastery lamps and candlesticks. The pedestrian mall of Voukourestiou has a number of the leading jewelry shops: **PentheRoudakiS** (Voukourestiou 19; Tsakalof 5); **Xanthopoulos** (No. 4); **J. Vourakis & Fils** (No. 8), who represent Piaget; and **Michalis** (No. 2). **Petra Nova** (No. 19) is noted for semiprecious stones set in pins, earrings, and pendants.

The world-famous **Lalaounis** (Panepistimiou 6) has branches in the Grande Bretagne and the Athens Hilton. His main competitor, **Zolotas** (Panepistimiou 10) is noted for superb museum copies. Other finely rendered copies of classical jewelry can be found at the shops of the **Benaki Museum** and **Goulandris Cycladic Museum** (*see* Tour 5 in Exploring Athens, *above*). The Benaki also has excellent copies of Greek icons at fair prices.

An inexpensive but unusual gift is a string of *koboloi*, or worry beads, in plastic, wood, or stone. You can pick them up very cheaply in Monastiraki or look in antiques shops for more expensive versions, with amber or black onyx beads. Coin and stamp collectors will want to check out the **Pylarinos** shops (Sofocleos 7–9, near Omonia and Stadiou 6). At Stadiou 17 is **Gold Coin Jewelry**, where you'll find decorative copies of ancient Greek coins.

Sports and Outdoor Activities

Participant Sports

Fitness Centers Health clubs abound these days, and you'll have little problem finding one near your hotel. The Athens Hilton, Inter-Continental, and Caravel hotels have excellent facilities with saunas and pools that can be used by the general public.

Golf **Glyfada Golf Course and Club** (Glyfada, tel. 01/894–6820 or 01/894–6834) has 18 holes and is open to the public.

Horseback Riding **Athens Riding Club** (Gerakas, Ayia Paraskevi, tel. 01/661–1088), **Attikos Riding Club** (Ekali, tel. 01/813–5576), **Hellenic**

Riding Club (Paradissou 18, Maroussi, tel. 01/681–2506 or 01/
682–6128), **Tatoi Riding Club** (Varybobi, tel. 01/801–4513 or 01/
808–3008), and **Varybobi Riding Club** (Varybobi, tel. 01/801–
9912).

Sailing and The **Greek Windsurfing Federation** (tel. 01/413–7351), **Pan-Hel-**
Windsurfing **lenic Open Sea Sailing Federation** (Microlimano, tel. 01/412–
3352 or 01/412–3357), and **Piraeus Sailing Federation**
(Microlimano, tel. 01/412–3352 or 01/417–7636) can give information and recommendations about where to wind-surf and
rent sailboats.

Swimming and The beaches at Paleo Phaleron and Piraeus have signs to
Diving warn you of the high levels of pollution. Believe them. **National**
Tourist Organization (GNTO) beaches have snack bars and
beach umbrellas, chairs, dressing rooms, and sports equipment for rent, plus windsurfing and waterskiing lessons. The
main ones close to Athens are **Alimos**, tel. 01/982–7064; **Porto**
Rafti, tel. 0299/72572; **Voula**, 1st beach tel. 01/895–1646, 2nd
beach tel. 01/895–9569); **Vouliagmeni**, tel. 01/896–0906; and
Varkiza, tel. 01/897–2102.

Scuba diving is heavily restricted, to protect underwater artifacts. A travel agent can steer you to a supervised diving trip.

Vouliagmeni Lake, whose spring-fed waters are reputed to
have curative powers, is popular with older Greeks. A number
of nice tavernas line the sandy shoreline. **Astir Beach,** in
Vouliagmeni, is very upscale, with full facilities, including
showers. You can take bus No. 117 from Zappion to both.

Tennis Call the **Tennis Federation** (Yassilis Olgas 2, tel. 01/324–8140,
01/921–5630, or 01/923–2872) for information on tennis courts.

Spectator Sport

Horse Racing Racing is held at the **Syngrou–Delta Phaleron** racetrack in
Tsitsifies Monday, Wednesday, and Friday 4–8:30.

Dining

Dining out in Greece is a leisurely, gregarious experience, a
celebration of life and good company. Meals are still a bargain
compared to other European countries, especially if you stick
to Greek cuisine and avoid the most touristy areas. If you're not
watching your budget, the foreign restaurants now offer dishes
of a world-class standard, with prices that you would expect in
any European capital.

Highly recommended restaurants are indicated by a star ★.

Category	Cost*
Very Expensive	over 8,000 dr.
Expensive	5,000 dr.–8,000 dr.
Moderate	3,000 dr.–5,000 dr.
Inexpensive	under 3,000 dr.

per person, excluding drinks, service, and sales tax

Although Athens is informal and few of the restaurants listed here requires jacket or tie, you'll feel more comfortable wearing one in the more expensive places (as noted). Conservative casual dress (not halter tops or shorts) is acceptable in most establishments. In the last two weeks of August, when the city empties out and most residents head for the seaside, more than 75% of the restaurants and tavernas catering to Greeks close, though hotel restaurants, seafood restaurants in Microlimano, and tavernas in Plaka usually remain open.

Eating places discussed below fall into several categories. Truly authentic **tavernas** have wicker chairs with a concave shape that inevitably pinches your bottom, checkered tablecloths covered with butcher paper, a wobbly table that needs a coin under one leg, and wine from the barrel served in little metal carafes. If a place looks inviting and is filled with Greeks, give it a try.

Greek restaurants offer a more sophisticated selection than tavernas and often some international dishes, too. *Ouzeries,* sometimes called *mezzodopoleon* (places that sell *mezze,* or appetizers), are friendly little publike establishments that serve tidbits for you to nibble on while sipping ouzo. A few years ago the category of **haute cuisine** would not have existed, but Athens now has restaurants of international standard, in both preparation and presentation. A number of **foreign restaurants** now thrive in this increasingly cosmopolitan capital that are not just inferior versions of the original ethnic cuisine. See restaurants listed under **Seafood** and **Fast Food** for something different from what you get at home, although if you *must* placate the children there are local McDonald's, Wendy's, and Pizza Huts.

Fast Food

The *souvlaki* joints in Monastiraki (*see* Tour 4 in Exploring Athens, *above*) provide a satisfying and cheap snack. **Ioannina Chicken,** a little hole-in-the-wall at 3 Kolonaki Square, serves succulent and tender roast chicken—a whole bird or half. You can eat it at the little tables outside or take it out for a picnic in the National Gardens a short distance away. Night owls looking for a snack will probably find something to their liking at **Everest Fast Food** (Tsakalof and Irakleitou, Kolonaki), where a wide menu is offered, including various *pittas* (pies) with meat, spinach, and cheese fillings; hamburgers; housemade ice cream; fresh strawberries with whipped cream; and pastries. It stays open until about 5 AM, and patrons spill out onto the pedestrian street leading to Kolonaki Square, which late in the evening is a huge social center for Athenian youth.

The **Neon** (Plateia Omonia 8), a newly remodeled cafeteria in a stunning 1920s building, is open until at least 2 AM, and a new Neon has opened in Pasalimani in Piraeus. The vast selection ranges from salad bar fare, pasta, and meat dishes to sandwiches, ice cream, and other desserts, and prices are moderate. The nonsmoking section may be unique in Athens restaurants.

For a trendy people-watching place open in the wee morning hours, try **Tea in the Sahara** (Laodikeias 18, Ilisia, near Holiday Inn). It serves cocktails, soft drinks, juice, coffee, and of course tea and cold plates until 6 AM. A DJ is on duty to play taped music, and there are live appearances by top Athenian and foreign performers and occasional "ethno" happenings.

Foreign

Very Expensive **Kona Kai.** A setting of tropical luxury and 54 Polynesian dishes make one feel pampered. The Aiga menu is an easy way to sample a cross-section of sumptuous fare, or try something from the Japanese *tepanyaki* menu, prepared in front of you. Hawaiian wonton puffs are filled with curried shrimp, and the *matsamon* beef has a strong coconut accent. *Ledra Marriott Hotel, Syngrou Ave. 115, tel. 01/934–7711. Reservations required. Jacket advised. AE, DC, MC, V. Closed Sun. and July–Aug.*

Expensive **Michiko.** This reliable favorite, set in a gracious Plaka mansion with a garden shaded by a giant fig tree, has been around for more than 20 years, serving decorative, meticulously prepared Japanese dishes. An authentic sushi and sashimi bar has its own chef. Special menus offer a sampling of some of the best dishes. *Kidathineon 27, Plaka, tel. 01/322–0980. Reservations advised on weekends. AE, DC, V. Closed Sat. lunch and Sun.*

Pane e Vino. A small trattoria-type eatery in a cheerful semibasement is currently in vogue with Kolonaki trendsetters. Rigatoni al Gattopardo has a rich sauce of tomato, mozzarella, olive oil, and basil, and the tangy Filetto Aphrodisiaco is liberally flavored with ginger and soy sauce. *Spefsipou 8, Kolonaki, tel. 01/722–5084. Reservations advised. AE, DC. Closed Sun. and July–Aug.*

Prunier. A cozy French bistro decorated with copper utensils, antiques, and tasteful art nouveau accents is imbued with a romantic glow. The cuisine ranges from solid French standards to such original recipes as Quail Salmi and Delice des Amoureaux (sautéed seafood in a vol-au-vent, laced with cognac). *Ipsilantou 63, Kolonaki, tel. 01/722–7379. Reservations required. AE, D, V. Closed Sun. and July–Aug.*

White Elephant. The Polynesian food here (in the Andromeda Hotel) is competition for Kona Kai. The small ground-floor dining room will be used as a bar with cold plates when the restaurant moves to larger quarters on the first floor. Fresh lobster is served—a rarity in Athens—as well as piquant Thai shrimp. Specialties include spicy Mandarin beef and aromatic, crispy duck with vegetable pancakes. *Andromeda Hotel, 22 Timoleontos Vassou St., next to American Embassy, tel. 01/ 643–7302. Reservations advised. Jacket advised. AE, DC, MC, V.*

Moderate **Bistro Seven Steps.** Run by an American couple, this delightful
★ little hideaway close to bustling Exarchia has a well-prepared eclectic cuisine: The potato-leek soup is velvety and the chili zesty but not lethal. Crunchy Chinese stir-fried chicken and vegetarian pizza are other good choices. The spicy carrot cake is divine, and the cheesecake makes even jaded diners swoon. *Arachovis 49, Exarchia, tel. 01/350–0874. Reservations required on weekends. No credit cards. No Sun. dinner. Open for occasional Sun. brunches.*

Bohemia. This unusual restaurant has a huge menu of authentic Czechoslovak fare. In cool weather it's in an old house with nostalgic murals of Czech scenes, and in the summer it moves to a huge canopied area in a pleasantly breezy square covered with greenery. Appetizers include tasty *trello* (which means "crazy"), baked cheese covered with a tangy tartar sauce; and *rolakia*, Emmentaler-type cheese wrapped around ham and asparagus. The salad Bohemia, a murky mixture of veal tongue

Athens Dining and Lodging

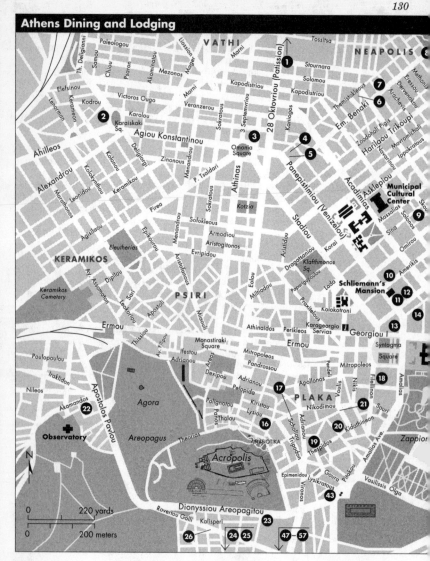

Dining

Apaggio, **50**
Apotsos, **11**
Athinaikon, **4**
Bajazzo, **31**
Balcony Tou
Immitou, **58**
Bistro Seven Steps, **7**
Black Goat, **54**
Bohemia, **35**
Boshetto, **39**
Courser, **51**
Delicious, **14**
Dourabeis, **53**
Eden, **17**

Everest Fast Food, **28**
Famagusta, **37**
Fourtouna, **34**
Gerofinikas, **15**
Ideal, **5**
Ioannina Chicken, **27**
Kafenio, **33**
Kona Kai, **48**
Manessis, **46**
Michiko, **20**
Neon, **3**
Pandelis, **49**
Pane e Vino, **30**
Perix, **29**

Premier, **56**
Prunier, **38**
Psara, **16**
Salamandra, **9**
Socrates Prison, **23**
Symposio, **26**
Syntagma
Syntrivani, **18**
Tea in the Sahara, **41**
Themistocles, **45**
Vasilenas, **52**
White Elephant, **37**
Xynou, **19**

Lodging

Acropolis House, **21**
Andromeda Athens
Hotel, **36**
Aphrodite Astir
Palace, **55**
Art Gallery Pension, **25**
Athenaeum
InterContinental, **56**
Athenian Inn, **32**
Athens Chandris, **57**
Athens Gate, **43**
Athens Hilton, **40**
Caravel, **44**

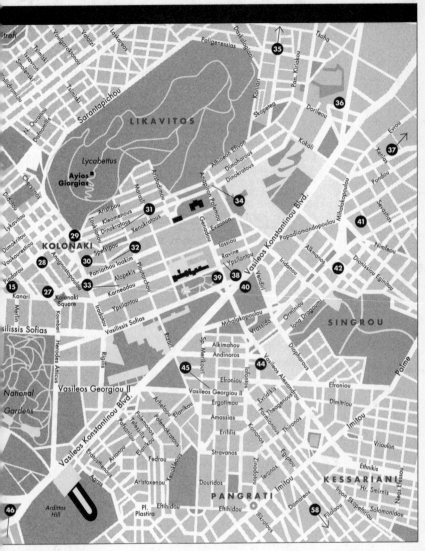

Divani Palace
Acropolis, **24**
Erechtheon, **22**
Exarchia, **6**
Grande Bretagne, **13**
Holiday Inn, **42**
Ledra Marriott, **47**
Lycabette, **12**
Orion and Dryades, **8**
Park, **1**
Stanley, **2**
XEN, **10**

and mushrooms in a sauce, is distinctive. Bohemia stocks Pilsner Urquell and Budvar, the original Budweiser. *Dimou Tseliou 5, Ambelokopi, tel. 01/642–6341. Reservations required on weekends. No credit cards. Closed late Aug., Sun. in summer, and Wed. in winter.*

Courser. Sophisticated decor with Oriental accents and a dignified garden set the tone for distinctive Chinese food. The wok dishes are particularly pleasing, and the "Chicken Hot Pot" abundant. The shrimp *pane* (with sesame) and Szechuan pork are memorable. At the reasonably priced Sunday brunch you can sample a variety of dishes. *Platia Esperidon 2, Glyfada, tel. 01/894–4905. Reservations advised on weekends. AE, V.*

Delicious. An intimate feeling engendered in this small room with burgundy walls and six tables is manifested in the homey Hamburg fare. Homemade black bread, a variety of sausages with sauerkraut, and sweet-and-sour marinated fish are only some of the highlights of an ample selection. *Zalakosta 6, Kolonaki, tel. 01/363–8455. No reservations. No credit cards. Closed Sun.*

★ **Famagusta.** The Mediterranean and Middle East have both influenced Cypriot cuisine, resulting in the tasty assortment of little tidbits known as *mezze*. Famagusta is romantic, the walls and candlelit tables decorated with Cypriot handicrafts: baskets, colorful weavings, and ceramics. Two guitarists discreetly sing Greek and Cypriot favorites, and later the dance floor is packed. A special plate with small portions of 14 mezze is a convenient way to sample a number of different dishes. Tabbouleh salad with cracked wheat, and *lounza*, a thick smoked pork fillet spiced with coriander, are two recommended dishes. *Zagoras 8 (end of Michalachopoulou), Ambelokopi, tel. 01/ 778–5259. Reservations required on weekends. No credit cards. Closed Mon. and July–Aug.*

Inexpensive **Eden.** This slightly cluttered, comfortable old neoclassical mansion with stained-glass wall decorations and overhead fans is the closest you'll come to dining in a Plaka family dwelling. The strictly vegetarian menu features vegetable burgers, lasagna with soya and cheese, and spring pie. An upstairs terrace catches breezes in summer, and in winter, there are three fireplaces to sit by. *Flessa 3, Plaka, tel. 01/324–8858. Reservations not necessary. No credit cards.*

Greek

Very Expensive **Premier.** This cheerful piano bar, with stylish wicker furniture and a stunning view, has created quite a stir with Chef Nikos's Friday night feast; he has developed extraordinary dishes in his Hellenized version of nouvelle cuisine: fillets of chicken and langoustine laced with brandy and served with pistachio cream sauce, and Samos pork fillets with walnuts and raisins. *Hotel Inter-Continental, Syngrou Ave. 89–93, tel. 01/902–3666. Reservations advised on weekends. Dress: casual. AE, DC, MC, V.*

Expensive **Gerofinikas.** Serving the epitome of the *politiki* cuisine (mean-
★ ing Greek cooking as evolved in Constantinople), this refined establishment takes its name (Palm Tree) from several that grow in the center of the dining room, once a barracks. It's perfect for a civilized business lunch or festive dinner, with specialties like Hunkar Beyendi (veal in eggplant puree), delectable lobster thermidor, and heavenly *ekmek kataifi*, a

dessert of shredded wheat soaked in honey and orange. *Pindarou 10, Kolonaki, tel. 01/362–2719. Reservations advised. AE, DC, MC, V.*

Moderate **Apaggio.** This unique establishment specializes in fastidiously prepared regional dishes you'll rarely find in any other restaurant. Standouts include Hunter's Plate, a pork cutlet in a vegetable-and-wine sauce with green olives, and spleen sausage with pine nuts and orange zest. *Megistis 8, Kalamaki, tel. 01/983–9093. Reservations advised. No credit cards. Closed Mon.*

Ideal. The original Ideal burned down after almost 70 years, and the new upmarket art deco interior is a distinct contrast to the former dark, rustic look. The best bets on the eclectic menu are such Greek and Turkish dishes as the piquant *mititei*, a mincemeat kebab; and baby lamb roasted with tomato and cheese. The service is fastidious, and almost everyone speaks English. *Panepistimiou 46, Omonia, tel. 01/361–4604. Reservations advised for groups and on weekends. AE, DC, MC, V. Closed Sun.*

Pandelis. The grandfather of owner-chef Pandelis owned the legendary Pandelis in Istanbul, and this one is a real find. The tables are set among greenery on a quiet side street, and the waiters are courteous and helpful. Among the entrées are an eggplant dish with garlic and tomato named *Imam Bayildi* ("the cleric fainted"—presumably because the dish was so delicious), and the pièce de résistance: *yaourtlu kebab*, skewered lamb and beef with a piquant yogurt sauce. Try *kavuk gogsu*, an unusual chicken-based dessert pudding. *Naidon 96, Paleo Phaleron, tel. 01/982–5512. Reservations not necessary. No credit cards. No lunch Mon.–Sat., no Sun. dinner.*

Haute Cuisine

Very Expensive **Bajazzo.** If you have only one big splurge in Athens, have it
★ here, one of the finest restaurants anywhere. The main dining room is a joyful explosion of scents and colors, and the menu constantly changes as Chef Klaus Feuerbach experiments with wildly imaginative creations. Samples are brought to your table in wicker baskets for your inspection: Appetizers include a heavenly seafood bisque; and strawberry salad with sweet corn, shrimp, and Emmentaler cheese. The veal fillet stuffed with yam, lobster, and green apple is an inspired combination; and the langoustine dumplings in peach champagne sauce are also delectable. Leave room for banana cake filled with cinnamon chocolate cream or the mango slices marinated in white wine and rum. *Ploutarchou 35 and Dinokratous, Kolonaki, tel. 01/729–1420. Reservations required for groups and on weekends. AE, DC, V. Closed Sun.*

Boshetto. Set in a romantic, largely glass pavilion in verdant Evangelismou Park, Boshetto serves Italian cuisine at its most refined. Standard dishes are given a new twist, such as John Dory with almond sauce and sautéed leeks and meat, and guinea hen with bacon and pomegranate sauce. Lavender ice cream or the *crema cotta* provides a sensual finish to the meal. Ask for the special lunch menu. *Alsos Evangelismou, opposite Hilton Hotel, tel. 01/721–0893. Reservations required for dinner. Jacket advised. AE, V. Closed Sun.*

Symposio. This restored 1920s house has a spacious garden, and the cheerful front bar is a popular late-night gathering place for the Athens intelligentsia. Symposio blends the familiar with the new in unexpected ways. The al dente *gnocchi* with Gorgonzola and smoked salmon, the baked Camembert with blueberry sauce, and the raspberry cheesecake are recommended. Iced strawberry schnapps makes a nice digestif. *Erechthiou 46, Makriyanni, tel. 01/922–5321. Reservations required. Dress: stylish. AE, MC, V. Closed Sun.*

Ouzeries

Moderate **Apotsos.** In this folksy old ouzerie the bentwood chairs, old posters, and early calendars will take you back to the 1930s. It's full of talkative journalists and politicians, the atmosphere is lively and crowded, and the food is almost secondary. *Saganaki* (fried cheese) and *gigantes* (lima beans in tomato sauce) are typical dishes. Get there early; Apotsos closes at 5. *Panepistimiou 10, in arcade, tel. 01/363–7046. No credit cards. Closed Sun.*

★ **Athinaikon.** This renowned establishment moved here after near 60 years near the law courts, and it is still a favorite of attorneys and local office workers. The decor is quintessential nononsense ouzerie, with rectangular marble tables, dark wood accents, framed memorabilia on the walls, and a checked floor. Crisp shrimp croquettes and tender fried calamari are recommended. *Themistocleos 2, Omonia, tel. 01/363–8485. No reservations. No credit cards. Closed Sun.*

Kafenio. This ouzerie is slightly upscale from the ordinary, with cloth napkins and a handsome dark wood interior. The menu is enormous, with many unusual concoctions; the tender marinated octopus and the cheese croquettes are good choices. *Loukianou 26, Kolonaki, tel. 01/722–9056. No reservations. No credit cards. Closed Sun.*

Perix. This is a good place to go after taking the funicular ride up Lycabettus. Tables are set under a canopy in Dexameni Square or in a nautical-style dining area across the street. Among the appetizers, fava salad Santorini style (mashed chickpeas with onions) and an exquisite *bourekakia melitzanes* (a wonderful eggplant and cheese pie) are outstanding. *Glykonos 14, Dexameni Sq., Kolonaki, tel. 01/723–6917. Reservations required for groups. No credit cards.*

Salamandra. In this bilevel house near Athens University, the seating is at wooden tables in cozy little nooks, and in winter the fireplace is lit. Salamandra has a reputation for well-prepared mezze, like the creamy Roquefort salad and the cheese croquettes. *Mantzarou 3, Kolonaki, tel. 01/361–7927. Reservations not necessary. No credit cards. Closed Sun. and July–Aug.*

Seafood

Expensive **Fourtouna.** In this restored 1930s house the handsome dining rooms on two levels are usually crammed with customers. A wood boat in the front hall serves as a buffet area, displaying the main dishes. Fourtouna really excels in fresh seafood. The splendid *karavides*, or crayfish, are steamed, tender-sweet morsels served simply with a butter sauce and lemon. *Thallasina*, fluted clamlike shellfish, are a rare treat. The barreled white wine from an Attic village has a fine bouquet. *Anapiron Polemou 22, Kolonaki, tel. 01/722–1282. Reservations required for dinner. No credit cards. No Sun. dinner.*

**Moderate–
Expensive**
Black Goat. This restaurant (also called Kavos) is one of few with a Greek clientele in the Microlimano area. Sitting here watching the colorful fishing boats in the little harbor is the next best thing to hopping on a ferry boat and heading for an island. There is a wide selection of such fresh fish and seafood as *barbouni* (red mullet), *lithrini* (sea bream), and calamari. Since grade-A fish and lobster are expensive, it's a good idea to make your choice from the refrigerated compartments, then have it weighed, so you'll know the exact price in advance. Specialties here include a thick seafood crepe and *garides yiouvetsi*, a shrimp casserole with cheese and tomato sauce. *Akti Koumoundourou 64, Piraeus, tel. 01/422–0691. Reservations advised on weekends. AE, DC, MC, V.*

Dourabeis. Favored by shipowners and other cognoscenti, this 50-year-old landmark with a fine sea view has earned its solid reputation for fresh, well-prepared seafood and gracious service. Its own boats supply a plethora of different fish, which are all there for your inspection. Try the sweet, tender, sautéed langoustine chunks or the house salad, a robust assortment of greens, radishes, leeks, and hot peppers. *Athena Dilaveri 29, Piraeus, tel. 01/412–2092. Reservations advised on weekends. No credit cards.*

Inexpensive
★ **Vasilenas.** Longtime residents and frequent visitors rejoice in this precious vestige of the good old days, a family-run taverna that is probably still as good a bargain now as it was 60 years ago. The decor is minimal, with walls lined with alternating Del Monte tomato cans and bottles of Megara wine. In summer the operation moves to the upper terrace. Come here ravenously hungry with friends, so you can do justice to the set menu of 16 dishes, brought in a steady stream to your table. Zesty shrimp *yiouvetsi* and prawn croquettes are two standouts. *Etolikou 72, Ayia Sophia, Piraeus, tel. 01/461–2457. Reservations required for groups and on weekends. No credit cards. Closed Sun.*

Tavernas

Moderate
Balcony Tou Immitou. This large, unpretentious place has a huge balcony on a hill, with panoramic views. It's known to few tourists, although the waiters speak some English. The extensive menu includes all the standards, plus such game dishes as rabbit stew, and *gardoumba* (innards stuffed in a skin), which tastes much better than it looks. *Pavlou Mela 11, Karea (take bus No. 203 from Acadimias), tel. 01/764–0240. Reservations required for groups. No credit cards.*

Manessis. One of the best of the old-time places, Manessis is set in a homey garden in the summer and several rooms of a little house with straw matting on the walls in the winter. A waiter brings you a long wooden tray with appetizers to choose from, including smoked herring, sausage (which he'll fry right at the table), and black-eyed peas. Specialties include Zakinthos-style veal, and chicken souvlaki. *Marko Mousourou 3, Mets, tel. 01/922–7684. Reservations required for groups. No credit cards. No lunch. Closed Sun.*

★ **Socrates Prison.** At this taverna, near the Herod Atticus Theater, you will often hobnob with the actors. Tables are set right at streetside in summer, but you can ask to be inside the little patio if you want to converse more quietly. In cooler months, the action moves inside, where there's a cozy room upstairs with a fireplace. Amiable owner Socrates makes many unusual dishes, including his own special salad with dill, eggs, and cheese; spicy stuffed pita bread; and pork rolls with carrots and celery in lemon sauce. *Mitseon 20, Makriyanni, tel. 01/922–3434. Reservations advised. No credit cards. Closed Sun.*

Xynou. At this 50-year-old Plaka taverna tables are set outside in summer, and three guitarists croon mellow Greek sing-alongs, much to the delight of the regulars, who come from all walks of life. Tender liver bits in egg-lemon sauce, and the dolmades are both well prepared, and the barreled retsina is invigorating. *Angelou Geronta 4, Plaka, tel. 01/322–1065. Reservations required. No credit cards. Closed Sat., Sun., and part of July.*

Inexpensive
★
Psara. This genuine neighborhood institution is especially popular for Sunday lunch. The tables are on a cobbled footpath, and the lively goings-on are as much a draw as the satisfying food. The juicy *ksifias* (swordfish) kebab and *soupies* (cuttlefish) in sauce are notable, and are best accompanied by the tangy retsina. *Erechtheos 16, Plaka, tel. 01/325–0285. No reservations. No credit cards. Closed winter.*

Syntagma Syntrivani. Ignore the kitschy sign and go down the hallway to the most reliable taverna in the area and the best bargain as well. You sit in a small dining room or in a flourishing garden under an awning with vines. The veal Perivolari (baked veal with vegetables) and a mixed grill, with liver, beefsteak, and ham, are two of the more unusual dishes. *Filellinon 5, Syntagma, tel. 01/322–5568. Reservations required for groups. AE, V. Closed Christmas.*

Themistocles. The taverna is in a little whitewashed house with a tile roof and a pleasant garden behind, where signs caution patrons to speak quietly after 11 PM. This venerable neighborhood landmark has a limited menu, but its food is always dependable, service is friendly, and it is open on Sunday, when most others are closed. *Bekri mezze* (drunkard's tidbits), marinated pork chunks with sauce; and *keftedakia* (fried meatballs) are two favorites. *Vassileos Georgiou 31, Pangrati, tel. 01/721–9553. Reservations not necessary. No credit cards.*

Lodging

Athens has true luxury hotels and many in the budget range, but a shortage of middle-rank family-style hotels. Staying in a seaside suburb or in Piraeus is a good way to beat the heat and smog of the city center in summer, although the traveling time and expense are a deterrent.

Some of the older hotels in Plaka and near Omonia are comfortable and clean, exuding the charm of age. But along with charm may come leaking plumbing and sagging mattresses—take a good look at the room. The thick stone walls of neoclassical buildings keep them cool in the summer, but few of the budget hotels have central heating, and it can be devilishly cold in the winter. You can expect to find air-conditioning in all hotels in the Very-Expensive and Expensive categories; it is unusual in moderate and inexpensive hotels.

Highly recommended lodgings are indicated by a star ★.

Category	Cost*
Very Expensive	over 25,000 dr.
Expensive	15,000 dr.–25,000 dr.
Moderate	8,000 dr.–15,000 dr.
Inexpensive	under 8,000 dr.

*All prices are for a double room, including tax, VAT, and service charges; breakfast is included unless noted otherwise.

Athens

Very Expensive   **Andromeda Athens Hotel.** Athens's newest luxury hotel caters to business travelers with a mixture of deluxe rooms, studios, suites, and penthouses. The spacious rooms have a salmon color scheme with quilted headboards, wall-to-wall carpeting, minibars, TV, and fax machines. The hotel is on a quiet street, and the bedrooms have double glazing. The White Elephant Polynesian restaurant is excellent. *Timoleondos Vassou St. 22, Mavilli Sq., 11521, tel. 01/643–0702, fax 01/646–6361. 30 rooms with bath. Facilities: restaurant, 2 banquet halls, health club, Jacuzzi, convention space, parking. AE, DC, MC, V.*

★ **Aphrodite Astir Palace.** There are actually three hotels at this exclusive seaside resort on a pine-covered peninsula, with a helicopter pad. Staying here in summer, among tycoons and celebrities at play, carries a certain cachet. The **Nafsika,** built into the hillside, has the loveliest location; the **Aphrodite,** with balconies on the sea, is the newest; and **Arion,** the oldest, is the most exclusive. The food in the restaurants is exquisite, and the rooms are large (especially in Arion) and tastefully furnished. *Vouliagmeni, 16671, tel. 01/896–0211, 01/896–0212, or 01/324–3961; fax 01/896–2579. Aphrodite Astir: 165 rooms with bath. Facilities: restaurant, bar, 2 lounges, private beach, outdoor pool. Nafsika: 165 rooms with bath. Facilities: restaurant, bar, indoor pool. Arion: 165 rooms with bath, 77 bungalows. Facilities: restaurant, bar, indoor pool. AE, DC, MC, V.*

Athenaeum Inter-Continental. One of Athens's plushest hotels, it has a marble atrium lobby with a central fountain, mirrored planters, and a private art collection. The rooms are very spacious, with separate marble-floor sitting rooms, and thick carpeting. The fourth, sixth, seventh, and ninth floors have been renovated, with brighter colors, cheerful quilted bedspreads, and carpeting throughout. The suites have pantries and dining nooks. The Rotisserie and Kubla Khan restaurants are reputed to be two of Athens's best. *89–93 Syngrou Ave., 11745, tel. 01/902–3666, fax 01/921–7653. 525 rooms with bath, 44 suites. Facilities: 4 restaurants, 2 bars, health club, outdoor pool, meeting rooms. AE, DC, MC, V.*

Athens Hilton. Several 200-year-old olive trees add an earthy touch to the glamorous entrance with its multilevel lobby of variegated marble. Built in 1963, this is still one of the top hotels in the city, giving an impression of calm confidence amid the comings and goings of many conventions, banquets, and meetings. The poolside restaurant is a favorite of Athenians, who come to swim and lunch; others choose the Byzantine Café for a light meal or the buffet. Ta Nissia Restaurant serves taverna fare, and often has "ethnic" weeks. The spacious rooms have a subdued color scheme, carpeting, and double doors that buffer the street noise. The huge balconies face either the Acropolis or Hymettos. *Vassilisis Sophias 46, 10676, tel. 01/ 722-0201 through 01/722-0209, fax 01/721-3110. 450 rooms with bath and shower, 3 suites with Jacuzzi. Facilities: 3 restaurants, 3 bars, outdoor pool, sauna, massage, convention space, secretarial and translation services. AE, DC, MC, V.*

Caravel. There's an enormous lobby with bronze and marble copies of classical statues, mosaics and Santorini frescoes. The rooms are ample, with small couches and minibars, and a fairly busy decor. The quiet rooms are the interior ones. The large heated pool and well-equipped health studio and sauna on the top floor have a view of the Acropolis. The Amalias Discotheque has a good selection of music played at a reasonable level. *Vassileos Alexander 2, 11610, tel. 01/729-0721 through 01/ 729-0729, fax 01/723-6683. 469 rooms with bath. Facilities: 3 restaurants, coffee shop, 3 bars, discothèque, health club, heated pool, conference space. AE, DC, MC, V.*

Divani Palace Acropolis. This recently renovated and upgraded hotel is ideally located. A new five-story wing has its own spacious lounge area leading to the turquoise tile pool. The newer rooms are very large and have marble floors, flocked wallpaper, dressing tables, and balconies, some with a view of the Acropolis. In the older wing, the Divani Roofgarden Restaurant has a panoramic view. *Parthenonou 19–23, Makriyanni, 11742, tel. 01/922–9650 through 01/922–9659, fax 01/921–4993. 206 rooms with bath. Facilities: reataurant, taverna, bar, pool, convention space. AE, DC, MC, V.*

★ **Grande Bretagne.** The GB, as it is called, is a truly grand landmark, the only deluxe older hotel in Athens. Built in 1842, its guest list over the years has matched its colorful history. The huge lobby's marble walls and floors are accented by antiques, plush sofas, Oriental rugs, tapestries, and ornate chandeliers. There's a bar behind the lobby furnished in dark wood that exudes the quietly elegant ambience of an English drawing room. At the Victorian GB Corner (complete with piano) you can get a full dinner or a gooey ice-cream sundae, although there have been recent complaints of overcharging and poor service. The most coveted rooms have huge balconies facing Syntagma, furnished with white wrought iron tables and chairs . The elegant lounge areas on each floor have velvet couches and antique furniture, with etchings on the walls. *Vassileos Georgiou A 1, Syntagma Sq., 10563, tel. 01/323–0251 through 01/323–0259 or 01/325–0701 through 01/325–0709, fax 01/322–8034. 355 rooms with bath and shower. Facilities: 2 restaurants, 2 bars, secretarial and translation services, convention space. AE, DC, MC, V.*

Ledra Marriott. The Ledra has earned a reputation as one of the most efficient and attractive hotels in this chain. The piano bar in the lobby has a spectacular 1,000-crystal chandelier; Kona Kai, the Polynesian restaurant, is excellent; and the Zephyros Café has a bountiful Sunday brunch. The rooftop pools, open only to guests, have a view of the Acropolis that is breathtaking at sunset. The rooms, newly renovated in 1990, have a lively color scheme, vast closet space, and armchairs and sofas. Some of them have views of the Acropolis. *Syngrou 115, Kalithea, 17675, tel. 01/934–7711 through 01/934–7719, fax 01/935–9153. 258 rooms with bath. Facilities: 4 restaurants, buffet, coffee shop, bar, outdoor heated pool, hydrotherapy pool, conference space. AE, DC, MC, V.*

Expensive **Athens Chandris.** This seaside hotel, which opened in 1977, is convenient to both Athens and the airport. The lobby is striking, with bold colors in an art-deco design and of course, lots of marble. The rooms have been upgraded with cubist, ultramodern Italian furniture. The Four Seasons restaurant serves Continental cooking. *Syngrou Ave. 385, Paleo Phaleron, 17554, tel. 01/941–4824, 01/941–4825, or 01/941–4826; fax 01/942–5082. 386 rooms with bath. Facilities: 2 restaurants, coffee shop, snack bar, 2 bars, outdoor pool, ballroom, meeting rooms. AE, DC, MC, V.*

★ **Athens Gate.** This fine hotel, now a Best Western, gives friendly, efficient service and is quite a bargain. The lobby has been smartly renovated with muted paisley couches, apricot rugs, and sleek glass-and-chrome tables. From the front rooms you see the Temple of Olympian Zeus, from the back rooms the Acropolis. The rooms have TVs but no minibars. The restaurant has a good buffet breakfast and the bar and restaurant on the breezy rooftop has a generous buffet table. *10 Syngrou, Syntagma, 11743, tel. 01/923–8302, 01/923–8303, or 01/923–8304; fax 01/923–7493. 106 rooms with bath. Facilities: restaurant, bar. AE, DC, MC, V.*

Holiday Inn. This favorite of business people had a recent facelift, and the lobby is quite striking with its rugs and furnishings in pale orange and green, a glass-enclosed shopping arcade, a coffee shop, and a monolithic sculpture in the center. The rooms, with minibars and small lounge areas, have soothing colors and floral bedspreads. Those on the fifth and sixth floors have balconies and are quieter. The rooftop pool has a pleasant garden with a cozy bar. *Michalakopoulou 50, Ilisia, 11528, tel. 01/7248–322 through 01/7248–329, fax 01/724–8187. 190 rooms with bath. Facilities: bistro, bar, swimming pool, garage, meeting and banquet facilities. AE, DC, MC, V.*

Park. The Park Hotel has a friendly, easygoing ambience, with a panelled lobby and leather furniture. The plush guest rooms have bars and minibars, and telephones in the marble bathrooms. The upper balconies and the bar on the roof have views of the park. The coffee shop is open 24 hours and the Latina Restaurant serves both Greek and international cuisines. *Alexandras 10, Areos Park, 10682, tel. 01/883–2712 through 01/883–2719, fax 01/823–8420. 146 rooms with bath. Facilities: restaurant, coffee shop, snack bar, bar, discothèque, pool, convention space. AE, DC, MC, V.*

Moderate **Athenian Inn.** The flowering plants, white stucco walls, dark ★ beams, terra-cotta tile floors, and watercolors of Greek scenes combine to give this well-located hotel the warmth and charm of a village inn. Opened almost 20 years ago, it has a loyal clientele of return visitors, so you must book well ahead. The lounge/breakfast room has an open fireplace. The rooms have traditional Greek spreads on the wood-frame beds, carpeting, and radios. The upper rooms in front have balconies, some with a view of Lycabettus. The street has little traffic, but there's occasional loud conversation from Ratka's popular bar. *Haritos 22, Kolonaki, 10675, tel. 01/723–8097, 01/723–9552, or 01/721–8756; fax 01/724–2268. 28 rooms with bath or shower. Facilities: air-conditioning. AE, DC, V.*

Lycabette. This small hotel has a gregarious atmosphere and pleasant service, but the "pedestrian" street is full of cars and motorbikes nowadays. The comfortable rooms all have balconies. The lobby is bright and cheerful, there's a tea room on the mezzanine and a pretty breakfast room/restaurant on the ground floor. *Valaoritiou 6, Syntagma, 10675, tel. 01/363–3514 through 01/363–3518, fax 01/363–3518. 39 rooms with shower or bath. Facilities: restaurant, bar, tearoom, air-conditioning. AE, DC, MC, V.*

Stanley. This large hotel, not far from the train station, is a favorite of Spanish and Italian groups. It has a bustling air, and the popular Tropicana bar. The cheerful apricot and gold rooms are of ample size and have radios but no TVs or balconies. The quieter rooms are in the back. *Odysseus 1, Karaiskaki Sq., 10437, tel. 01/522–0011 or 01/524–1611 through 01/524–1618, fax 01/524-4611. 395 rooms with bath or shower. Facilities; taverna, 2 bars, air-conditioning, pool, gift shop, hairdresser. AE, V.*

Inexpensive **Acropolis House.** This landmark family-run villa on the edge of Plaka with Belle Epoque accents is a favorite of visiting students and faculty. The decor is somewhat cluttered, although some of the rooms have new spreads and curtains, and they are all clean. There's elderly wallpaper and tattered airline posters in the halls. But this makes it all the more endearing to its clients, who feel the hotel's nurturing service and friendly atmosphere more than compensate. *Voulis and Kodrou 6–8, Plaka, 10558, tel. 01/322–2344 or 01/322–6241. 23 rooms, 20 with shower or bath. V.*

★ **Art Gallery Pension.** On a quiet side street near the Acropolis, this friendly place, much prized by visiting students and single travelers, draws a congenial crowd. The handsome house has an old-fashioned look with family paintings on the muted white walls, earth-tone spreads on the comfortable beds, hardwood floors, and overhead fans. Most rooms have balconies with views of Filopappou or the Acropolis. *Erechthiou 5, Veikou, 11742, tel. 01/923–8376 or 01/923–1933. 18 rooms with shower or bath, 2 suites. Facilities: bar. No credit cards.*

Erechtheon. This quiet hotel off busy Apostolou Pavlou is convenient for visiting ancient Athens. The rooms are air-conditioned, they have rugs on the floor, and all doubles have a view of the Acropolis. Off the lobby are a TV room and a small breakfast room, where a buffet is served in the morning. *Flamarion 8, Thission, 11851, tel. 01/345–9606. 22 rooms with bath. Facilities: TV room. AE.*

Exarchia. Seasoned tourists often choose this hotel in the heart of the student area and near the National Museum, but the area has many late-night bars and cafés, and periodic demonstrations that often erupt into violence. That said, people who stay here are generally satisfied. The rooms are basic, with modern pine furnishings, and most have a balcony. The rooftop bar on the sixth floor has a good view of the Acropolis and the nearby hills. *55 Themistokleous, Exarchia, 10683, tel. 01/360–1256, 01/360–0731, or 01/360–3296; fax 01/360–3296. 50 rooms with bath. Facilities: bar. No credit cards.*

Orion and **Dryades.** These two hotels in a quiet area near a park on the craggy peak of Lofos Strefis (the Poor Man's Acropolis) are heavily booked by local fashion agencies who house their models there. Orion is the humbler, with smaller rooms and shared baths between two rooms. Dryades' rooms all have balconies; all but five of Orion's have balconies. At both, rooms are white or have wood paneling, the wood furniture is new and modern, the spreads and accents are in earth tones. Orion has a third-floor roof garden, with a lovely view, that is the breakfast area, and both have kitchens that guests can use. The atmosphere is congenial, the help very friendly, and the hotels attract a young, lively crowd. *Emmanuel Benaki 105 and Anexartisias, 11473, tel. 01/362-7362 or 01/362-0191, fax 01/360-5193. Orion: 20 rooms share bath. Facilities: kitchen. Dryades: 15 rooms with bath. Facilities: kitchen. No credit cards.*

XEN (YWCA). This modern building close to Syntagma has a hairdresser, a library, kitchens, laundry facilities, and a cafeteria (closed for renovation at press time), but no breakfast. Most rooms use the communal bathroom although three doubles and one single have private baths. The marble floors have rugs in winter; sheets and blankets are provided. The rooms are not air-conditioned; those at the back are cooler and quieter. Aside from one double room set aside for couples, only women are allowed. *Amerikis 11, 10672, tel. 01/362-4291. 52 beds. Facilities: cafeteria, hairdresser, kitchen and laundry facilities, library. No credit cards.*

Piraeus

Moderate **Castella Hotel.** Beautifully located on the hill above Mikrolimano, Castella is under new management and has upgraded its image. The rooms are sizable and the decor is pleasant; some rooms on high levels have a sea view. The spacious roof garden is landscaped with flowering plants and has a splendid view of Mikrolimano and the yacht club. *Vassileos Pavlos 75, Castella, 18533, tel. 01/411-4735, fax 01/412-2223. 30 rooms with bath. Facilities: restaurant, bar. DC, MC, V.*

★ **Mistral Hotel.** This pleasant new Piraeus hotel, at the top of the moderate range, is quite suitable for families. The rooms are attractively designed, and all have balconies. The furniture is modern wood, and there are marble-top tables, blue spreads and curtains, and tile floors. A pool is expected to be completed in 1993. *Vassileos Pavlos 105, Castella, 18533, tel. 01/412-1425, 01/412-6589, 01/411-0175, or 01/411-5887; fax 01/412-2096. 74 rooms with bath. Facilities: restaurant, cafeteria, bar, air-conditioning in bedrooms, conference room, pool under construction. AE, MC, V.*

Inexpensive **Scorpios.** The view of the Makra Teixoi (Long Walls of Themistocles) is the draw at this little hotel in Piraiki, not far from Zea Marina. The rooms are small but attractive, with wood furniture and brown decor; the balconies in front have fine views of the harbor and ancient walls. The roof garden lounge area is cooled by a fresh sea breeze and overlooks Microlimano and the Saronic Gulf. *Akti Themistokleous 156, Piraiki, 18539, tel. 01/451-2172. 24 rooms with bath. Facilities: breakfast room. AE, MC, V.*

The Arts and Nightlife

The Arts

The weekly magazine *Athinorama* (in Greek) gives detailed information about current performances, gallery openings, and films. *The Greek News*, an English-language weekly, has an arts section, as does *Greece's Weekly*. *The Athenian*, the English-language monthly, has a thorough calendar section with good background details on exhibits and performances.

Athens Festival and Other Shows

The city's primary summer artistic event, the **Athens Festival,** held in Herod Atticus, draws performers like Pavarotti and Diana Ross; such dance troupes as Martha Graham and Maurice Béjart; symphony orchestras; and local groups doing ancient Greek drama. It is a delightful setting, the Roman arches making a stunning backdrop for the performers, but the upper-level seats have no cushions, so you should bring one, along with a light wrap. Tickets sell out quickly for popular shows; they are on sale in the arcade at Stadiou 4, tel. 01/322–1459. Prices vary from about 2,000 dr. to as high as 20,000 dr. for the big names.

Other events are held at the modern **Lycabettus Theater,** set on a pinnacle of Lycabettus, with wooden bleacher seats and a glorious panoramic view. The specialty here is popular concerts, with such performers as B.B. King, Ravi Shankar, and Nina Simone. Bus No. 23 gets you only to the bottom of the hill, and taxi drivers often can't drive to the top. Buy a one-way ticket on the funicular and walk about 10 minutes down to the theater.

Events at the **Athens Concert Hall** have usually played to sell-out crowds since it opened in 1991. Tickets are sold at the box office at Vassilis Sophias and Kokkalis, next to the American Embassy, and for most events are very difficult to get. Try going to the theater just before the performance, although the scalpers may ask hefty prices.

From April through October, **Sound and Light Spectacles,** with a recorded text reciting the history of the Acropolis, are given every evening. The English-language version is at 9 PM, (8 PM in Oct.). Seating is on the Pnyx hill opposite the Acropolis, a great place to view the sunset before the show. Tickets are sold at the arcade at Stadiou 4 (tel. 01/322–1459) or at the Pnyx (tel. 01/922–6210) before showtime.

The Dora Stratou Group, a lively young dance troupe with great spirit, is well worth seeing. They perform a fine selection of **Greek folk dances** from all regions, as well as Cyprus, in eye-catching authentic costumes. Two performances are held every summer evening at the Filopappou Theater near the Pnyx (tel. 01/324–4395 or 01/921–4650).

Film

Films are shown in original-language versions with subtitles (except for major animated films), a definite boon for foreigners. Check the *Greek News* or the *Athens News* for programs, schedules, and addresses and phone numbers of theaters (including those of the Hellenic-American Union and the British Council, which both screen films free).

The **outdoor cinema,** a charming, uniquely Greek entertainment, opens in summer (it supposedly ranks second to the Acropolis as an Athens attraction). About 50 of them operate in vine-covered empty lots and on rooftops (with customers sitting on lawn chairs), and in traditional theaters with roofs or walls that open. A disadvantage is the mandatory lower sound level at the second screening, so audiences have to resort to lip reading (especially at comedies, when the laughter drowns out the lines). These are some of the best: **Cine Paris** (Kidathineon 22, Plaka); **Athenian** (Haritos 50, Kolonaki) has good toasted sandwiches and imported beer; **Riviera** (Valtetsiou 46,

Exarchia); **Vox** (Exarchia Sq.); **Amaryllis** (Ayios Ioannou 2, Ayia Paraskevi) serves mezze at little tables; **Zephyros** (Troon 36, Thisio) is known for its art films; and **Cine Paradisos** (Ayios Giorgiou and Zappa 4, Korydallos, suburb of Piraeus), shows distinguished top-notch films in a renovated cinema resembling a whitewashed Cycladic courtyard; the trip is worth the taxi fare.

Galleries A pleasant way to get a feel for contemporary Athenian life and get acquainted with leading figures on the arts scenes (ideally through some conversation) is to attend the opening nights of art exhibits (most of the top galleries serve complimentary wine and snacks). Many of the galleries close in July and August. Some of the top ones are **Dada, Epoches, Gallery 3, Ileana Tounda, Jill Yakas, Nees Morphes, Zouboulakis,** and **Zygos.** Information about the dates of openings, gallery addresses, and phone numbers appear in *The Athenian*, the *Greek News*, and the *Athens News*.

Nightlife

Athens is a sociable, late-night town where people love to see and be seen, and the action goes on until the wee morning hours. Neither high inflation and frozen wage scales, nor a government campaign to get people to pay their taxes seem to slow down the social life, and clubs and restaurants are usually packed. Credit cards are not commonly accepted.

Bars Bars not in hotels, a relatively new development in Greece, are now popular with young and old alike. Since the belief is that drinking without eating is bad for the stomach, most of these places serve snacks and cold plates. Overimbibing, especially by women, is frowned upon. According to Greeks, if you want to guard against a hangover, go to **To Monastiri,** a taverna in the central market on Athinas Street, for *patsas*, a murky tripe soup that is said to be infallible.

Art Café (Vasileos Pavlou 61, tel. 01/413–7896) is a restaurant-bar housed in a beautifully restored old mansion in Kastella, Piraeus, and has a view of Microlimano below. It serves chicken with vegetables and trout salad, and its music is an interesting eclectic mix.

Booze (Kolokotroni 57, tel. 01/324–0944), featuring progressive music, is in a three-story building frequented by serious bohemians, who are distinguished by their black turtlenecks.

Dada (Arachovis 57, Exarchia, tel. 01/360–7751) is an attractive old-time favorite of the intellectual crowd. It's in a neoclassical house and has a good selection of discreet piped-in music.

Loutro (Ferron 18, tel. 01/883–3685) has an old apricot-color Turkish bath, or *loutro*, in the center. It serves a large selection of fine wines to an interesting crowd.

Gregarious **Memphis** (Ventiri 5, Ilisia, behind Hilton, tel. 01/724–1562), popular with Greek Yuppies, features live jazz Tuesday and Wednesday.

Rhythm and Blues (Tositsa 11, Exarchia, tel. 01/822–8870) is a friendly place that features recorded blues and jazz, and has live music on Thursday and Friday.

Bouzoukia Many tourists think Greek social life centers around large clubs where live bouzouki music is played and patrons get their kicks by smashing up the plates. This practice, called *spasta*, is now prohibited. A few clubs provide specially made light plates that are harmless when smashed. In others, flowers are sold for showering your companions when they take to the dance floor. The clubs listed below have standard performers but are very expensive, and the waiters are expert in hustling drinks and mediocre meals, but if you feel you must go, you have been warned. Wear your glitziest clothes and you'll still feel modest by comparison. Try **Allegro** (Patision 208, Patissia, tel. 01/862–4941), **Iphigenia** (Syngrou 201, tel. 01/934–9444), or **Panorama** (Acharnon 77, tel. 01/881–4427).

An upmarket form of the above type of club is found at and near the airport, where top entertainers deservedly command top drachmas. Some of the most popular are **Diogenis Palace** (Syngrou 259, tel. 01/942–4267), **Fantasia** (Hellenikon Airport, tel. 01/982–0300), **Nea Delina** (Glyfada seaside, tel. 01/894–1300), and **Posidonio** (Possidonos 18, Hellenikon Airport).

Discothèques **Aftokinesi.** This modern night spot (Kifissias 7, Filothei, tel. 01/681–2360) attracts a smart, young crowd which really comes to boogie the night away. **Alexander's** (Anagnostopoulou 44, Kolonaki, tel. 01/364–6660) caters to a gay male crowd, though straights also come here to dance. The selection is good, the music is very loud, and the room very smoky, but that doesn't keep it from being packed every night. **Kalua** has two branches. The Syntagma one is a tastefully decorated semibasement with two main bars, frequented by lively people who crowd the dance floor. The Glyfada one is known as a place for wild abandon, where you can really let your hair down. *Amerikis 6, Syntagma, tel. 01/360–8304; Possidonos 2, Glyfada, tel. 01/894–1300. Closed fall–spring.*

Mercedes (Asteria Beach, Glyfada, tel. 01/894–6898), the in place along this busy seaside strip, has a stimulating, eclectic, music selection and is frequented by all age groups. The crowd at **Wild Rose** (Panepistimiou 10, Syntagma, tel. 01/364–2160) is older here than at most of the discos, and studded with celebrities and Beautiful People.

Jazz Clubs **Blue Velvet** (Ermou 116, Monastiraki, tel. 01/323–9047) plays recorded jazz and pop in the evenings and has great brunches with live jazz Sunday 1 PM–8 PM. Known as the venue of noteworthy groups, especially European ones, the **Half Note** (68 Fthiotidos, tel. 01/644–9236) is the hangout of serious jazz fans and the atmosphere is casual. **Jazz Club 1920** (Ploutarchou 10, Kolonaki, tel. 01/721–0533) is an upmarket club in a cozy semibasement that features a quintet, interspersed with recorded music that includes retro rock-and-roll from the '60s.

Live-Music Bars **Guilietta e Romeo** (Athimou Gazi 9, behind Kolokotronis statue on Stadiou, tel. 01/322–2591) is like a cozy inn, with tables outdoors on a lovely little square not far from the central telephone office. Italian troubador Umberto Giardi sings romantic ballads accompanied by a piano, while diners sit at candlelit tables.

Prova (Patriatch Ioakim 43, tel. 01/723–3773) is an offbeat bar that on Tuesday features *proves* (improvisations) on an open stage at which anyone from gypsies to classical violinists may take their turn. A tiny place with only five tables and a few bar stools, it's informal and lots of fun.

The Latin-American band Hasta Banana performs at **Snob** (Anapiron Polemou 10, Kolonaki, tel. 01/722–9943) Wednesday–Saturday. Drinks cost 1,300 dr.

Plaka Tavernas with Music
Dionysos (Lysiou 7, tel. 01/322–7589) has a floor show featuring Greek popular music and is distinguished by the fact that some of its waiters can pick up tables with their teeth. **Klimataria** (Klepsidras 5, tel. 01/324–1809) is an authentic old taverna with music, in an old house without a roof, and has been around for many years. It features two guitarists and a pianist, who play sing-along favorites much appreciated by the largely Greek audience. This slice of old-style Greek entertainment is surprisingly reasonable.

Palea Taverna Kritikou (Mniskleos 24, tel. 01/322–2809) specializes in distinctive Cretan music featuring the *lyra*, a bowed instrument, and a spirited dance group wearing authentic costumes. This is a good way to see regional dancing. **Yeros tou Morea** (Mniskleos 27, tel. 01/322–1753), a vine-draped outdoor club that has stood for almost 150 years at the top of a steep pedestrian street, features pleasant popular Greek music and satisfactory food. Prices are reasonable, and the mostly Greek crowd is usually in a festive mood.

Rembetica Clubs
At the thriving clubs that play this popular form of Greek urban blues you can catch a glimpse of Greek social life and perhaps even get out and join the dances (but remember, it is considered rude to join a group of people dancing without being asked, and worse yet to interrupt a solo dance). Most of the clubs are closed during the summer, so call in advance. They have reasonable prices for an evening of live entertainment, but the food is often expensive and not very good.

Anifori is a friendly club that plays both Rembetica and popular music. *Vassileos Yiorgiou 47, Piraeus, tel. 01/411–5819. Closed Sun.–Thurs.*

Frankosyrianni is run by dedicated musician Nikos Argyropoulos, with a group specializing in the songs of Markos Vamvakaris, a Rembetica great. *Arachovis 57, Exarchia, tel. 01/360–0693. Closed Mon.–Tues.*

Stoa Athanaton, in a renovated warehouse right in the Central Market, is a joy. The authentic music is enhanced by an infectious, devil-may-care mood and the enthusiastic participation of the audience. The small dance floor is jammed; the food is delicious and reasonable, but liquor is expensive. *Sofolkeous 19, central market, tel. 01/3214–362. Reservations required for evenings. Closed Sun.*

Taximi, one of the older clubs, features Bobis Goles, a gravelly voiced entertainer, who's one of the best of the bouzouki players. *Harilaou Trikoupi and Isavron 29, tel. 01/363–9919. Closed Sun.*

4 Attica, the Saronic Islands, and Delphi

By Catherine Vanderpool

Catherine Vanderpool of the American School of Classical Studies has written on art, history, archaeology, and travel.

Since the first millennium BC, the story of Attica has been almost inextricably bound to that of Athens, the most powerful of the villages that lay scattered over the peninsula. Athens brought these towns together, by force and persuasion, into a unit that by the 5th century BC had become the center of an empire. The bulk of Attica, which stretches southeast into the Aegean, lies east and north of Athens. Separated from Central Greece by mountains—Pateras, Kithairon, Aigaleo, and Parnis—and bordered by the sea, Attica was easily defensible. It also had several fertile plains, well watered with rivers and seasonal streams, and its coves and natural harbors encouraged the development of seafaring and trade.

Athens lies in a basin defined by three mountain masses: Hymettos to the east, Parnis and Aigaleo to the west, and Pendeli to the north. East of Hymettos stretches the Mesogeion, or "middle territory," those gently undulating hills and fields laced with vineyards and dotted with olive trees, source of Attica's most characteristic products and of the sweet-smelling thyme, food for the bees whose hives in blue boxes were once a familiar sight along any country road. Northeast of Pendeli, between the slopes and the sea, lies the fabled plain of Marathon, its flat expanse now dotted with small agricultural communities and seaside resorts, second home to many Athenians.

In this chapter we will also explore areas that are outside the modern political entity of Attica, which is a *nome*, or province. We will follow geography and history rather than political logic. Closely tied to Attica, both historically and geographically, are the nearby islands of Salamis, Aegina, and, to a lesser extent, Poros, Hydra, and Spetses. Today the latter, known as the Saronic Islands, are easily visited on day trips from Piraeus. Delphi can also be seen in a long day trip from Athens, but because the ancient site and its museum are probably the high point of any trip to Greece, our tour presupposes at least one overnight, so you can visit the sites one day and the museum the next.

Essential Information

Important Addresses and Numbers

See Essential Information in Chapter 3. **Tourist Police:** in Attica, tel. 171; in Delphi, tel. 0265/82220.

Arriving and Departing

For information on arriving in and departing from Attica, *see* Essential Information in Chapter 3.

Getting Around

By Car Points in Attica can be reached from the main Thessaloniki–Athens highway without ever having to go into Athens itself. From the Peloponnese, you can drive east via Corinth to Athens, or from Patras, take the Rion–Antirion ferry and the coast road, visiting Delphi first. Most of the roads are two-lane secondary arteries; a few of them (notably from Athens to Delphi and Itea and to Sounion) have been recently upgraded, are very good, and often spectacularly scenic. Expect heavy traffic to Delphi in summer and ski season, and to and from Athens on weekends. Cars are not allowed on Hydra and Spetses.

Car and Scooter Rentals
Most international agencies have offices in Athens and desks at the airport, including **Avis** (airport tel. 01/322–4951 through 01/322–4955), **Budget** (airport tel. 01/961–3634 or 01/984–5538), **Hertz** (airport tel. 01/961–3625 or 01/981–3701), **Interrent-Europcar** (airport tel. 01/961–3424 or 01/982–9565), and **Thrifty** (20 Hatzichristou and Syngrou, Athens, tel. 01/923–8842). On the islands of Aegina and Spetses, many people rent scooters, mopeds, and bicycles from shops along the harbor, but extreme caution is advised: The equipment may not be in good condition, roads can be narrow and treacherous, and many drivers scorn your safety. Wear a helmet, and drive defensively.

By Bus
If you are not renting a car, the next most efficient mode of travel (as usual in Greece) is the bus. An extensive network of public buses serves all points in this itinerary from Athens, and local buses connect the smaller towns and villages at least daily. For **Attica,** buses leave frequently from 29 Mavromateon (tel. 01/821–0872) for Marathon, Nea Makri, and Rafina; and from 14 Mavromateon (tel. 01/821–3203) for Sounion. For the closer suburbs, including Glyfada (Nos. 128 and 129), Varkiza and Vouliagmeni (Nos. 116 and 117), and Voula (No. 122), buses depart from stops along Vassilissis Olgas and Syngrou approximately every 20 minutes. Nos. 853 and 862 depart for Eleusis (45 minutes), every 20 minutes from Eleftherias Square. To **Delphi,** there are five departures per day from 260 Liossion (tel. 01/831–7096), beginning at 7:30 AM.

By Boat
The islands of Poros and Spetses are so close to the Peloponnese mainland that you can drive there, park, and ferry across the channel in any of a number of little skiffs (price negotiable), but to get to them from Athens or to visit the other Saronic Islands, you must take to the sea in a ship. The **Argossaronikos Line** will take you (and your car) from the main port in Piraeus to Aegina (1½ hours) and Poros (3 hours 40 minutes), or you alone to Hydra (4 hours 10 minutes) and Spetses (5 hours 25 minutes). There are approximately half a dozen departures per day, and fares range from 674 dr. per person for Aegina to 1,532 dr. for Spetses. Car rates start at 2,474 dr. for Aegina to a top of 8,420 dr. for Spetses. These ferries are the leisurely—meaning *very* slow—and cheap way to travel. Most people now prefer the speedier **Flying Dolphins** (tel. 01/453–6107 or 01/453–7107, no cars carried), hydrofoils that depart from the harbor of Zea, also in Piraeus. They are more expensive and look and feel like prop planes, with assigned seating in a claustrophobic cabin watched over by nattily garbed flight attendants. There are about half a dozen departures daily, and it is advisable to make reservations ahead of time—they book up quickly. The cost ranges from 1,080 dr. for Aegina to 2,796 dr. for Spetses. You can also reserve through a travel agent.

Exploring Attica, the Saronic Islands, and Delphi

Athens itself is a good base for exploring Attica; most of the tours described below can be done in a day, or at most, two days. But if you wish to stay outside Athens, then there are several alternatives. On the mainland, Sounion and Marathon offer good locations and comfortable hotels; for the Saronic Islands, Hydra or Spetses would be the first choice: Each is worth extra exploration time and each offers adequate accommodations and good food. On a trip to Delphi you can stay in the town itself or next-door Arachova, both of which offer access to the shore areas of Itea and Galaxidi and to Mt. Parnassos.

Tour 1 takes you southeast along the Apollo Coast to Sounion, at the tip of the Attic peninsula, which is crowned by the 5th-century-BC Temple of Poseidon. **Tour 2,** also archaeological in nature, explores the Sanctuary of Artemis at the seaside site of Brauron, the plain of Marathon, and the ancient city of Rhamnous. **Tour 3** takes you around the northern flank of Pendeli to the enchantingly rural archaeological site at the Amphiareion. **Tour 4** takes in the Fortress of Phyle, on the slopes of Parnis; the Sanctuary of Demeter and Kore at Eleusis; and the Monastery of Daphni. **Tour 5,** which will take several days, introduces you to the Saronic Islands of Aegina, Poros, Hydra, and Spetses. A short **Tour 6** takes you to the Monastery at Kaisariani, on the slopes of Hymettos. Finally, **Tour 7** is an excursion to Delphi and its surroundings.

Highlights for First-Time Visitors

Delphi (*see* Tour 7)
Galaxidi (*see* Tour 7)
Hydra (*see* Tour 5)
Monastery of Daphni (*see* Tour 4)
Temple of Aphaia on Aegina (*see* Tour 5)
Temple of Poseidon at Sounion (*see* Tour 1)

Tour 1: To Cape Sounion and Back

Numbers in the margin correspond to points of interest on the Attica and the Saronic Islands map.

From the center of Athens, take Vouliagmeni Boulevard past Athens International Airport, and connect at Glyfada with Poseidonios Boulevard, the shore road to Sounion, 68 kilometers (42 miles) from town. The road leads you through Glyfada, Voula, and Vouliagmeni, all fashionable seaside resorts. Once located well beyond the city boundaries, they have now been virtually absorbed into the urban sprawl, and the water lapping at the broad sandy beaches regularly fails pollution tests. If you stay at a hotel in this area, stick to the swimming pool.

Glyfada, site of Athens International Airport, was also home to many American families during the years when the United States maintained a major base at the airfield. Perhaps as a direct result, Glyfada was one of the first Athenian suburbs to give birth to fast-food restaurants and malls, now endemic to the city. Beyond **Vouliagmeni,** the road, recently widened to four lanes, threads along a rocky coastline dotted with inlets. Intrepid bathers swim off the rocks, leaving their cars in the frequent roadside parking areas and scrambling down paths to the inviting coves below. If you join them, take along your snorkels, fins, and masks so you can enjoy the underwater scenery (as rocky and barren as the dry land above) and, most important, avoid the sea urchins clinging to the shoreline. The drive beyond Vouliagmeni now leads through one of the most heavily developed seacoasts in Greece. The former fishing villages, built over with apartments, condominiums, hotels, villas, and qvillettas, retain nothing of their earlier charm; only the many tavernas proclaiming *Psari fresca* (fresh fish) remind us of their past.

At **Legrena,** approximately 60 kilometers (37 miles) from Athens, the road skirts the last headland before the cape. Just offshore is the uninhabited islet of Patroklou, and ahead the steep-walled promontory of **Sounion** itself, the **Temple of Poseidon** clearly visible. The road leads you, off a right fork, directly to the parking lot east of the temple hill. Passing through the gate, you climb a rocky path which follows, roughly, the ancient approach, through the scanty remains of the ancient *propylon* (gateway) into the sanctuary itself. On your left are the remains of the *Temenos* (precinct) of Poseidon, on your right a stoa and rooms. The temple itself may have been designed just after the middle of the 5th century BC by the same architect who built the Temple of Hephaistos in the Agora of Athens: The people who lived in Sounion were considered Athenian citizens, the sanctuary was Athenian, and Poseidon occupied a position in Athenian foundation mythology second only to Athena herself. Since the temple is now off limits to tourists, you won't be able to see what used to be one of the highlights of a visit here— Lord Byron's signature, carved into a column in the east facade. Situated on the highest point of the acropolis, the temple was built on the site of an earlier cult to Poseidon, and two colossal statues of youths (perhaps votives to the god), carved well over a century before the temple's construction, were discovered in early excavations. Both are now in the National Museum in Athens. The remaining columns, some of which have recently been re-erected, now stand sentinel over the Aegean, visible from miles away. The view from the summit is spectacular. Particularly in the slanting light of the late afternoon sun, the land masses to the west stand out in sharp profile: the tip of Hydra, the bulk of Aegina backed by the mountains of the Peloponnese. And just offshore to the east lies the narrow island of Makronissos (literally, "long island"). *Tel. 0292/39363. Admission: 600 dr. Open Mon.–Sat. 9–sunset, Sun. 10–sunset.*

On the land side, the slopes of the acropolis retain traces of the fortification walls. Sounion was also a seaport, with a well-protected harbor, where today there's a beach, a hotel, and several tavernas.

Time Out A converted fisherman's shack, **Restaurant Ilias,** on the beach below the Temple of Poseidon, serves a selection of fresh fish, simple salads, and greens at lunch and dinner, indoors or outdoors. Fish is always expensive, so do not be surprised at the size of the bill, even in these humble surroundings (but it is still less than in Athens). In winter, try *gopes*, or red mullet, and

Attica and the Saronic Islands

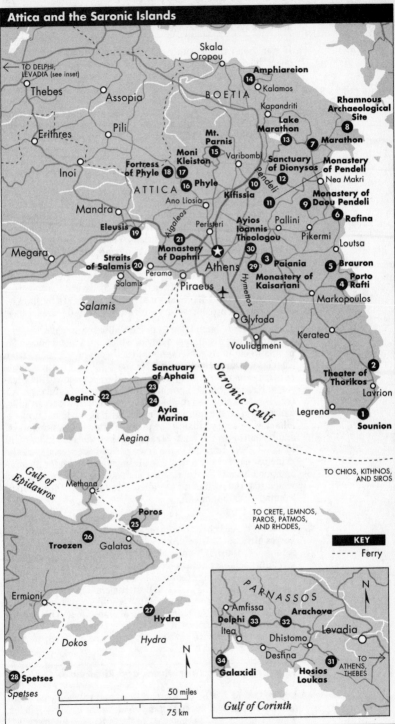

TO DELPHI;
LEVADIA (see inset)

Thebes

Assopia

Erithres

Pili

Inoi

Mandra

Megara

Skala
Oropou

14 Kalamos

B O E T I A

Kapandriti

**Rhamnous
Archaeological
Site**
8

**Mt.
Parnis**
15 Varibombi

**Moni
Kleiston**
17

**Fortress
of Phyle** **18**

16 **Phyle**

Ano Liosia

ATTICA

Peristeri

Aigaleos

Eleusis
19

**Straits
of Salamis** **20**

Salamis

Perama

**Monastery
of Daphni**
21

Athens ★

Piraeus

Glyfada

Vouliagmeni

**Lake
Marathon**
13 **7** **Marathon**

**Sanctuary
of Dionysos**
12

10

Pendeli

Kifissia

11

Pallini

**Ayios
Ioannis
Theologou**
30

29

**Monastery of
Kaisariani**

Hymettos

**Monastery
of Pendeli**

Nea Makri

**Monastery of
Daou Pendeli**
9

6 **Rafina**

Pikermi

Loutsa

3 **Paiania**

5 **Brauron**

4 **Porto
Rafti**

Markopoulos

Keratea

2

**Theater of
Thorikos**

Lavrion

Legrena

1
Sounion

Salamis

Saronic Gulf

TO CHIOS, KITHNOS,
AND SIROS

TO CRETE, LEMNOS,
PAROS, PATMOS,
AND RHODES,

**Sanctuary
of Aphaia**
23

Aegina **22**

24
**Ayia
Marina**

Aegina

*Gulf of
Epidauros*

Methana

Poros
25

26
Troezen Galatas

Ermioni

27 **Hydra**

Dokos

Hydra

28 **Spetses**

Spetses

N

0   50 miles

0   75 km

KEY

- - - - - Ferry

P A R N A S S O S

N

Amfissa

Delphi **33**

32 **Arachova**

Itea

Dhistomo

Levadia

Destina

34
Galaxidi

31
**Hosios
Loukas**

TO
ATHENS,
THEBES

Gulf of Corinth

remember, the shrimp and squid, cheaper than the fish, are almost always imported "fresh frozen."

If you spend the morning at Sounion and have lunch on the beach below, you may also want to take a swim, although the sandy strip becomes uncomfortably crowded in summer. If you do make a day of it, stay on for the sunset, but be warned that it is heavily promoted by tour agencies, so you will share the experience with hundreds of others. An alternative is to head back to Athens after lunch via a different route and explore the inner reaches of Attica. Return to the main road and continue along the shore northeast of the temple. Pass through **Lavrion,** a post-industrial town with a few remnants of Belle Epoque architecture.

Continue north past a large electrical plant at the end of a long sweep of public beach. Visible just to the right of the road as it turns inland are the remains of the 4th-century BC **Theater of Thorikos,** cut into the hill of Velatouris, acropolis of the ancient town. The silver mines of ancient Thorikos, along with the more significant mines at ancient Lavrion, exploited since prehistoric times but worked principally in the 5th century BC, provided the wherewithal for Athens' astounding growth. Several thousand ancient shafts have been discovered in the area, perpendicular and diagonal bores that were worked by slave labor controlled by contractors with state-granted leases.

The road winds inland, through bare hilly country now spoiled by cement box dwellings, many of which are second homes for people living in Athens. **Keratea,** 10 kilometers (6 miles) from Thorikos, is an agricultural center now built over with a jumble of beige cement two-story buildings interspersed with an occasional Neoclassical village house from a more graceful past. After Keratea, a series of small factories dot the barren hills, which yield to the Mesogeion plain, with Pendeli and its foothills now clearly visible to the north, Parnis in the northwest, and Hymettos to the west. Straddling the road at 10 kilometers (6 miles) from Keratea is the town of **Markopoulos,** one of the principal market centers of the Mesogeion, known for its wine and good bread. Continuing through stands of olive trees and vineyards, the road now runs almost due west, with Hymettos looming straight ahead.

At Koropi the inland road joins the major north–south road at **Paiania,** site of a cave tricked out with music and lights and the **Vorres Museum of Greek Art** (tel. 01/664–2520 or 01/664–4771. Admission: 100 dr. Open weekends 10–2), which holds some interesting folk art and a collection of contemporary Greek works, all in buildings restored in traditional style by a Greek-Canadian collector. Paiania is best remembered as the birthplace of Demosthenes, whose oratory could not prevent Athens from falling under the rule of Philip of Macedon and his son Alexander. After Paiania, the route connects with the Mesogeion Road and returns to Athens through the suburb of Ayia Paraskevi.

Tour 2: Brauron, Marathon, and Rhamnous

Leave Athens by the Mesogeion Road and retrace your steps (*see* Tour 1, *above*) via the inland road, as far as Markopoulos, where you pick up the road east to **Porto Rafti,** 5 kilometers (3 miles) away. This seaside town is notable for a colossal ancient statue on an islet just offshore. This seated figure long ago was nicknamed the *rafti*, or "tailor." The town, with its fine natural harbor, is given over to summer homes for Athenians.

5 From Porto Rafti, retrace your steps toward Markopoulos, turn right at the crossroads, and continue about 3½ kilometers (2 miles) toward the sea to the town of **Brauron.** The **Sanctuary of Artemis** lies in a waterlogged depression at the foot of a small hill. Built on the site of an earlier shrine, the sanctuary consists of a 5th-century-BC temple and horseshoe-shaped stoa. Here, the virgin huntress Artemis was worshiped in her function (ironically) as protectress of childbirth. Every four years, the Athenians celebrated the Brauronia, in which young girls between the ages of 5 and 10 took part in arcane ceremonies, including (among other rites) a dance in which they were dressed as bears. In the museum next to the site are statues of these little girls, as well as many votive offerings. *Tel. 0294–710221. Admission: 400 dr. Open 8:30–3, closed Mon., Thurs., Fri.*

6 From Brauron, continue north along the coast road, which skirts an extensively (and badly) developed coastline. Loutsa's pleasant beach, framed by a backdrop of umbrella pines, has shallow waters perfect for families with small children, but it is very crowded in the summer. The road continues to **Rafina,** a busy port that serves Evia and the Cyclades. On weekdays it is a joy to sit in one of the many seaside tavernas and watch the bustle of arrival and departure, or to wander along and examine the fresh catch just off the numerous fishing boats, but it is too crowded on weekends and holidays. Ferries leave from Rafina for Karystos on the southern end of Evia and for the Cyclades, a shorter sea passage than from Piraeus but only convenient if you are traveling by car.

From Rafina, drive inland 3 kilometers (2 miles) to the intersection of the main road to Marathon. Turn right and drive north, and in 5 kilometers (3 miles) you will come to Nea Makri, a busy seaside resort, the site of a former U.S. military base that the municipality plans to turn into a sports or cultural center.

Time Out   One kilometer (½ mile) beyond **Nea Makri** turn at a partially obscured sign for **Zoumberi** and follow the road approximately 1 kilometer (⅔ mile) until it ends at the beach. On the right is **To Delphini** (the Dolphin, tel. 96645), a pleasant taverna in neat rustic style, with a fireplace for the winter dining room and a large terrace on the beach. Best of all, a peculiar flat rock formation at the edge of the beach forms miniature tidal basins, where even the smallest children can splash safely while parents are served fresh fish and a glass of wine. Prices are moderate and the service warm and friendly.

7 Just north of Nea Makri, you pass Mt. Agiliki on the left and enter the fabled plain of **Marathon.** Here, in 490 BC, a numerically superior Persian force was soundly defeated by Athenian hoplites aided by their Plataian allies. Some 6,400 invaders were killed fleeing to their ships, while the Athenians lost just 192 warriors. This, their proudest victory, became the stuff of Athenian legends; the hero Theseus was said to have appeared himself in aid of the Greeks, along with the god Pan. Just after you enter the plain, a sign for the **Marathon Tomb** directs you to the right, to the ancient mound built over the graves of the

Athenian dead. Return to the main road, and continue for another 1½ kilometers (1 mile) to a fork, where the left branch leads to the **Museum of Marathon,** in the village of Vrana. At the entrance to the village, another large tumulus, excavated in 1969–70, is thought to mark the **Tomb of the Plataians.** The museum contains objects from excavations in the area, including those of the mound of the Athenians. *Marathon Tomb and Museum, tel. 0294–55155. Admission: 400 dr. Open Tues.– Sun. 8:30–3.*

Although it is a push to include Rhamnous in this same tour, owing to the 3 PM closing of many archaeological sites, it is most easily reached from Marathon. You might consider spending the night in this area (*see* Dining and Lodging, *below*). Continue north on the main road 1 kilometer (½ mile) beyond the Vranas turnoff. Just before the modern town of Marathon, in view of the starting point of the modern Marathon run (*see* Sports and Outdoor Activities, *below*), a road branches right, leading to ⑧ the **Rhamnous archaeological site,** 16 kilometers (10 miles) farther along, at the end of the road. *Tel. 0294–63477. Admission: 400 dr. Open daily except Mon. 8:30–3.*

An isolated, romantic place, Rhamnous occupies a small promontory over the sea. From at least the Archaic period, Rhamnous was known for the worship of Nemesis, the great leveler, who brings down the proud and punishes the arrogant. Excavated over many years, the site preserves traces of temples from the 6th and 5th centuries BC. The later temple (perhaps by the same architect who built the Temple of Poseidon at Sounion and of Hephaistos in Athens) housed the cult statue of Nemesis, envisioned as a woman and carved by Agorakritos, the famous Athenian pupil of Pheidias. This work is of extraordinary interest because it is the only cult statue (even fragmentary) we have left from the High Classical period. Exploration and excavation have turned up many fragments, including the head, which was shipped off to the British Museum in the years before the establishment of the modern Greek state. The pleasure of wandering over this usually serene, and always evocative, site is greatly enhanced by discovering the little coves at its edge, where, time permitting, you can take a swim.

On the way back to Athens via the Marathon road, 3 kilometers (2 miles) past the Rafina turnoff, a road branches right to the ⑨ village and **Monastery of Daou Pendeli,** another 5 kilometers (3 miles) into the hilly Attic countryside. Halfway, you pass the singularly unattractive apartment buildings that comprise Kallitechnoupolis, or Artists' Town, where some of Greece's notables in music and art have banded together in a joint building project. The road ends in the village of Daou Pendeli, which in spite of its accessibility manages to preserve the humble charm of a herders' settlement from long ago. Turn right at the crossroads, and within a few hundred feet you reach the monastery, set in a glen with water and a thick stand of enormous maple trees and Aleppo pines. A drive lined with cypresses leads to the fortresslike building, protected, peaceful, and secluded from virtually all modern construction and noise. As you enter the large garden, the fragrance of jasmine and roses rises to meet the delicate scent of the nearby pines and cypresses. To the left are the main living quarters, and at the center is the church, dating from the 17th century.

Time Out Return now to the village for dinner at **The Philosopher's,** a taverna (tel. 01/6677–263) owned by the Papakyriakos family, on your right as you face uphill (avoid its competition across the street). The taverna serves good country fare indoors and outdoors year-round at lunch and dinner. The food has hardly changed in anyone's memory: rabbit stew, goat soup, chicken on the grill, fried cheese, grilled lamb chops by the kilo, and the good, lightly resinated house wines.

Returning to the main road back to Athens, you continue through the village of **Pikermi,** the site of a great fossil find in the last century. These fossils from the neo-Tertiary period, now in Athens University's natural history museum, show the existence in Greece of saber-toothed tigers, mammoths, miniature horses, and a dinotherium (a huge proto-elephant with down-turned tusks). After Pikermi, the main road continues through the market town of Pallini and returns to Athens through Ayia Paraskevi.

Tour 3: Pendeli, Amphiareion, and Parnis

A circuit that can been done in one long day, this tour takes you to the Sanctuary of Amphiareos via Pendeli, returning via Parnis. From Athens follow Kifissia Boulevard north, passing through the fashionable suburbs of Psihico and Maroussi to **Kifissia,** about 14½ kilometers (9 miles) from Athens itself on the southwest side of Pendeli. In ancient times, Kifissia provided a cool, leafy refuge from the summer heat of the city. Today it is still one of the most desirable addresses in this part of Attica. The **Goulandris Natural History Museum** (13 Levidou, tel. 01/808–6405; admission: 200 dr.; open daily except Fri. 9–2:30) gives an excellent introduction to the flora and fauna of Greece.

From Kifissia, a secondary road leads southeast to the large and lavishly endowed **Monastery of Pendeli,** established in 1578 on the southern slopes of the mountain. Little is left of the original architecture, but there are some 17th-century paintings in the chapel. **Pendeli** was extensively exploited in antiquity, as now, for marble, prized for its whiteness and fine grain by Athenian architects and artists of the 5th century BC and later. Unfortunately, modern mining operations have made terrible scars on this southern slope, visible from almost everywhere you go on the plain of Athens.

If you retrace your steps to the main road north out of Kifissia, you continue through suburbs of elaborate apartment houses and expansive villas. North of Ekali, a road on the right leads to the village of Dionysos, where 2 kilometers (1 mile) farther, a turnoff on the left leads to the romantic, overgrown ruins of the **Sanctuary of Dionysos,** which was excavated by a team from the American School of Classical Studies in the late 19th century.

Returning to the main road, you continue northeast, parallel to the National Road on your left (resist joining it). In the distance on your right, you can discern **Lake Marathon,** a man-made reservoir formed by the Marathon Dam, constructed by an American company in 1925–31. The dam and its small park are about 9 kilometers (5½ miles) down a side road from the village of Ayios Stefanos. Walk or drive across the dam for a picnic in the cool park.

Approximately 10 kilometers (6 miles) north of Ayios Stefanos the road diverges from the National Road and begins the gentle climb to **Kapandriti**, a fast-developing country village with a wonderful restaurant.

Time Out

At the top end of Kapandriti's tiny square is the simplest of inexpensive village tavernas, known by its owner's name, **Nikos Skintzos** (tel. 0295–528290). There's a pot-bellied stove and a large open grill, from which wonderfully tasty and delicate baby goat (kid) chops are served on sheets of butcher paper. The potatoes are truly home-fried, and the lightly resinated local wine is an essential part of the meal.

From Kapandriti continue north toward Kalamos, about 8 kilometers (5 miles) beyond, where a road veers left toward the **Amphiareion.** Cradled in a hidden valley at a bend in the road, the Sanctuary of Amphiareos is a quiet, well-watered haven, blessed with green bushes and trees. It is startlingly different from the surrounding countryside, where overgrazing and development have destroyed most of the trees. Amphiareos was a mortal transformed after death into a healing divinity. In the sanctuary are the remains of a 4th-century-BC Doric temple, the long stoa, the **Enkimiterion** (literally, "dormitory"), where patients stayed awaiting their cure, and a miniature theater. There is also a small museum containing finds from early excavations. *Tel. 0295-62144. Admission: 400 dr. Open daily 8:30–3. (At press time, however, the museum was closed for renovation, but was scheduled to reopen in 1993.)*

Continue to the crossroads approximately 3 kilometers (2 miles) beyond, turn left and drive south to the National Road, which leads back to Athens. On the drive back take a detour to **Mt. Parnis**. Watch for exit signs for **Tatoi** and **Varybobi**, which will connect you to a long and winding road leading to the tiny resort of Ayia Trias. On the right is the Grand Hotel Mont Parnes, which contains one of Greece's only casinos. From the parking area and the hotel itself there's a splendid view of the plain of Athens cradled by Pendeli and Hymettos. Once the heavily wooded habitat of wolves and bears, Parnis provided fuel for the charcoal burners of Archanes in the days before oil. The rugged heights of the Parnis massif, often snow-clad in winter, make a natural barrier dividing Attica and the lands claimed by Athens from Boeotia in central greece.

Time Out

If you're ready for dinner by now, try **Leonidas** (tel. 01/801–0000), near the entrance to the former royal estates at Tatoi. This longtime favorite of Athenians serves traditional Attic grilled meat, indoors and outdoors, at moderate prices. The restaurant is crowded on weekends.

Tour 4: Phyle, Eleusis, Daphni

This itinerary follows the old road from Athens over the southern shoulder of Parnis to Eleusis, with a stop at the fortress of Phyle on the way, returning via the Monastery at Daphni. Cross the National Road at Peristeri and head north for Ano Liosia, beyond which the road leads through a narrow pass. Suddenly Athens disappears and the country town of **Phyle** improbably takes its place. Evidence of its source of wealth—livestock—is everywhere, in the dozens of whole lambs, pigs, and goats strung up in front of butcher shops; in the numerous tavernas lining the main street; in the many window displays of fresh sheep yogurt. Continue through town and in approximately 2 kilometers (1 mile) you come to the turnoff for **Moni Kleiston,** a tiny monastery perched over a steep, densely wooded gully. Dating mainly from the 17th century, the neatly maintained monastery, home still to a handful of nuns, was partially renovated in the recent past. Some of the tiny 14th-century chapel, rebuilt in the 17th, is carved out of a cave. Across a gully, another cave, on a perilously steep slope above the rushing waters of the gorge, is full of votives placed there by nimble worshipers.

From the monastery the road loops back and around the flank of Parnis, climbing slowly through rugged, deserted country all the more spectacular and evocative for its proximity to the teeming Attic plain and the industrial expanse of Eleusis. In antiquity, this was the most direct route to the Boeotian city of Thebes. The Athenians built several fortresses along the way, including the fine example whose walls still stand 7 kilometers (4 miles) beyond Moni Kleiston, on a high bluff just west of the road. The **Fortress of Phyle** was built in the 4th century BC of rugged polygonal masonry, much of which still stands or lies on the site, a stony cliff that falls off abruptly into a steep ravine, explored by an occasional sheep or goat.

Time Out   If you visit the fortress on a weekend, be sure to lunch at **To Frourio** (the Fort, tel. 01/241–1172, open weekends) several hundred feet beyond the turnoff to the ruins. You can dine inexpensively indoors next to a fireplace on cold days, or outdoors on a terrace, on lamb, potatoes, and salad in an unforgettable setting. *Note:* when it snows on Parnis, the road up here may be closed, so call before setting out.

Take a deep breath of fresh air here and enjoy your last glimpse of unsullied nature, for on the next leg of the tour we descend through Athens's rather messy backyard. From the town of Phyle head west to **Eleusis,** through the **Aspropyrgos** (white tower) wasteland of abandoned cars and city dump, which is the shortest route. As the road leaves the foothills of Parnis, it enters the fabled **Thriaisian Plain,** whose fertile soil, watered by mountain streams coursing down from Parnis and the mountains to the northwest, fed the ancient city of Athens.

The modern city of Athens, once it had exhausted the land along the Kifissos River in its own plain, co-opted the land around **Eleusis,** placing shipyards in the pristine gulf and steel mills and petrochemical plants along its shores. It is hard to imagine that once there stretched in every direction fields of corn and barley sacred to the goddess Demeter, whose sanctuary now lies in the heart of the new town. The legend of Demeter and her daughter Persephone (also called Kore) explained for the ancients both the cause of the seasons and the origins of agriculture.

It was to Eleusis that Demeter traveled in search of Persephone after the girl had been kidnapped by Hades, god of the underworld. Zeus himself interceded to restore her to the distraught Demeter, but succeeded only partially, giving mother and daughter just half a year together. Nevertheless, in gratitude to

King Keleos of Eleusis, who had given her refuge in her time of need, Demeter presented his son Triptolemos with wheat seeds, the knowledge of agriculture, and a winged chariot so he could spread them to mankind. Keleos built a megaron (large hall) in her honor, the first Eleusinian sanctuary.

The worship of Demeter took the form of mysterious rites, the nature of which were never to be revealed to any but the initiates. Both the Lesser and the Greater Eleusinian rituals closely linked Athens with the sanctuary. The Lesser mysteries, preliminary initiation ceremonies, took place in Athens, and the procession for the Greater Eleusinia began and ended there, following the route of the Sacred Way. The sanctuary lies on the east slope and at the foot of the acropolis, which is hardly visible amid the modern buildings of Eleusis. Much of what we see now in the sanctuary is of Roman construction or repair, although physical remains on the site date back to the Mycenaean period. The modern entrance to the site follows the old Sacred Way to the **Great Propylaea** (Gates), which closely resembled the Athenian Acropolis's Propylaea. The modern path continues on to the **Precinct of Demeter,** which in antiquity was strictly off limits on pain of death to any but the initiated. The **Telesterion,** or Temple of Demeter, now a vast open space surrounded by battered tiers of seats, was a roofed hall which could accommodate 3,000 people. At its center was the innermost sanctuary, the Anaktoron, forbidden to all but the priests. The **museum,** just beyond the Telesterion, contains an array of pottery and sculpture, particularly of the Roman period. *Tel. 01/554–6019. Admission: 400 dr. Open Tues.–Sun. 8:30–3.*

The main road back to Athens leads along the coast, past oil refineries and across the Aspropyrgos shoreline. On the left are a pond and salt marsh known in antiquity as the Rheitoi streams, where the Eleusinian priests had what were in essence fish farms. These streams, the borderline between Eleusis and Athens, were crossed by a narrow landbridge in ancient times. At the far end of the modern causeway, a road to the right leads in approximately 8 kilometers (5 miles) to **Perama,** where ferries every half hour will take you to the island of **Salamis.** In the **Straits of Salamis,** lying between Perama and the island, the desperate and wily Athenians aided by Sparta, Corinth, and Aegina, trapped and destroyed the Persian fleet. After their defeat at Marathon in 490 BC, the Persians had returned to exact revenge in 480 BC, attacking and burning the Acropolis. The Athenians, told to protect themselves with "wooden walls," interpreted this to mean their ships. Evacuating their women and children to Troezen, opposite Poros (*see Tour 5, below*), they drew up their wooden boats and, by a ruse, were able to draw the Persians into a trap. So sure were the Persians of a devastating victory that Xerxes the king had set up a fine silver throne on the hill of **Aigaleo** overlooking the strait, to watch his troops thrash the Greeks. He witnessed instead a disaster that, even more than Marathon, put a definitive end to Persian ambitions in the western Aegean.

Return the way you came, and turn right on the main road to Athens, which takes you first to the **Monastery of Daphni.** Established probably in the 6th century, the Orthodox Christian church and monastery buildings were rebuilt in the late 11th century, only to be sacked in 1205 by a different set of Christians, the Crusaders. For years in the hands of the Roman Catholic order of Cistercians, the monastery was not reoccupied by Orthodox monks until the 16th century. After a turn as barracks and then as a lunatic asylum in the 19th century, the monastery and, in particular, the church were restored extensively in several phases. The miraculously preserved mosaics are among the finest extant from the golden age of Byzantine art: powerful portraits of figures from the Old and New Testaments, images of Christ and his mother, and in the golden dome, a stern Pantokrator, "ruler of all." The monastery's name means "laurel tree," sacred to Apollo, which reminds us that once his sanctuary occupied this site. It was destroyed in AD 395 after the anti-pagan edicts of the Emperor Theodosius. *Tel. 01/581–1558. Admission: 500 dr. Open daily 8:30–3.*

The main road leads back into Athens along a route almost parallel to that of the Sacred Way, approximately 1 kilometer (½ mile) to the south.

Tour 5: The Saronic Islands

Although you can visit the islands in one day on an organized tour, it is far more rewarding to spend two to three days exploring them. This can be done without a car because of the frequent ferry and bus service, not to mention taxis. In spite of their accessibility, they have managed to retain a flavor and color uniquely their own.

Aegina, the closest to Piraeus, roughly 30 kilometers (19 miles) offshore, has become an inexpensive resort area primarily for Athenians. The boats and hydrofoils dock at the main town, also called Aegina, a busy little harbor city on the western side of the island, where a few surviving Neoclassical buildings mingle with a modern cement and cinder-block sprawl. Its seaside location and some fine town gardens make Aegina an attractive place. This side of the island is more fertile and less mountainous than the east side; its gardens and fields are blessed with grapes, olives, figs, almonds, and above all, the treasured pistachio trees. The eastern side is rugged and sparsely inhabited, except for a major tourist development at the harbor of **Ayia Marina** below the **Temple of Aphaia.**

Settled since prehistoric times, Aegina emerged from the Greek "Dark Ages" and rose to preeminence in the Aegean as a prosperous maritime center, well positioned on the trade routes. The Aeginetans were first among the peoples of Greece to mint their own coins (often of fine silver, stamped on one face with the image of a turtle), which for generations were common tender throughout the Greek world. They created a standardized system of weights and measures, and Aegina became a major trader in grain, wine, oil, and slaves during Greece's Archaic period, her ships plying from the Black Sea to the coast of Egypt.

Much of the ancient city lies under the modern, with public buildings and sanctuaries built on the promontory just north of the modern town. Still visible on this hill (known as Kolonna, or "column") is a single column of a late Archaic Temple of Apollo. By the 6th century BC, Aegina, the commercial entrepôt, had become a major art center, known in particular for bronze foundries, worked by such sculptors as Kallon, Onatas, and Anaxagoras.

This powerful island, lying so close off the coast of Attica, could not fail to come into conflict with Athens. Even though the Aeginetans had fought on the side of the Greek fleet and Athens in the decisive battle of Salamis, as Athens's imperial ambitions grew, Aegina became a thorn in its side. In 458 BC Athens laid siege to the city, eventually conquering the island, and in 431 BC, Athens actually exiled the entire population. The citizens were allowed to return some years later, but the island's power and significance were broken. In the 19th century, it experienced a remarkable rebirth when its location, its fertility, and its easily defensible island position made it an important base in the Greek War of Independence from Turkey. It was briefly the capital of the new Greek state, from 1827 until 1829, when the capital was transferred to Nafplion.

② As you approach from the sea, your first view of the town of **Aegina** takes in the sweep of the harbor, punctuated by the tiny white Chapel of **Ayios Nikolaos.** The numerous cafés and restaurants lining the harbor face a road along the water teeming with horse-and-carriage traffic, trucks, and taxis. Take a stroll around town before heading to the eastern shore.

The main road to Ayia Marina and the Temple of Aphaia begins near the **Archaeological Museum,** which is housed in a building of the early 19th century. Next door is the **cathedral,** dating to 1806, and farther along the same road, you pass Aegina's **prison,** in a 19th-century building designed as an orphanage. The road continues east, through gardens of pistachio, almond, and olive trees. At 6 kilometers (4 miles) from town, you pass the **Monastery of Ayios Nektarios,** the island's patron saint (canonized in 1961; his relics lie in this and more than a dozen other churches throughout Greece). On the rocky barren hill above the monastery are the sprawling remains of the medieval **Palaiochora** ("old town"), built in the 9th century by islanders whose seaside town was the constant prey of pirates. Palaiochora still has over 30 churches in various stages of decay, some still in use, amid the rubble of its houses and streets.

㉓ At 12 kilometers (7 miles) from Aegina, the road ends at the **Sanctuary of Aphaia,** situated on a promontory with superb views of Athens and Piraeus across the water. This site has been occupied by many sanctuaries to Aphaia; the ruins visible today are those of the temple built in the early 5th century BC. Aphaia was apparently a prehellenic deity, whose worship eventually converged with that of Athena. The temple, one of the finest extant examples of Archaic architecture, was adorned with an exquisite group of pedimental sculptures that are now in the Munich Glyptothek.

㉔ A paved road and a path wind down to the small port of **Ayia Marina,** which has many hotels, cafés, and restaurants as well as a beach.

㉕ The island of **Poros,** the next leg of the tour, lies due south of Aegina, separated from the Peloponnese by a narrow strait less than 450 yards across at its narrowest. The town itself, draped over the promontory guarding the strait, has a long attractive waterfront skirting the base of the hill. Its history is closely connected with Troezen, on the mainland, opposite. Poros (or Kalauria in antiquity) was the site of an important Sanctuary of Poseidon, whose scrappy remains can be seen at the approximate center of the island. It was at the sanctuary that the Athenian orator and politician Demosthenes committed suicide in 323 BC. Many of the blocks from the 6th-century-BC temple were carried off to build the monastery on nearby Hydra during the 18th century.

26 To reach the ancient town of **Troezen,** you cross to Galatas on the mainland in one of the numerous little boats or ferries that regularly run back and forth. From Galatas, a bus takes you the 9 kilometers (6 miles) through delightful countryside to the town of **Dhamala,** lying over part of the ancient city, of which there is little left but crumbling walls entwined with olive trees. Troezen, supposedly the birthplace of Theseus, first king of Athens, provided refuge for Athenians who fled from the Persians just before the battle of Salamis (*see* Tour 4, *above*).

27 Returning to Poros, you can continue on to **Hydra** by hydrofoil or ferry. As you clear the narrow straits of Poros and head south, you will see on your left the 18th-century monastery of **Zoodochos Pighi** (Life-giving Spring), situated on a pine-clad hillside just east of the town of Poros.

As the ferry leaves Poros behind, it rounds the tip of the mainland, and before you stretches the full length of Hydra, mountainous and barren, the town itself invisible at first. As you travel along the island, the town of Hydra gradually reveals itself, with gray and white houses climbing steep slopes surrounding a nearly round harbor. There is little doubt that the town's prosperity in the late-18th and early 19th centuries was largely owing to its easily defensible position, which allowed its merchant fleet to flourish unthreatened. The modern town looks much as it did from 1821 to 1826, when Hydra was a leader in the Greek struggle for independence.

Although there are traces of ancient settlement, the island was sparsely inhabited until the Ottoman period. In the 16th century, its rugged slopes offered a haven for refugees from the Peloponnese during the constant wars between the Ottomans and the Venetians. The settlers turned to the sea and began building boats, and by the early 18th century, their trade routes stretched from the mainland to Asia Minor and Constantinople. By its end, the fleet, profiting by the Napoleonic Wars, had captured much of the lucrative grain trade between the Ukraine and western Europe, earning great fortunes and much notoriety in blockade-running. After the Greek Revolution, Hydra sank into relative obscurity until well past the middle of this century, when it was discovered by outsiders; its noble port and houses have since been rescued and placed on the Council of Europe's list of protected monuments. The town has now passed strict ordinances regulating construction and renovation, and all motor traffic is banned from the island (except for a lone garbage truck).

Most of Hydra's houses and public buildings were constructed between 1770 and 1821. Many of the houses consist of a rectangular basic unit two to three stories tall, with the upper floor set back to create a terrace on the roof of the lower level, and most have courtyards with large subterranean cisterns, which are essential on this dry island. (People claim that the cisterns were also used to hide gold and treasure in the 18th and 19th centuries, and that eels were introduced to keep the water clean and drinkable.) In the early 19th century, the tremendous surge in disposable wealth enabled shipowners to build the characteristic *archontika* ("great houses"), massive gray stone mansions facing the harbor, with forbidding, fortresslike exteriors. Good examples include the **Tsamados House,** now the Merchant Marine Academy, on the harbor opposite the ferry landing; the **Tombazi House,** now the School of Fine Arts, halfway up the west side of the harbor; the **Voulgaris (Merikles-Oikonomou) House,** on the west harbor; and the **Koundouriotes House,** looming on the west headland over the harbor. Along the central section of the harbor is the **Monastery of the Panaghia,** built in the late 18th century partly of stone taken from the Sanctuary of Poseidon on Poros. The monastery's bell tower is a fine example of the early 19th-century marble-carving done by a guild of traveling artisans (perhaps from the island of Tinos) who left their mark all over the Aegean in this period.

In the years leading up to the revolution, Hydra's great rival and ally was the island of **Spetses.** Lying at the entrance to the Argolic Gulf, just off the mainland, Spetses was known even in antiquity for its hospitable soil and verdant, pine-clad slopes. Now the pine trees are far fewer, but the island is still well watered, and the many prosperous Athenians who have made Spetses their second home compete in making beautiful gardens and terraces. The island shows sporadic evidence of continuous habitation through all of antiquity. From the 16th century, settlers came over from the mainland, and as on Hydra, they soon began to look to the sea, building their own boats. They became master sailors, successful merchants, and later, in the Napoleonic wars, skilled blockade runners, earning fortunes that they poured into bigger boats and bigger houses. With the outbreak of the War of Independence in 1821, the Spetsiotes dedicated their best ships and brave men (and women) to the cause. Bravest of all was Laskarina Bouboulina, daughter of an Hydriot sea captain, and the wife, then widow, of two more sea captains. Left with a considerable inheritance and nine children, she dedicated herself to increasing her already substantial fleet and fortune. On her flagship, the *Agamemnon*, the largest in the Greek fleet, she sailed into war against the Ottomans at the head of the Spetsiote ships. Shortly thereafter she met her end, but not in war. She was shot by the outraged relative of a girl with whom her son had just eloped.

To explore the town, begin at the **Dapia,** the jetty overlooking the modern harbor. Fortified with cannons dating to the War of Independence, it overlooks an attractive waterfront, full of outdoor cafés and restaurants with front-row seats on the harbor activity. The harbormaster's offices, to the right as you face the sea, occupy what was the chancellery at the time of the revolution, a building designed in the simple two-story, center-hall architecture typical of the period and this place. Just behind the Dapia is Bouboulina's house (not open to the public). Following a diagonal road from the Dapia almost due south into the town itself, you come to the **museum,** in a fine late-18th-century *archontiko* built in a style that could be termed Turko-Venetian. The museum preserves many articles of artistic, historic, and folkloric interest from the period of Spetses' greatness. Bouboulina's casket rests here in a room festooned with the island's revolutionary flag.

Return to the waterfront and walk southeast toward the Old Harbor, past a promontory with the little 19th-century **Church of Ayios Mamas** and the headland bearing the **Monastery of Ayios Nikolaos,** now the episcopal seat. Its lacy white marble bell tower recalls that of Hydra's port monastery. The road continues past many fine 19th-century houses to the Old Harbor itself, dominated by the gray stone mansion of the Botassis family, one of the earliest to settle on Spetses. Northwest from Dapia, in the opposite direction, you pass the newly renovated **Posidonion Hotel.** Opened in 1914, it was the scene of a glittering social life in the era between the two world wars. You then come to several well-built mid-19th century houses, testimony to a solid prosperity even after the revolution. Continuing west, you pass near another of Bouboulina's houses, where she was shot in 1825. After passing the Spetses Hotel, you reach the **Anargyrios School,** established as an English-style boarding school for the children of Greece's anglophilic upper class; it is known as the inspiration for the school in John Fowles's *The Magus.*

Back in town, you may wish to walk up to **Kastelli,** the original settlement of Spetses, of which little remains but four churches: the **Panaghia** or *Koimisis tis Theotokou* (the Assumption of the Virgin Mary), from the 17th century; **Ayios Vassilis** (Saint Basil); the **Taxiarchoi** (Archangels), early 19th century; and **Ayia Triada** (Holy Trinity), late 18th century. The churches are kept locked, but ask for the property owner or the guardian, who has a key.

Tour 6: The Monasteries of Hymettos

The itinerary of this easy, short tour takes you to the slopes of **Hymettos,** the eastern "wall" of Athens, which yields up the sun each morning and catches its last purple shadows at night. Denuded of its pine forests, mainly in the terrible years of deprivation during World War II, the mountain has been partially reforested by Friends of the Trees, Greece's first private-initiative environmental association. Leaving Athens by Alexander Boulevard, head east through the neighborhood of Kaisariani, settled by refugees from the disastrous Turkish-Greek War of 1922 (and also an incubator for Greece's communist and left-wing political movements). In 5½ kilometers (3 miles), the road reaches the **Monastery of Kaisariani,** cradled in a glen of pine, cypress, and plane trees fed by a copious flow of water. A temple of Aphrodite stood on the hill just above the present-day monastery, which dates to the 11th century. The buildings surround a central court, including, besides the church, a refectory, mill, and bakery, all restored in 1956–57. Most of the frescoes are from the 17th and 18th centuries. Follow the road beyond the monastery for another 3½ kilometers (2 miles) to the **Moni Asteriou,** also dating to the 11th century. At this point, you can park your car along the road and walk down to the chapel of **Ayios Ioannis Theologou,** a pleasant 1½-kilometer (1-mile) detour that gives you a view of Athens, which stretches west toward the Aigaleo hills and Parnis. It also lets you sniff at close hand the tiny aromatic shrubs—above all sage, which once fed the bees of Hymettos, giving that special taste to its famous honey. Now there are few bees here, and few beekeepers. If you continue up the mountain to the end of the public road, from here, too, there is a splendid view of the Athenian basin. The summit (which is off limits) was the site of an altar to Zeus.

Tour 7: Delphi

Delphi, one of the most important sanctuaries of ancient Greece, lies 189 kilometers (117½ miles) northwest of Athens. The preferred route to Delphi follows the National Road to the Thebes turnoff, at 74 kilometers (46 miles). Take the secondary road south past Thebes and continue west through the fertile plain, now planted with cotton, to the busy agricultural and commercial center of Levadia, capital of the nome of Boeotia.

Time Out Many people break their trip here in the central square, which fairly floats on the odor of sizzling souvlaki. It is served on slim wood skewers and wrapped in butcher paper for carry-out.

In antiquity, Levadia was the site of the oracle of Trophonios, which was influential in the later Greek and Roman periods. All that remains of the sanctuary, on Mt. Ayios Ilias west of town, are scrappy traces, mainly in the form of blocks built into later constructions. The city flourished during the Ottoman period, and at the time of the Greek War of Independence its strategic position made it the second most important city on the mainland.

Beyond Levadia the road climbs gradually, twisting through shallow valleys and foothills. After 21 kilometers (13 miles), bear left just before Schiste to the town of Dhistomo, where you turn east; in another 8 kilometers (5 miles) you come to **31** **Hosios Loukas,** set on a prominent rise in the midst of a sparsely inhabited, fertile valley. This important monastic complex is still inhabited by a few monks. Named for a local Luke, not the Evangelist, the monastery was founded by the emperor Romanos II in 961. The Katholikon dates from the early 11th century and can be compared to the Church at Daphni (*see* Tour 4, *above*) in the beauty of its architecture and quality of the mosaics in the narthex and in portions of the domed nave. The tomb of Hosios Loukas is set in the crypt, which is covered by lively and colorful 11th-century frescoes.

From Dhistomo an alternate, less-traveled route to Itea and Delphi climbs over the plain of Desfina and descends sharply to the sea just east of Itea. This route is slightly longer but more pleasant and lets you stop in Itea for a seaside lunch. The conventional route ignores Dhistomo and continues west past the Schiste turnoff, climbing ever higher as it nears Parnassos. At 157 kilometers (97 miles) from Athens, you reach the village of **32** **Arachova,** whose gray-stone houses with red-tile roofs cling to the steep slopes. Parnassos, the highest mountain range in Greece after Olympos, has since 1980 been developed for skiing and is now transformed into a winter resort, which may have spoiled its pristine calm but has brought new life and money. The sophisticated newcomers (mostly Athenians) have preserved and restored many otherwise doomed houses. Arachova's main street is lined with shops selling rugs and weavings; the town was known even in pre-ski days as a place to shop for handicrafts, honey, and wine. Now it has several good tavernas and cozy hotels.

The road from Arachova descends slightly as it winds toward **Delphi.** To the left the ground drops sharply to the narrow valley of the Pleistos River, obscured by vineyards and olive trees, and on the right rise the stony cliffs of Parnassos. After nearly 10 kilometers (6 miles) the road skirts one last outcropping and brings you to great twin cliffs, the **Phaedriades** (the Bright Ones), which glow with reflected light, particularly in late afternoon. These form the eastern gate, so to speak, of Delphi, whose ancient ruins lie cradled in a theatrical curve between the Phaedriades and Mt. Ayios Ilias to the west. Below Delphi the valley of the Pleistos opens into the plain of Krisa (named for a powerful 7th-century-BC city) and the modern town of Chrissa, close to the floor of the plain. A sea of olive trees flows almost unbroken from the Pleistos valley to the edge of Itea, on the shore of the Gulf of Corinth.

Home to Apollo and to the most famous oracle of antiquity, Delphi is one of the most evocative and enchanting sites in Greece. Its history reaches back at least as far as the Mycenaean period, and in Homer's *Iliad* it is referred to as Pytho. At first the settlement probably was sacred to a female deity; toward the end of the Greek Dark Ages (ca. 1100 BC–800 BC), the site incorporated the cult of Apollo. According to Plutarch, who was a priest of Apollo at Delphi, the oracle was discovered by chance, when a shepherd noticed that his flock went into a frenzy when it came near a certain chasm in the rock. When he approached, he also came under a spell and began to utter prophecies, as did his fellow villagers. They chose from among their number a woman to sit over the chasm on a three-footed stool and to prophesy.

Traditionally, the Pythia was a woman over 50, who, upon her anointment, gave up normal life and lived thereafter in seclusion. On oracle day, the seventh of the month, the Pythia prepared by washing in the Castalian Spring and undergoing a purification involving barley smoke and laurel leaves. If the male priests of Apollo determined the day was propitious for prophecy, she entered the Temple of Apollo to sit on the tripod, presumably by that time in a trance. Questions presented to her received strange and garbled answers, which were then translated into verse by the priests. Those citizens who wished to consult the oracle took their place in a line that might form days in advance, and after an animal sacrifice each questioner was admitted to the Adyton. A number of the lead tablets on which questions were inscribed have been uncovered, but the official answers were inscribed only in the memories of questioners and priests. Those that have survived, from various sources, suggest the equivocal nature of these sibylline emanations: Perhaps the most famous is the answer given to King Croesus of Lydia, who asked if he should attack the Persians. "Croesus, having crossed the Halys River, will destroy a great realm," said the Pythia. Thus encouraged, he crossed it, only to find his *own* empire destroyed.

From its earliest years, Delphi was the center of the Amphictyonic League, made up of 12 tribes, including Athens and Sparta. During the 8th and 7th centuries BC, the oracle's advice played a significant role in the colonization of southern Italy and Sicily (Magna Graecia), and as the league grew in stature and significance so did the potential for conflict over its control. In the early 6th century BC, members of the league embarked

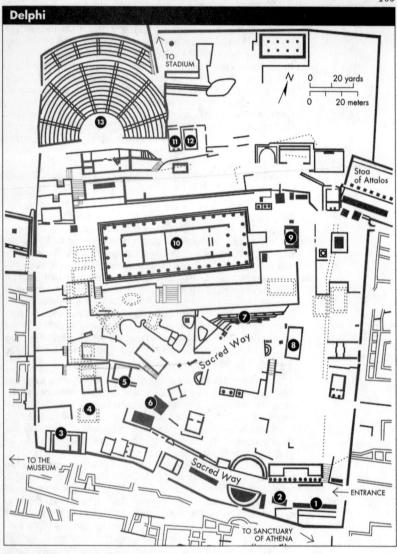

Delphi

TO STADIUM

Stoa of Attalos

0 20 yards
0 20 meters

Sacred Way

TO THE MUSEUM

Sacred Way

ENTRANCE

TO SANCTUARY OF ATHENA

Spartan Monument, **1**
Base of Marathon Monument, **2**
Theban Treasury, **3**
Treasury of the Boeotians, **4**
Treasury of the Athenians, **5**
Syracusan Treasury, **6**
Stoa of the Athenians, **7**
Treasury of Corinth, **8**
Altar of Apollo, **9**
Temple of Apollo, **10**
Dyonisian Shrine, **11**
Dyonisian Shrine, **12**
Theater, **13**

on the First Sacred War, against the town of Krisa. The town was leveled, and the plain, declared sacred to Apollo, was left uncultivated.

Beginning in 582 BC the Pythian Games became a quadrennial festival similar to that held at Olympia. Increasingly an international center, Delphi attracted supplicants from beyond the Greek mainland, including such valued clients as King Midas of Phrygia and King Croesus of Lydia, both wealthy kingdoms of Asia Minor. During this period of prosperity many cities built treasure houses at Delphi. The sanctuary was threatened during the Persian War but never attacked, and it continued to prosper, in spite of the fact that Athens and Sparta, two of its most powerful patrons, were locked in war. In 373 BC an earthquake damaged the site and destroyed the temple. Delphi came under the influence first of Macedonia and then of the Aetolian League (290 BC–190 BC) before yielding to the Romans in 189 BC. Although the Roman general Sulla plundered Delphi in 86 BC, there were at least 500 bronze statues left to be collected by Nero in AD 66, and the site was still full of fine works of art when Pausanias visited and described it a century later. The emperor Hadrian restored many of the cities and sanctuaries of Greece, but within a century or two the oracle was silent. The town survived, but by the 7th century, after the barbarian invasions, it had become a small village known as Kastri. Probably little changed until the late 19th century, when French excavators began to uncover the site of Apollo.

Begin your tour at the **Sanctuary of Athena,** just below the Arachova road before you reach the Phaedriades. The most notable among the numerous remains on the terrace is the **Tholos,** or Round Building, a graceful 4th-century-BC ruin of Pentelic marble, whose purpose and dedication are unknown. Return to the road, and walk beneath the Phaedriades. In the cleft between the rocks a path leads to the **Castalian Fountain,** a spring where visitors bathed to purify themselves before approaching the sanctuary.

Just beyond the spring, on the main road, is the modern entrance to the sanctuary. Passing through a square surrounded by late-Roman porticoes, the path leads through the main gate onto the Sacred Way. On its way up the hill the Way passes between building foundations and bases for votive dedications, stripped now of ornament and statue, mere scraps of what was one of the richest collections of art and treasure in antiquity. Thanks to the 2nd-century-AD writings of Pausanias, archaeologists have identified treasuries built by the Thebans, the Corinthians, the Syracusans, and others, a roster of 6th- and 5th-century BC powers. Just after the first bend in the road, on the left, stands the Treasury of the Athenians, built with money from the victory over the Persians at Marathon. As you approach the Temple of Apollo, on your left are the remains of the **Stoa of the Athenians,** which housed, among other objects, an immense cable with which the Persian king Xerxes roped together a pontoon bridge for his army to cross the Hellespont from Asia to Europe.

The **Temple of Apollo** visible today (there were six successive temples built on the site) is that of the 4th century BC. Although ancient sources speak of a chasm within, there is no trace of that opening in the earth from which emanated trance-inducing vapors. Above the temple is the well-preserved **Theater** (which seated 5,000); it was begun in the 3rd century BC, completed in about 160 BC, and later restored by the Romans. The view from the theater is worth the climb, as is that from the **Stadium,** still farther up the mountain, at the highest point of the ancient town. Built and restored in various periods and cut partially from the living rock, the stadium underwent a final transformation under Herodes Atticus, the Athenian benefactor of the 2nd century AD. It lies cradled in a grove of pine trees, a quiet refuge removed from the sanctuary below and backed by the sheer, majestic rise of the mountain. *Sanctuaries of Apollo and Athena Pronaia, tel. 0265/82313. Admission: 1,000 dr. Open weekdays 8–6, weekends and holidays 8:30–3.*

Retrace your steps through the sanctuary, exit, and walk along the Arachova road toward modern Delphi. Almost immediately you reach the **Delphi Museum,** which contains a wonderful collection of art and architectural sculpture principally from the Sanctuaries of Apollo and Athena Pronoia. Among the masterpieces are the twin statues of Kleobis and Biton, stylized representations of young brothers who were given the gift of eternal sleep by Hera and of whom it was said, "those whom the gods love die young." Dating to the first half of the 6th century BC, these statues are related to the series of *kouroi* (stylized statues of young men) in the National Museum in Athens. There are fragments of a silver bull of the 6th century BC, the largest example we have from antiquity of a statue in precious metal. In the same room are the remarkable remains of a seated male figure executed in the chryselephantine technique, which used gold (*chrys*) and ivory (*elephantine*). The museum's chief masterpiece is the famous bronze *Charioteer,* a delicate, diminutive work, whose size is surprising if you are seeing it for the first time. Created in about 470 BC to commemorate the victory of a Syracusan prince in the chariot races, the statue is one of the few ancient bronzes to survive pillage and war. Its strength and quality remind us of what we have lost. *Tel. 0265/82313. Admission: 1,000 dr. Open Mon. 11–6, Tues.–Fri. 8–6, weekends and holidays 8:30–3.*

The road west from Delphi winds down into the Sacred Plain, passing the modern village of Chryssa and leading through olive groves to the seaside port of **Itea.** Follow the road west from Itea around the gulf to a small promontory and the harbor town of **Galaxidi,** which retains traces of classical masonry. Galaxidi enjoyed its heyday in the 19th century, thanks to shipbuilding and a thriving mercantile economy. After the invention of steamships, the town faded until its recent discovery by outsiders, who appreciated the sea captains' fine houses and the evocative atmosphere. Now a historical monument, Galaxidi is undergoing renovation and restoration. If you are a shore person rather than a mountain person, Galaxidi is a good alternative to Delphi as a base for exploration of the area. It's rewarding to stroll the narrow streets, there are places to swim nearby, and you'll find several tavernas on the harbor (where the food doesn't always live up to the environment).

Time Out   For an evening drink, try the **Omilo** (Yacht Club), at the entrance to the main harbor. The few chairs and tables on a little beach make a simple setting, and one of the best bartenders in town provides exceptional service. The view is unforgettable, especially at sunset: The Gulf of Itea stretches before you and the peaks of Parnassos tower in the background, with the little gray houses of Delphi clustered on its slopes. You can swim off the beach here, and midnight dips are encouraged.

What to See and Do with Children

The **Koutouki cave** above the village of Paiania (*see* Tour 1), discovered in 1926, is just the right depth and darkness to awe young children into silence without frightening them. High on the eastern slopes of Hymettos, connected to the village by a good paved road, the cave has been rigged out with paths, lights, and sound. *Tel. 01/664–2910. Admission: adults 300 dr., students 150 dr. (children often free). Open year-round (call ahead for hours).*

A **cruise through the Saronic islands** (*see* Tour 5). The ships of **Cycladic Cruises** (tel. 01/822–9468, 01/883–2111, or 01/883–2112) usually depart from Piraeus about 8:30 AM and touch in at Poros, Hydra, and Aegina before returning about 8 PM. The tours can include pick-up at your hotel in Athens, a visit to the Temple of Aphaia at Aegina, a beach stop (although some boats have pools), and meals. It is best to book through a travel agency.

A day on the beach at **Zoumberi** (*see* Tour 2).

Kifissia's **Goulandris Natural History Museum** (*see* Tour 3).

Swimming in the shallow water at **Itea** (*see* Tour 7).

Shopping

Just about every town sells tourist trinkets, but surprisingly these are usually cheaper in the **Monastiraki** district of Athens (*see* Shopping in Chapter 3). Pottery is a specialty of **Maroussi,** where many pottery shops line the road to Kifissia (*see* Tour 3, *above*). In **Spetses** and in **Hydra,** a number of elegant shops (some of them offshoots of Athens stores) sell fashionable and amusing clothing and jewelry, though you won't save anything by shopping here. In **Arachova,** the modern mass-produced bedspreads and kilim-style carpets sold today are colorful and reasonably priced. If you poke into dark corners in the stores, you still might turn up something made of local wool, though anything that claims to be antique brings a higher price. Here you'll also find delicious Parnassos honey, a local mild sheep cheese called *formaella,* and *chilopites,* or "thousand pies," thin homemade noodles cut into thousands of tiny squares, often served with chicken and lamb.

Sports and Outdoor Activities

Participant Sports

Golf   The **Glyfada Golf Course and Club,** at the east end of Athens International Airport, has many distinguished politicians, businessmen, and members of the diplomatic community on its roster. It is open to travelers. *Tel. 01/894–6820 or 01/894–6834.*

Hiking   The summit of Parnassos (8,061 feet) is now easily accessible, thanks to roads opened up for the ski areas. The less hardy can drive to within 45 minutes of the summit. You can also drive to the Hellenic Alpine Club's refuge at 6,201 feet to spend the night and then walk to the summit in time to catch the sunrise—the only way to climb Parnassos! For information on the refuge, contact the **Greek Skiing and Alpine Federation** in Athens (7 Karageorgi Servias, tel. 01/323–4555). For guides in Arachova and detailed maps, contact the **Greek Touring Club** (12 Polytechniou, Athens, tel. 01/524–8600 or 01/524–8601) or the **Federation of Excursion Clubs** (4 Dragatsaniou, Athens, tel. 01/323–4107).

Horseback Riding   Riding is a popular sport in Athens, and a number of clubs are located in Attica. At the **Gerakas Riding Club** (Aghia Paraskevi, tel. 01/661–1088), one of the oldest, there are few trails left because of the spread of the suburbs. You are mostly confined to the ring. The **Hellenic Riding Club** in the inner suburb of Maroussi (18 Paradissou, tel. 01/681–2506) is also confined mainly to the rings. The **Tatoi Riding Club** has some fine trails in the area around the former royal summer estate in Tatoi. (Varybobi, tel. 01/801–4513 or 01/808–3008).

Running   Every year in October the **Athens Open International Marathon** is run over the same course taken in 490 BC by Pheidippides, when he carried to Athens the news of victory over the Persians. The 42.2-kilometer race, open to men and women of all ages, starts in Marathon and finishes at the Olympic Stadium in Athens. There is no entry fee. To apply, write to SEGAS, Race Organizers, 137 Sygrou Ave., 17121 Athens; tel. 01/935–9302, telex 219844.

Sailing, Scuba Diving, and Windsurfing   Many yacht brokers charter boats and organize underwater "safaris," scuba tours, and "flotilla" cruises around the islands in small rented sailboats. Try **Ghiolman Yachts & Travel** (7 Fillelinon, tel. 01/323–3696, 01/323–0330, or 01/322–8530), **Valef Yachts** (22 Akti Themistokleous, tel. 01/452–9571 or 01/452–9486), **Vernicos Yachts** (4 Marina, Glyfada, tel. 01/894–6981), or **Nereus Yachting** (2 Afendouli, tel. 01/452–4842), among others, and shop around. Most of the large seaside resort hotels rent windsurfing equipment and arrange lessons, usually for guests only. For further information, contact the **Greek Windsurfing Association** (7 Fillelinon, tel. 01/323–3696 or 01/323–0068).

Skiing   If you hear that the snow is good on Parnassos, go for it. Ski with the gods and the muses, just 40 minutes from Arachova, at **Kelaria** and **Fterolakas** ski centers, which have 12 lifts including a gondola. Kelaria has more challenging runs; Fterolaka better restaurants and beginners' slopes. Rental equipment is available there and in Arachova. Contact the **Greek Skiing and Alpine Federation** (*see above*).

Tennis   The large resort hotels have tennis courts, which are sometimes open to the public, and there are public courts on the shore opposite the airport in Voula, on Leoforos Posidoniou.

Beaches

Attica's eastern coast is mainly rock, with some short sandy stretches, as in **Glyfada, Vouliagmeni,** and **Voula,** that have been made public beaches. These have full facilities for a day in the sun, but the water is not very clean. The coves at **Rhamnous** are delightful (*see* Tour 2, *above*), but beware of sea urchins when swimming off the rocks. Aegina's beaches near town are pleasant enough, though crowded; Hydra has only a small one at the little harbor called **Miramare; Spetses's** (*see* Tour 5, *above*) best beaches are on the south side of the island, in **Ayioi Anargyroi** and **Ayia Paraskevi.**

Dining and Lodging

Dining The cuisine of Attica resembles that in Athens, central Greece, and the Peloponnese. Local ingredients predominate, with fresh fish perhaps the greatest (if expensive) delicacy. Since much of Attica used to support herds of sheep and the omnivorous goat, the meat of both animals is also a staple in many country tavernas. It is becoming increasingly difficult, particularly in areas close to Athens, to find the traditional Greek taverna with large stewpots full of today's hot meal, or big *tapsis* (casseroles) of eggplant moussaka or *pastitsio*. Always ask to see the *kouzina* (kitchen), to look at the day's precooked dishes, or even to get a glimpse inside the pots. Informal dress is appropriate at all but the very fanciest of restaurants, and unless noted, reservations are not necessary.

Highly recommended restaurants are indicated by a star ★.

Category	Cost*
Very Expensive	over 8,000 dr.
Expensive	6,000 dr.–8,000 dr.
Moderate	2,000 dr.–6,000 dr.
Inexpensive	under 2,000 dr.

*per person for 3-course meal, including VAT and 10% service (most Greeks add 5%–10% of bill in addition to that)

Lodging Many of the hotels in Attica are resorts catering to Greek families, from which the father (and/or mother) can commute to the city. Many have been built recently of reinforced concrete slabs, with spindly metal balconies and diverse arrays of facilities, but the decor, which varies little from one to the next, tends to be a modern "Greek island" look: simple pine furnishings, tile floors, and, at most, a colorful bedspread. Be forewarned: Some of the large hotels ask you to take half board, particularly in high season. If you know your plans ahead of time, you should book through a travel agent, who can negotiate a good price and eliminate the half-board requirement, if you wish. Delphi and Arachova, which have had recent minibooms in hotel construction, have a number of appealing small hotels, with fresh and cheerful rooms and public spaces, but elsewhere, picturesque, cozy family-owned country inns and pensions are rare. Note also that many hotels close in late fall and reopen usually around Easter week, except in Delphi and Arachova, which are open all year.

Highly recommended lodgings are indicated by a star ★.

Category	Cost*
Very Expensive	over 20,000 dr.
Expensive	15,000 dr.–20,000 dr.
Moderate	10,000 dr.–15,000 dr.
Inexpensive	5,000 dr.–10,000 dr.

*All prices are for standard double room for 2, excluding taxes
and breakfast.*

Aegina, Ayia
Marina
Lodging

Apollo. This hotel has a good location on the beach, at the foot of
the Temple of Aphaia. The former fishing hamlet is now completely given over to tourism, but the view of the temple as you
paddle out from the Apollo's beach is unforgettable. The satisfactory service here outweighs the hotel's plain rooms and
baths. *Ayia Marina beach, 18010, tel. 0297/32281 or 0297/32271
through 0297/32274. 107 rooms with bath. Facilities: restaurant, bar, pool, water sports. AE, MC, V. Moderate.*

Aegina Town
Dining and Lodging

Aegina Maris. This hotel and bungalow complex, 8 kilometers
(5 miles) from town, is a self-contained resort convenient for
families. The rooms have the standard island decor. *Perdica
Beach, 18010, tel. 0297/251300, 0297/251301, 0297/251302, or
0297/61341. 164 rooms with bath. Facilities: restaurant, bar,
discothèque, pool, tennis court, water sports. DC. Moderate.*
Moondy Bay Hotel. This hotel 6 kilometers (4 miles) outside Aegina sits next to a pleasant beach. One of the older of the "modern" hotels (built in 1967), it has simple, comfortable rooms and
a relaxing setting. *Moondy Bay Beach, 18010, tel. 0297/25147,
027/61146, or 027/61147; in Athens, 01/360–3745 or 01/360–
3746. 78 rooms with bath. Facilities: restaurant, taverna, bar.
No credit cards. Moderate.*

Lodging

Eginitiko Archontiko Traditional Settlement. This jewel of a
pension is in a restored 19th-century mansion of Neoclassical
inspiration. The owner has lavished attention on every detail of
public rooms and private, preserving the original painted walls
and ceilings and furnishing every nook and cranny in period
style. Its in-town location, next to the first Parliament building, is very convenient. *Ayiou Nicolaou and 1 Thomaidou,
18010, tel. 0297/24156 or 0297/24968. 10 rooms. No credit cards.
Moderate.*

Arachova
Dining

Taverna P. Thasargiris (Barba Yannis). For many years this
busy taverna, the first in Arachova, was run by Barba Yannis
(Uncle John), who has handed on the management to his son.
Summer or winter, it is always full, which can cause occasional
surliness in the staff, but the food is good. As befits a mountain
town that once counted its wealth by the size of its flocks, it
serves standard meat dishes and, above all, lamb. For starters,
try the fried *formaella*, a bland sheep's milk cheese. Greek patrons tout the *splinendera* (politely translated as "innards"), a
tasty mix of various sheep organs. Also highly recommended is
kokkoretsi, intestine stuffed with more chopped innards; and
mayeritsa soup, absolutely delicious, and full of the same. Try
Barba Yannis' own wine, a light, non-acidic *kokkineli* (rosé),
which cuts right through the cholesterol. *56 Delphi Rd., 32004,
tel. 0267/31291. No credit cards. Inexpensive.*

Lodging

Arachova Inn. Most of this newly built inn's small, efficient,
blue-and-white guest rooms have a view of the lower town and

valley. They have rustic wood furnishings, and the sitting rooms and dining area are decorated with touches of local handicrafts. In winter the dining room is warmed by a large fireplace. *Delphi Rd., 32004, tel. 0267/31353, 0267/31497, or 0267/32195; fax 0267/31134. 42 rooms with bath. Facilities: restaurant, bar, parking. MC, V. Moderate.*

★ **Hotel Anemolia.** At this hotel on a bluff above the Delphi road at the western edge of Arachova, almost all the guest rooms have a view of the plain of Amphissa; on a clear day you may be able to see as far as the Peloponnese. The cozy, recently renovated hotel has pleasant rustic furnishings in its guest rooms, country antiques in the public rooms, and a large fireplace in the lobby. The covered swimming pool (the only one in Arachova) is usable year-round. *Delphi Rd., 32004, tel. 0267/31640 through 0267/31644. 52 rooms with bath. Facilities: restaurant, bar, pool, sauna, exercise room. AE, DC, MC. Moderate.*

Apollo Inn. This inn makes up for its claustrophobic location in the center of town with neat pine-furnished rooms, pretty bedspreads, and lovely terraces. *106 Delphi Rd., 32004, tel. 0267/31057 or 0267/31073. 19 rooms with bath. Facilities: breakfast room. MC, V. Inexpensive.*

Parnassos. This little family-run hotel offers a rock-bottom solution to the housing problem and is comfortable for the price. The bedrooms in the old family home are of various sizes (most are large), have high ceilings, and are neatly if plainly furnished. *Delphi Rd., 32004, tel. 0267/31307. 7 rooms share 4 baths. Facilities: breakfast room. No credit cards. Inexpensive.*

Delphi Dining

Iniohos Restaurant. With its turn-of-the-century touches the Iniohos offers Delphi's most elegant dining. The large dining room has the requisite fine view, and there's an enormous veranda for outdoor dining. The restaurant offers good seafood in season, as well as home-made *dolmadaki* (stuffed vine leaves), *saganaki* (a dish of fried cheese), and wine-stewed rooster. Try the house wine, a light rosé. Evening meals are accompanied by a piano and guitar duo. *Vassilisseos Pavlou and Frederiki. AE, DC, MC, V. Moderate.*

Lodging

★ **Apollo Hotel.** Owned and operated by a husband-and-wife team ("She's the decorator, I do the public relations," says he), this hotel is new and delightful. The cheerful rooms have light-wood furniture set off by blue quilts and striped curtains. Many have wood balconies with black-iron railings. The wife has added hair dryers (a rare amenity in Greece) and pretty tiles in the bathrooms. The *saloni* (living room) displays traditional wall hangings and carefully selected furnishings. *598 Vassileos Pavlou and Friderikis, 33054, tel. 0265/82580 or 0265/822442. 17 rooms with bath. Facilities: breakfast room. MC, V. Moderate.*

Hotel Castalia. The Castalia and its sister, **Hotel Fedriades,** are owned and operated by the Maniati family. Both have been recently rebuilt in the traditional style that has taken over Delphi and injected an element of charm into streets that for a time looked doomed to anonymous cement-block modernism. The Castalia's rooms are decorated with touches of red, those at the Fedriades with brown. The views from some of the rooms and from the public rooms are spectacular. *Vasileos Pavlou and Friderkikis 13, 33054, tel. 0265/82205, 0265/82206, or 0265/82207. fax 0265/82208. 26 rooms with bath. Facilities: restaurant. AE, DC, MC, V. Moderate.*

Hotel Delphi-Panorama. Living up to its name, the Panorama has a splendid view from its perch on the highest road in town, looking out to the mountains of the Peloponnese. The spotless, cheerful rooms and living area make up for the nondescript furnishings. *Ados Hosios Loukas and Ionos, 33054, tel. 0265/ 82437 or 0265/82061. 20 rooms with bath. Facilities: breakfast room. MC, V. Moderate.*

Pension Delfini. The rooms are truly tiny in this basic accommodation with the most modest amenities. But the warmth of the owners, who have run this pension in their home for years, provides a singular experience. The street is noisy, however, and the rooms are not equally pleasant, so carefully check what is available before moving in. *4 Dimo Frangou, 33054, tel. 0265/ 82202. 13 rooms with bath. No credit cards. Inexpensive.*

Galaxidi
Dining

To Derveni. The tiny main port of Galaxidi is lined with restaurants, bars, and cafés, but perhaps the best food in town can be found a few blocks inland, at To Derveni. The restaurant has a big covered garden for outdoor dining and serves a range of excellent standard taverna fare. The service is good and the staff pleasant. *Gourgouris St. next to OTE. No credit cards. Closed Dec.–Mar. Moderate.*

Lodging

Hotel Galaxidi. The newly opened Galaxidi lies just two blocks from the busy port. Although the building is entirely modern, it has taken its style, outside and in, from the traditional Galaxidi captains' houses. The rooms are small but bright, and they open onto balconies with views of narrow streets lined with typical Galaxidi houses. *11 Sigrou Ave., 33052, tel. 0265/ 41850 or 0265/41851. 18 rooms with bath. Facilities: breakfast room. V. Moderate.*

Pension Ganimede. One of the few truly comfortable bed-and-breakfasts in all of Greece, the Ganimede has recently been remodeled, and owner-manager Bruno Perocco has taken full advantage of the elegant spaces provided by a typical 19th-century Galaxidi mansion. Best of all is having breakfast in the shade of the lushly planted garden, accompanied by Bruno's gentle multilingual humor. Book ahead in high season; the few rooms go fast. *Gourgouris St. opposite OTE, 33052, tel. 0265/ 41328. 6 rooms with bath. Facilities: breakfast room, garden. No credit cards. Moderate.*

Glyfada
Dining

Antonopoulos. This is one of several large, charmless, but very popular fish restaurants on the Glyfada waterfront. *Opposite Glyfada Marina, tel. 01/894–5636. No credit cards. Expensive.*

★ **Psaropoulos.** A favorite with Athenians from way back, Psaropoulos continues to dish up excellent fish in an informal, family-style setting. It is always crowded on weekends and holidays, especially at lunchtime. *Opposite Glyfada Marina, tel. 01/894–5677. No credit cards. Expensive.*

Loxandra. Known for home-style Greek cuisine, Loxandra also gives you a piano accompaniment to your meal. You will find here all the classics of Greek *mayirefta* ("cooked" as opposed to grilled) specialties, from *bourekakia* (cheese rolls in flaky pastry), to *spanikopita* (spinach pie) and *yiouvetsi loxandra* (pork on a spit with miniature macaroni). *31 Eleftherios Venizelou, Glyfada, tel. 01/963–1731. No credit cards. Moderate.*

Lodging

Palace Hotel. The Palace was recently renovated, and its rooms, baths, and public spaces are attractively contemporary in appearance. Although it is 55 yards from the sea (not swimmable here), it's just 20 minutes or so from the center of

Athens. This is a good compromise for those who want a first-class city hotel that's not quite in the city. *4 V. Georgiou, 16675, tel. 01/894–8361. 80 rooms with bath. Facilities: restaurant, bar, pool. AE, DC, V. Expensive.*

Hotel Fenix. This is a recent addition to the Best Western chain, with comfortable, recently updated rooms and facilities at a good price. It's near Athens and the airport, and the Glyfada Golf Club is practically next door. *1 Artemisiou, 16675, tel. 01/898–1255. 138 rooms with bath. Facilities: restaurant, bar, cocktail lounge, pool, air-conditioning. AE, DC, MC, V. Moderate.*

Hydra
Dining

Drousko's. This restaurant on the main street leading up from the east end of the port serves good traditional Greek home cooking: *mayirefta* as well as grilled meat. *1 block inland from e. end of port, no tel. No credit cards. Moderate.*

Dining and Lodging

Miramare Beach. This small, simple hotel could be just what you need if you are in Hydra with small children. All the rooms open directly onto the little beach, the only stretch of sand in or near the town of Hydra. The attached restaurant has expensive food that's not particularly exciting, but at least it's convenient, if you are spending the day on the beach. *Mandraki Beach, 18040, 2 km (1¼ mi) from main harbor; walk or take a taxi boat; tel. 0298/52300 or 0298/25301. 28 rooms with bath. Facilities: restaurant. AE, DC, MC. Expensive.*

Lodging

Miranda Guest House. A traditional Hydriote home was renovated to create an art gallery, in addition to artistically decorated rooms and public spaces. The location and setting just a few steps up from the port area are also commendable. *2 blocks inland from center of port, 18040, tel. 0298/52230. 14 rooms with bath. No credit cards. Expensive.*

Mistral Hotel. This recently (1988) renovated archontiko offers you cozy rooms in simple, traditional style and fine views over the town from those in front. It is small and fills up quickly in summer. *Above port, 18040, tel. 0298/52509 or 0298/53411. 18 rooms with bath. No credit cards. Expensive.*

Leto Hotel. The Leto makes up for the plainness of its rudimentary design and furnishings with its location just behind the port of Hydra and its very pleasant staff. Hydra's narrow streets can be noisy, so ask for a room on the upper floors, away from the alleys. *1 block inland from center of port, 18040, tel. 0298/52280. 31 rooms. Facilities: breakfast room. No credit cards. Moderate.*

Itea
Dining

Dolphin Restaurant. If you are near Itea around mealtime—lunch or dinner—try a seaside stop at the Dolphin, located on the waterfront at the east end of town. Itea's shorefront is land-locked and protected from wind, so even in winter, if it's a sunny day you can probably eat outdoors. The proprietor will be happy to set up a table for you on the beach. The family-owned taverna offers fresh fish at reasonable prices as well as their own lightly resinated house wine, made from grapes grown at Desfina, high on the plateau east of Itea. *E. end of port, tel. 0265/33202 or 0265/33510. No credit cards. Inexpensive.*

Lagonissi
Dining and Lodging

Xenia Lagonissi. This hotel (part of the government-owned Xenia chain), which dates to 1963, has recently undergone some renovations. A splendid location and artfully designed rooms opening into the gardens, make this big beach resort appealing if you are looking for a virtually self-contained holiday. *Lagonissi, 19013, tel. 0291/23911 or 0291/23933. 357 rooms with bath. Facilities: 2 restaurants, taverna/nightclub, bars, discothèque, pool, minigolf, tennis, cinema, shopping center, sauna, water sports. DC, MC, V. Very Expensive.*

Lavrion
Lodging

Belle Epoque Hotel. Not even the inhabitants of Lavrion know about this little in-town hotel, recently opened in a renovated Belle Epoque mansion. The outside is much better done than the inside, which now has cell-like rooms and baths, but the public areas have been lovingly decorated with the owners' collections of minerals, shells, and bric-a-brac. It is a comfortable alternative to some of the high-priced resort hotels in the area. *23 Pleionai, 19500, tel. 0292/27130, 0292/26564, or 0292/26059. 28 rooms with bath. Facilities: breakfast room. No credit cards. Inexpensive.*

Marathon
Dining and Lodging

Golden Coast Hotel and Bungalows. Located right on the beach, the Golden Coast has the kind of simple, functional rooms and facilities that are perfect for families. Although the beach is narrow and rocky—as on most of this coast—children have a choice of two pools, and the adults can go in a third. The restaurant's food is unusually good. *Marathon Beach, 19007, tel. 0292/92102 or 0292/92920. 242 rooms with bath, 254 bungalows, 45 apartments. Facilities: 2 restaurants, 4 bars, taverna, discothèque, pools, minigolf, tennis, water sports. AE, DC, MC, V. Expensive.*

Sounion
Dining and Lodging

Cape Sounion Beach. The rooms at this self-contained complex, designed as individual little bungalows, are tastefully fitted out with solid furniture and attractive Greek island colors. All open into a garden setting, and face southeast toward the Temple of Poseidon. The hotel has its own fine little sand beach on a cove that would be idyllic, except for the nearby road. *Leoforos Posidonion, 19500, tel. 0292/39391 through 0292/39394; in Athens, 01/861-7837 or 01/865-5516. 188 rooms. Facilities: 2 restaurants, cafeteria, taverna, 3 bars, discothèque, pool, tennis, gym, private beach, water sports. Expensive.*

Egeon Hotel. This hotel has seen much better days and is in dire need of renovation, but nothing can beat its location on *the* beach below the Temple of Poseidon, on the very harbor where ancient ships once anchored. Even the rooms in back, which look up the slopes flanking the acropolis, have a good view, but the ones in front are better. Be warned: the beach will be crowded in high season, the heat may not work in the winter, and environmentalists and archaeologists object to its location. *Sounion Beach, 19500, tel. 0292/39200 or 0292/39234. 45 rooms with bath. Facilities: restaurant, bar. No credit cards. Expensive.*

★ **Hotel Posidonion.** This glorious fin-de-siècle waterfront hotel has views across Spetses harbor to the mainland opposite. The public rooms with their belle époque furnishings have recently been renovated floor to ceiling; they have the grace of an earlier age and an air of grandeur unusual in Greece. The guest rooms are furnished more modestly than the public rooms, although those at the front have wonderful views and tall windows. *Dappia waterfront, 19500, tel. 0298/72006, fax 0298/72208. 55 rooms with bath. Facilities: breakfast room, bar-lounge. AE, DC, MC, V. Expensive.*

Surf Beach Club. This self-contained family resort, another alternative to the Cape Sounion Beach, also has its own beach.

The rooms and bungalows are comfortably and efficiently arranged in a fresh, spare, island style, and the activities are varied. *Sounion Beach, tel. 0292/25778, 0292/22363, or 0292/22364; in Athens, 01/323–7640. 236 rooms with bath, 156 bungalows. Facilities: restaurant, taverna, 2 bars, discothèque, pools, water sports, tennis, volleyball, basketball. AE, DC, MC. Moderate.*

Spetses
Dining and Lodging

Kastelli Hotel. This ordinary hotel, with rooms and baths of standard shape and decor, derives its appeal from the location right on the beach and proximity to the town of Spetses. *Spetses Beach, 18050, tel. 0298/72311, 0298/72312, 0298/72313, or 0298/72161. 79 rooms with bath. Facilities: restaurant, bar, tennis, water sports. AE, DC. Expensive.*

Spetses Hotel. Because this self-contained resort is close to Spetses you can also enjoy the urban life of this delightful town. The rooms and baths were renovated in 1988 and are comfortably fitted. All of them have a sea view. *Spetses Town Beach, 18050, tel. 0298/72602, 0298/72603, or 0298/72604. 77 rooms with bath. Facilities: restaurant, 2 bars, private beach, water sports. AE, DC. Expensive.*

Vouliagmeni
Dining

Moorings. Perched above Vouliagmeni's elegant little marina, this international-style restaurant is equally elegant. The food is European, the piano accompaniment tasteful, and the menu is highlighted by lobster flambé. *Marina Vouliagmeni, tel. 01/896–1310 or 01/896–1113. AE, DC, MC, V. Expensive.*

Lodging

Astir Palace Hotel. The grand old lady of Greek hotels (built in 1967), has housed many of Greece's rich and powerful, not to mention some international stars, and its name was synonymous with resort heaven. The complex, occupying a large portion of the wooded peninsula of Vouliagmeni, offers an ocean-liner-size main building, with rooms in modern international-hotel style, and a few dozen bungalows, seasonal tenancy of which is something of a local status symbol. *Vouliagmeni Beach, 16671, tel. 01/896–0211 or 01/896–0219. 422 rooms with bath, 77 bungalows. Facilities: restaurant, bar, pool, private beach, tennis, water sports. AE, DC, MC, V. Very Expensive.*

Armonia. Most guest rooms in the Armonia have sea views and private terraces, and all are done in impeccable Greek island style. The hotel was built in 1986 on the beach, but whether the water is swimmable depends on pollution levels in the Saronic Gulf. In any case, there are pools for adults and children. *1 Armonias, 16671, tel. 01/896–0030, 01/896–0105, 01/896–2656, or 01/896–3184. 105 rooms with bath, 25 suites. Facilities: restaurant, bars, pool, children's pool. AE, DC. Expensive.*

Margi House. A slightly less expensive alternative in this very expensive resort suburb is the Margi, which was just renovated. The guest rooms and baths are comfortably, if plainly, furnished in "Greek modern," and the pool is adequate if you decide not to walk the 110 yards to the beach. *11 Letous, 16671, tel. 01/896–0812 or 01/896–2061 through 01/896–2065. 110 rooms with bath, 10 suites. Facilities: restaurant, bar, discothèque, pool. AE, DC, V. Moderate.*

The Arts and Nightlife

The Arts

During the summer, the Pendeli Festival offers evening performances in the courtyard of the Duchess de Plaisance's home in Kifissia. Built in 19th-century Gothic style by the architect Kleanthes for this eccentric lady, it belonged for a time to the former Greek royal family. For information on the festival, contact the Greek National Tourism Organization in Athens.

Nightlife

Perhaps it is the daytime heat through so many months of the year, perhaps it is an excess of energy, perhaps it is their intense sociability, unrequited during the work day, but whatever the reason, Greeks love going out at night. Traffic can be as bad at 3 AM as in the morning rush hour. Greeks also like to combine food with their entertainment and there are many ways to do it. Some emphasize the show over the cuisine, others do the opposite, and they range from the simplest taverna with a bouzouki trio to fancy nightclubs with elaborate floor shows.

The **Nea Deilina,** for example, has top Greek entertainers and dinner, for an evening that may seem expensive, until you consider that the performers begin warming up around 9 PM and finish well after midnight (Glyfada, tel. 01/894–1300, reservations required). Other well-known nightspots include the **Neraida** (Vassiliou Georghiou 2, Kalamaki, tel. 01/981–2004), **Posidonio** (18 Posidonios, Hellenikon, tel. 01/894–1033 or 01/894–1035), and **Show Center** (5 Posidonios, Ayios Kosmas, tel. 01/894–5723). All are very expensive and all require reservations. Among less expensive restaurants with less-established (but often surprisingly good) performers, try **Apofili** (15th km. National Rd., Kifissia, tel. 01/807–6720); **Embati** (Varybobi Circle, tel. 01/807–5598 or 01/807–1468); and **Laleousa** (16th km. National Rd., Kifissia, tel. 01/807–5336). You'll need reservations on weekends. Of the music restaurants, another notch down in price and usually with just one or two performers, try **Alt Berlin** (35 Kolokotroni, Kefalari, tel. 01/801–5792) for a Greek-German trip into nostalgia; **Voukouresti-Gypsy Violins** (1 Penteli, Kefalari, tel. 01/808–0338); **La Gondola** (52 Ayiou Konstantinou, Maroussi, tel. 01/689–6730), **El Greco** (20 I. Metaxa, Glyfada, tel. 01/894–3165 or 01/894–3011), and the elegant **La Belle Epoque** (Hotel Pentelikon, 66 Deliyianni, Kefalari, tel. 01/801–9223 or 01/808–0311). All these range from moderately expensive to expensive; reserve on weekends.

For dancing, the discos at most large resort hotels are usually open to outsiders as well as guests. **Oui** has a retro music disco, a retro disco plus restaurant, and a jazz and soul music club (disco alone at 33 Vassileos Georghiou, Glyfada, tel. 01/894–1456; disco restaurant and jazz at 81 Vassileos Georghiou, Glyfada, tel. 01/894–9585 or 01/894–1456), reserve on weekends; expensive. In the northern suburbs, try the **Agora Herodium** (12 Kifissias, Maroussi, tel. 01/684–6139) or **Vogue**

(25 Eleftherotrias, Politeia, tel. 01/808–1794). Of the islands, Hydra and Spetses offer the most sophisticated bars and discos. In Hydra, there is **Lagoudera,** on the port; **Cavos,** high above the east side of the port; and the boisterous **Sirocco,** halfway between the town and the hamlet of Kaminia. Spetses offers the **Twins Disco** in Ayia Marina, the **Karnayo** in the Old Harbor, and the **Delphinia.**

5 Corfu

By Daniel Gorney

Daniel Gorney, a
former New
Yorker, has lived
and worked in
Athens for 20
years.

Corfu (Kerkyra), the northernmost of the seven major Ionian Islands, lies in the Ionian Sea off the west coast of Greece near the Albanian border. The other Ionian Islands, spreading southward, include Paxi, Lefkada, Ithaka, Kefallonia, Zakynthos, and Kythera, which stands alone off the southeast tip of the Peloponnese. The Ionians' proximity to Italy and Europe and their sheltered position on the East–West trade routes made them prosperous; both their wealth and strategic position assured them a lively history of conquest and counter-conquest. The classical remains have suffered from this history and also from earthquakes; architecture from the centuries of Frankish and Venetian rule is most evident, leaving the islands with a strong Italian flavor.

On the island of Corfu, Corcyra, a mistress of Poseidon, bore a son named Phaex, the first of the Phaeacians, who inhabited the island. According to Homer, at the time of the Trojan War, when Odysseus, King of Ithaca, was shipwrecked on his long voyage home, he came ashore on Corfu and was befriended by the Princess Nausicaa (daughter of Alcinous, king of the Phaeacians), who was playing ball with her maidens near Ermones.

In Classical times, Corinth colonized the northern islands, but Corfu, growing powerful, revolted and allied itself with Athens, a fateful move that triggered the Peloponnesian War. There followed a period of subjection to the tyrants of Syracuse, the kings of Epirus and of Macedonia, and in the 2nd century, Roman rule.

After the Byzantine Empire broke up, the islands fended for themselves against sporadic Germanic and Saracen invasions, and from the 11th to the 14th century were ruled by Norman and Angevin kings. Then came the Venetians, who protected Corfu from Turkish occupation and provided a period of peace for the flowering of arts and letters. Venice also made Italian the official language. Napoleon took the islands after the fall of Venice, lost them briefly to a Russo-Turkish fleet (though Corfu was never occupied by the Turks), and for a short time a Greek-run republic was formed, which whetted local appetites for the independence that was to come later in the 19th century.

In 1814 the islands came under British protection. Corfu was ruled by a series of Lord High Commissioners, beginning with the much hated Sir Thomas Maitland, and then by Sir Frederick Adam, who married a Corfiote lady with a heavy mustache. Nationalism finally prevailed, and the islands were ceded to Greece in 1864.

The climate of the Ionian islands is rainier (in fall and winter) than that of the rest of Greece, which makes them green and gives them well defined seasons. Corfu's wildflowers are spectacular. It is a delectable island, perhaps the most beautiful in Greece—Homer's "well-watered gardens"—moderated by westerly winds, scored with fertile valleys, and punctuated by enormous, ancient, gnarled olive trees. Figs, oranges, lemons, grapes, and corn are otherwise the chief produce. The mild climate keeps visitors coming from May through November: about 1.2 million each year. Corfu has been a resort of the storm-tossed British from time immemorial, and it is the most developed of the Ionians, with a population of about 100,000.

The lovely Italianate town of Corfu is one of its chief draws, and its greenness must have made the English feel at home.

The down side of the picture is that tourism has dramatically affected the local population, who, extremely poor for centuries, now live very well on what they earn in the tourist season. The odor of greed wafts in the breeze, mixed with the scents of jasmine and sea salt. Some of the merchants have forgotten that tourists can be customers who return to one's shop over and over, and noticing that many visitors shop and eat at a different place each day, try to squeeze as much money as possible out of each one. Certainly this is not true everywhere, but it must be mentioned. Be aware that at the most scenic spots, the rents, and therefore the prices, are the highest. Note, also, that considerably reduced prices are widespread in the two months that precede and follow the June–August high season.

Essential Information

Important Addresses and Numbers

Tourist Information The **Greek National Tourist Office** on Corfu is at Kapodistriou 1, tel. 0661/37520, 0661/37638, or 0661/37639, fax 0661/30298.

Tourist Police: Kapodistriou 1, tel. 0661/30265

Emergencies **Police:** Alexandros Avenue 19, tel. 100

Medical: The hospital is on Polychronioukostanda Street, tel. 0661/45811 through 0661/45815; the Polyclinik is just outside town on the road to Palaeokastritsa, tel. 0661/22946.

Arriving and Departing by Plane

Olympic Airways has three flights a day from Athens that land at Corfu's airport, a few miles south of Corfu town. Fare: 11,300 dr. each way.

Arriving and Departing by Boat, Bus, and Car

By Boat Passenger ships stop at Corfu twice a week, April–October. **Minoan Lines** (Akti Posidonos 28, Piraeus, tel. 01/411–8211 through 01/411–8216, fax 01/411–8631) runs the *Festos*, which connects Corfu with Ancona, Igoumenitsa, Heraklion, and Piraeus. The *Ariadne* connects Corfu with Kusadasi (Turkey), Samos, Paros, Kephallonia, and Ancona.

Ferries from Igoumenitsa on the mainland leave every hour in summer and every two hours off-season, landing in Corfu town (two hours) and in Lefkimi, at the southern tip of Corfu (45 minutes).

By Bus **KTEL Corfu** buses (tel. 0661/39985 or 0661/37186) leave Athens (tel. 01/512–9443) daily at 8 AM (twice daily in summer), arriving in Corfu at 6 PM, via Patras and the ferry from Igoumenitsa. The fare is approximately 5,500 dr. each way.

By Car The best route from Athens is the national road via Corinth to the Rion/Antirion ferry, then to Igoumenitsa (472 kilometers/ 274 miles), where you take the ferry to Corfu. In winter, severe weather conditions often close the straits at Rion/Antirion, and the ferries from Igoumenitsa can also stop running. Call the **Touring Club of Greece** (ELPA, tel. 104) for information.

Getting Around

By Motorbike and Car The gentle climate and rolling hills make Corfu ideal motorbike country, but you must drive very slowly until you feel comfortable, and be extremely cautious. There is little system to Greek driving, and "Depend on the other guy's brakes" best expounds the basic philosophy of the road—this is very different from defensive driving at home. The road surfaces deteriorate as the tourist season progresses, and potholes abound. Helmets are rarely provided, and then only on request. Check the lights, brakes, and other mechanics before you accept a machine. Be warned and be careful.

A 50cc motorbike can be rented for 2,500 dr. a day (100cc for 5,000 dr.), but you can bargain, especially if you want it for two or more days. Rentals are available in even the most remote villages. In Corfu town, try **George's Bikes** (El. Venizelou 38, tel. 0661/32727).

Car rental can be considerably more expensive, starting about 7,500 dr. a day for a Fiat 127 (100 kilometers/62 miles minimum) plus insurance, delivery, and so forth. A four-wheel-drive Jeep, with the extras, can run to 15,000 dr. a day. In Corfu town you can try **Olympus Rent-a-Car** (29 National Stadium, tel. 0661/36147) or **Suncars, Ginargirou Brothers Ltd.** (40 Alexandras Ave., tel. 0661/31565).

By Bus Bus travel on Corfu is inexpensive, and the bus network covers the island. Buses tend to run fairly close to their schedules, and you can get timetables and information at the depots of the two bus companies and at many other places, for example, in the free 16-page *What's On—Corfu*, which can be found in hotel lobbies. The depot of the **Old Port** (Spilia) bus company (tel. 0661/39985) is at the New Fort, behind the Old Port. The **San Rocco** bus company's depot (tel. 0661/31595) is at San Rocco Square.

By Taxi Radio-controlled taxis (0661/33811) are available 24 hours a day, and rates, which are set by the government, are reasonable. Many drivers speak English and they know the island in a very special way. If you want to hire a cab and driver on an hourly or daily basis, you must negotiate the fee; ask for advice at your hotel's front desk.

Guided Tours

Many agencies run a half-day tour of Old Corfu town, and tour buses go daily to all the sights on the island. Tickets and information are available at travel agencies all over town. **Vaba Travel** (Ethnikis Antistaseos [New Port], tel 0661/44455, fax 0661/22174) is a reliable agency.

Most agencies offer an evening tour to **Danilia Village** (To Horio or "the village," tel. 0661/91621, fax 0661/91485), the fairly accurate reconstruction of an entire 17th-century Corfiot settlement, located in the mountains on the road to Afra, 16 kilometers (10 miles) from Corfu town. This Corfu-style Disneyland gives an interesting picture of how people lived at that time, and the tour includes live Greek and foreign music, dancing, food, and wine. You can order a set menu with barrel wine included, choose from the à la carte menu, or just have a drink and watch the show in a relaxed, informal atmosphere.

Exploring Corfu

Corfu Town

Numbers in the margin correspond to points of interest on the Corfu Town map.

Corfu town sticks off the east coast of the island like a shoe pointing south. The toe is the ancient town, **Paleopolis,** the heel is the main part of town, and the shoe's high heel, separated from town by a deep canal, is the Old Fortress. If you arrive from Igoumenitsa or Patras, on mainland Greece, your ferry will dock at the **Old Port** on the north side of town, below the hill of the **New Fortress** (1577–1578), which was built by the Venetians and added to by the French and the British. It was a Greek naval base until 1992, when it was opened to the public. Tourists can now wander through the fascinating maze of tunnels, moats, and fortifications, which makes you wonder at the imagination of the builders. A classic British citadel stands at its heart, and there are stunning views of the town, the sea, and the countryside in all directions. The best time to come here is early morning or late afternoon, out of the noonday sun.

Follow the road east along the water, around the corner toward the Old Fortress, up through the arch of St. George, and you will come to the **Esplanade (Espiande),** the huge open parade-ground on the land side of the canal, which is central to the life of the town. It is bordered on the west by a street lined with a row of tall houses and arcades, called the **Liston** (modeled on the Rue de Rivoli), which was once the exclusive preserve of Venetian nobility: The name means "of the list," and the local population was actually forbidden to walk on the street. Now the arcades are lively with souvenir shops and cafés that spill out onto the square in the evening, when the flower beds, trees, and monuments are illuminated. Cricket matches are played on the northern half of the Esplanade, and on the southern half there's a bandstand, an Ionic **Rotunda** in honor of Sir Thomas Maitland, and a statue of Ioannou Capodistria, a Corfiot, the first president of Greece.

At the north end of the Esplanade stands the **Palace of St. Michael and St. George,** an elegant, colonnaded Regency structure built as a residence for the Lord High Commissioner and headquarters for the order of St. Michael and St. George. The State Rooms are now open to the public, and one wing contains a notable collection of Asian porcelains and bronzes, along with mosaics and icons. In 1994 an EC conference will take place on Corfu, and because the palace will be the site of many meetings, it is scheduled for renovations. The work will begin sometime during 1993. *Tel. 0661/23124. Admission 500 dr. Open Tues.–Sun 8:45–3.*

As you walk east along the central path of the Esplanade you pass the **Statue of Count Schulenburg,** the hero of the siege of 1716, the Turks' last attempt to conquer Corfu. Take the bridge across the canal onto the promontory of the **Old Fortress,** or Citadel, which now houses the Ionian University. The promon-

Corfu

Avliotes
Sidari
Kavadades
Karoussades
Roda
Pelekito
Episkepsi
Kassiopi
Mount Pantokrator ▲
Ayios Stefanos
Makrades
Ano Korakiana
Lakones
Barbati
Koulori
Paleokastritsa
Skripero
Pirgi
24
Ipsos
Nissaki
Sgombou
Dassia
Gianades
Gouvia
Kondokali
Ermones
Ptihia
Myrtiotissa ■
Pelekas
Airport ✈ ☆ Corfu
Kanoni
Kinopiastes
Perama
Pondikonissi
Sinarades
Gastouri
Achilleion ■
Pendati
Benitses
Ayios Matheos
Strongili
Korissia
Hlomos
Boukari
Argirades
Lefkimi
Perivoli
Neohori
Paleohori
Dragotina
Kavos

TO IGOUMENITSA

TO PIRAEUS

N

KEY
----- Ferry

0   6 miles
0   9 km

Corfu Town

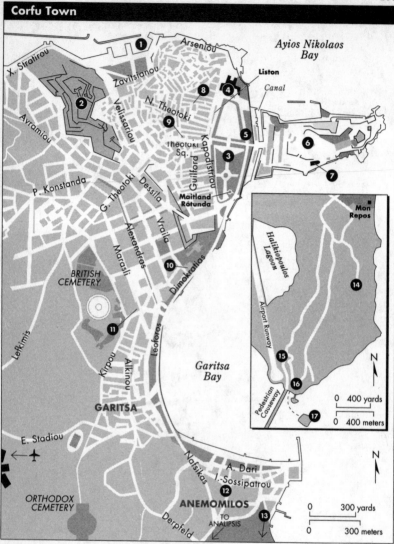

Analipsis, **14**
Archaeological
Museum, **10**
Church of Ayios Iason
and Ayios Sosipater, **12**
Church of St.
Spyridon, **8**
Esplanade, **3**
Garrison Church of St.
George, **7**
Kanoni, **16**
Mon Repos, **13**
New Fortress, **2**

Old Fortress, **6**
Old Port, **1**
Palace of St. Michael
and St. George, **4**
Pontikonisi, **17**
Statue of Count
Schulenburg, **5**
Temple of Artemis, **15**
Tomb of
Menekrates, **11**
Town Hall, **9**

tory, mentioned by Thucydides, has two heights, or *corypho*, which gave the island its Western name. Most of the fortifications were blown up by the British when they left, but it's interesting to wander through the parts that remain and to visit the

⑦ **Garrison Church of St. George** (1830), with its Doric portico. In summer there's folk dancing, and in August sound-and-light shows relate the fortress's history. The views from here, east to the Albanian coast and west over the town, are splendid.

The narrow streets that run west from the Esplanade take you into the medieval part of the city, where Venetian buildings stand cheek-by-jowl with the 19th-century ones built by the British, and where you can buy anything on earth you need. Be

⑧ sure to visit the **Church of St. Spyridon** (1596): The saint's remains—brought here after the fall of Constantinople and contained in a silver reliquary—are carried in procession several times a year to commemorate the miraculous protection this

⑨ popular patron has given the town. The 17th-century **Town Hall,** on Theotoki Square, was built as a Venetian loggia and later converted into a theater, before becoming the town hall early in this century.

Walk south of the Esplanade along Leoforos Dimokratias just past the Corfu Palace Hotel, turn inland, and you'll come to the

⑩ **Archaeological Museum,** where finds from the ongoing excavations at Palaeopolis are displayed. The most notable exhibit here is the Gorgon from the pediment of the 6th-century BC Temple of Artemis (*see below*). *Tel. 0661/30680. Admission 400 dr. Open Tues–Sun. 8:30–3.*

Continue south around Garitsa Bay, a pleasant walk, with the gardens of the Garitsa neighborhood on your right. If you turn right at the obelisk dedicated to Sir Howard Douglas, you come

⑪ to the **Tomb of Menekrates** (items from which are in the museum), part of an ancient necropolis. At the south end of the bay is the suburb of Anemomilos ("windmill"), crowned by the ruins

⑫ of the Palaeopolis church and the Byzantine **Church of Ayios Iason and Ayios Sosipater,** but no longer by a windmill. A short

⑬ distance east is the palace of **Mon Repos,** surrounded by gardens, which was built by Sir Frederic Adam for his bearded spouse. It was later the summer residence of the Lord High Commissioners, and Prince Philip, Duke of Edinburgh, was born here. Now the property of the former King Constantine of Greece, it is closed to the public.

Time Out | There are cabins and a café at the beach of Mon Repos, where it is pleasant to sit in the shade of large plane trees and have a drink.

⑭ A bit farther south, the village of **Analipsis** crowns the site of the ancient town's acropolis, and a path leads to a spring where the Venetians watered their ships. The road continues through

⑮ gardens and parks to the ruins of the Archaic **Temple of Artemis** and past the lagoon of Halikiopoulou to the tip of the peninsula,

⑯ called **Kanoni,** one of the world's most beautiful spots. A French cannon once stood in this sublimely peaceful landscape, where you see against the backdrop of the green slopes of Mount Ayia Deka a tiny islet with a white convent and beyond,

⑰ tall cypresses guarding the chapel on **Pontikonisi** (Mouse Island).

Elsewhere on the Island

The Achilleion Leave Corfu town by the southwest road and drive south, past the airport. One branch of the road climbs inland to the village of Gastouri, nestled among trees, and arrives at the **Achilleion**, 19 kilometers (12 miles) from town, a remarkable monument to bad taste, redeemed by lovely gardens stretching to the sea. This palace was built in the late 19th century by an Italian architect for the Empress Elizabeth of Austria. After Elizabeth was assassinated, Kaiser Wilhelm II bought it. He lived here full-time until the outbreak of World War I and throughout the war used it as a summer residence. After the armistice the Greek government received it as spoils of war.

The street facade is fairly inoffensive, but the interior is a preposterous hodgepodge of a pseudo-Byzantine chapel, a pseudo-Pompeian room, and a pseudo-Renaissance dining hall, culminating in a hilariously vulgar fresco of *Achilles in His Chariot*. Worse is to come on the terrace, which commands a superb view over Kanoni and the town. In what was seriously intended as an Ionic peristyle stand a bewildering number of statues, in various degrees of undress, but uniformly depressing or funny, according to your mood. One of the best is *The Wounded Achilles*, Elizabeth's favorite hero, for whom the palace was named. In 1962 it was restored and leased as a gambling casino, and the renovation carefully preserved all the historic monstrosities. The casino has now moved to the Corfu Hilton and is closed for major repairs. A museum on the ground floor contains mementoes and portraits. *Tel. 0661/56210. Admission: 400 dr. Open 8:30–7 in season, 8:30–1 off-season.*

Before returning to Corfu town, make a short detour south to the former fishing village of Benitses, now overrun with tourists and pubs, which has an interesting **Museum of Sea Shells.** *Tel. 0661/55895. Open summer, daily 10–7.*

Palaeokastritsa To reach the resort and monastery at **Palaeokastritsa,** take the **and the West Coast** road bearing northwest out of town, hugging the coast for a few miles, with the mountains of Epirus a backdrop on your right, across the waters of the narrow strait. Pass the bay at Gouvia, turn inland on Route 24, and drive through the small farms in the fertile Ropa plain. Hairpin bends take you through orange and olive groves, over the mountainous spine of the island to the rugged bays and promontories of the west coast. Where the road descends to the sea, two headlands, 130 feet high and covered with trees and boulders, form a pair of natural harbors.

Palaeokastritsa's popularity has brought hotels, tavernas, bars, and shops to the hillsides above the bays, and the beaches swarm with hordes of people on day trips from Corfu town. It is nevertheless a spectacular spot and certainly worth a visit.

On the northern headland stands the **Byzantine Monastery,** set in terraced gardens facing the Ionian Sea. Its treasure is a 12th-century icon of the Virgin Mary, and there's a small museum with some other early icons. Be sure to visit the inner courtyard (reached through the church), built on the edge of the cliff. It's dappled white and green and black by sunlight on the stonework, the vine leaves, and the habits of the hospitable monks. Under a roof of shading vines you look precipitously down to the green and placid cove and to the torn coastline stretching south.

The village of Lakones on the steep mountain behind the monastery is crowned by the grim ruins of **Angelokastro,** built in the 13th century by a despot of Epirus, during his brief rule over Corfu. The road to this spot was reputedly built by British troops in part to reach the bearded Lady Adam's favorite picnic place, the **Bella Vista terrace,** to which Kaiser Wilhelm also came to enjoy the magnificent view.

Time Out Though it may be crowded, having a drink and seeing the view at the **Bella Vista Café** is worth the wait.

South of Palaeokastritsa are the towns of **Ermones** and **Glyfada,** both with good beaches, plentiful (if expensive) fish, and resort hotels. Still farther south you come to **Pelekas,** with a famous lookout point called the **Kaiser's Throne,** a beach that's packed with busloads of bathers and sun worshippers on day trips from Corfu, and tavernas and discos galore. Pelekas is 13 kilometers (8 miles) due west of Corfu town.

Another monastery on the west coast that should be visited for its lovely site is the hermitage of the **Myrtiotissa,** an hour's walk from Pelekas (below Mt. Ayios Georgios) or a half-hour from Vathos.

North from Corfu After the turnoff for Palaeokastritsa (*see above*), the coast road continues north and northeast around the bay, through a string of highly developed towns, with beaches, hotels, restaurants, and many campsites: **Dassia, Ipsos, Pirgi,** and **Nissaki,** where the urban sprawl begins to thin out. You are now driving east around **Mt. Pantokrator,** which forms the northeast lobe of the island. At **Koulouri,** the Albanian coast is only about 1 kilometer (½ mile) away. This is the part of Corfu immortalized by Gerald Durrell in *My Family and Other Animals* and by his brother Lawrence in *Prospero's Cell;* a taverna in Kalamai called the **White House** was where the latter was written.

Kassiopi, farther north around the mountain, occupies a promontory between two bays. It was once an important town, with a shrine to Zeus that Nero visited, and later fortifications. A church with a 17th-century icon and frescoes now occupies what was probably the site of the shrine. When Kassiopi's fortress was finally destroyed by the Venetians, the town declined. But now the fishing village has discovered the tourist trade and become a busy resort. On the north coast, **Roda** and **Sidari** have good beaches and plenty of tourists, and though some spots farther west are less crowded, the roads to them are not good. At Sidari, there are unique striated cliffs that are constantly being eroded into tunnels and caves, notably the "tunnel of love," which keeps changing its location.

Sports and Outdoor Activities

Boating

Sailors can moor boats at the New Port in Corfu town, at Couvia Marina on the east coast, and at Paleokastritsa on the west coast. Boats can be rented at the Old Port in Corfu town,

at Kassiopi, at Paleokastritsa, and at Kondokali, north of town.
For information tel. 0661/25759.

Golf

A well kept 18-hole golf course (tel. 0661/94220) is open to the
public near Ermones Bay in the Ropa Valley.

Tennis

There are tennis courts in Corfu town, between I. Romanou
and Kalosgourou Streets, west of the Corfu Palace Hotel, and
in Kefalomandouko, where you can play and take lessons. Some
hotels also have courts (*see* Dining and Lodging, *below*).

Water Sports

Skin diving is possible on both west and east coasts, and
Paleokastritsa has a diving school where you can take lessons
and rent equipment. The winds on the west coast are best for
windsurfing, although the water on the east coast is calmer.
Sailboards are available, and pedal and rowboats can be rented
at many beaches.

Dining and Lodging

Dining   Restaurants all over the island cater to every taste, and prices
vary widely depending upon what is ordered, the season, and
the location. As elsewhere in Greece, the demand for fresh fish
often exceeds the supply, and it is usually priced as a luxury
item—sometimes according to the waiter's gut feeling as he
sizes up a particular tourist. Be aware that lobster and seafood
are often priced by the kilo, and injudicious ordering can easily
produce an expensive meal in a moderate restaurant. Always
ask the price before ordering a dish, even if the waiter suggested it. And remember that the same bottle of cheap wine
can cost from 2,000 drachmas on up through the roof.

Speaking of wine, the Greeks have been successfully storing
grape juice in barrels for thousands of years, producing wonderful wines. But it seems that the secret of bottling, a completely different process, has not been discovered here. There
are certainly some great Greek whites (try Hadjimichailis or
Strofilia), but consistency is a problem: The same label does not
guarantee the same quality from one bottle to another. If the
house wine from a barrel (*hima*) is available, go for it, and you'll
rarely be disappointed.

Unfortunately, barrel wine isn't readily available in Corfu, as
there are too few vineyards and too many tourists. Also, since
the price of barrel wine is fixed per liter by the government,
owners of restaurants tend to put up a barrel or two for their
own use and sell the bottled stuff (for which they can charge
whatever they like) to tourists. Bottled water can be bought
everywhere, and you'll want to order it because Corfu's tap water tastes atrocious.

Sweets and coffee are not always available at restaurants; they
are traditionally taken after a meal at a *zaharoplastic* (literally,
"sugar seller"), which specializes in baklava or *kadaiffi* (pastry
with nuts and honey), ice cream, and various types of coffee.

Drinking coffee is a Greek national pastime and requires a few notes. The classic thick (Turkish) coffee is always served in a demitasse with a glass of cold water, and should be allowed to settle for a few minutes. It is then sipped very slowly, sometimes over an entire afternoon. One orders Greek coffee *sketo* (no sugar), *metrio* (medium: one spoonful of sugar), or *gliko* (sweet). In the last 10 years, instant coffee, called *Nescafé Frappee* has become popular. It is shaken and served cold or hot (*Nescafé zesto*), sketo, metrio, gliko, or even *me gala* (with milk). Good coffee shops serve espresso, cappuccino, and even drip coffee, sometimes called *Americaniko* and sometimes *Galliko* (French).

Some Corfiot specialties available at most restaurants and tavernas and all worth a try are: *Sofrito:* veal cooked in a sauce of white wine, herbs, and plenty of garlic; served with rice or potatoes. *Pastitsada:* beef cooked in a rich and spicy tomato sauce; served with spaghetti (always called "macaroni" in Greece). *Bourdetto*: firm-fleshed fish stewed in tomato sauce with lots of paprika. *Bianco*: whole fish stewed with potatoes, herbs, black pepper, and lemon juice.

It is customary to leave about 5% of the bill if the service has been satisfactory, since a service charge is always included in the prices.

Category	Cost*
Very Expensive	over 6,000 dr.
Expensive	3,500 dr.–6,000 dr.
Moderate	2,000 dr.–3,500 dr.
Inexpensive	under 2,000 dr.

for appetizer, entrée, and salad, including modest service charge and tax and not including wine

Lodging   Corfu offers accommodations to fit every taste and budget. If it's peace and quiet, you can find it; but if disco, drink, and crowds are your dish, they're readily available too. The lodgings can be elegant luxury hotels or clean, simple rooms; expect air-conditioning only in the Very Expensive category. The explosion of tourism in recent years has created an abundance of inexpensive rooms-to-let as well as enormous problems. Tour operators with their own or leased jumbo jets fly in large groups on prepaid, low-priced package tours. Many of these tourists are "lager louts," who arrive on the island with little or no cash to spend and do nothing but drink beer and send postcards home. It is easy to recognize their haunts and move on a few miles to find peace and quiet.

Don't neglect the "Rooms" signs that cover the countryside; there are actually more rooms than tourists. They are always clean, comfortable, and relatively inexpensive. Rates are negotiable, which means you should nogotiate—that is, bargain. The variables are the amenities, view, distance to the sea, and Continental breakfast, which is often included but should always be mentioned. Comparison shopping and a healthy attitude toward protracted negotiation over coffee can result in excellent bargains and sometimes lasting friendships, but only if you enjoy the process.

Category	Cost*
Very Expensive	over 25,000 dr.
Expensive	10,000 dr.–25,000 dr.
Moderate	6,000 dr.–10,000 dr.
Inexpensive	under 6,000 dr.

*All prices are for standard double room, usually including Continental breakfast and not including tax.

Corfu Town
Dining

Albatros. A meal here in the grill room on the terrace of the Corfu Palace Hotel—or at the hotel's **Panorama Restaurant**—is almost anyone's definition of "style": Both have Swiss chefs, perfect service, and international as well as local specialties. Sitting in Albatros's comfortable white-metal armchairs on the terrace overlooking the pool, Garitsa Bay, and the gardens is an excellent way to pamper yourself. The Saturday night barbecue here is a tradition with locals and tourists alike (8,000 dr.; book well in advance). You'll be amazed at the incredible buffet display of seafood, while the smell of meat cooking over charcoal will whet your appetite. In the luxurious Panorama, peace, quiet, and dignity reign, and even the silverware and sparkling china proclaim ease and comfort. The local specialties, done to perfection, are particularly recommended (why come to Corfu for steak and potatoes?), but if you want international cuisine, this is the place to have it done beautifully. Expensive restaurants should be marvelous in every aspect; Albatros and Panorama both measure up. *Leoforos Democratias 2, tel. 0661/39485. Reservations advised. Dress: casual but neat. AE, DC, MC, V. Very Expensive.*

Aegli. This restaurant (pronounced *Egg-lee*) on the Espianda (the Venetian promenade) offers more than 100 different meals, both local and international. The owner claims that everything, even the dessert, is made on the premises. It has been operating for more than 35 years in the same location—and what a location. The tables in front, with comfortable armchairs and spotless tablecloths, give a marvelous view of the nonstop parade on the promenade. The swordfish with red-pepper sauce is a treat, if a bit expensive. For a more private meal, choose one of the 40 or so tables with white pine chairs inside, under a wood ceiling. This is a place to enjoy your meal in leisure. *Espiande, tel. 0661/31949. Reservations advised in high season. Dress: casual. AE, DC, MC, V. Closed Dec.–Feb. Expensive.*

Quattro Stagioni. Although hard to find in the twisting, narrow streets of the old town, this place offers a light and airy old-world setting of marble tables, bronze light fixtures, and faded prints on the walls. It also has a covered veranda area across the street, where you can watch the tourists pass during your meal. Try the snails with butter and garlic sauce for starters, or the baked feta cheese for the less adventurous. A large variety of salads and pastas is served, which make a nice change from the heavier Greek meals. It's also a good place to try such local dishes as sofrito, pastitsada, bourdetto, or bianco. The moussaka and pepper steak are tempting. Dessert might be yogurt and honey, cakes, or ice cream. *Maniarisi and Arlioti 16, Kaduni Bisi, tel. 0661/43956. Reservations advised in high season. Dress: casual. AE, DC, MC, V. Closed Dec.–Feb. Expensive.*

The Rex Restaurant. "We have air-conditioning," the waiter said, pointing out a huge fan turning languidly on the ceiling. Classic Greek Taverna is the style of The Rex, which has 25 sturdy wood tables and the usual wood chairs with woven seats. Tables also line the wall outside, for those who like to watch the passing crowds. This clean and simple place on a corner just west of the Espiande serves only Greek and local specialties— at the same price to tourists and residents alike. It also serves red or white wine from a barrel. Try the *steffado*, meat stewed with small, sweet onions; or the *laxhana tholmadas*, cabbage leaves stuffed with seasoned ground meat and rice. The *stamna*, lamb baked in a ceramic bowl with potatoes, rice, beans, and cheese, is absolutely delicious. Breakfast, lunch, and dinner are served: Greek food at its best in a comfortable, friendly atmosphere. *Kapodistriou 66, tel. 0661/39649. Reservations not required. Dress: casual. No credit cards. Closed 4:30 PM–8:30 PM and Sun. Moderate.*

2M. This is a real find, in the commercial center (*emboriko kentro*) of Corfu, a place where you can feel at home and really enjoy the food—a full range of pasta, chops, and seafood—the service, the decoration, and even the bill. It has 10 modern, tubular steel tables and easy chairs on the veranda; clean, plain tablecloths; pink-flowered china; and a pleasant view of the small yacht harbor across the road. You won't be disappointed here or ripped off: You are treated as a welcome guest who will be back. Babis, the owner, worked at major Athens hotels before opening his own place, and his good training shows. *Main rte. n., past port; Ethniki Antistasis 34, tel. 0661/46030. Reservations recommended in high season. Dress: casual. AE, DC, MC, V. Moderate.*

O Yiannis. This taverna is one of the nicest places in Corfu. It offers barrel wine—white (retsina) or a nice rosé—and the food and wine are wonderful. Go right into the kitchen, lift the lids of the steaming pots, and savor the smells. Try the steffado, the pork with sprouts, or the dolmades. For the bold, there's also *hordi*, intestines baked with a flavorful sauce. Make sure you order an ample supply of starters, hima wine, and eat in good company. There's nothing pretentious about Yianni's. The walls are covered with black and white photographs of old Corfiots: the butcher, the baker, and a singer or two. Straw baskets covering the light bulbs disperse the light but don't pretend to be chandeliers. The place is full of local residents (and any tourists lucky enough to have found it). You'll be hard pressed to eat and drink your way through 2,000 drachmas. *Sophia Kremona and Iassonos-Sossipatrou 30, Anemomilos, tel. 0661/31066. No reservations. Dress: casual. No credit cards. Inexpensive.*

Lodging **Astir Palace.** On a 14-acre peninsula jutting into Komeno Bay, 10 kilometers (6 miles) north of town, is a resort complex with luxury rooms and bungalows, whose balconies all have sea views. The rooms are comfortable and functional rather than elegant and attractive: The brown molded plastic chairs and tables and the plastic light fixtures work, but they're not very appealing. There's a private beach with a variety of water sports. *Komeno Bay, Corfu 49100, tel. 0661/91481, fax 0661/91881. 176 rooms and 124 bungalows with bath. Facilities: restaurant, taverna, 2 bars, disco, card room, TV lounge, shopping arcade, hairdresser, laundry service, pool, 2 floodlighted tennis courts, water sports. AE, DC, MC, V. Very Expensive.*

Corfu Hilton International. This hotel near the airport provides almost all the facilities offered by the Corfu Palace (no room TV, no hair dryers), though it is nowhere near as elegant and has a rather dark lobby. It does have lovely modern wood-panelled rooms (it was built in 1976) and a beautiful private beach, with a restaurant/bar, a snack bar, and water sports. The less expensive "lake view" rooms in back look over the lagoon and the airport: Ask for a room on the front for the panoramic view. *On beach at Kanoni, Corfu 49100, tel. 0661/36540, fax 0661/36551. 255 rooms with bath. Facilities: 2 restaurants, health club, gambling casino, 2 seawater pools, sauna, 2 lighted tennis courts, room service, bowling center, jogging track. AE, DC, MC, V. Very Expensive.*

Corfu Palace. Overlooking the bay, 100 yards from the center of town, this hotel is without a doubt one of the most beautiful—not only in Corfu but in all of Greece. "Elegant" best describes its Venetian grandeur; it's surrounded by tropical gardens, and offers taste, beauty, and comfort. Guests can play tennis at the four courts of the nearby Corfu Tennis Club and are also welcome to use the facilities of the Corfu Yacht Club. The spacious rooms, furnished in various styles (including Louis XIV, Empire, and rustic), have wide balconies with tables and chairs and splendid views of the bay. They also have telephones, TV, and minibars; the bathrooms have hair dryers and telephones, and it is evident that attention has been paid to every detail. *Leoforos Democratias 2, Corfu 49100, tel. 0661/39485, fax 0661/ 31749. 110 rooms with bath. Facilities: 2 restaurants, 2 bars, outdoor and indoor seawater pools, room service, health club, shops, conference rooms, baby-sitting service. AE, DC, MC, V. Very Expensive.*

Kontokali Bay. When you tire of exploring the Venetian streets and museums in town, this hotel about 6½ kilometers (4 miles) north of town is just the place to relax. The bright guest rooms have modern dark wood furniture that matches the woodwork and are done in pleasant pastel shades that look cheerful in the daylight streaming through the doors. All have direct-dial phones, radios, and hair dryers, and large balconies facing the sea, the mountains, or the lake. There's a buffet/grill restaurant with acres of plants hanging from the ceiling, where Tuesday is Greek night and Wednesday Italian night (call for the schedule). The private beach has thatch umbrellas and deck chairs. *Kontakali Bay, Corfu 49100, 0661/38736, fax 0661/ 91901. 234 rooms with bath. Facilities: restaurant, bar, disco, room service, 2 tennis courts, water sports, marina. AE, DC, MC, V. Very Expensive.*

Cavalieri Hotel. In this ancient, eight-story building on the arcade of the Liston, rooms on the fourth and fifth floors whose numbers end in 2, 3, or 4 offer an absolutely incredible view of the Old Fort, which goes far to offset the worn carpets and noisy bedsprings. The building has style, grace, and history, but it needs some renovation, some paint, and new furnishings in the guest rooms to justify its classification and its rates. It has a charming English-style wood paneled bar that no one uses, a large lovely room at the back that doubles as breakfast room and restaurant, and a tiny elevator. The guest rooms have telephones and radios. *4 Kapodistriou St., Corfu 49100, tel. 0661/39041, fax 0661/39336. 50 rooms with bath. Facilities: restaurant/breakfast room, bar. AE, DC, MC, V. Expensive.*

Hotel Bella Venezia. This two-story Venetian building just behind the main square in the center of town was operated as a hotel as early as the 1800s. It was renovated in 1988, but because it has no restaurant (and also no view) it falls into a lower classification (with rates to match) than its perfectly beautiful building would warrant. There's a large lobby with a marble floor and a wood-paneled ceiling, and a huge back garden where breakfast is served and where you can relax in lounge chairs and make use of the snack bar. Its rooms are small but charmingly furnished, and they have radios, telephones, and TV (a rarity on the island). All in all, it's good value for the money. *4 Zambelli St., Corfu 49100, tel. 0661/46500. 32 rooms with bath. Facilities: snack bar, lounge. AE, DC, MC, V. Moderate.*

Hotel Cyprus. The rooms are clean in this lodging in the old town, and there are two toilets and a shower for every five rooms. The ancient building dates back to who-knows-when, as do the locks and fixtures and the odds and ends of furnishings. It's next to a historic church that's undergoing reconstruction, and seems to need some help itself for its missing chunks of masonry and cracked plaster. But as with all historic buildings, special permits from the Ministry of Culture are needed before any work can be done. Staying here would be an adventure, and the price is certainly right. *13 Agion Pateron St., Corfu 49100, tel. 0661/30032. 16 rooms with shared baths. No credit cards. Inexpensive.*

Hotel Konstantinoupoulis. From this Venetian building, opposite the dock for car-ferries to the islands, there's a great view of the old port. The structure has been a hotel for more than 200 years and was last renovated 20 years ago. The rooms could be called, at best, "traditional," but it's clean and acceptable if you're short of cash. There's a bank of toilets and showers on each floor and about seven rooms to a floor. Long-distance phone calls can be made in the lobby, a rarity in low-cost hotels. *Zavitsianou 11, Old Port, Corfu 49100, tel. 0661/39826. 44 rooms share communal baths. Facilities: exchange office with bank rates, free luggage storage for guests. No credit cards. Inexpensive.*

Out of Town Dining

Taverna Tripas. People drive about 13 kilometers (8 miles) south of town, to the mountain village of Kinopiastes, to go to the most famous restaurant on the island. You might go to satisfy curiosity or to say you had gone, but it's terribly touristy (be sure to book your table in advance in high season); and you might find yourself sitting next to members of Parliament, well-known artists, or even the prime minister. There's an impressive array of *menzedakia*, a selection of delicious tidbits brought to you more or less at the waiter's discretion. The meal, a set menu, is described as "a delicious range of unique specialities." Out-of-season fruit is one of the specialties, which seems silly in a country full of fresh produce. A variety of live music and traditional Greek dances are performed while you dine, and there's fine retsina in those barrels. *Kinopiastes, tel. 0661/56333. Reservations required in high season. Dress: casual. AE, DC, MC, V. Expensive.*

Fish Taverna Roula. Follow the signs to the Kondakali Bay Hotel and continue on, keeping your eyes open for a sign to "Roula's." This is the place to order fresh fish; you can come in the morning, if you like, and pick out your favorite kind from the catch. Sit on the balcony under an enormous, ancient olive tree, and watch the boats on the bay. In high season, remember to book a table and reserve your fish early because when the fish runs out, Roula stops serving. *Kondokali, tel. 0661/91832.*

Reservations not necessary. Dress: casual. No credit cards. Moderate–Expensive.

Chez George. Sitting on the rock of the bay in Palaeokastritsa, in the middle of a postcard view where a bright blue sea kisses forest green mountains, Chez George can provide a sublime experience or a very expensive and depressing tourist mistake. Order simply and don't buy wine. The pork chops are delicious and the *Horiaktico* (village salad), though expensive, contains carrot and onion as well as tomato, cucumber, feta, olives, and all sorts of other good things. But remember that moderate prices seldom go along with gorgeous views. *The Rock, Paleokastritsa, tel. 0663/41233. Dress: casual. MC, V. Moderate.*

The Nornberg. Everybody in the area knows this restaurant as Mihali's in Livadi Ropa, about 13 mountainous kilometers (8 miles) west of town. It's a *psystaryia* (grill taverna) specializing in meat over charcoal, and one of the best. First let them bring you an assortment of appetizers: fried eggplant, *tsatsiki* (yogurt, chopped cucumber, and garlic), fresh salad, and a lovely feta cheese. Then have them charcoal broil you some *paidakia* (lamb chops) or a pork chop. First of all, Michail Moumouris knows just how and where to choose the best local meat; he bastes it with lemon juice and local olive oil, sprinkles salt and fresh oregano over it, and something extremely special comes off his grill: a meal you'll remember. And don't forget to order some of his homemade retsina. *Livadi Ropa, tel. 0661/51473. Reservations not necessary. Dress: casual. No credit cards. Moderate.*

Lodging **Corfu Chandris** and **Dassia Chandris Hotels.** These two hotels next to each other at Dassia, 11 kilometers (7 miles) north of town, create a huge complex, with private chalet/bungalows also for rent. Stretching in front of both hotels is a wide, private sandy beach, but each has its own swimming pool. The public areas in both are gloriously marbled and full of light and color; the guest rooms, furnished in what might be called Functional Modern style, are comfortable but not luxurious. They have large, sea-view balconies, radios, and telephones, but are done in dark brown or drab blue and gray, and the bulbous plastic sculptures that serve as lamps and light fixtures are reminiscent of a student dormitory. *Dassia, Corfu 49100, tel. 0661/33871 through 0661/33875, fax 0661/93458; or Akto Miaouli, Piraeus 18536, tel. 01/452–4934, fax 01/453–7916. 526 rooms with bath. Facilities for each: restaurant, bar, lobby, card room, TV room, air-conditioning, room service, swimming pool, tennis court, hairdresser, shops, playground, water sports. AE, DC, MC, V. Expensive.*

Apraos Bay Hotel. On the northern tip of the island, about 32 kilometers (20 miles) from Corfu town, sits a small, utterly charming hotel, built in 1992 in the traditional Venetian style. It's 30 yards from a private beach, with a fantastic view of the sea and the Albanian coast: a perfect place to relax in friendly atmosphere, far from the noise of discos, bars, and machines. Though it's almost completely isolated, just a mile away in the village of Kassiopi is all the action anyone could want. Each of the fresh and airy modern rooms has a balcony with a phenomenal view and is full of light. *Apraos, Corfu 49100, tel. and fax 0662/81350; or Golden Key Col, 31 Thisseos St., Athens 17671, tel. 01/956–4206, fax 01/958–7531. 16 rooms with bath. Facilities: restaurant, piano bar, TV lounge, play-*

ground; tennis court and pool were planned at press time. AE, DC, MC, V. Closed Dec.–Feb. Moderate.

Lodging **Fundana Villas.** And now for something completely different: 10 villas built in and around a 17th-century stone-and-mortar Venetian storehouse. Some of the villas were converted from outbuildings and some are in the ground floor of the old structure, whose walls are almost a yard thick. The common room/bar still contains the huge olive press and a stone mill with three five-foot grindstones. Set on a hilltop in the mountains west of town, surrounded by gardens and by olive and orange groves, the complex provides a panoramic view. You can really imagine what it was like hundreds of years ago, and at the same time enjoy the modern baths and kitchens of the villas. It's an ideal place for families interested in biking, exploring, and history, and is a short drive from the Paleokastritsa beaches. You will need your own transportation. *Spyros Spathas, Box 167, Corfu 49100, tel. 0663/22532, fax 0663/22453. 10 villas. Facilities: playground. No credit cards. Moderate.*

The Arts and Nightlife

At press time the **Art Gallery** (0661/42602) of the Municipality of Corfu is closed for major repairs. Its collection of paintings spans five centuries, from 1400 to 1900.

In the village of Sinarades on the west coast, south of Glifada, there's a **Folk Art Museum** (tel. 0661/35673; open Tues.–Sun 9:30–12:30), exhibiting a private collection of local costumes, embroidery, furniture, and pottery.

Just past the Commercial Center, 3 kilometers (2 miles) from town is a string of discos that really don't start swinging till after midnight. They have names like **Sax, Slik, Electron, bora bora, Slaze, Astral, Rondo, Mobile Club, Interview, Hippodrome,** and **LA Boom,** and they throb with with all the latest international sounds and styles, from heavy metal to rap, techno, and fusion. Incredibly loud sound systems are just what the young T-shirted crowd needs to dance into the wee hours of the morning. A drink costs about 1,000 dr.

Bill's Bar, on the main drag of the Commercial Center, has a quieter scene, with a definite trend toward music from the '60s, slower dancing, and even a taste of blues.

At the end of the disco strip turn left at the sign for the Paleokastritsa road, and you'll come to the **Ekati.** Evening dress is the norm at this Greek nightclub (*skiladiko*, which translates roughly as "dog party"), and there's an older, more sophisticated atmosphere, but the volume is nevertheless high as live entertainers perform the latest popular songs backed by a live band. This is where people flaunt gold chains, diamond necklaces, and Paris designer fashions. Whiskey by the bottle at your table is the height of status here. Buy a plate of carnations to throw at your favorite performer, or even break a plate or two if you're in the mood. You're charged by the flower and the plate, and it's good clean fun. Drinks cost 1,500 dr.–2,000 dr.; prices for flowers and plates on request.

6 The Northern Peloponnese

With Bassae, Mystras, and Monemvassia

By Mark J. Rose
and Toula
Bogdanos

*Toula Bogdanos,
who lives in
Athens, writes for
the New York
Times and the
Daily Telegraph,
among others, and
lectures on writing
and journalism.*

The hand-shaped Peloponnese, the southern peninsula of Greece, is linked to the north by a narrow isthmus, from which the Gulf of Corinth leads west to the Adriatic, and the Saronic Gulf opens eastward into the Aegean. Named for Pelops, son of the mythical Tantalos, this ancient land offers magnificent scenery; massive mountains covered with low evergreen oak and pines surround coastal valleys and loom above rocky shores and sandy beaches. Over the millennia this rugged terrain nourished kingdoms and empires and witnessed the birth of modern Greece. Traces of these lost realms—ruined Bronze Age citadels, Greek and Roman temples and theaters, and the fortresses, churches and mosques of the Byzantines, Franks, Venetians, and Turks—attest the richness of the land. It comprises the Argive peninsula, jutting into the Aegean, and runs westward past the isthmus and along the Gulf of Corinth to Patras and the Adriatic coast. (The modern administrative districts, or nomes, are Argolis, Corinthia, Achaea, and Elis.)

The fertile Argive plain was the heart of Greece in the Late Bronze Age and the home of the heroes of Homer's *Iliad.* Walking through the lion gate to Mycenae, the citadel of Agamemnon, brings the Homeric epic to life, and the massive walls of nearby Tiryns remind us of that age when might was right. The thriving market town of Argos, the successor to Mycenae and Tiryns, engaged in a long rivalry with Sparta, generally getting the short end of the stick. Corinth, the economic superpower of the 7th and 6th centuries BC, dominated trade and established colonies abroad. Although eclipsed by Athens, Corinth earned a reputation for wealth and soft living. Modern Corinth is a bustling, if unremarkable, regional center. Not far from Corinth is Epidauros, the sanctuary of Asklepios, god of healing, where Greek dramas are re-created in the ancient theater during summer. Far to the west lies Olympia, the sanctuary of Zeus and home of the Olympic games.

After the armies of the Fourth Crusade (in part egged on by Venice) captured Constantinople in 1204, they conquered the Peloponnese, which became the Frankish principality of Achaea. The Franks settled in for the long haul, the Villehardouin family establishing the impressive castle of Chlemoutsi near Killini, but their dominion was brief, and Byzantine authority was restored under the Palaiologos dynasty at Mystras and Monemvassia. Soon after Constantinople fell in 1453, the Turks, taking advantage of an internal rivalry, crushed the Palaiologoi and helped themselves to the Peloponnese. In the following centuries the struggle between the Venetians and the Ottoman Turks for control of the eastern Mediterranean was played out in Greece, and largely in the northern Peloponnese. The two states alternately dominated the region until the Ottomans ultimately prevailed, as Venetian power declined in the early 1700s. The Turkish mosques and fountains and the Venetian fortifications of Nauplion recall this epic struggle. The Peloponnese played a key role in the Greek War of Independence, and from 1829 to 1834 Nauplion was the capital of Greece.

Today Patras is the chief city of the region, and the third largest in Greece. Agriculture and tourism are the economic bases of the northern Peloponnese. Citrus, grapes (and wine), and currants are grown, as well as the ubiquitous olive. Modern resorts like Porto Heli in the east and Killini in the west attract crowds seeking sun, sand, and sea.

Essential Information

Important Addresses and Numbers

Tourist Information The regional office of the **Greek National Tourist Organization** is in Patras (110 Iroon Polytechniou St., Glyfada, tel. 061/423866, fax 061/429046). There are city offices in Nauplion (Iatrou Sq., tel. 0752/24444) and Olympia (Praxitileous Kondili St., tel. 0624/23100 or 0624/23125) and a privately run tourist office (tel. 0754/51052) in Porto Heli.

Emergencies For help with any emergency you can contact the **Tourist Police** in Patras (tel. 061/220903), Corinth (tel. 0741/23282), Nauplion (tel. 0752/27776), and Olympia (tel. 0624/22550). There is also a 24-hour **help-line** (English spoken): tel. 031/922777.

Late-Night Pharmacies Pharmacies, clearly identified by red cross signs, take turns staying open late. A listing is published in the local newspaper; it is best to check at your hotel to find out not only which pharmacy is open but how to get there.

Arriving and Departing by Car, Train, Bus, and Boat

There is no plane service to the northern Peloponnese.

By Car Most people take the toll highway from Athens to the Isthmus of Corinth (84 kilometers/52 miles, 1¼ hours). Others take the car ferry from Italy (Ancona, Bari, or Brindisi); contact the Sea Connection Center (757 Deep Valley Drive, Rolling Hills Estates, CA 90274, tel. 310/544–3551 or 800/367–1789, fax 310/541–0166) for information and reservations. An alternate route from Athens to Patras is via Delphi and the Rion–Antirion ferry.

By Train Traveling by train is convenient for the northern Peloponnese and relatively inexpensive. Trains from Athens depart from the Peloponnissou station (take bus 057 from Panepistimiou St., fare: 75 dr.); there are 13 departures daily, eight to Patras and five to Argos. For schedule information call 01/513–1601 (English spoken).

By Bus The regional bus associations (KTEL) provide frequent direct service at reasonable prices to Patras, Pyrgos (for Olympia), Corinth, Argos, Epidauros, Kranidi, Nauplion (for Mycenae), and Xylokastro. Buses leave from the terminal at 100 Kifissou Street on the outskirts of Athens (take bus 51 at the corner of Vilara and Meandrou Sts. near Omonia Sq.).

By Boat **Ceres** (8 Themistokleous St., Piraeus, tel. 01/452–7107) operates the Flying Dolphin hydrofoils (passengers only) from Zea Marina in Piraeus to ports on the east coast of the Peloponnese, sailing daily to Porto Heli (1 hour, 55 minutes), daily (April 15–October 15) to Nauplion (3 hours), and once or twice a day (3 hours 10 minutes) to Monemvassia (*see* Off the Beaten Track, *below*).

Nauplion (port authority, tel. 0752/27372) and Patras (tel. 061/277622) are ports of entry and exit for yachts arriving in and departing from Greece. The GNTO (tel. 061/420303) maintains a Frontier Post at the port of Patras.

Getting Around

By Car   The roads are good in the northern Peloponnese, and driving can be the most enjoyable (if not the most economical) way of seeing the region. **The Greek Automobile Touring Club (ELPA)** has an office in Patras (Astingos and 127 Korinthou Sts., tel. 061/425411 or 061/ 425141) and can assist with repairs and information. During the Epidauros Festival ELPA road assistance vehicles patrol the roads around there.

By Train   Trains run from Athens to Corinth and then the route splits; you can go southwest to Argos and Tripolis en route to Kalamata in the southern Peloponnese or west along the coast to Patras and then south to Pyrgos and Kalamata. From Argos you can easily reach Nauplion by bus or taxi. On the western route the train stops at Kiato, Xylokastro, Diakofto (where a narrow-gauge branch line heads inland to Kalavrita; *see* Off the Beaten Track, *below*), and Aigion, before arriving in Patras. (In high summer the trains between Patras and Athens can be crowded with young people arriving from or leaving for Italy on ferries from Patras.) Branch lines leave the main line at Kavassilas for Killini and at Pyrgos for Olympia.

By Bus   In addition to serving major centers, like Nauplion, Argos, Corinth, and Patras, the blue-green coaches of the regional bus associations (KTEL) travel to virtually every village in the northern Peloponnese. The bargain price and the extensive network makes bus travel a viable alternative to renting a car, although frequency decreases off the beaten track. Schedules are posted at local KTEL stations, usually on the main square or main street.

Guided Tours

Many companies offer bus tours from Athens to the major archaeological sites in the northern Peloponnese. Typically they are four days and three nights, and include accommodations, breakfast, lunch, and entrance fees. The itinerary usually includes Epidauros (possibly a performance at the ancient theater), Nauplion, Mycenae, Corinth, and Olympia. If you take a tour that returns to Athens via Delphi you will have covered the most spectacular and most important sites of ancient Greece. Combined with a few days in Athens, it's a very good introduction for the first-time visitor. Many local travel agents offer whirlwind day trips to sites, especially Epidauros (usually including the performance and stopping at some combination of Nauplion, Mycenae, and Corinth) and Olympia. These basic, no-frills tours are for those who don't expect a lot of hand holding and have trouble planning in advance. They can be booked at travel agencies, at larger hotels, and sometimes at the KTEL bus stations in smaller towns.

Exploring the Northern Peloponnese

Tour 1 is a trip from the Isthmus of Corinth through the heart of the Argolid, including the sites of Argos, Tiryns, and Mycenae. Tour 2, a walking tour of Nauplion, takes in the Turkish and Venetian architecture of its old quarter and the Neoclassical buildings from its years as the capital. Tour 3 goes to ancient Corinth, its modern counterpart, Patras, and the ruins of Olympia, the sanctuary of Zeus. An excursion from Olympia takes in the Temple of Apollo at Banae, and excursions off the beaten track go to Kalavrita, to ancient Mystras, and to the walled town of Monemvassia.

Highlights for First-Time Visitors

Ancient Corinth (*see* Tour 3)
Greek dramas performed at Epidauros (*see* Tour 1)
Monemvassia (*see* Off the Beaten Track)
Mycenae and **Tiryns,** home of Homer's Heroes (*see* Tour 1)
Old Nauplion and **the Palamidi** (*see* Tour 2)
Sanctuary of Zeus at Olympia (*see* Tour 3)

Tour 1: From the Isthmus through the Argolid

Numbers in the margin correspond to points of interest on the Northern Peloponnese map.

Were it not for the Isthmus of Corinth, a narrow neck of land less than 7 kilometers (4 miles) across, the waters of the Gulf of Corinth and the Saronic Gulf would meet, making the Peloponnese an island; the name, in fact, means "Pelop's island." The tragic myths and legends surrounding Pelops and his family provided the grist for poets and playwrights from Homer to Aeschylus and enshroud many of the region's sites to this day.

For the ancient Greeks the isthmus was strategically important for both trade and defense; Corinth, with harbors on either side of the isthmus, grew wealthy on the lucrative east–west trade. Ships en route from Italy and the Adriatic to the Aegean had to go clear around the Peloponnese, so in the 7th century BC a paved roadway was constructed across the isthmus on which ships were hauled using rollers. Nero was the first to begin cutting a canal, supposedly striking the first blow with a golden pickax in AD 67. But the canal died with Nero the following year, and the roadway was used until the 13th century. The modern canal, built 1882–93, was cut through 280 feet of rock to sea level. The impressive sight goes by quickly if you are traveling by bus, so keep a sharp lookout. The isthmus was not only a barrier to sea trade, but also a choke point on north–south land routes. As early as the Late Bronze Age (13th century BC) a wall was constructed across the isthmus, apparently to keep out invaders from the north, and throughout history other fortifications were erected, which generally failed when actually put to the test. Today there are no walls, but the line of rest-stop restaurants at the isthmus may be a more effective defense than the walls ever were. Be wary of those restaurants: It is better to enter the Peloponnese hungry than to eat the souvlaki there.

Turn left immediately after crossing the isthmus, and pick up the scenic secondary road that runs along the coast of the Saronic Gulf, making a brief stop at the site of **Isthmia,** an ancient sanctuary dedicated to Poseidon, scarcely a mile from the canal. It isn't much to look at today, largely because its buildings were dismantled for stone to repair the Isthmian wall and to build a large fortress. Better preserved, not surprisingly, are the remains of the fortress, called the Hexamilion, and of the wall (east of the sanctuary is a stretch that rises more than 20 feet). Ancient Isthmia was an important place, the site, from 580 BC, of the Isthmian Games, biennial athletic and musical competitions on a par with those at Nemea, Delphi, and Olympia.

Continue south for about 5 kilometers (3 miles) and, rounding the bend, you'll pass the remains of **Kenchreai,** Corinth's eastern port. Much of the site is underwater, including a sanctuary of Isis, from which excavators retrieved the unique glass panels depicting Nile scenes and Greek philosophers now on display at the Isthmia museum. It was from Kenchreai that Paul sailed for Ephesus, having his hair cut before departure (Acts 18: 18). Leaving Kenchreai the road climbs into more rugged countryside, on the steep slopes overlooking small fjordlike inlets and the open waters of the Saronic Gulf. On the left you pass first the small post-Byzantine church of the Odigitria (Virgin Indicator of the Way) and second the 14th-century Monastery Agnounda.

As you head south on Highway 70 you'll find the names confusing. You first pass a sign for Nea Epidauros, then 6½ kilometers (4 miles) later there's a turnoff marked for Palaio Epidauros. After this seaside village the road turns inland and gradually the tall pines give way to scrubby vegetation. Keep going—the Epidauros you want is about 8 kilometers (5 miles) farther, about 3 kilometers (2 miles) south of Ligourio.

The **Sanctuary of Asklepios** at **Epidauros** is world renowned for one thing: its theater, whose extraordinary qualities were recognized even in the 2nd century AD. Pausanias of Lydia, an early traveler and geographer, writes, "The Epidaurians have a theater in their sanctuary that seems to me particularly worth a visit. The Roman theaters have gone far beyond all the others in the world…but who can begin to rival Polykleitos for the beauty and composition of his architecture?" Extolled for its acoustics, it is also the best-preserved Greek theater anywhere. Built in the 4th century BC with 14,000 seats, it was never remodeled in antiquity, and being rather remote, its stones were never quarried for building material. The summer drama festival staged in the theater is "worth a visit," as Pausanias might say. The quality of the theater, the setting, and the productions are outstanding, which cannot be said of any other festival in Greece. The rest of the site does not match the standard set by the theater. The temple of Asklepios is not well preserved; some copies of its sculptures are in the site museum, but the originals are in the National Museum in Athens. An exhibit of ancient medical implements is of interest, as are models of the sanctuary. The reconstruction of the *tholos,* a circular building also possibly by Polykleitos, is noteworthy.

From Epidauros, head south toward the resort town of Porto Heli. After 16½ kilometers (11 miles), just beyond the village of Trahia, the road divides. Follow the left fork as it swings east to

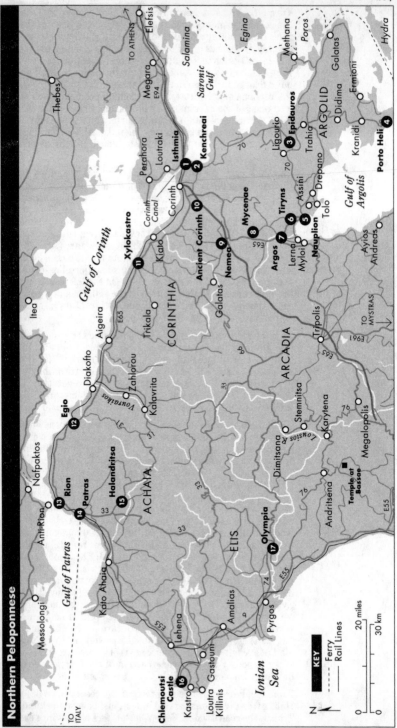

the coast, with a beautiful view across the Saronic Gulf to Aegina. After 30 kilometers (18 miles), a left turn takes you to the peninsula known as **Methana,** where a spa in the small port of the same name will treat you for rheumatism and skin disorders with hot sulfurous water. Continuing past Methana on the main road brings you to Galatas, overlooking the island of Poros. The road sweeps around the end of the peninsula and runs west along the coast to Ermioni, opposite Hydra, then to the beach at Kosta, opposite Spetses, and finally to Porto Heli. Ferry service and infrequent hydrofoils connect the Saronic Islands (*see* Essential Information in Chapter 4) with Methana, Ermioni, Kosta, and Porto Heli. A booming summer resort,

④ Porto Heli is well supplied with tavernas, restaurants, souvenir shops, and discos. If you want traditional Greek culture, look elsewhere. Although its beach is not as good as others in the near vicinity, Porto Heli's circular bay offers sheltered water for windsurfing, waterskiing, and other aquatic sports, and a safe harbor for sailboats. On the south side of the bay are the submerged ruins of the ancient city of Halieis.

The road north passes through Kranidi, a conservative town with plenty of good pre–concrete slab architecture, and Didima, a small town in a large flat depression below the hulking mass of Mt. Didima. Perhaps because the sheer bulk of the mountain highlights its insignificance, Didima itself is depressing, and the long climb up the mountain, with many switchbacks and a steep grade, is like feeling the wind after being trapped in a closed room with stale air. At the top you can continue onward, through Trahia again and to Nauplion via Ligourio, or turn left and take the coast road to Nauplion, past the villages and beaches of Iria, Kandia, and Drepano along the Gulf of Argos.

⑤ *Oreia* (beautiful) is the word Greeks use to describe **Nauplion** (*see* Tour 2, *below*). They say the word with assurance and enthusiasm, wanting to convince you of Nauplion's beauty but knowing that it is self-evident and that you share their recognition of it. The town's old section, on a peninsula jutting into the Gulf of Argos, mixes Greek, Venetian, and Turkish architecture; narrow streets—often just broad flights of stone stairs—climb the slopes beneath the walls of Acronauplia; statues honoring heroes preside over tree-shaded plazas surrounded by neoclassical buildings, and the elegant Venetian fortress draped over the high cliff guards the town. The Greeks are right; Nauplion is beautiful. It deserves at least a leisurely day of your undivided attention.

On a low hill, scarcely past the suburbs of Nauplion, partly obscured by citrus trees, are the well-preserved ruins of the My-

⑥ cenaean acropolis of **Tiryns.** Some tours skip the site in their mad dash to cover everything in a single day, but if you see this citadel, with its massive walls and its palace, before touring Mycenae, you can understand those rambling ruins more easily. Homer describes Tiryns as "the wall-girt city," the only ancient literary reference to it, and Henry Miller was repelled by the place, as he records in *The Colossus of Maroussi*: "Tiryns is prehistoric in character. . . . Tiryns represents a relapse. . . . Tiryns smells of cruelty, barbarism, suspicion, isolation." Today the site seems harmless, home to a few lizards who timidly sun themselves on the Bronze Age stones and run for cover if you approach. Archaeological exploration of the site—begun in

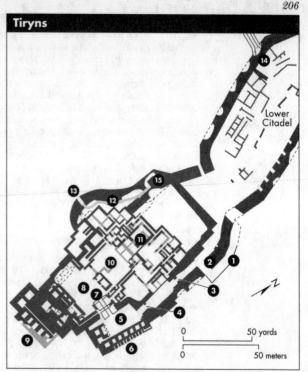

Tiryns

Lower Citadel

0 — 50 yards

0 — 50 meters

1876 by Schliemann, continued by Dorpfeld and later by the German Archaeological Institute, which still continues—shows that the acropolis was occupied in Neolithic times.

The citadel, the legendary birthplace of Herakles, makes use of a long, low outcrop, on which was set the circuit wall of gigantic limestone blocks (of the type called "cyclopean" because the ancients thought they could have been handled only by the giant *cyclopes*—the largest block is estimated at more than 15 tons). It was entered on the east side, through a gate leading to a narrow passage between the outer and inner walls. One could then turn right, toward the residential section in the lower citadel (now usually closed to the public) or to the left toward the upper citadel and palace. Two heavy gates blocked the passage to the palace and trapped attackers caught between the walls. After the second gate, the passage opens onto a rectangular courtyard, whose massive left-hand wall is pierced by a gallery of small vaulted chambers, or casemates, opening off a long narrow corridor roofed by a corbeled arch. (They were possibly once used to stable horses, and the walls have been worn smooth by the countless generations of sheep and goats who have sheltered there.) This is one of the famous galleries of Tiryns; another such gallery at the southernmost end of the acropolis also connects a series of five casemates with sloping roofs.

An elaborate entranceway leads west from the court to the upper citadel and palace, sited at the highest point of the acropolis. The complex included a colonnaded court; the main hall, or *megaron*, opened onto it and held the royal throne. Surviving

fragments suggest that the floors and the walls were decorated, the walls by frescoes (now in the National Archaeological Museum of Athens) depicting a boar hunt, women riding in
chariots, and a procession of women. Beyond the megaron, a
large court overlooks the houses in the lower citadel; from here,
a long stairway descends to a small postern gate in the west
wall. At the excavated part of the lower acropolis (which can't
be visited) a significant discovery was made; two parallel tunnels, roofed in the same way as the galleries on the east and
south sides, start within the acropolis and extend under the
walls, leading to subterranean cisterns that ensured a continuous water supply.

From the palace you can see how Tiryns dominated the flat, fertile land at the head of the Gulf of Argos. The view would have
been different in the Late Bronze Age: the ancient shoreline
was nearer to the citadel, and outside the walls there was an
extensive settlement. Profitis Ilias, the prominent hill to the
east, was the site of the Tiryns cemetery.

On the western edge of the Argive plain, about 11 kilometers (7
miles) from Nauplion by a flat road through citrus groves, sits
❼ the city of **Argos** (population 21,000), the economic hub of the
region. The fall of Mycenae and Tiryns at the close of the Late
Bronze Age was like the opening of a door for Argos. Built first
on a low, round hill called the Aspis, the city later expanded to
the adjacent peak of Larissa, a second, more formidable, acropolis. Under King Pheidon, Argos reached its greatest power in
the 7th century BC, becoming the chief city in the Peloponnese
and defeating the Spartans at Hysiae in the opening battle of a
centuries-long rivalry. In the mid-5th century, it consolidated
its hold on the Argive plain by eradicating Mycenae and Tiryns.
But like Corinth, Argos was never powerful enough to set its
own course, following in later years the leadership of Sparta,
Athens, and the Macedonian kings. In the Peloponnesian War,
Argos sided with Athens when it was convenient and when it
enabled her to inflict damage on Sparta. Twice in its history,
women are said to have defended Argos: once in 494 BC when
Telesilla the poetess (who may be mere legend) armed old men,
boys, and women to hold the walls against the Spartans; and
again in 272 BC when Pyrrhus, king of Epiros, who was taking
the city street by street, was felled from above by an old woman
armed with a tile.

Remains of the classical city are scattered throughout the modern one, and along Tripoleos Street you can see in a small area
the extensive ruins of the Roman bath, theater, odeon, and agora. Like many medieval fortresses in Greece, the Kastro on top
of Larissa is a Byzantine and Frankish structure incorporating
remnants of classical walls, which was later expanded by the
Turks and Venetians. The strength of its defenses held the
Franks back for seven years, until 1212. Argos was twice captured by the Turks, first in 1397, then during the War of Independence. A small archaeological museum on the main plateia,
Ayios Petros, has well-displayed finds from Argos and nearby
sites. On Saturday morning, the plateia is a huge open house-
hold-merchandise-and-produce market (dwarfing that at
Nauplion). It's more fun to wander through than to visit yet another tourist shop, and you can often find good souvenirs, like
wooden stamps used to impress designs on bread loaves, at
prices that haven't been inflated.

North of Argos, the road gradually rises and leaves the citrus orchards of the flat plain for olive groves and tobacco fields; after 9 kilometers (about 5 miles), it arrives at the turnoff for the ancient citadel of **Mycenae,** which Homer describes as "rich in gold." It stands on a low hill, wedged between the sheer, lofty peaks of Mt. Zara and Mt. Profitis Ilias, separated from them by two deep ravines. It commanded both the greater part of the plain stretching southward to the sea and the exit from the Pass of Dervenakia; the Perseia Fountain, close to the entrance of the acropolis, ensured a continuous water supply; the fertile Argive plain provided food. The site's natural advantages thus enhanced its strategic position. It was inhabited very early in Neolithic times, but the period of its greatest power came at the close of the Late Bronze Age (1600 BC–1100 BC), also known as the Mycenaean. Many tales and legends originated in the internal strife and dissension of these years.

Mycenae was founded by Perseus, son of Zeus and Danae, and the Perseid dynasty provided many of its rulers. After the last of them, Eurystheus (famous for the labors he imposed on Herakles), the Mycenaeans chose Atreus, son of Pelops and Hippodamia, as their ruler. But Atreus hated his brother, Thyestes, so much that he offered Thyestes his own children to eat, thereby incurring the wrath of the gods. Thyestes pronounced a fearful curse on Atreus and his progeny; Atreus's heir, the renowned and energetic Agamemnon, was murdered on his return from the Trojan War by his wife, Clytemnestra, and her lover, Aegisthus (Thyestes's surviving son). Orestes and his sister Electra, the children of Agamemnon, took revenge for this murder, and Orestes became king of Mycenae. During the rule of his son, Tisamenus, the descendants of Herakles returned and claimed their birthright by force, thus satisfying the wrath of the gods and the curse of Atreus.

In the 17th century BC, Mycenae began an extraordinary growth in wealth and power that was to influence all of the eastern Mediterranean. The Mycenaean civilization, at first heavily influenced by that of Minoan Crete, spread throughout Greece, and by 1400 BC Mycenaeans controlled the mainland and the Aegean, including Crete. Clay tablets inscribed with Mycenaean Greek writing have provided us with information about the society. At its height, it centered on palaces, from which kings or princes governed feudally, holding sway over various bakers, bronze workers, carpenters, masons, potters, and shepherds. And there were merchants, priests, or priestesses, possibly a military leader, the nobility, and, of course, slaves. Some tablets record commodities (grain, bronze, livestock, wool, and oil) and palace possessions (swords, textiles, furniture, and chariots). The dwellings of the elite were decorated with wall paintings depicting processions of court ladies, hunting scenes, oxhide shields, heraldic griffins, and such religious activities as priestesses bearing stalks of grain.

From their recorded offerings, it seems that the Mycenaeans worshiped familiar classical deities, but the bizarre figurines found in a shrine at Mycenae (Now in the Nauplion Museum)—along with models of coiled snakes—are scarcely human, let alone godlike in the style of classical statuary. Myceneans usually buried their dead in chamber tombs cut into the sides of hills, but rulers and their families were interred more grandly, in shaft graves at first and later in immense *tholos* tombs—cir-

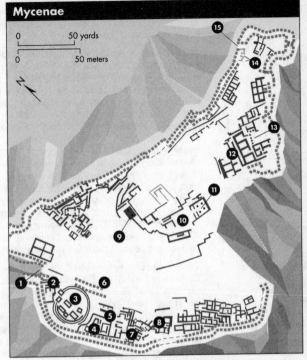

Mycenae

cular vaults, a hallmark of Mycenaean architecture, made by overlapping successive courses of stones, while reducing the diameter of the opening, until it was closed with a single stone on top. The tholos was built into a hillside, like a chamber tomb, entered by a long passage or *dromos*, and covered with a mound of earth. Doors at the end of the dromos allowed the tomb to be opened and reused—not a bad feature, since the average life expectancy of a Mycenaean was about 36 years.

Massive fortification walls and gateways, also Mycenaean specialties, were necessary defenses in a culture whose economy of agriculture and trade was supplemented by occasional raiding and intercity warfare. The Mycenaeans had widespread trade contacts—their fine pottery has been found in Cyprus, southern Italy, Egypt, and the Levant. Wrecks of trading ships apparently headed toward Greece have yielded oxhide-shape bronze ingots, aromatic resin, logs of ebony and ivory, and blue glass for jewelry. But the heyday of the Mycenaeans did not last. Drought, earthquake, invasion, and economic collapse have all been suggested individually and in combination for their fall. Around 1300 BC, arrangements were made to secure the water supplies at Mycenae itself as well as at Tiryns and Athens. Coincidence? Some time around 1200 many sites, but not all, seem to have suffered some destruction. An uprising, invasion, or earthquake? Recovery and rebuilding took place, but it is likely that the palaces were no longer used, and it is certain that a major shift in political and economic administration was underway. By 1100, when there may have been another round of destruction, Greece was heading into a Dark Age.

Writing became a lost art, connections beyond the Aegean were nearly severed, and many sites were abandoned. Whatever the cause, or causes, the lights went out.

In 1841, soon after the establishment of the Greek state, excavations of the Archaeological Society uncovered the parts of the Lion Gate that lay below the surface, and in 1874, Schliemann began to dig. In 1876, he discovered Grave Circle A, five of whose graves he excavated. In the following years, systematic explorations laid bare the palace on the summit of the Acropolis, foundations of two-story houses, the underground spring, and many tombs outside the walls. The citadel of Mycenae was protected by a cyclopean wall, whose huge, irregularly shaped blocks—some worked, some unworked—were placed in regular courses. The first and therefore the oldest wall was built around 1340 BC, enclosing only the summit of the hill. Grave Circle A lay outside it. The **Lion Gate** was erected in 1250 BC, together with the western and southern sections of the wall, which now enclosed the Grave Circle. A little later (circa 1200 BC), the defenses were extended at the northeast angle to enclose and protect the subterranean spring.

Today's visitors enter the citadel from the northwest through the famous Lion Gate. The triangle in relief above the lintel carries two lions, whose heads, probably of steatite, are now missing. They stand facing each other, their forepaws resting on a high pedestal representing an altar, above which stands a pillar ending in a uniquely shaped capital and abacus. Above the abacus are four sculptured discs, interpreted as representing the ends of beams that supported a roof. The gate was closed by a double wooden door sheathed in bronze. The two halves were secured by a wooden bar, which rested in cuttings in the jambs, still visible. The holes for the pivots on which it swung can still be seen in both sill and lintel.

Just inside on the right stands the **Granary,** which was in continuous use until the destruction of the citadel. Between it and the Lion Gate a flight of steps used to lead to the top of the wall; today you see a broad ramp leading steeply up to the palace; the staircase is modern. We come next to **Grave Circle A,** which contains six royal graves, encircled by a row of upright stone slabs interrupted on its northern side by the entrance. Above each grave stood a vertical stone stele. The "grave goods" buried with the dead were a selection of personal belongings including gold face masks, gold cups and jewelry, bronze swords with ivory hilts, and daggers with gold inlay, now in the National Archaeological Museum of Athens. South of the Grave Circle lie the remains of the **House of the Warrior Vase,** the **Ramp House,** the **House of Tsountas,** and others; farther south is the **cult center** of Mycenae.

The palace complex covers the summit of the hill and occupies a series of terraces; one entered through a monumental gateway in the northwest side and, proceeding to the right, beyond it, came to the **Great courtyard** of the palace. The ground was originally covered by a plaster coating above which was a layer of painted and decorated stucco. East of the Great Court is the **Megaron** with a porch, a vestibule, and the throne room itself, with its four columns supporting the roof and the circular hearth in the center. Remains of an archaic and a hellenistic temple can be seen north of the palace, and to the east on the right, on a lower level, are the workshops of the artists and craftsmen employed by the king. On the same level, adjoining the workshops to the east, is the **House of the Columns,** with a row of columns surrounding its central court. The remaining section of the east wall consists of an addition made at the end of 13th century BC to ensure free communication from the citadel with the subterranean reservoir cut at the same time.

On the hill of Panagitsa, below the citadel, lies another Mycenaean settlement, with, close by, the most imposing example of Mycenaean architecture, the **Treasury of Atreus,** also known as the Tomb of Agamemnon. Its construction is placed around 1250 BC, contemporary with the Lion Gate and after Grave Circle A was no longer used for burials. Like the other tholos tombs, it consists of a passageway built of huge squared stones, which leads into a domed chamber. The facade of the entrance had applied decoration, but only small fragments have been preserved. Traces of bronze nails suggest that similar decoration once existed inside. The tomb was found empty, already robbed in antiquity, but it must at one time have contained rich and valuable grave goods. Pausanias tells us that the ancients considered it the "Treasury of Atreus."

Rejoin the main road north, which now climbs more sharply; 19 kilometers (12 miles) from Argos it enters the narrow Dervenakia pass, between the summits of Mt. Tretos. Near this pass, the revolutionary leader Theodorus Kolokotronis defeated the Turks in 1822. Four thousand Turks were slain in the battle and an additional 1,000 perished as they desperately tried to fight their way out of the Argolid. A statue of Kolokotronis near the Nemea–Dervenakia train station commemorates the victory. Beyond the station, the road branches to the left and leads to the site of ancient **Nemea,** near the village of Heraklion and modern Nemea, 10 kilometers (6 miles) farther on. Set in an upland valley, ancient Nemea was the site of a sanctuary of Zeus and the home of the biennial Nemean games, a panhellenic competition like those at Isthmia, Delphi, and Olympia.

Lykourgos and Eurydike, late in life, finally had a son whom they named Opheltes. They asked the Pythian oracle how to ensure the child's health and happiness, and were told not to let their son touch the ground until after he learned to walk. Hypsipyle, the couple's slave, was approached by seven thirsty heroes, marching from Argos against Thebes to support the claim of Oedipus's son Polyneikes to the throne. Leading them to a spring, Hypsipyle set the baby down among some wild celery to fetch the water, unaware that a serpent was fatally biting the baby. To honor the child and to propitiate the gods in the face of this bad omen, the heroes initiated the games.

In the athletic contests at Nemea—footraces, boxing and wrestling, the pentathlon, and chariot and horse races—the victors were crowned with wild celery. The main monuments at the site are the temple of Zeus (built about 330 BC to replace a 6th-century structure), the stadium, and an early Christian basilica of the 5th–6th century. Three columns of the temple still stand, and efforts have begun to re-erect two more. An extraordinary feature of the stadium, which dates to the last quarter of the 4th century BC, is its vaulted tunnel and entranceway. The evidence indicates that the use of the arch in building may have been brought back from India with Alexander, though arches were previously believed to be a Roman invention. A spacious museum displays finds from the site, including a bronze figurine of the baby Opheltes, pieces of athletic gear, and coins of various city-states and rulers. Around Nemea, keep an eye out for roadside stands where local growers sell the famous red wine of this region.

As the road comes out of the hills and into the flatter terrain around Corinth, the massive rock of Acrocorinth rises nearly 1,900 feet on the left. The ancient city sat at the foot of this imposing peak, its long walls reaching north to the harbor of Lechaion on the Gulf of Corinth. The modern city of Corinth is on the coast about 8 kilometers (5 miles) beyond the turnoff for the ancient town (*see* Tour 3, *below*).

Tour 2: Nauplion

Numbers in the margin correspond to points of interest on the Nauplion map.

Nauplion, known to the Venetians as Napoli di Romania, has an exquisite natural setting. On the north side of a rocky peninsula that juts into the Gulf of Argos is the oldest section of town, where the narrow streets are lined with the buildings of Greeks, Venetians, Turks, Franks, and Byzantines, and the stones are worn smooth by their feet. A central swath of flat land, given over to shady parks and plazas, lies below the sheer cliffs of a massive peak adorned with the Palamidi fortress, an elegant display of Venetian might from the early 1700s.

Though it's hard to imagine anyone not liking Nauplion, Henry Miller, in the late 1930s, whined about it at length in *The Colossus of Maroussi*. "Nauplia," he writes, "is dismal and deserted at night. It is a place which has lost caste, like Arles or Avignon. In fact, it is in many ways suggestive of a French provincial town, at night more particularly. There is a little military garrison, a fortress, a palace, a cathedral—and a few crazy monuments. There is also a mosque which has been converted into a cinema. By day it is all red tape, lawyers and judges everywhere, with all the despair and futility which follows in the train of these blood-sucking parasites. The fortress and the prison dominate the town. Warrior, jailer, priest—the eternal trinity which symbolizes our fear of life. I don't like Nauplia. I don't like provincial towns. I don't like jails, churches, fortresses, palaces, libraries, museums, or public statues to the dead."

If you spend at least a day or two in Nauplion, your impression may be more positive.

Little is known about ancient Nauplion, although Neolithic pottery has been found in the vicinity and the peninsula may have had a defensive wall in the Late Bronze Age. It grew in importance in Byzantine times, and was fought over by the Byzantines and the Frankish crusaders. In 1210 Villehardouin captured Nauplion and gave it and Argos to Otho de la Roche, the Duke of Athens. In 1388 the Venetians bought Nauplion from Marie d'Enghien and held it until 1540, when they finally ceded it to the Turks in compliance with a treaty. It remained under Turkish authority (except for 30 years, when the Venetians returned) until the War of Independence, when the

Greeks besieged Nauplion and eventually captured the Palamidi and liberated the city. Serious rifts later developed among the former allies, and Ioannis Kolettis, a war hero, with French support seized Nauplion, Argos, and Tripolis. He convened the National Assembly in 1832 and orchestrated the approval of the Bavarian prince, Otho, as the king of Greece. Although the capital was moved to Athens in December 1834, Nauplion remained the administrative and cultural center of the region. But the city revolted against Otho's rule in 1862, which led to his abdication. During the Second World War, German troops occupied Nauplion from April 1941 until September 1944. Today it is once again just a "provincial town," busy only in the tourist season.

Before beginning the tour, drive out the Epidauros road and turn right after 1 kilometer (⅝ mile), to visit the fine Byzantine convent and church of **Ayia Moni,** a place of Christian devotion with a pagan twist. It was built in 1149 by Leo, the Bishop of Argos and Nauplion, and an inscription on the west gate records his efforts in building it and hopefully expresses the possibility that the Virgin will reward him by absolving him of his sins. In the monastery garden is a fountain said to be the spring Kanathos, where Hera annually renewed her virginity. On the way back to town, be sure to stop and see the **Bavarian Lion,** a beast of more than life size carved into a rock outcrop in the Pronoia section, Nauplion's modern suburb. The sleeping lion, a memorial to the Bavarian troops who died of typhus while serving King Otho, is a sad symbol of mortality compared to the invincible Venetian lions on Nauplion's fortresses.

Seen from the old part of Nauplion, the **Palamidi,** on its 700-foot peak is elegant, with the red stone bastions and flights of steps that zigzag down the cliff face. A modern road lets you drive up the less precipitous eastern slope, but if you are in reasonable shape and it isn't too hot, try climbing the stairs. Most guidebooks will tell you there are 999 of them, but 892 is closer to the mark. From the top you can see the entire Argive plain and look across the gulf to Argos or down its length to the Aegean.

Palamidi, built in 1711–14 by Agostino Sagredo, the Venetian governor, comprises three forts, originally named San Girardo, San Nicolo, and Sant'Agostino, and a series of freestanding and connecting defensive walls. Sculpted in gray stone, the lion of St. Mark looks outward from the gates. The Palamidi fell to the Turks in 1715 after only eight days, and if you climbed the stairs, you can feel the desperation of the fleeing defenders racing down the stairs with the Turks in hot pursuit. After the war, the fortress was used as a prison. On summer nights the Palamidi is illuminated with floodlights, a beautiful sight from below.

At the foot of Palamidi, the flat ground between the Pronoia and the old part of Nauplion is occupied by a pleasant series of tree-shaded plateias, all the nicer since King Constantine Street was closed to automobile traffic. A playground and duck pond, as well as some small aviaries with songbirds, offer entertainment for children. Benches here are perfect for sitting in the evening before dining. In **Kolokotronis Park,** on the north side of King Constantine Street, a bronze equestrian statue surrounded by four small Venetian cannons commemorates the revolutionary hero. South of the street is the old train station

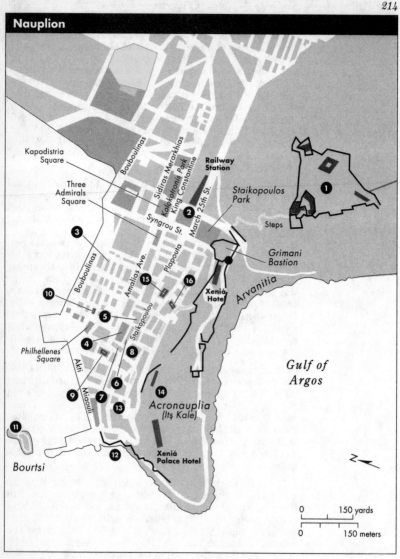

Nauplion

Kapodistria Square

Three Admirals Square

Bouboulinas

Sidiras Merarkhias

Kolokotroni Park
King Constantine

Railway Station

Staikopoulos Park

March 25th St.

Syngrou St.

Steps

Grimani Bastion

Bouboulinas

Amalias Ave.

Plapoula

Xeniá Hotel

Arvanitia

St. Spyridon, **15**

Staikopoulou

Gulf of Argos

Philhellenes Square

Alti

Miaouli

Acronauplia
(Its Kale)

Bourtsi

Xeniá Palace Hotel

| 0 | 150 yards |
| 0 | 150 meters |

Acronauplia (Its Kale), **14**

Archaeological Museum, **7**

Bourtsi, **11**

Catholic Church of the Transformation, **16**

Church of the Virgin Mary's Birth, **9**

"Cinémosque", **5**

The Five Brothers, **12**

National Bank, **6**

Palace of Justice (Nikitaras Park), **2**

The Palamidi, **1**

Peloponnesian Folklore Foundation Museum, **3**

Psaromachalas, **13**

Saint Nicholas' church, **10**

St. Spyridon, **15**

Syntagma Square, **4**

Turkish Mosque (former Parliament), **8**

with a steam engine and vintage freight and passenger cars. In front of the station is a new statue of Bouboulina, the heroine of the revolution, shown with an alarming hair style the sculptor must have adapted from the *Bride of Frankenstein*. This is not to be confused with the bust of Bouboulina on Bouboulina Street, which is a much better, if more traditional, representation.

Walking west, you arrive in **Kapodistria Square,** with its marble statue of the Corfiote diplomat and father of modern Greece, standing statesmanlike, oblivious of the noise from the playground at his feet, from the tavernas across the street, and from the taxis and buses turning left onto Amalias Avenue. Across Syngrou Street from the KTEL bus station two blocks down is a square with yet another hero, Nikitaras the Turk-Killer, who directed the siege of Nauplion. In the same square, beyond the Turk-Killer's statue, is the **Palace of Justice.** If Henry Miller loathed Nauplion for its lawyers and public buildings, you have to believe that he must have spent much of his time staring at the Palace of Justice, a building whose ugliness is magnified by its large size. This monumentality makes it useful as a landmark, however, since the telephone company (OTE) office and pay phones are in the next building.

South of the Palace of Justice, across Staikoupolos Street, is a small sun-drenched open area with a few benches, **Staikopoulos Park.** It is named for the conqueror of the Palamidi; if you are collecting revolutionary heroes (this part of Nauplion is where to pursue them, as they are mercifully rarer in the old town), head back down Syngrou Street. Across from Kapodistria Square you will find **Three Admiral Square,** named for the English, French, and Russian admirals who sank Ibrahim Pasha's fleet in 1827 and centered upon the memorial to **Demetrios Ypsilantis,** a leading general in the War of Independence.

Heading north toward the quayside along Syngrou Street, past the post office on the corner of Sidiras Merarkhias Street, you come to a miniature triangular park that contains, inevitably, a **monument** to a revolutionary hero, admiral **Konstantinos Kanaris;** across from its far end is the **bust of Laskarina Bouboulina.** Twice widowed by wealthy shipowners, she built her own frigate, the *Agamemnon.* Commanding it herself, along with three small ships captained by her sons, Bouboulina blockaded the beleaguered Turks by sea, cutting off their supplies. Turn the corner on which Bouboulina's pedestal sits and walk one block from the harbor along Sophoni Street to the **Peloponnesian Folklore Foundation Museum,** an exemplary small museum that focuses on textiles. *1 King Alexander St., tel. 0752/28379. Open Mar.–Jan., Wed.–Mon. 9–2:30.*

Walk south and turn right on Amalias or King Constantine Street to reach **Syntagma (Constitution) Square,** the center of the old town. King Constantine is more picturesque and takes in older buildings, while the more commercial Amalias is lined with butcher shops and grocery stores. In summer, the restaurants and patisseries along the west and south sides of Syntagma Square—a focal point of Naupliote life—are boisterous with the shouts and laughter of children and filled with diners well into the evening.

Immediately to the left as you enter Syntagma from King Constantine street is the **mosque-turned-movie-theater** (cinémosque?) that Henry Miller took as an example of Nauplion's crassness. He neglected to point out that its course had always been unsteady—before becoming a theater, which at one point showed kung fu movies dubbed into German and subtitled in Greek, it had been successively mosque, church, court, and school. Today it houses city offices.

Walking from the cinémosque, at the southeast corner of Syntagma, along the south side, you pass a café and a store called **Odyssey,** the best place in Nauplion for newspapers and books in English; the owners are very helpful if you need advice ❻ or directions. Continue past the **National Bank,** whose union of Mycenaean and modern Greek architectural elements with concrete is amusing. (The Mycenaeans covered their tholos tombs with mounds of dirt; the bank's ungainly appearance may explain why.) On the square next to the bank are sculptures of a winged lion of St. Mark (which graced the main gate in the city's landward wall, long since demolished) and of Kalliope Papalexopoulou (a leader of the revolt against Otho), whose house once stood in the vicinity.

❼ The **Archaeological Museum,** a red stone building on the west side of Syntagma, was built in 1713 by Augustine Sagredo to serve as the storehouse for the Venetian fleet. The ground floor is occupied by administrative offices, the upper floors by galleries. To say that it is "well-constructed" is an understatement; its arches and windows are nicely proportioned. It has housed the archaeological museum since 1930, and artifacts from such sites as Mycenae, Tiryns, Asine, and Dendra are exhibited here. Of special interest are the Mycenaean suit of armor from Dendra; figures of deities or worshipers and of coiled snakes from the Citadel House shrine at Mycenae and from Tiryns; jewelry from Mycenaean tombs in the area; and 7th-century gorgon masks from Tiryns. *Syntagma, tel. 0752/27502. Admission: 1,500 dr. Open weekdays 8:30–7, weekends 8:30–6.*

Next to the museum and behind the National Bank is a Turkish ❽ mosque, which was the **Parliament** (*Vouleftiko*) from 1827 to 1834, and its seminary (*medressa*), now used for storage by the Archaeological Museum. The mosque is well built of carefully dressed gray stones. Legend has it that the lintel stone from the Treasury of Atreus was used in the construction of its large square-dome prayer hall. The mosque now serves as a music school, and occasionally the sound of a Rossini overture played on a piano can be heard.

It is said that this mosque and the cinémosque on Syntagma were built to expunge the guilt of a murderer. Peter Loderano, a wealthy Venetian merchant, hid his treasure in the basement of his house before fleeing from the Turks in 1715. His sons, Andreas and Guido, returned in 1730 to recover the treasure, and unwisely told Aga Pasha Delviniotis, who then lived in the house, about it. Delviniotis let them search, and killed them after they found it, but his ill-gotten wealth came with a guilty conscience, so he later built the mosque to expiate his crime. The medressa attached to the Parliament was used as a prison earlier in this century. Built in three stories around a paved courtyard, its low-arched colonnades are reminiscent of the fanciful buildings in prints by Dutch artist Maurits Escher.

❾ Next to the **Church of the Virgin Mary's Birth,** west of Syntagma, is an ancient olive tree, where, according to tradition, Saint Anastasius, a Naupliote painter, was killed in 1655 by the Turks. Anastasius was supposedly engaged to a local girl, but abandoned her because she was immoral. Becoming despondent as a result of spells cast over him by her relatives, he converted to Islam. Returning to his senses, he cried out, "I was a Christian, I am a Christian, and I shall die a Christian." A Turkish judge ordered that he be beheaded, but the mob, outraged by the insult to Islam, stabbed Anastasius to death. A local tradition holds that he was hanged on this olive tree, and it never again bore fruit. (Theologians debate whether such a miracle, minor at best and perhaps even dubious, is adequate recompense for Anastasius' unmerited martyrdom.) The church, a post-Byzantine three-aisle basilica, was the main Orthodox church during the Venetian occupation. It has an elaborate wooden reredos carved in 1870.

Continuing north past the church and tree you come to the quayside at the **Philhellenes Square**, named for the memorial erected in 1903 to honor French fighters in the revolution. The French, Germans, English, Swiss, and Americans who fought with the Greeks are called philhellenes, or "friends of Greece." Off Philhellenes Square stands the church of **St. Nicholas**, built in 1713 for the use of sailors by Augustine Sagredo, the prefect of the Venetian fleet. The facade seen today and the belfry are recent additions. Inside, the church is furnished with a Venetian reredos and pulpit, and a chandelier from Odessa. From St. Nicholas westward along the quayside (*paralia*, called Akti Miaouli) is an unbroken chain of restaurants, most just average, and, farther along, more successful patisseries. It is pleasant in the afternoon for postcard writing, an iced coffee or ouzo, and conversation. Sparrows looking for handouts will flit around your feet; the air is warm and the sky blue; and Larissa, Argos's high acropolis, is clearly visible across the smooth sea.

If you like the view to distant Argos, the sight of the **Bourtsi**, Nauplion's pocket-size fortress in the harbor, will captivate you. Built in 1471 by Antonio Gambello, one of those industrious Venetians, the Bourtsi (or Castelli) was at first a single tower on a speck of land generously called St. Theodore's Island. Morosini is said to have massacred the Turkish garrison when he recaptured it for Venice in 1686. A tower and bastion were then added, giving it the shiplike appearance it has today. In 1822, after it was captured in the War of Independence, it was used to bombard the Turks defending the town. In the unsettled times after the revolution, the government retreated to the Bourtsi for a while; after 1865, it was the residence of the town executioners; and from 1930 until 1970 it was run as a hotel. During the day the Bourtsi is no longer menacing; a tree blooms bright red in its courtyard during spring. You can take a small boat out to it for spectacular views of the old part of Nauplion and the Palamidi. Illuminated by floodlights at night in summer it is beautiful at dusk but becomes grimmer as darkness falls. Extending from the extreme end of the paralia is a large breakwater, the west mole, built by the Turks as the anchor point for a large chain that could be drawn up between it and the Bourtsi, blocking the harbor completely.

Farther along toward the promontory of the peninsula is the bastion known as the **Five Brothers**, the only remaining part of the wall built around Nauplion in 1502. The name comes from the five guns placed here by the Venetians; there are five here today, all from around 1690 and all bearing the winged lion of St. Mark. From here follow the broad, winding Kostouros Street up to the large asphalt parking lot below the Xenia Palace hotel and explore **Psaromachalas,** the fishermen's quarter, a small district of narrow, alley-like streets running between cramped little houses that huddle beneath the walls of Acronauplia. The old houses, painted in brownish yellow, green, and salmon, have had all sorts of additions and overhangs added to the original buildings. The walk is enjoyable, but it is a poor neighborhood, and it's easy to feel like a voyeur studying the private lives of the locals.

Now take a moment to look at the pretty miniature whitewashed chapel of **Ayios Apostoli,** just off the nearby parking lot, where six small springlets trickle out of the side of Acronauplia. Return to the Five Brothers to continue the promenade around the peninsula (or go through the tunnel that looks like a James Bond movie set, from the parking lot and take the elevator to the top of Acronauplia).

Time Out A little beyond the Five Brothers is a small, nameless **taverna** that opens in the afternoon. It's a great place to sit with an ouzo and watch the sun set behind the mountains across the gulf. Keep an eye out for the arrival of the evening *Flying Dolphin,* the hydrofoil from Piraeus, as it comes up the gulf to Nauplion.

The promenade, once a simple gravel pathway, is now paved with reddish flagstones and graced with an occasional ornate lamppost. Here and there a flight of steps goes down to the rocky shore below. (Be careful if you go swimming here, since the rocks are infested with sea urchins.) Just before you reach the very tip of the peninsula, marked by a ship's beacon, there is a little shrine at the foot of a path leading up toward the Acronauplia walls above; the end is the diminutive church **Ayia Panagitsa** (Little Virgin Mary), which hugs the cliff on a small terrace and is decorated with an array of icons. Two other terraces, like garden sanctuaries, have a few rose bushes and the shade of olive and cedar trees. They are very restful places to sit and not much frequented.

Along the south side of the peninsula, the promenade runs midway along the cliff—it's 100 feet up to Acronauplia, 50 feet down to the sea. Some go swimming here, but since there is the danger of being slammed into the rocks by a wave, it's safer to swim farther along, at a slightly broader area of pine trees and prickly pear at the foot of the cliff; there is a pay beach with a small playground, but it may not be in usable condition. All along the promenade there are magnificent views of the cliff on which the Palamidi sits and the slope below, known as the Arvanitia.

From the huge parking lot at Arvanitia, you can walk back to town, between the Acronauplia and the Palamidi, or walk up the road toward the Xenia Hotel and explore the **Acronauplia,** which the Turks called Its Kale. Until the Venetian occupation, it had two castles: a Frankish one on the eastern end and a Byzantine one on the west. The Venetians added the massive Castello del Torrione (or Toro for short) at the eastern end around 1480. If you have trouble locating the Toro, look under the Xenia Hotel (not the Xenia Palace), which was built on part of it. During the second Venetian occupation, the gates were strengthened and the huge Grimani bastion was added (1706) below the Toro.

Returning to town via the hotel road, pick up Plapouta Street and head west, stopping first at the square dominated by **Ayios Georgios,** a Byzantine church set at an angle, with five domes dating from the beginning of the 16th century. Around the square are several high-quality neoclassical houses—the one opposite the church is especially classy. Note the fine palmette centered above the door, the pilasters on the third floor with Corinthian capitals, the running Greek key entablature, and the end tiles along the roofline. This house is matched perhaps by the one at the intersection of Plapouta and Tertsetou streets, whose window treatments are especially ornate. Nauplion has many other fine neoclassical buildings; keep your eyes open and don't forget to look up once in a while.

The intersection of Plapouta and Terzaki streets is marked by a jog in the road and a coffee store. Turn left on Terzaki and walk **15** up to the gray square of **St. Spyridon,** a one-aisled basilica with a dome (1702). It has a special place in Greek history, for it was at its doorway that the statesman Ioannis Kapodistria was assassinated in 1831. The mark of the bullet can be seen next to the Venetian portal. On the south side of the square, opposite St. Spyridon, are two of the four Turkish fountains preserved in Nauplion. A third is a short distance east (away from St. Spyridon) on Kapodistria Street, at the steps that constitute the upper reaches of Tertsetou Street.

Potamianou Street, actually a flight of stone steps, ascends from St. Spyridon Square toward Acronauplia. A bit more than **16** halfway up you'll find the Venetian **Catholic Church of the Transformation,** which Otho returned to Nauplion's Catholics. It is best known for the wooden arch erected inside the doorway in 1841, with the names carved on it of philhellenes who died during the War of Independence (Lord Byron is number 10). Note also the evidence of its use as a mosque by the Turks: an elaborate stone portal at the entrance and the amputated stub of a minaret. Descending to Staikopoulos Street and walking west, you pass the fourth Turkish fountain and a series of good restaurants behind Syntagma and the National Bank. From Syntagma you can head back to the waterfront, explore higher up beyond the Catholic church, find a café, try the tourist shops in the vicinity, or go back to your hotel and collapse.

Tour 3: Corinth–Patras–Olympia

Numbers in the margin correspond to points of interest on the Northern Peloponnese map.

This trip is most conveniently made by car, but there is good bus and train service that, combined with local buses or taxis, will do just fine. It will take two days, assuming a half day tour of ancient Corinth, an evening and overnight at Patras, followed by a morning's drive and half-day tour of Olympia. You can return to Athens by retracing the coastal route, cutting across the mountains of Achaia, or crossing the gulf and going via Delphi.

West of the isthmus, the countryside opens up into a low-lying coastal plain around the head of the Gulf of Corinth. Modern Corinth, near the coast, is a regional center of some 23,000 inhabitants. Concrete pier-and-slab is the preferred architectural style, and the city is under a seismic curse: Periodic earthquakes knock the buildings down before they develop any character. It was founded in 1858 after one of these quakes leveled the old village at the ancient site; another flattened the new town in 1928; and yet another in nearby Megara destroyed many of its buildings in 1981. Most tourists avoid the town altogether, visiting the ruins of ancient Corinth and moving on.

⑩ Ancient Corinth, at the base of the massive Acrocorinth peak (1,863 feet) was blessed: It governed the north–south land route over the isthmus and the east–west sea route. The fertile plain and hills around the city (where currants are grown, which are named for Corinth) are extensive, and the Acrocorinth afforded a virtually impregnable refuge. It had harbors at Lechaion on the Gulf of Corinth and at Kenchreai on the Saronic Gulf. Corinth was a wealthy city with a reputation for luxury and vice and a Temple of Aphrodite with sacred prostitutes. These facts are emphasized too often today, and amid the titillation the real story of Corinth is lost.

The city came to prominence in the 8th century BC, becoming a center of commerce and founding the colonies of Syracuse in Sicily and Kerkyra on Corfu. The 5th BC century saw the rise of Athens as the preeminent economic power in Greece, and Athenian "meddling" in the Gulf of Corinth and in relations between Corinth and her colonies helped bring about the Peloponnesian War. After the war, Corinth made common cause with Athens, Argos, and Boeotia against Sparta, later remaining neutral as Thebes and then Macedonia rose to power.

In the second half of the 4th century, Corinth became active once more; in 344 the city sent an army to rescue Syracuse, which was threatened by local tyrants allied with the Carthaginians. Timoleon, the aristocrat who led the army, was in self-imposed exile after killing his own brother, who had plotted to become tyrant of Corinth. Corinthian opinion was divided as to whether Timoleon was the savior of the city or merely a fratricide, so no one objected to Timoleon's appointment to this dangerous mission (he wasn't present at the time). The Corinthian statesman Teleclides understood the challenge facing Timoleon perfectly, saying, "We shall decide that he slew a tyrant if he is successful; that he slew his brother if he fails." The tyrants were suppressed and Carthaginian armies expelled from Sicily; Timoleon, declared a hero, retired to a small farm outside Syracuse, where he died two years later.

Corinth was conquered by Philip II of Macedon in 338 BC, but was named the meeting place of Philip's new Hellenic confederacy. After Philip was assassinated, Alexander immediately swooped down on Corinth to meet with the confederacy, to confirm his leadership, and to forestall any thoughts of rebellion. It's said that outside the gates Alexander encountered the philosopher Diogenes the Cynic, who espoused a creed of living as simply and cheaply as possible. When not carrying a lantern around in broad daylight on his quest for an honest man, he lived in a large storage jar, which is where Alexander found him. When Alexander the Great asked Diogenes if there was anything he could do for him, "Only step out of my sunlight," was the curt reply.

After the death of Alexander, the climate continued profitable for trade, and Corinth flourished. When the Roman general Flamininus defeated Macedonia in 198–196 BC, Corinth became the chief city of the Achaean confederacy, in fact the chief city of Greece. Eventually the confederacy took up arms against Rome, attacking with more impetuosity than brains or training, and was crushed. The Romans under Lucius Mummius marched to Corinth and defeated a second Greek army, and Pausanias says: "...Two days after the battle he took possession in force and burnt Corinth. Most of the people who were left there were murdered by the Romans, and Mummius auctioned the women and children." Corinth was razed and its wealth sent back to Rome, and for nearly 100 years the site was abandoned. In 44 BC, Julius Caesar refounded the city, and under *pax romana* Corinth prospered as never before; its population (about 90,000 in 400 BC) was recorded as 300,000 plus 450,000 slaves.

The apostle Paul lived in Corinth for 18 months (AD 51–52), working as a tent maker or leather worker, making converts where he could. The city received imperial patronage from Hadrian, who constructed an aqueduct from Lake Stymphalos to the city, and Herodes Atticus made improvements to its civic buildings. Corinth survived invasions but was devastated by earthquakes and began a long decline with further invasions and plague. After 1204, when Constantinople fell to the Fourth Crusade, Corinth was a prize sought by all, but it eventually surrendered to Geoffrey de Villehardouin (the subsequent Prince of Achaea) and Otho de la Roche (soon to be Duke of Athens). Corinth was captured by the Turks in 1458, the Knights of Malta won it in 1612, the Venetians took a turn from 1687 until 1712, when the Turks returned, and it finally came into Greek hands in 1822.

The ancient city was huge. Excavations, which have gone on since 1896, have exposed ruins at several locations: on the height of Acrocorinth and on the slopes below, the center of the Roman city, and northward toward the coast. Most of the buildings that have been excavated are from the Roman era; only a few from before the sack of Corinth in 146 BC were rehabilitated when the city was refounded.

Walking from the parking lot, you pass the **Glauke Fountain** on the left and beyond it the **museum** (tel. 0741/31207; admission 1,500 dr.; open weekdays 8:30–7, weekends 8:30–6), which displays examples of the pottery decorated with friezes of panthers, sphinxes, bulls, and such, for which Corinth was famous; some fine mosaics from the Roman period; and a variety of marble and terra-cotta sculptures. The remains of a temple (Temple E) adjoin the museum, and steps lead from there left toward the **Temple of Apollo.**

Seven of the original 38 columns of the Temple of Apollo are still standing and it is by far the most striking of Corinth's ancient buildings, as well as being one of the oldest in Greece (mid-6th century BC). Beyond the temple are the remains of the **North Market,** a colonnaded square once surrounded by many small shops. Retracing your steps south, walk along the row of shops that formed the western boundary of the Forum, turn left, and pass through a series of small temples into the forum's main plaza. A long line of shops runs lengthwise through the **Forum,** dividing it into an upper (southern) and lower (northern) terrace, in the center of which is the *bema*, a large podium.

The southern boundary of the Forum was the **South Stoa**, a 4th-century building, perhaps erected by Philip II to house delegates to his Hellenic confederacy. There were originally 33 shops across the front, and the back was altered in Roman times to accommodate such civic offices as the council hall, or *bouleterion,* in the center. The road to Kenchreai began next to the bouleterion and headed south. Farther along the South Stoa were the entrance to the **South Basilica** and, at the far end, the **Southeast Building,** which probably was the city archive.

In the lower Forum, below the Southeast Building, was the **Julian Basilica**; under the steps leading into it were found two starting lines (an earlier and a later one) for the course of a foot-race from the Greek city. Continuing to the northeast corner of the Forum, we approach the facade of the **Fountain of Peirene.** Water from a spring was gathered into four reservoirs before flowing out through the arcadelike facade into a drawing basin in front. Frescoes of swimming fish from a 2nd-century refurbishment can still be seen. Leaving the Forum via the Lechaion road, we come to a colonnaded courtyard (on the right), the **Peribolos of Apollo,** and beyond it a public latrine, with toilets in place, and the remains of a Roman-era bath, probably the Baths of Eurykles described by Pausanias as Corinth's best-known.

Along the west side of the Lechaion road (on the right as we head back to the Forum) is a large basilica entered from the Forum through the **Captives' Facade,** named for its sculptures of captive barbarians. West of the Captives' Facade the row of **Northwest Shops** completes the circuit.

Heading past the parking lot we come to the Odeum and Theater. The **Odeum,** cut into a natural slope, was built during the 1st century, but it burned down around 175. Around 225 it was renovated and used as an arena for combats between gladiators and wild beasts. Just north of the Odeum is the **Theater** (5th century BC), one of the few Greek buildings reused by the Romans, who filled in the original seats and set in new ones at a steeper angle. By the 3rd century they had adapted it for gladiatorial contests and finally for mock naval battles.

North of the theater, just inside the city wall are the **Fountain of Lerna** and the **Asklepieion,** the sanctuary of the god of healing, a small temple (4th century BC) set in a colonnaded courtyard, and a series of dining rooms in a second courtyard. Terracotta votive offerings representing afflicted body parts (hands, legs, breasts, genitals, etc.) were found in the excavation of the Asklepieion, and many of them are displayed at the museum; similar votives of body parts can be purchased and blessed at some Orthodox churches in Greece today. A stone box for offerings was found at the entrance to the sanctuary. Off the lower courtyard are the drawing basins of the Fountain of Lerna.

From the museum you can drive to the base of Acrocorinth, though die-hard hikers take a path that leads south. On the slope is the **Sanctuary of Demeter,** a small shrine and a series of dining rooms with couches. The climb up to Acrocorinth is worth the effort for both the medieval fortifications and the view, one of the best in Greece. The entrance is on the west, guarded by a moat and outer gate, middle gate, and inner gate. Most of the fortifications are Byzantine, Frankish, Venetian, and Turkish—but the right-hand tower of the innermost of the three gates is apparently a 4th-century BC original.

⑪ Xylokastro, a pleasant little town 34 kilometers (21 miles) west, is perfect if you want to soak your feet after trudging around Corinth. A wide, paved promenade along the shore, with a beautiful view of the mountains across the gulf, leads to a good if somewhat pebbly beach beyond the east end of town. If mountains are what you want, take the road that climbs up to **Ano Trikala,** an alpine landscape where the peak (second-highest in the Peloponnese) stays covered with snow into June. **Diakofto** (81 kilometers [50 miles]) is the railway junction for the narrow-gauge line to Kalavrita (*see* Off the Beaten Track, *below*).

⑫ Egio (94 kilometers [57 miles]), a regional agricultural and commercial center, has always suffered from competition with Patras and Corinth. The meeting place of the Achaean League after 276, it went into a decline when Augustus reconstituted Patras.

⑬ Rion is distinguished by the **Castle of the Morea,** built by Sultan Bayazid II in 1499, which sits as forlorn as a castle can be amid a field of oil storage tanks. With the **Castle of Roumeli** on the opposite shore, it guarded the narrows leading into the Gulf of Corinth. A half-hourly car ferry connects Rio with Antirion, linking the Peloponnese with central and northwestern Greece. Of the titanic bridge proposed during the Papandreou administration, there is no trace.

⑭ Patras, the third largest city in Greece, begins almost before Rion is passed. Like all respectable Greek cities, it has an ancient history. Off its harbor in 429 BC Corinthian and Athenian ships fought inconclusively, and in 279 BC the city helped defeat an invasion of Celtic Galatians. Its losses then and at the debacle at Corinth in 146 BC brought the city in danger of abandonment until Augustus brought the Achaeans together to form a new colony at the site. Its acropolis was fortified under Justinian in the 6th century, and Patras withstood an attack by Slavs in 805. Silk production, begun in the 7th century, brought renewed prosperity, but control passed successively to the Venetians, the Franks, and the Turks, until the War of Independence.

Thomas Palaiologos, the last Byzantine to leave Patras before the Turks took over in 1458, carried an unusual prize with him—the skull of the apostle St. Andrew, which he gave to Pius II in exchange for an annuity. St. Andrew had been crucified in Patras and was the city's patron saint. In 1964 Pope Paul VI returned the head to Patras (apparently thinking that Pius II had gotten his money's worth, or that it had been a while since Thomas last collected his annuity). Today it graces St. Andrew's Cathedral, seat of the Bishop of Patras.

The major western port for freighters carrying the all-important currants, and for passenger and car ferries sailing to Italy, thoroughly modern Patras has the international, outward-looking feel common to port cities. The waterfront is pleasant enough, though not very interesting; you'll find lots of mediocre restaurants, a range of hotels, the bus and train stations, and numerous travel agents (caveat emptor). Back from the waterfront, the town gradually rises along arcaded streets, which provide welcome shade and rain protection but make some feel claustrophobic. Of the series of large plateias, tree-shaded Queen Olga Square is the nicest. A good walk is to take Ayios Nikolaos Street upward through the city until it comes to the long flight of steps leading to the ruined castle overlooking the harbor. There isn't much to do up there, but the panoramic view can be beautiful in the evening when lighted ferry boats are moving in and out of the port. Descend the steps and then take an immediate left, to arrive at the Plateia 25 Martiou and the restored Roman odeum (circa AD 160), where performances are given in late summer. On the northern side of the plateia are the steps at the head of Gerokostopoulou Street. Closed to traffic along its upper reaches, this street's myriad cafés and music bars make it a relaxing place to spend an evening.

Time Out Greek vintners, faced with EC competition, are producing better wines than ever before. Some are opening up their wineries for tours, among them **Constantine Antonopoulos Winery** (19 km [12 mi] s. of Patras on Tripolis Rd., tel. 061/277723; open daily 9–4) and **Achaia Clauss** (9 km [6 mi] west of Patras, tel. 061/325051; open daily 7–2:30). It is best to call ahead for tours and tastings.

If you take an easy detour south from Patras on Highway 33 and turn left after 16 kilometers (10 miles), you come to 15 **Halandritsa**, seat of a prosperous Frankish barony, whose early stone churches and narrow streets make it a worthwhile stop. There are beautiful views across the coast to the open sea. Back on the coast road from Patras toward Olympia, after Kato Ahaia, you come to the plains and wooded hills of Elis. About 40 kilometers (25 miles) farther on, a brief side trip can be made by turning toward the sea at Lehena and driving to **Kastro** at 16 the foot of **Chlemoutsi Castle**, the best-preserved Frankish monument in the Peloponnese. Geoffrey I de Villehardouin, who built it from 1220 to 1223, named it Clairmont. The Venetians called it Castle Tornese, perhaps on account of the Frankish coins (*tournoi*) minted in nearby Glarentza. The Byzantine despot Constantine Palaiologos captured it in 1427 and used it as a base from which to attack Patras, the last Frankish stronghold. The castle has a huge hexagonal keep, with vaulted galleries around an open court. After 1460 the Turks strengthened the gate and altered the galleries. It was captured by the Venetians in 1687, and shortly thereafter was ceded to the Turks. On the southwest side you can see a breach made by Ibrahim Pasha's cannon during the War of Independence.

The coast south of Kastro toward **Loutra Killinis** is a beach resort area. Heading southeast again to Olympia via Gastouni and Pyrgos, you encounter other fine beaches off Highway 9, at Katakolo and Spiantza. Just before Pyrgos, a thriving regional center, take Highway 74 to the left for the final leg into Olympia. The modern village of Olympia is a one-street town (Kondilis Street to be exact) and consists largely of hotels and tourist shops with a scattering of tavernas. It's good for a stopover, but has little to offer except the pleasant hilly countryside (for once, in southern Greece, well watered and green).

Just across the Kladeos River at the east end of town is 17 **Olympia**, the ancient Sanctuary of Zeus, one of the most popular sites in Greece. Two hours is a minimum for seeing the ruins

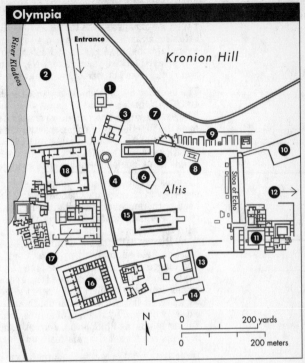

and the fine museum, and three or four would suffice. The ancient sanctuary occupies a compact, flat area at the base of the Kronion hill (on the north), where the Kladeos and Alpheios rivers join. It comprised the sacred precinct, or Altis, a large rectangular enclosure south of the Kronion, with administrative buildings, baths, and workshops on the west and south, and the Stadium and Hippodrome on the east. In 1829, a French expedition investigated the Temple of Zeus and removed a few metope fragments to the Louvre. The systematic excavation begun by the German Archaeological Institute in 1875 has continued intermittently to this day.

Although the first Olympiad is thought to have been in 776 BC, bronze votive figures of the Geometric period (10th–8th centuries) reveal that the sanctuary was in use before that date. The festival took place every four years over a five-day period in the late summer during a sacred truce, observed by all Greek cities. Initially only native speakers of Greek (excepting slaves) could compete, but Romans were later admitted. Foreigners could watch, but married women, Greek or not, were barred from the sanctuary during the festival on pain of death. The events included the footrace, boxing, chariot and horse racing, the pentathlon (combining running, jumping, wrestling, and both spear and discus throwing), and the *pankration* (a no-holds barred style of wrestling in which competitors could break their opponent's fingers and other body parts).

By and large the Olympic festival was peaceful, though not without problems. The Spartans were banned in 420 BC for breaking the sacred truce; there was fighting in the Altis between the Eleans and the Pisans and Arcadians; the Roman dictator Sulla carried off the treasure to finance his army and five years later held the games in Rome itself. The 211th festival was delayed for two years so that Nero could compete, and despite a fall from his chariot, he was awarded the victory.

The long decline of Olympia began after the reign of Hadrian. In 267 AD, under threat of an invasion, many buildings were dismantled to construct a defensive wall; Christian decrees forbade the functioning of pagan sanctuaries and caused the demolition of the Altis. Earthquakes settled its fate, and flooding of the Alpheios and the Kladeos, together with landslides off the Kronion hill, buried the abandoned sanctuary.

Olympia's ruins are fairly compact, so it's easy to get a quick overview in an hour and then investigate specific buildings or head to the museum. The site is very pleasant, with plenty of trees providing shade. Entering the site and heading south with the Kronion hill on your left, you pass the remains of a small **Roman bath** and the **Gymnasion,** essentially a large open practice field surrounded by stoas (long, narrow porticoes). The large complex opposite the Gymnasion was the **Prytaneion,** where the *prytaneis* (magistrates in charge of the games) feted the winners and where the Olympic flame burned on a sacred hearth. Continue south and turn left through a gateway marked by two sets of four columns to enter the Altis. To the right is the **Philippeion,** a circular shrine started by Philip II and completed after his death by Alexander the Great.

Directly in front of you is the large Doric temple of Hera, the **Heraion** (circa 600 BC). It is well preserved, especially considering that it is constructed from the local coarse, porous, shell limestone. At first it had wooden columns, which were replaced as needed, so although they are all Doric, the capitals don't exactly match. Three of the columns have been set back up. A colossal head of a goddess, possibly from the statue of Hera, was found at the temple and is now in the site museum. Just south of the Heraion are the remains of a sixth-century BC pentagonal wall built to enclose the **Shrine of Pelops,** at the time an altar in a sacred grove. According to Pausanias, the **Altar of Zeus** was southeast of the temple of Hera, but no trace of it has been found. Some rocks mark its supposed location.

There is no doubt about the location of the **Nymphaion,** or **Exedra,** which brought water to Olympia from a spring to the east. A colonnade around the semicircular reservoir had statues of the family of Herodes Atticus and his imperial patrons. The 4th-century **Metroon,** at the bottom of the Nymphaion terrace, was originally dedicated to Cybele, Mother of the Gods, and was taken over by the Roman imperial cult. At the foot of the terrace wall were 16 bronze statues of Zeus, called the Zanes, bought with money from fines levied against those caught cheating at the games. Bribery seems to have been the most common offense, steroids not being available. Olympia also provides the earliest case of the sports-parent syndrome: In the 192nd Olympiad, Damonikos of Elis, whose son Polyktor was to wrestle Sosander of Smyrna, bribed the latter's father in an attempt to buy the victory for his son.

On the terrace itself are the city-state **Treasuries,** which look like small temples and were used to store valuables, such as equipment used in rituals. Walking along the row of Treasuries, leave the northeast corner of the Altis and enter the **Stadium.** At first it ran along the terrace of the Treasuries and had no embankments for the spectators to sit on; embankments were added later, but never given seats, and 40,000–50,000 spectators could be accommodated.

A 1st-century villa off the southeastern corner of the Altis was the **House of Nero,** near which was found a lead water pipe marked NER. AUG. Beyond this villa, running parallel to the Stadium, was the **Hippodrome,** where horse and chariot races were held. It hasn't been excavated, and much has probably been eroded away by the Alpheios. Leaving the Altis by the large southeastern gate, you see, appended to its southern wall, the **Bouleuterion** and, just south of it, the **South Hall.** The Bouleuterion consisted of two rectangular halls on either side of a square building that housed the Altar of Zeus Horkios, where athletes and trainers swore to compete fairly.

Returning to the Altis, we approach the **Temple of Zeus.** Only a few column drums are in place, but the huge size of the temple platform is impressive. Designed by Libon, an Elean architect, it was built from about 470 to 456 BC. The sculptures from the pediments are on view in the Olympia Museum. A gilded bronze statue of Nike (Victory) stood above the east pediment, matching a marble Nike (in the site museum) that stood on a pedestal in front of the temple. Both were the work of the sculptor Paionios. The cult statue inside the temple, made of gold and ivory, showed Zeus seated on a throne, holding a Nike in his open right hand and a scepter in his left. It was created in 430 BC by Pheidias, sculptor of the cult statue of Athena in the Parthenon, and was said to be seven times life size; it was one of the seven wonders of the ancient world. It is said that Caligula wanted to move the statue to Rome and replace the head with one of his own, but the statue laughed out loud when his men approached it. It was removed to Constantinople, and destroyed by fire in AD 475. Pausanias relates that behind the statue there was "a woolen curtain...decorated by Assyrian weavers and dyed with Phoenician crimson, dedicated by Antiochos." It is possible this was the veil of the Temple at Jerusalem (Antiochos IV Epiphanes forcibly converted the Temple to the worship of Zeus Olympias).

Just outside the gate at the southwestern corner of the Altis stood the **Leonidaion,** at first a guest house for important visitors and later a residence of the Roman governor of the province of Achaia. Immediately north of the Leonidaion was the **workshop of Pheidias,** where the cult statue of Zeus was constructed in a large hall of the same size and orientation as the interior of the temple. Tools, clay molds, and Pheidias's own cup (in the museum) make the identification of this building certain. It was later used as a Byzantine church. As you head north, toward the entrance, you pass the **Palaestra,** built in the 3rd century BC, for athletic training. The rooms around the square field were used for bathing and cleansing with oil, for teaching, and for socializing.

The "new" museum at Olympia, officially opened in 1982, is northwest of the site. In its collections are the sculptures from the Temple of Zeus, the Nike of Paionios, and the Hermes of Praxiteles. Also of note are a terra-cotta group of Zeus and Ganymede, the head of the cult statue of Hera, statues of the family and imperial patrons of Herodes Atticus, and the many bronzes found at the site, including votive figurines, cauldrons, and armor. Of great historical interest are a helmet dedicated by Militiades, the Athenian general who defeated the Persians at Marathon, and a cup owned by the sculptor Pheidias. The central gallery of the museum holds the pedimental sculptures and metopes from the Temple of Zeus. *Tel. 0624/22529. Admission: 1,500 dr. Open weekdays 8:30–7, weekends 8:30–6.*

Excursion from Olympia

The Apollo Temple at Bassae
Leave Olympia and, following signs for Krestena, take the road leading southeast for 57 kilometers (35 miles) to **Andritsena,** for a visit to the temple of Apollo at Bassae. An ice-cold stream tumbling down from Mt. Minthis waters **Andritsena** and accounts for its many fountains. Once a major hillside town, its claim to fame today is a collection of 15th-century Venetian and Vatican first editions and documents relating to the War of Independence. The books are now in storage, but the new library should be finished by early 1993. *On main rd., 100 yds past sq., tel. 0626/22242. Admission free. Open weekdays 8:30–3.*

Time Out
Join the old men relaxing under the plane tree at **Kafenion Apollon** in Andritsena's main square. Order a cool *frappe*, iced coffee Greek-style. Be sure to have it with milk (*me gala*).

Outside Andritsena, turn left and follow the signs 14 kilometers (9 miles) to the **Temple of Apollo Epikourios at Bassae.** The cragged, uncompromising scenery all around may leave you unprepared for the elegant, spare building, which has not yet fallen prey to vandalism or commercialism, perhaps because of its remoteness. Pausanias believed this temple was designed by Iktinos, the Parthenon's architect. Although this theory has recently been disputed, it is nevertheless one of the best-preserved Classical temples in Greece, superseded in its state of preservation only by the Hephaisteion in Athens. The residents of nearby Phygalia built it atop an older temple in 420 BC to thank Apollo for delivering them from an epidemic; *epikourious* means "helper."

The Bassae temple, made of local limestone, has some unusual details: exceptional length compared to its width; a north–south orientation rather than the usual east–west (probably because of the slope of the ground); and Ionic half-columns linked to the walls by flying buttresses. It had the first known Corinthian column sporting the characteristic acanthus leaves—only the base remains now—and the earliest example of interior sculptured friezes, which illustrated the battles between the Greeks and Amazons and the Centaurs and Lapiths. The friezes now hang in the British Museum.

Take the time to climb to the summit northwest of the temple for a view overlooking the Nedas River, Mt. Lykaeon, and on a clear day, the Ionian Sea. Despite its splendid setting, the temple loses some of its impact because it is veiled by a canopy to protect it from acid rain. *Tel. 0626/22254. Admission free. Open daily 8:30–3.*

Rather than retrace your steps, you can continue on to Tripolis and thence back to Athens via the Isthmus.

Off the Beaten Track

Kalavrita Express One of the most enjoyable side trips in the northern Peloponnese begins in Diakofto, a bit more than halfway along the road from the isthmus to Patras, at a small switchyard, where, on a narrow-gauge branch line, the *Kalavrita Express* heads up into the mountains through the Vouraikos Gorge, a fantastic landscape of towering pinnacles and precipitous rock walls. The diminutive train, a cabless diesel engine sandwiched between two small passenger cars, crawls upward, clinging to the rails in the steeper sections with a rack and pinion. After 45 minutes the train pauses at Zakhlorou, where you can hike up a steep path through evergreen oak, cypress, and fir to the monastery of **Mega Spileo** (altitude 3,117 ft). This 45-minute trek offers superb views of the Vouraikos valley and distant villages on the opposite side. The occasional sound of bells carries on the wind from flocks of goats grazing on the steep slopes above. The monastery, founded in the 4th century, sits at the base of a huge curving cliff face and incorporates a large cavern (the monastery's name means "large cave"). You can tour the monastery to see an icon of the Virgin supposedly painted by St. Luke, vellum manuscripts of early gospels, and the heads of the founding monks. Beyond Zakhlorou, the gorge widens into a steep-sided green alpine valley for the last 11 kilometers (7 miles) to Kalavrita, a small town of about 2,000, where the ruins of a Frankish castle, the Church of the Dormition, and the small museum are worth seeing.

The *Kalavrita Express* makes the round trip from Diakofto four times daily; the first trip is at 7:45 AM, the last return at 5:25 PM. *Fare: 600 dr. first class, 400 dr. 2nd class (a fairly meaningless distinction considering the small size of the coaches). Although the trip can be made directly from Athens (round-trip fare, Athens–Kalavrita: 2,640 dr. first-class, 1,760 dr. 2nd class) it may be best enjoyed as a break in the journey between Corinth and Patras.*

To Sparta and Mystras In the south central Peloponnese (116 kilometers [72 miles] from Argos, via Tripolis) lies modern-day Sparta, and just west of it, on a wooded foothill of Mt. Taygettos, the ancient city of **Mystras.** There are hotels and restaurants in Sparta, but most visitors come here on their way to Mystras (take Lycourgou Street west for about 5 kilometers [3 miles]), since there isn't much to see except, at the end of Konstandinou Street, the stern **statue of Leonidas,** the Spartan king. When his army of 8,000 was ordered by the advancing 30,000 Persians to lay down its arms, he sent back the challenge "Come and get them."

Enjoy an hour in the city's **archaeological museum,** tucked into a cool park. Its eclectic collection reflects Lakonia's turbulent history: Neolithic pottery; jewels and tools excavated from the Alepotrypa cave; Mycenaean tomb finds; bright Roman mosaics (4th and 5th centuries); and objects from Sparta, including an expressive clay woman's head, a Parian marble statue of Le-

onidas (490 BC), prizes given to the Spartan youths, and ritual
dance masks. Most characteristic of Spartan art are the bas reliefs with deities and heroic figures; note the one depicting a
seated couple bearing gifts and framed by a snake (540 BC). *Ag.
Nikonos between Dafnou and Evagelistrias, tel. 0731/28575.
Admission: 400 dr. adults, 200 dr. students. Open Tues.–Sun.
8–3.*

Time Out   If you should find yourself waiting for a bus out of Sparta, cross
the street to **Parthenon** (Vrasidou 106, tel. 0731/23767) for the
best gyro you may ever eat. The meat, which has a local reputation for being a cut above the ordinary, is served in pita that has
just the right amount of chew, with generous doses of onion,
tomato, and a garlic-yogurt sauce.

Ethereal Mystras, with its abandoned golden-stone palaces,
churches and monasteries lining winding paths, is eerie. The
scent of herbs and wildflowers permeates the air, goat bells tin-
kle from far off, and the silvery olive trees glisten with the
slightest breeze. It seems appropriate that this place was the
last hurrah for the Byzantine emperors in the 14th century, an
intellectual and cultural center where philosophers like
Chrysoloras, "the sage of Byzantium," held forth on the good
and the beautiful.

In 1249 William de Villehardouin built the **castle** in Mystras in
an attempt to control Lakonia and establish Frankish supremacy over the Peloponnese. He held court here with his beautiful
Greek wife, Anna Comnena, surrounded by knights of Champagne, Burgundy, and Flanders, but in 1259 he was defeated
by the Byzantines. As the Byzantines gradually built a palace
and numerous churches (whose frescoes exemplified several
periods of painting), the town grew down the slope.

At first the seat of the Byzantine governor, Mystras later became the capital of the Despotate of Morea. It was the despots
who made Mystras a cultural phenomenon, and it was the despots—specifically Emperor Constantine's brother Demetrios
Palaiologos—who surrendered the city to the Turks in 1460,
signaling the beginning of the end. For a while the town survived because of its silk industry, but after repeated pillaging
and burning by bands of Albanians, by Russians, and by Ibrahim Pasha's Egyptian troops, the inhabitants gave up and
moved to modern Sparta.

Among the most important buidings in the lower town (Kato
Chora) is **Ayios Demetrios,** the *mitropolis* (cathedral) founded
in 1291. Set in its floor is a stone with the two-headed Byzantine eagle marking the spot where Constantine, the last emper-
or of Byzantium, was consecrated. The cathedral's brilliant
frescoes include a vivid depiction of the Virgin and Child on the
central apse and a wall painting in the narthex of the Second
Coming, its two red-and-turquoise winged angels sorrowful as
they open the records of Good and Evil. One wing of the church
houses a museum that holds fragments of Byzantine sculptures, including an eagle seizing its prey (11th century), later
Byzantine icons, jewels, decorative metalwork, and coins.

Farther along the path to the right in the Vrontokion monas-
tery are **Ayios Theodoros** (AD 1295), the oldest church in
Mystras, and the 14th-century **Church of Virgin Odegetria,** or
Afendiko, which is decorated with remarkable murals. These

include, in the narthex, scenes of the miracles of Christ: the Healing of the Blind Man, the Samaritan at the Well, and the Marriage of Cana. The fluidity of the painting, its subtle but complicated coloring, and its resonant expressions suggest the work of extremely skilled artists. The nearby **Pantanassa monastery** is a visual feast of intricate tiling, rosette-festooned loops like frosting on a wedding cake, and myriad arches. It is the only inhabited building in Mystras: the hospitable nuns still produce embroidery for sale. Step out on the east portico for a view of the Evrotas river valley below.

Every inch of the tiny **Perivleptos monastery** (meaning "attracting attention from all sides") is covered with exceptional 14th-century illustrations from the New Testament, including the Birth of the Virgin—in a lush palette of reds, yellows, and oranges—the Dormition of the Virgin above the entrance (with Christ holding his mother's soul represented as a baby), and immediately to the left of the entrance, the famous fresco of the Divine Liturgy. Perivleptos is in the southernmost corner of the lower town.

In the upper town (Ano Chora) where most aristocrats lived, stands a rare Byzantine civic building, the **Palace of Despots,** home of the last emperor. To get to the Palace, backtrack from Perivleptos to Pantanassa, where the path ascends to the upper town. The older, northeastern wing contains a guardroom, a kitchen, and the residence. The three-story northwest wing holds an immense reception hall on its top floor, lit by eight Gothic windows and heated by eight huge chimneys; the throne probably stood in the shallow alcove that's in the center of a wall.

In the palace's **Ayia Sofia chapel,** the Italian wives of emperors Constantine and Theodore Palaiologos are buried. Note the polychromatic marble floor and the frescoes that were preserved for years under whitewash, applied by the Turks when they transformed this into a mosque. Continue the climb to the castle and look down into the gullies of Mt. Taygettos, where it's said the Spartans, who hated weakness, hurled their malformed babies.

In spring Mystras is resplendent with wildflowers and with butterflies like brimstones and swallowtails, but it can be oppressively hot in summer, so get an early start. Bring water and sturdy shoes for the slippery rocks and the occasional snake. *Tel. 0731/93377. Admission 1,000 dr. adults, 500 dr. students. Open winter, daily 8–3; summer, daily 8–7.*

To the Byzantine Gibraltar **Monemvassia,** 96 kilometers (59 miles) from Sparta, near the southeast tip of the Peloponnese, can also be reached from Athens by ferry—the *Ionian* (tel. 01/412–4800 or 01/451–1311 for Port Authority) arrives twice weekly from Athens (once a week in winter)—and by Flying Dolphin (tel. 01/453–6107 or 01/453–7107) six times per week in summer (twice weekly in winter, weather permitting). The Byzantine town, often called the Gibraltar of the East, clings to the side of a 350-meter (1,148-foot) rock that seems to blast out of the sea; in AD 375 it was cut off from the mainland by an earthquake. Like Gibraltar, Monemvassia once controlled the sea lines from western Europe to the Levant. If you come from Athens by ferry or hydrofoil, you'll get the most spectacular view; if you walk or take a taxi down the causeway from the adjoining town of Gefira, the rock looks uninhabited until you suddenly see castellated walls with an opening only wide enough for one. The name *moni emvasia*, or single entrance, refers to the narrow passage to this walled community.

The town was first inhabited in the 6th century by Lakonians fleeing from Arab and Slav raiders. During its golden age in the 1400s under the Byzantines, Monemvassia was the home of wealthy families who had inland estates from which they exported malmsey wine, a sweet variety of Madeira praised by Shakespeare. When the area fell to the Turks, Monemvassia ended up under the Pope's control and then came under the sway of the Venetians, who built the citadel and most of the fortifications. Well-to-do Greeks once again live on the rock in houses they have restored as vacation homes. Summer weekends are crowded, but the rest of the time Monemvassia is nearly deserted. Empty houses are lined up along streets often only wide enough for two people abreast, and remnants of another age—escutcheons, marble thrones, Byzantine icons—evoke the sense that time has stopped. It's worth a splurge to spend the night here.

After passing through the gate to the Lower City, walk left up to the main street, where most of the restored houses are. It runs into a small square (Platia Tzamiou) where **Christos Elkomenos** (Christ in Chains) stands, the largest medieval church in southern Greece. Its carved peacocks are symbolic of the Byzantine era, while the detached bell tower—like those of Italian cathedrals—is a sign of Venetian rebuilding in the 17th century. Across from the square is the 10th-century **Ayios Pavlos**, which, though converted into a mosque, was allowed to function as a church under the Ottoman occupation, an unusual indulgence.

Bear right to the south ramparts to visit the **Panagia Hrissafitissa**, a third church restored by the Venetians (note the framed doorway with an oculus). A tiny chapel is built over the "sacred spring" (the only spring on the rock), believed locally to be effective against sterility, especially when sons are desired. For solitude and a dizzying view, pass through the upper town's original wooden entrance gates, complete with their iron reinforcements. Up the hill is a rare example of a domed octagonal church, **Ayia Sofia,** founded in the 13th century by Emperor Andronicus II and patterned after Dafni monastery near Athens. Follow the path to the highest point on the rock for a view of the coast, then return to the main gate along the sentry walk (but not after dark—you could tumble down the cliff or into one of the open cisterns).

Shopping

Many stores in Nauplion and Olympia have the reproductions of bronzes, frescoes, and vase paintings, the T-shirts and worry beads that your family, friends, and coworkers crave. Nauplion is better for antiques, especially toward the end of Staikopoulos Street in the old part of town; Olympia has many shops specializing in big-ticket gold jewelry—some very nice, some very gaudy. Patras is the best bet for fashion, especially downtown around Korinthos and Maizonos streets. If you are traveling by car, be on the lookout for roadside stands selling the wonderful peaches and apricots—dead ripe and far superior to grocery-store fruit. Look for red wines from the region around Nemea, between Corinth and Argos, and the sweet mavrodaphne from the Patras area.

Sports and Outdoor Activities

Participant Sports

Hiking and Climbing
The **Greek Skiing and Alpine Federation** (7 Karageorgi Servias St., Athens, tel. 01/323-4555) operates five huts in the Achaean mountains that are open to the public. On Mt. Ziria, in the east, there are huts at Megali Vrissi (capacity 50) and Portes (capacity 20). The Pouliou Vrissi hut (capacity 16) is near Kalavrita on Mt. Helmos. For information on these three call 01/323–4555 in Athens. On Mt. Panahaiko there are huts at Psarthi (capacity 50) and Prassoudi (capacity 16); for information on these, call 061/273912 in Patras.

Tennis
Some luxury hotels in Olympia and Porto Heli have courts, as does the **Kyllini Camping Ground** (tel. 0623/96270, 0623/96275, or 0623/96278.) The **Patras Tennis Club** (12 Amalias and Othonos Sts., Patras, tel. 061/277776) is open to the public.

Water Sports
The popular beaches are well provided with water sports: Paddle boats can be hired, and windsurfing lessons are available at small "beach-bum" operations at many beaches, such as Tolo. In some resorts, like Port Heli, jet skis are making an appearance. Waterskiing lessons are given at the **Kymata Club** (formerly the PLM Hotel), in Porto Heli, tel. 0754/51546).

Beaches

The beach at **Kosta,** in the south of the Argolid, is more pleasant than at Porto Heli itself. Farther north, toward Nauplion, are **Drepano** and **Tolo**. There is frequent bus service from Nauplion's KTEL station to Tolo, which has a warm aquamarine bay, a fine sandy beach, seafood tavernas supplied by the local fleet, and discothèques. Just before Tolo the road takes a sharp turn at the Bronze Age and Classical site of **Asine,** which has a fine beach less crowded than Tolo's. Closer to Nauplion is the beach at **Karathona** (bus and taxi service), the equal of those at Tolo and Asine but favored by Greek families with children and picnic baskets. In Nauplion, there's the **Arvanitia Beach** (tel. 0752/28991). There are good beaches along the Gulf of Corinth with spectacular views of the opposite shore, but some are of cobbles rather than sand. **Xylokastro,** for example, starts out cobbly but farther from town becomes sandy. The wide, sandy beaches of **Loutra Kyllini** and **Glifa** on the Adriatic are among the best in Greece.

Dining and Lodging

Dining
One of the greatest simple pleasures of Greece is a late dinner of traditional Greek food with good Greek wine, preferably "from the barrel." In the small towns of the northern Peloponnese, any restaurant that pretends to offer more than this should be viewed with suspicion—none are included here. Not

all restaurants listed below have phones, but dress is always casual and reservations unnecessary, although you might have to wait for a table if you're dining with the majority at 9:30 or later. Unless otherwise noted, credit cards are not accepted. Keep freshness and the change of seasons in mind; if you order fish, have a look at it before it's cooked—there's no reason to buy something frozen. Grape leaves are best early in the season, no later than early July, when they're young and tender. Ask to visit the kitchen; any chef worth his salt will tell you what's good and what's left over from lunch.

Highly recommended restaurants are indicated by a star ★.

Category	Cost*
Very Expensive	over 6,000 dr.
Expensive	4,000 dr.–6,000 dr.
Moderate	2,000 dr.–4,000 dr.
Inexpensive	under 2,000 dr.

for 3-course meal, including tax, service, and beer or small carafe of barrel wine

Lodging Travelers should not expect to find the amenities customary in the United States or in Europe, such as phones or television, much less VCRs in bedrooms, or invariable air-conditioning. These are noted if present. Radios are sometimes provided, and unless noted a Continental breakfast is included. Renovations are usually done in winter, when many hotels close down; hotels here are open year-round unless noted.

There are youth hostels in Nauplion (Synikismos Neo Vyzantio, tel. 0752/27754), Mycenae (Ifigenias St. 20, tel. 0751/66224),Patras (Heroon Polytechniou 60, tel. 061/427278), and Olympia (Praxitileous-Kondili St. 18, tel. 0624/22580).

Campgrounds run by the Greek National Tourist Organization (GNTO) are located in Patras (tel. 061/424–131, 061/424–132, or 061/424–133) and Kyllini (tel. 0623/96270, 0623/96275, or 0623/96278).

Highly recommended lodgings in all price categories are indicated by a star ★.

Category	Cost*
Very Expensive	over 25,000 dr.
Expensive	18,000 dr.–25,000 dr.
Moderate	13,000 dr.–18,000 dr.
Inexpensive	under 13,000 dr.

All prices are for 2 people in a standard double room, excluding 8% government tax and 4½% local tax and including service and Continental breakfast.

Monemvassia **Marianthi.** You'll feel like you're dropping in on someone at din-
Dining ner here: Family photos of stern mustachioed ancestors hang on the walls along with Monemvassia memorabilia; someone's aunt is doing the cooking, and the service is down-home. Order the wild mountain greens, any of the fish—especially the fresh

You've Let Your Imagination Go, Now Get Up And Follow Your Dreams.

For The Vacation You're Dreaming Of, Call American Express® Travel Agency At 1-800-YES-AMEX.*

American Express will send more than your imagination soaring. We'll fly you, sail you, drive you to any Fodor's destination and beyond. Because American Express believes the best vacations happen from Europe to the Orient, Walt Disney®World to Hawaii and everywhere in between.

For dependable service, expert advice, and value wherever your dreams take you, call on American Express. After all, the best traveling companion is a trustworthy friend.

It's easy to recognize a good place when you see one.

American Express Cardmembers have been doing it for years.

The secret? Instead of just relying on what they see in the window, they look at the door. If there's an American Express Blue Box on it, they know they've found an establishment that cares about high standards.

Whether it's a place to eat, to sleep, to shop, or simply meet, they know they will be warmly welcomed.

So much so, they're rarely taken in by anything else.

Always a good sign.

red mullet—the addictive potato salad (you may have to order two plates), and the marinated octopus sprinkled with oregano. *Old town, tel. 0732/61371. No credit cards. Moderate.*

Matoula. This is the first restaurant you come to on the old town's main street and the least charming, but it serves the staples of Greek cooking in large portions. The cramped low-ceiling room is packed with people who all seem to know each other, and the kitchen is across the street. Although the service is without finesse, the dishes are nicely turned out. Especially good are the *bifteki* (beef patties) with their cinnamony taste, *paidakia* (ribs), and the roasted chicken basted with lemon and oil. *Old town, tel. 0732/61660 or 0732/61154. No credit cards. Moderate.*

To Kanoni. After you roll out of bed, wander over to the Kanoni, which serves breakfast on a terrace overlooking the square's cannon, for which the restaurant is named. Choose from omelets, ham and eggs, bacon, or thick, creamy yogurt and honey in a parfait glass. If you want to sit inside, you'll find red-and-white checked tablecloths, 19th-century prints of Greece, and the same glorious sea view, accompanied by calming wave music. If you miss breakfast, you can always order a "toast" (Greek for a grilled ham and cheese sandwich), a burger, or *giouvetsi*—special tiny noodles and beef cooked in a clay pot. *Old town, tel. 0732/61387. Moderate.*

Lodging
★ **Byzantinon.** When you walk the lamp-lit vaulted streets of the old town, you get a feeling of medieval Greece (particularly in spring before the crowds arrive). The Byzantinon is housed in an old building; the requirement that owners get permission from the archaeological bureau before making any changes explains the rudimentary showers in some rooms. All the rooms are shaped differently, with beautiful decorations: a carved marble tile depicting a scale set in the floor; a Greek costume sketch adorning an alcove; sailor's lanterns for illumination. The best room is No. 1, a perfect hideout suite with an antique radio, a marble bath, a balcony, a hidden kitchen, and a large cozy bed. *Old town, 23700, tel. 0732/61351. 14 rooms with bath. No credit cards. Expensive.*

★ **Malvasia.** Staying in this hotel is like living in a fairy tale; it is so engaging you may prolong your stay just to wallow in its comforts. Rooms are tucked into nooks and crannies and under cane-and-wood or vaulted brick ceilings. Each is decorated with bright patchwork rugs, embroidered tapestries, antique marble, and dark antique wood furniture. The hotel is in three buildings; the best is the one on the main street. Many of the rooms have sea views, some have fireplaces; suites are also available. *Old town, 23700, tel. 0732/61323, fax 0732/61722. 33 rooms with bath. Facilities: bar, breakfast room. AE, V. Expensive.*

Ta Kellia. Built in an old monastery (*kellia* means "cells"), this establishment is now run by Greece's tourist organization. It sits on the lower square opposite the church of Panagia Chrissafitissa. Though it's not as glamorous as Byzantinon or Malvasia, the rough-hewn rooms are a good choice when the others are full. Only a few rooms on the second floor have ocean views, and they can be quite hot in summer. *Old town, 23700, tel. 0732/61520. 20 rooms with bath. Facilities: breakfast room. No credit cards. Expensive.*

Nauplion
Dining
With one or two exceptions you'll eat better for less in the restaurants on Syntagma Square or just beyond on Staikopoulos

Street than in the ones strung out along the waterfront. After dining you might have dessert at **Fantasia** (Staikopoulos 42), at **Stratos'** (on the south side of Syntagma), or in one of the patisseries on the harbor.

Hellas. This reliable restaurant is one of the most popular in Nauplion. Ask to go back in the kitchen and see what's cooking, and if moussaka or pastitsio has just finished baking, you're in luck. Both are outstanding, especially the pastitsio. The tomatoes stuffed with rice, and the grape leaves are also very good. *West side of Syntagma Sq., opposite Archaeological Museum, no tel. Moderate.*

Psarotaverna Onikolas. The specialty here is fish grilled individually on a small open hearth in the center of the room. It's always fresh, and seasoned just right. The decor is pleasant, the staff friendly. *Staikopoulos 12, no tel. Moderate.*

Taverna O Moustakias. There's no better place in town for grilled meats, like lamb chops (*brizoles*), or souvlaki. The simple fare is especially satisfying if you've spent the day trudging around ancient sites and need refueling. *Philhellenes Sq., no tel. Moderate.*

Palaia Taverna. Traditional Greek food—chicken or beef with pasta, and vegetables—is on the menu here, served in generous amounts. Excellent Nemean wine in wooden casks sets this unpretentious restaurant above most in Nauplion. *Staikopoulos 6, no tel. Inexpensive.*

★ **Phanaria.** This is the finest restaurant in Nauplion. You should arrive late, sit at one of the tables in the narrow alley beside the restaurant, and ask what's best that night. Follow the advice and enjoy. Of the traditional fare, the grilled chicken is always excellent, the salads are generous, and the wine is good. *Staikopoulos 13, no tel. Inexpensive.*

Lodging   **Xenia Palace.** The view from the rooms in the Xenia Palace—of the picturesque Bourtsi fortlet in the harbor—is exceptional; it appears in GNTO television advertisements, and is possible only because the hotel was built on the ruins of the Frankish fortification atop Acronauplia. Modern art adorns the lobby, the relatively spacious rooms have exposed stonework, and the marble bathrooms are, without qualification, among the best in Greece. Lighting in the rooms is dim, however, and the slightly shabby furniture is in need of reupholstering. An elevator cut through the rock to a tunnel straight out of a James Bond movie takes you to and from town, below. *Acronauplia, 21100, tel. 0752/28981 or 0752/28983. 48 rooms, 3 suites. Facilities: restaurant, air-conditioning, disco in summer, minibars, parking, pool. AE, MC, V. Very Expensive.*

★ **Amphitryon.** Everything about the Amphitryon is better than average. The double rooms are fairly large, and the wood floors and historic prints on the walls give a pleasant ambience. The tile bathrooms of the double rooms have tubs. Amphitryon's prime location near the sea provides the rooms with harbor views. *Akti Miaouli, tel. 0752/27366 or 0752/27367. 48 rooms. Facilities: restaurant, parking, adjacent playground. DC, MC, V. Expensive.*

Xenia Acronauplia. The worn carpeting of the Xenia Acronauplia is redeemed by the fact that all rooms have balconies and those facing the gulf have spectacular views of the Venetian fortress above the city. Like the Xenia Palace, it is built within the Frankish walls (some feel the Xenia Acronauplia, or "Holiday-Inn-on-the-heights," is intrusive and spoils the view of Acronauplia from below). The bedrooms have couches. *Acronauplia, tel. 0752/28981 or 0752/28983. 58 rooms. Facilities: restaurant, bar, air-conditioning, disco in summer, parking. AE, MC, V. Expensive.*

★ **Dioscuri.** This nice hotel is nothing fancy but well looked after, and if you don't have piles of money but want a decent room, this could be it. From the small balconies there is a good view of the harbor, and the staff is especially helpful. *Zigomala 6 and Vyronos, tel. 0752/28550 or 0752/28644. 51 rooms. Facilities: restaurant, bar, parking. No credit cards. Inexpensive.*

Leto. There is a certain randomness about the Leto. No two rooms are the same and not all rooms have baths, but they are all clean and well kept. The neighborhood, just below the walls of Acronauplia, is quiet and sees less tourist traffic than the town below. *Zigomala 28, tel. 0752/28093. 11 rooms. Facilities: parking. No credit cards. Inexpensive.*

Victoria. A fairly new hotel, the Victoria has nothing plush about it except for the red carpets. But it is spotless, and the pink-and-green wallpaper is as new as the furnishings. So what that the bathrooms are on the small side; the location in the heart of old Nauplion is hard to beat. *Spiliadou 3, tel. 0752/27420. 36 rooms. Facilities: air-conditioning, parking. V. Inexpensive.*

Olympia
Dining

Taverna Pritannio. This unpretentious taverna in the center of the modern town has satisfying fare. The grilled meat and chicken are both good bets. *Praxitileous Kondili, no tel. Moderate.*

★ **Pete's Den.** Traditional Greek and German cooking come together at Pete's Den, which is owned by a Greek-German couple. The *saganaki* (baked cheese) and garlic bread are both tasty. *On main st., Praxitileous Kondili, no tel. Inexpensive.*

Lodging

Antonios. The fairly spacious rooms here have newish upholstered wood furniture, and all have balconies overlooking the modern village of Olympia and its cemetery. The hotel operates the adjacent Touris (sic) Club, which has a restaurant, bar, discothèque, and pool. *Kondulis St., 27065, tel. 0624/22348 or 0624/22349, fax 0624/22112. 70 rooms. Facilities: restaurant, air-conditioning, parking. V. Very Expensive.*

★ **Europa (Best Western).** Olympia's best, if you can afford it, the Europa combines white stucco, pine, and red tiles in a traditional style but with high ceilings and large windows. The newly furnished rooms have small terraces, some overlooking the town and the hills in the distance. Set well back and above the cheesy modern town, it is close to the ancient site. *Drouva 1, tel. 0624/22650 or 0624/22700, fax 0624/23166. 42 rooms. Facilities: restaurant, air-conditioning, parking, pool, riding stable, telephones and radios in rooms, tennis. AE, V. Closed Oct.–Mar. Expensive.*

Altis. Built in 1987, the Altis covers all the bases, with a letter-writing lounge, an ouzo bar, and a tourist shop. Its cafeteria-style restaurant and salad bar is undoubtedly enjoyed by the large groups that use the hotel and by those who wonder what Denny's would be like in Greece. The rooms are average; some of the marble-and-tile bathrooms have showers, some have tubs. Altis is very near the ancient site. *Praxitileous and Kondili St., tel. 0624/23101. 61 rooms. Facilities: restaurant, air-conditioning, parking. AE, DC, MC, V. Closed Oct.–Mar. Moderate.*

Apollon. Although the rooms at the Apollon are not exceptional, the wood furnishings and white walls do produce a cheerful beach bungalow atmosphere. The carpets are a little worn, but the bathrooms have new fixtures. Apollon is in the center of the modern town, convenient to both bus and train stations. *Douma 13, tel. 0624/22513 or 0624/22522. 96 rooms. Facilities: restaurant, parking, pool. AE, DC, MC, V. Closed Oct.–Mar. Moderate.*

Xenia. Rooms at the Xenia call for workmanlike adjectives: basic, clean, and, perhaps more appropriate, Spartan. Overlooking the main street and a gas station, the Xenia is the closest hotel to the ancient site. *Praxitileous and Kondili St., tel. 0624/22510. 40 rooms. Facilities: restaurant, parking. AE, DC, MC, V. Closed Oct.–Mar. Moderate.*

Kronion. The rooms at the Kronion are uniform in many crucial respects: They're clean, and they have private baths, balconies, and high ceilings. The decor varies wildly, without apparent rhyme or reason; but the rationale for faux granite here or patterned wallpaper there is a matter for contemplation, not a drawback. The train station is close at hand. *Tsoureka 1, tel. 0624/22502. 32 rooms. Facilities: restaurant, parking. AE, DC, MC, V. Closed Oct.–Mar. Inexpensive.*

Pelops. A pleasant edition of the standard cubical Greek hotel, Pelops is a nice place to stay. It's away from the main street and fairly quiet and has a vine-shaded terrace. The rooms are more than adequate but not fancy: clean and well kept, with plain wood furnishings and telephones. Shaggy throw rugs are scattered on the tile floors. *Varela 2, tel. 0624/22543. 25 rooms. Facilities: restaurant, bar, parking. MC, V. Inexpensive.*

Patras **Dining**
Avoid the indifferent restaurants along much of Patras's waterfront. For lighter fare or coffee and pastry or ice cream after dinner, choose one of the cafés along upper Gerokostopoulou Street, which is closed to traffic.

★ **Evangelatos.** If it's been a long day, or you simply want a little elegance at dinnertime, Evangelatos is the restaurant for you. The ornate ceiling, chandeliers, and courteous waiters set the tone, and a wide selection of traditional food is meticulously served. The lamb is very good; the bread is unfortunately made with refined white flour. *7 Ayios Nikolaos, no tel. AE, DC, V. Moderate.*

★ **Taverna Restaurant.** This less-than-pretentious spot is not on the tourist trail, but if you want solid food that your Greek grandmother would be proud to serve, seek it out. The regulars might wonder aloud in a friendly way who the foreigners are, but don't worry, they need something new to talk about. The selection is limited—meat and pasta, chicken, salad—but the local red and white wines drawn from wooden barrels perfectly complement every selection. It's like having a meal in a rural village right in the middle of Patras. *Alexander Ypsilantis 161, off Gerokostopoulou St., no tel. Inexpensive.*

Lodging
★ **Astir.** Near the Patras waterfront, the genteel Astir is a classy hotel in a convenient location, whether you are traveling by car, bus, or train. While the decor is a bit mid-'60s, the rooms are nice, there are plenty of public lounges, and the staff is well trained. But what really sets it apart is the rooftop view over the quayside. As dusk gives way to night you can watch the brilliantly lighted ferries for miles as they sail northwest toward Brindisi. It's all perfect after a less-than-perfect day. *Ayiou Andreou 16, 26221, tel. 061/276311 or 061/277502, fax*

061/271644. 121 rooms. Facilities: restaurant, bar, air-conditioning, parking, pool. AE, DC, V. Expensive.

Galaxy. The Galaxy is dependable. Its clean, gray rooms have clean gray-tile bathrooms with tubs, and there is no hokey decor or overdone anything. Near, but not on the waterfront, this hotel will give you a good night's sleep without frills or annoyances. *Ayiou Nikolaou 9, 26221, tel. 061/27815. 53 rooms. Facilities: air-conditioning, parking. V. Moderate.*

Rannia. This is an adequate hotel. Rooms could be larger, but they have pine furniture, and all have balconies; the view varies—some overlook Queen Olgas Square, the nicest plaza in Patras. The location isn't bad; it's a few blocks in from the waterfront, walkable from the train station and the bus station. *Riga Fereou 53, 26221, tel 061/220114. 30 rooms. Facilities: bar. MC, V. Moderate.*

Acropole. If your budget is nonexistent, the Acropole is for you. The rooms aren't great—some open onto light wells rather than the outside world—but most of the lights work and some sort of furniture is provided. If you've been lugging a backpack around for days, the Acropole can be a welcome sight. On the waterfront opposite the train station. *Othonos 39 at Amalias, tel. 061/279809. Facilities: restaurant. MC, V. Inexpensive.*

★ **Adonis.** The Adonis has, for its class, very good rooms. They are well taken care of, and nothing about them is shabby or in need of work. The TV and air-conditioning are amenities you would expect in a more expensive hotel. All rooms have a balcony, and those facing the gulf and the Adriatic have nice views. On the down side, the bathrooms are not spacious, and the shower is of the curb-and-curtain variety. Adonis adjoins the bus terminal, and some rooms may be noisy during the day; ask for one on the opposite side or facing the sea. *Zaini and Kapsali 9, tel. 061/226715. 33 rooms. Facilities: bar, air-conditioning, parking, tel. and TV in rooms. AE, MC, V. Inexpensive.*

Mediterranee. Many of the drawbacks you'd expect in a middle- to lower-class Greek hotel are present at the Mediterranee: worn carpeting, framed pictures cut from magazines, closetlike bathrooms. But there are hints of an effort being made to please—the rooms are clean, and much of the space in the bathrooms is taken up by an abundance of towels. Not bad; not great. Some rooms look out to sea, others look into adjacent buildings so close that asking if the residents have any Grey Poupon may not seem an insane suggestion. *Ayiou Nikolaou 18, tel. 061/279602, fax 061/223327. Facilities: restaurant, bar, parking, TV lounge. AE, DC, MC, V. Inexpensive.*

Porto Heli
Dining

Papadias. In a town of undistinguished dining options, this taverna near the church in the older part of Porto Heli stands out. The seafood is good, and in general fish is the high-water mark of Porto Heli cuisine. *No tel. Moderate.*

Dining and Lodging

Porto Heli. This lodging of the Kymata Club (formerly PLM), like the other resorts around the sheltered bay, offers more than just a room for the night: The nearby beach has a range of water sports like wind surfing and paddleboating. The reasonably large white-stucco rooms have phones, stone floors, and, as wall decorations, colorful Byzantine-style plates. *Waterfront, 21300. Porto Heli, 21300, tel. 0754/51490 or 0754/51494. 210 rooms, 8 suites. Facilities: restaurant, air-conditioning, minibar and TV in suites, beach, minigolf, nightclub, parking, playground, pool, tennis. AE, DC, MC, V. Expensive.*

La Cité. The buildings climbing the hillside behind the beach here resemble gigantic white stucco Lego blocks. Inside, wood-frame furniture fills the rooms that, although clean and well kept, aren't as large as you might like. They do have balconies overlooking the beautiful bay. In addition to the built-in activities, there are water sports and rental bicycles and mopeds at the beach opposite. *Porto Heli, 21300, tel. 0754/51265. 164 rooms. Facilities: restaurant, bar, beach, minigolf, parking, pool, radios in rooms, tennis. DC, MC, V. Moderate.*

Rozos. An alternative to the giant resorts, Rozos is synonymous with the words *character* and *budget.* The rooms are clean. Some of the furniture in each room matches, perfectly complementing the framed magazine illustrations on the walls. Large ceiling fans, like salvaged propellers from B–29 bombers, ensure good air circulation. A saving grace for this establishment, if you think it needs one, is the front terrace, shaded by grape vines, lemon trees, and olive trees. *Waterfront, tel. 0754/51416. 21 rooms. Facilities: restaurant, parking. No credit cards. Inexpensive.*

Sparta
Dining

Diethnes. Considered by locals to be one of Sparta's best restaurants, Diethnes has been around for more than 30 years, serving classic Greek food and local specialties. It recently moved several blocks and became a slightly more upscale dining room, with pink tablecloths and a courtyard that opens in summer. People love the special fish dish made with garlic, parsley, wine, oil, and rusks; the eggplant stuffed with onions; sliced pork; and local chicken *bardouniotiko,* made with onions, the hard white cheese from Kalamata called sfela, and red sauce. Occasionally, Diethnes has delicacies like sheep's heads or *kokoretsi* (entrails wrapped around pieces of heart or liver), cooked on a spit until crunchy, which taste much better than they sound. *Paleologou 105, tel. 0731/28636. No credit cards. Moderate.*

Elysse. The new restaurant in town, with wallpaper, carpeting, and flowers, is a bit fancier than Diethnes but serves essentially the same cuisine. Here you can get large portions of chicken *bardouniotiko, perka* (a fish prepared in oil and lemon), excellent local sausage made with bits of orange, *moschari* (beef) ragout, and Continental dishes like pepper steak, *filet madera* (in Madeira sauce), and veal scallopini. The barrel wine is a smooth red. In summer you dine outdoors on the sidewalk. *Paleologou 113, tel. 0731/29896. No credit cards. Moderate.*

★ **Semiramis.** This underground restaurant, with its fluorescent lighting, linoleum floor, and old calendars, is not much to look at, but the cooking is wonderful. The simple Greek dishes like *gemista* (stuffed tomatoes), pork with eggplant, *stifado* (beef with pearl onions), and seasonal vegetables are perfectly cooked. In spring, try the wild artichokes with red sauce (*anginares antidia*), in summer the stuffed squash. Their barrel wine (at something like $1.50 a kilo) is light and fragrant but strong. For dessert try the rich sheep yogurt with honey before you stagger outdoors. *Palaeologou 48, tel. 0731/26640. No lunch alternate Sun. Inexpensive.*

Dining and Lodging
★ **Hotel Maniatis.** It's hard to believe this hotel is so reasonably priced. It's been completely renovated in mauve and baby blue geometrics reminiscent of L.A. 1980s design; it is air-conditioned; and it is run better than many hotels of higher class. The staff pays attention to details: the lounge is relaxing, with subdued lighting and large plate-glass windows; fresh-cut

flowers adorn the dining room; the dapper waiter sports a paisley vest. Rooms on the front above the third floor have an excellent view of Mt. Taygettos; those in back are quieter and look out on the less impressive Mt. Parnonas. If you need a bathtub, ask for a corner room. The hotel's new Dias restaurant has elegant decor, and the chef was lured from Athens's St. George Lycabettus hotel. Try the local speciality, *arni araxobitiko* (lamb with onions, cheese, red sauce, and walnuts), the chicken liver Madagascar, or *bourekakia* pastries. *Paleologou 72, 23100, tel. 0731/22665, fax 0731/29994. 75 rooms with bath. Facilities: restaurant, bar. V. Moderate.*

Lodging **Lida.** This hotel away from downtown traffic, though expensive for its category, provides flawless service and a lobby decorated with antique treadles, the stones from flour mills and olive presses, and lithographs of Greek revolutionary heroes (the owner's wife is an interior designer). The rooms have new furnishings and tapestries; many above the third floor have a view of Mt. Taygettos. *Ananiou and Atreidon, 23100, tel. 0731/23601 or 0731/23602. 37 rooms with bath. Facilities: restaurant, bar. AE, MC, V. Closed mid-Nov.–Feb. Expensive.*

Dioskouri. This hotel and **Lida,** the one next door, are owned by the same family. While this one is more modest, it's a good deal at the lower price. The bathrooms are a bit smaller than Lida's, there are paint blisters here and there, and the furnishings in the lobby are not as carefully selected, but it offers the same excellent service. *Lykourgou 94, 23100, tel. 0731/28484. 30 rooms with bath. Facilities: breakfast room. No credit cards. Moderate.*

Menelaion. Sparta's dowager hotel sits in state, presiding over the main strip. To its old-fashioned lobby (check out the phone booths) and the lounge with worn velvet chairs come the town's old gents to sip coffee, play cards, and chat over local affairs. With their high ceilings and dark furniture, the guest rooms are just the place to settle down with a dog-eared copy of *The Magus. Paleologou 91, 23100, tel. 0731/22161 through 0731/22165. 50 rooms with bath. Facilities: restaurant, bar. MC, V. Moderate.*

Sparta Inn. The rooms here have no frills; ask for one with a view of Taygettos, though these are on the noiser side of the hotel. If you need a bathtub, ask for a suite. The two pools (and the air-conditioning, if it's on) make a stay in summer bearable, as does the roof bar, which has a large terrace. Inside it, a slightly kitsch painted mountain view and a Parthenic frieze (plus painted flames over the lamps) may make you feel like a god sipping nectar atop Mt. Olympus. *Thermopylon 105, 23100, tel. 0731/25021, fax 0731/24855. 177 rooms with bath. Facilities: restaurant, bar, 2 pools, conference room. V. Moderate.*

Tolo Most of the restaurants in Tolo are unremarkable, but the town
Dining has an active fishing fleet that supplies the many tavernas—usually a few small tables set out on a patio separated from the beach by a low fence or wall. The fresh fish available on any given day is usually posted on a chalkboard at the taverna entrance. Ask for sea bream (*tsipoura, lithrini,* or *fagri*) or grouper (*rofos*), and look the fish over before deciding where to dine.

Lodging **Aris.** The matched pine furniture and popular blue and white decor add to the neat impression given by the clean rooms.

All of them have balconies but not all face the sea—ask for one that does. Not all rooms have bathtubs. *Aktis 28, 21056, tel. 0752/59231, fax 0752/59510. 30 rooms. Facilities: restaurant, air-conditioned bar, parking. V. Inexpensive.*

Minoa. The relatively large, clean rooms of the Minoa are decorated blue and white—the national color scheme of Greece. This pleasant hotel is near the end of the town, so it's a little walk to the wide, sandy beach for which Tolo is known. *Aktis 56, 21056, tel. 0752/59207, fax 0752/59707. 44 rooms. Facilities: restaurant, bar, air-conditioning, radios in rooms, TV lounge. No credit cards. Inexpensive.*

★ **Tolo** and **Tolo II.** These two hotels run by the same family are opposite each other on the town's main street. The rooms are straightforward in decor and well kept—nothing fancy. Tolo, in particular, has immediate access to the nicest part of the beach. *Bouboulinas 15, 21056, tel. 0752/59248 or 0752/59464, fax 0752/59689. 59 rooms. Facilities: restaurant, bar, air-conditioning, parking, tennis. No credit cards. Inexpensive.*

Nightlife

The innumerable discos catering to tourists come and go from one year to the next, so a recommendation of Romantic Hill in Porto Heli or Disco Memory in Tolo may be of little value. It's best to ask around. The **Artemis Boite** in Nauplion seems more durable, producing bouzouki music year after year from the same location on Konstantinoupoleos Street in the old quarter above the archaeological museum. Nightlife in Patras is a bit livelier, and in addition to the inviting cafés along Gerokostopoulou Street below the ancient theater are such music clubs as **Prive** (55 Germanou St.), **Café Rallis** (14 Aratou St.), **Dust Rythym & Blues** (Germanou and 12 Eunardou Sts.), **Utopia Music Hall** (91 Ayiou Andreou St.), **Memphis** (148 Alexander Ypsilantis St.), **Peripou Jazz-Rock Club** (5 Aratou and Ayiou Andreou Streets), and **La Boum** (34 Gounari St.).

7   The Cyclades

Andros, Mykonos, Naxos,
Paros, Santorini, and Siros

By Melissa Dailey

Melissa Dailey, a resident of Athens, is editor of Greek American Trade.

The six major stars in this constellation of islands in the central Aegean Sea—Andros, Mykonos, Naxos, Paros, Santorini, and Siros—are the most famous, and the most visited—the archetype of the islands of Greece. In a magnificent fusion of sunlight, stone, and sparkling, aqua sea, they offer both culture and hedonism: ancient sites, Byzantine castles and museums, lively nightlife, shopping, dining, and beaches plain and fancy. On many of them the chief town, officially named Chora (meaning "town"), has come to be called by the name of the island.

These arid, mountainous islands are the peaks of a deep submerged plateau, and their composition is rocky, with few trees. The summer heat is modified by northern winds, the *tramontana* and the gustier *meltemi*, and the weather is reliably sunny. Some of the other Cyclades are Tinos, Ios, and Milos.

Well-to-do **Andros,** where ship-owning families once lived, retains an air of dignity, and its inhabitants go about their business largely indifferent to the visitors. It's a good place for adults in search of history, fine museums, and quiet evenings. On the island of **Mykonos,** in the classic town of that name, the whitewashed houses huddle together against the meltemi winds, and backpackers rub elbows with millionaires in the mazelike white marble streets. The island's sophistication level is high, the beaches fine, the shopping varied and upscale, and it's the jumping-off place for a mandatory visit to tiny, deserted **Delos.** That windswept dot, birthplace of Apollo, watched over now by a row of marble lions, was once the religious and commercial center of the eastern Mediterranean.

Naxos, greenest of the Cyclades, makes cheese and wine, raises livestock, and grows potatoes, olives, and fruit. For centuries a Venetian stronghold, it has a large Roman Catholic population, Venetian houses and fortifications, and a wealth of Cycladic and Mycenaean sites. **Paros,** the hub of the ferry system, has reasonable prices and is a good center from which to make trips to other islands. It's also good for lazing on long, white-sand beaches and visiting fishing villages.

Crescent-shape **Santorini** (Thera), southernmost of the Cyclades, is the rim of an ancient drowned volcano that exploded about 1500 BC. The sensational views across its flooded caldera would be worth a visit even if it didn't have fascinating excavations and a dazzling white town where the shopping is great and tourism highly developed. Ermoupolis, the chief city of **Siros** and administrative capital of the Cyclades, used to be a shipbuilding town. Though its commercial and industrial presence and its neoclassical architecture give Siros a different feel from the fishing and agricultural islands, its southern part is green and fruitful and its beaches are wonderful.

Essential Information

Important Addresses and Numbers

Tourist Information
Andros

The Tourist Information office is in Gavrion, on the road to Batsi (tel. 0282/71282); the **police station** (Gavrion, across from the ferry dock, tel. 0282/71220) lists available accommodations. To locate a room, call one of the four travel agencies in Batsi: **Dolfin Hellas** (tel. 0282/41185), **Greek Sun** (tel. 0282/41239), **An-**

dros Travel (tel. 0282/41252), or **Andrina Tours** (tel. 0282/41064).

Mykonos **Tourist police** (harbor, near departure point for Delos, tel. 0289/22482 or 0289/22716).

Naxos The **Tourist Information Center** (waterfront, tel. 0285/24525, 0285/24358, or 0285/22993) has free booking service, bus and ferry schedules, international dialing, luggage storage, and foreign exchange at bank rates.

Paros In Paroikia, the **Tourist Information Bureau** (tel. 0284/22079) is inside the windmill on the harbor; in Naoussa, try the **Nissiotissa Tourist Office** (off the main square, opposite the pastry shop, tel. 0284/51480).

Santorini There's no National Tourist Office on Santorini, but at **X-Ray Kilo** (Etkostis Pemptis Martiou St., Fira, tel. 0286/22624 or 0286/23243), English-speaking agents book ferries, sell plane tickets, and represent American Express. Another reputable office is **Nomikos Travel** (tel. 0286/23660), which has offices in Fira and Perissa.

Siros Ermoupolis has the **National Tourist Office of the Cyclades** (Town Hall, tel. 0281/22375 or 0281/26725), the **National Tourist Organization** (harbor, tel. 0281/22375 or 0281/26725), and the **Municipal tourist office** (harbor, tel. 0281/27027).

Emergencies **Andros:** in Gavrion tel. 0282/71220; in Batsi, tel. 0282/41204;
Police and in Andros town, tel. 0282/22300. **Mykonos:** tel. 0289/22235. **Naxos:** in Chora, tel. 0285/22100 or 0285/23280; in Filoti, tel. 0285/31244; **Paros:** in Paroikia, tel. 0284/21221; in Naoussa, tel. 0284/51202). **Santorini:** in Fira, tel. 0286/22649. **Siros:** in Ermoupolis, tel. 0281/22160 or 0285/81247.

Medical Assistance **Andros:** If you cannot find a doctor, contact the local police (Batsi medical assistance, tel. 0282/41326; Gavrion, tel. 0282/71210; and Andros town, tel. 0282/23000, 0282/22344, or 0282/22758). **Mykonos:** In Mykonos town, the hospital (tel. 0289/23994) has 24-hour emergency service with pathologists, surgeons, pediatricians, dentists, and X-ray technicians; first aid, tel. 0289/22274; in Ano Mera, first aid, tel. 0289/71395). **Naxos:** The Health Center just outside Chora (tel. 0285/23333 or 0285/23550) is open 24 hours a day. **Paros:** Paroikia health clinic, tel. 0284/21235, in Naoussa tel. 0284/51216; in Antiparos, tel. 0284/61219. **Santorini:** for first aid in Fira, tel. 0286/22237; in Oia, tel. 0286/71227. **Siros:** Ermoupolis hospital, tel. 0281/22555.

Arriving and Departing by Plane

There is no airport in **Andros**. Most European countries now have charter flights to **Mykonos: Olympic Airways** (in Athens, tel. 01/966–6666) is the only domestic carrier. It has seven flights daily to Mykonos (10 daily during peak tourist season); in July and August you should make reservations a few days before departure. There are also flights between Mykonos and Santorini, Heraklion (on Crete), and Rhodes. The Olympic Airways offices in Mykonos are at the port (tel. 0289/22490 or 0289/22495) and at the airport (4 km or 1½ mi southwest of Mykonos town, tel. 0289/22327).

Naxos airport (tel. 0285/23292), a few kilometers outside Chora, was finished in 1992; Olympic Airways has two flights daily to and from Athens. There are four daily flights to **Paros**

from Athens and a number of flights there from Rhodes, Heraklion, and Santorini. The Paros airport is in Alyki village, 9 kilometers (6 miles) south of Paroikia; the Olympic Airways office (tel. 0284/21900) is in Paroikia. There are four flights daily to **Santorini** from Athens in peak season. From Santorini daily flights go to Athens and Mykonos, and there are flights to Heraklion (Crete) and Rhodes about three times per week. The airport (tel. 0286/31525), is in Monolithos, on the east coast, 8 kilometers (5 miles) from Fira, and the Olympic Airways office (tel. 0286/22493 or 0286/22793) is on Ayia Athanassiou Street, in Fira. From Athens to **Siros** there are two daily flights; the airport (tel. 0281/27025) is in Manna, 4½ kilometers (3 miles) south of Ermoupolis.

Arriving and Departing by Boat

Many visitors use the extensive ferry network to the Greek islands. If you are not in a hurry and the weather is favorable, sitting in the sun on deck will get you in the island mood. Ferries and the faster catamarans and Flying Dolphin hydrofoils sail from Piraeus (Port Authority, tel. 01/451–1311 or 01/417-2657) and from Rafina, 35 kilometers (22 miles) northeast of Athens (Port Authority, tel. 0294/23300 or 0294/22700). Leaving from Rafina cuts traveling time by a half an hour to Andros, Siros, and Mykonos; there are buses every hour from Athens. Traveling time from Piraeus to Mykonos, for example, is six hours; to Santorini, 12 hours.

Third-class boat tickets cost roughly one-third the airfare, and passengers are restricted to snack bar services, seats in the deck areas, and often-crowded indoor seating areas. A first-class ticket, which buys a private cabin and restaurant services, costs about the same as an airplane ticket. For information on interisland connections, contact the port authorities on the various islands (*see below*). The tourist season is April through October; boats are less frequent in the off season.

Andros   Ferries to **Andros** leave from Rafina, usually three times a day in summer (about two hours). From Andros (Port Authority, Gavrion, tel. 0282/22250) boats leave twice daily for Tinos and Mykonos and once daily for Siros. An excursion boat goes daily to Mykonos and Delos, returning in late afternoon.

Mykonos   In summer, three ferries daily go from Piraeus to **Mykonos** and three ferries a week from Rafina. From Mykonos (Port Authority: harbor, above National Bank, tel. 0294/22218) there are daily departures to Paros, Tinos, Siros, and Andros and five to seven departures per week for Santorini, Naxos, Ios, and Crete.

Naxos   In summer, ferries leave Piraeus for **Naxos** four to eight times a day (about seven hours); from Rafina, three times a week. A boat goes daily from Naxos (port police, tel. 0285/22300) to Mykonos, Ios, and Santorini; six times a week to Siros.

Paros   Ferries leave for **Paros** at least twice daily from Piraeus and once a day from Rafina. Paros (Port Authority, tel. 0284/21240) has daily ferry service to Santorini, Ios, and Naxos. Cruise boats leave daily from Paroikia and Naoussa for excursions to Mykonos.

Santorini   **Santorini** is served at least twice daily from Piraeus and four times a week from Rafina; from Santorini ferries make frequent connections to the other islands—to Mykonos four times weekly. Almost all ferries dock at Athinios port, where taxis and buses take passengers to Fira, Kamari, and Perissa Beach. Travelers bound for Oia take a bus to Fira and change there. The port below Fira is used only by small ferries and cruise ships. Passengers disembarking here face a 45-minute hike, or they can ride up on a mule (traditional mode of transport) or take the cable car. The port police (tel. 0286/22239) can give information on ferry schedules.

Siros There are 19 ferries per week to **Siros** from Piraeus and five per week from Rafina. Siros (Port Authority: harbor, tel. 0281/22690) is still a focal point of interisland trade, and there is a daily boat in summer to Tinos and Mykonos, and at least two tourist boats per week to Santorini, Andros, Paros, Naxos, and other islands.

Getting Around

By Moped and Car Travelers can take their cars on most of the ferries for an additional fee; it is wise to make reservations in advance. All the major islands have car and moped rental agencies at the ports and in the business districts. Car rental starts at about 7,500 dr. per day, with unlimited mileage and third-party liability insurance. Full insurance costs about 2,000 dr. a day more. Small motorbikes start at 2,000 dr. a day, including third-party liability coverage. Jeeps and dune buggies are also available in Santorini, Mykonos, Paros, and Naxos. Choose a dealer that offers 24-hour service and a change of vehicle in case of a breakdown. Many foreigners end up in Athenian hospitals after moped accidents, brought about in part by the narrow, winding roads on the islands, but often because the moped has not been maintained properly. When renting cars and motorbikes pay attention to traffic regulations.

On the large and mountainous island of **Andros,** though there is bus service, it is much more convenient to travel by car. Cars can be rented at the Hotel Aegli (tel. 0282/22303) in the center of Andros town or from the **Rent-A-Car** agency (tel. 0282/41418) in Batsi behind the beachfront Hotel Lykaion. In **Mykonos** and other heavily visited towns, motor vehicles are not allowed in the shopping districts, and police may confiscate the license plates and fine you for violations. In **Naxos** the roads don't go everywhere and are sometimes poor. Often it's easier just to take the bus, especially to places like Apollonas, where the road is steep and twisting. Still, if you drive carefully, you shouldn't have any problem. In **Paros** it is a good idea to rent a vehicle because the island is large, there are many beaches to choose from, and it can be difficult to find taxis. Extreme caution is advised on **Santorini,** the car- and moped-accident capital of the Cyclades; the narrow roads are extremely crowded with inexperienced (and often drunk) drivers. Cars can be rented at **Avis** (tel. 0286/23742) or at **Hertz** (tel. 0286/22221) in Fira. **Siros** is a small island with good public transportation; buses and taxis are plentiful.

By Taxi On **Andros,** there's a taxi stand (tel. 0282/22171) off the main street near the bus station in Andros town. In **Mykonos** the taxi stand (tel. 0289/22400 or 0289/23700) is on the harbor near the Mando Mavroyennis statue. Meters are not used; standard fares for each destination are posted on a notice board. In

Naxos the taxi stand (tel. 0285/22444) is near the harbor. In **Paros** there is a taxi stand (tel. 0284/21500) across from the windmill on the harbor, but the island is known for infrequent taxi service, and you may have to wait. On **Santorini** the taxi station (tel. 0286/22555) is near Fira's central square on Eikostis Pemptis Martiou Street. A line of taxis waits in front of Miaouli Square in **Siros** (tel. 0281/26222).

By Bus On **Andros,** about six buses a day from Andros town (to the right of marble walkway, tel. 0282/22171) go to Gavrion and back, in conjunction with the ferry schedule; all buses stop in Batsi. Daily buses also go to and return from Stenies, Apoikia, Strapouries, Pitrofos, and Korthion.

In **Mykonos** town the Ayiou Louka station near the Olympic Airways office is for buses to Ornos, Ayios Ioannis, Plati Yialos, Psarou, the airport, and Kalamopodi. Another station near the archeological museum is for connections to Ayios Stefanos, Tourlos, Ano Mera, Elia, Kalafatis, and Kalo Livadi. For bus information, dial 0289/23360.

The bus system in **Naxos** is reliable and fairly extensive. Daily buses go from Chora (waterfront, tel. 0285/22291) to Engares, Melanes, Sangri, Filoti, Apeiranthos, Koronida, and Apollonas. In summer there is added daily service to the beaches, including Ayia Anna, Pyrgaki, Agiassos, Paxia Ammos, Xilia Brisi, Ayia Mama and Abram. In **Paros,** the Paroikia bus station (tel. 0284/21133) is to the left of the windmill on the central square. There is service every hour to Naoussa, and less frequent service to Alyki and to the beaches at Piso Livadhi, Chrissi Akti, and Drios.

Buses on **Santorini** are frequent and fairly reliable. From the main station in central Fira (Deorgala Street, no phone) buses leave periodically for Perissa and Kamari beaches, Oia, Pyrgos, and other villages. In **Siros** buses depart daily from the station at the harbor (tel. 0281/22575) for all towns.

Guided Tours On **Andros,** try **Andrina Tours** (tel. 0282/41064) or **Greek Sun Holidays** (tel. 0282/84503), both in Batsi.

On **Mykonos, Delos Tours** (Fabrica Sq., tel. 0289/24459) takes a group every morning for a day tour of Delos; it has half-day guided tours of the Mykonos beach towns, with a stop in Ano Mera for the Panagia Tourliani Monastery. Another rewarding all-day excursion (about 6,000 dr.) goes to nearby Tinos to visit the marble studios, monasteries, and a Venetian castle.

On **Naxos, Zas Travel** (Chora, tel. 0285/23330 or 0285/23115, fax 0285/23419; Ayios Prokopios, tel. 0285/24780) runs two good one-day tours of the island sights with different itineraries, each costing about 2,300 dr., and one-day trips to Delos/ Mykonos (4,500 dr.) and Santorini (6,000 dr.).

On **Paros,** day trips around the island to such places as the Golden Beach, the Valley of the Butterflies, and the cave in Antiparos are organized by **Paros Travel** (tel. 0284/21582) and **Nissiotissa** (tel. 0284/51480 or 0284/51474). Buses leave at about 10 AM from Paroikia and Naoussa; tours cost 2,000 dr.—4,000 dr. **Glaraki,** in Naoussa (tel. 0284/51101 or 0284/51748) and in Paroikia (tel. 0284/22335 or 0284/21668), runs one-day cruises to Delos, Santorini, Tinos, and Naxos on air-conditioned boats with lounges and TV.

In **Santorini, Bellonias Tours** (Fira, tel. 0286/22469 or 0286/23604; Kamari, tel. 0286/31721) runs coach tours to Akrotiri, Ancient Thera, and Oia and daily boat trips to the volcano and Thirassia and also arranges private tours. **X-Ray Kilo** (tel. 0286/22624 or 0286/23243) has tours to the same sights, and to the island's wineries and the Monastery of Profitis Elias.

On **Siros, Team Work Travel** (near the port, 10 P. Ralli St., Ermoupolis, tel. 0281/23400 or 0281/22866) runs half-day bus tours around the island, six-hour nighttime-entertainment bus tours, and full-day beach tours by motorboat.

Exploring the Cyclades

Andros

The northernmost and second-largest of the Cycladic islands, Andros is about 32 kilometers by 16 kilometers (nearly 20 miles by 10 miles), and its rugged, mountainous geography is best seen by car. The highest peak, Mt. Kouvari, is 3,260 feet. An array of springs gives birth to streams, which whirl down from the mountaintops, feeding lush valleys, so, unlike most of the Cyclades, Andros is green with pines, sycamores, mulberries, fig trees, and lemon and lime trees. In ancient times it was called Hydroussa, or "Watery Isle." Not only do the springs and streams have a cooling effect, but the prevailing northern wind, called the *meltemi*, which sweeps across Andros throughout the summer, ameliorates the scorching heat. Locals say that when the meltemi subsides, the gentler, *notias* winds arrive from the south, bringing more humid weather and bothersome jellyfish.

Tourism is in an early stage on Andros, and most of the islanders are indifferent to it. Perhaps the reason for this snobbishness toward tourists is that Andros is historically a wealthy island. The well-known Goulandris shipping family from Andros founded two museums of modern art and the archaeological museum in Andros town, arguably the best in the Aegean. Among Greeks, Andros is considered an island for the cultured elite. Prices are, surprisingly, still in line with the Greek economy, and restaurants and hotels are less expensive than they are in Mykonos or Santorini.

Our tour begins on the northwest coast in **Gavrion,** where the ferries arrive and depart. Although there are some accommodations here, most people stay 8 kilometers (5 miles) south of town in Batsi, the island's only resort, or around Andros town, on the opposite side of the island. It's a good idea to buy a map.

Few visitors are adventurous enough to take the small dusty roads north of Gavrion. In the remote mountain villages live ethnic Albanians, the descendants of Orthodox Albanians who left their native Epirus in the 14th century and found a safe haven here. Many of them still speak an Albanian dialect. But before leaving Gavrion you may want to take a short detour northeast on a side road shown on the island map, to see the round watchtower of Ayios Petros. The hike from Gavrion takes about one hour. The tower is built of enormous brown blocks 6½ feet long, fitted without mortar. You have to bend down to get through the low entranceway, and, once inside, you can attempt to climb the stone steps 65 feet to the top. It is

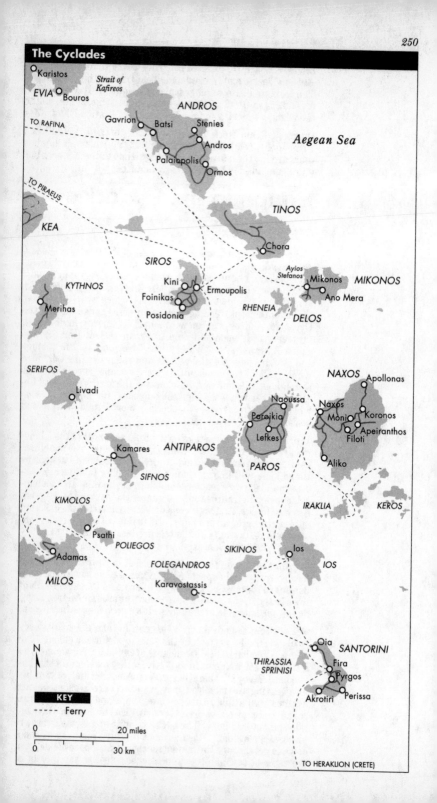

The Cyclades

Strait of Kafireos

EVIA
Karistos
Bouros

ANDROS
TO RAFINA
Gavrion
Batsi
Stenies
Andros
Palaiopolis
Ormos

Aegean Sea

TO PIRAEUS

KEA

TINOS
Chora

KYTHNOS
Merihas

SIROS
Kini
Foinikas
Posidonia
Ermoupolis

Ayios Stefanos
Mikonos
Ano Mera
MIKONOS

RHENEIA
DELOS

SERIFOS
Livadi

NAXOS
Apollonas
Naxos
Moni
Koronos
Apeiranthos
Filoti
Aliko

ANTIPAROS
Naoussa
Paroikia
Lefkes
PAROS

Kamares
SIFNOS

KIMOLOS
Psathi
POLIEGOS

IRAKLIA
KEROS

SIKINOS
Ios
IOS

Adamas
MILOS

FOLEGANDROS
Karavostassis

SANTORINI
Oia
THIRASSIA SPRINISI
Fira
Pyrgos
Akrotiri
Perissa

N

KEY
- - - Ferry

0   20 miles
0   30 km

TO HERAKLION (CRETE)

thought to be one of a series of signal towers used during the Byzantine era to communicate across long distances, or perhaps to protect nearby mines from pirates. It can be seen far up in the hills above the road between Gavrion and Batsi.

Take the main road south out of Gavrion, and as you approach **Batsi** the road splits; the low road is more direct, immediately winding down toward the seaside town; the high road that goes to the left travels around the back of Batsi and enters from the south. Originally a little fishing village, Batsi has developed only over the last 10 years, and as a new resort town, many of the businesses have a friendly, almost innocent nature; Athenian hustlers have not yet arrived. On the hillside, a few lovely houses from a century ago look down to the promenade along the sea, where Athenian and foreign visitors stroll, patronizing the new restaurants, shops, and bars. Many people stay here because the social life is a bit more lively than in Andros town and because of the beach, where windsurfing, paddleboats, and canoes can be rented.

Heading south along the coast you will see signs after 9 kilometers (6 miles) that you are coming into **Palaiopolis,** the ancient capital of Andros. Unfortunately, most of the ancient city lies beneath the sea, destroyed either by an earthquake or a landslide during the 4th century. The town today is a quiet but gorgeous village that stretches down the slope of Mt. Kouvara to the shore. The road cuts through the middle of the town, where there are a roadside taverna and café. From the taverna you can look up to the hill and see the site of an ancient acropolis 984 feet above the sea, now occupied by a small Orthodox chapel. In 1832 a farmer turned up the famous statue of Hermes in this area, which is now on display in the archaeological museum in Andros Town.

Opposite the café, 1,039 steps lead down through the lower village, in the shade of flowering vines and trees heavy with lemons and limes. Scattered about the beach are marble remnants of early buildings and statues. Though it has not been systematically excavated, archaeologists did enough digging around here in 1956 to conjecture that the bits and pieces are remains from the ancient agora.

South of Palaiopolis you soon come to a fork, where a sign marks the road east through the interior of the island, to **Andros town.** Across the entire landscape of Andros you will notice an interesting network of stone walls that mark boundaries between the fields of different owners. In a building style unique to Andros, the walls are interrupted at regular intervals, and each gap is filled with a large flat slab set on its edge longitudinally. Not only did this save stone and labor, but it also allowed herders to lay the large slab flat temporarily, to allow the passage of animals.

Another common feature of Andros (also seen on Mykonos and Siros) are the dovecotes: square towers whose pigeonholes form decorative geometric designs. The Venetians introduced them in the 13th century, when keeping doves, traditional symbols of love and peace, was fashionable. Eventually the dovecotes fell into disuse, but when hard times struck the islands in this century, local farmers started breeding the pigeons and preserving and selling them abroad as a delicacy. Today only a few of the dovecotes are inhabited and cared for.

Time Out Stop in **Menites** (½ kilometer or ⅓ mile off the main road, half-way between the fork and Andros town) to see the **sacred springs** and have a glass of local wine and a bite to eat at one of two shaded tavernas. Mineral spring water tumbles from a series of spouts along a stone wall, and hidden by greenery in the background is **Panayia tis Koumulous,** an Orthodox church supposedly built on the site of a major temple to Dionysos. According to legend, these are the very springs whose water turned to wine each year on the god's feast day.

Andros town (or Chora) has been the capital of the island since the Venetian occupation in the 13th century. The city is built on a long, narrow peninsula, with a small island at its tip, on which are the remains of a Venetian castle built about 1220. Overlooking the castle is the statue of *The Unknown Sailor,* by Michael Tombros, whose works are exhibited in the sculpture museum (*see below*). After parking in the public lot at the head of town (cars are not allowed in the center), take a leisurely stroll down the marble promenade, past the impressive 13th-century **Palatiani Church** and the interesting gift shops that sell local Andros pottery. Handsome stone mansions of the 19th century line the streets, and over their doors are carved galleons, large three-masted sailing ships, indicating that the original owners were shipowners or sea captains. The tidy appearance of the town and the distinction of its neoclassical houses bear witness to its long-standing prosperity.

The main street leads to **Kairis Square,** at the tip of the peninsula, where in the center stands a bust of Theophilos Kairis, a local hero. Born in Andros town in 1784, Kairis was educated in Paris and returned to Andros in 1821 to become one of the leaders in the War of Independence. A philosopher, scholar, and social reformer, he toured Europe to raise money for an orphanage and school, which he founded in 1835. The school became famous in Greece, and enrollment eventually rose to 600, but the Orthodox church closed it down and tried Kairis as a heretic for his individualistic religious beliefs. He died in a Siros prison in 1852.

Turn left on the side street at Kairis Square and a short distance on is the **Museum of Modern Art,** the first of the three museums on Andros funded by the Goulandris Foundation. It stages exhibitions of such notable international and Greek artists as the sculptor Alberto Giacometti (whose work was shown in 1992). *Admission: 200 dr. (free Sun.). Open daily 10–2 and 6–9 (except Tues. and Sun. afternoon).*

The **Museum of Sculpture,** across the street, displays rotating exhibitions by Greece's best modern painters and a permanent collection of the works of sculptor Michael Tombros (1889–1974), whose parents were born on Andros. *Tel. 0282/22444. Admission free. Same hrs as Museum of Modern Art (see above).*

The pride of Andros's **Archaeological Museum** is a statue of Hermes discovered in Palaiopolis, thought to be a copy of a Praxiteles original. The museum presents sculpture from the Archaic through the Roman periods on the lower floor. Upstairs is an extensive display on Zagora, the earliest known settlement in Andros, a town built during the Geometric Period on the southwest coast, on a promontory 529 feet above sea level, surrounded by jagged cliffs. It was the main settlement from

900 BC to 700 BC, before the rise of Palaiopolis. The Athens Archaeological Society and the University of Sydney are excavating Zagora. The site is not open, but the museum provides a model of the town and displays many of the archaeological finds. *Kairis Sq., tel. 0282/23664. Open Tues.–Sat. 8:45–3, Sun. and holidays 9:30–2:30. Admission: 250 dr. adults, 100 dr. children, under 12 free.*

Off the Beaten Track South of Andros town (22 kilometers or 14 miles) is the Bay of Korthion, where a pretty village extends down to a beach on a deep indentation of the sea. High on a hill above the bay are the ruins of the medieval Venetian fortress called **Kastro tis Grias** (the Castle of the Old Woman). A legend says that an old Greek woman tricked the guard into allowing her access to the castle gate, which she later opened to the waiting Ottoman Turks. After the soldiers slaughtered the Venetians, the old woman, filled with remorse, leapt to her death from a cliff now known as **Tis Grias to Pidema,** or Old Lady's Leap.

Mykonos and Delos

Numbers in the margin correspond to points of interest on the Mykonos Town map.

Mykonos The dry and rugged island of Mykonos is one of the smallest of the Cycladic group: It's only 16 kilometers (10 miles) long, 11 kilometers (7 miles) wide, and its two highest peaks, both named Profitis Ilias, are less than 1,197 feet above sea level. An ancient myth tells us that the rocks strewn across its barren landscape are the solidified remains of the giants slain by Hercules. Despite its deserted appearance, Mykonos has become one of the most popular (and expensive) of the Aegean islands. Tourists from all over the world are drawn by its vast stretches of sandy beaches and the upscale bars and restaurants crowded into the port town—also called Mykonos. The town's whitewashed streets, its cubical houses and churches with their dashes of sky-blue doors and domes, are the stereotype of classic Cycladic architecture.

The islanders seem to have been able to fit the tourists gracefully into their way of life. You'll often see, for example, an old island woman leading a donkey laden with vegetables through the narrow streets of the town, greeting the suntanned vacationers walking by. But Mykoniots regard a good tourist season as a fisherman looks at a good day's catch. For many, the money made in July and August is the money they will live on for the rest of the year. Not long ago Mykoniots had to rely on what they could scratch out of the island's arid land for sustenance, and some remember the time of starvation under Axis occupation during World War II. In the 1950s a few tourists began trickling into Mykonos on their way to see the ancient marvels on the nearby islet of Delos. There are no restaurants or hotels on Delos, and so they came to know Mykonos and to appreciate its appeal.

For almost 1,000 years Delos was the religious and political center of the Aegean, host every four years to the Delian games, the region's greatest festival. The population of Delos actually reached 20,000 at the peak of its commercial period, and throughout antiquity Mykonos, eclipsed by its holy neighbor, depended on this proximity for income, as it does today. Visitors interested in antiquity should plan to spend a day on Delos, an excursion described below. You can go with a guided tour or hire a small boat at the port to take you over for about 1,500 dr.

1 Those with limited time might want to start their tour of Mykonos with a quick visit to the **Archaeological Museum,** for some insight into the intriguing history of the shrine. The museum houses Delian funerary sculptures discovered on the neighboring islet of Rhenea, many with scenes of mourning. The most significant work from Mykonos is a 7th-century BC *pithos*, or storage jar, showing the Greeks emerging from the Trojan horse. *Ayios Stefanos Rd., n. end of port, tel. 0289/22325. Admission: 250 dr. Open Wed.–Mon. 9–3, Sun. 9:30–2.*

2 Turn right from the museum onto Polykandrioti, and walk past the post office and the Olympic Airways office to the central harbor. The best time here is in the cool of the evening, when the islanders promenade down the **esplanade** to meet friends and go to the numerous cafés. A bust of Mando Mavroyennis, the island heroine, stands on a pedestal in the **main square.** In the War of Independence the Mykoniots, known for their naval and seafaring skills, volunteered an armada of 24 ships, and in 1822, when the Ottomans later landed a force on the island, Mavroyennis and her soldiers forced them back to their ships.

Along the waterfront where the boats dock, the town mascot, Petros the Pelican, can be seen preening himself. In the 1950s a group of migrating pelicans passed over Mykonos, leaving behind one exhausted bird. Vassilis the fisherman nursed it back to health, and locals say that the pelican in the harbor is the original Petros. Chances are, it is his successor, enjoying the spotlight and carrying on tradition.

Perpendicular to the harbor runs the main shopping street, **Matogianni Street,** which is lined with jewelry stores, clothing boutiques, chic cafés, and sweetshops.

Time Out Try the island's traditional almond biscuits. Though most of the sweetshops carry this specialty, the best can be found on Matogianni Street at **Skaropoulos** (tel. 0289/71550 or 0289/24983). Nikolaos Skaropoulos started the family business in 1921, and his grandson claims that their cookies were a favorite of Winston Churchill.

Any visitor who has the pleasure of getting lost in the narrow, whitewashed streets of Mykonos town will appreciate the fact that its confusing layout was designed to foil attacking pirates. After Mykonos fell under Turkish rule in 1537, the Ottomans allowed the islanders to arm their vessels against pirates, which had a contradictory effect: Many of them found that raiding other islands was more profitable than tilling arid land. At the height of Aegean piracy, Mykonos was the principal headquarters of the corsair fleets—the place where pirates met their fellows, found willing women, and filled out their crews. Eventually the illicit activity evolved into a legitimate and thriving trade network.

3 At the end of Matoyianni Street, turn right onto Enoplon Dynameon, and you will soon see the **Aegean Maritime Museum** on the right. This charming museum houses a collection of model ships, navigational instruments, old maps, prints, coins, and nautical memorabilia. The backyard garden displays some old anchors and ship wheels and a reconstructed lighthouse from

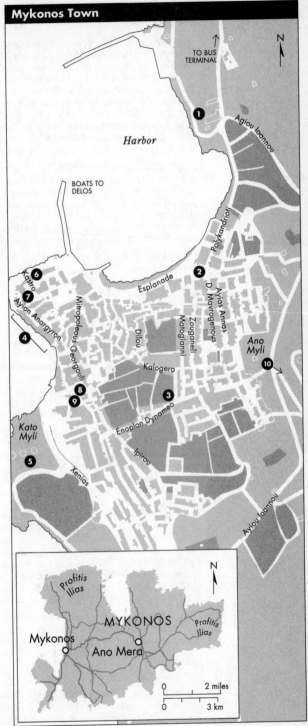

Mykonos Town

Aegean Maritime
Museum, 3

Archaeological
Museum, 1

Folk Museum, 6

Greek Orthodox
Cathedral, 8

Little Venice, 4

Main Square, 2

Monastery of the
Panayia Tourliani, 10

Mykonos Windmills, 5

Paraportiani Church, 7

Roman Catholic
Cathedral, 9

TO BUS
TERMINAL

N

Harbor

Agiou Ioannou

Polykandrioti

BOATS TO
DELOS

Esplanade

Kastro

Ayion Anargyron

Mitropoleous Georgouli

Dilou

Kalogera

Ayias Annas

D. Mavrogenous

Zouganeli Matogianni

*Ano
Myli*

*Kato
Myli*

Enoplon Dynameo

Ipirou

Xenias

Ayiou Ioannou

N

*Profitis
Ilias*

MYKONOS

Mykonos

Ano Mera

*Profitis
Ilias*

| 0 | | 2 miles |
| 0 | | 3 km |

1890, which once used oil for illumination. *Tel. 0289/22700. Admission: 125 dr. Open daily 10:30–1 and 6–9.*

Continue west on Enoplon Dynameon Street, turn right on Mitropoleos Georgouli, and walk a few blocks toward the water. Many of the early ship captains built distinguished houses directly on the sea here, with wooden balconies over the water. Today this neighborhood, at the southwest end of the port, is **④** called **Little Venice.** A few of the old houses have been turned into stylish bars, which offer a romantic atmosphere at twilight. In the distance across the water, lined up like toy soldiers **⑤** on the high hill, are the famous **Mykonos windmills,** echoes of a time when wind power was used to grind the island's grain.

Around the corner from Little Venice, south of the boat dock, is **⑥** the **Folk Museum,** housed in an 18th-century house. One bedroom has been furnished and decorated in the fashion of that period, and on display are looms and lace-making devices, Cycladic costumes, old photographs, and Mykoniot musical instruments that are still played at festivals. *Tel. 0289/22591 or 0289/22748. Admission free. Open Mon.–Sat. 4–8, Sun. 5–8.*

Mykoniots claim that exactly 365 churches and chapels dot their landscape, one for each day of the year. The most famous **⑦** of these, the **Church of Paraportiani** (beyond the walls) is on Ayion Anargyron Street, near the Folk Museum. The sloping, whitewashed conglomeration of four chapels, mixing Byzantine and vernacular idioms, has been described as "a confectioner's dream gone mad," and its position on a promontory facing the sea sets off the unique architecture. Continue south on Ayion Anargyron to the square off Odos Mitropolis and the **⑧** **Greek Orthodox Cathedral of Mykonos,** which has a number of old icons of the post-Byzantine period, and right next to it the **⑨** **Roman Catholic Cathedral,** from the Venetian period. The name and coat of arms of the Ghisi family, who took over Mykonos in 1207, are inscribed in the entrance hall.

Travelers interested in monasteries will find it worthwhile to make the 7-kilometer (4-mile) excursion from town to **Ano** **⑩** **Mera,** in the central part of the island. The **Monastery of the Panayia Tourliani,** founded in 1580, dedicated to the protectress of Mykonos, stands on the town's central square. Its massive baroque iconostasis (altar screen), made in 1775 by Florentine artists, has small icons carefully placed amid the wooden structure's painted green, red, and gold-leaf flowers. At the top are carved figures of the apostles and large icons of New Testament scenes. The hanging incense holders with silver molded dragons holding red eggs in their mouths show an eastern influence. In the hall of the monastery, an interesting museum displays embroideries, liturgical vestments, and wood carvings. To see the monastery's interior and the museum, you must call 0289/71249 in advance for an appointment.

Delos The obvious question that arises regarding Delos is how such a small islet, with virtually no natural resources, could have become the religious and political center of the Aegean. The answer is that Delos, shielded on three sides by other islands, provided the safest anchorage for vessels sailing between the mainland and the shores of Asia.

The great Zeus fell in love with gentle Leto, the Titaness, and she became pregnant. When Hera discovered this infidelity, she forbade Mother Earth to give Leto refuge and ordered the

Delos

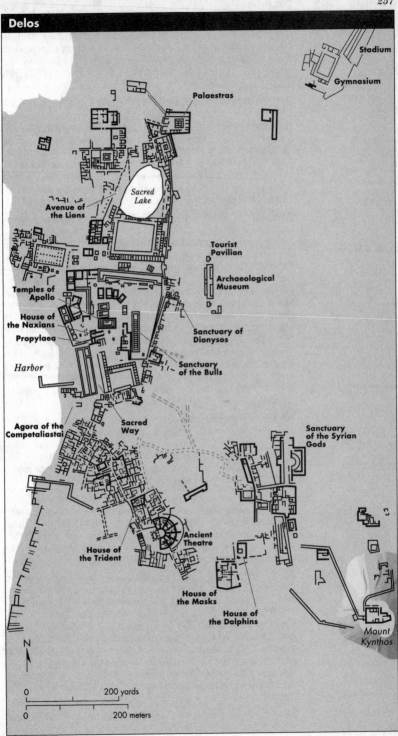

Stadium

Gymnasium

Palaestras

Sacred Lake

Avenue of
the Lions

Tourist
Pavilion

Archaeological
Museum

Temples of
Apollo

House of
the Naxians

Propylaea

Sanctuary of
Dionysos

Sanctuary
of the Bulls

Harbor

Agora of the
Competaliastai

Sacred
Way

Sanctuary
of the Syrian
Gods

House of
the Trident

Ancient
Theatre

House of
the Masks

House of
the Dolphins

*Mount
Kynthos*

N

| 0 | 200 yards |
| 0 | 200 meters |

serpent Python to pursue her. Poor Leto wandered the earth,
and finally Poseidon, taking pity on her, anchored the floating
island of Delos with four diamond columns to give her a place
to rest. She gave birth first to Artemis, goddess of the hunt and
virginity, and nine days later, to Apollo, god of truth and light,
while Zeus looked down from nearby Mt. Kynthos.

By 1,000 BC the Ionians, who inhabited the Cyclades, had made
Delos their religious capital, introducing the cult of Apollo. A
Homeric hymn mentions this cult in the 7th century BC. A difficult period began for the Delians when Athens rose to power
and developed aspirations to Ionian leadership, seeking to conquer the political and religious center. In 543 an oracle at
Delphi conveniently decreed that the Athenians must purify
the island by removing all the graves to Rhenea, a dictate designed to alienate the Delians from their past.

After the defeat of the Persians in 478 BC, the Athenians organized the Delian alliance, with its treasury and headquarters at
Delos (in 454 the funds were transferred to the Acropolis in
Athens). The Delians paid a yearly tax and supplied ships to the
Athenian fleet in exchange for protection. A second "purification" was ordered in 426 BC, and in 422 Athens forced the entire
population of Delos to move to Asia Minor. Delos had its second
and perhaps greatest period in the late Hellenistic and Roman
times, when an international merchant community grew up. It
was declared a free port and quickly became the financial center of the Mediterranean, the focal point of trade, and a slave
market, where 10,000 people were said to be sold every day.
Foreigners from as far apart as Rome, Syria, and Egypt lived
in this cosmopolitan port, in complete tolerance of one another's religious beliefs, and each group built its various
shrines.

In 88 BC Mithridates, the king of Pontus, in a revolt against Roman rule, ordered an attack on the unfortified island. The entire population of 20,000—natives and foreigners—was killed
or sold into slavery. Delos never fully recovered, and later Roman attempts to revive the island failed because of pirate raids.
After 70 BC the island was gradually abandoned.

In 1872, the French School of Archaeology began excavating on
Delos—a massive project, considering that much of the island's
4 square kilometers (1½ square miles) is covered in ruins. Their
work continues today. The archaeological site (tel. 0289/22259,
admission 1,000 dr.) is open late March–early October, weekdays 10–4, Sunday and holidays 10–3.

On the left as you walk from the harbor is the **Agora of the
Competaliastai** (ca. 150 BC), members of Roman guilds, mostly
freedmen and slaves from Sicily, who worked for Italian trad-
ers. They worshiped the *lares competales*, the Roman "crossroads" gods; in Greek they were known as Hermaistai, after the
god Hermes, protector of merchants and the crossroads. Beyond the agora, turn left onto the Sacred Way, which was the
route, during the holy Delian festival, of the procession to the
sanctuary of Apollo. The pilgrimage, or *theoria*, was made by
dignitaries, two choirs, poets, actors, and athletes who would
compete in gymnastic and running events.

At the end of the walkway is the **Propylaea,** once a monumental
white marble gateway with three portals framed by four Doric

columns, which leads to the **Sanctuary of Apollo.** Though little remains today, when the Propylaea was built in the mid-2nd century BC, the sanctuary was crowded with altars, statues, and temples—three of them to Apollo. Just inside and to the right is the **House of the Naxians,** a 7th- to 6th-century BC structure with a central colonnade. Items dedicated to Apollo were stored in this shrine. Outside the north wall is a massive rectangular pedestal, once supporting a colossal statue of Apollo (one of the hands is in Delos's archaeological museum, and a piece of a foot is in the British Museum). Near the same spot a bronze palm tree was erected in 417 BC by the Athenians to commemorate the palm tree under which Leto gave birth. According to Plutarch, the palm tree toppled in a storm and brought the statue of Apollo down with it.

Southeast of the temples of Apollo are the ruins of the **Sanctuary of the Bulls,** an extremely long and narrow structure built, it is thought, to display a trireme, an ancient boat with three banks of oars, dedicated to Apollo by a Hellenistic leader thankful for a naval victory. Maritime symbols were found in the decorative relief of the main halls, and the head and shoulders of a pair of bulls were part of the design of an interior entranceway. A short distance north is an oval indentation in the earth where the **Sacred Lake** once sparkled. It is surrounded by a stone wall that shows the original periphery. According to islanders, the lake was fed by the River Inopos from its source high on Mt. Kynthos until 1925, when the water stopped flowing and the lake dried up. Along the shores are two ancient **palaestras,** buildings for exercise and debate.

One of most evocative sights of Delos is the 164-foot-long **Avenue of the Lions.** The five Naxian marble beasts crouch on their haunches, their forelegs stiffly upright, vigilant guardians of the Sacred Lake. They are the survivors of a line of at least nine lions, perhaps as many as 16, erected in the second half of the 7th century BC by the Hellenistic kings. One was removed in the 17th century and now stands before the arsenal of Venice. A short walk northeast, past the palaestras, will bring you to a large square courtyard, nearly 131 feet on each side, which once was the **gymnasium.** The long, narrow structure farther northeast is the stadium, the site of the athletic events of the Delian Games, and east of there, by the seashore, are the remains of a synagogue built by Phoenician Jews in the 2nd century BC.

A road south from the gymnasium leads to the **tourist pavilion** (which has a restaurant and bar) and the **Archaeological Museum,** which contains most of the antiquities found in excavations on the island: monumental statues of young men and women, steles, reliefs, masks, and ancient jewelry. The museum has the same hours of operation as the site.

Immediately to the right of the museum is a small **sanctuary of Dionysos,** erected about 300 BC; outside it are several monuments dedicated to Apollo by the winners of the choral competitions of the Delian festivals. Each is decorated with a huge phallus, emblematic of the orgiastic rites that took place during the Dionysian festivals. Around the base of one of them is carved a lighthearted representation of a bride being carried to her new husband's home. A marble phallic bird, symbol of the body's immortality, also adorns this corner of the sanctuary.

Heading south down the path that leads to the southern part of the island, you arrive at the **ancient theater,** built in the early 3rd century BC in the elegant residential quarter inhabited by Roman bankers and Egyptian and Phoenician merchants. The one- and two- story houses were typically built around a central courtyard, sometimes with columns on all sides, and they were floored with decorative mosaics, which channeled rainwater into cisterns below. The colorful mosaics show fantastical natural themes: panthers, birds, and dolphins; the best preserved can be seen in the **House of the Dolphins,** the **House of the Masks,** and the **House of the Trident.** A dirt path leads to the base of Mt. Kynthos, where there are remains from many **Middle Eastern shrines,** including the Sanctuary of the Syrian Gods, built in 100 BC. A flight of steps continues upward (112 m, 368 ft) to the summit of **Mt. Kynthos,** where the sunset is unforgettable.

Naxos

Numbers in the margin correspond to points of interest on the Naxos map.

"Great sweetness and tranquillity" is how Nikos Kazantzakis, premier writer of Greece, described Naxos, and indeed your first impression as you step off the boat is of abundance, prosperity, and serenity. The greenest, most fertile of the Cyclades, Naxos, with its many potato fields, its livestock and thriving cheese industry, its fruit and olive groves framed by the pyramid of Mt. Zas (3,295 feet, the Cyclades' highest), is practically self-sufficient. Inhabited for 5,000 years, the island offers today's visitor memorable landscapes—abrupt ravines, hidden valleys, long sandy beaches—and towns that vary from a Cretan mountain stronghold to the seaside capital, strongly evoking its Venetian past.

❶ As your ferry chugs into the harbor, you see before you the white houses of **Chora,** the capital, on a hill crowned by the one remaining tower of the Venetian castle. Perched on a rock beside the waterfront, the tiny church of Panayia Myrtidiotissa watches over the local sailors, who built it for divine protection. At the harbor's far edge looms Naxos's most famous landmark, the **Portara,** a massive doorway that leads to nowhere. Once you've settled in, this should be your first stop. It stands on the islet of **Palatia,** which was once a hill (since antiquity the Mediterranean has risen quite a bit) and in the 3rd millennium BC was the acropolis for a nearby Cycladic settlement. The Portara is believed to be the entrance to an unfinished Temple of Apollo (it faces exactly toward Delos, Apollo's birthplace), begun about 530 BC by the tyrant Lygdamis, who said he would make Naxos's buildings the highest and most glorious in Greece. He was overthrown in 506 BC and the temple was never completed; by the 5th and 6th centuries AD it had been converted into a church; and under Venetian and Turkish rule was slowly dismembered, so the marble could be used to build the castle. The gate, built with four blocks of marble, each 16 feet long and weighing 20 tons, was so large it couldn't be demolished, so it remains today, along with the temple floor. Palatia itself has come to be associated with the tragic myth of Ariadne, princess of Crete.

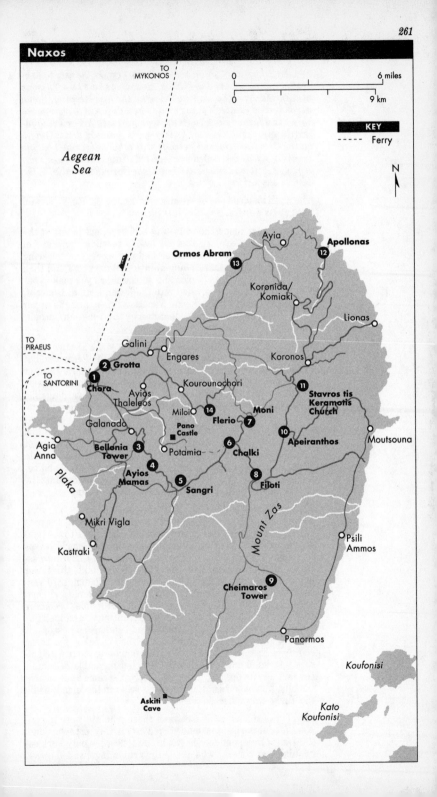

Naxos

TO
MYKONOS

0   6 miles

0   9 km

KEY
- - - - Ferry

N

*Aegean
Sea*

TO
PIRAEUS

TO
SANTORINI

Ayia

Apollonas

Ormos Abram ⑬   ⑫

Koronida/
Komiaki

Lionas

Galini

Engares   Koronos

② **Grotta**
①   Kourounochori
Chora

Ayios
Thaleleos   Miloi   ⑭   **Moni**

Galanado   **Flerio** ⑦   ⑪ **Stavros tis
Keramotis
Church**

Pano
Castle   ⑩ **Apeiranthos**

**Bellonia
Tower** ③   ⑥ **Chalki**   **Moutsouna**

Agia
Anna   Potamia

④   **Ayios
Mamas**   ⑤   ⑧ **Filoti**

Plaka   **Sangri**

Mikri Vigla   *Mount Zas*

Kastraki   Psili
Ammos

**Cheimaros
Tower** ⑨

Panormos

Koufonisi

**Askiti
Cave**   *Kato
Koufonisi*

Ariadne, daughter of King Minos, helped Theseus escape the labryinth of Knossos (where he slew the monstrous Minotaur), and in exchange, he promised to marry her. On the way to Athens the couple stopped in Naxos, and it was here that Theseus abandoned Ariadne, sailing away as she was sleeping. Some say his jilted fiancée's curse made Theseus forget to change the ship's sails from black to white, which caused his grieving father to jump into the sea, believing his son was dead. Others claim Ariadne drowned herself; still others describe how the great Dionysos descended in a leopard-drawn chariot to marry Ariadne, setting her bridal wreath, the Corona Borealis, in the sky, in eternal token of his love.

The myth inspired one of Titian's best-known paintings, as well as Strauss's opera, *Ariadne auf Naxos.*

As you return along the causeway to Chora, cut in left at the first square to explore the **old town**'s bewildering maze of twisting cobblestone streets, arched porticoes, and towering doorways, where you're plunged into cool darkness and then suddenly into pockets of dazzling sunshine, as you make your way. The old town is divided into the lower section, **Bourgos**, where the Greeks lived during Venetian times, and the upper part, called **Kastro** (castle), inhabited by the Venetian Catholic nobility.

No matter how you ascend, sooner or later you will come to the gates of the castle. The south gate is called the **Paraporti,** but it's more interesting to enter through the northern gate, or **Trani** (strong), via Apollonos Street. Note the vertical incision in the gate's marble column—it is the Venetian yard against which drapers measured the bolts of cloth they brought the noblewomen. Just outside the gate is the rust-colored **Glezos tower,** home to the last dukes, with its coat of arms: a pen and sword crossed under a crown. Step through the Trani and enter another age, where around silent courtyards still stand sedate Venetian houses, emblazoned with their coats of arms and bedecked with flowers, the only sign of present-day occupants the drying clothes fluttering occasionally from a balcony.

The citadel was built in 1207 by Marco Sanudo, a Venetian who, three years after the fall of Byzantium, landed on Naxos as part of the Fourth Crusade. For two months he laid siege to the Byzantine castle at t'Apilarou, and upon its downfall made Naxos the headquarters of his duchy. He divided the island into estates, distributing them to his officers, who built the tower houses (*pirgi*) that still dot the countryside. When in 1210 Venice refused to grant him independent status, Sanudo switched allegiance to the Latin Emperor in Constantinople, becoming Duke of the Archipelago. Under the Byzantines, "archipelago" had meant "chief sea," but after Sanudo and his successors, it came to mean "group of islands," i.e. the Cyclades. For three centuries Naxos was held by Venetian families, who resisted pirate attacks, introduced Roman Catholicism, and later rebuilt the castle in its present form. In 1564 Naxos came under Turkish rule, but even then, the Venetians still ran the island, while the Turks only collected taxes.

Few Turks settled on Naxos, and those who did were in constant fear of the pirates, who preyed exclusively on them; when the War of Independence began in the 1820s, the only Turk remaining was a clerk, who at the first rumblings, sailed away.

The only reminder of Turkish rule is a ruined fountain on the road from Chora to Engares, although it was the lack of schools under Turkish rule that led to the founding of the Kastro's Ursuline convent and the commercial school.

In the Kastro you'll first come upon the **cathedral,** built by Sanudo in the 13th century and restored by Catholic families in the 16th and 17th centuries. The marble floor is paved with tombstones bearing the coats of arms of the noble families. Venetian wealth is evident in the many gold and silver icon frames. The icons reflect a mix of Byzantine and Western influences: The one of the Virgin Mary is unusual because it shows a Byzantine Virgin and Child in the presence of a bishop, a cathedral benefactor. Another 17th-century icon shows the Virgin of the Rosary surrounded by members of the Sommaripa family.

A few steps beyond the cathedral are the **convent and school of the Ursulines** begun in 1739. In a 1713 document, a General of the Jesuits, Francis Tarillon, mentions that the proposed girls' school should be simple; grandeur would expose it to the Turks' covetousness. Over the years, extensions were added, and the Greek state has now bought the building for cultural purposes. The nearby **French School of Commerce** is marked by an escutcheon bearing a fleur-de-lis surrounded by the collar of the Order of the Holy Spirit. The school was run in turn by Jesuits, Lazarists, and Salesians. Under the latter it enjoyed its most distinguished period (1891–1927); the Cretan writer Nikos Kazantzakis attended the school for two years. Its library, archives, and opulent furnishings were destroyed during the German–Italian occupation, but it's easy to imagine rows of schoolboys traipsing to class as you enter its vast, cool halls. Today it houses the archaeological museum.

The **museum** is best known for its Cycladic and Mycenaean finds. During the Early Cycladic period (3200 BC–2000 BC), there were settlements along Naxos's east coast and just outside Chora at Grotta. The finds are from these settlements and graveyards scattered around the island. Many of the vessels exhibited are from the Early Cycladic I period, made of coarse-grained clay, sometimes decorated with a herringbone pattern. Gradually, the variety of shapes and decoration increased—new forms appeared, like candlesticks, wine pourers, and sauce boats inscribed with spiral patterns, fish, or the typical many-oared boat. One common vessel unearthed is known, from its shape, as the "frying pan," though archaeologists are uncertain of its use. Some believe it held water and served as a mirror; others think that skins were stretched across the pan to make a drum for funeral processions.

The museum has so many items in its glass cases that it's difficult to examine them, but you should try not to miss the white marble Cycladic statuettes, which range from the early "violin" shapes to the more detailed female forms with their tilted flat heads, folded arms, and legs slightly bent at the knees. The male forms are slightly more complex and often appear sitting. Again, some archaeologists have suggested these correspond to heroes and nymphs; others believe they represent such divinities as gods of fertility and were meant to protect the dead on their journey to the underworld.

A period of notable prosperity in Naxos was the Late Mycenean period (1400 BC–1100 BC), and much of the museum's collection comes from a Mycenaean settlement near Grotta. The finds include seal rings, false-necked amphoras, water pitchers with sculpted snakes, and many vessels with the octopus motif, the spaces between the tentacles filled with designs of plants and animals. In the museum's courtyard there is a mosaic pavement from a 4th-century BC house depicting a Nereid astride a bull rising from the sea. *Kastro, tel. 0285/22725. Admission: 400 dr., free Sun. Open Tues.–Sun. 8:30–3.*

If you want to see Grotta, descend from the Kastro in the direction of the Portara through the Bourgos section. You will pass the **Greek Orthodox cathedral** built in 1789 on the site of a church called Zoodochos Pigis (Life-giving Source). The cathedral was built from the materials of ancient temples: The solid granite pillars are said to be from the ruins of Delos. Amid the gold and the carved wood, there is a vividly colored iconostasis painted by a well-known iconographer of the Cretan school, Dimitrios Valvis, and the Gospel Book is believed to be a gift from Catherine the Great of Russia.

Next to the cathedral are the ruins of the **agora,** the center of the ancient city. Excavations have revealed a 167-foot-by-156-foot square closed on three sides by Doric stoas, so that it looked like the letter π. A shorter fourth stoa bordered the east side, leaving room at each end for an entrance. The *heroon* (shrine for a hero or demigod) and bases for statues stood in front of the stoas; the inscriptions recovered indicate Artemis was worshiped here.

② In **Grotta,** just a few steps northeast along the coast, you can sometimes see **underwater remains of the Cycladic buildings** strewn along an area of about 134 feet, a series of large worked stones that are perhaps the remains of the mole, and a few steps that locals say go to a tunnel leading to the islet of Palatia.

The island flourished from the 7th to the 6th centuries BC, and for a time, Naxiots were the administrators of the Delos sanctuary. The wealthy island was one of the first to become a center of marble sculpture: The famous Delos lions and several large kouros were done here (*see below*). Gifts from Naxian donors were found in many sanctuaries of that period, such as the temple of Apollo at Delphi and the temple of Athena on the acropolis at Athens.

That was the time of the oligarchs, known as the *pachis,* or fat ones, after which one-man rule was established by Lygdamis during the latter 6th century BC. When he was overthrown, the Persians destroyed the island in 490 BC and sold off the inhabitants as slaves. Naxos never recovered its former splendor, and in 471 came under Athenian rule, beginning its decline during the Classical age. The island passed successively from Macedonian to Egyptian to Rhodian rule, and in 41 BC became a Roman province. When the Romans were succeeded by the Byzantines in the 5th century, Naxos regained some importance as the seat of the provincial governor who controlled one-third of the Aegean. Then, after the fall of Constantinople in 1204, the Byzantines lost the island to the Venetians, as mentioned above.

To explore the rest of the island, leave Chora by the main road, going southeast past Galanado, and drive through the reeds, cacti, and plains of the Livadi Valley 5 kilometers (3 miles) to **③** the graceful **Bellonia tower** (Pirgos Bellonia). It belonged to the area's ruling Venetian family, and like other fortified houses, was built as a refuge from pirates and as part of the island's alarm system. The towers were located strategically throughout the island; if there was an attack, a large fire would be lit on the nearest tower's roof, setting off a chain reaction from tower to tower and alerting the islanders. Bellonia's thick stone walls, its lion of St. Mark emblem, and flat roofs with zigzag chimneys are typical of these pirgi. In front of it is the unusual 13th-century **"double church" of St. John,** exemplifying Venetian tolerance. On the left side is the Catholic chapel, on the right, the Orthodox church, separated only by a double arch. The mansion and the church are closed, but take a moment to gaze across the peaceful fields to Chora and imagine what the islanders must have felt when they saw pirate ships on the horizon.

❹ As you continue toward Sangri, keep a lookout for one of the island's oldest churches, **Ayios Mamas,** which sits just off the road on the left after about 3 kilometers (2 miles). St. Mamas is the protector of shepherds and is regarded as a patron saint in Naxos, Cyprus, and Asia Minor. Built in the 8th century, the stone church was the island's cathedral under the Byzantines. Though it was converted into a Catholic church in 1207, it was neglected under the Venetians and is now falling apart.

❺ The name **Sangri** is a corruption of Sainte Croix, which is what the French called the town's 16th-century monastery of Timios Stavros (Holy Cross). The town, about 6 kilometers (4 miles) from Galanado, is actually three small villages spread across a plateau. During the Turkish occupation, the monastery served as an illegal school, where children met secretly to learn the Greek language and culture. Sangri is the center of an area with so many monuments and ruins spanning the Archaic to the Venetian periods, it is sometimes called "little Mystras." Above the town on Mt. Profitis Ilias, you can make out the **ruins of t'Apilarou,** the castle Sanudo first attacked. Just outside Sangri is the underground cavern **Kaloritisa,** which contains three small frescoed churches; above the cave are the ruins of the 13th-century monastery, Panayia Kaloritisa, built on the spot where an icon of the birth of Christ was found by a shepherd.

❻ You are now entering the heart of the lush Tragaia Valley, where in spring the air is heavily scented with honeysuckle, roses, and lemon blossoms, and many tiny Byzantine churches hide in the dense olive groves. One of the most important of them is the bright white, red-roof **Panayia Protothronos** (Virgin of the First Throne), in **Chalki** (5 kilometers/3 miles from Sangri). Restoration work has uncovered frescoes ranging from the 9th through the 13th centuries. The older layers depict such decorative motifs as crosses, birds, and fish. The church is also of interest to historians: the 9th-century sanctuary has seats for senior clergy, a custom that was believed to have been typical only in early Christian times. Chalki itself is a pretty town, known for its neoclassical houses in shades of pink, yellow, and gray, which are oddly juxtaposed with the spare but stately 17th-century Venetian **Frangopoulos tower.** Both the church and the tower are usually open to visitors in the morning.

❼ From Chalki, take a winding detour 8 kilometers (5½ miles) north to **Moni** and one of the Balkans' most important churches, **Panayia Drossiani,** which has rare early Byzantine frescoes from the 6th and 7th centuries. Its name means Our Lady of Refreshment, because once during a severe drought, when all the churches took their icons down to the sea to pray for rain, only this church's icon got results. The frescoes are visible in layers: To the right when you enter are the oldest— one shows St. George the dragon slayer astride his horse, along with a small boy, an image one usually sees only in Cyprus and Crete. According to legend, the saint saved the child, who had fallen into a well, and there met and slew the giant dragon that had terrorized the town. Opposite him is St. Dimitrios, shown killing barbarians. The church is made up of three chapels— the middle one has a space for the faithful to worship at the altar rather than in the nave, as was common in later centuries. Next to that is a very small opening that housed a secret school during the revolution. Walk to the back of the church for a view of its odd configuration; the undulating curves are reminiscent of a Gaudi building. If the church is closed when you arrive, ring the bell loudly, and a local woman who is usually in the fields or in town will come to open it.

8 After returning to Chalki, continue southeast 7 kilometers (4½ miles) to **Filoti,** a peaceful village on the lower slopes of Mt. Zas and the interior's largest. Nothing much seems to happen here, but if you're lucky, you may see a festive bridal procession. According to custom, the groom, accompanied by musicians, goes to the bride's house to collect her and her family, and then the party strolls through the village picking up well-wishers. In the center of town is another Venetian tower that belonged to the Barozzis and the main church with its fine marble iconostasis and carved bell tower. Filoti, however, is better known as the starting place for several **walks** in the countryside, for example, the climb up to Zas Cave, where obsidian tools and pottery fragments have been found. Mt. Zas has been associated with Zeus, and on the path to the summit lies a block of unworked marble that reads *Oros Dios Milosiou,* or "boundary of the temple of Zeus Melosios." (Melosios, it's thought, is a word that has to do with sheep.) The islanders say that under the Turks the cave was used as a chapel, and two stalagmites are called the Priest and the Priest's wife, who are said to have been petrified by God to save them from arrest by the Turks. It's best to ask directions for the start of the path, which is southeast of town off a small dirt track.

9 For less determined walkers, there is a flatter 3½-hour walk with excellent views of the island, which culminates at the **Cheimaros tower** (Pirgos Chimarou), built by Ptolemy, a cylindrical 40-foot Hellenistic tower, its marble blocks perfectly aligned. It sits next to two chapels, the pagan side by side with the Christian. The tower, which also served as a lookout post for pirates, is often celebrated in the island's poetry: "O, my heart is like a bower/And Cheimaros's lofty tower!" The path begins on a dirt track off the main road to Apeiranthos, just outside Filoti.

Time Out Take an iced-coffee (*frappe*) break under the plane tree in Filoti's square at **Gratzias** kafeneion, where the owner's name and the date of its founding (1926), are inscribed over the doorway, so you don't confuse it with the other two competing kafeneions.

519 M.P.H.

190 M.P.H.

75 M.P.H.

0 M.P.H.

WE LET YOU SEE EUROPE AT YOUR OWN PACE.

Regardless of your personal speed limits, Rail Europe offers everything to get you over, around and through anywhere you want in Europe. For more information, call your travel agent or **1-800-4-EURAIL.**

Rail Europe

MCI brings Europe and America closer together.

Call the U.S. for less with MCI CALL USA®.

It's easy and affordable to call home when you use MCI CALL USA!

- Less expensive than calling through hotel operators
- Available from over 65 countries and locations worldwide
- You're connected to English-speaking MCI® Operators
- Even call 800 numbers in the U.S.

Call the U.S. for less from these European locations.

Dial the toll-free access number for the country you're calling from. Give the U.S. MCI Operator the number you're calling and the method of payment: MCI Card, U.S. local phone company card, Telecom Canada Card or collect. Your call will be completed!

Austria	022-903-012	Hungary	00*800-01411	Poland	0*-01-04-800-222
Belgium	078-11-00-12	Ireland	1800-551-001	Portugal	05-017-1234
Czechoslovakia	00-42-000112	Italy	172-1022	San Marino	172-1022
Denmark	8001-0022	Liechtenstein	155-0222	Spain	900-99-0014
Finland	9800-102-80	Luxembourg	0800-0112	Sweden	020-795-922
France	19*-00-19	Monaco	19*-00-19	Switzerland	155-0222
Germany	0130-0012	Netherlands	06*-022-91-22	United Kingdom	0800-89-0222
Greece	00-800-1211	Norway	050-12912	Vatican City	172-1022

* Wait for 2nd dial tone. Collect calls not accepted on MCI CALL USA calls to 800 numbers

MCI®

Call **1-800-444-4444** in the U.S. to apply for your MCI Card® now!

⑩ **Apeiranthos,** 4 kilometers (2 miles) farther on, is known as the marble village because of its marble-paved streets and the marble-edged buildings that are lined up between two Venetian towers, the Zevgolis and Bardanis houses. As you walk through the arcades and alleys, notice the unusual chimneys—no two alike. The elders sit in their doorsteps chatting, while packs of children shout "Hello, hello" at any passerby who looks foreign. Off the main square a very small archaeological **museum,** established by a local mathematician, Michael Bardanis, displays Cycladic finds from the east coast. The most important of the artifacts are unique gray marble plaques from the 3rd millenium BC that are carved with scenes of daily life: hunters and farmers and sailors going about their business. Hours vary according to the guard's schedule, but in summer the museum is usually open in the morning. If it's closed, ask in the square for the guard. *No tel. Admission free.*

The villagers of Apeiranthos have always been considered somewhat a breed apart because they are of Cretan origin. Indeed, travel literature of the late 1800s mentions that other islanders hesitated to travel in the north, fearing the thievery of Apeiranthiotes! Today the local dialect still resembles Cretan, and the people preserve many Cretan traditions, like the singing of *kotsakia*, rhyming eight-syllable couplets that praise virtue and condemn infidelity, desertion, and the like:

Oh, you have made me lose my mind
And babble in the street;
My love is such that I dissolve
Whene'er we chance to meet.

During festivals, the singing often develops into a poetic contest between boisterous bards. Apeiranthos also has a strong weaving tradition; most families have their own loom, and until recently the women made clothing for their families, along with decorative tablecloths and curtains. Although these last are usually not for sale, more and more often you may find women spreading out their wares for tourists near the local sights.

From here you may want to return to Chora, as the road to Apollonas, a small resort on the northern tip of Naxos, is winding and narrow in places, and it's just as easy to catch a bus for the two-hour trip there from Chora the next day. If you proceed cautiously, however, and have reliable transportation, it's a magnificent ride through the mountains. After 9 kilometers **⑪** (6 miles) on the right you come to the **Stavros tis Keramotis church,** the only point from which you can see both the east and west coasts of Naxos. After Koronos, when you arrive in the adjoining towns of Koronida/Komiaki (7 kilometers or 4½ miles farther), consider walking the rest of the way to Apollonas if it's not too hot. Just out of town past the cemetery, a sign marks the beginning of a trail that snakes down the mountainside, leading you through wildflowers, past goats and running streams and small stone houses, with the sea stretched out before you. The walk takes about 1½ hours, and from Apollonas, you can catch a bus back up to your car.

Time Out Before setting out on the walk, stop at **Apollon** kafeneion in Komiaki for a piece of homemade baklava and a view down the mountain from the terrace.

⑫ Just before you arrive in **Apollonas** (12 kilometers or 7½ miles via the road), you will see steps on the left leading to the unfinished 28-foot-long **kouros** of Apollonas, which lies in an ancient quarry. It's thought to represent Dionysos. Initially, the Greeks represented gods with small idols, but after the Homeric epics, the gods were seen as anthropomorphic, though much larger than a tall man, and were depicted by these giant, highly stylized statues. This kouros was probably abandoned because cracks developed in the marble while the work was in progress. It lies on its back, eroded by the winds, but still, somewhat eerily, in the shape of a man. *No tel. Admission free.*

You can continue along the coast back to Chora on a rather poor road that just outside Apollonas passes the **Ayia tower**, the lookout post for northwestern Naxos, and the simple **Ayia monastery** with its running springs tucked among the plane trees. Here, during the feast of the Assumption (August 15), women who had taken a vow to the Virgin used to attend the service after walking barefoot from Apollonas along the rough paths. The road continues along the steep cliffs traversing inlets and ⑬ secluded beaches; the most accessible is **Ormos Abram** (5 kilometers or 3 miles from Apollonas), which is pleasant when the north winds aren't blowing.

At Engares (11 kilometers or 7 miles), turn off for Miloi and the ⑭ island's second famous **kouros**, at **Flerio**, which, although smaller (17½ feet), is more detailed and lies in a beautiful private orchard. (If you're returning to Chora on the main road from Apollonas, turn right at Chalki and take the road via Potamia.) Archaeologists think the 7th-century statue was abandoned either because the artist made a mistake or because the client who commissioned it died. Also, when the tyrant Lygdamis came to power, he confiscated all the orders of the rich that were still in the quarries. When he couldn't find a way to dispose of some of the kouros, he tried to sell them back to former owners. Turn right just before the small white shack, pass through the small gate, and you will suddenly come upon the silent kouros, like Ozymandias, a reminder of a once-glorious age. *No tel. Admission free. Open May–Oct., daily 8–sunset.*

Time Out | After seeing the kouros, relax in the **garden**, among bougainvillea and lilac and order the local family's homemade citron (*kitro*) preserves or a shot of citron liqueur.

From Miloi return to Chora, and if there's still light, head for one of the west coast's sandy **beaches**, where you may be just in time to catch the setting sun. The best are the mile-long **Plaka**, about 8 kilometers (5 miles) south of town, and then **Mikri Vigla**, and **Kastraki**, with its creamy white marble sand.

Paros

Paros lacks the chic of Mykonos and has fewer top-class hotels, but at the height of the season it often gets Mykonos overflow, and people are delighted by the island's lower prices, golden sandy beaches, and sleepy fishing villages. It is large enough to accommodate the traveler in search of peace and quiet, yet the port towns of Paroikia and Naoussa also have an active nightlife. Paroikia is a focal point of the ferry network, and many people stay here for a night or two while waiting for a connection. It's particularly good for bars and discos, though Naoussa has a more authentic island atmosphere.

Paroikia   There's a tourist information center (with free maps) in the windmill on the harbor and a multitude of car and motorbike rental agencies nearby (finding a taxi in Paros can be difficult, and the public buses to and from the beaches are infrequent). If you walk east on the harbor road you will see a lineup of bars, fast-food restaurants, and coffee shops—most owned by Athenians who come to Paros to capitalize on tourism during the summer. The better restaurants and the shopping district are in the interior of the town, where it is easy to get lost in the maze of narrow, stone-paved streets that intersect with the streets of the quiet residential areas. The tourist culture has not blended as naturally here as it has in Mykonos and Santorini; this sense of separation is evident in the neglected state of the town, where municipal gardens are untended, sidewalks crumbling, and historic fountains ignored and left dry. But you should not miss two important sites in Paroikia that are very near each other: the church of Our Lady of the Hundred Portals and the Archaeological Museum.

Take the road leading northwest a short way up from the windmill on the port to a shady park of pine trees, all growing diagonally from the strong Aegean winds. You will see a white gate, the front of the former monastic quarters that surround the magnificent **Panayia Ekatontapyliani** church, the greatest of the remaining Byzantine sanctuaries in Greece. According to legend, 99 doors have been found in the church and the 100th will be discovered only after Constantinople has been returned to the Greek nation. Inside, the subdued light mixes with the cream, reddish, and green stonework, creating an emerald glow. At the corners of the dome are two fading Byzantine icons depicting angels. The 17th-century iconostasis is adorned with ornately carved and gilded woodwork and is divided into five frames by marble columns. One panel holds a silver icon of the Virgin Mary, the object of veneration, which is carried through the town on August 15, the Feast of the Assumption.

According to legend, St. Helen, the mother of Constantine the Great, sought refuge from a storm in Paros on her way to the Holy Land. Islanders claim that here she had a vision of finding the true cross and vowed to build a church on the site. It was not until 200 years later, however, that Justinian the Great, who ruled the Byzantine Empire 527–565, fulfilled her vow and built the church. The emperor appointed Isodorus, one of the two chief architects of the famous Ayia Sophia in Istanbul, to design it; and the master architect sent an apprentice, Ignatius, to Paros to build the church. Upon its completion Isodorus arrived in Paros for an inspection and found such a magnificent church that he was consumed by jealousy. He pushed the young apprentice off the top of the dome, but Ignatius grasped his master's foot as he fell, and the two tumbled to their death together. Carved into the column base at the left entrance of the church is a frieze that portrays an old man kneeling beside a young man who holds a cracked head in his hands, presumably Isodorus and Ignatius. *Admission free. Open daily 8–1 and 5–8.*

Up the street from the church is the **Archaeological Museum.** In the room to the left is a fragment of the famed Parian chronicle, which recorded cultural events in Greece from about 1500 BC until 260 BC (a much larger section is in the Ashmolean Museum in Oxford). What has interested scholars is the fact that the historian inscribed valuable information about only the lives of artists, poets, and playwrights, completely ignoring wars and shifts in government.

In the large room to the right is a carved marble funeral monument dedicated to the poet Archilochus, who is pictured in a banquet scene, lying on a couch as slaves serve him. Archilochus, the inventor of iambic meter, is ranked second only to Homer among ancient Greek poets. When he died in battle against the Naxians, his conqueror was cursed by the oracle of Apollo for putting to rest one of the faithful servants of the muse. *Tel. 0284/21231. Admission: 300 dr. Open Tues.– Sun. 8:30–3.*

The tour of Paros is divided into three excursions from Paroikia. One goes northeast to the town of Naoussa; another winds through the mountainous center of the island past the ancient marble quarries to Lefkes; and the third travels south to Petaloudes, better known as the Valley of the Butterflies, and on to the undiscovered village of Alyki. None is longer than 8 kilometers (5 miles).

To Naoussa Just off the northern road to Naoussa, built on the side of a mountain, is the **Monastery of Longovardes,** whose well-known icon-painting school continues today, though only 15 monks reside there. Founded in 1683, the monastic community farms the local land, cooks, and makes wine and olive oil. Only men, dressed in conservative clothing, are allowed inside the gates, where there are post-Byzantine icons, 17th-century frescoes depicting the Twelve Feasts in the Life of Christ, and a library of rare books.

As you approach Naoussa, half-finished buildings on the outskirts of town are evidence of the recent construction boom, since the once-quiet fishing village has just discovered the benefits of tourism. Along the harbor, red and navy-blue boats knock gently against each other as fishermen repair their orange and yellow nets and foreigners relax in the ouzeries lined up along the water's edge. Navies of the ancient Persians, flotillas from medieval Venice, and the imperial Russian fleet have anchored in this harbor. The half-submerged ruins of the Venetian fortifications still remain, and are even more intriguing in the evening when they are lit. Each year on August 23 Naoussa celebrates the heroic naval battle against the Turks, with children dressed in native costume, great feasts, and traditional dancing. The day ends with 100 boats illuminated by torches converging on the harbor.

To Lefkes During the Classical period the island of Paros had an estimated 150,000 residents, many of them slaves who worked the marble quarries. The island grew rich from the export of the white, granular marble known among ancient architects and sculptors for its ability to absorb light. They called it *lychnites,* which means "marble won by lamplight." Four kilometers (2½ miles) east of Paroikia, in **Marathi,** are the ancient marble quarries. If you take a short walk beyond the village you will see three caverns cut into the hillside, the largest of them 300 feet deep. The most recent quarrying done in these mines was in 1844, when a French company cut marble here for Napoleon's tomb.

After another 4 kilometers (2½ miles) you come to the scenic village of Lefkes, built on a hillside in the protective mountains. In the 18th century rampant piracy forced thousands of people from the coastal regions to move inland, and for many years Lefkes was the capital of the island. Today it is still the largest village in the interior and has maintained a sedate, Old European feeling. Farming is a major source of income, as you can tell from the fields of wheat sectioned off by stone walls, and dotted by rectangular bundles of golden hay. Walk along the narrow streets where the balconies are overhung with jasmine and honeysuckle. Ceramics is the second strongest industry in Lefkes, and most craftsmen will welcome you into their shops to watch them work. Two 17th-century churches of interest are Ayia Varvara (St. Barbara) and Ayios Sotiris (the Savior). The 1830 neo-Renaissance Ayia Triada (Holy Trinity) is the village's largest church.

The road continues past Lefkes to **Piso Livadi,** the ancient port for the marble quarries and today a small resort town at the center of Paros's main beach colony. (You can also get to the east coast beaches by driving south from Naoussa. Beware of maps that show the road south from Paroikia reaching the east side of the island. After Alyki, the paved road ends and a rough dirt road begins.) The island's best beach, **Chrysi Akti** (the Golden Beach), a long stretch of sand with sparkling, clear waters, is a bit farther south.

To the Valley of the Butterflies About 4 kilometers (2½ miles) south of Paroikia, signs in English direct tourists to a dirt road leading left toward **Petaloudes,** the Valley of the Butterflies, where a species of nocturnal butterfly returns year after year to mate in a lush oasis of greenery in the middle of this dry, barren island. In May, June, and perhaps July, you can watch them as they lie dormant during the day, their chocolate brown wings with yellow stripes lying still against the ivy leaves. In the evening they flutter upward to the cooler air, showing the coral red undersides of their wings as they rise. A notice at the entrance asks visitors not to disturb them by taking photographs or shaking the leaves.

Time Out Even when the butterflies are not there, it is pleasant to have coffee in the small **kafeneion** near the entrance to the park and enjoy the shade of the cypress, olive, chestnut, mulberry, and lemon trees.

The pathways of Petaloudes are protected on one side by the towering archways of a former Venetian castle, and in the distance is its tower, on the summit of a nearby hill. A local legend has grown up around the castle's founder, Iakovos Alisafis, whose name and the date 1626 are inscribed on the tower. It's said that during the Ottoman period, when the Turks ruled Paros from Istanbul, appearing once a year to collect taxes, the lack of a continuous military presence allowed piracy to spread, and Algerian corsairs raided south Paros. The 12 Alisafis brothers barricaded themselves in their castle with a large supply of food and access to a secret spring outside the tower, but when the pirates discovered the spring, the brothers knew they were doomed. They killed their sister rather than let her be taken and waged a valorous battle before they were killed.

A 15-minute walk up the dirt road from the Valley of the Butterflies leads to the convent known as **Christos sto Dasos,** or Christ of the Wood, where there's a spectacular view of the Aegean. The 15 elderly nuns who run the convent are a bit leery of tourists. If you want to go into the church to see the icons, be sure to wear long pants and a shirt that covers your shoulders, or the sisters will offer you makeshift black-and-white striped skirts that look like prison uniforms. The convent is known among the Parians as the burial place of Ayios Arsenios (1800–1877), their patron saint, who was a schoolteacher, an abbot, and a prophet; the Parians say he was also a rainmaker and that his prayers ended a long drought and saved Paros from starvation.

Though south Paros is barren and sparsely inhabited, it is worthwhile driving another 8 kilometers (5 miles) to the remote fishing village of **Aliki.** Few foreigners have discovered this quiet town, where tourism is just a rumor and where at sunrise fishermen can be seen in the distant sea, hauling in the day's catch. South of the port is a smooth pebble beach that's a favorite spot among locals for a chilly early morning swim.

Off the Beaten Track On the little islet of **Antiparos,** southwest of Paros, an enormous cave descends 230 feet into the earth. Boats from Paroikia take passengers directly to the landing stage on the shore below the cave, and drivers wait there with donkeys for those who want a ride up the hill of St. John to the cave's entrance. Even in August, travelers will feel damp and chilly as they descend the 400 cement steps into the cave. Famous visitors have carved their names on the walls, including Lord Byron and King Otho, the King of Greece in 1840. On three occasions the French ambassador, Count M. de Nouantelle, celebrated midnight mass here, using the enormous truncated stalagmite at the end of the subterranean chapel as an altar. At its base is this inscription: *Hic ipse Christus/Ejus natalie die media celebrato/ MDCLXXIII* ("Here midnight mass was celebrated on Christmas, 1673"). Islanders claim an older inscription that has been lost was written by runaways who had been wrongfully accused of attempting to assassinate Alexander the Great and were hiding in fear of retribution.

Santorini

Santorini is undoubtedly the most extraordinary island in the Aegean, as well as one of the most crowded in summer. If you arrive by boat you will be met by one of the world's most breathtaking sights—a crescent of cliffs, striated in black, pink, brown, white, and pale green, rises 1,100 feet, with the white clusters of the towns of Fira and Oia perched along the top. The encircling cliffs are the ancient rim of a still-active volcano, and you are sailing east across its flooded former caldera. Santorini and its four neighboring islets are the fragmentary remains of a larger land mass that exploded in about 1625 BC: The core of the island volcano blew up, and the sea rushed into the abyss to create the great bay, which measures 10 kilometers by 7 kilometers (6 miles by 4 miles) and is 1,292 feet deep. The other island pieces of the rim, which broke off in later eruptions, are Thirassia Sprinisi, home to a few hundred people, and deserted little Aspronissi (The White One). In the center of the bay, black and uninhabited, are two still-smoldering cones, the "Burnt Isles" of Palea Kameni and Nea Kameni,

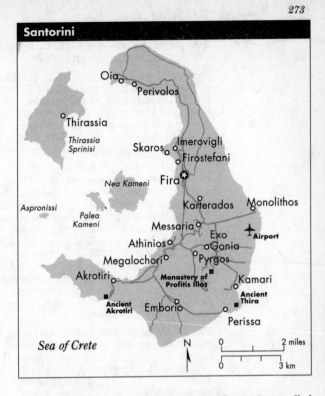

Santorini

Oia
Perivolos
Thirassia
Thirassia Sprinisi
Skaros
Imerovigli
Firostefani
Nea Kameni
Fira
Aspronissi
Palea Kameni
Karterados
Monolithos
Messaria
Athinios
Exo Gonia
Airport
Megalochori
Pyrgos
Akrotiri
Monastery of Profitis Ilias
Kamari
Ancient Akrotiri
Emborio
Ancient Thira
Perissa
Sea of Crete
N
0   2 miles
0   3 km

which appeared between 1573 and 1925. The ancients called Santorini's island group Stronghyle (The Round One) and Kalliste (Most Beautiful); although the island is officially named Thera, the alternate name of Santorini stems from that of its patron, Saint Irene.

There has been a great deal of speculation about the possible identification of Santorini with the mythical Atlantis, mentioned in Egyptian papyri and discussed by Plato, but as yet the subject is moot. This is not true of arguments about whether or not tidal waves from Santorini's cataclysmic explosion destroyed the Minoan civilization on Crete. The latest carbon-dating evidence clearly indicates that the Minoans outlasted the eruption by a couple of hundred years.

Since antiquity, Santorini has depended on rain collected in cisterns for drinking and irrigation—the well water is mostly brackish—and the serious shortage is alleviated by the importation of water from other islands. The fertile volcanic soil produces cherry tomatoes with tough skins and concentrated flavor (used to make tomato paste); the famous Santorini fava beans, which have a light, fresh taste; barley; wheat; pistachio nuts; and white-skinned eggplants. The locals say that in Santorini there is more wine than water, and it may be true; wine is the island's largest export. The volcanic soil, high daytime temperatures, and humidity at night produce 36 varieties of grape, and these unique growing conditions are ideal for the production of a strong, sweetish red wine that is gaining international recognition. All over the countryside you see vines growing in a basketlike configuration that protects the grapes from the wind: Farmers wind the vines into a bowl-like shape, and the bunches of grapes grow inside.

Tourism, the major industry, adds more than 1 million visitors per year to the island's population of 7,000. As a result, **Fira,** the capital, midway along the west coast of the east rim, is no longer just a picturesque town but a major tourist center, overflowing with discos, shops, and restaurants. The vast majority of its employees don't speak a word of Greek; they are young travelers extending their summer vacations.

The modern Greek Orthodox cathedral of **Panayia Ipepantis** is a major landmark in the southern part of town (the local priests, with somber faces, long beards, and black robes, look strangely out of place in summertime Fira). East of here, along Eikostis Pemptis Martiou (25th of March) Street, is where you'll find inexpensive restaurants and accommodations. To the west is the blocked-off Hypapantis Street, leading to Kato Fira (Lower Fira), built into the cliffside overlooking the caldera, where prices are higher and the vista wonderful. For centuries the people of the island have been digging themselves rooms with a view right in the cliff face—many bars and hotel rooms have actually been made out of caves—which lowers building costs and provides constant temperatures.

The **Ghyzis Palace,** Fira's cultural museum, is housed in a restored 17th-century mansion once owned by the Catholic church. The collection includes old maps, engravings, photographs, and paintings by 20th-century Greek artists. *Stavrou and Ioannis Sts., tel. 0286/22244 or 0286/22721. Admission: 100 dr. Open daily 10:30–1:30 and 5–8.*

The **Museum of Historic Cultures,** one block away, displays an interesting but limited collection of pottery, statues, and grave artifacts found at excavations on the island (mostly from Ancient Thera), which represent the Archaic, Classical, Hellenistic, Roman, and Byzantine periods. *Stavrou and Nomikos Sts., tel. 0286/2217. Admission: 100 dr. Open Wed.–Sat. and Mon. 8:45–3, Sun. 9:30–2:30.*

Diehard archaeology buffs may want to visit the site of **Ancient Thera.** There are relics of a Dorian city, with 9th-century BC tombs, Hellenistic houses and public buildings, and traces of Byzantine fortifications and churches. At the sanctuary of Apollo, graffiti dating to the 8th century BC record the names of some of the boys who danced naked at the god's festival. To get there, take a taxi part way up **Mesa Vouna,** a mountain in the southeast corner of the island, which overlooks Perissa and Kamari, then hike to the summit to see the scattered ruins, excavated by the German school of archaeology around the turn of the century.

At the tip of the northern horn of the island, 14 kilometers (9 miles) away, sits **Oia** (pronounced Ía), Santorini's second-largest town. Its cubical white houses stand out against the green, brown, and rust-color layers of rock, earth, and solid volcanic ash that rise from the sea. The most recent eruption, in 1956, caused tremendous earthquakes (7.8 on the Richter scale) that left 48 people dead and hundreds injured and toppled 2,000 houses. The island's west side—especially Oia, until then the largest town—was hard hit, and many residents emigrated to

Athens, Australia, and America. And although Fira, also damaged, rebuilt rapidly, the people from Oia proceeded slowly, sticking to the traditional architectural style. The perfect example of that style is the restaurant 1800, a renovated ship-captain's villa *(see* Dining and Lodging, *below).*

Oia has a cultural classiness that Fira lacks, and visitors who like a lot of activity might feel isolated at the tip of the island. But every summer evening, travelers from all over the world congregate at the caldera's rim—sitting on whitewashed fences, staircases, and beneath the town's windmill—each looking out to sea in anticipation of the performance: the Oia sunset.

About 11 kilometers (7 miles) southeast of Fira is the **Monastery of Profitis Ilias**, at the highest point on Santorini. Follow signs for Pyrgos, then bear right around the town and follow the road to the summit (1,856 feet). From here you can see the surrounding islands and, on a clear day, the mountains of Crete, more than 100 kilometers (66 miles) away. (You may also be able to spot Ancient Thera on the peak below Profitis Ilias.) Unfortunately, radio towers and a NATO radar installation provide an ugly backdrop for the monastery's wonderful bell tower.

Founded in 1711 by two monks from Pyrgos, Profitis Ilias is cherished by islanders because here, in a secret school, the Greek language and culture were taught during the dark centuries of the Turkish occupation. A museum in the monastery contains a model of the secret school in a monk's cell, another model of a traditional carpentry-and-blacksmith shop, and a display of ecclesiastical items. The only way to get in, however, is to arrive early in the morning and hope that one of the remaining caretakers will open the doors for you. There are no longer any set visiting hours, and the monastery's future is in doubt because there are so few monks left.

On your way back to Fira stop in **Pyrgos** to see its medieval houses, stacked on top of one another and back to back for protection against pirates. And you can also see the crumbling walls of the old Venetian castle here.

To reach the excavations at **Akrotiri** (13 kilometers, or 8 miles, from Fira), near the tip of the southern horn of the island, you can take a public bus, a guided tour, or drive yourself.

Time Out En route from Fira, stop at **Boutari** in Megalochori (tel. 0286/ 81011), Santorini's largest winery, and take a tour of the modern facility. An oenologist leads a wine-tasting, and a slide show describes local wine production.

In the 1860s, in the course of quarrying tephra (volcanic ash) for use in making water-resistant cement for the Suez Canal, workmen discovered the remains of an ancient town, frozen in time by layers of pumice that buried it at the time of the eruption, 3,600 years ago. In 1967 Spyridon Marinatos of the University of Athens began excavations, which are continued today by his students and successors. But it is thought that the 40 buildings that have been uncovered are only one-thirtieth of the huge site and that excavating the rest will probably take a century. You enter from the south, pass the ticket booth, and walk 100 yards or so up a stone-paved street to a vast metal shed that protects 2 acres of the site from wind and sun. A path punctuated by explanatory signs in English leads through the ancient town.

Marinatos and his team discovered great numbers of extremely fine and well-preserved frescoes depicting all aspects of Akrotiri life. Now displayed in the Archaeological Museum in Athens, they are eventually to be moved to a new museum in Fira. Meanwhile, postcard-size pictures of them are posted outside the houses where they were found. The antelopes, monkeys, and wildcats they portray suggest trade with Africa. One notable example, apparently representing a trading expedition to Libya, shows two ports, one with dark-skinned people and a lion running across a mountain, and the other full of women in long dresses welcoming the adventurers back home; in the center is a fleet of sailing ships at sea, with playful dolphins swimming alongside. Another fresco shows that Akrotirian ladies wore makeup and jewelry and ornate two-piece garments that revealed their breasts.

There is general agreement that Akrotiri was an outpost of the Minoan civilization on Crete. Although it was settled as early as 3,000 BC, it was not until about 2,000 BC that the civilization reached its height and developed its trade and agriculture and settled the town being uncovered today. The inhabitants cultivated olive trees and grain, and their advanced architecture—four-story frescoed houses faced with fine masonry (some show signs of having had balconies) and public buildings of sophisticated construction—is evidence of an elaborate lifestyle. A sanitary system emptied into drains beneath the streets; ceramic storage jars in 50 shapes were made (many have been left in situ); and many of the houses had wood posts inserted in their stonework to make the walls more flexible in case of earthquakes (the mortar that held the beams in place was decorated with seashells and pebbles). The town is often compared to Herculaneum, but here no human remains, gold, silver, or weapons were found. It appears that the earthquakes preceding the eruption gave enough warning to enable the inhabitants to pack their belongings and flee. After the explosion Santorini was uninhabited for about two centuries while the land cooled and plant and animal life regenerated.

Off the Beaten Track If you'd like to peer down into a live, smoldering volcano, join one of the popular excursions to **Nea Kameni,** the larger of the two Burnt Isles (*see* Getting Around in Essential Information, *above*). After disembarking, you hike 430 feet to the top, to walk around the edge of the crater and wonder if the volcano is ready for its fifth eruption in this century—after all, it has been quite some time since the last, in 1956.

Siros

Stand on the deck of the ferry as it approaches Ermoupolis, and take in the wide-angle view of the fine harbor and the two conical hills, with tiers of houses that spread upward to the summits, crowned by two churches, one Catholic and the other Orthodox.

When the Venetians conquered the Cyclades in the 13th century they knew that Siros's location and its harbor made it ideal for east–west trade; they built their city on the higher hill, farther from the port, where they would have time to prepare defenses against invading pirates. The strong Catholic tradition they established there in Ano Siros (upper Siros) is evident today; Ermoupolis is the seat of the Catholic and Orthodox archbishops of the Cyclades, and Siros has a larger percentage of Catholics than any other island in the archipelago.

During the War of Independence in the early 19th century the new town, closer to the port, was established. Refugees from Turkish-occupied islands sought asylum in Siros and built on Vrontado hill. They named their town Ermoupolis after Hermes, the god of commerce, an appropriate choice. Once called the Manchester of Greece, Ermoupolis was the country's premier port and commercial center in the 19th century. The imposing shipyards in the harbor remind islanders of a time when coal-powered steamships, traveling between western Europe and the Black Sea, would stop to refuel or to store their Egyptian cotton and spices from the East. Britain and nine other nations established consulates in Ermoupolis, and a prosperous bourgeoisie organized a chamber of commerce, insurance companies, newspapers, and charitable institutions—at a time when these were almost unknown in the rest of Greece. Great fortunes were raised to construct neoclassical buildings for a high school (claimed to be the first in Greece), a town hall, law courts, and churches. For 50 years the shipping flourished, but by the 1870s oil had replaced coal and Ermoupolis was no longer used as a fueling station. The port of Piraeus gained the business that Siros lost, and a period of economic decline followed.

Ermoupolis has not lost its air of sophistication, and it remains the administrative center of the Cyclades. Its law courts serve the entire archipelago and the robust island population of 23,000, and the floating docks still build small vessels and repair domestic and foreign ships. The Greek government has designated Ermoupolis a national historic landmark.

Walk along the harbor, past the tavernas, cafés, and shops, and take a left onto Venizelou Street. It leads to the grand 19th-century square, **Plateia Miaoulis.** It is desolate in the heat of the day, but on cool summer evenings the townspeople promenade across the marble pavement, surrounded by stately buildings, a clock tower, and palm trees. On special occasions, local musicians perform on the marble bandstand, which is carved with the faces of the muses. The square is named for Admiral Andreas Vokos Miaoulis, a patriot in the War of Independence, whose statue stands in front of the town hall.

Ernst Ziller, an Austrian architect who fell in love with a Greek woman and settled permanently in Greece, designed the **Town Hall,** a stately neoclassical building on the north side of the square. Though it is under renovation, visitors are welcome to go in to see the full-length portraits of King George I and Queen Olga or to visit the central tourist office for the Cyclades.

To the west of the Town Hall and up a few steps is a small **Archaeological Museum.** Three rooms contain finds from Siros and neighboring islands, notably marble burial figurines from the 3rd millennium BC. Other finds include two miniature Hellenistic marble heads, and an ancient relief of a boar hunt. *Tel. 0281/28487. Admission free. Open daily 8:30–3.*

To the right, behind the square, is the **Apollon,** the first theater built in Greece since ancient times; a miniature version of La Scala in Milan, it supported a regular Italian opera season until

1914. European Community funding is helping to renovate the interior, and it's expected to open for a new season in 1993 (*see* The Arts and Nightlife, *below*). Walk northeast up Nikolao Street a few blocks to one of the city's most elegant churches, **Ayios Nikolaos** (St. Nicholas), on the square of the same name. Near the entrance is a garden where you will see a pedestal topped by a lion, the world's first monument to the unknown soldier, carved by the 19th-century sculptor Vitalis, as was the green marble iconostasis inside the church. A short walk above the square brings you to the Vaporia quarter, with its mansions from the time of the town's great prosperity.

On the west side of Plateia Miaoulis there are two other churches of interest: **Ayia Koimesis** (St. Prioiou St., next to the European Hotel) has an icon, *The Assumption of the Virgin Mary*, painted by the renowned Cretan painter Dominicos Theotokopoulos, better known as El Greco. The **Church of the Metamorphoseos** holds the tomb of Anthimios Gazis (1758-1828), a hero of the War of Independence; during that war it was a temporary shelter for hundreds of refugees, who slept on the floors and in the courtyard and held meetings in the nave, where they voted to name their town Ermoupolis.

Time Out   Stop at one of Ermoupolis's many sweetshops and ask for *loukoumia*, gummy squares smothered in powdered sugar. Greeks claim that the best Turkish delight comes from Siros. If you don't acquire a taste for it, try *halvadopites*, round sandwiches of sweetened sesame pulp and almonds, introduced to Greece from the Middle East.

It takes about one hour to climb the 800 steps that wind from Omirou Street to the top of Ano Siros. Many people take a taxi or a bus to the summit and walk down through the stone-walled alleyways and little squares that are reminiscent of the Middle Ages. The Catholic quarter is dominated by the **Cathedral of St. George,** founded early in the Venetian period and rebuilt in 1843. Notice the icon of the *Virgin Mary of Hope*, who holds a small gold anchor in one hand, representing a prayer for Siriot sailors. Beneath the icon is a case of gold and silver votive offerings, miniature models of hands, hearts, babies, ears, and breasts that the donors hoped would be healed by the Virgin. Also on the summit is **Moni Kapoutsinon,** the monastery of the Capuchins founded by Louis XIII of France.

The Catholics of Ano Siros are called *Frankosyrianni*, a word that has become familiar to most Greeks through a famous love song by Markos Vamvakaris, who is known as the father of *rembetika*, the traditional Greek urban blues. Born in 1905 in a poor village on Siros, the young Vamvakaris earned a few drachmas playing a dog-skin drum beside his father, who played the *gaida* (Greek bagpipes). At this time the island was rich in musicians, with violinists, drummers, and bouzouki players showing off their talents during Carnival, in the weeks before Lent. The entire family was arrested for selling tobacco and sugar on the black market and were sent to prison. At the age of 15 Vamvakaris escaped on a ship for Piraeus, the town where rembetika was born, and at 31 he wrote "Sweet Frankosyrian Girl." His portrait hangs in Ano Siros's restaurant and music hall, Lilis (*see* Dining and Lodging, *below*).

Halfway down the hill, beside the Orthodox Church of Ayios Yiorgios, is the **British Military Cemetery,** where 111 British and Allied servicemen are buried, many of them killed when the British ship *Arcadia* was torpedoed and sank in the Aegean in 1917.

Time Out   Stop at **Café No. 9** on the port and order jasmine tea or the non-alcoholic Yin Yang cocktail, made from the fruits of the season. The owner may let you read a book from his collection; many are antiques from the attics of Sirian homes.

Take the road from Ermoupolis that runs along the mountainous spine of the island to **Chalandriani.** The northern landscape, unlike the green southern part of the island, has little vegetation, few inhabitants, and a meager supply of water. A short walk northwest of Chalandriani will take you to the hill of **Kastri,** the remains of one of the earliest fortified settlements in the Cyclades, with crumbling walls, house foundations, and an overgrown necropolis. This area was inhabited from the Early until the Late Bronze Age. Another excavation on the northwest coast uncovered an early Cycladic cemetery with 97 graves and evidence that the area was inhabited until the Late Bronze Age.

After returning to the main road, turn toward Kampos, the northernmost village on the island. West of Kampos, halfway between the village and the sea, is Spilia tou Ferekidou, the Cave of Pherecydes, believed to be where the ancient philosopher Pherecydes lived and taught philosophy in summer, moving in winter to another cave at Alythini in the southern part of the island. Born in Siros in the 6th century BC, he was one of the world's first astronomers and is credited with the invention of the sundial. His most renowned student, Pythagoras, traveled throughout Greece and Italy teaching the immortality and transmigration of souls. Local legend has it that Pherecydes made a pilgrimage to Delos to spend his last days and, strangely enough, was eaten alive by lice, but that before he died he was visited by his old student Pythagoras.

To reach the greener part of the island you must return to Ermoupolis and take one of the western or southern routes. Twelve kilometers (7½ miles) southwest of the capital is Dellagratia, better known as **Posidonia,** whose nearby sandy beaches make it one of the island's most popular resort areas. Wealthy Siriotes build their summer villas here, where the mountain streams flow toward the bay, irrigating the pine forests, palm trees, and wild flowers. Some 6,000 species of *louloudia* (flowers) flourish in Greece and most of these can be found in the Cyclades. In July look for golden thistle, oleander, aloe flowers, and blossoming pear trees.

Two kilometers (1¼ miles) north along the coast from Posidonia is **Foinikas,** named for the Phoenicians, who are thought to be Siros's first inhabitants. They settled in these two cities and called the island *usyra*, which means "happy."

Eumaeus, son of Ktesius, the king of Siros, was captured by pirates and sold to Odysseus, King of Ithaca. He grew up to become the faithful swineherd to the king. When the hero returned to Ithaca in disguise, according to Homer, Eumaeus said to him: "You are asking me about my early days. Let me give you this tale. There is an island named Syrie . . . where the sun

*turns its course . . . famine is unknown and there is no dis-
ease. No dreadful scourges spoil the islanders' happiness, but
when the men of each generation grow old in their homes, Apollo of the Silver Bow comes with Artemis, strikes them with silver darts and lays them low. There are two cities on the island,
which is divided between them. My father, Ktesius, was king of
them both."*

It is apparent that Homer too believed Siros to be a rich, fertile
land where people lived long, healthy lives and died not of ill-
ness or misfortune, but in the dignified autumn of old age.

**Off the
Beaten Track** From the fishing village of Kini, due west of Ermoupolis, adventurous travelers can take a boat to Grammaton Bay, a gulf
near the northwestern tip of the island. There you can see ancient inscriptions carved into the marble cliff by sailors from
the Hellenistic age, apparently thanking the gods for saving
them from a shipwreck. The bay takes its name from the Greek
word *grammata*, which means "letters."

Shopping

Mykonos, with Santorini taking a close second, is the best island in the Cyclades for shopping. You can buy anything from
Greek folk items to Italian designer clothes, cowboy boots, and
leather jackets from the United States. Although island prices
are better than in the expensive shopping districts of Athens,
there are many tourist traps in the resort towns, with high-
pressure sales tactics and inflated prices for inferior goods.
The Greeks have a word for naive American shoppers—
Americanaki. It's a good sign if the owner of a shop selling traditional crafts or art lives on the island and is not a hotshot
Athenian over for the summer to make a buck.

Each island has its unique pottery style that reflects its individ-
uality: In Siros, for example, the colors are brown and earthy,
while in Santorini they are the bright shades of the setting sun.
Island specialties are handpainted icons copying Byzantine
originals; flokati rugs; embroidered linens; local wines; and
gold worked in ancient and Byzantine designs.

Don't be surpised when the stores close between 3 and 5 in the
afternoon and reopen in the evenings; even on the chic islands
everybody takes a siesta.

Andros

At **Batsi Gold** (Harbor St., Batsi, tel. 0282/41575) skillful and
imaginative goldsmiths sell a collection of jewelry (including
bracelet, necklace, and ring sets) designed with such ancient
symbols as honey bees, bull's horns, and the Macedonian star.
In Andros town **Roio** (no phone), a gift shop on the main street
near Kairis Square, has a wide selection of native pottery, embroidery, ship models, and other handmade objects. Notable
are the ceramic bowls in bright colors with flowers molded in
the centers.

Mykonos

Crafts **Pandora** (Laka Sq., tel. 0289/24754) is a new art gallery that exhibits the paintings of many of the artists living in Mykonos.

You may see owner Chris Christos sculpting a block of Tinos marble in front of his store. His sculptures cost from 30,000 to 2,000,000 drachmas. **The White Shop** (Metropoleos St., tel. 0289/22612) sells embroidery and lace made by nuns in monasteries throughout Greece. Owner Anna Ykelou carries bedcovers and curtains, decorated with flowers, birds, and small ships. A tablecloth of delicate lace costs 75,000 dr. Ask to see Ms. Ykelou's mother's traditional Mykonos stitch.

Fashion Yiannis **Galatis** (near taxi sq., opposite Lalaounis, tel. 0289/ 22255) has dressed such famous women as Elizabeth Taylor, Ingrid Bergman, and Jackie Onassis. It is likely that he will greet you personally and show you some of his coats and costumes, hostess gowns, and long dresses. He also has men's clothes. **Pan Boutiques** (29 Matogianni St., tel. 0289/24114) has designer clothes for men and women, including Molinari, Moschino jeans, Fendissimi, Armani, Gianni Versace, and Enrico Coveri. **Armonia** (Laka Sq., tel. 0289/23930) carries a more risqué, racier selection of men's and women's fashions by such designers as Gottex, Plus Zero, Daniel Hechter, and Options. **Mardoules** (89 Efthmiou St., near bus station, tel. 0289/ 24132) is the place to go for children's shoes and garments.

Gold and Silver Ilias **Lalaounis** (Polykandrioti St., near taxi sq., tel. 0289/ 22444) is known internationally for jewelry in ancient Greek and Byzantine designs. It also carries silver bowls, candlesticks, and decorative objects—some with semiprecious stones. **Delos Dolphins** (Zanni Pitaraki St., Limni Sq., tel. 0289/22765) is becoming known also for handmade jewelry based on Greek museum pieces.

Leather **Apollon Leather** (17 Mavrogenous St., tel. 0289/24496) carries a wide selection of jackets, handbags, briefcases, and luggage.

Rugs **Karamichos-Mazarakis** (harbor, near Delos boats, tel. 0289/ 22463) sells a wide range of handwoven Greek carpets, including virgin wool flokati rugs, and ships anywhere in the world.

Naxos

Books At **Zoom** (Chora waterfront, tel. 0285/23675 or 0285/23676) there's an excellent selection of English-language history and picture books about Naxos.

Food and Wine Visitors might also think about stocking up on local cheeses like *mizithra* and *kefalotiri*, and savory olives called *throubes*. A large selection of the famous citron liqueur (*kitro*) and preserves, as well as Naxos wines, can be found at **Promponas Wines and Liquors** (Chora waterfront, tel. 0285/22258), which has been around since 1915.

Hand Knits The embroidery and knit items made by women in the mountain villages are known throughout Greece; they can occasionally be bought in a Chora tourist shop like **Old Market Naxos** (Old Town, tel. 0285/24767) or from villagers hawking their wares in front of tourist sites.

Jewelry For unusual jewelry in gold and silver at reasonable prices try **Takis'** (Chora waterfront, tel. 0285/23045), where the owner and a German goldsmith create good luck talismans in different settings that feature a "Naxos eye," which is the operculum, or door of a seashell, in red or white, with a spiral design. The workshop-gallery of **Angelos V** (Exarchopolou, Old Town, tel.

0285/23187) sells one-of-a-kind pieces distinguished by their
fluid shape and bold design.

Marble Since ancient times the island has been lauded for its marble.
For an unusual gift, pick up some tiles, art items, or designs for
a marble fireplace at **Naxos Marble** (Chora New Town, tel 0285/
24747).

Paros

At **Yria Pottery** (in the mountains above Kostos village), local
craftsmen can be seen at work in their studio. Both the table
wares and the works of art make use of Cycladic island motifs in
their designs, and some pieces incorporate Parian marble.
Many organized tours stop here, or you can take a taxi. **Raku**
(near the central square, Naoussa, tel. 0284/51052) is named for
the fragile, difficult type of ancient Far Eastern ceramic sold
here. "Raku" means happiness, but the potters must have tremendous patience to endure the frustration of having large
numbers of pieces break during firing. Owner Katerina
Fotopoulou uses maroons and deep blues in the glazes of her
wares—an array of unique sculptures, bowls, and platters, and
she is an acknowledged expert.

Santorini

The best town for finding locally made items is Oia. The inhabitants are sophisticated, and here you will find the best art galleries, antiques shops, crafts shops, and stores that sell
reproductions of Byzantine icons.

Art **Art Gallery** (main shopping st., Oia, tel 0286/71448) sells large
three-dimensional representations of Santorini architecture
by Bella Kokeenatou and Stavros Galanopoulos. Their lifelike
depth invites the viewer to walk through a door or up a flight of
stairs. **Art Gallery Oia** (main shopping st., Oia, tel. 0286/71463)
is the place to find a watercolor to take home; painter Manolis
Sivridakis understands how to capture the special light of
Santorini.

Clothing **Meteo** (main shopping st., Oia, no phone). This white store with
purple trim has the best hats in the Cyclades—in many colors
and shapes, with various ribbons and dangling decorations—
whatever the heart desires. Check out too the handmade silk
and cotton shawls and the funky dresses from the 1950s. At
Gemini (Hypapantis Walkway, Fira, tel. 0286/23242), passers-
by are irresistibly drawn by the display of geometric patterned
Thio Peppe sweatshirts in the window. These Italian-
designed, Greek-made shirts seem to blow right out of the
store when the meltemi winds begin. Gemini also carries Italian Diesel jeans, American Levis, and Camomilla women's
clothes.

Jewelry **Kostas Antoniou Jewelry** (Ayiou Ioannou, Fira, tel. 0286/
22633). *Vogue* and *Marie Claire* have taken photographs of the
pieces displayed in this shop, which is a favorite among cruise-
ship passengers. Imagine the magnificence of solid gold necklaces named Earth's Engravings, Ritual, and Motionless
Yielding! Antoniou also carries a selection of Van Cleef &
Arpels watches from Paris.

Souvenirs **Yordani** (Near main sq., Oia, tel. 0286/71490) is the perfect shop for inexpensive handmade souvenirs, like shiny ceramic apples, hand-painted tiles, and gold jewelry, all made in Greece. The delicate blown-glass chandeliers are spectacular, but not so easy to take home in your suitcase.

Wine and Liquor **Kava Liquor Store** (Aghiou Ioannou, Fira, tel. 0286/22593) carries 10 kinds of ouzo, including the sweet Canava from Santorini and a local brand that comes in a hand-painted bottle, and 12 kinds of Metaxa (another Greek liqueur)—not to mention the numerous Santorini wines.

Siros

The sign in front of **Milo** (Platia Vardava, next to Apollon theater, Ermoupolis, tel. 0281/27203) spells out the name in large letters—it means "apple" in Greek. The colorful store is crammed with dried flowers, soaps, candles, baskets, silk scarves, pillows, and quilted children's backpacks. The most appealing items are handmade marionettes and dramatic masks used in the October carnival's masquerade parades. **Kira** (Proio St., near corner of Filini, Ermoupolis, no tel.) sells Siros pottery, in royal blue and cream, antique linens and statuettes, dolls and paintings.

Sports and Outdoor Activities

Andros

The mountainous geography and lush greenery make Andros a pleasant island for **hiking**, especially around Andros town and near Messaria, Apoikia, and Stenies. The 5-kilometer (3-mile) hike from the little village of Lamira to Andros town is popular. The **Andros Naval Club**, where you can go **rowing** and **sailing**, is at the port of Nimborio, just north of Andros town. The **Andros Holiday Hotel** in Gavrion (tel. 0282/71384 or 0282/71433) has **tennis courts** open to the public. For **water sports**, try Batsi Beach, where windsurfing equipment, jet skis, canoes, and pedal boats can be rented by the hour. More adventurous travelers might want to try waterskiing or parasailing behind a motorboat.

Mykonos

The **Aphroditi Hotel** on Kalafati Beach (tel. 0289/71367 or 0289/71380) and the **K Hotels** (tel. 0289/22929 or 0289/22107) on the hill above Mykonos town, among others, have **tennis courts**. You can work out at the **Body Work Gym** (from taxi sq. go to Alexis Snack Bar and turn right, no tel.) and **Style Workout Gym** (tel. 0289/24270), both of which have weights, aerobics, and saunas. Travel agencies in the town can arrange **sailing** trips and charters: Try **Ecotourism** (19 Ayiou Efthimiou St., tel. 0289/24415). For **water sports**, the windy northern beaches on Ornos Bay are best; you can rent surfboards and take lessons. There's windsurfing and waterskiing at Ayios Stefanos, Plati Yialos, and Ornos. The **Psarou Diving Center** (in Hotel Psarou, tel. 0289/23579) offers certification programs for beginners and wreck dives and cave dives for the advanced. **Lucky Divers** at Ornos Bay (tel. 0289/23220) also gives lessons and runs daily dive excursions.

Naxos

The best **spear fishing,** for rockfish and blackfish, is off the cape at Ayios Prokopios and along the northern coast, although night fishing is forbidden, as is diving with air tanks. For **fishing with a line,** try Apollonas Bay. The areas around Xirokabos, Ayios Xrisostomes, and Ai Fokas and the southeast side of Mt. Zas are good for hunting partridge, snipe, quail, turtledove, and hare. For wild duck, local hunters go to Stelidas Lake in the south, but look out for NO HUNTING signs. To rent a **sailboat,** contact the **Rental and Travel Center** in Chora (tel. 0285/23395 or 0285/23396), where a Drimor Discovery 3,000 or a Beneauteau Oceanis is available, with a skipper or bare-boat. Call the port authority (tel. 0289/22300) for information about where to go in Chora for gas, water, and repairs. The **Mathiassos Village Hotel,** just outside the new section of Chora, has a **tennis court** open to the public. At Ayios Prokopios and Ayia Anna beaches the wind and water conditions are ideal for inexperienced **windsurfers,** and there's also **water skiing,** equipment rentals, and instruction for both sports. **Jet skis** can also be rented at Ayios Prokopios. The **Mikri Vigla hotel complex** south of Chora has a **windsurfing center** (tel. 0285/75240, 1285/75241, or 0285/75242), but experienced windsurfers prefer Kastraki, Pyrgaki, Moutsouna, and Agiassos beaches, where wind speeds can reach 7 on the Beaufort scale.

Paros

You can play **tennis** at the **Hotel Contaratos** in Naoussa (tel. 0284/51693) and the **Hotel Yria** outside Paroikia (tel. 0284/24154 through 0284/24158). Many of the beaches on Paros have various **water sports:** For waterskiing lessons, equipment, and organized groups, contact the **Ipanema Water Sports** office in Paroikia (tel. 0284/51544 or 0284/51476). For windsurfing lessons and rentals, try the **Santa Maria Surf Club,** on the beach of the same name about 4 kilometers (2½ miles) north of Naoussa.

Santorini

The **Santorini Sailing Center** in Merovigli (tel. 0286/23059 or 0286/22895) arranges charters and runs weekly 2- to 3-day sailing trips around the Cyclades for groups of up to 10. The **Santorini Tennis Club** (tel. 0286/22122) at the hotel complex of the same name, in Kartaradoes, has two concrete courts where two can play in high season for the equivalent of $75 (open Apr.–Oct.). The **Santorini Image Hotel** in the middle of the island (tel. 0286/31874 or 0286/31875) also has a court. **Windsurfing** and **waterskiing** are available on Kamari and Perissa beaches, and Kamari also offers **parasailing.**

Siros

Teamwork Travel (near the port, 10 P. Ralli St., tel. 0281/23400 or 0281/22866) charters sailboats that accommodate four to 12 people. For fuel, contact Vasilis Vergos at the Mobil station (tel. 0281/22369) and for repairs, charts, parts, and the like, contact

Makis Stathopouros (tel. 0281/22478). The **Dolphin Bay Hotel** in Galissas (tel. 0281/42924) has **tennis courts** open to the public. For **windsurfing** and **waterskiing**, try Foinikas Beach.

Beaches

Andros

The beach in **Batsi** is sandy, accessible, and offers some protection from the winds. Adjacent to Andros town is another beach that provides a view of the castle ruins, but the nearby road and development in the area are distractions. There's a nice sandy beach at **Nimborio Bay** about 2 kilometers (1¼ miles) north of Andros town, and another in the bay below Korthion and Yialia, near the village of **Stenies.**

Mykonos

There is a beach for every taste in Mykonos. Within walking distance of Mykonos town are **Tourlos, Ayios Stefanos,** and **Ayios Ioannis.** Ayios Stefanos has a mini-golf course, water sports, restaurants, and umbrellas and lounge chairs for hire. **Psarou,** on the south coast, protected from wind by hills and surrounded by restaurants, offers a wide selection of water sports and is considered the finest beach. Nearby **Plati Yialos,** popular for families, is also lined with restaurants and dotted with umbrellas for rent. From here you can take a small boat to **Paranga, Paradise, Super Paradise,** and **Elia,** on all of which nude bathing is common. All have tavernas within walking distance. At the farthest end of this sandy stretch is **Kalafatis,** known for package tours, and between Elia and Kelafatis there's a remote beach at **Kato Livadhi,** which can be reached by taxi. The great indentation on the north coast of the island, called Panormes Bay, has unprotected sandy beaches that can get windy.

Naxos

Venture past Chora's beach, **Ayios Georgios,** to the long, mostly sandy stretches farther south. **Ayios Prokopios** has a small leeward harbor and gives way to the small cape of **Ayia Anna,** followed by **Plaka,** ringed by sand dunes and bamboo groves. Farther south are **Mikri Vigla** and **Kastraki,** sandy beaches edged by cedar trees. Next is **Pyrgaki,** ideal with its crystalline water. In the northeast, **Apollonas** is a spread-out beach with small white marble pebbles; much more rewarding are the bays of **Abram, Ayias Mamas, Xilia Brisi,** and **Paxia Ammos,** small sand beaches to the west that are seldom crowded. Most of these can be reached by bus.

Paros

The best beaches are on the southeast coast of the island; the **Golden Beach** is a long stretch of white sand, with a few tavernas to choose from; **Chrysi Akti** is a popular place for sailboarding; **Pounda beach** is nudist. There are also a number of spots to swim from along the bay east of Naoussa. The best is **Langheri,** a long sandy beach with dunes. **Kolimbithres,** in the bay south of Naoussa, has water sports and a choice of tavernas. Avoid the beaches on the waterfront in Paroikia; their proximity to the port makes the water murky. It is better to take a boat (they leave about every 20 minutes) across the bay to sandy **Livadhia** or the quieter and more remote **Krios** beach.

Santorini

There are no worthwhile beaches close to the main towns of Fira and Oia, although from Fira you can easily get a bus to the beaches on the south or east coast. If you hike down the cliffside in Oia to the port of Armenti, you can catch a bus to the small sand beach of **Baxedes**, and there's a quiet beach on the southwest shore just below Akrotiri that's known for its red sand. If you're a beach bum, it's better to stay in Kamari or Perissa, which both have long, black beaches. A mixture of sand and volcanic ash, the black beaches are a natural treasure of Santorini, but some stretches are becoming polluted with cigarette butts and garbage left by tourists. Deck chairs and umbrellas can be rented at both beaches, and tavernas and *cantines* (drink stands) abound.

Siros

In sharp contrast to the seaside resort towns is the inviting fishing village of **Kini,** where locals rent bamboo umbrellas on the cozy beach and where you can escape from the crowds. To the south is **Galissas,** a long, oval sandy beach considered the best on the island, which is protected on both sides by hills and has pleasant natural surroundings. Farther south is **Foinikas**, with the port's bright boats bobbing in the distance. Conditions here are suitable for windsurfing and water skiing. Cafeterias and restaurants are a short walk away. **Megas Yialos beach** at Bounta Bay is a family beach with a row of trees that provide shade.

Dining and Lodging

Dining

Eating is a lively social activity in the Cyclades, and the friendliness of most taverna owners compensates for the lack of formal service. Except in the top-flight restaurants of Mykonos and Santorini, you can forget white linen and candlelight, and don't expect leisurely three-course meals. In most tavernas, plastic covers the table, and a basket contains your forks and knives, napkins, and bread. Unless you order intermittently, the food comes all at once. Reservations are not required unless otherwise noted, and casual dress is acceptable.

If you don't like the taste of garlic and olive oil, order the grilled seafood and meat (try grilled octopus with ouzo). A typical island lunch is fresh fried calamari with a salad of tomatoes, peppers, onions, white goat cheese, and olives. Lamb on a skewer and *keftedes* (spicy meatballs) are a couple of other favorites. The volcanic soil of Santorini is hospitable to the grape, and Greeks love the Santorini wines. Try to be there on July 20 for the celebration of St. Elias's name-day, when a traditional pea and onion soup is served, followed by walnut and honey desserts and folk dancing.

Highly recommended restaurants are indicated by a star ★.

Category	Cost (all islands)*
Very Expensive	over 6,000 dr.
Expensive	3,000 dr.–6,000 dr.
Moderate	2,000 dr.–3,000 dr.
Inexpensive	under 2,000 dr.

per person for 3-course meal, including tax, service, and beer or barrel wine

Lodging

Island accommodations range from run-down pensions or an extra bedroom in a private house to first-class hotels. It is customary to leave your passport with the proprietor when you check in (to ensure payment). If you're on a budget, walk around town and ask villagers where you can rent a room, but before paying any money, be sure to look at the room, check that the bathroom is clean, and make sure the door locks. If there are extra beds in the room, clarify in advance that the amount agreed on is for the entire room—owners sometimes try to put another person in the same room later in the day.

The best rooms and service (and noticeably higher prices) are on Mykonos and Santorini, but even there many hotels don't have telephones in the rooms, and the presence of air-conditioning and TV cannot be taken for granted. But in order to do the Cyclades properly, you should not go seeking technological amenities; make a room with a view your priority—preferably one with a balcony that overlooks the sea. Avoid hotels on main roads or near all-night discos, and try to locate one with a freshwater pool. An evening dip in "sweet water" after swimming in the sea is a luxury.

Only the most expensive hotels provide hot water 24 hours a day; in some hotels you must turn on a thermostat for a half hour to heat water for a shower (not forgetting to turn it off). Signs tell you that water is in short supply in the Cyclades, reminding you to conserve it, and that the delicate sewage systems require that toilet paper go in the wastebasket. Fresh water is often shipped from the mainland, and though faucet water is generally potable, you should not drink from fountains or springs. Most people drink bottled water, which can be found everywhere.

Highly recommended lodgings are indicated by a star ★.

Category	Cost (all islands)*
Very Expensive	over 25,000 dr.
Expensive	10,000 dr.–25,000 dr.

| Moderate | 6,000 dr.–10,000 dr. |
| Inexpensive | under 6,000 dr. |

All prices are for a standard double room.

Andros

Dining
★
Stamatis. Batsi's high-class taverna has been serving tradition-al Greek cooking since 1965. It's a homey, rustic place for din-ing, with a fireplace and a wall display consisting of a stuffed falcon, deer antlers, hunting knives, and an old clarinet. The chef invites customers to go behind the counter and have a look at the selection of special dishes for the evening. Try the fresh roasted chicken filled with a mixture of mushrooms, peas, and cheese; or the tender lamb chops cooked in foil with a special Andros stuffing. For dessert, try the scrumptious milk pie, *galactobouriko*. *On side st. to right of Dolphins taverna, tel. 0282/41283. Reservations advised Aug. MC, V. Expensive.*

The Dolphins. This popular taverna in Batsi has outdoor seat-ing that overlooks the harbor; inside, a colorful mural depicts the local fishing scene. The owners Jannis Fotiou and his German wife Gesa both cook and wait on tables. Try their spe-cialty—onion stew loaded with chunks of tender veal—or the liver or grilled filet mignon. The seafood includes lobster, blacktail, and fish soup that locals claim is the best in town. *S. end of harbor, tel. 0282/41568. No credit cards. Moderate.*

Parea. This shaded taverna perched high above a windswept beach is the perfect place to try the island's special omelette, the *fourtalia.* It is packed with potatoes, cheese, sausage or ba-con, a handful of broad beans, and herbs and is cooked in the oven. Other favorites are veal in lemon sauce, and long, round fresh *kannelonia* stuffed with mincemeat. At the end of a meal Andriotes like their local cheese, *dopio* (like feta), with fresh fruit. You will, too. *Kairis Sq., Chora, tel. 0282/23721. V. Inexpensive.*

Lodging
Epaminondas. This newly opened complex has spacious rooms and a quiet atmosphere within walking distance of the center of Batsi. Though the stark exterior architecture, with brown stone and small windows, may remind you of a dormitory, all the rooms in this hotel have balconies that overlook Batsi Bay. The freshwater pool is lit all night for those who want a moon-light swim. There's a variety of room sizes for two to six people, some with kitchenettes, and some are duplexes, with an up-stairs and downstairs. *En route to lower Batsi, on l. before hairpin turn, 84500, tel. 0282/41682, 0282/41683, or 0282/41177. 33 rooms with bath. Facilities: kitchenettes, freshwater pool. No credit cards. Expensive.*

Paradise Hotel. This white colonial-style hotel is just outside the center of Andros town, within walking distance of the shops and museums. The best rooms have white lacy curtains and canopy double beds; all have balconies overlooking the sea or the mountains. You can walk 10 minutes to the main town beach, or take the hotel van to better beaches. *Main st., on r. side before entering center, 84500, tel. 0282/22187, 0282/22188, or 0282/22189. 41 rooms with bath. Facilities: TVs and minibars in rooms. MC, V. Expensive.*

Hotel Pighi Sarisa. This white three-story hotel flies the EC, United States, British, and Greek flags. It's on a mountain road near the Sarisa mineral springs, and is wonderful if you're looking for a break from the heat. The air is cool, there's a freshwater pool, and you can take mountain hikes on the many trails near the hotel. Rooms are clean and simple, with TVs and minibars. The restaurant has an international menu. *Left side of Apoikia Rd. 3 km (2 mi) n. of Andros town, 84500, tel. 0282/ 23799, 0282/23899, or 0282/23999. 42 rooms with bath. Facilities: restaurant, sauna, games room, minibus to beach. DC, V. Moderate–Expensive.*

Camping **Camping Andros** (tel. 0282/71444) is situated in a grove of olive trees 328 yards from the port of Gavrion and 273 yards from the beach. A minimarket and a snack bar add to its convenience.

Mykonos

Dining **Chez Cat'rine.** This restaurant is hidden at a quiet intersection
★ of Mykonos's narrow, stone-paved alleyways, but the Greek and French cuisine is worth the search. A host will greet you at the entrance and formally present a display of fresh meats and fish from which you may choose. Although there is no outdoor seating, the splendid interior mixes the whitewashed walls and archways of the Cyclades with the feeling of a French château. An old stove has been transformed into a wine display. Candles, classical music, and a faded 16th-century mural from Istanbul (still Constantinople to Greeks), add to the restaurant's warm formality. For an appetizer try baby squid stuffed with rice and Greek mountain spices, or cheese soufflé, puffed to perfection and loaded with mussels, prawns, carrots, and potatoes. Favorite entrées include grilled swordfish, leg of lamb, and tournedos langoustine—a beef fillet with lobster sauce, flamed with cognac. After dinner try the strawberry pie or *popanisi*, the island's special cheese, served with fresh fruit. *Ayios Gerasimos St., tel. 0289/22169. Reservations required on weekends. AE, MC, V. Expensive.*

Edem. The painting of Adam and Eve embracing, with the motto "You will wish you never had to leave" is undeniably tacky. And just ignore the fact that the waiters are dressed like Cycladic chapels, in light blue vests and white shirts. The truth is that Edem offers two pleasant garden spots for dining: on the rooftop lined with flowerpots, and on the ground floor, where blooming vines hang overhead and a 16-foot cactus guards the door. Though not designed for intimacy, Edem manages its large clientele with prompt service and good-quality food. Of five lamb dishes, the specialty is Vine Grower's Lamb, baked with cheese inside and white wine sauce. Try lobster cooked over charcoal and braised in *ladolemono*, a tangy lemon and oil sauce. For appetizers, choose from dolmades, baked potatoes filled with spiced meat and cheese, and Edem shrimp cooked in a garlic, olive oil, and tomato sauce. *Turn off Matogianni onto N. Kalogera St., tel. 0289/22855 or 0289/23355. Reservations advised. Dress: casual but neat. AE, MC, V. Moderate–Expensive.*

Nikos and Maria's King Pizza. Since 1975 this couple has been blending the tastes of Italy with the culinary traditions of Greece. Pizza Mykonos is perfect for a light lunch: Homemade dough is warmed in the oven and topped with crumbled feta cheese, tomatoes, fresh oregano, and olive oil. Pizza Siciliana features olives, tomatoes, anchovies, and green peppers. Nikos and Maria serve warmed, whole-grain rolls with their pasta dishes and place a generous chunk of white, creamy feta on top of their salads. (Beware of other Italian places that serve the lighter, inexpensive white bread and Greek salads strangely devoid of feta cheese.) Two blocks from the harbor on a quiet, private square, King Pizza offers a nice respite from the shopping crowds. The restaurant's white facade is lined with royal blue doors and window frames. You can sit on the front porch under a shady grape trellis at tables with peppermint-stripe tablecloths and carnations. The humble decor inside features a painting of Nikos's mother and a few model ships beside the whiskey bottles. *Ayia Anna Sq., tel. 0289/22840. No credit cards. Inexpensive.*

Dining and Lodging

Petinos. This group of three hotels on Plati Yialos beach is owned and managed by the same family. People on extended vacations and those with children especially like the convenience of this casual resort community, where all facilities are open to all guests. The beach, dotted with umbrellas and lounge chairs, is protected from the wind; there are water sports, an arcade of snackbars and restaurants, and a boat that goes to five other beaches. Plati Yialos is 4 kilometers (2½ miles) from Mykonos town and the airport, but the frequent buses stop in front of Petinos Hotel. At the seaside taverna, which comes to life two nights a week with Greek music and dancing, pink tablecloths and flower arrangements decorate the painted wooden tables. Choose your own fresh fish or meat, or have a lobster cooked to order. The moussaka, with fried eggplant and beef topped with cream sauce, is baked in individual casserole dishes. You must reserve on weekends. **Petinos Beach,** the star and most popular of the three hotels, is yards away from the beach and has a saltwater pool. **Petinos Hotel,** a short walk up the street, has less expensive, smaller rooms, with showers instead of bathtubs, and studios with kitchenettes upstairs. **Hotel Nissaki,** on a hillside above a smaller beach, is set off from the crowds and is a little more quiet. Request a room on a top floor with a balcony. All the hotels have the standard wooden beds with multicolored spreads, a desk, and chairs. *Plati Yialos Beach, 84600, tel. 0289/22913, 0289/ 23903, or 0289/23680. 100 rooms with bath. Facilities: restaurant, 2 bars, money exchange, laundry, TV rooms, saltwater pool. AE, MC, V. Petinos Beach, Very Expensive; Petinos Hotel and Hotel Nissaki, Expensive.*

Lodging

★ **Cavo Tagoo.** This hotel perched above Ayios Stefanos beach seems to emerge from its cliffside backdrop and reach out to the sea below. Recognized for its unique architecture in a national competition sponsored by the National Tourist Organization, this medley of cream cubical suites features roof terraces for watching the sunset and an attractive saltwater pool. The reception area, restaurant, and guest rooms all have marble floors, dark beamed ceilings, and matching wooden furniture. Double beds are available here, instead of the two singles provided in many island hotels. It's a 10-minute walk to the harbor. Be aware that there is another hotel nearby with the exact same name but lower standards. *Follow Polykandrioti St. n. from port, 84600, tel. 0289/23692, 0289/23693, or 0289/23694. 58 rooms with bath. Facilities: restaurant, bar, snack bar, TV room, pool. AE, MC, V. Very Expensive.*

★ **Golden Star.** After the day's island excursion, you can laze by a freshwater pool overlooking the sea and sip a cocktail from the bar or sink into one of the soft leather chairs in the TV room.

Designed by Mykonos's mayor, an architect, this new hotel modernizes traditional Cycladic architecture. The reception, bar, and breakfast areas are built on three levels that step down to the pool patio, and windows on the sea add to the sense of space. Each room has a balcony or veranda, a full-size bathtub, and two single beds. The windmill outside is actually a three-story apartment with a kitchenette that can be rented for twice the price of a double room (about 40,000 dr. in peak season). This family-run hotel is a friendly place where the owners take the time to answer questions. The hotel is on a hill above the town of Mykonos, five minutes' walk from a beach, one of the bus stations, and the shopping district. Reservations are advised in July and August. *Despotiko area, Xenias, 84600, tel. 0289/23883 or 0289/24921. 20 rooms with bath. Facilities: bar, TV room, breakfast area, freshwater pool. AE, MC, V. Expensive.*

Camping **Paradise Beach Camping** (tel. 0289/22852), near one of the best beaches, is popular among young backpackers. It has a restaurant, bar, store, and hot showers and offers bungalows for rent. **Mykonos Camping** (tel. 0289/24578) at Paraga Beach, a 10-minute walk from Platis Yialos, has a restaurant, bar-café, minimarket, and cooking and laundry facilities.

Naxos

Apollonas **Apollon.** In this small resort town, where the pickings are slim,
Dining this is the best, though haphazard in appearance, of the tavernas encircling the harbor. It is run by the Vigileos family, who leave the cooking to their grandmother. Between frying potatoes and garnishing the Greek salad, this sweet-faced lady can often be found sitting down to chat (or gesture) with customers or joining a table of local women stringing garlic in the corner. Her food is basic—fresh fish like red mullet perfectly grilled, bite-size rib lamb chops (*paidakia*) with oregano, *dolmades* (grape leaves stuffed with rice and laced with nutmeg), juicy chicken souvlaki, and *pastitsio* (layers of macaroni and ground meat baked with a light bechamel sauce). *Apollonas waterfront, tel. 0285/81324. No credit cards. Closed Oct.–Apr. Inexpensive.*

Lodging **Flora's.** The apartments and rooms at Flora's, the best bet in Apollonas, overlook the owner's fields and the tiny bay below. To get to the hotel, you must trek through the potato patch, fording irrigation rivulets, which can be a bit annoying, but the spacious apartments all have marble floors, comfortable beds, and the usual pine furniture. Most have a bedroom and a sitting area with a kitchenette, and are large enough for a family of four. Kitchen utensils and sheets are provided, but no maid service. *Apollonas above waterfront, 84300, tel. 0285/81270. 9 rooms. Facilities: washing machines. No credit cards. Closed Oct.–Mar. Moderate.*

Chora **Faros.** The opening of Faros has meant that tourists need never
Dining again suffer an unrelenting diet of moussaka and pastitsio. The
★ owner, who moved to Naxos from Berlin, serves so many interesting dishes, you may return repeatedly just to work your way through the menu. Most people sit out on the harborfront veranda, but the small rooms inside are covered with beer decals and barrel spigots. German dishes predominate, but there is something for every foodie. For appetizers, try the smoked

trout on toast, the homemade liver sausage, or the fried Camembert and cranberries topped with a sprig of deep-fried parsley. Entrées range from prawns wrapped in bacon to the traditional steak Jaeger (hunter style), with button mushrooms and roast potatoes. The steaks are quite large and are served with piquant sauces—roquefort, garlic, onion, and mustard; liver served with tangy onions and apples is another favorite. For dessert there are seven kinds of pancakes, like apple-cinammon-raisin and yogurt-cherry and there's a half-dark, half-white mousse that will elate chocolate lovers. *Chora waterfront, tel. 0285/23325. No credit cards. Closed Nov.–Mar. Expensive.*

Apolafsi. Along with Nikos around the corner (*see below*), this is the best Greek taverna in Naxos. The sparkling view of the bay from the second floor offsets the rather drab interior. Regardless of the surroundings, the food is excellent, relying heavily on local meats, for which Naxos is famous. Try the lemony goat (*katsiki fricasee*) or the rabbit *stifado*, plump morsels simmered in red sauce. Among the grilled meats are *kontosouvli* (lamb and pork on a short spit) and juicy beefsteaks. A specialty here is *tilixto*, a dish you don't see very often—phyllo dough wrapped around beef slices, feta, bacon, and a hard-boiled egg—filling enough to be an entrée. Apolafsi (which means "enjoyment" in Greek) also serves fresh fish daily and a few Continental dishes like chicken Marengo with mushrooms. *Chora waterfront, tel. 0285/22178. No credit cards. Closed Nov.–Mar. Moderate.*

I Apothiki tou Ballidras/Kraemerladen. Though the service may be slow, this taverna is worth the wait, for the traditional and local specialties you don't usually find. After the fried zucchini appetizer, for instance, sample the *boxa*: lamb, mountain greens, and a lemon sauce cooked slowly in a ceramic pot; the Macedonian eggplant stuffed with tomatoes, onions, and feta, then baked and sliced thinly so it won't overwhelm; or the *kouneli krasato*, hare in red wine. I Apothiki also serves several of the well-known local cheeses like the salty *kefalograviera* and a creamy, almost sweet, *mizithra*—perfect after your meal. Most dishes come with the island's delicious potatoes, lightly covered with olive oil and dill. Fresh fish is also available, as are some non-Greek dishes like garlic steak and curried chicken. *Chora waterfront, tel. 0285/23675. MC, V. Closed Nov.–Apr. Moderate.*

Nikos. Don't be fazed by the 30-pound fish hanging in the glass case, along with eels, sharks, and any other kind of seafood you can imagine. You haven't even begun to examine the possibilities at Naxos's finest Greek restaurant; as you step inside, you're met with an array of 20–25 mayirefta dishes. From the ocean view to the fresh carnations on the tables and the prompt service, Nikos has done everything to earn its enthusiastic clientele. Start your meal with *kakavia*, a delicate fish soup made from small catch, and a plate of grilled octopus. For an entrée, you might try the *bitock*—beefsteak with an egg on top—*moschari stamnas* (beef and carrots cooked in a clay pot), or hearty octopus macaroni cut into bite-size chunks. The steaks are quite good, and there's a "ramsteak" studded with garlic. Black-eyed peas (*fassolia mavromati*) cooked in fragrant olive oil, and fava dip are good side dishes. The wine list is long and varied, with Cycladic wines as well as Italian selections. Finish off your meal with a piece of apple pie, Greek style. *Chora wa-*

terfront above Commercial Bank, tel. 0285/23153, 0285/23381, or 0285/24529. V. Moderate.

Meltemi. At the far end of the harbor sits a typical Greek restaurant with fluorescent lighting and plastic-wrap tablecloths. What Meltemi lacks in looks, however, it makes up for in food; it's known locally as the place to go for inexpensive Greek staples. Some of these include souvlaki—chicken, swordfish, or pork—lamb *exohiko* (meat cooked in paper with vegetables), and pans and pans of such mayirefta as stuffed peppers, *gigantes* (giant white beans in olive oil), and *tsoutsoukakia* (meat patties made from spicy sausage). A more unusual dish is *kalogiero*—eggplant with ham and bechamel. You can also order barbecued fillets of the daily catch (swordfish is almost always available), local cheeses, and a lovely *creme caramele*, made with fresh eggs and milk from the owner's village. The gentlemanly, ever-so-jaded waiters are fast and efficient, even when the place is packed. *Chora waterfront, tel. 0285/22654. No credit cards. Closed Nov.–Mar. Inexpensive.*

Lodging
★ **Chateau Zevgoli.** This fairy-tale pension is in a Venetian house in the heart of the old town. Its charm is owing not only to its lovely surroundings but also to its co-owner Despina Kitis, a cosmopolitan islander who creates an ambience of comfort and tradition within exacting standards. The living room is filled with dark antique furniture, gilded mirrors, old family photographs, and locally woven curtains and tablecloths. Each room is different—in one of the nicest, which has a private bougainvillea-covered courtyard, the pillows were handmade by Kitis's great-grandmother. Another room to ask for is the honeymoon suite, with a canopy bed, a spacious balcony, and a view of the Portara. All guest rooms have showers and central heating. Rooms can sometimes be had off-season for half price, making this without a doubt the most appealing place to stay in Chora. *Chora old town (follow signs stenciled on walls), 84300, tel. 0285/24525 or 0285/24358; in Athens, tel. 01/651–5885. 10 rooms. Facilities: breakfast room. No credit cards. Closed Nov.–Mar. Expensive.*

Chora Beach Area
Dining
O Kontos. If you're staying at Orkos Village or visiting the Plaka–Mikri Vigla beach stretch, south of Chora, stop here for a bite. The enclosed veranda overlooks the windswept bay, and proprietor Maria Salteri-Antoniou runs the spacious kitchen as though she were at home. The main dish might be an irresistible plate of *fassolia* (green beans cooked in oil), *kokkinisto* (beef in red sauce), or grilled fish basted in lemon and oil: red mullet, boce (*gopa*), and pandora (*lithrinia*). The retsina barrel wine is so good, it usually runs out by summer, but ask anyway. Beach goers may also fortify themselves for a long day in the sun with breakfast. *Central rd. between Orkos and Mikri Vigla beaches, tel. 0285/75278. No credit cards. Closed Oct.–May. Moderate.*

Panorama. This new seaside taverna is ideal for those frequenting the popular Ayia Anna beach, just south of town. The taverna is easygoing, with a crowd that ranges from German dreadlocked couples toting their babies in backpacks, to local patriarchs twirling their worry beads. It has a large shaded terrace brightened with blue-and-white checked tablecloths. You can get a hefty lamb chop sprinkled with oregano, crisp roast chicken, or fresh fish barbecued over charcoal, all well cooked and low priced. The messy but delicious crab, served in a mustard-lemon-olive oil sauce, is an especially good deal, and another fine appetizer is the garlicky *tzatziki*, made with the local strained yogurt. Panorama also has Greek standbys like meatballs and eggplant, as well as breakfast: omelets, yogurt with honey, toast, and coffee. *Beach rd. into Ayia Anna from Chora, no tel. No credit cards. Closed Nov.–Mar. Inexpensive.*

Lodging **Galaxy.** As you approach this hotel, it seems to shimmer in the distance, all whitewash and marble. Its three buildings rather resemble grand pueblos, except that they have wide stone arches; wooden doors in shades of green, purple, and turquoise; and balconies with grillwork depicting swans. Archways also span the large rooms, which have beamed ceilings and trim orange accessories, plants, kitchenettes, and dining areas. Most rooms have ocean views (the beach is about 110 yards away); all have balconies. Though they lack any shade, the carefully tended grounds are a pleasure, with yellow roses, a fountain, and a midsize pool. *Ayios Georgios Beach, 84300, tel. 0285/ 23581 or 0285/23582, fax 0285/22889. 60 rooms. Facilities: snack bar, pool, playground. V. Closed Nov.–Apr. Expensive.*

Orkos Village. When Norwegian doctor Kaare Oftedal first saw Orkos beach years ago, he fell in love with the almost isolated strand ringed by sand dunes and cedars. Today he returns from Norway every spring to open his small, popular hotel, whose guests seem perfectly content never to leave their idyllic surroundings to go to town. The hotel's white cubist bungalows that stagger down the hillside to the sea's edge are simply furnished and decorated (dried flowers and blue wooden shutters just about cover it). They all have kitchenettes, sea views, and verandas; a few have an additional sitting area. Guests love to hang around the friendly stone bar, where the doctor's wife Katerina leads Greek dances and serves up classic Greek meals, and to ramble downhill to the unspoiled beach. The hotel shuttle goes into town every other day. *Orkos beach between Plaka and Mikri Vigla, 84300, tel. 0285/75321, fax 0285/75320 (Nov.–Mar. tel. in Norway, 033/90919, fax 033/91596. 26 rooms with bath. Facilities: restaurant, bar, minimarket. No credit cards. Closed Nov.–Apr. Expensive.*

Glaros. Walk into this friendly pension and you may find people sitting around listening to the owner's son playing guitar and a guest in the kitchen making himself a coffee with just the right amount of sugar. The lobby reinforces this air of informality, with its rattan furniture, travel posters, and unruly banana plants. The pension is a nice balance between the larger, more impersonal package hotels and the rundown smaller places, in this popular beach area of Chora. Owner George Franjescos makes improvements every year, like furnishing a small single with a canopy bed draped in blue and yellow flowers. The rooms are simple and extremely clean; all those in front have balconies and a sea view, and the beach is just 30 feet away. *Ayios Georgios beach, 84300, tel. 0285/23131 or 0285/23533. 13 rooms. Facilities: bar. AE. Closed Nov.–Feb. Moderate.*

★ **Iria Beach.** The newest of the Ayia Anna establishments, this hotel echoes Chora's old town, with its stucco arches, peaceful nooks and crannies, sunlit courtyard, and bright red and blue shutters. The reception area smacks of luxury with its huge glass doors, cool marble floor, and brass details. More than half the hotel's apartments have an ocean view, and the owners, who also run Zas Travel in Chora, have eschewed the usual Greek hotel furniture for unlacquered wood with a gray wash and an interior color scheme of light blue, gray, and white. The spacious one- and two-room apartments all have kitchenettes, but guests will also enjoy hanging out in the shady bar/restaurant on the beach. *Ayia Anna, 84300, tel. 0285/24178, 0285/ 24488, 0285/24489, or 0285/23988; fax 0285/23419. 21 rooms. Facilities: restaurant, bar. MC. Closed Nov.–Apr. Moderate.*

Nissaki. Just across the street from Glaros, Nissaki is slightly more expensive but much grander in feel. Everything is built on a larger scale—from the low-ceiling dining room to the grapevine-shaded courtyards, with their massive teal ceramic vases. Though the hotel is often booked by agencies, it seldom feels crowded, and the staff takes even the busiest days in stride, making time to cater to guests' requests. The quiet rooms are done in cool blues and whites with dark furniture; all have telephones and access to a balcony, and most have showers rather than tubs. The beach is just steps away. *Ayios Georgios beach, 84300, tel. 0285/22876 or 0285/23102, fax 0285/23876. 40 rooms. Facilities: restaurant, bar. AE, DC, MC, V. Closed Nov.–late Mar. Moderate.*

Camping **Camping Apollon** (tel. 0285/24117), between Ayios Georgios and Ayios Prokopios, sits near windsurfers' hangouts about 3 kilometers (2 miles) outside Chora. It has a friendly staff and a good cafeteria, and many of the sites have excellent views of the Kastro. The camp arranges transfers from town in their buses. If a better beach means more to you than proximity to town, try **Maragas** (tel. 0285/24552), in Ayia Anna, which has room for about 100 people. Both camps are closed November–April.

Paros

Dining **Lalula.** The delicious Mediterranean cooking and fine service
★ induce some people to dine in this restaurant every evening of their vacation. Lalula is owned and managed by two German women, Sigi Koyhler and Ruth Wagner, who oversee every step, from the selection of fresh produce to the seating of guests. You can dine in the small garden in back of this homey restaurant, but if it fills before you arrive don't fret. The interior has calm aqua walls, subdued lighting and colorful modern artwork, and Koyhler and Wagner suit the mood of the moment with the music, playing old Greek tangos, for example, at festive times and baroque music at sunset. The menu changes frequently, but two tasty first courses stand out: the orange-carrot soup, and smoked trout mousse with horseradish cream and lemon. Featured entrées are butterfly shrimp fried in sesame sauce and roast leg of lamb stuffed with soft goat cheese, herbs, and French mustard. Vegetarians like the *tain de courgettes*, and the baked vegetables with bread crumbs and cheese, and everybody will like the dessert of seasonal fruit crumble with whipped cream. *Naoussa, opposite Minoa Hotel (from village, take left at post office), tel. 0284/51547. Reservations required. Dress: casual but neat. No credit cards. Expensive.*

May-Tey. Established 13 years ago, this was the first Oriental restaurant in the Cyclades. The menu changes every day, and there are four traditional Thai, Indian, and Chinese entrées to choose from. For starters try the Thai salad with shrimp and peanut sauce or the chicken and sweet corn soup. Specialties include king prawns with sweet and sour sauce, crispy duck with red honey sauce, and stir-fried beef and peppers topped with crisp noodles. The contrast of the China red tablecloths against Cycladic white walls is softened by indirect lighting, and the five small dining areas give the place a sense of intimacy. Kimonos with pelican and flower designs hang on the walls from bamboo rods. *Parikia, take Market St. from main sq.; on right at bend in rd.; tel. 0284/22693. AE, MC, V. Closed Wed. Expensive.*

Taverna Christos. Most tavernas toss a basket on the table containing the silverware, bread, and napkins. Christos distinguishes itself with crisp white tablecloths neatly set, a bright, fresh atmosphere, and good service. For a first course try the octopus salad, avocado vinaigrette, or mushrooms with cream sauce. One special entrée is poached fillet of perch smothered with herb cream; another is grilled pork with a sauce of seasonal vegetables. The menu is distinctly Greek, but there are pasta dishes and wiener schnitzels, too. *Naoussa, bear right at pastry shop on central sq., walk up hill; restaurant on left; no tel. No credit cards. Moderate.*

The Balcony. Perched above the hustle and bustle of the crowds, this creperie, fitted cozily into the second floor of a sophisticated old house, shows French influence not only in the food but also in the atmosphere. Walk up the stairs and through the front door, with its dash of red and green stained glass, and sit at one of the marble-topped tables. The floors are dark-stained wood, and the decorations include a gold-frame mirror and an antique radio and guitar. Have a champagne breakfast with a savory ham-and-pineapple crepe, and instead of orange juice try a health drink of carrot milk and honey. The favorite sweet crepes are the apple, walnut, and raisin one and one with chocolate cream, nuts, and Cointreau. An entrée for a candlelight dinner might be pork with a mustard cream sauce served with herbed potatoes and ratatouille. *Market St. off main sq., Parikia, tel. 0284/22074. Inexpensive.*

Lodging **Yria.** This beachside hotel built in 1992, the only one on Paros with an A rating, is about five minutes by car from Paroikia. A little oasis of luxury, it has two tennis courts, a freshwater pool, and a sandy beach; its rooms have plush carpeting, TVs, and balconies or verandas. The "double deluxe" bungalows have two levels. The staff has been trained in hotel management, which has produced a pleasing professionalism. *S. of Paroikia on Paros Pouros beach, 21009, tel. 0284/24154 through 0284/24158, fax 0284/21167. 70 rooms with bath. Facilities: restaurant, bar, barbecue area, freshwater pool, 2 tennis courts. AE, DC, MC, V. Expensive–Very Expensive.*

★ **Hotel Contaratos.** The hotel is east of Naoussa, steps away from one of the best sandy beaches, so the sound of gentle waves will lull you to sleep at night. Each room has a view of the sea from a balcony or a veranda. The modern, Cycladic white suites are built in a horseshoe, around a patio and pool, where you can have a drink from the outdoor bar. With the beach, a tennis court, and a taverna within the hotel, everything you need is in reach. *Ayia Anargirie beach, 21009, tel. 0284/51693, fax 0284/51740. 33 rooms with bath. Facilities: taverna, bar, saltwater pool, tennis court, TV in rooms. V. Expensive.*

Kalypso Hotel. The hotel's three floors surround a lovely garden courtyard dripping with bright purple morning glories, and the spacious lobby has white Cycladic archways and an ornately carved wooden mezzanine balcony. Open the shutters in the airy, immaculate rooms or walk out onto the private balconies and you will have a spectacular view of the sea. Guests sit outside reading and talking at tables beneath the shade of some olive trees, or sun themselves on the nearby sand beach. *Ayia Anargirie beach, Naoussa, 21009, tel. 0284/51488 or 0284/ 51259, fax 0284/51607. 41 rooms with bath. Facilities: bar, breakfast area, kitchenettes in 5 rooms. V. Moderate.*

Xenia Hotel. If you expect a good night's sleep, avoid the hotels in downtown Paroikia, where young partygoers can be heard almost all night long. Xenia is built on a hill overlooking the sea, far away from the noisy nightlife. Outside there's a renovated windmill and a little park surrounding the chapel of Ayia Anna. The hotel lobby looks like an enormous living room, with low, cushioned seats around circular wooden tables, a stone fireplace decorated with antique keychains, and a cozy bar. The veranda off the lobby is perfect for sunset watching. The rooms are sparsely decorated; 12 have balconies and shower stalls in the bathrooms; the other 12 have bathtubs but no balconies. *E. of Paroikia, up hill at Ayia Anna church, 21009, tel. 0284/ 21394 or 0284/21643, fax 0284/23501. 24 rooms with bath. Facilities: bar, breakfast area. AE, MC, V. Moderate.*

Camping
Three campgrounds near beaches are **Camping Koula** (tel. 0284/22082), about 1 kilometer (½ mile) northwest of Paroikia's harbor; **Parasporos** (just south of Paroikia, tel. 0284/21944), which is newer and larger; and **Santo Maria Campgrounds** (within walking distance of Naoussa, tel. 0284/51013 or 0284/ 51181), with a minimarket, public phone, and taverna.

Santorini

Dining
Alexandria. No international kitchen here. The menu of Greek dishes lists many special recipes of the islands. As an appetizer try the mushrooms stuffed with crabmeat, the eggplant with vinegar, or a salad of beets, eggs, capers, and anchovies. Stuffed lamb cutlets, with cumin, mushrooms, and wine, is a specialty. Alexandria is right on the rim of the old volcano in a remodeled aristocratic house with high ceilings and a great veranda. The young Athenian owners' sense of humor runs to such art as a giant donkey sculpture with a misplaced part and framed children's paintings. *S. end of Hypapantis Walkway, Fira, tel. 0286/23673. AE, MC, V. Expensive.*

★ **1800.** The goal here is to revive the special homelike atmosphere of a captain's house. Indeed this historic Venetian-style building, with tall windows and a cathedral *volda cruchera* ceiling, was owned by a sea captain. It was abandoned after the 1956 earthquake until its purchase (with antique furniture intact) and restoration a few years ago. Try the zucchini pie with onions, eggs, and cheese, or the veal cooked in tomato sauce and served with smashed eggplant. There's occasional live music, with flute and oboe duets. *Main St., central Oia, tel. 0286/ 71485. AE, MC, V. Expensive.*

Kastro. There's very little here that's authentically Greek, but the expansive outdoor dining area is usually packed throughout the evening, which lends the place a festive atmosphere. Kastro's rather European menu caters to those who have not acquired a taste for olive oil and garlic. Hors d'oeuvres include Danish or Russian caviar and prosciutto with melon; the wine list offers Dom Perignon. You can have your filet mignon done in seven ways, including the special: topped with sautéed onions, green peppers, madeira cheese, and bacon. The light, scrumptious soufflés come with a choice of five stuffings.

Grilled shrimp, lobster, and swordfish are sold by the kilo. Upstairs there's a cafeteria that serves American breakfasts and fast food. *Ayios Ioannis Walkway, Fira, tel. 0286/22503. AE, MC, V. Expensive.*

Kyklos. This restaurant invites you to explore its intersecting caverns, with arched ceilings, black slate floors, and no windows. Ursula Deneke, the German chef, searches the countryside for wildflowers for her arrangements and mushrooms and herbs for her dishes. Notice also the fresh local capers in the Greek salads. Try the appetizer plate of varied dips made from local yellow lentils, eggplant, and garlic with yogurt. The *graviera* cheese dipped in beer, floured, and fried crisp is worth the calories, and the Santorini lamb with rosemary is delicious. *Follow signs in Oia, tel. 0286/71145. V. Expensive.*

Archipelago. The food is delicious; the inside atmosphere dreary, but if you arrive early, there may be room on the small balcony overlooking the caldera. If you sit inside, go straight for the menu and ignore the tacky movie posters. For a change from Greek salads, try "The Archipelago" of shredded chicken, ham, corn, cheese, and a special dressing. The "something like ratatouille" listed on the menu is really a traditional Greek dish called *briam* made with seasonal vegetables, spices, and olive oil. Another good entree is the *yiartou* (meatballs and yogurt served in a warmed pita). *Entrance on Hypapantis Walkway, Fira, take staircase down, tel. 0286/23673, AE, MC, V. Moderate.*

Lodging **Atlantis Hotel.** One of the oldest, most distinguished and most expensive hotels in Santorini, the Atlantis is perched on Fira's volcanic rim, and all the rooms have balconies. The floors and staircases are white marble. The decor throughout is coordinated, with curtains and walls both depicting lush bamboo shoots and cheerful flowers. Unfortunately, beer is delivered for Fira's bars outside the hotel in the wee hours of the morning. *S. end of Hypapantis Walkway, Fira, 84700, tel. 0286/22232 or 0286/22111. 22 rooms with bath. Facilities: lounge, bar. AE, MC, V. Very Expensive.*

Hotel Aressana. The only drawback to Fira's newest hotel, which opened in 1992, is that being behind another major hotel it has no view of the volcano. Its advantages are its freshwater pool (with classical music piped in) and its location, a short walk from Fira's business district. If you want a spanking new room with white tile floors, a balcony, and a spotless bathroom, this is your best bet. *S. end of Hypapantis Walkway, Fira, 84700, tel. 0286/23900 or 0286/23901. 50 rooms with bath. Facilities: bar, TV room, swimming pool. AE, MC, V. Very Expensive.*

Delphini I and **II.** Owner-manager Vassilis Rousseas says he has "prices for everyone." The more expensive Delphini II has spacious apartments, all different in architecture and decor, that once were village homes. (Ask to see the one with the old stove.) The less-expensive Delphini I lacks a view. *Delphini I: Near hospital in central Fira, 84700, tel. 0286/22371. 10 rooms with bath and refrigerator. No credit cards. Moderate–Expensive. Delphini II: Down hill in front of Atlantis Hotel, Fira, tel. 0286/22780. 7 studios and apartments with bath, all with refrigerator or kitchenette. No credit cards. Expensive.*

Oia's Sunset. This modern hotel looks like a castle made from miniature Cycladic chapels. The rooms, decorated in traditional style, all have balconies. *Central Oia, near main sq., Fira, 84700, tel. 0268/71420 or 0268/71490. 8 rooms and 7 2-bedroom*

American Express offers Travelers Cheques built for two.

American Express® Travelers Cheques *for Two*. The first Travelers Cheques that allow either of you to use them because both of you have signed them. And only one of you needs to be present to purchase them.

Cheques *for Two* are accepted anywhere regular American Express Travelers Cheques are, which is just about everywhere. So stop by before your next trip and ask for Cheques *for Two*.

 **Travelers Cheques**

2½ Hours
VHS-C

2½ Hours
8mm

SONY

PACK WISELY.

Given a choice, the seasoned traveler always carries less.
Case in point: Sony Handycam® camcorders, America's most
popular. They record up to 2½ hours on a single tape.
VHS-C tapes record only 30 minutes.* And why carry five tapes
when you can record everything on one? Which brings us
to the first rule of traveling: pack a Sony Handycam camcorder.

Over 1500 Great Weekend Escapes...

in Six Fabulous Fodor's Guides to
Bed & Breakfasts, Country Inns, Cottages,
and Other Weekend Pleasures!

The
Mid-Atlantic
Region

The
South

New
England

The
West Coast

England
and
Wales

Canada

Fodors
Where the best memories begin

apartments with bath. Facilities: freshwater pool. AE, MC, V. Expensive.

Panorama Hotel. From the cliffside of Fira, this hotel provides a breathtaking view of the caldera. The rooms have seaside verandas, telephones, mini-bars, FM radios, and fresh white linens. A local travel desk in the reception area can book tours, rent cars and exchange money. *Hypapantis Walkway, Fira, 84700, tel. 0286/22481, 0286/22479, or 0286/22271. 23 rooms with bath. Facilities: café, travel desk. AE, MC, V. Expensive.*

Sellada Beach. Right on the black-sand beach of Perissa, this small hotel is perfect for sunbathers. The new, three-story building, done in modernized Cycladic style, is surrounded by a green lawn, a rarity on this dry island. There's a homey, friendly feeling here, and all the rooms have verandas, TV, and air-conditioning. *On the beach in Perissa, 84700, tel. 0268/81492. 7 studios, 7 apartments. V. Expensive.*

Traditional Settlements. Eight neoclassical ship-owners' houses have been converted into guest houses by the GNTO. The bedrooms are charming, with arched ceilings, and are decorated in traditional Cycladic style, with handwoven rugs, painted woodwork, and plates with nautical designs on the walls. *On the cliffside, Oia, 84700, tel. 0286/71234. 31 rooms with bath. Expensive.*

Hotel Astro. This hotel, in the resort town of Kamari, is a short walk to the black sandy beach and minutes away from the local nightlife. Rooms have phones, and those on the lower level have verandas; those on the second floor have balconies facing the mountains or the Aegean. After spending the day at the sea, it's great to take a dip in the pool in the evening. *Central Kamari, 84700, tel. 0286/31366. 36 rooms with bath. Facilities: coffee shop, TV lounge, freshwater pool. No credit cards. Moderate.*

★ **Hotel Kavalari.** This architectural wonder is built in layers down the side of the volcano's rim. The rooms are cozy, and their colorful Santorini rugs and bedcovers are brilliant against the whitewashed walls. All have telephones and refrigerators. There are numerous accessible patios with deck chairs and tables where you can sit in the sea air and watch the fiery sunsets. *Look for sign on Hypapantis Walkway, Fira, 84700, tel. 0286/22455 or 0286/22347. 18 rooms with bath (5 with kitchenettes). AE, MC, V. Moderate.*

Camping **Camping Perissa Beach** (tel. 0286/81343), right next to the beach, is the most popular site, with a restaurant, minimarket, hot water, and a lively disco. **Kamari Camping** (tel. 0286/31451 or 0286/31453), right off the main road to Kamari, 875 yards from the beach, has a restaurant, cafeteria, minimarket, laundry, and hot water.

Siros

Dining **Halatis.** The dining room here is pleasant, but its historical appeal was lost in the renovation of the neoclassical house. High ceilings, navy blue floral wallpaper, and large windows provide a nice lunchtime ambience. Evenings on the roof are more festive; local musicians play Greek and Latin music (June–Oct.), and people like the view of the harbor. The varied menu lists Italian dishes, German schnitzels, and an array of Greek foods. For an appetizer, try spinach crepes or dip fresh bread into some *tzatziki*, a blend of yogurt, cucumber, and garlic. Ringlets of calamari delicately fried in olive oil or octopus cooked in white wine are good seafood choices, and the chef recommends the veal with mushrooms. *Kanari Sq., next to Hermes hotel, Ermoupolis, tel. 0281/25786. Reservations required on weekends. Jacket advised. MC, V. Moderate–Expensive.*

★ **Lilis.** Built on the side of a hill in the Catholic quarter of Ano Siros, this spacious restaurant has picture windows and a veranda that overlook the Ermoupolis harbor. Locals go for the view and the outstanding *keftedes* (meatballs), which are flavored with onion, fresh parsley, and mint, lightly fried, and served with tasty fried potatoes. Other specials are the *moschari riganato*, veal with oregano, and such fresh fish as red mullet, red snapper, or blacktail. This is a well-known gathering place, with live folk music on Saturday nights in fall and winter, when the windows are closed and the sound doesn't carry. Note the two portraits of Markos Vamvakaris, known throughout Greece as the father of rembetika. *On pathway below St. George's church, Ermoupolis (taxi drivers can drop you off and direct you), tel. 0281/28087. No credit cards. Moderate.*

Taverna Mykonos. After cooking for five years at the Petinos Taverna on Mykonos, Evangelos Paterakes moved to Siros. He started his own operation and with his son painted a lifesize pelican and a windmill, symbols of home, on the back wall of the taverna. He brought a flair for seasoning fish and likes to take customers into the kitchen to see the day's selection. Larger fish may be poached, with vegetables, lemon, and dried rosemary or dill weed. Small smelt, fried crisp in oil, or fried cod with garlic sauce are favorites with the locals. You can sit outside and watch the boats come in, or inside, where a large orange buoy from a Russian ship is proudly displayed. For six months Evangelos fed the crew, and every member signed the buoy as a token of gratitude. The crew's favorite dish? Fried pork chops with a unique concoction of wine, cognac, Tabasco, and mustard. *Akti Papagou 36 (near ferry dock), Ermoupolis, tel. 0281/25752. No credit cards. Moderate.*

Lodging **Dolphin Bay Hotel.** This hotel on the sandy beach of Galissas is a resort unto itself. You can go to the relaxing piano bar or the lively disco for entertainment, and the rooms are equipped with conveniences rarely found in Greece: satellite TV, minibars, and hair dryers. The more expensive suites are decorated with pastel carpeting, and when you sit back on the cushioned couches and close your eyes, it won't matter that the flowers are plastic and the pictures look as if they were bought in an Athenian grocery store. The balconies overlooking the sea are furnished with chairs and a table. *On beach in Galissas, 84100, tel. 0281/42924, fax 0281/42843. 141 rooms with bath. Facilities: restaurant, snack bar, disco, piano bar, conference room, seawater swimming pool, children's pool, tennis court, minigolf, in-room movies. No credit cards. Expensive.*

Adriadni. This new hotel in a remodeled three-story classical Ermoupolis house is bright and cozy. The suites on top are the most appealing, with spectacular views and convenient kitchenettes. A first-floor room with a spiral staircase leading up to a loft and a second double bed, is perfect for a family. Guest rooms have standard furniture, with light blue tile floors and roomy bathrooms. *As you leave ferry, turn inland (left) on Filini St.; Adriadni is 2 blocks up on left; 84100, tel. 0281/*

25851 or 0281/27039. 10 rooms with bath. No credit cards. Moderate.

The Europe Hotel. Although officially rated C, this old hotel has a special historic appeal. It was built in 1823, as Ermoupolis was just beginning to boom, and in 1837 it was turned into a hospital. On the patio a spectacular black-and-white stone mosaic laid in 1861 has geometric and floral designs and two lions in the center, holding a double-headed eagle. There are no balconies on the exterior, but guests can relax in the spacious open verandas overlooking the patio's greenery, red hibiscus flowers, and aromatic white jasmine. Today the hotel is owned by the town and managed by Teamwork travel agency. The modest rooms have maroon carpets, sparse furniture, and showers. *Proious St., Ermoupolis, 84100, tel. 0281/28771. 28 rooms with bath. Facilities: bar, breakfast room. MC, V. Moderate.*

Camping **Yianna Campground** (330 feet from Galissas Beach, tel. 0281/42418 or 0281/42447) has 30 campsites, a disco, snack bar, and minimarket. The **Two Hearts Campground** (tel. 0281/42052) is also near Galissas Beach.

The Arts and Nightlife

Andros

Ano Approvato, a village south of Batsi, holds a **paneyiri** (festival) on August 15, the feast of the **Assumption of the Virgin Mary,** with feasting and dancing along with the religious rites. On nearby Tinos (another of the Cyclades) thousands of the faithful come from all over the country on the feast of the Assumption of the Virgin to see the icon of the Panayia Evangelistria, which is said to work miracles.

On the perimeter road of Batsi you'll find the popular **Blue Sky disco** and the open-air **Sunrise** nightclub; more remote but livelier is the **Marabout,** on the main road halfway between Batsi and Gavrion. The **Panorama** in Palaiopolis features live bouzouki shows.

Mykonos

The **Anemo Theatre** (Steno Roharis, tel. 0289/23944) is a non-profit open-air center for the performing arts set in a unique olive garden in the center of town, where distinguished international artists present an eclectic array of concerts, performances, and seminars. A second Anemo Theater box office is on the harborfront (for information and reservations, call daily 11–1 or from 7:30 PM at theater).

Little Venice is a good place to begin an evening, and the **Caprice Bar,** with whitewashed low ceilings, blown-glass chandeliers, a piano, and an elegant atmosphere, is full of the romance of the neighborhood. The same is true of **Kastro** (tel. 0289/23070), near the Paraportiani Church, and the distinguished **Montparnasse** (tel. 0289/23719), which has Toulouse-Lautrec posters. At **Thalami,** a small underground bar near Paraportiani Church, there's Greek dancing in a cozy nightclub atmosphere. As the night goes on you feel the heightened energy level, which continues to build as dawn approaches. **Mykonos Club** (tel. 0289/23291), opposite the Caprice Bar in Little Venice, is a larger, more expensive bouzouki center that's popular among locals and tourists. **Rainbow Disco,** also in Little Venice (43 Mitropoleos St., no tel.), draws a young Euro-pop crowd, and at the famous **Pierro's** (Matoyianni St., no tel.) you can find late-night wild dancing to American and European rock.

Naxos

Chora celebrates the **Dionysia** festival during the first week of August, with concerts, folk dancing in costumes, and free food and wine in the square. At other times, feast days are marked with local bashes (*paneyiri*). For example, during Carnival, "bell wearers" take to the streets in **Apeiranthos** and **Filoti,** running from house to house, making as much noise as possible with strings of bells tied around their waists. They're a disconcerting sight in their hooded cloaks, with scarves concealing their faces, as they ritually escort a man dressed as a woman around the houses collecting eggs. In Apeiranthos also, you can hear villagers square off in **rhyming-verse contests:** On the last Sunday of Greek Orthodox Lent, the *paliomoskari*, their faces blackened, challenge each other in improvising satirical couplets called *kotsakia*. At the **May Day Festival** in Koronis, wildflower garlands are made, and there's lively dancing. On July 14, **Ayios Nikodemos Day** is celebrated in Chora with a procession of the patron saint's icon through town, but the Assumption of the Virgin on August 15 is, after Easter and Christmas, the festival most widely celebrated, especially in Sangri, Filoti, and Apeiranthos.

Nightlife in Naxos is quieter than on Santorini or Mykonos, but there are several popular bars in Chora. **Veggera** (Chora waterfront near Ayios Georgios Beach, tel. 0285/23567) has a garden that's a respite from the rap and rock music inside. Next door, in a small white house, is **Ecstasis** (no tel.), which has a spacious bar, happy hours, strong drinks, all kinds of music from surf to blues, and a terrace overlooking the sea.

Paros

The group **N.E.L.E.** (tel. 0284/51082 or 0284/51480) formed in 1988 to preserve the traditional dances and music of Paros, performs all summer long in Naoussa in the traditional costumes of the 16th century and has participated in dance competitions and festivals throughout Europe. Keep an eye open for posters, or ask travel agents about times and locations of performances.

The **Aegean School of Fine Arts,** at the end of Market Street in Paroikia, sometimes stages exhibitions of students' work. It was founded by Brett Taylor, an American artist, and offers summer courses in writing, painting, and photography, among other disciplines.

Turn right from the port in Paroikia and take your choice of the many bars lining the walkway. The **Piano Bar** has a relaxing view and classical music; **Saloon D'Or** is for the 30-something crowd. At the far end of the Paralia is the laser-light-and-disco section of town, with a **Hard Rock Cafe** among the selection of buzzing bars. In Naoussa the liveliest bars are the **Paracato Disco** and the **Banana Moon,** both on the main street, up the hill from the town square.

Santorini

The **International Santorini Music Festival** (tel. 0286/22220) takes place in late August–early September in Estis Hall in Fira. The roster of well-known classical artists who will perform in solo recitals and small ensembles is announced during the summer and posted in tourist shops. You can see the best traditional Greek music and dancing at **Canava Roussos Winery** (the oldest on the island, founded in 1838), where professional and local dancers in costume perform nightly 8–midnight. Call 0286/31276 for reservations.

As the sun sets on the caldera, **Palia Kameni** (tel. 0286/22430) is the relaxing place to go for well-selected jazz, classical, and passionate Greek music. Try a strawberry margarita or one of the other reasonably priced drinks. **Franco's Bar** in Fira (tel. 0286/31462) provides calm, classical music; **Bar 33** (tel. 0286/23065) has bouzouki music and a celebratory atmosphere; and the **Koo Club** (tel. 0286/22025) is Fira's most popular outdoor disco by far. In Kamari the younger set heads for the **Yellow Donkey** disco (tel. 0286/31462) and the other bars along the beach promenade. In Oia, sophistication and architectural interest are the selling points of the **1800** bar and restaurant (*see* Dining and Lodging, *above*), and those in search of a happy hour beer go to **Zorba's,** on the Oia cliffside.

Siros

The **Apollon Theater,** a 19th-century miniature of Milan's La Scala opera house, is being renovated with EC funding, and the work is scheduled for completion by 1993. Call the GNTO (tel. 0281/22375 or 0281/26725) for information.

Both Ermoupolis and Ano Siros celebrate Carnival with masquerade parades and feasts in local tavernas during the three weeks before Lent. Every other year (in either the last week of July or the first week of August) the municipality of Ano Siros organizes the **Apanosyria Festival,** with exhibitions of crafts and antiques, dancing, lectures, and folkloric performances. To honor Greek seamen, every two years the first week of July is celebrated as **Naval Week,** with fireworks, sailing, and rowing regattas, and swimming games organized by the Naval Club of Siros.

Ermoupolis nightlife is centered at Miaoulis Square, where people of all ages gather for coffee and conversation. **Café No. 9** (tel. 0281/22018) has a broad selection of live music, from jazz to classical to traditional Greek. For funky music and a swinging singles crowd, try the **Dolphin Bay Hotel's** disco (tel. 0281/42924) in Galissas.

8 Crete

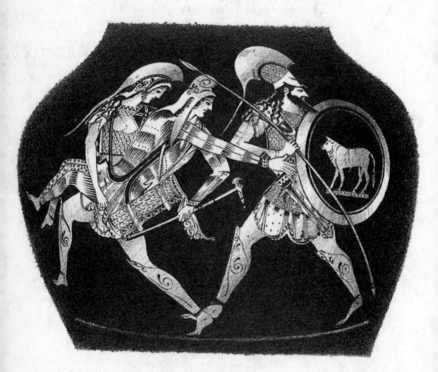

By Kerin Hope

Kerin Hope, an archaeologist, works in Athens as correspondent for the Financial Times *in Greece.*

The mountains, blue-gray and barren, split with deep gorges and honeycombed with caves, define both landscape and life-style in Crete. In the south and west they rise in sheer walls from the sea; along the north coast they loom as a backdrop, snowcapped for much of the year, to long stretches of sandy beach, vineyards, and olive groves. No other Greek island is so large or so rugged. To Greeks, Crete is known as the Megalonissi, the Great Island, where rebellion was endemic for centuries—against Arab invaders, Venetian colonists, Ottoman pashas, and German occupiers in World War II. The mountains were a refuge for outlaws or resistance fighters—the names changed with the times—and a spirit of defiant ingenuity survives in upland villages, maybe in stealing a sheep for a wedding feast, or in transporting crates of soft drinks down a mountainside to a remote beach. Hospitality is still important, despite the growth of mass tourism; off the beaten track, you may be offered as much *tsikouthia*—the local firewater—as you can drink, and be sent on your way with a bag of grapes or oranges.

As the cradle of European civilization, Crete holds a special place in history. The Minoans, prehistoric Cretans, founded Europe's first urban culture as far back as the third millennium BC, and its rich legacy of art and architecture strongly influenced both mainland Greece and the Aegean islands in the Bronze Age. From around 1900 BC the Minoan palaces at Knossos (near present-day Heraklion), at Mallia, Phaistos, and elsewhere were hubs of political power, religious authority, and economic activity—all concentrated in one sprawling complex of buildings. Their administration seems to have had much in common with contemporary cultures in Egypt and Mesopotamia. What set the Minoans apart from the rest of the Bronze Age world was their art. It was lively and naturalistic, and they excelled in miniature techniques. From the scenes illustrated on their frescoes, stone vases, seal-stones, and signet rings, it is possible to build a picture of a productive, well-regulated society. Yet new research suggests that prehistoric Crete was not a peaceful place; there may have been years of warfare before Knossos became the island's dominant power, around 1600 BC. It is now thought that political upheaval, rather than the devastating volcanic eruption on the island of Santorini, triggered the violent downfall of the palace civilization around 1450 BC.

From the glossy beach resorts along the north coast—with the faint echoes of Minoan hedonism in their stunning settings—to the backpackers' haunts in the south, there are destinations to suit every tourist's taste. The rooms, restaurants, and other facilities at first-class hotels now compare with the best of southern Europe, though dozens of dull concrete blocks built in the 1970s, with indifferent plumbing and service, are still around. In the west especially, old houses, Venetian mansions, and 19th-century consulates are being sensitively restored as small hotels. English is spoken everywhere. Local travel agents offer an increasingly imaginative range of tours, to frescoed Byzantine churches deep in the countryside, beaches reachable only by boat, or offshore islets inhabited mostly by birds and sheep. Keep in mind, though, that in July and August the main Minoan sites and the coastal towns come close to overflowing. Places like Mallia town and Limin Hersonissos, where bars and pizzerias fill up with hard-drinking northern Europeans, should be avoided. Driving can be hazardous amid the profusion of buses, jeeps, and motorbikes, not to mention the impatient Cretan drivers. The most pleasant times of year for visiting Crete are April and May, when every outcrop of rock is ablaze with brilliant wildflowers, or October, when the sea is still warm and the light golden but piercingly clear.

Essential Information

Important Addresses and Numbers

Tourist Information The **Greek Tourist Organization** (EOT) offices are in Heraklion (Xanthoudidou 1, tel. 081/228225) and Hania (Kriari 40, tel. 0821/26426), which are open year-round, in winter 8–2 and in summer until 6. There are community-run information offices in Rethymnon (Venizelou 20, tel. 0831/29148), Ayios Nikolaos (Akti Koundourou 20, tel. 0841/22357), Ierapetra (Town Hall, tel. 0842/28658), and Siteia (Iroon Polytechneiou Square, tel. 0843/24955).

Tourist police. Heraklion (tel. 081/282243), Hania (tel. 0821/24477), Rethymnon (tel. 0831/28156), Ayios Nikolaos (tel. 0841/22244), Ierapetra (tel. 0842/24200), and Siteia (0843/24200).

Emergencies Tel. 100 for police, fire, or ambulance services. Your hotel will call an English-speaking doctor. Pharmacies stay open late on a rotation basis, and a list of those open late is displayed on the door or window of every pharmacy.

Hospitals Heraklion: Venizeleion Hospital (Knossos Road, tel. 081/231931); Apolloneion General Hospital (Albert and M. Moussourou Street, tel. 081/229713); Hania: General Hospital (tel. 0821/27231); Rethymnon: town hospital (tel. 0831/22261); Ayios Nikolaos: town hospital (tel. 0841/22369); Ierapetra: town hospital (tel. 0842/22488); Siteia: town hospital (tel. 0843/24311).

English-Language Bookstores In Heraklion, you can find English-language books at **Kouvidis-Manouras** (Daidalou 6, tel. 081/220135) or **Astrakianakis** (Plateia Venizelou, tel. 081/284248). Newspapers and magazines are available in Plateia Venizelou. In both Hania and Rethymnon, one or two souvenir stores on the waterfront sell English-language books and newspapers.

Post Offices and Telephones Post offices are open weekdays 8–8. The main post office in Heraklion is in Plateia Daskaloyianni; in Hania, at Tzanakaki 3. You can sometimes buy stamps at a kiosk. To avoid heavy surcharges imposed by hotels on long-distance calls, you can make them from a post office, known as OTE. In Heraklion, the main OTE office is in El Greco Park. In Hania, it is at Tzanakaki 5. In Rethymnon, both the post office and OTE are in Koundourioti Street. You can often make metered calls overseas from kiosks and kafeneions (coffee shops), even in small villages.

Arriving and Departing by Plane

The principal arrival point on Crete is **Heraklion airport** (tel. 081/228402) in the center of the island, 5 kilometers (3 miles) east of the city, where up to six flights daily arrive from Athens and two flights weekly from Rhodes. There are also several daily flights from Athens to **Hania airport** (tel. 0821/63224) in the west, 15 kilometers (10 miles) east of town, and flights two or three times weekly to **Siteia airport** (tel. 0843/24424) in eastern Crete, 2 kilometers (1¼ miles) west of the town. Twice-weekly flights from Rhodes via Karpathos also land in Siteia.

Bewteen the Airport and Heraklion A municipal bus outside Heraklion airport will take you to Plateia Eleftherias in the center of town (known locally as Treis Kamares). Tickets are sold from a kiosk next to the bus stop; the fare is 105 dr. From Hania and Siteia airports, Olympic Airways buses take you to the airline office in the town center. The fare is 250 dr. from Hania airport and 100 dr. from Siteia airport. Cabs are lined up outside Heraklion and Hania airports; the fare into town is 600 dr. from Heraklion and 1,200 dr. from Hania. Taxis usually turn up to meet flights into Siteia airport, but if there are none to be seen, ask the information desk to call one from town. The fare will be approximately 500 dr.

Arriving and Departing by Ship

Heraklion and Souda Bay (5 kilometers [3 miles] east of Hania) are the island's main ports. Two Cretan shipping companies, **Anek** (25th Avgoustou 33, Heraklion, tel. 081/222481) and **Minoan Lines** (25th Avgoustou 78, Heraklion, tel. 081/229646) have daily ferry service to both ports from Piraeus year-round. **Rethymniaki Lines** (Arkadiou 250, Rethymnon, tel. 0831/21518) has service from Piraeus to Rethymnon three or four times a week. The overnight crossing takes 10–12 hours. You can book a berth in a first-, second-, or tourist-class cabin or an aircraft-style seat. Make reservations for summer crossings through a travel agent several days in advance. At other times of the year, you can buy a ticket from a dockside agency in Piraeus an hour before the ship sails. When buying your ticket make sure your cabin is air-conditioned; older vessels may have no air-conditioning in tourist-class cabins. There are self-service cafeterias in second and tourist classes and a comfortable dining room in the first-class section. All ferries take cars: A discount may be available if you buy a round-trip ticket for the car. In summer, you should make your return-trip reservation several days in advance at the shipping company: Both Anek and Minoan Lines have offices in all the main towns on the island. A one-way first-class fare costs about 9,000 dr., second-class about 7,000 dr., and tourist class 5,000 dr., with little or no discount for round-trips. Car fares range from 10,000 dr. to 14,000 dr., one way, depending on size. Other ferry services change from year to year, but there are weekly sailings in summer from Piraeus to Siteia and to Kastelli Kissamou in western Crete. A small ferry links Siteia with the Dodecanese islands of Kassos, Karpathos, and Rhodes, and both ferries and catamarans operate in summer between Santorini and Heraklion. There is also a weekly sailing from Heraklion to Limassol in Cyprus, and Haifa, Israel. Ferry service is sometimes available to Kusadasi, Turkey, and Alexandria, Egypt. Travel agents in Crete can advise you on the schedules.

Getting Around

By Car Roads on Crete are uncongested but, apart from the north coast highway, tend to be winding and narrow. Most are now asphalt, but dirt tracks between villages are still found in mountainous regions. Towns, archaeological sites, and larger villages have signs in English, but you will have to decipher

Greek signs in remote districts. Gas stations are not plentiful outside the big towns, and road maps are not always reliable, especially in the south. Driving in the main towns can be nerve-racking, especially during the lunchtime rush hour. Drive defensively wherever you are, for Cretan drivers are aggressive and liable to ignore the rules of the road. In summer, tourists on motor scooters can be a hazard. Sheep and goats frequently stray onto the roads, with or without their shepherd or sheep-dog. Night driving is not advisable.

You can rent cars, jeeps, and motorbikes in all the island's towns, or you can arrange beforehand with a major agency in the United States or in Athens to pick up a car on arrival in Crete. **Hertz** (tel. 081/229702) and **Avis** (tel. 081/225421) have offices at Heraklion airport as well as in the city, but other reliable companies, like **Hellascars** (tel. 081/223240) and **Thrifty** (tel. 081/288395), have cheaper rates. A medium-size, four-door car costs about 12,000–15,000 dr. a day with 100 kilometers (63 miles) of free mileage (extra mileage costs about 50 dr. per kilometer) including insurance and taxes. Weekly prices are negotiable, but with unlimited mileage they start at about 50,000 dr.

By Bus The public bus companies (KTEL) have regular, inexpensive service between the main towns. You can book seats in advance at whichever bus station is the terminus for the district of the island you're going to. The efficient village bus network operates similarly, from the bus station in each *komopolis*, or market town. In Heraklion, the bus station for western Crete (tel. 081/221765) is opposite the Historical Museum; the station for the south (tel. 081/283287) is just outside the Hania Gate to the right; and for the east (tel. 081/282637), just east of the traffic circle at the end of Leoforos D. Bofor, close to the old harbor .

Guided Tours

Resort hotels and large travel agents organize guided tours by air-conditioned bus to the main Minoan sites; excursions to spectacular beaches like Vei in the northeast and Elafonisi in the southwest; and trips to Santorini and to some offshore islands like Gaidouronisi, south of Ierapetra, and Spinalonga, a former leper colony off Ayios Nikolaos. From Heraklion, **Creta Travel** (Epimenidou 20–22, tel. 081/227002) and **Adamis Tours** (25th Avgoustou 23, tel. 081/246202) both offer a wide range of island tours. In Hania, **G.A. Travel** (Halidon 25, tel. 0821/24965), **Canea Travel** (Tzanakaki 28, tel. 0821/28817), and **El Greco Tours** (Theotocopoulou 63, tel. 0821/21829) organize hikes through the Samaria Gorge and other local excursions. For example: a tour of the Heraklion Museum and Knossos costs 4,500 dr.; a tour of Phaistos and Gortyna plus a swim at Matala costs 6,000 dr.; a trip to Omalos and the Samaria Gorge, returning to Sfakia by boat, about 9,000 dr. Travel agents can arrange for personal guides, whose fees are negotiable.

Exploring Crete

Highlights for First-Time Visitors

Ayios Nikolaos and the **Gulf of Mirabello** (*see* Tour 2)
Hania old port (*see* Tour 4)

Heraklion Archaeological Museum and Knossos (*see* Tour 1)
Kato Zakro (*see* Tour 2)
Phaistos (*see* Tour 3)
Vei beach (*see* Tour 2)

Tour 1: Heraklion and the Palace of Knossos

Numbers in the margin correspond to points of interest on the Western Crete, Eastern Crete, and Heraklion maps.

This tour explores **Heraklion,** Crete's largest city, and introduces the Minoans in their palace at Knossos. Heraklion's narrow, crowded alleys and thick stone ramparts recall the days when soldiers and merchants clung to the safety of a fortified port. In Minoan times, this was a harbor for Knossos, the largest palace and effective power center of prehistoric Crete. But the Bronze Age remains were built over long ago, and now Heraklion, with more than 120,000 inhabitants, stretches far beyond even the Venetian walls. But its center is the same: a few traffic-jammed streets around the open-air market and the

❶ marble Renaissance fountain, **Ta Leontaria** (the lions), where we begin this tour.

Officially, this triangular pedestrian zone filled with cafés is **Eleftheriou Venizelou Square,** named after the Cretan statesman who united the island with Greece in 1913. But for hundreds of years it had been the heart of the colony founded in the 13th century, when Venice bought Crete, and Heraklion became an important port of call on the trade routes to the Middle East. The city, and often the whole island, known then as Candia, was ruled by the Duke of Crete, a Venetian administrator.

❷ The 13th-century church of **Ayios Markos,** now an exhibition center, is named for Venice's patron saint, but, with its modern portico and narrow interior, it bears little resemblance to its grand namesake in Venice. Around the corner on 25th August

❸ Street stands the **Loggia,** a gathering place for the island's Venetian nobility. Built in the early 17th century by Francesco Basilicata, an Italian architect, it was recently restored to its former Palladian elegance. Adjoining it is the old Venetian Armory, now the City Hall.

Going north toward the harbor down 25th Avgoustou, you pass travel, shipping, and car-rental agencies and come to the

❹ church of **Ayios Titos,** the island's patron saint, set back from the street on the right. A chapel to the left of the entrance contains the saint's skull, set in a silver-and-gilt reliquary. Ayios Titos is credited with converting the islanders to Christianity in the 1st century AD on the instructions of St. Paul. At the bottom of the street, you cross a busy roundabout and come to the inner harbor, the old Venetian port, where fishing boats land their catch and yachts are moored. To the right rise the tall vaulted tunnels of the Arsenal; here, Venetian galleys were repaired and refitted and timber, cheeses, and sweet Malmsey wine were loaded for the three-week voyage to Venice. A

❺ miniature fortress, known now by its Turkish name of **Koules,** dominates the old port. It was built by the Venetians, and three stone lions of St. Mark, symbol of Venetian imperialism, decorate the exterior. The panoramic view from its battlements takes in both the outer harbor, where freighters and passenger ferries drop anchor, and the sprawling labyrinth of concrete apartment blocks that is modern Heraklion. To the south rises

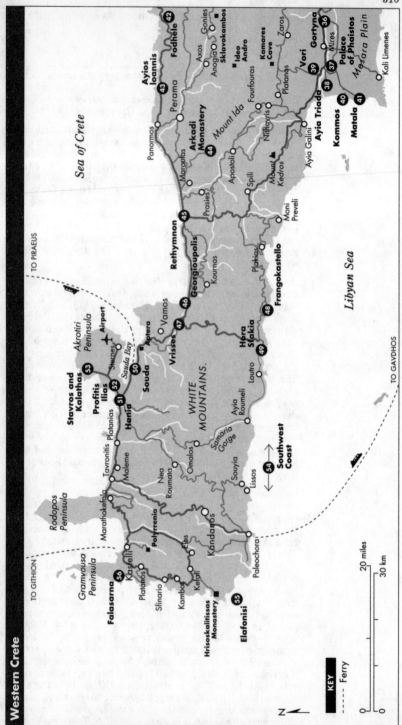

Western Crete

Sea of Crete

Libyan Sea

TO PIRAEUS

TO GITHION

TO GAVDHOS

Rodopos Peninsula

Gramvousa Peninsula

Akrotiri Peninsula

WHITE MOUNTAINS.

Samaria Gorge

Mount Ida

Mount Kedros

Mesara Plain

Falasarna 56
Kastelli
Platanos
Sfinario
Kambos
Kefali
Elos
Polyrrenia
Kandanos
Paleochora
Hrisoskalitissas Monastery
Elafonisi 55
Marathokefala
Tavronitis
Platanias
Maleme
Nea Roumata
Omalos
Souyia
Lissos
Southwest Coast 54
Ayia Roumeli
Loutro
Stavros and Kalathas 53
Profitis Ilias 52
51 **Hania**
Airport
Sternes
Souda
Sauda Bay
Aptera 50
Vrisses 47
Vamos
Souda
Georgioupolis 46
Kournas
Rethymnon 45
Panormos
Margolas
Prasies
Perama 43
Ayios Ioannis
Fodhele 42
Panormos
Arkadi Monastery 44
Apostoli
Spili
Plakias
Moni Preveli
Frangokastello 48
Hora Sfakia 49
Axos
Gonies
Anogia
Sklavokambos
Ideo Andro
Kamares Cave
Zaros
Fourfouras
Platanos
Nithavris
Ayia Galini
Vori 39
Mires
Gortyna 36
37 **Palace of Phaistos**
38 **Ayia Triada**
40 **Kommos**
Matala 41
Kali Limenes

KEY
----- Ferry

N

0   20 miles
0   30 km

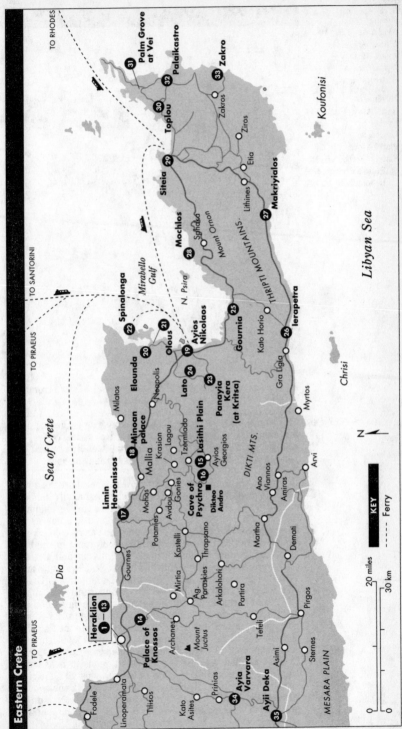

Eastern Crete

KEY

— Ferry

TO PIRAEUS

TO RHODES

TO SANTORINI

TO PIRAEUS

TO PIRAEUS

Sea of Crete

Libyan Sea

Dia

Fodele

Linoperamata

Tilisos

Gournes

Heraklion **1 — 13**

14 Archanes

Mount Juchus

Kato Asites

Prinias

34 Ayia Varvara

Asimi

Sternes

35 Ayii Deka

Tefeli

MESARA PLAIN

Pirgos

Demati

Martha

Arkalohori

Partira

Ag. Paraskies

Mirtia

Kastelli

Thrapsano

Potamies

Mohos

Avdou

Gonies

17 Limin Hersonissos

Mallia

18 Minoan palace

Milatos

Neapolis

20 Elounda

22 Spinalonga

21 Olous

19 Ayios Nikolaos

24 Lato

23 Panayia Kera (at Kritsa)

Lasithi Plain **15**

16 Ayios Georgios

Dikteo Andro

Cave of Psychro

Tzermiado

Lagou

Krasion

DIKTI MTS.

Ano Viannos

Amiras

Arvi

Myrtos

Chrisi

Gournia **25**

Kato Horio

Gra Ligia

26 Ierapetra

27 Makriyialos

THRIPTI MOUNTAINS

Mount Ornon

Sphaka

N. Psira

Mochlos **28**

Mirabello Gulf

Siteia **29**

30 Toplou

31 Palm Grove at Vei

32 Palaikastro

33 Zakro

Zakros

Ziros

Etia

Lithines

Koufonisi

N

20 miles

30 km

0

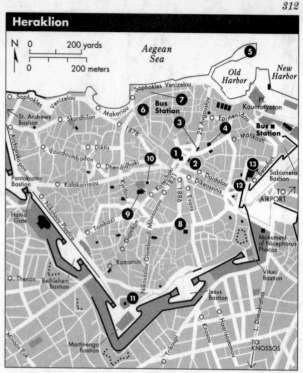

Heraklion

Mt. Iuktas and to the west, the pointed peak of Mt. Stromboli. *Admission: 500 dr. Open Tues.–Sun. 8:30–3.*

Time Out   The **Marina Café** in the old harbor is a favorite gathering place for young Herakliots. It serves cakes, ice cream, coffee, and cold drinks. Even in high summer there is usually a breeze, and you can watch the comings and goings of the fishermen.

Return to the roundabout and follow the seashore road west **6** past the medieval shell of **St. Peter's church,** heavily damaged during World War II in the bombing before the German invasion in 1941. Opposite, an imposing mansion houses the **7** **Historical and Ethnological Museum.** The varied collection includes early Christian and Byzantine sculptures in the basement and several rooms filled with Venetian and Ottoman stonework. Look out for a splendid lion of St. Mark, with an inscription that says in Latin "I protect the kingdom of Crete," and some striking tombstones of Ottoman officials, topped with stone turbans. Left of the entrance is a room stuffed with memorabilia from Crete's bloody revolutionary past: weapons, portraits of mustachioed warrior chieftains, and the flag of the short-lived independent Cretan state set up in 1898. The 19th-century banner in front of the staircase sums up the spirit of Cretan rebellion against the Turks: It reads in bold letters *Eleftheria i Thanatos* (Freedom or Death). Upstairs, look in on a room arranged as the study of Crete's most famous writer, Nikos Kazantzakis, the author of *Zorba the Greek* and an epic poem *The Odyssey, a Modern Sequel.* The top floor contains a stunning collection of Cretan textiles, including the brilliant scarlet weavings typical of the island's traditional handwork, and another room arranged as a comfortable domestic interior of the early 1900s. *Sophocleou Venizelou, tel. 081/226092. Admission: 500 dr. Open Tues–Sun. 8–3.*

Time Out   Back at Ta Leontaria, stop for a *bougatsa*, an envelope of flaky pastry stuffed with a sweet creamy filling dusted with cinnamon and sugar, or with soft white cheese. A double portion served warm with Greek coffee makes a change from a hotel breakfast, especially if you've just arrived off the ferry from Piraeus. There are two **bougatsa shops,** side by side, on the square.

Starting out again from Ta Leontaria, head south and, at the traffic lights, cross Kalokairinou into Odos 1866, the lively open-air market. Fruit and vegetable stalls alternate with butchers' displays of whole lambs and pigs' feet. You can stock up here for a picnic: Grocers sell cheese (you can taste a sliver before buying), wine, and olives; or you can eat a hearty lunch at one of the tavernas in Meat Alley, on the left of Odos 1866. ⑧ The square at the top of the street is **Plateia Cornarou,** which is graced with a Venetian fountain and an elegant Turkish stone kiosk.

From the plateia walk west to Kyrillou Loukareos, the main road that leads to the huge unprepossessing 19th-century ca- ⑨ thedral, **Ayios Minas.** Nestled in its shadow is one of Crete's ⑩ most attractive small churches, **Ayia Aikaterina of Sinai,** built in 1555. It is now a museum of icons by Cretan artists, who traveled to Venice to study with Italian Renaissance painters. Look for six icons (Nos. 2, 5, 8, 9, 12, and 15) by Michael Damaskinos, who worked in both Byzantine and Renaissance styles in the 16th century. *Admission: 500 dr., Open 9:30–1; closed Tues. and Sun.*

Heading back along Kyrillou Loukareos, turn south down N.G. Mousourou, leading directly to the **Martinengo Bastion,** the ⑪ **burial place of Kazantzakis.** The grave is a plain stone slab marked by a weathered wooden cross. The inscription, from his writings, says: "I fear nothing, I hope for nothing, I am free."

The Martinengo is the largest of six bastions shaped like arrowheads that jut out from the well-preserved Venetian walls. Designed by Micheli Sanmicheli, they were built in the 16th century to keep out Barbary pirates and Turkish invaders. When the Turks finally overran Crete in 1648, the garrison at Heraklion held out for another 21 years in one of the longest sieges in European history. General Francesco Morosini finally surrendered the city to the Turkish Grand Vizier in September 1669. He was allowed to sail home to Venice with the city's archives and such precious relics as the skull of Ayios Titos— which was not returned until 1966.

Starting once again from Ta Leontaria, walk east into Daidalou, just south of Ayios Markos. This street, which follows the line of an early fortification wall, is now a pedestrian walkway lined with tavernas, boutiques, jewelers, and souve- ⑫ nir shops. It ends in **Plateia Eleftherias,** the city's biggest square (known to residents as Treis Kamares), just opposite ⑬ the **Archaeological Museum.**

In summer the best time for visiting the Archaeological Museum is early in the morning, before tourist buses start disgorging their passengers. The museum is in the process of being equipped with air-conditioning and an up-to-date security system; some galleries may be closed or prize exhibits removed while the renovations are carried out. Whatever the confusion, visiting the Minoan collection compares with a visit to any of the great museums of western Europe. Even before the great palaces were built, around 1900 BC, the prehistoric Cretans excelled at metalworking and in carving stone vases (like the box in Gallery I with a lid whose handle is in the shape of a lazing dog). They were also skilled at producing fine pottery, such as the eggshell-thin Kamares ware decorated in delicate abstract designs (in Gallery III), and miniature work like the superbly crafted jewelry (in Galleries VI and VII) and the colored sealstones (in Gallery III) that are carved with lively scenes of people and animals.

Though naturalism and an air of informality distinguish much Minoan art from that of contemporary Bronze Age cultures elsewhere in the eastern Mediterranean, you will also see a number of heavy, rococo set-pieces, like the fruitstand with a toothed rim and the punchbowl with appliqué flowers (both in Gallery III). The Linear B script, inscribed on clay tablets (Gallery V) is now recognized as an early form of Greek, but neither the earlier Linear A script (Gallery V) nor that of the Phaistos Disk (Gallery III) has yet been deciphered.

The Minoans' talents at modeling in stone, ivory, and a kind of glass paste known to archaeologists as faience peaked in the later palace period (1700 BC–1450 BC). A famous rhyton (vase for pouring libations) carved from dark serpentine in the shape of a bull's head had eyes made of red jasper and clear rock crystal with horns of gilded wood (Gallery IV). An ivory acrobat—perhaps a bull-leaper—and two bare-breasted faience goddesses in flounced skirts holding wriggling snakes (both Gallery IV) were among a group of treasures hidden beneath the floor of a storeroom at Knossos. Bull-leaping, whether religious rite or a favorite sport, inspired some memorable Minoan art. Three vases of serpentine (probably covered originally in gold leaf) from Ayia Triada (Gallery VII) are carved with scenes of Minoan life thought to be by artists from Knossos: boxing matches, a harvest-home ceremony, and a Minoan official taking delivery of a consignment of hides. The most stunning rhyton of all, from Zakro, is made of rock crystal (Gallery VIII). Commodities were stored in the palaces: An elephant tusk and bronze ingots (Gallery VIII) were found at Zakro and Ayia Triada. Make sure to save some time and energy for the fresco galleries upstairs. Dating from the later palace period, they show both the Minoans' preoccupation with religious ritual and enjoyment of their island's natural beauties. *Plateia Eleftherias, tel. 081/226092. Admission: 1,000 dr. Open Mon. 11–5, Tues.–Fri. 8–7, weekends 8:30–3.*

14 Bus No. 2 leaves every 15 minutes from Odos Evans, close to the market, for the Minoan **Palace of Knossos** just 5 kilometers (3 miles) south of Heraklion. If you are driving, follow the signs south from Plateia Eleftherias to Leoforos Dimokratias, and follow a busy road lined with garages, supermarkets, and nightclubs. Bear left at the cemetery and again at the turning for the north coast highway. Heraklion spreads almost as far as

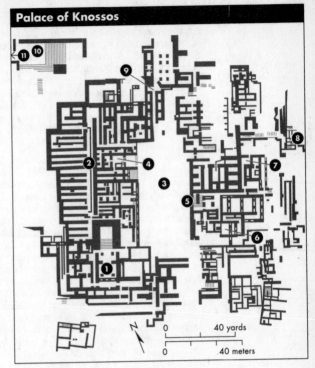

Palace of Knossos

Knossos; as you leave the straggling village the palace is on your left and there is a large parking area.

The palace of Knossos belonged to King Minos, who kept the Minotaur, a hybrid monster of man and bull, in an underground labyrinth.

A low hill at the site was occupied from Neolithic times, and the population spread to the land around. Around 1900 BC, the hilltop was leveled and the first palace constructed; around 1700 BC, after an earthquake destroyed it, the later palace was built, surrounded by houses and other buildings. Around 1450 BC, another widespread disaster occurred, perhaps an invasion: Palaces and country villas were razed by fire and abandoned, and though Knossos remained inhabited, the palace suffered some damage. But around 1380 BC the palace and its outlying buildings were destroyed by fire, and, at the end of the Bronze Age, the site was abandoned. Still later, Knossos became a Greek city-state. Fine houses with mosaic floors and statuary have been excavated. Evidence of the Minoan civilization was unearthed in the early 1900s, when Crete had just achieved independence after centuries of foreign rule by Venice and then by the Ottoman Turks.

You enter the palace from the west, passing a bust of Sir Arthur Evans, the British archaeologist who excavated at Knossos on and off for more than 20 years after 1900. Opinions vary about his concrete restorations and copies of the frescoes. But without them, it would be impossible to experience, even at second hand, the ambience of a Minoan palace, with its long pillared halls, narrow corridors, deep stairways and light wells, and curious reverse-tapering columns. But the restorations themselves are in need of renovation; some areas of the palace are now closed off. A path leads you around to the monumental south gateway; go through, then head into the west wing and take a look at the lines of long narrow storerooms where the true wealth of Knossos was kept in tall clay jars: oil, wine, grains, and honey. Work your way back to the central court, about 164 feet by 82 feet and go into the cool, dark throne room complex, with its griffin fresco and tall, wavy-back gypsum throne.

The most spectacular piece of palace architecture is the Grand Staircase, on the east side of the court, leading to the domestic apartments. Four flights of shallow gypsum stairs survive, lit by a deep lightwell. Here you get a sense of how noble Minoans lived; rooms were divided by sets of double doors, giving privacy and warmth when closed, coolness and communication when open. The Queen's Megaron (apartment) is decorated with copies of the colorful Dolphin fresco and furnished with stone benches. Beside it is a bathroom, complete with a clay tub, and next door a toilet, whose drainage system permitted flushing into a channel flowing into the Kairatos stream far below. The east side of the palace also contained workshops. Look for the staircase leading down to the east bastion: Beside the steps is a stone water channel made up of parabolic curves and settling basins: a Minoan storm drain. Back in the central court head for the north entrance, guarded by a relief fresco of a charging bull. Beyond is the Theatral Area, shaded by pines and overlooking a shallow flight of steps leading down to the Royal Road. This was perhaps the ceremonial entrance to the palace. *Admission: 1,000 dr. Call Archaeological Museum in Heraklion (tel. 081/226092) for information in English on hours open.*

Tour 2: Eastern Crete—Mallia, Ayios Nikolaos, Ierapetra, and Zakro

From Plateia Eleftherias follow the signs for the north coast highway, still labeled "new road," though it was built more than 20 years ago. It is a good idea to fill up with gas beforehand. The highway east runs parallel to the coast; you pass the radio masts of the U.S. air base at Gournes before reaching, at 24 kilometers (15 miles), a right turn marked for Kastelli Pediada.

From here the road winds steadily upward for 25 kilometers (16 miles), toward a wall of barren mountains; behind them lies **⑮** the **Lasithi plain**, 2,800 feet above sea level. It is covered with mechanical windmills pumping water for fields of potatoes and for apple and almond orchards that are a pale haze of blossom in early spring. Lasithi, the biggest of the upland plains of Crete, has a remote atmosphere: It is sometimes cut off in winter by **⑯** heavy snowfalls. At the **Cave of Psychro** (admission 500 dr.; open daily 8–5), a slippery descent takes you into an impressive cavern hung with stalactites, which was once a Minoan sanctuary. It's where Zeus, the king of the gods, was supposedly born, and it is well worth a visit. You can get a meal at **Tzermiado,** 52 kilometers (32 miles) from Heraklion, but there is no comfortable hotel in any of the villages around the plain.

(17) Backtrack down to the north coast, and turn east; you'll reach **Limin Hersonissos** after 26 kilometers (16 miles) on the main road. Once an important Roman port, it is now a flourishing but charmless tourist resort, with dozens of souvenir shops, pizzerias, pubs, discos, jostling cafés, and tavernas. **Mallia,** 34 kilometers (21 miles) farther on, is much the same, its character submerged to serve mass tourism, and its sandy beach, overlooked by the brooding Lasithi mountains, backed by a solid line of hotels and vacation apartments. Just past the town, a
(18) sign to the left of the road directs you to the **Minoan palace.** Like Knossos and Phaistos, the palace at Mallia was built around 1900 BC, but it was less sophisticated both in architecture and decoration. The layout, however, is similar. You approach the palace across the west court, along one of the paved raised walkways, passing a double row of round granaries sunk into the ground, which were almost certainly roofed. Entering through the south doorway, notice the large, circular limestone table, with a large hollow at its center and 34 smaller ones around the edge. This was a *kernos*, on which were placed offerings to a Minoan deity. The central court has a shallow pit at its center, perhaps the location of an altar. Opening off it to the west are the remains of an imposing staircase leading up to a second floor, and a terrace, most likely used for religious ceremonies. Behind is a long corridor with storerooms to the side. In the north wing is a large pillared hall, part of a set of public rooms. The domestic apartments appear to have been in the northwest corner of the palace, entered through a narrow dogleg passage. They are connected by a smaller northern court, through which you can leave the palace by the north entrance, passing two giant *pithoi*, or storage jars. Much excavation has been done nearby, but only a few of the sites are open to the public. *Tel. 0841/22462. Admission: 500 dr. Open Tues.–Sun. 8:30–3.*

(19) Continue along the highway, which now turns inland, and drive about 24 kilometers (15 miles) to **Ayios Nikolaos** on the **Gulf of Mirabello,** a dramatic composition of bare mountains, islets, and deep blue sea. The town was built just over a century ago by Cretans from the southwest of the island. Behind the crowded harbor lies a natural curiosity, tiny Lake Voulismeni, linked to the sea by a narrow channel. Before visiting the town,
(20) detour north around the gulf to **Elounda,** 11 kilometers (7 miles) farther on, along a narrow corniche road with spectacular views across the sea. This is not an area renowned for beaches, which tend to be narrow and pebbly, but the water is crystal clear and sheltered from the *meltemi*, the fierce north wind that blows in summer. Elounda village is becoming a full-scale resort, serving the dozens of villas and apartment hotels dotting the surrounding hillsides. You can escape the crowds
(21) by following signs for **Olous,** an ancient city whose sunken remains are still visible beneath the sea as you cross a causeway to Spinalonga. There is good swimming off the rocks.

(22) You can also take an excursion boat from Ayios Nikolaos to **Spinalonga,** a small, narrow island in the center of the Mirabello Gulf where the Venetians built a huge, forbidding fortress in the 17th century. In the early 1900s it became a leper colony, and it is a fascinating if somewhat macabre place to visit. Ask at the harbor; there are two or three trips every day in summer, some including a midday beach barbecue and a swim on a deserted islet. As you cruise past the islet of Ayioi

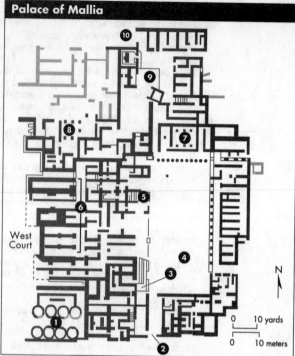

Round Granaries, **1**
South Doorway, **2**
Kernos, **3**
Central Court, **4**
Staircase, **5**
Storerooms, **6**
Pillared Hall, **7**
Domestic
Apartments, **8**
Northern Court, **9**
North Entrance, **10**

Palace of Mallia

West
Court

N

0   10 yards

0   10 meters

Pantes, look for the *agrimi*, the Cretan wild goat, with its impressive curling horns. The islet is a reserve for about 200 of this protected species.

Back in Ayios Nikolaos, visit the **museum,** which displays some unique finds. The *Goddess of Myrtos,* an Early Minoan rhyton from a site on the southeast coast, is an appealing figure cradling a large jug in her spindly arms. There are some fine examples of Late Minoan pottery in the naturalistic marine style, with lively octopus and shell designs. The Triton stone vase found at Mallia is carved with an unusual scene of a Minoan religious ritual. A Roman cemetery on the edge of the town yielded a rare find: a skull adorned with a gold wreath, perhaps an athlete who died young. *Odos Palaiologou, tel. 0841/22462. Admission: 500 dr. Open Tues.–Sun. 8:30–3.*

Time Out   The quietest place to stop for a coffee or cool drink is one of the **cafés** overlooking the Kitomilia beach south of town, with a spectacular view of the island of **Pseira** and the **Thripti** mountains.

If you visit only one Byzantine church in Crete, it should be **Panayia Kera** at **Kritsa,** 9 kilometers (6 miles) west of Ayios Nikolaos. From the central square with its grove of palm trees, follow the signs for Siteia to the bypass road and head straight across: The road to Kritsa is well marked. After 7 kilometers (4 miles) turn right for the whitewashed church (admission 200 dr.; open Sat.–Thurs. 9–3). It is an unusual shape, with three naves supported by heavy triangular buttresses. Built in the early years of Venetian occupation, it contains some of the liveliest and best-preserved medieval frescoes on the island, painted in the 13th century. The village of Kritsa is renowned for its weaving tradition; among the tourist items, you can usually find a rug or bag in natural wool—cream, gray, or brown.

Time Out For one of the best views in Crete, turn north down a dirt track (24) (1 kilometer [½ mile] beyond the church) leading to **Lato,** an ancient city built in a dip between two rocky peaks. Make your way over the ancient masonry to the far end of the site: On a clear day, you can see the island of Santorini, about 135 kilometers (84 miles) across the Cretan Sea.

Back on the main highway, head east for Siteia. The road winds around the south side of the Mirabello Gulf. At 18½ kilometers (25) (12 miles) the Minoan site of **Gournia** lies spread out on a low hillside to the right. It was excavated in 1904 by Harriet Boyd Hawes, the first woman archaeologist to work here (along with her team of Cretan workmen came a chaperone). Most of what you see dates from the later Palace period, though Gournia boasted only a small mansion set among dozens of small houses. Finds indicated that Gournia was a fishing and weaving community. It was destroyed around 1400 BC and never resettled. *Admission free. Open Mon.–Sat. 8:30–3, Sun. 9:30–2:30.*

About 3 kilometers (2 miles) farther on, a road branches right (26) for **Ierapetra,** 35 kilometers (22 miles) away across the narrowest part of the island. Ierapetra, the only town on the south coast, is a flourishing agricultural center, its prosperity based on the plastic-covered greenhouses where early tomatoes and cucumbers are grown and exported all over Europe. The climate in this part of Crete is north African; you are nearer to Libya than to mainland Greece. Tourism is fast developing to the east of Ierapetra, where there are some fine sandy beaches. (27) Head for the village of **Makriyialos** and take your pick; even in high summer you might have most of a cove to yourself.

Back on the gulf coast, the road from Gournia to Siteia narrows and winds between the base of the mountains and the sea. If you feel like a swim, or a leisurely taverna meal, turn left at the (28) village of Sphaka and head down to **Mochlos.** After 1 kilometer (½ mile), fork right, and the narrow coastal plain comes into view, with the island of Mochlos at the far end, separated from shore by a swimmable channel. On it is a Minoan cemetery excavated early in this century. Mochlos is a good place for lazing in the hottest part of the day; there are several pleasant tavernas on the shore and, if you want to stay longer, rooms to rent.

Back on the highway, the road skirts Mt. Ornon before rising to a ridge crowned with a row of impressive stone windmills— (29) the last crest before you descend to the coastal plain of **Siteia.** Like Ierapetra, it is an unpretentious town where agriculture is at least as important as tourism: Raisins and, increasingly, bananas are the main crops. The waterfront, lined with cafés and tavernas, is lively in summer, and a long sandy beach stretches to the east. From Siteia you can take a plane or ferry to Rhodes via the small islands of Kassos and Karpathos. A Venetian fort, the **Kazarma,** overlooks the town from a height on the west: It offers a spectacular view across the bay. The **archaeological museum,** on the outskirts of town, contains a unique find: a Minoan ivory and gold statuette of a young man, found at Palaikastro on the east coast. The figure dates from around 1500 BC and though incomplete, is a masterpiece of Minoan carving. *Admission: 500 dr. Open Tues.–Sun. 9–3.*

East of Siteia, you take the road for Palaikastro and Zakro. At 12½ kilometers (8 miles) turn left to the fortified monastery of **30** **Toplou,** set among barren hills where the sparse trees are twisted into strange shapes by the fierce north winds that sweep this region. Only a few monks live here now, though the monastery is slowly being renovated. Inside the tall loggia gate, built in the 16th century, the cells are arranged around a cobbled courtyard with a 14th-century church at its center. It contains a famous icon, composed of 61 scenes, each inspired by a phrase from the Orthodox liturgy.

31 To reach the beach and **palm grove at Vei,** go northeast from Toplou for 6 kilometers (4 miles), turn left at the T-junction and after another 1½ kilometers (1 mile), take a right leading down to the beach. The palm grove at Vei existed in classical Greek times; it is unique in Europe. The sandy **beach** with offshore islets set in clear turquoise water is one of the most attractive in Crete, but in summer it is also one of the most crowded.

32 More repose is to be found at **Palaikastro,** 9 kilometers (6 miles) south, where the sandy beach is rarely crowded and service is friendly at the waterside tavernas. In the village, take a left at the sign for Marina Village. Follow a dirt track through olive groves to the sea. The sprawling Minoan town, currently being excavated by British and American archaeologists, lies off to the right.

Back at Palaikastro village, take the road south for Ano Zakro, 20 kilometers (12 miles) away. From here you can walk down to **33** the Minoan palace site at **Kato Zakro,** through a deep ravine with caves on either side, used for burials in early Minoan times. Ask at one of the cafés for directions to the start of the path. The walk down takes about one hour. You can also drive 9 kilometers (6 miles) down to the site by a circuitous but spectacular route. The village of Kato Zakro, on a fine beach, is a cluster of tavernas with a few rooms to rent. The **Minoan palace,** smaller than those of Knossos, Phaistos, and Mallia, is surrounded by a terraced town with narrow cobbled streets, like Gournia. You enter along a paved Minoan road, which leads up from the harbor through what was once a covered gateway, reaching the northeast court down a stepped ramp. A roofed area to the right covers a bathroom, suggesting that visitors to the palace may first have undergone a ritual cleansing. The splendid rock-crystal rhyton and other treasures now in the Heraklion Museum were found in a treasury in the west wing. The kitchen area was in the north section of the west wing, and the east wing contained a large cistern. The site is badly in need of conservation but, by climbing up to the town above, you can get a clear idea of its ground plan. *Tel. 0841/22462. Admission: 500 dr. Open Tues.–Sun. 8–3.*

Tour 3: Phaistos and Central Crete

South of Heraklion lies the traditional agricultural heartland of Crete: long, narrow valleys where olive groves alternate with vineyards growing sultana grapes for export. The landscape seems unchanging; but in fact, the arrival of phylloxera, a disease that dries up the roots of the vine, has meant that the vineyards are gradually being uprooted and, in many cases, replaced with olives. The olive is less time-consuming to cultivate, which makes it possible for members of a village family to combine farming with summer jobs in the tourist industry.

Leave Heraklion by the Hania Gate and head for the north coast highway. After 2½ kilometers (1½ miles) you turn left, following signs to Mires and Phaistos, and take a narrow road climbing slowly through a vine- and olive-clad valley. Thirty kilometers (19 miles) farther on, you reach the village of **Ayia Varvara,** where the whitewashed church of Profitis Ilias, built high on a rock, is said to mark the center of Crete. The road swings left around the rock, and the Mesara plain comes into view, filled with silver-gray olives, interspersed with plastic greenhouses for growing early tomatoes and cucumbers. The plain spreads down to the craggy Asterousia Mountains; beyond them is the Libyan Sea. In summer especially, the temperature rises sharply as you descend.

In 14 kilometers (8 miles) you come to the village of **Ayii Deka,** built largely of stones removed from the Greco-Roman city of **Gortyna,** a huge expanse of scattered ruins a bit farther south. The 13th-century village church has been restored, but you can still see fragments of sculpture and inscriptions on stones that are part of the walls. Gortyna was made capital by the Romans in 67 AD. The main road slices through the ruins; the best place to stop is at the church of **Ayios Titos,** an early Christian basilica from the 6th century that is supposed to be the saint's burial place. Follow a path to the Odeion, a small amphitheater where musical recitals were staged in the 1st century AD. In the brick building behind it the Gortyna Law Code is displayed, inscribed on a set of stone blocks. This is Europe's earliest code, dating from the first half of the 5th century BC. In 600 lines it details the laws concerning marriage, divorce, inheritance, adoption, assault and rape, and the status of slaves. Another path climbs to the acropolis, which has a fine view across the plain. Italian archaeologists, who have dug here since the 1880s, recently completed a detailed topographical survey. A plan is posted at several points on footpaths around the site, enabling you to find your way through the olives to several temples, a small theater, and the public baths. The city was destroyed by Arab raiders in the 7th century AD and never rebuilt.

Drive west through Mires, a flourishing market town, and turn left for Phaistos and Ayia Triada. You cross the Geropotamos river and climb the hill to the Minoan palace, which is superbly situated, with a panoramic view across the Mesara plain, north to twin-peaked Mt. Ida, Crete's highest mountain (8,058 feet), known locally as Psiloritis. A gray blur beneath the right-hand peak marks the **Kamares Cave,** which gave its name to the delicate Minoan pottery first found there.

Like Knossos and Mallia, the **palace of Phaistos** was built around 1900 BC and rebuilt after a disastrous earthquake around 1650 BC. It was burned and abandoned in the wave of destruction that swept across the island around 1450 BC. You enter down a flight of steps leading into the west court, and climb a grand staircase. From here you pass through the Propylon porch into a lightwell and descend a narrow staircase into the central court. Much of the southern and eastern sections of

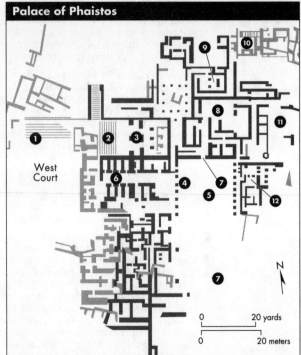

West Court, **1**
Grand Staircase, **2**
Propylon Porch, **3**
Narrow Staircase, **4**
Central Court, **5**
Storerooms, **6**
Elaborate Doorway, **7**
North Court, **8**
Domestic
Apartments, **9**
Phaistos Disk
found, **10**
Palace Workshops, **11**
Domestic
Apartments, **12**

Palace of Phaistos

West
Court

N

0		20 yards
0		20 meters

the palace have eroded away. But there are large *pithoi*—storage jars—still in place in the old palace store-rooms. On the north side of the court is an elaborate doorway, whose recesses bear a rare survival: red paint in a diamond pattern on a white ground. A passage leads to the north court and the domestic apartments, now roofed and fenced off. The Phaistos Disk was found in 1903 in a chest made of mud brick at the northeast edge of the site. East of the central court are the palace workshops, with a metalworking furnace fenced off in the east court. South of there lies a set of domestic apartments, including a clay bath. They have a memorable view across the plain. *Tel. 0892/22615. Admission: 500 dr. Open daily 8–5.*

Time Out You can enjoy as good a view as the Minoans had from the **Phaistos tourist pavilion,** which serves snacks, coffee, and cold drinks.

38 The road to **Ayia Triada** winds around the western end of the Phaistos hill, past a small church. The site dates from the later palace period and was destroyed at the same time as Phaistos. It was once believed to have been a summer palace for the rulers of Phaistos, but now is thought to have been a group of villas and warehouse areas. There's another magnificent view toward the Paximadia islets in the Mesara Gulf. Rooms in the L-shape complex of buildings were paneled with gypsum slabs and decorated with frescoes: Two now in the Heraklion Museum show a woman in a garden and a cat hunting a pheasant. A road from the upper courtyard leads to the sea. *Admission: 500 dr. Open daily 8–5.*

39 Drive back to the main road and turn off for the village of **Vori,** where a well-arranged museum in an old house illustrates Cretan farm life before mechanization started in the 1950s. *Admission free. Open daily 10–6.*

However, if you feel ready for a swim, turn right on the way back to Phaistos from Ayia Triada and head for the coast. After 3 kilometers (2 miles), you hit the main road from Mires to Matala; turn right toward the village of Pitsidia. After 1 kilometer (½ mile), a track to the right leads down to a long sandy beach, one of the best on the south coast and rarely crowded. Above it is the recently excavated Minoan harbor site of **40 41** **Kommos.** The road continues to **Matala,** now a popular resort but renowned in the 1960s as a stopover on the hippie trail across the eastern Mediterranean. The 2nd-century AD Roman tombs cut in the cliffside (where the hippies lived) are now fenced off, but there's good swimming from the rocks below.

Tour 4: Western Crete—Hania and Rethymnon

Western Crete, with soaring mountains, deep gorges, and rolling green lowlands planted with olives and oranges, is much less affected by the growth of mass tourism than the rest of the island. There are no important Minoan sites to visit but, for the independent traveler, a wealth of interesting byways to be explored. This region is rich in Byzantine churches, Venetian monasteries, and friendly upland villages. There are some outstanding beaches on the west and south coasts.

Leaving Heraklion by the Hania Gate, you turn left toward Mires and almost immediately right for the north coast highway. Follow the signs for Rethymnon and Hania. The broad corniche road climbs away from Heraklion bay and then hugs the coastline: There are plenty of places to turn off the road and go for a swim. At 22 kilometers (14 miles) you turn south to **42** **Fodhele,** a straggling village set among orange groves, said to be the birthplace of Domenico Theotocopoulos, the 16th-century Cretan painter known as El Greco. This is a pleasant place for a coffee beneath a spreading plane tree. After 23 kilometers (14 miles) you reach the monastery of **Ayios Ioannis, 43** dedicated to John the Baptist. It is just above the highway, with a spectacular view from its terrace across the Cretan Sea. The White Mountains that dominate western Crete come into view 15 kilometers (9 miles) later, as you drive down toward the coastal plain of Rethymnon. Oddly, they are named for their pale appearance in summer, when the sun glints off bare limestone slopes, rather than for the snow that clings to their summits between December and June.

Soon the old Heraklion–Hania road begins to parallel the coast **44** highway. Make a detour to **Arkadi Monastery** by doubling back along the old road for 3 kilometers (2 miles) from Perivolia, and take a right at the village of Platanias. The road follows a gorge inland before emerging into flat pastureland, part of the monastery holdings. Arkadi is a place of pilgrimage for Cretans and one of the most stunning pieces of Renaissance architecture on the island. Built in the 16th century, of honey-color local stone, it has an ornate facade decorated with Corinthian columns and an elegant belfry above. In 1866, the monastery was besieged during a major rebellion against the Turks, and Abbot Gabriel and several hundred rebels, together with their wives and children, refused to surrender. When the Turkish forces broke through the gate, the defenders set the gunpowder store afire, killing themselves together with hundreds of Turks. *Admission free. Open daily 8–5.*

Time Out Zissi's Taverna (tel. 0831/28814), 3 kilometers (2 miles) outside Rethymnon on the old Heraklion road, is a friendly, family-run place, well known for its spicy homemade sausages and strong local wine.

45 After Heraklion and Hania, **Rethymnon** is the island's next-largest town. As the population (about 30,000) steadily increases, villagers move into new houses on the outskirts of town; the old Venetian quarter is being restored; and the port has been expanded, allowing Rethymnon to have its own ferry service. The town is dominated by the huge Venetian castle at its western end known as the **Fortetsa.** High, well-preserved walls enclose a large empty space occupied by a few scattered buildings and filled with wildflowers in spring. Forced labor from the town and surrounding villages built the fortress from 1573 to 1583, but it never fulfilled its purpose of keeping out the Turks: Rethymnon surrendered after a three-week siege. The **archaeological museum** next to the fortress entrance is in what used to be a Turkish prison. Look for the collection of beautifully made bone tools from a Neolithic site at Yerani, west of Rethymnon. An unfinished statue of Aphrodite, the goddess of love, is interesting: The ancient chisel marks show clearly. *Tel. 0831/29975. Admission: 500 dr. Open Tues.–Sun. 8:30–3.*

The long, sandy beach at Rethymnon is one of its main attractions; you can step out of a hotel on the seafront and jump into the sea. But the town's real charm lies in the old section. Wandering through the narrow alleyways you come across handsome carved-stone Renaissance doorways belonging to vanished mansions, fountains, archways, wooden Turkish houses, and one of the few surviving minarets in Greece. It belongs to the **Neratzes mosque,** now a concert hall, and you can climb its 120 steps for a panoramic view. Don't miss the carefully restored **Venetian loggia,** the clubhouse of the local nobility. The small **Venetian harbor,** with its restored 13th-century lighthouse, comes to life in summer, with restaurant tables cluttering the quayside.

The north coast highway continues west toward Hania. At 21½ kilometers (13 miles) from Rethymnon, you can turn right for **46 Georgioupolis,** named for Prince George of Greece, the high commissioner of Crete from 1898 to 1906, who built a shooting lodge here, where migrating birds gather, at the mouth of the Vrysanos river. There are several good fish tavernas and a wide choice of rooms to rent.

Time Out Back on the main road, after 5 kilometers (3 miles) you reach **47 Vrisses,** famous throughout Crete for its thick, creamy yogurt, served in the cafés beneath the plane trees as you come into the village. It's best eaten with a large spoonful of honey on top.

Vrisses is also the turnoff point for a spectacular detour, a drive across Crete to Hora Sfakia and Frangokastello on the south coast. The road south winds up the Askyphou plain, overlooked by an Ottoman fort on a knob-shaped hill, and then descends to the Libyan Sea, following the line of the **Nimbros gorge.** After 36 kilometers (22½ miles) take a left turn for **Frangokastello,** a medieval Venetian fort (with rooms to rent), overlooking a fine sandy beach. Backtrack west about 10 kilometers (6 miles) to **Hora Sfakia,** the landing point for the boat trip from the mouth of the Samaria Gorge, farther west. It gets crowded with buses and walkers in the early evening, but is otherwise a tranquil place where you can find a taverna.

Drive back to Vrisses, where the road to Hania climbs across the Vamos peninsula, and **Souda Bay** comes into view. This deep inlet, considered the best harbor in the eastern Mediterranean, can shelter the entire U.S. Sixth Fleet. Looking north across the bay to the Akrotiri peninsula, you can spot a small islet topped with a Venetian fort, guarding the harbor's inner reaches, which is now part of a large Greek naval base with installations all around the harbor. Taking photos is forbidden around Souda Bay, a regulation to be taken seriously: If you are caught doing so you may be charged with spying. At the top of the bay, turn right for **Souda** port, where passenger ferries from Piraeus dock, and on to Hania.

A long avenue lined with eucalyptus trees takes you to the outskirts of Hania, where signs lead you around the one-way system to the large cross-shaped covered market in the town center. With its well-preserved Venetian harbor and old quarter, **Hania** is one of the most attractive towns in Greece. It was here that the Greek flag was raised in 1913 to mark unification with Greece, and until 1971 it was the island's capital. On Sunday the flag-raising ceremony is repeated at the **Firka,** the old Turkish prison, now the naval museum, on the waterfront (check the opening hours with the EOT information office). Take a stroll through the **covered market,** where local merchants sell rounds of Cretan cheese, jars of golden honey, lengths of salami, salt fish, lentils, and other pulses from sacks. Then work your way through a maze of narrow streets to the waterfront, which is a pedestrian zone in summer. Walk around the inner harbor, where the fishing boats moor, past the **Venetian arsenals** and around to the **old lighthouse,** for a magnificent view of the town with the imposing White Mountains looming beyond. The **Janissaries mosque,** now a tourist information center, was built when the Turks captured the town in 1645 after a two-month siege. The Kastelli hill above the harbor, where the Venetians first settled, remained the quarter of the local nobility, but it had been occupied much earlier; parts of what may be a Minoan palace have been excavated at its base.

Behind the outer harbor, either Theotocopoulou or Zambeliou street will lead you into the narrow alleyways where almost all the houses are Venetian or Turkish. In Parodos Kondylaki, look for an old synagogue, formerly the Venetian church of St. Catherine and now a warehouse. The **archaeological museum** occupies the Venetian church of St. Francis. Finds on display come from all over western Crete: The painted Minoan clay coffins and elegant Late Minoan pottery indicate that the region was as wealthy as the center of the island in the Bronze Age, though no full-scale palace has yet been located. *Tel. 0821/20334. Admission: 500 dr. Open Tues.–Fri. 8:30–3.*

East of town is the Halepa suburb, whose fine neoclassical mansions date from the turn of the century, when Britain,

France, Russia, and Italy were active in Cretan politics. Follow airport signs on the Akrotiri road, and turn left after 4½ kilometers (3 miles) for **Profitis Ilias,** the burial place of Eleftherios Venizelos, Crete's great statesman. A panoramic view from here takes in Hania and its surrounding villages, along with much of the northwest coast.

There are good beaches at **Stavros** and **Kalathas** on the Akrotiri peninsula, about 10 kilometers (6 miles) farther out. Or you can head south or west (the main roads are narrow and twisting but fairly well-surfaced). In summer, a boat service operates along the **southwest coast** from Hora Sfakia to Loutro, Ayia Roumeli, Souyia, Lissos, and **Paleochora,** the main resort on the southwest coast. You can easily rent a room for the night in these towns. The islet of **Elafonisi,** close to the southwest corner of Crete, has white sand beaches and black rocks set in a turquoise sea (to get there, you wade across a narrow channel). A good road that now traverses the west coast from Elafonisi north has opened up access to beaches that are rarely crowded even in summer. One of these is the fine beach at **Falasarna,** near Crete's northwest tip.

What to See and Do with Children

There is practically no provision made on Crete for the specific amusement of children, but people take them everywhere, and Cretans will welcome yours. Just remember that there is a limit to most children's tolerance for ruins, which can be greatly extended by frequent administrations of ice cream and cold drinks, and many dunkings in the sea, a pleasure in itself.

Off the Beaten Track

The **Samaria Gorge,** at 17 kilometers (10½ miles), is the longest in Europe. It starts at **Xyloskala** (wood staircase), 44 kilometers (27½ miles) south of Hania, and descends in a steep curve to the Libyan Sea. The hike down it takes six hours and is one of the most memorable experiences you can have on Crete. You start early in the morning, descending the precipitous staircase from the high Omalos plain. The going is stony in places: Wear tough shoes, and take a water bottle and a swimsuit—the reward at the end is a dip in the sea. From Ayia Roumeli, where the gorge debouches on to the coast, you take a boat to Hora Sfakia and make the return trip to Hania by bus. Unless you are prepared to wrestle with local bus timetables, it is best to go with an organized tour; avoid Sunday in summer, when the gorge is overcrowded. Late June and October are the best times of year.

The triangular **island of Gavdhos,** the southernmost point of Europe, is a two-hour boat journey from Paleochora at the western end of the south coast.

On Gavdhos, covered with juniper bushes, the beautiful sorceress Calypso seduced Odysseus, who was on his way home from Troy, and kept him prisoner for seven years.

More prosaically, Gavdhos was a prison island in the 1920s and 1930s for political exiles, who built some of the rough stone houses scattered across the island. Now there are just 60 residents, who rely on an experimental solar power station for electricity—enough is generated to keep drinks cool at the two fish tavernas where you can also find rooms to rent. There are superb sandy beaches at Korfos, Sarakiniki, and Potamos. For the boat timetable, check with the Paleochora harbor authority (tel. 0823/41214) or Sfakia harbor authority (tel. 0825/91292).

To get to **Tylissos** and the **Nidha Plateau,** leave Heraklion by the Hania Gate and take the old road to Rethymnon. At 10½ kilometers (6½ miles) turn left; the road winds uphill through vineyards to the village of Tylissos. The Minoan site lies to the left of the road at the 14-kilometer (9-mile) mark; there are three later Palace-period buildings in the pine-shaded complex: workshops, living quarters, and storerooms. *Admission: 500 dr. Open Tues.–Sun. 8:30–3*.

Five kilometers (3 miles) beyond Tylissos the road cuts through another Minoan building of the same period, the villa of **Sklavokampos,** and 11 kilometers (7 miles) farther on you reach **Anoyia,** in the foothills of Mt. Ida, a sprawling mountain village with a tradition of weavings done in bright colors. Its buildings are modern because Anoyia was razed during World War II in reprisal for the capture of the commander of the German occupying force.

From Anoyia drive south across the **Nidha plateau** 4,600 feet above sea level, where the scenery is magnificently wild and dotted with shepherds' stone huts. There is a newly discovered Minoan villa at **Zominthos,** 15 kilometers (9 miles) on, which is now being excavated by Greek archaeologists. Continue on and take a left fork to the **Idaean cave** (IdeoAndro), which was a place of pilgrimage for thousands of years, from Minoan through Roman times.

When Zeus was a baby he was hidden in the Idaean cave to protect him from his jealous father, Kronos.

After you park outside the café at the base of the slope, a 15-minute walk takes you up to the cave. It is now fenced off to protect the antiquities inside, but the air is invigorating and the view superb.

Shopping

Crete is a serendipitous place for the shopper. Little serious attempt has been made to adapt the island's traditional crafts to the demands of foreign customers, but by poking around the back streets of **Heraklion, Rethymnon,** and **Hania,** you can find things both useful and exotic—and sometimes even beautiful. Crete was famous even in Minoan times for its weaving. You still occasionally come across the heavy scarlet-embroidered blankets and bedspreads that formed the basis of a traditional dowry chest. Woven wool rugs in plain geometric designs from the village of **Axos** on the slopes of Mt. Ida are attractive, as are heavy sweaters in natural oily wool. Local craftsmen produce attractive copies of Minoan jewelry in gold and silver, as well as some with original modern designs. A shepherd's kit, a striped woven haversack and a staff, comes in useful for the hiker. Bootmakers in **Heraklion** and **Hania** will make you a pair of heavy Cretan leather kneeboots to order. A Cretan knife, whether plain steel or with a decorated blade and handle, makes a handy kitchen or camping implement. In the village of **Thrapsano,** 20 kilometers (12½ miles) southeast of Heraklion, at one of the potteries you can choose a new *pithos,* the tall Ali

Baba–style jar used by the Minoans for storing wine and oil and still popular today (often as a flower pot): Have it air-freighted home. Also, some Cretan produce travels well: perhaps a can of olive oil, or of Cretan olives, a packet of dittany (a tangy herb used for making tea), or a supply of crunchy barley rusks, and in cool weather a small *graviera* cheese (check customs regulations about importing foodstuffs).

Sports and Outdoor Activities

Bird-Watching

Bird-watchers have access to a huge variety of bird life, though most species are not resident. A bird sanctuary is being set up at the Gouves estuary east of Heraklion, which is a stopover for a large range of migratory birds. Details are available from the Grecotel group, which runs the Creta Sun Hotel (tel. 0831/71602), next door to the site. Mt. Iuktas, south of Heraklion, is the place to spot vultures.

Bicycling

Bicycle rentals are available in all Cretan towns. Mountain bikes for cycling in the uplands are now easier to find; ask at the **G & A Travel Agency** (Halidon 25, tel. 0821/28817) in Hania or at the **Grecotel Rithymna Beach** hotel in Rethymnon (*see* Dining and Lodging, *below*). Crete is rewarding biking country. Though the White Mountains of the west are for hardened addicts, there is plenty of pleasant riding in the gentler landscapes of eastern Crete. Ask at the **Creta Tours** (Epimenidou 20–22, tel. 081/227002) travel agency in Heraklion.

Hiking

Crete provides both the casual walker and the experienced hiker with challenging opportunities. There are no island-wide trails yet, but the **Greek Mountaineering Association** operates refuges in the White Mountains (tel. 0821/24647) and on Mt. Ida (tel. 081/267110), and has marked numerous paths, especially in the south of the island. Trekking can be arranged from Hania; ask for details at the Greek Tourist Organization office.

Water Sports

Water-sports enthusiasts will find Windsurfers available for rent on any beach frequented by tourists. Scuba diving, snorkeling, dinghy sailing, and yacht rentals are available at large resort hotels or can be arranged through local travel agencies; ask at an EOT or municipal-information office.

Dining and Lodging

Dining   Crete cannot claim to be a center of gastronomy, but ingredients are always fresh, and the family-run tavernas take pride in their cooking. The island produces top-quality fruit and vegetables—cherries from the Amari valley in June, oranges from the groves around Hania in winter, tomatoes and cucumbers all year round, and, increasingly, avocados and bananas. The Cretans enjoy grilled meat, generally lamb and pork, but there is also plenty of fresh fish. Cretan *graviera* cheese is prized, along with *mizythra*, a creamy white variety. Cretan olive oil is famous throughout Greece, though it's heavier than other varieties. The island's wines are improving fast: Look for Boutari Kritikos, a crisp white, and Minos Palace, a smooth red. Wine from the barrel is best in eastern Crete, where local growers produce full-bodied reds. Retsina is not part of the Cretan tradition, but can be found in town restaurants.

In restaurants, oven-cooked dishes (*mayirefta*) are prepared in the morning and are best eaten at lunch. Never feel shy about looking them over in the kitchen. In a fish taverna, you will be expected to select your own fish from the ice tray: To check its freshness, make sure the eyes gleam brightly and lift the gills to see if they are a healthy pink. As a rule, it is hard to go hungry in Crete; in a village *cafeneion*, you can almost always order salad and an omelet or eggs fried with graviera cheese. Make sure you try *tsikouthia* (also known as *raki*), the Cretan firewater, which is drunk at any time of day, sometimes accompanied by a dish of raisins, or walnuts in a pool of honey.

You will almost certainly eat better in a taverna or restaurant than at a hotel, where (unless you are staying at a first-class resort) the menu is usually of the bland "international" variety. Hotel desk clerks understand this and willingly recommend a choice of tavernas. Dress is invariably casual, though shorts are not worn in the evenings, and reservations are unnecessary unless noted. Credit cards are usually accepted only in more expensive restaurants.

Highly recommended restaurants are indicated by a star ★.

Category	Cost*
Very Expensive	over 8,000 dr.
Expensive	5,000 dr.–8,000 dr.
Moderate	3,000 dr.–5,000 dr.
Inexpensive	under 3,000 dr.

per person for a 3-course meal, including tax and service and excluding drinks

Lodging Crete offers a wide range of accommodation, from luxury hotels with sports and entertainment facilities that compare with anywhere in the Mediterranean, to simple whitewashed, cement-floor rooms in seaside villages. Many moderately priced hotels are undistinguished concrete blocks with little character, though this is starting to change.

Unless the months of closing are noted, a hotel is open year-round. Prices rise sharply in June and come down again in mid-September, but even in high season you can often negotiate a discount at medium-priced hotels if you are staying more than a night or two. Resort hotels sometimes require half-board (MAP); many will give substantial discounts at the beginning and end of the season. If you are staying in Hania or Heraklion in July or August, you may want to pay a little more for a room with air-conditioning. Travel agencies, the local Greek Tourist Organization (EOT) offices, and the tourist police all will help you find accommodation at short notice. In villages, ask at the *kafeneion* about rooms for rent. Standards of cleanliness are high in Crete and service is friendly.

Category	Cost*
Very Expensive	over 20,000 dr.
Expensive	14,000 dr.–20,000 dr.
Moderate	9,000 dr.–14,000 dr.
Inexpensive	under 9,000 dr.

All prices are for a standard double room including breakfast and tax.

Ayios Nikolaos
Dining

Itanos Restaurant. This old-fashioned taverna is patronized by locals, as it offers much better value than most seafront establishments. The wine comes from a row of barrels in the kitchen. In summer you dine on a terrace above the square with a view of the town's comings and goings around the formal arrangement of palm trees at its center. The oven-cooked meatballs, *soutzoukakia*, are tender and spicy, and vegetable dishes like braised artichokes or green beans with tomato are full of flavor. *Plateialroon. No credit cards. Inexpensive.*

Lodging
★

Elounda Beach. This is one of Greece's most renowned resort hotels, set in 40 acres of gardens looking across the Mirabello Gulf. Built in 1973 and renovated regularly since then, it has inspired imitations on a half dozen other Aegean islands. The architecture reflects Cretan tradition: whitewashed walls, shady porches, and cool flagstone floors. You can have a room in the central block or a bungalow at the edge of the sea. The hotel has two sandy beaches and a wide range of beach and water sports, from windsurfing and dinghy sailing to scuba diving and para-sailing. There is a miniature Greek village, complete with cafeneion and church, and an open-air amphitheater for movies and dancing. Meals are lavish and the wine list varied. The Dionysos Taverna offers a successful mixture of Greek and French cooking—its specialty is lobster flambée with ouzo. *Elounda 72053, tel. 0841/41412 or 0841/41413, fax 0841/41373. 150 rooms with bath, 150 bungalows. Facilities: air-conditioning, satellite TV, sauna, Jacuzzi, Turkish bath, tennis, minigolf, water sports. AE, DC, MC, V. Closed Nov.–Mar. Very Expensive (steep reductions Apr. and Oct.).*

Akti Olous. This friendly, unassuming hotel on the edge of the Mirabello Gulf is just a step away from a strip of sandy beach and a short swim from the sunken city of Olous—its remains are easy to spot while snorkeling. Manolis Zervos and his family can organize anything from lessons in Cretan dancing to a squid-fishing trip on a local boat. The rooftop bar has a stunning view across the gulf, especially at sunset. The rooms, decorated with Cretan weavings, are small, but all have balconies overlooking the sea. *Elounda, 72053, tel. 0841/41270, fax 0841/41425. 65 rooms with shower. No credit cards. Closed Nov.–Mar. Inexpensive.*

Hania
Dining

An almost unbroken row of tavernas lines the old harbor in summer. Their menus are nearly identical and almost all offer grills and fresh fish at reasonable prices. Among those frequented by Haniots are **Ta Kavouria,** on the ground floor of the Plaza Hotel opposite the Turkish kiosk; **Dinos,** which spreads onto the waterfront from a barrel-shape Venetian vault on the inner harbor, and almost next door, **Apostolis.** On the outer harbor is **Karnagio,** where Cretan specialties are served. *No credit cards. Inexpensive.*

Dining and Lodging   **Doma.** This converted 19th-century mansion on the outskirts of town has the welcoming atmosphere of a private house. Once the Austrian consulate and later the British vice-consulate, it now belongs to Rena Valyrakis. The sitting room, complete with fireplace, is in traditional Cretan style: The comfortable armchairs and settees have embroidered scarlet bolsters, and there are exotic artifacts such as fragments of marble with Ottoman and Hebrew inscriptions. The top-floor dining room, decorated with old family photos, has a memorable view across the bay to the old town. Bedrooms are cozy, but the front rooms can be noisy in summer; ask for one overlooking the garden. Breakfast includes homemade jams and yogurt with a Turkish topping: a delicious mix of spices, quince preserve, and honey. Mrs. Valyrakis will prepare a traditional dinner on request; a popular Cretan specialty is lamb roasted in red wine. *124 Eleftherios Venizelou St., 73100, tel. 0821/21772 or 0821/21773, fax 0821/23040. 28 rooms with shower. DC, MC, V. Closed Nov.–Mar. Moderate.*

Lodging   **Villa Andromeda.** This elegantly restored neoclassical mansion in the suburb of Halepa, with gleaming marble floors, painted ceilings, and period furniture, was formerly the German consulate. It belongs to the Naxakis family, who now live next door and offer friendly, helpful service. The rooms all have views of the sea or the mountains, and are luxuriously furnished. Next to the swimming pool in the garden is a curious historical remnant: a much smaller pool built for General Rommel in World War II. *150 Eleftherios Venizelou, 73133, tel. 0821/45263 or 0821/45264, fax 0821/45265. 8 rooms with bath. Facilities: satellite TV, air-conditioning. AE, DC, MC, V. Closed Nov.–Mar. Very Expensive.*

★ **Casa Delfino.** A unique small hotel in the heart of the old town, this was once part of a Venetian Renaissance palace. The rooms are set behind graceful stone archways surrounding a courtyard paved in pebble mosaic, with a huge urn filled with greenery at its center. It belongs to two descendants of Pedro Delfino, an Italian merchant who lived in the house in the 1880s. Most rooms are on two levels, with a sleeping area above and bathroom and sitting room below. The view takes in the medieval harbor and the old town, but you are protected by thick stone walls from the noise of nearby bars and tavernas. The rooms are done in cool pastels with stylish modern furniture. *Theofanous 9, Palio Limani, 73100, tel. 0821/42613, fax 0821/46500. 12 rooms with bath. Facilities: minibar, air-conditioning. DC, MC, V. Expensive.*

Porto Veneziano. This modern block on the waterfront of the inner harbor is considered an eyesore by locals. But if you are staying in it you are immune to its appearance; your balcony looks out over one of the best-preserved medieval harbors in the Mediterranean, filled with fishing boats and guarded by a Venetian lighthouse. Breakfast is served on a landing stage where you can watch the fishermen hanging out freshly caught octopus to soften in the sun. The hotel belongs to the Platsidakis family, who are friendly and knowledgeable about the local scene. The rooms have little character and could do with some refurbishing, but the air-conditioning is welcome in the height of a Cretan summer. *Palio Limani, 73100, tel. 0821/ 29311, 0821/29312, or 0821/29313, fax 0821/27470. 60 rooms with bath or shower. DC, MC, V. Moderate.*

Pension Eva. This is one of a growing number of small pensions in renovated Venetian houses in the old town. The wooden ceilings, small deep-set windows, and flat terraced roof recall the past; there are large brass beds, and the walls are hung with faded pictures of 19th-century Cretan revolutionaries. Each room has a refrigerator and a gas burner for making coffee. *Theofanous and Zambeliou Sts., 73100, tel. 0821/55319. 6 rooms with shower. No credit cards. Closed Dec.–Mar. Inexpensive.*

Heraklion
Dining

La Parisienne. Heraklion's popular French restaurant, in a narrow street behind Ayios Titos church, is the place to enjoy a change from taverna fare. The proprietor, Pierre Miessen, offers traditional dishes like boeuf Bourguignonne and coq au vin. His fondue, made with Cretan cheeses, is a favorite for parties of four or more. The setting is almost medieval, with candlelight flickering over antique Flemish furniture. *Ayiou Titou 7, tel. 081/240966. Reservations advised. DC, MC, V. No lunch. Closed Wed. Moderate–Expensive.*

Kyriakos. With its pink tablecloths and green chairs, this is no ordinary taverna. Just a short walk from the Galaxy Hotel, Kyriakos offers a wide range of well-prepared salads, grills, and fish dishes. Watch for seasonal Cretan specialties, such as snail stew in summer and *volvi*, baked iris bulbs in olive oil and vinegar, in spring. There is a good wine list, with Cretan and mainland wines. *Leoforos Dimokratias 43, tel. 081/224649. Reservations advised for dinner. AE, DC. Moderate.*

Nea Ionia. Frequented by villagers doing business in town, this old-fashioned restaurant near the open-air market offers a variety of mayirefta, like lamb fricassee and lamb *youvetsi*, Greek lunchtime staples that are hard to find in the tourist resorts. *Odos Evans. No credit cards. Inexpensive.*

Terzakis. This unassuming establishment behind Ayios Dimitrios church is one of Heraklion's most popular *meze* houses, where you choose half a dozen or more dishes from a long list of fish, dips, and salads. Traditionally *meze* is accompanied by ouzo, but beer or wine are equally acceptable. *Loh. Marineli 17, tel. 081/221444. No credit cards. No Sun. dinner. Inexpensive.*

Yacoumis. This is reputed to be the best of the small restaurants in the covered alley leading off the market. You find Meat Alley by following the aroma of roasting meat and clouds of steam wafting out between the stalls. Sizzling chunks of spit-roasted lamb and pork are sold by weight, accompanied by salads of roughly sliced tomatoes and onions, drenched in thick Cretan olive oil. *No credit cards. Closed Sun. Inexpensive.*

Lodging

Galaxy. This modern hotel just outside the city center is efficiently run and popular with Greek businessmen, but its decoration and furnishings are on the drab side. To avoid traffic noise, make sure you ask for an inside room on an upper floor. But apart from the Galaxy's convenient location on the road to Knossos, there are two good reasons for making it your base—the swimming pool and the coffee shop, which offers the best patisserie in town. *Leoforos Dimokratias 67, 71306, tel. 081/ 232157 or 081/238812, fax 081/211211. 120 rooms with bath. Fa-*

cilities: restaurant, coffee shop, air-conditioning, pool, sauna. DC, MC, V. Expensive.

Astoria Capsis. Conveniently located opposite the archaeological museum in the liveliest area of the city, this old-fashioned hotel is overdue for refurbishment and can be noisy, but it has a rooftop swimming pool and is fully air-conditioned. *Plateia Eleftherias, 71201, tel. 081/229002, fax 081/229078. 120 rooms with bath. Facilities: restaurant, coffee shop, air-conditioning, bar, swimming pool. AE, DC, MC, V. Moderate.*

Amnisos. This beach hotel 7 kilometers (4 miles) east of Heraklion is a convenient place to avoid the city heat and crowds. The long sandy beach at Amnisos, backed by the ruins of a Minoan port, gets crowded in the afternoons, but there is plenty of space early and late in the day. The hotel, set in attractive gardens, has a slightly dilapidated air, but the simply furnished rooms are spotlessly clean. There are tennis and volleyball courts, water sports, and a fair-size pool. *Karteros, 71500, tel. 081/240012 or 081/240034, fax 081/223008. 60 rooms with shower. Facilities: restaurant, pool, bar, playground, tennis and volleyball courts. No credit cards. Closed Oct.–Mar. Inexpensive.*

★ **Atrion.** This well-run hotel tucked away in a quiet street behind the Historical Museum is fully air-conditioned. There is a generous breakfast buffet, and drinks are served in the evening in a tiny patio-garden. *Palaiologou 9, 71202, tel. 081/229225 or 081/242830, fax 081/223292. 50 rooms with bath or shower. Facilities: restaurant, air-conditioning, parking. DC, MC, V. Inexpensive.*

Daedalos. On a pedestrian street of the same name in the city center, this small hotel is shabby but extremely friendly. The owner, Takis Stoumbidis, used to run an art gallery, and the rooms and corridors are lined with Cretan landscapes. The ground-floor bar is a local gathering place, where you may run into a distinguished archaeologist or folklorist downing a glass of *tsikouthia*. *Daidalou 15, 71202, tel. 081/224391 through 081/224395. 60 rooms with shower. DC, MC, V. Inexpensive.*

Ierapetra
Dining and Lodging
★

Lyktos Beach. This luxury resort hotel, 7 kilometers (4 miles) east of Ierapetra, has put southeast Crete on the map. The Lyktos has the best sports facilities on the island, with seven floodlit tennis courts. It is decorated in cool blues with dark polished wood floors, and the rooms have broad balconies for breakfasting with a view. Entertainment is lavish, with satellite TV, a video library, a nightclub, disco, and piano bar. The three restaurants offer taverna-style cooking, international fare, and French cuisine. *Koutsounari 72200, tel. 0842/61280, 0842/61740, or 0842/61745, fax 0842/61318. 250 rooms with bath. Facilities: 3 restaurants, 6 bars, air-conditioning, satellite TV, sauna, massage, Jacuzzi, tennis, water sports, gymnasium, video library, card room. AE, DC, MC, V. Closed Nov.–Apr. Very Expensive.*

Lodging **Astron.** Opened in 1992, this comfortable hotel overlooks a quiet stretch of waterfront at the edge of town. The beach is just a minute away. All rooms have balconies with a sea view. The coffee shop looks onto a pleasant interior courtyard with a fountain. *Mihail Kothri 56, 72200, tel. 0842/25114 through 0842/25117, fax 0842/25917. 70 rooms with bath. Facilities: air-conditioning, minibar, restaurant, coffee shop, snack bar. V. Closed Nov.–Apr. Moderate.*

Rethymnon
Dining
★

Cava D'Oro. This is the most stylish of the handful of fish restaurants around the tiny Venetian harbor that offer air-conditioned dining. The long wood-panel room was once a medieval storeroom, and there are tables on the cobbled waterfront as well. Lobster and a wide range of fresh fish are always available. *Nearchou 42–43, tel. 0831/24446. DC, MC, V. Expensive.*

Taverna George. Just down from the Venetian Fortetsa, this pleasant taverna well above the noisy beachfront catches a welcome evening breeze in summer. The menu is a combination of traditional Greek cooking and some international dishes. George's specialties are pepper steak and *stifado*, a rich stew sometimes made with hare. *Heimaras St., no tel. No credit cards. Inexpensive.*

Dining and Lodging
★

Grecotel Rithymna Beach. On a long sandy beach 7 kilometers (4 miles) east of town, this comfortable old resort hotel offers excellent food and service and features an in-house children's camp. A meal at the taverna beside the swimming pool is a feast of traditional dishes, beautifully presented. A typical lunch might begin with a series of dips—creamy *taramosalata* and *tzatziki*—and different kinds of miniature cheese pies, followed by spicy village sausage or fresh-grilled sea bass, and salads. The French restaurant, Le Gourmet (also open to nonresidents) offers a range of classics, from sole meunière to veal with calvados, and chateaubriand. The wine list includes Cretan, mainland Greek, Cypriot, and French wines. *Rethymnon, 74100, tel. 0831/71002 or 0831/29491, fax 0831/71668. 414 rooms with bath. Facilities: 3 restaurants, cafeneion, air-conditioning, satellite TV, 2 pools, fitness club, water sports, tennis, bridge and video rooms, children's camp. AE, DC, MC, V. Closed Nov.–Apr. Expensive.*

Lodging
★

Porto Rethymno. This strikingly designed hotel on the town waterfront opened in 1992. You enter through a shopping mall, whose facade is of the same creamy local stone used by the town's medieval builders. Ask for a room high up (to escape street noise), with a view across the bay to the old Venetian fortress. The hotel has its own beachfront and most of the facilities of a resort, despite being only five minutes from the town center. Tennis and other sports are available at the Grecotel Rithymna Beach (*see above*), a sister hotel in the Grecotel chain. *Paralia, 74100, tel. 0831/20821, fax 0831/27825. 200 rooms with bath. Facilities: restaurant, snack bar, air-conditioning, swimming pool, water sports, fitness club, Jacuzzi, Turkish bath. AE, DC, MC, V. Expensive.*

Kyma Beach. This comfortable hotel overlooking the town beach has a ground-floor café-restaurant that's a popular gathering place for young Rethymnians. To avoid traffic noise, ask for a room on an upper floor. *Plateia Iroon, 74100, tel. 0831/21503 or 0831/21504, fax 0831/22353. 40 rooms with shower. DC, MC, V. Moderate.*

Liberty. This quiet, friendly, family-owned hotel opposite a park has a roof garden with an attractive view up to the hills overlooking the town. The rooms are small but comfortable. *Themis Moatsou 8, 74100, tel. and fax 0831/21850. 24 rooms with shower. DC, MC, V. Inexpensive.*

Siteia
Lodging

Itanos. In a town that still lacks a comfortable modern hotel, this friendly but characterless establishment is the best bet if you decide to make an overnight stop on the way to Zakro.

Eleftheriou Venizelou, 72300, tel. 0843/22146, fax 0843/22915. 72 rooms with shower. AE, DC, V. Inexpensive.

The Arts and Nightlife

The Arts

Crete has few serious arts activities and events. Though the island attracts painters from all over Europe, they rarely exhibit locally. In Heraklion, Rethymnon, and, occasionally, Hania, however, local authorities sometimes organize concerts, theater, and folk dancing events during the summer. Athenian and even some foreign musical groups stage open-air performances in the Koules fort at Heraklion and the Fortetsa at Rethymnon. Ask at the Greek Tourist Organization offices for up-to-date booking information. In winter, both local and visiting choirs and chamber music groups perform occasionally. The town hall will have information on times and bookings.

Nightlife

An evening out in Crete is generally spent in a *kentron*, a taverna that features traditional Cretan music and dancing. The star performer is the *lyra* player, who can extract a surprisingly subtle sound from the small pear-shape instrument, held upright on his thigh and played with a bow. Cretan dances range from monotonous circling to astonishing displays of athletic agility, but much depends on the *kefi* (enthusiasm) of the participants. In winter, the Kentron moves indoors and becomes a more typical bouzouki joint. Ask at your hotel where the best-known lyra players are performing.

There are discos in every resort hotel and almost every seaside village. Heraklion and Hania have a wide variety of bars: Check with your hotel to find out which are the hot places. Most resort hotels organize weekly displays of Cretan dancing; many also offer lessons, so guests can join in. But the most spontaneously enjoyable events of this kind are village *panayiria*, the festivals of local saints, when everyone gets drunk and dances into the early hours. If you are lucky, you may be invited to a *glendi*, a local party, or even a traditional Cretan village wedding, where the celebrations can last 24 hours.

9 Rhodes and the Dodecanese

Kos, Patmos, and Symi

*By Catherine
Vanderpool*

At the eastern edge of the Aegean Sea, rimming the west coast of Asia Minor, lies a string of Greek islands, many just a few kilometers or less offshore. The southernmost group is called the Dodecanese (Twelve Islands), sometimes known as the Southern Sporades. Of them, the largest by far is Rhodes, for many years one of the most popular vacation spots in the Mediterranean; best known of the others are Kos, Patmos, and Symi. The dozen islands, plus additional tiny members of the archipelago (the administrative Nome of the Dodecanese), have long shared a common history and fate. The landscapes, however, are sharply contrasting. Patmos, Karpathos, and Kassos, for example, resemble in some ways the Cycladic islands: rugged hills and mountains almost devoid of vegetation, with villages and towns clinging in picturesque disarray to craggy landscapes. Rhodes and Kos unfold in fertile splendor, creased with streams and dotted with large stretches of green; their major towns lie on almost flat land next to the sea, embracing exceptionally large and well-protected harbors facing the mainland of Asia Minor. Leros, perhaps the greenest, is seldom visited by foreigners; its splendid harbor is adorned with monumental examples of Italian fascist architecture constructed in the 1930s in expectation of a glory that never came. Kalymnos, home to what was once one of the main sponge-diving fleets of the Mediterranean, still shows traces of its former prosperity, and its native sons have done well by their island and their town, whose colorfully painted houses ornament the amphitheatrical harborside. At the very edge of the archipelago, connected only administratively, is Kastellorizo, a lonely outpost that has lost much of its population to emigration.

Of the Twelve Islands, strategically located Rhodes has played by far the most important role in history, with Kos coming second, particularly in antiquity, when its famous Sanctuary of Asklepeios, a center of healing, drew people from all over the ancient world. Both islands are worth visits of several days each. Symi, easily accessible from Rhodes, is a virtual museum of 19th-century neoclassical architecture, and Patmos, where St. John wrote his Revelations, became a renowned monastic center during the Byzantine period and continues as a significant focal point of the Greek Orthodox faith.

Essential Information

Important Addresses and Numbers

Tourist
Information

The Greek National Tourist Organization in **Rhodes** (Archbishop Makarios and Papagou, in the new city, close to the medieval walls, tel. 0241/23655, 0241/23255, 0241/27466, or fax 0241/26955) is one of the largest and most efficient in Greece; there are also GNTO offices in **Kos** (Koundouriotis, tel. 0242/28724 or 0242/24460) and **Patmos** (Skala, tel. 0247/31166 or 0247/31158).

Emergencies

Kos: police, tel. 0242/22222, tourist police, tel. 0242/28227. **Patmos:** hospital, tel. 0247/31211; police, tel. 0247/31100 and 0247/31303. **Rhodes:** hospital, tel. 166 or 0241/22222; police, tel. 100; tourist police, tel. 0241/27423.

Late-Night
Pharmacies

As elsewhere in Greece, pharmacies post in their windows a list showing which ones are open 24-hours, on which days, under the rotating system.

Travel Agencies **Kos:** Aeolos Travel, 17 Artemisias, tel. 0242/26203, 0242/24310, or 0242/21549; fax 0242/25948. **Patmos:** Apollon Travel, Skala Harbor, tel. 0247/31324, 0247/31356, or 0247/31724; fax 0247/31819. Astoria Travel, Skala Harbor, tel. 0247/31205 or 0247/31208; fax 0247/31975; **Rhodes:** Triton Holidays, 25 N. Plastira, tel. 0241/21778, 0241/21690 or 0241/21691; fax 0241/31625. **Symi:** Symi Tourist & Travel Agency, Symi Harbor, tel. 0241/71307 or 0241/71689, fax 0241/72292. Both Aeolos in Kos and Triton in Rhodes are large travel agencies with extensive networks in the Dodecanese, and will be very helpful in arranging travel to other, less-frequented islands.

Car Rental **Rhodes:** AI-Ansa International Rent-A-Car (45 Organidou, tel. 0241/31895 or 0241/31811); Eurodollar (7 Ioannis Kazouli, tel. 0241/91718); Interrent-EuropCar (18 28th October, tel. 0241/21958, fax 0241/30923 or Rhodes Airport, 0241/93105). **Kos:** Interrent-EuropCar (28 El. Venezelou, tel. 0242/24070, 1; fax 0242/25180).

Arriving and Departing by Plane

Olympic Airways (in Athens tel. 01/966–6666, fax 01/961828; at Rhodes airport, tel. 0241/92981, 0241/92982, or 0241/92983) has at least five flights per day to **Rhodes** from Athens, and extra flights are added during high season. The flight takes less than an hour and costs 15,300 dr. one way, 30,600 dr. round-trip. You can also fly to Rhodes from Heraklion twice a week. It is possible to fly directly to Rhodes from a number of European capitals, especially on charters. The airport is about 20 minutes from Rhodes town, and it's best to take a taxi (about 1,000 dr.) because you'd have to carry your luggage to the local bus stop, where the service is infrequent. **Kos** has daily flights from Athens, and several of the smaller islands have less frequent service. Taxis meet incoming flights, and there is occasional bus service.

Arriving and Departing by Car and Boat

By Car If you drive to Greece, you may take your car to the Dodecanese on one of the large ferries that sail daily from Piraeus to Rhodes and less frequently to the smaller islands.

By Boat Of the several ferryboat lines serving the Dodecanese, the **Dane Sea Line** (tel. 01/429–3240) has the largest boats and the most frequent service, sailing daily out of Piraeus. Boats leave Monday and Friday at 6 PM and arrive early the next morning. On Tuesday, Wednesday, Thursday, and Saturday they sail at 1 PM (also arriving the next morning), stopping at Patmos, Leros, Kalymnos, and Kos. To Patmos, fares are 2,830 dr.–5,125 dr., cars 11,160 dr.–14,650 dr.; to Rhodes, fares are 3,765 dr.–6,500 dr., cars 11,130 dr.–14,610 dr., not including taxes). The Sunday boat, a local that stops at 11 islands en route, sails at 6:30 PM.

Getting Around

By Plane **Olympic Airways** (9 Ierou Lochou, Rhodes town, tel. 0241/24571 through 0241/24575) runs two flights a week to Kos (30 minutes, 7,400 dr.) and other flights to less-visited islands (Karpathos, Kassos, and Kastellorizo) that are not served directly from Athens.

By Bus There is a good bus network on all the islands. Buses from the town of Rhodes, on the northern tip of the island, leave from the bus stop on Alexander Papagou street, near Mandraki Harbor for points on the east side of the island, and from Averoff Street beside the new market for the west side of the island.

By Boat There are frequent local boats, and in summer, hydrofoils connect the Dodecanese with each other. For information, contact the **Piraeus Port Authority** (tel. 01/417–2657) or **Rhodes Port Authority** (tel. 0241/22220).

By Car and Bicycle On **Rhodes,** the roads are good, there are not many of them, and good maps are available. It is only possible to tour the island in one day if you rent a car. Traffic is likely to be heavy only from Rhodes town to Lindos, and again as you near Kameiros. In **Kos,** a car is advisable only if you are very pressed for time; most of what you want to see in Kos can by reached by bicycle or public transportation. Bicycle shops are plentiful. In **Patmos,** there is no point in renting a car unless you want to explore the outer edges of the island, since both monasteries are easily reached by bus, on foot, or even by taxi. There are no roads suitable for cars on **Symi,** and exploration is done on foot or by boat. The other Dodecanese islands are also best visited by public transportation.

Guided Tours

A wide variety of local boat and land tours offered in Rhodes, Kos, Patmos, and Symi will take you to the usual sites (which you can probably reach by yourself anyway), and will give you a day picnicking on a remote beach, or even visiting the shores of Turkey. **Triton Holidays** in Rhodes, for example, organizes a visit to Lindos by boat; a caique leaves Mandraki Harbor in Rhodes in the morning, sails to Lindos (2½ hours; 7,000 dr.), deposits you there for a day of sightseeing and beaching, and returns you to Rhodes in the evening. In Kos, **Aeolos Travel** organizes seven-day cruises by 30-passenger caique to Samos and other islands, for about $80 per person per day. **Symi Tours** will take you on a boat trip to the magical islet of Seklia (with a barbecue) for about 1,000 dr., or on a round-the-island trip for 2,000 dr.

Exploring Rhodes and the Dodecanese

If you have a few weeks, exploring the entire Dodecanese by boat would make a marvelous, and unusual, holiday, particularly if you head for the less-visited islands. Especially in winter, inter-island boats may leave just once a day (or not at all if the weather is bad), so you have to allow time for getting stranded. We concentrate here on the four most interesting islands: Rhodes, the largest, is also the richest, culturally and in every other sense. **Tour 1** takes in the city of Rhodes; **Tour 2** explores the island; in **Tour 3** you spend a day in Symi; Kos is the subject of **Tour 4**; and Patmos of **Tour 5**.

Highlights for First-Time Visitors

Asklepieion and **Archaeological Museum of Kos** (*see* Tour 4)
Medieval town of Rhodes (*see* Tour 1)
Monastery of St. John the Thelogian (*see* Tour 5)
Symi town (*see* Tour 3)

Tour 1: Rhodes Town

Numbers in the margin correspond to points of interest on the Rhodes and the Dodecanese map.

The island of Rhodes (1,400 square kilometers, or 540 square miles) is, after Crete, Evia, and Lesbos, the largest Greek island and, along with Sicily and Cyprus, one of the great islands of the Mediterranean. Rhodes is a country and almost a continent unto itself, and in the years before tourism, was easily self-sufficient. It lies almost exactly halfway between Piraeus and Cyprus, 18 kilometers (11 miles) off the coast of Asia Minor, and was long considered a bridge between Europe and the East. Geologically similar to the Turkish mainland, it was probably once a part of it, separated by one of the frequent upheavals this volatile region produces. A central mountain range thickly forested with pine and cypress stretches roughly northeast–southwest along its westernmost half. Most of the rainfall spends itself against the northwestern flank of the range; yet the runoff makes the island's eastern side also extremely fertile. Rhodes has almost twice as much rainfall as Athens and Attica, and the climate is extremely mild.

Rhodes saw successive waves of settlement, culminating with the arrival of the Dorian Greeks from Argos and Laconia some time early in the first millenium BC. They settled in Ialysos, Lindos, and Kameiros, and together with Dorians from Kos, and from Knidos and Halicarnassos in Asia Minor, formed a kind of loose confederation, later known as the Hexapolis ("Six Cities"). From the 8th to the 6th centuries BC the three Rhodian cities established settlements in Italy, Sicily, France, Spain, and Egypt, and actively traded with mainland Greece, exporting pottery, oil, wine, and figs.

By the end of the 6th century BC, the independence, creativity, and expansion came to an abrupt halt when the Persians took over the island, later forcing Rhodians to provide ships and men for King Xerxes' attack on the mainland in 480 BC. The Persian failure resulted in their final expulsion from the mainland and the creation of a league of city-states under Athenian leadership. In 408 BC the inhabitants of the three cities established the united city of Rhodes, on the site of the modern town; much of the populace moved there, and the earlier towns eventually became mainly religious centers.

The new city grew and flourished, and its political organization was the model for the city of Alexandria in Egypt. At the end of the 4th century BC the Rhodians commissioned the sculptor Chares, from Lindos, to create the famous Colossus, a huge bronze statue of the sun god, Helios, which stood astride the harbor, one of the Seven Wonders of the ancient world. The next two centuries were great years; thanks to its superb location on trade routes, Rhodes's economy flourished. In 227 BC, when an earthquake leveled the city, help poured in from all quarters of the eastern Mediterranean, attesting to the city's importance. After the calamity the Delphic oracle advised the Rhodians to let the great Colossus lie where it had been toppled in the quake. So it lay, for some eight centuries, until AD 654, when it was sold as scrap metal and carted off to Syria by a caravan of 900 camels. After that, we know nothing of its fate.

In 42 BC, Rhodes came under the hegemony of Rome, and through the years of the empire, it was fabled as one of the most beautiful of cities, with parks and gardens and the straight streets that had been laid out in the 4th century BC. The roads were lined with porticoes, houses, and gardens, and according to Pliny, who described the city in the 1st century AD, it possessed some 3,000 statues, at least 100 of them colossal.

The sculptural school flourished through the Hellenistic period, and one of its most famous exemplars—probably executed in the 1st century BC—was the *Laocöon*, showing the Trojan priest who warned the Trojans to beware of Greeks bearing gifts and his sons, in their death struggles with a giant serpent, a work that Pliny reports having seen in Rome in the 1st century AD. Excavations in Rome in 1506 uncovered the statue, which stands in the Vatican today. The intellectual life of Rhodes was also dazzling, and attracted students and visitors from around the Mediterranean; its schools of rhetoric and philosophy found great favor among young Romans.

Of all this ancient glory, there is almost nothing left in the modern town; the city was ravaged by Arab invaders in AD 654 and again in 807, and only with the expulsion of the Arabs, and the reconquest of Crete by the Byzantine emperors, did Rhodes begin to revive. During the Crusades, it was a crucial stop on the road to the Holy Land. It came briefly under Venetian influence, then Byzantine, then Genoese, but in 1309, when the Knights of St. John took the city from its Genoese masters, its most glorious modern era began.

The Knights of St. John, an order of Hospitalers organized in Jerusalem to protect and care for Christian pilgrims, were grouped into "Tongues" by country of origin. Each Tongue's Inn, its place of assembly, was under the orders of a bailiff; the bailiffs were ruled by an elected Grand Master. By the beginning of the 12th century the order had become military in nature, and after the fall of Acre in 1291, the knights fled from Palestine, withdrawing first to Cyprus, and then capturing Rhodes. In 1312, the Knights inherited the immense wealth of the Templars (another religious military order, which had just been outlawed by the Pope), and used it to fortify Rhodes.

But for all their power and the strength of their walls, the Knights could not hold back the Turks. By the 16th century they manned the last bastions against the Turks in the eastern Mediterranean, as one by one the towns and cities of Byzantium fell. In preparation for the attack they knew would come, the Knights continually enlarged the moats and reinforced the sea walls, building new towers, fortifying gates, and installing artillery of all sizes. In 1522, the Ottoman Turks, with 300 ships and 100,000 men under Süleyman the Magnificent, began what was to be the final siege, taking the city after six months. During the Turkish occupation, Rhodes became a possession of the Grand Admiral, who collected taxes but left the Rhodians to pursue a generally peaceful and prosperous existence. They continued to build ships and to trade with Greece, Constantinople (later Istanbul), Syria, and Egypt. The Greek mainland was liberated by the War of 1821, but Rhodes and the Dodecanese remained part of the Ottoman Empire until 1912, when the Italians took over. After World War II, the Twelve Islands were formally united with Greece in 1947.

❶ Early travelers described **Rhodes** as a town of two parts: a castle or high town (Colacchium); and a lower city. In the castle area, a city within a city, the Knights built most of their monuments. The best place to begin a tour of Rhodes is the **Palace of the Grand Master.** At the highest point of the medieval city, it offers an advantageous point for orienting yourself before wandering through the labyrinthine old town. Also a great help is the permanent exhibition on the downstairs level, with extensive displays on the building, and maps and plans of the city. A large rectangular building with a broad central courtyard, the palace was so solidly built that it withstood unscathed the events of 1522, but in 1856, an explosion of ammunition stored in the basement of the Church of St. John devastated church and palace; the present buildings are Italian reconstructions. Note the Roman mosaic floors throughout, which came from the Italian excavations in Kos. *Tel. 0241/21954. Admission: 800 dr. Open Tues.–Sun. 8:30–3.*

In front of the court of the palace is the **Loggia of St. John** (it too, almost totally rebuilt by the Italians), which led to the destroyed Church of St. John (something of the church's appearance is known from early drawings; under the pavement of the lavishly decorated interior were the tombs of the Grand Masters). From the Loggia, the Street of the Knights descends toward the Commercial Port, bordered on both sides by the Inns of the Tongues, where members ate and held their meetings. Approximately halfway down the street is the **Inn of France,** the largest, whose architecture is typical of many buildings in Rhodes. The ground floor is occupied by vaulted utility areas opening onto the road; the first floor is reached by a stairway rising from the central courtyard. The facade is carved with flowers and heraldic patterns, and bears an inscription that dates the building between 1492 and 1509.

At the end of the street stands the **Hospital,** completed in 1489, the largest of the Knights' public buildings. The imposing facade opens into a courtyard, where there are quantities of cannonballs from the siege of 1522, and a wide staircase leads to the main floor. The building now houses the **Archaeological Museum,** which contains a collection of ancient pottery and sculpture, including two well-known representations of Aphrodite, one in a crouching pose, perhaps washing her hair, and the other a standing figure, known as *Aphrodite Thalassia,* or "of the sea," since she was found in the water off the northern city beach. *Museum Sq., tel. 0241/21954. Admission: 600 dr. Open Tues.–Sun. 8:30–3.*

To the left of the Hospital, the road leads toward Liberty Gate, passing the **Inn of Auvergne,** which now houses the Market Police, and entering Plateia Symi (or Arsenal Square), just inside the gate. Continue south to Hippokratous Square, just inside Arsenal Gate, where you will see at the far side the impressive **Palace of Castellania,** an early 16th-century building that was the Court House of the Knights. The road leaving the square on the south takes you to the southernmost side of the old city, once the Jewish Quarter, where there is still a dilapidated **syn-**

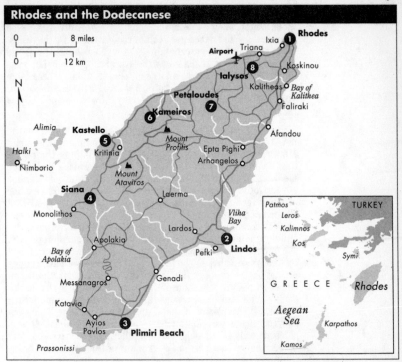

Rhodes and the Dodecanese

0   8 miles

0   12 km

N

Rhodes **1**
Ixia
Triana
Airport
Koskinou
Ialysos **8**
Kalitheas
Bay of Kalithea
Petaloudes
Kameiros **7**
Faliraki
6
Kastello
5
Kritinia
Mount Profilis
Epta Pighi
Afandou
Alimia
Arhangelos
Halki
Nimborio
Mount Ataviros
Siana
4
Laerma
Vliha Bay
Monolithos
Lardos
2 Lindos
Apolakia
Pefki
Bay of Apolakia
Genadi
Messanagros
Katavia
Ayios Pavlos
3 Plimiri Beach
Prassonissi

Patmos
Leros
TURKEY
Kalimnos
Kos
Symi
G R E E C E   Rhodes
Aegean Sea
Karpathos
Kamos

agogue, usually kept closed. At this end of the city Süleyman and his forces were able to breach the walls and end two centuries of the Knights' rule. Just inside the remains of the wall are the ruins of a magnificent Gothic cathedral, **Our Lady of the Bourg,** whose soaring vaults are a startling reminder of this city's Frankish past. Nearby is St. Catherine's Gate, which opens onto the **Commercial Harbor,** Rhodes's largest.

Return to Museum Square, and head west to the intersection of Sokratous Street, the old city's shopping center, which is lined with boutiques selling furs, jewelry, and other high-ticket items. At the top of Sokratous is the **Mosque of Süleyman,** built soon after 1522 and rebuilt in 1808. Just opposite is the **Turkish Library,** dating from the late 18th century. These striking reminders of the Ottoman presence are still used by those members of Rhodes's Turkish community who stayed behind after the population exchange of 1922.

The medieval town also contained numerous Orthodox and Catholic churches (many of which have disappeared), and fine houses lined the streets, some of which follow the ancient orthogonal plan. All the public buildings are similar in style, creating a harmonious whole, which has been enhanced in recent years by careful reconstruction. Staircases are on the outside, either on the facade or in the court; the facades are elegantly constructed of well-cut limestone from Lindos. Windows and doors are often outlined with strongly profiled moldings and surmounted by arched casements.

The **walls** of Rhodes in themselves are one of the great medieval monuments in the Mediterranean. Wonderfully preserved (even before the extensive Italian reconstruction), they illustrate the engineering capabilities as well as the financial and human resources available to the Knights. A road that runs along the top for the entire 4 kilometers (2½ miles) is accessible through municipal guided tours. *Tel. 0241/21954. Admission: 800 dr. Tours Mon. and Sat. 3–5; departure from courtyard of the palace.*

The old city of Rhodes is now completely surrounded by the new city. North of the medieval walls, rimming the small Mandraki Harbor, are many of the official buildings, their style heavily influenced by the Grand Master's Palace and other medieval monuments, and making abundant use of Lindos stone, Gothic architectural detail, and crenellation. The harbor is dominated by the **cathedral,** modeled after the destroyed Church of St. John in the Colacchium. Next door is the **Governor's Palace,** constructed in an arcaded Venetian Gothic style. Other buildings include the port authority and customs offices, the municipal buildings, and a huge open-air bazaar now faced by fancy sweetshops. The main shopping areas of new Rhodes lie just behind these buildings. To the west rises Mt. Smith, on whose slopes are still some of the villas and gardens that in the early part of this century made Rhodes look like a miniature Italian Riviera. Many of them, unfortunately, have been torn down to make way for modern apartment buildings. It is a pleasant walk up through this neighborhood to the top of Mt. Smith, where there are many **remains of the ancient town,** including a heavily restored theater, a stadium, the three restored columns of the Temple of Apollo Pythios, and scrappy remains of the Temple of Athena Polias. For a dramatic view, walk to the westernmost edge of Mt. Smith, which drops in a sharp and almost inaccessible cliff to the shore below, now lined with enormous hotels. *Acropolis, theater, and stadium, tel. 0241/21954. Admission free. Open daily 8:30–3.*

Tour 2: Around the Island

The island's east coast, particularly the stretch between Rhodes town and Lindos, is blessed with white sandy beaches and dotted with copses of trees, interspersed with fertile valleys full of figs and olives. Unfortunately, its beauty has meant that long stretches of this country are now given over to vast resort hotels and holiday villages. Take the road east out of Rhodes, following signs to Faliraki Beach and to Lindos, and after about 10 kilometers (96 miles), the road passes a group of buildings that look as if they've been transplanted from Morocco. In fact, this is a modern spa built by the Italians in the 1920s, now much neglected. Farther on, you pass **Faliraki Beach,** a splendid strip of sandy beach now ringed by hotels.

Time Out A right turn 30 kilometers (19 miles) from Rhodes leads in about 2 kilometers (1¼ miles) to a footpath that's an easy, uphill walk through a pleasant ravine to a deeply shaded glen surrounding Epta Pighi, or Seven Springs. Here an enterprising local shepherd began serving simple fare to visitors about 40 years ago, and his sideline turned into the busy taverna of today. He imported peacocks and turned them loose in the woods, where they pierce the silence with their scratchy shrieks and flaunt their bright plumage high up in the trees. If you arrive before mealtime, you can have a glass of orange juice, freshly squeezed by a family member.

At 60 kilometers (37 miles) from Rhodes town, you reach **②** **Lindos,** which lies cradled between two harbors. The modern town is on the land side of the Acropolis, which can be reached only on foot, after you have left bus or car in the parking lot. Like Rhodes town, Lindos is enchanting off-season and almost unbearably crowded otherwise, since it is a focus of every day trip from Rhodes. To reach the Acropolis, you pass through the center of town, along a street lined with shops selling clothes and trinkets of all types; the streets are medieval in their narrowness and twisting course, so the passage slows to a snail's pace, and is as crowded as a subway at rush hour. Donkeys can be hired for the 15-minute climb, for 500 dr. The winding path leads past a gauntlet of Lindian women who spread out their lace and embroidery over the rocks like fresh laundry. The final approach ascends a steep flight of stairs, past a marvelous representation of a Lindian ship, carved into the rock on the left, and through the main gate of the Crusader castle.

Lindos had a particular importance in antiquity. Before the existence of Rhodes, it was the island's principal maritime center. Perhaps the poverty of Lindos's land (which could barely support a few fig trees and vines), in combination with the fine harbor, forced the Lindians to turn outward for survival and led to their maritime success. Lindos possessed a revered sanctuary, consecrated to Athena, whose cult probably succeeded that of a pre-Hellenic divinity named Lindia, and in fact the sanctuary was dedicated to Athena Lindia. By the 6th century BC, an impressive temple was raised, and after the foundation of Rhodes, the Lindians set up a *propylaia* (monumental entrance gate) on the model of Athens's. In the mid-4th century BC, the temple was destroyed by fire and almost immediately rebuilt, with a new wood statue of the goddess, covered by gold leaf and with arms, head, and legs of marble or ivory. In the Hellenistic period, the Acropolis was further adorned with a great portico at the foot of the steps to the propylaia. Lindos prospered into Roman times, during the Middle Ages, and under the Knights of St. John. Only at the beginning of the 19th century did the age-old shipping activity cease. The population decreased radically, reviving only with the 20th-century influx of foreigners.

The entrance to the **Acropolis** takes you through the medieval castle, with the Byzantine chapel of St. John on the next level above. On the upper terraces are the remains of the elaborate porticoes and stoas, initially restored by the Italians and once again being restored. As is the case with Sounion (*see* Exploring Attica, the Saronic Islands, and Delphi in Chapter 4), the site and temple command an immense sweep of sea, making a powerful statement on behalf of the deity and city to which they belonged; the forests of white columns on the summit must have presented a magnificent picture. The main portico had 42 Doric columns, at the center of which an opening led to the staircase up to the propylaia. The temple at the very top is surprisingly modest, given the drama of the approach. It is not peripteral; that is, unlike most Greek temples, there is no encircling colonnade. Instead, both the front and the rear are flanked by four Doric columns, like the Nike Temple on the

Acropolis of Athens. Numerous inscribed statue bases were found all over the summit, attesting in many cases to the work of Lindian sculptors, who were clearly second to none.

From the southwest side of the Acropolis you have a good view over the small harbor—where St. Paul supposedly landed bringing his message to Lindos. At the foot of the slope you can see the remains of the ancient theater and, slightly to its right, the ancient agora. The town itself is remarkably well preserved, and many 15th-century houses are still in use. Everywhere are examples of the Crusader architecture you saw in Rhodes town: substantial houses built of finely cut rectangles of grayish Lindos limestone, the facades pierced by doors and windows crowned with stone arches, often elaborately carved in the characteristic rope patterns, and inner courtyards containing stairs to the upper level. Many of their floors are paved with the typical Rhodian black and white pebble mosaics. Intermixed with these Crusader buildings are other houses of almost Cycladic appearance: white geometric shapes pierced by plain square windows framed with blue shutters are nestled in gardens filled with bougainvillea and hibiscus. *Acropolis of Lindos, tel. 0241/21954. Admission: 800 dr. Open Tues.–Sun. 8:30–3.*

Returning to the village, take some time to wander through the residential area. Near the main plateia, you'll come to the **Church of the Panayia,** a graceful building with a fine bell tower, now in perilous condition. The body of the church probably antedates the Knights, although the bell tower bears their arms with the dates 1484–1490. The interior is painted with frescoes executed in 1779 by Gregory of Symi.

The area south of Lindos is less traveled than the rest of the island. The land is not as attractive as in the north, the sandy beaches are fewer, and the soil is less fertile, so there is much less development. The village of Genadi, approximately 20 kilometers (12 miles) from Lindos, offers some inexpensive pensions and rooms for rent, as well as tavernas. Push on 10 kilometers (6 miles) farther on a detour to **Plimiri Beach,** a good place for a swim to break the long drive.

Time Out A turnoff takes you along a narrow country road to the **Plimiri Beach** taverna (tel. 0244/43250; closed Nov.–mid-Apr.), on a splendid, deserted beach. The food is very simple—though expensive if you have fish—but the location is hard to beat.

Return to Genadi and turn inland on a road that leads across the island, through a river valley dotted with curious hillocks, to the town of Apolakia, where you bear right at the crossroads to begin your return trip north. The road climbs through spectacularly wooded hills, and after 15 kilometers (10 miles), passes through the town of **Siana,** perched above a vast, fertile valley and shadowed by a rock outcropping crowned with the ruin of a castle. Siana is known for *souma,* a local drink resembling unflavored schnapps, and for its honey and walnuts, which can be obtained at **Tasia's Cafeneion,** on the main road just past the town's church.

Beyond Siana, the road continues on a high ridge through thick pine forests, which carpet the precipitous slopes dropping toward the sea. To the right looms the bare stony massif of Mt. Ataviros, Rhodes's highest peak (1,215 m, or 3,985 ft). At the town of Kritinia, 12 kilometers (7½ miles) from Siana, there is a ⑤ turnoff for **Kastello,** a fortress built by the Knights in the late-15th century. It is an impressive ruin, situated high above the sea with fine views in every direction. Approximately 17 kilometers (10 miles) from Kastello, a road leads to the site of ancient ⑥ **Kameiros,** one of the three ancient cities of Rhodes, excavated by the Italians in 1929. The apparently unfortified ruins lie on a slope above the sea, and most of what is visible today dates to the Classical period and later, including some impressive remains of the early Hellenistic period. If you want to visit the site on a one-day tour around the island, remember that it closes at 3 PM. *Kameiros archaeological site, tel. 0241/21954. Admission: 400 dr. Open Tues.–Sun. 8:30–3.*

On the way back to Rhodes town, after 15 kilometers (9 miles) a ⑦ side road leads south 7 kilometers (4 miles) to **Petaloudes,** the Valley of the Butterflies, which lives up to its name, especially in July and August. The butterflies cluster by the millions around the low bushes of the pungent storax plant, which grows all over the area. Back on the main coast road, a turnoff at Triana leads south for 5 kilometers (3 miles) to Mt. ⑧ Phileremos, capped by the site of **Ialysos,** the third of the ancient Rhodian cities. There are some remains of an early Hellenistic Temple of Athena, as well as a Byzantine church. Because of its strategic position, Phileremos also was used by the Knights for a fortress, which stands above a monastery of Our Lady of Phileremos. *Acropolis of Ialysos, tel. 0241/21954. Admission: 400 dr. Open Tues.–Sun. 8:30–3.*

Tour 3: Symi

The island of Symi, a wonderful day trip from Rhodes, is an enchanting place, with a 19th-century town that was built up in just a generation or two, and then virtually abandoned almost as quickly. Fortunately, the island has no beaches—in fact almost no flat land—so it is not attractive to developers. Homer writes of Nireus, the king of Symi, who sailed with three vessels to assist the Greeks at Troy. Symi was later part of the Dorian Hexapolis dominated by Rhodes, and continued under Rhodian dominance throughout the Roman and Byzantine periods.

The island has good natural harbors, and the nearby coast of Asia Minor had plentiful timber. The Symiotes were fine shipbuilders, fearless seafarers and sponge divers, and finally, rich and successful merchants. Under the Ottomans their harbor was proclaimed a free port and attracted the trade of the entire region. Witness to their prosperity are the fine neoclassical mansions that were fashionable elsewhere in Greece at the same time. The Symiotes' continuous travel and trade and their frequent contact with Europe led them to incorporate foreign elements in their furnishings, clothes, and cultural life. At first they lived in Chorio, high on the hillside above the port, and in the second half of the 19th century spread down to the seaside at Yialos. There were some 20,000 inhabitants at its acme, but under the Italian occupation at the end of the Italo-Turkish war in 1912, the island declined; the Symiotes lost their holdings in Asia Minor and were unable to convert their fleets to steam. Many emigrated to work elsewhere, and now there are just a few thousand inhabitants in Chorio and Yialos.

The boat from Rhodes usually stops first at the inlet of **Pedhi,** a small village from which you can walk, in about a half hour, up to Chorio and from there in another 10 minutes, down into the main harbor of Yialos. It is a pleasant walk, but if you prefer, you can stay aboard and visit **Yialos** first. Rounding the last of many rocky barren spurs, the boat suddenly comes in view of the town, at the back of a deep, narrow harbor. The shoreside is lined with shops and houses; the esplanade at the head of the harbor, once the site of shipyards, is now full of cafés. Nearby is the **Church of Ayhios Ioannis,** built in 1838 and incorporating in its walls fragments of ancient blocks from a temple that apparently stood on this site.

To visit **Chorio,** leave the square of Skala on the main road of the town—actually a staircase of some 500 steps, known as **Kali Strata** (Good Road). It is flanked by many elegant pastel stucco houses of neoclassical design, characterized by fine stonework around windows and doors, sometimes elements of classical orders, the lavish use of pediments, and intricate wrought-iron balconies. Just before the top of the stairs, to the left, a line of windmills crowns the hill of Noulia.

In Chorio, alleys branch out in every direction from Kali Strata, winding through neighborhoods in various states of repair. Many of the houses, older than the neoclassical mansions, are built in typical Aegean style, occasionally modernized by a bit of neoclassical ornament. Passing through the **Laikos Milos Square,** you come to the **Archaeological Museum,** whose collection includes Hellenistic and Roman sculptures and inscriptions; and more recent carvings, icons, costumes, and handicrafts. Most of Chorio's many churches date from the 18th and 19th centuries, and many are ornamented with richly decorated iconostases and ornate bell towers. At the top of the town is the **Kastro,** on the ancient Acropolis, incorporating fragments of Symi's history in its walls. The view from here takes in the village of Pedhi as well as both Chorio and Yialos.

Many day trips from Rhodes also visit the **Monastery of Taxiarchis Michael Panormitis,** located in another near-perfect harbor, on the south side of the island. (It is also possible to get there on foot: the five-hour hike along the island's only road offers an opportunity to enjoy the scenery and the smell of the fennel, thyme, rosemary, and basil growing in great profusion.) Surrounded by atypically green, pine-covered hills, the little gulf of **Panormitis** is adorned by a shrine to Taxiarchis Michael, Symi's patron saint, and also the protector of sailors. In recent years, inns, cafés, and restaurants have been built near the monastery to accommodate the many pilgrims and tourists.

The entrance is surmounted by an elaborate bell tower, of the multilevel wedding-cake variety already seen in Yialos and Chorio. In the courtyard, which is surrounded by a vaulted stoa, the floor is adorned with a black-and-white pebble mosaic. The interior of the church, entirely frescoed in the 18th century, contains a marvelously ornate wooden iconostasis, flanked by a heroic-size 18th-century representation of Michael, completely covered with silver. Note also the collection of votives, including ship models, gifts brought from all over, and a number of bottles with money in them, which according to local lore traveled to Symi on their own after having been thrown into the sea. *Monastery of Taxiarchis Michael*

Panormitis, tel. 0241/71354. Admission free. Open daily. Some rooms available.

Tour 4: Kos

The island of Kos, third largest in the Dodecanese, is certainly one of the most beautiful, with verdant fields and tree-clad mountains, surrounded by miles of sandy beach. Its highest peak, part of a small mountain range in the northeast, is less than 3,280 feet.

In Mycenaean times and during the Archaic period, the island prospered. In the 6th century BC it was conquered by the Persians, but later joined the Delian League, supporting Athens against Sparta in the Peloponnesian War. Kos was invaded and destroyed by the Spartan fleet, ruled by Alexander and various of his successors, and has twice been devastated by earthquakes. Nevertheless the city and the economy flourished, as did the arts and sciences. The painter, Apelles, the Michelangelo of his time, came from Kos, as did Hippocrates, father of modern medicine. Under the Roman Empire, the island's Asklepieion and its renowned healing center drew emperors and ordinary citizens alike. The Knights of St. John arrived in 1315 and ruled for the next two centuries, until they were replaced by the Ottomans. In 1912, the Italians took over, and in 1947, the island was united with Greece.

The modern town lies on a flat plain surrounding a spacious, round harbor called Mandraki. Begin your visit at the fortress crowning its west side, where Hippocrates is supposed to have taught in the shade of a large plane tree. On one side of Plateia Platanou, the little square named after the tree, stands the graceful **Loggia** (actually a mosque), built in 1786. A bridge from the square leads you to the entrance to the **Castle of the Knights,** built mostly in the 15th century and full of ancient blocks from its Greek and Roman predecessors. The castle is a repository of fragments of ancient inscriptions, funerary monuments, and other sculptural material. A walk around the walls affords fine views over the town, whose flat skyline is pierced by a few remaining minarets and many palm trees. *Tel. 0242/28326. Admission: 400 dr. Open Tues.–Sun. 8:30–3.*

Just behind the castle, excavations have uncovered the Roman agora and harbor, as well as portions of 4th-century BC and Hellenistic buildings. The area, which is not fenced, blends charmingly into the fabric of the modern city; it's a shortcut for people on their way to work, a place to sit and chat, an outdoor playroom for children. The ruins are now overgrown, and in spring are covered with brightly colored flowers, which nicely frame the ancient gray and white marble blocks tumbled in every direction.

Go west from the agora through the gate leading to the main square, to the **Archaeological Museum,** which contains extremely important examples of Hellenistic and Roman sculpture by Koan artists. Among the treasures is a group of sculptures from various Roman phases, all found in the House of the Europa Mosaic, and a remarkable series of Hellenistic draped female statues mainly from the Sanctuary of Demeter at Kyparissi and the Odeion. *Plateia Eleftherias, tel. 0242/28326. Admission: 400 dr. Open Tues.–Fri. 8:30–3.*

Beyond the museum and the large Roman House (built to protect the numerous mosaics found inside) are the West Excavations, which lie just below the ancient Acropolis. A portion of
one of the main Roman streets has been uncovered, with many
houses, including the **House of the Europa Mosaic.** Part of the
Roman baths nearby has been converted into a basilica. Also of
interest is the ancient gymnasium, distinguished by its partly
reconstructed colonnade, and the so-called **Nymphaion,** a lavish public latrine that's been restored.

You can reach the **Asklepieion,** one of the great healing centers
of antiquity (4 kilometers or 2½ miles west of the town), on foot,
by bicycle, or by bus or taxi. It is framed in a thick grove of cypress trees and laid out on several broad terraces connected by
a monumental staircase. Reminiscent of the Sanctuary of Athena Lindia in Rhodes, it is typical for this period. The lower terrace probably held the Asklepieian Festivals. On the middle
terrace is an Ionic temple, once decorated with paintings by
Apelles, including the renowned depiction of Aphrodite often
written about in antiquity and eventually removed to Rome by
the emperor Augustus. On the uppermost terrace is the Doric
Temple of Asklepeios, once surrounded by colonnaded porticoes. *Tel. 0242/28763. Admission: 600 dr. Open Tues.–Sun.
8:30–3.*

Drive southwest from the town of Kos on the main road tran-
secting the island lengthwise, and after 25 kilometers (15
miles) turn left onto a dirt track leading to the magnificent **Castle of Antimacheia.** Built by the Knights, along with the Castle
at Kardamena, it is actually a large town, which because of its
isolation has not been quarried for stone. Most of its buildings
lie where they have fallen, in heaps of rubble picturesquely
shrouded in thick vegetation. Two small churches still stand at
the center of the site, one built in 1494, according to an inscription over its door, the other, a Latin-type basilica—with a single nave and no transept—now dedicated to Ayia Paraskevi
and still in use. Continue along the main road another 10 kilometers (6 miles), and you reach the **Bay of Kamares.** Close to
shore is a little rock formation holding a chapel to St. Nicholas,
and opposite, on the mainland, are the ruins of a magnificent
5th-century Christian basilica, perched on the edge of a public
beach, a good chunk of which is now occupied by a Club
Méditerranée. The town of **Kephalos,** just beyond, sits on a
height that also holds the ruins of a castle.

Tour 5: Patmos

The small island of Patmos, rocky and barren, is the site of the
famed Monastery of St. John the Theologian, high above the
modern port town of Skala. Most of the island's approximately
2,500 people live in three villages: Skala, medieval Chora, and
the small rural settlement of Kambos. Skala, the island's main
port, is its commercial center and the location now of almost all
the hotels and restaurants. There is not much to see in the
town, but strict building codes have been enforced and even
new buildings have traditional architectural detail. The village
of Chora, clustered around the walls of the monastery, has become a preserve of international wealth; many of the houses,
now exquisitely restored, are owned by Athenians and foreigners, who discovered the settlement some years ago.

The early history of Patmos remains shadowy, for classical references are few and the area has not been the object of extensive excavation. There is scattered evidence of Mycenaean presence, and walls of Classical date indicate the existence of a town near Skala. In AD 95, during the emperor Domitian's persecution of Christians, St. John was banished to Patmos, where he lived until his reprieve two years later. He writes that it was on Patmos that he "heard...a great voice, as of a trumpet," commanding him to write a book and "send it unto the seven churches."

Patmos was virtually abandoned after the 6th century, and re-emerges in history at the end of the 11th century with the founding of the Monastery of St. John the Theologian by Hosios Christodoulos, a man of education, energy, devotion, and vision. Born in Bythynia in Asia Minor, he had spent some years as a hermit, then built the Theotokos Monastery in Kos, and came to Patmos in 1088. He wrote, "My ardent desire was to possess this island at the edge of the world, for there were no people, all was tranquillity, no boats dropped anchor here." So he traveled to Constantinople for permission to set up a monastery, receiving Patmos in exchange for his holdings on Kos.

Take the cobbled road between Skala and Chora from the west side of town to reach both the Monastery of the Apocalypse and the Monastery of St. John. According to tradition, St. John wrote the text of Revelations in the little cave, the Sacred Grotto, now built into the **Monastery of the Apocalypse** (tel. 0241/ 31234). It is decorated with wall paintings of the 12th century and icons of the 16th. The monastery, constructed in the 17th century from architectural fragments of earlier buildings, and further embellished in later years, also contains chapels to St. Artemios and St. Nicholas.

The **Monastery of St. John the Theologian** is one of the finest extant examples of a fortified medieval monastic complex. From its inception, it attracted monks of education and social standing, who made sure that it was ornamented with the best sculpture, carvings, and paintings. It was an intellectual center, with a rich library and a tradition of teaching, and by the end of the 12th century, it owned land on Leros, Limnos, Crete, and Asia Minor, as well as ships, which carried on trade exempt from taxes. A broad staircase leads to the entrance, which was fortified by towers and buttresses. The complex consists of buildings from a number of periods: in front of the entrance is the 17th-century Chapel of the Holy Apostles; the main church dates from the time of Christodoulos; the chapel of the Virgin, the refectory, kitchen, and some of the cells are 12th century.

The monastery contains three of the most important cultural treasures of the Orthodox Church: the library, the archives, and the treasury. The **library,** with a wonderful series of illuminated manuscripts, approximately 1,000 codices, and more than 3,000 printed volumes, was first catalogued in 1200; of the 267 works of that time, the library still has 111. Later catalogues make it possible to reconstruct the library's history and the monastery's intellectual life. The oldest codices, dating to the early 6th and the 8th centuries, contain parts of the Gospel of St. Mark and the Book of Job.

The documents in the **archives** (not open to the public) preserve a near-continuous record, down to the present, of the history of the monastery as well as the political and economic history of the region. The **treasury** contains a wide range of relics, icons, silver, and vestments, most dating from 1600 to 1800. Many of the objects are votives dedicated by the clerics, nobles, and wealthy individuals: One of the most beautiful is an 11th-century icon of St. Nicholas, executed in the finest of mosaics, in an exquisitely chased silver frame. The more than 600 vestments are of luxurious fabrics, elaborately embroidered with gold, silver, and multicolored silks. *Monastery of St. John, Treasury, Library, tel. 0241/21954. Admission free. Open Tues.–Fri. 8:30–3.*

What to See and Do with Children

A walk around Rhodes' medieval **fortification wall** (Tour 1); a visit to Petaloudes, the **Valley of the Butterflies,** in Rhodes (Tour 2); and an excursion to the fortifications at **Kastello** (Tour 2).

The flat island of Kos, particularly the area around the town, is good for **bicycle riding.**

Ride to the **Asklepieion** for a picnic, or visit the **Castle of Antimacheia** (Tour 4). Note: Be aware of such danger points as cistern openings; very few have fences around them.

Shopping

Although **Rhodes** is no longer a duty-free port, some people still regard it as one big shopping center. In the old town, particularly on Sokratous Street, upscale shops sell furs and jewelry as well as more ordinary trinkets. While the styling of the jewelry can be extremely attractive, the prices are no better than in Athens and often even higher, and in any case, the relative weakness of the dollar and the pound sterling means that Greek furs and jewelry are no longer the bargain they once were to American and British shoppers. In both Rhodes town and in Lindos, you can buy good copies of Lindos ware, a fine pottery decorated with green and red floral motifs. **Patmos,** an upscale tourist island, has some elegant boutiques selling jewelry and crafts, including antiques mainly from the island. In **Chora,** on the main road to the monastery, **Katoi** (tel. 0247/31487 or 0247/32107) has a wide selection of ceramics, icons, and silver jewelry of traditional design.

Sports and Outdoor Activities

Participant Sports

Bicycling   Kos's north coast is perfect for bicycling: in a word, flat. You can rent bicycles everywhere; in Kos town and at the more popular resorts. Try the many shops along Eleftherias Venizelou Street in town. Renting a bike costs about 400 dr. per day; scooter rentals begin at about 1,500 dr.

Golf   There is an 18-hole golf course (tel. 0241/51255) at the village of Afantou, approximately 20 kilometers (12 miles) outside Rhodes town.

Sailing and Water Sports   Information can be obtained from the **Nautical Club of Rhodes** (9 Kountouriotou Sq., tel. 0241/23287). The larger resort hotels offer windsurfing, waterskiing, and in some cases, jet-skiing and parasailing.

Tennis   Several first-class and luxury hotels have courts, where equipment can be rented and where nonguests can usually play. The **Rhodes Town Tennis Club** (tel. 0241/25705) is open to nonmembers.

Beaches

Kos   On the north coast, **Tingaki,** a highly developed little resort town, has a sandy beach with showers, and umbrellas and sun beds for rent. At **Mastichari,** another resort, farther from Kos town, there's a wide sand beach, tavernas, rooms for rent, and a pier where boats sail on day trips to the uncrowded islet of Pserimos. **Paradise Beach** has plenty of parking, and thus crowds, but the broad, sandy beach is magnificent, curving around an enchanting bay. In **Kos** town, if you must get wet and can't leave town, try the narrow pebbly strip just south of the main harbor.

Patmos   In the morning, caiques make regular runs from Skala to the beaches, and prices vary with the number of people making the trip (or with the boat). Ask for several "bids" to find out the going rate and the time of return, and remember to negotiate. Most of Patmos's beaches are coarse shingle, but a 20-minute walk north of Skala (or a caique) will bring you to **Melloi Beach,** a sand and pebble strip with cafés and tavernas nearby. The beach at **Kambos Bay,** mostly fine pebble and sand, is the most popular on the island. It's accessible by caique from Skala (15–25 minutes), has nearby tavernas, and you can windsurf, water ski, and rent pedal boats. On the south shore, **Psiliamo** and **Little Psiliamo** have fine sand, but they are hard to get to: 45 minutes by caique from Skala or a two-hour walk.

Rhodes   Rhodes town and the east coast have exquisite stretches of tawny, fine-sand beach. Unfortunately, much of the coast is developed, so you can reach some of the best beaches only through the hotels that occupy them. **Sandy Point** beach in town has fine sand, an easy slope, chairs and umbrellas for rent, showers, pedal boats, and windsurfers.

Dining and Lodging

Dining   Although Dodecanese cooking doesn't differ significantly from that of the mainland, there are some restaurants whose location makes them delightfully different and whose chefs' imagination provides memorable meals. Rhodes produces most of its own foodstuffs, so you can count on fresh fruit and vegetables and, of course, an array of fish (as everywhere, very expensive). Kos, too, is a garden island with lush fields, so fresh vegetables are easy for chefs to come by and even simple salads can be delicious. Eating well is not quite so easy on Patmos and Symi, neither of which have much homegrown produce; the lack seems to have dulled the senses of the cooks, so the fare in tavernas tends toward the mediocre. Always check the food on display in the kitchen, and find out what is the specialty of the day.

Highly recommended restaurants in each price category are indicated by a star ★.

Category	Cost*
Very Expensive	over 8,000 dr.
Expensive	6,000 dr.–8,000 dr.
Moderate	3,000 dr.–6,000 dr.
Inexpensive	under 3,000 dr.

*per person for 3-course meal, including house wine or beer and excluding service (usually 10%)

Lodging Except for Athens, Rhodes probably has more hotels per capita than anywhere else in Greece. Almost all of them are resort or tourist hotels; a few of the most luxurious cater to conference and incentive business as well. Some of the most elaborate, at the edge of town, have sea views and easy access to the beach (extremely crowded in high season). Many have pools as well. Large resort hotels also cluster along the east coast as far as Lindos—many catering to families and groups, who come for several weeks at a time, on half or full board. Individuals may have difficulty finding a room in Rhodes; it is best to book through an agent in high season.

Kos presents a similar picture, although its hotels tend to be more modest in size and facilities. Symi and Patmos offer a greater number of small hotels with charm, since neither island has encouraged the development of mammoth caravansaries. For a cozy few days for two, try one of the small bed-and-breakfasts on Symi or Patmos.

Note: Many of the hotels, large and small, on all these islands are closed in winter. From November through April, contact a local travel agent for the latest information on what is open.

Highly recommended lodgings in each price category are indicated by a star ★.

Category	Cost*
Very Expensive	over 20,000 dr.
Expensive	15,000 dr.–20,000 dr.
Moderate	10,000 dr.–15,000 dr.
Inexpensive	5,000 dr.–10,000 dr.

*All prices are for a standard double room, excluding taxes and breakfast.

Kos **Panorama.** You will need a car to get here, but it is worth mak-
Dining ing an evening's excursion to sit in the large paneled dining
★ room with its exposed beams and fireplace or on the terrace—with a splendid view from either over the northwest side of the island. You'll enjoy the delicately fried *kolokithakia tiganita* (summer squash), octopus with oil and vinegar, fluffy *tiropitakia* (little cheese pies), and the marvelous salads with

subtly flavored tomatoes. Even if you think you don't like retsina, try the local Theokritos; it may convert you. *Bagiati-Asfendiou, tel. 0242/29367. Reservations Fri. and Sat. in high season. Dress: casual. No credit cards. Closed Nov.–Dec. Moderate.*

★ **Aklipios.** A memorable meal in Kos can be had at a little restaurant near the Asklepieion, in the village of Platani. Sit in the shade of an ancient laurel tree, and try the exquisite selection of *meze*: home-prepared *dolmadakia* (stuffed vine-leaves), *bourekakia* (cheese wrapped in fine pastry), *imam bayaldi* (baked eggplant), or a main course of grilled chicken and superb pilaf accompanied by artichokes with beans. Even the boiled cauliflower is perfect. *Platanio, tel. 0242/25264. No reservations. Dress: casual. No credit cards. Inexpensive.*

Lodging **Ramira Beach.** This is one of the better resort hotels for family holidays, just outside Kos town. Most of the white-and-blue rooms have sea views. *Psalidi Beach, tel. 0242/22891 through 0242/22894. 268 rooms. Facilities: restaurant, bar, pool, children's pool, tennis. AE, DC, MC, V. Closed Nov.–Mar. Expensive.*

Astron Hotel. This in-town hotel is located almost on the water, but it has a pool as well. Most of the rooms, which are sparsely decorated in white with touches of brown, have balconies and a view over the town's main harbor. *Akti Kountouriotou, tel. 0242/22814 or 0242/23704 through 0242/23707. 58 rooms. Facilities: cafeteria, bar, pool. AE, V. Moderate.*

Sevasti Hotel. The well-kept garden and the arches over the balconies lend a certain charm to this medium-size hotel in Kos town. The garden theme is carried over into the dining room, which has cane furniture, and in the guest rooms, with light wood furniture and white draperies and spreads. *El. Venizelou, tel. 0242/23896 or 0242/23897. 193 rooms. Facilities: restaurant, taverna, bar, pool. AE, DC, V. Closed Nov.–Mar. Moderate.*

Titania Hotel. This in-town hotel, right on the sea, offers good quality at a good price. The newly built structure is modern, outside and in, with plainly furnished but comfortable rooms. Because it is on the main road, the rooms may be noisy in high season, but to offset this, you are within walking distance of everything in town, and there's a little strip of beach right across the street. *1b Korai, tel. 0242/22556. 29 rooms. Facilities: lounge, bar. No credit cards. Closed Nov.–Mar. Moderate.*

Patmos **Grigoris.** This old favorite near the ferry landing is a good place
Dining to wait for the night boat to Athens. You can have grilled fish and meat, or a selection from the mayirefta arrayed in impressive display just outside the kitchen. Although the interior is carefully decorated in rustic taverna style, sitting outdoors is much more pleasant: Take a table under the spreading laurel tree, and enjoy the passing (and noisy) scene. *Skala, tel. 0247/31515. No reservations. Dress: casual. No credit cards. Inexpensive.*

O Kipos. The tiny hole-in-the-wall really comes to life in warm weather, when tables are pulled out into the street across the way, next to a large garden (*kipos*). Try the *kolokithopita* (squash pancakes), the delicious boiled octopus in vinegar, or *koukia* (flat beans), among other well-prepared traditional dishes. The restaurant is distinguished by the small boat and nets the owner has hung in the tree just outside, a memento of his previous life as a sailor. *Skala, tel. 0247/31279 or 0247/31884. No reservations. Dress: casual. No credit cards. Inexpensive.*

Pandelis Restaurant. Situated just a few steps back from the port, Pandelis offers good taverna-style cooking, with plenty of selection from whatever traditional Greek dishes the chef decides to do that day. Sit outside at one of the tables set up in the little sunny alley in front of the restaurant, or move inside, but not too close to the noisy TV. *Emmanuel Xenou, no tel. No reservations. Dress: casual. No credit cards. Inexpensive.*

Lodging **Blue Bay Hotel.** An enterprising Greek-Australian family has
★ returned to open this new hotel just outside Skala but within a 10-minute walk of everything. Its location, with a view over the open sea (shared by all but two of the rooms), is one of its great charms, as are the neatly decorated, immaculate rooms. *Skala, tel. 0247/31165. 21 rooms. Facilities: breakfast room. No credit cards. Closed Nov.–Mar. Inexpensive.*

★ **Captain's House.** One of the very special places to stay in Patmos (all the more because the owners are so pleasant), the Captain's House faces the sea at the edge of Skala. The atmosphere of old Patmos has been re-created with stone arches accenting the white-painted rooms and simple wood furniture. *Skala, tel. 0247/31793, fax 0247/32277. 13 rooms. Facilities: breakfast room. DC, MC. Closed Nov.–Apr. Inexpensive.*

Delfini. The bright and cheerful interior of this hotel reflects the taste of the owner's Swiss wife. Half the rooms look out to the sea, the other half toward the monastery and the hotel's lovely inner garden and patio. *Skala, tel. 0247/32060, fax 0247/32061. 12 rooms. Facilities: breakfast room. No credit cards. Closed Dec.–Mar. Inexpensive.*

Rhodes **Kontiki.** Located on a barge floating in Mandraki Harbor, this
Dining is one of the best known and most expensive places in town. The charm of its location is undeniable: In winter, the harbor lights twinkle outside the glassed-in, garden-style dining room; in summer the windows are removed, and you seem to be dining alfresco. The cuisine is international, with some house specialties: lobster thermidor, coquilles St. Jacques, shrimp Kontiki (made with bacon and mushrooms), and fillet Valeska (rolled with shrimp and lobster and sautéed au gratin). A seafood platter for two people, recommended by the chef, has scallops, lobster, swordfish, mussels, shrimp, and octopus, and costs 14,800 dr. *Mandraki Harbor, tel. 0241/22477. Reservations advised. Jacket advised. AE, DC, MC, V. Very Expensive.*

★ **Ta Kioupia.** Just outside Rhodes town in a group of humble farm buildings, Ta Kioupia is anything but humble inside. The three white-stucco rooms with exposed ceiling beams are elegantly adorned: Antique farm implements hang on the walls, there are linen tablecloths and napkins, fine china, and crystal. Don't bother to look at the menu; food arrives on large platters and you select what pleases your eye: pine-nut salad, cheese salad with garlic, *tiropita* (four-cheese pie), *bourekakia* (stuffed wafer-thin pastry) with clotted cream and nuts, *korkorosouvlaki* (rooster kebab)...the list goes on—and the food is extraordinary in its variety and quality. *Tris Periochi, tel. 0241/91824. Reservations advised. Jacket advised. AE, DC, MC, V. No lunch; closed Sun. Very Expensive.*

★ **Dinoris.** This family-owned and -run establishment is set in a great hall built in 1530 as a stable for the Knights. The food and service draw appreciative and demanding clients, from the mayor to hotel owners and visiting VIPs. Decorated in rustic style, with embroidered tablecloths, brightly painted pottery, and thick, seemingly handwoven draperies at the windows, Dinoris has long specialized in fish only. For mezes, try the variety platter, which includes *psarokeftedakia* (fish balls made from a secret recipe) as well as mussels, shrimp, and lobster. *Museum Sq., tel. 0241/35824 or 0241/35530. Weekend reservations advised in high season. Dress: casual but neat. AE, MC, V. Expensive.*

★ **Vlachos.** This restaurant, in the new town, may be slightly out of the way, but because it offers just about the best genuine home-style taverna cooking in Rhodes, and at very good prices, it is worth the taxi ride. Go to the kitchen display and see what mayireftas the chef has prepared for today: perhaps the stewed lamb with peas, or mountain-fresh *horta* (wild greens), a charcoal-broiled chicken, or just plain fresh feta cheese. The decor is nondescript modern, but the same cannot be said about the food. *90 Michael Petrides, tel. 0241/63287. No reservations. Dress: casual. No credit cards. Moderate.*

Kavo d'Oro. This simple taverna is one of the few places in the old town where you can get a good, inexpensive meal. The fare includes roast chicken, veal, lamb, and grilled meat. The decor is "taverna": plain whitewashed walls, with the typical rush-seat, straight-back chairs, and a garden at the back for warm-weather dining. *Sokratous 41, tel. 0241/36181. No reservations. Dress: casual. No credit cards. Closed Nov.-Mar. Inexpensive.*

Lodging **Rodos Palace Hotel.** At this giant resort set in gardens just outside town, everything is top of the line. It even has a pool covered with a transparent ribbed dome that's "unique in Europe." The guest rooms—some done in shades of ochre, orange, and brown, others in blue and green—are in bungalows and an 18-story tower, and many have views of the sea. *Ialysos Beach, tel. 0241/25222. 610 rooms, including suites, apartments, and bungalows. Facilities: 3 restaurants, coffee shop, 3 bars, disco, 3 pools (covered, outdoor, children's), bowling, shopping arcade, bank, convention center, scuba facilities, golf. AE, DC, MC, V. Very Expensive.*

Ibiscus Hotel. Superbly located on Sandy Point's legendary beach, the Ibiscus is good for families who want the beach and also the convenience of being close to monuments and museums. Many of the plain, beige-and-white rooms make up for their lack of charm with the wonderful views from their balconies. *17 Nisyrou, tel. 0241/24421, 0241/24422, or 0241/24423; fax 0241/27283. 206 rooms. Facilities: restaurant, bar, TV room. AE, DC, MC, V. Expensive.*

Lomeniz Hotel. This pleasant, family-style resort hotel on the eastern edge of town offers easy access to the sea, just across the street. The rooms are done in fresh sea-blue and white, the public areas are crisply and simply designed, with almost Scandinavian restraint. *Claudiou Peper and Konstandinidi, tel. 0241/35831 through 0241/35835. 207 rooms. Facilities: restaurant, 2 bars, snack bar, pool. AE, DC, MC, V. Moderate.*

St. Nikolis Hotel. Owned and run by an enterprising young family, the St. Nikolis is within the old city, away from the most crowded tourist area. The rooms are small, fitted out with dark, rusticated furniture, and look out either toward a little garden or toward the old city wall, while the roof terrace lets you breakfast with a view over the entire town with the sea in the distance. The owner also has four efficiency apartments in a newly renovated house down the street. *61 Hippodamou, tel. 0241/34561 or 0241/36238, fax 0241/32034. 10 rooms. Facilities: breakfast room, bar. V. Moderate.*

Spartalis Hotel. The hotel lives up to its name: It is Spartan, plain, and simple, but it has a wonderful location just off Mandraki Harbor, a few minutes from the gates of the old city. Insist on a room with a harbor orientation; the rooms on the street are noisy. *2 Plastiria, tel. 0241/24371 or 0241/24372. 79 rooms. Facilities: breakfast room, bar. AE, V. Moderate.*

Rooms to Let Sofia. The old town is full of rooms to rent, but Sofia's are pleasant, newly redone, and each has a little bath. *27 Aristofanous, tel. 0241/36181. 10 rooms. No credit cards. Closed Dec.–Mar. Inexpensive.*

Symi
Dining

Trawlers. Expect to eat simply in Symi; Trawlers does plain cooking better than most places on the island, and is reasonably priced. *Yialos, no tel. No reservations. Dress: casual. No credit cards. Inexpensive.*

Lodging

Aliki Hotel. Right on the water at the edge of town, the Aliki has been converted from a traditional 19th-century structure into a comfortable, modern facility. The rooms are simply furnished in island-rustic style, as are the public areas; for those who love sea views, the Aliki's can't be beat. *Yialos, tel. and fax 0241/71665. 15 rooms. Facilities: breakfast room, bar. No credit cards. Closed Dec.–Mar. Moderate.*

★ **Dorian Hotel Apartments.** You can cook your own meals in these small efficiency apartments, where the miniature living/dining rooms are fitted out with dark wood furniture, as are the cozy loft-style bedrooms. *Yialos, tel. 0241/71181, 0241/71811, or 0241/71307. 2 rooms, 7 suites. No credit cards. Closed Nov.–Mar. Moderate.*

★ **Village Hotel.** Spotlessly restored in 1992, the Village Hotel is set in a traditional neoclassical mansion that's been enlarged. Located in Chora, it has good views in all directions . . . and a steep climb home after you've had a morning coffee in the port. All the rooms open onto a balcony or terrace. *Chora, tel. 0241/71307. 17 rooms. Facilities: breakfast room. No credit cards. Closed Nov.–Mar. Inexpensive.*

10 The Northern Islands

Chios, Lesbos, Limnos, and Samos

By Toula Bogdanos

It's hard to categorize this group of northern islands off the coast of Asia Minor. When someone says "Cyclades," we instantly envision those islands with white cubist houses, sparkling sea, and often barren landscape. But these four are distinct, each with a strong identity. There's **Samos**—lush, seductive, a dizzying landscape of greens and blues and site of one of the seven wonders of the ancient world; **Limnos**—with its mournful volcanic outcroppings; **Chios**—recently ravaged by fires, but extraordinary for the historic interest of its *mastichochora* (mastic villages), engraved with geometric patterns; and **Lesbos**—Greece's third-largest island, birthplace of artists and writers inspired by its beauty, its quirkiness, its variety.

Although these islands fell into obscurity in later centuries, especially under the Ottoman empire, in the ancient world they prospered gloriously as important commercial and religious centers. They also were cultural hothouses, producing geniuses like Pythagoras, Sappho, and probably Homer.

One thing they do have in common is their proximity to Turkey, which accounts for the large military presence (most visible in Limnos) and the occasional acid remark about the neighbors to the east. After Turkey's invasion of Cyprus in 1974, tension mounted, and it was aggravated by the squabble over oil deposits in the straits between the islands and Turkey. Despite the rhetoric—mostly supplied by the two governments—islanders don't hesitate to shuttle people back and forth to Turkey. And why not, when tourism has at last arrived?

These were the last islands to be discovered by travelers; most people haven't even heard of them. They are not "party" islands that come alive only in summer, but working islands year-round, where people go about their business as they have for centuries, with that gratifying island temperament of open-mindedness and optimism.

Essential Information

Important Addresses and Numbers

Tourist Information

Chios

Tourist information office, 18 Kanari, Chios, tel. 0271/24217 or 0271/20324. **Tourist police,** 37 Neoriou, Chios, tel. 0271/26555. The **Women's Agricultural Tourist Collective** (main square, Pirgi, tel. 0271/72496) finds rooms with local families, as will Mesta's **tourist information office** (main square, tel. 0271/76319).

Lesbos

There are several **information offices,** in Eressos (main square, tel. 0253/53214), Molyvos (Possidonios near bus stop, tel. 0253/71347), Mytilini (harbor, tel. 0251/28199; airport, tel. 0251/61279), and Plomari (harbor, tel. 0252/32535). **Tourist police,** harbor, Mytilini, tel. 0251/22776. The **Women's Agricultural Tourist Collective** (Molyvos, tel. 0251/42787) finds rooms with farming families; you may help with chores, although it's not expected.

Limnos

Tourist police, 66 Garrufalini, tel. 0254/22200.

Samos

Tourist information: in Vathi, Th. Sofouli at harbor, tel. 0273/28530, and March 25th St. 4, tel. 0273/28–582; in Pythagorio, Logothetis, 1 block up waterfront, tel. 0273/61022; in Kokkari, across from OTE, tel. 0273/92333. **Tourist police:** Vathi harbor, tel. 0273/27333.

Emergencies **Chios,** tel. 0271/25914. **Lesbos,** Mytilini, tel. 0251/22–776;
Police Molyvos, tel. 0253/71222. **Limnos,** tel. 0254/22200. **Samos,** Vathi, tel. 0273/27980; Pythagorio, tel. 0273/61100; Karlovassi, tel. 0273/31444).

Medical Assistance **Chios,** tel. 0271/23488. **Lesbos,** tel. 0251/28457. **Limnos,** tel. 0254/22222 or 0254/23333. **Samos,** tel. 0273/27407.

Arriving and Departing by Plane

Airports and Even if they have the time, most people avoid the 10- to 12-hour
Airlines ferry ride from Athens and start their island-hopping trip by air. Most flights are 45 minutes or less. **Olympic Airways** (tel. 01/961–6161) has at least a dozen flights a week from Athens to each of the islands in summer.

Chios Olympic Airways has offices in the port town of Chios (Prokymeia midport, tel. 0271/24515) and at the airport (tel. 0271/23998), which is 4½ kilometers (3 miles) from town. To reach the airport, call 0271/24546.

Lesbos Olympic Airways offices are in Mytilini (44 Kavetsou, tel. 0251/28659) and at the airport (tel. 0251/61490). The airport (tel. 0251/61212) is 7 kilometers (4¼ miles) from Mytilini.

Limnos Call the Olympic office in Myrina (Garofalidi 6, tel. 0254/22214 or 0254/22215) or at the airport (tel. 0254/31204). The airport (tel. 0254/31294 or 0254/31202) is near Moudros Bay, 9 kilometers (5½ miles) from Myrina.

Samos The busiest airport (flight information, tel. 0273/61219) is here, 17 kilometers (10½ miles) from Vathi. More than 35 international charters arrive every week in midsummer. Olympic's offices are in Vathi (5 Kanari, tel. 0273/27237), in Pythagorio (Lykourgos 90, tel. 0273/61213), and at the airport (tel. 0273/61269).

Arriving and Departing by Boat

If you can't get on a flight, there's always the extensive ferry network, offering the consolation that you'll travel for a third of the airfare. The national tourist office in Athens distributes weekly ferry schedules. For last-minute departure times, call the Athens port authority (tel. 01/451–1311).

To reach the **Chio's** port authority, call 0271/22837. Boats arrive daily from Piraeus, and three ferries a week leave from Athens's backdoor port at Rafina (tel. 0284/22300). On **Lesbos** the port authority (tel. 0251/28827) is in Mytilini. There are at least four boats per week from Piraeus and two per week from Rafina. On **Limnos,** call 0254/22225; there are four arrivals weekly from Piraeus. **Samos** has port-authority offices in Vathi (tel. 0273/27318) and Pythagorio (tel. 0273/61225). Boats arrive six–eight times per week from Athens, stopping at Paros and Naxos, and in summer boats leave Pythagorio almost daily for Patmos.

Getting Around

By Plane   Other than four flights weekly between Limnos and Lesbos, there are no direct flights between these northern islands; it's best to go by ferry.

By Boat   There are several boat connections weekly between Samos, Chios, and Lesbos. From Limnos a boat goes once or twice a week to Lesbos and back.

By Car and Moped   A car is handiest on Lesbos, the biggest island, but costs about $70 a day. Mopeds (about $18 a day) are the ideal way to see the smaller islands. You won't have any trouble finding a rental agency.

By Bus   Buses leave the town of Chios several times per day for Mesta
Chios   and Pirgi, once daily for Volissos. For information call the KTEL station (Vlatarias 6, tel. 0271/27507).

Lesbos   Lesbos's bus system (KTEL, Platia Constantinopoleos, tel. 0251/28873) is expensive and infrequent, though there are several buses a day from Mytilini to Molyvos via Kalloni, and you can also get to Mandamados, Plomari, Eressos, and Sigri.

Limnos   On Limnos the few buses from Myrina (Platia KTEL, tel. 0254/22464) depart early and occasionally don't return the same day. You can, however, go from Myrina to Moudros and all points in between quite easily.

Samos   Samos has excellent bus service (KTEL, Ioannou Lekati and Kanari, near the Olympic Airways office, tel. 0273/27262), with frequent trips between Pythagorio, Samostown, Kokkari, and Karlovassi. Buses also travel frequently to Ireon, Pirgos, Marathokambos, and Votsalakia beach.

Guided Tours

El Travel (Xristodoulidou 10, Myrina, tel. 0254/24988, fax 0254/22697), on **Limnos,** gives English tours to the archaeological museum and to various villages and interesting sites.

On **Lesbos, Aeolic Cruises,** with branches in Mytilini (Prokimea, tel. 0251/23960 or 0251/23266, fax 0251/43694) and Plomari (Agios Isidoros, tel. 0251/32009), offers a variety of island tours. In Molyvos, **Panatella Tours** (Possidonion at town entrance, tel. 0253/71520 or 0253/71643 or 0253/71644, fax 0253/71680) has two tours that take in villages, monasteries, and other sights.

On **Chios, Ionia Touristiki** (Rodokanaki 17, tel. 0271/41047 or 0271/22034, fax 0271/41122) organizes excursions to the mastichochora and other sights (one is a four-wheel-drive tour).

On **Samos,** most of the branches of **Samina** (main office, Th. Sofouli 67, Vathi, tel. 0273/28841 or 0273/28842 to find a branch near you) run an island tour, a one-day trip to Patmos, and a picnic cruise.

Exploring the Northern Islands

Tour 1 is a quick stopover in Limnos, since there isn't much to see, except Myrina port and the Cabiri and prehistoric Poliochni sites (only for archaeological diehards). **Tour 2** covers Lesbos, moving from the capital Mytilini to northern villages like Petra and dreamy Molyvos, to Sappho's birthplace in Eressos, to Agiassos and Plomari, a fishing hamlet starting to go glitzy. **Tour 3** begins in the Turkish quarter of Chios and travels to Teacher's Rock, where Homer is said to have taught. It continues to Nea Moni monastery, with its fine mosaics and tragic history, to the southern mastichochora (mastic villages) of stenciled Pirgi and labyrinthine Mesta, and to the volcanic beach at Emborio. **Tour 4** circles Samos, from pretty Pythagorio to the Temple of Heraion, one of the seven Ancient Wonders, through mountain villages like Pirgos to the tiny harbor of Ormos Marathokambos, and the fishing village of Kokkari, ending at Vathi, the capital.

Highlights for First-Time Visitors

Agiassos, Lesbos (*see* Tour 2)
Kouros in archaeological museum, Vathi, Samos (*see* Tour 4)
Molyvos, Lesbos (*see* Tour 2)
Nea Moni monastery, Chios (*see* Tour 3)
Pirgi and Mesta mastichochora, Chios (*see* Tour 3)
Road from Ayios Konstantinos to Kokkari, Samos (*see* Tour 4)
Temple of Heraion, Samos (*see* Tour 4)

Tour 1: Limnos

Numbers in the margin correspond to points of interest on the Limnos and Lesbos map.

Lying low and flat on the Aegean, Limnos is essentially a garrison island guarding the entrance to the Black Sea; the military installations are the first thing one notices. On the way to nowhere, the island gets few tourists, with the exception of Greek families who come for the beaches, and British subjects on cruise ships, who want to see Moudros Bay, an important site of the Gallipoli campaign. The population, dependent on the military and farming, is dwindling rapidly. The island is divided into west and east by deeply indented Moudros Bay on the south and Pournias Bay on the north. Tiny villages of stone houses punctuate a checkerboard of hay and tobacco fields decorated with gaudy scarecrows; calm plains give way to dark volcanic rocks and remote sandy beaches. Once well wooded, the island's interior is now so barren that, when giving directions, villagers might tell you to turn at "the tree." Green enough in spring, the island becomes crackling brown in summer, and villages often shut off water in the evenings to conserve.

The god Hephaistos (Vulcan in Roman mythology) landed on Limnos when Zeus, his father, furiously hurled him from Mt. Olympus for daring to defend Hera, his unruly mother. At his foundry on Limnos, Hephaistos made a race of cast-gold maidens, who stoked the furnace, causing the disturbances that ruptured the island. When his wife Aphrodite left him for Ares, the

*strapping god of war, Limnian women flung her statue into the
sea. The miffed Aphrodite retaliated by giving the women body
odor, which drove their men into the arms of captive Thracian
women. The frustrated wives then poisoned their husbands'
wine, slit their throats, and threw them into the sea. They then
lived alone until the arrival of Jason and the Argonauts, who
helped them repopulate the island.*

Today Limnos's volcanic origins are evident in its hot springs
and the once famous Limnian earth. From antiquity, the soil,
high in sulfur, was exported in limited amounts to heal fester-
ing wounds and snakebite. Once a year on August 6 the precious earth is still dug up under the surveillance of a priest, who
allows only one wagonload to be carted off. Islanders use it, and
you can buy it from pharmacies in Myrina or Moudros.

❶ In **Myrina,** on the west end, the 13th-century Genoese-Turkish
fortress melds with the rust-brown rock formations cleaving
the bay in two. It's a short hike to the top, and although there's
not much except some cisterns, from the castle at sunset Mt.
Athos seems to rise out of the western sea, shimmering in the
distance. The castle belonged to Byzantium in the Middle
Ages, then fell to the Venetians, the Genoese, and finally in
1479 to the Turks. *No tel. Admission free. Open daily 8:30–2.*

Backing up to the castle are white, wind-hammered houses
with wood balconies, many of them mariners' homes, interspersed with the occasional Turkish house. The city **museum**
chronicles the island's history with finds from Poliochni,
Hephaestia, the Cabiri sanctuary (*see below*), and ancient
Myrina. *Romaiko Gialo beach, tel. 0254/22990. Admission
free. Open Tues.–Sun. 8:30–3.*

❷
❸ Southeast of Myrina are two lovely beaches—at **Plati,** about 2
kilometers (1¼ miles) down the road, and **Thanos,** 4 kilometers
(2¼ miles) away, but they're easiest to reach by caïque from the
harbor.

The east side of the island, with streams and fruit groves, is
more attractive than the barren west. On your way to Moudros
you first take the road to Repanidi, 26 kilometers (16 miles)
❹ from Myrina, where you can turn off for **Kotsinos village** and its
view of Pournias Bay. At Kondopouli, 6½ kilometers (4 miles)
past the turnoff, archaeology buffs should watch for signs to
❺ the ruins of ancient **Hephaestia** (sometimes called Paliopoli), inhabited since prehistoric times. Excavations here uncovered
houses, a 6th-century BC sanctuary, a cemetery, and a Roman
theater.

Across the silted-up bay, 3 kilometers (2 miles) from
❻ Hephaestia, is **Cabirion,** near Chloi, and the ruins of one of the
oldest sanctuaries of the Cabiri cult, which worshiped the underworld gods. Archaeologists found a large stoa and many inscriptions giving clues to early Limnian life. Both Hephaestia
and Cabirion are informal sites—without any entrance fee and
usually open in the morning, depending on the guard. (According to legend, Chloi is the site also of the famous **cave of Philoc-
tetes,** whose story is detailed in Sophocles' play).

Return from Chloi to the main road by way of Repanidi, and
❼ continue south to **Moudros,** the island's second biggest town.
Here in 1915 the Allies launched an attack on the Dardanelles,
and in 1918 the British signed an armistice with Turkey after

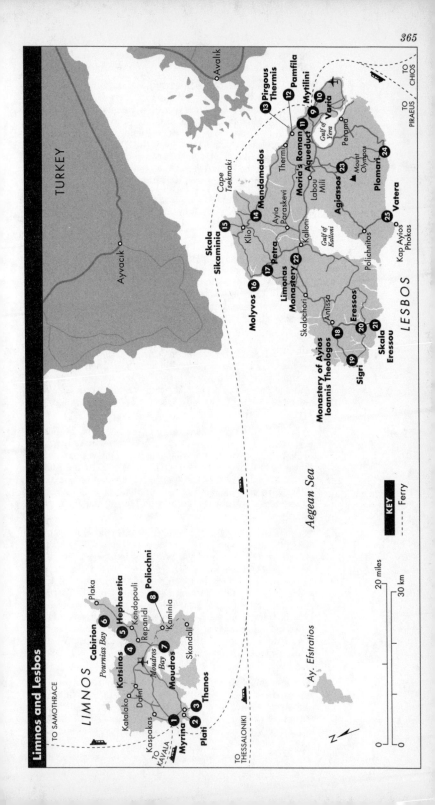

Limnos and Lesbos

TURKEY

Ayvalık

LIMNOS

TO SAMOTHRACE

Plaka

Cabirion **6**

Katalako

Kaspakas

Dafni

Poumias Bay

5 Hephaestia

Kondopouli

Repanidi

Kaminia

4 Kotsinos

Myrina **1**

Moudros Bay

7 Moudros

Plati **2**

Thanos **3**

Skandali

8 Poliochni

TO KAVÁLA

TO THESSALONIKI

Ay. Efstratios

Aegean Sea

Ayvacık

Cape Tsekmaki

Skala Sikaminia **15**

Mandamados **14**

Klio

Ayia Paraskevi

Petra **17**

16 Molyvos

Limonas Monastery **22**

Skalochori

Antissa

Monastery of Ayios Ioannis Theologos

Sigri **19**

18

Eressos **20**

Skala Eressou **21**

Thermia

Maria's Roman Aqueduct **11**

13 Pirgous Thermis

Pamfila

12 Mytilini

Vatia **9** **10**

Gulf of Yera

Perama

Labou Mili

Kalloni

Gulf of Kalloni

23 Agiassos

Mount Olympos

24 Plomari

Polichnitos

Vatera **25**

Kap Ayios Phokas

LESBOS

TO PIRAEUS

TO CHIOS

N

0   20 miles

0   30 km

KEY

----- Ferry

the disaster at Gallipoli. Only the Allied war graves hint at this dull town's former importance.

8 Southeast of Moudros lies **Poliochni,** signposted from Kaminia, 12 kilometers (7½ miles) from the bay. Here Italian archaeologists have uncovered four layers of settlement; the oldest predating the Minoan kingdoms in Crete. The only architectural remnants—an extremely thick wall and house foundations—come from the second oldest level, the 2000 BC city where the Italians also found the oldest baths in the Aegean. The third city dates to the Late Bronze Age, and the last settlement is a contemporary of Mycenae (1500 BC–1100 BC).

From Poliochni return 24 kilometers (15 miles) to Myrina, where you can catch the ferry or fly to Lesbos.

Tour 2: Lesbos

When you first land, Lesbos, with its rocky landscape, may not strike you as particularly interesting, but it will grow on you. The island was once a major cultural center, known for its Philosophical Academy, where Epicurus and Aristotle taught; it was the birthplace of the philosopher Theophrastus, who presided over the Academy in Athens; of the great lyric poet Sappho; of Terpander, the "father of Greek music"; and of Arion and Alcaeus, inventors of the dithyramb (a short poem with a wild erratic strain). Even in modernity, artists emerged from Lesbos: Theophilos, a poor villager who earned his ouzo by painting some of the finest primitive art modern Greece has produced; novelists Stratis Myrivilis and Argyris Eftaliotis; and more recently, Greece's latest Nobel prizewinner, poet Odysseus Elytis.

Greece's third-largest island, after Crete and Evia, Lesbos has more islanders than either Corfu or Rhodes, with only a smattering of the tourists. It looks like a giant jigsaw-puzzle piece, carved by two large sandy bays, the gulfs of Yera and Kalloni. The Turks called Lesbos the "garden of the empire" for its fertility: Olive trees abound on the undulating hills, while the higher peaks wear wreaths of wildflowers and dark green pines.

9 The main town, **Mytilini,** sprawls across two bays and an intervening headland, supporting a Genoese fortress. The bustling waterfront just south of the headland is where most of the town's sights are clustered. Stroll the main street, Ermou, past the fish market, where men haul in their sardines, mullet, and octopi, and the enormous baroque **church of St. Therapon,** which dominates the landscape. In front of the Mitropoleos cathedral, there is a **traditional Lesbos house,** restored and furnished in 19th-century style, that people are permitted to visit, so call to arrange a time with owner Marika Vlachou. *Mitropoleos 6, tel. 0251/28550. Admission free. By appointment only.*

The **archaeological museum,** in the newer part of town, will help you fathom Lesbos's past; its holdings include finds from prehistoric Thermi and reliefs of comic scenes from the 3rd-century AD Roman House of Menander. *Argiri Eftaliotis 7, tel. 0251/28032. Admission: 400 dr. adults, 200 dr. students. Open Tues.–Sun. 8:30–3.*

The only vestiges of ancient Mytilini are a Hellenistic theater in the pine forest northwest above town, one of the largest in ancient Greece. Pompey admired it so much, he copied it for his theater in Rome.

Also above town looms the stone **castle** built by the Byzantines on a 600 BC temple of Apollo. It was repaired using available material (note the ancient pillars crammed between the stones) by Francesco Gateluzzi of the famous Genoese governing family. Look above the gates for the two-headed eagle of the Palaiologos emperors, the horseshoe arms of the Gateluzzi family, and inscriptions made by Turks. Inside the castle is a crumbling prison and a Roman cistern, but you should make the visit for the fine view. *Tel. 0251/27297. Admission: 400 dr. adults, 200 dr. students. Open Mon.–Sat. 7:30–2:45, Sun. 8:15–2:45.*

Mytilini was the scene of one of the most dramatic moments in Greek history. Early in the Peloponnesian War, it revolted against Athens but surrendered in 428 BC. The Athens assembly decided to kill all men in Lesbos and enslave all women and children as punishment, and a boat was dispatched to carry out the order. The next day a less vengeful mood prevailed and the assembly repealed its decision and sent a second ship after the first. Its crew worked in shifts, eating and drinking as they rowed. Picture the second ship, pulling into the harbor just as the first commander finished reading the death sentence. Mytilini was saved.

⑩ One of Greece's best **art museums** is at **Varia,** 4 kilometers (2½ miles) south of Mytilini. Here, in the 19th-century painter Theophilos's former home, hang 80 of his whimsical paintings: great washes of color detailing the everyday life and the fantasies of another age. He painted airplanes—which he'd never seen—and exotic cities—where he'd never been—but most compelling are his scenes from daily life that evoke the island's charm. *Tel. 0251/28179. Admission: 100 dr. Open Tues.–Sun. 9–1 and 5–8.*

Next door are the **Teriad Library** and the **Museum of Modern Art,** home of Stratis Eleftheriadis, better known by his French name, Theriade. He rose to fame as the foremost publisher of graphic art in Paris and the exhibit includes his publications—*Minotaure* and *Verved* magazines—and his collection of works (mostly lithographs) by Picasso, Matisse, Chagall, and Miró. *Tel. 0251/28179. Admission: 250 dr. Open daily 9–5.*

⑪ Just outside Mytilini to the north is **Moria's Roman aqueduct,** from the 2nd century. It was in Lesbos that Julius Caesar first made his mark. Sent to Bythinia to drum up a fleet, he hung around so long at King Nicodemus's court he was rumored to be having an affair with the king, but in Lesbos he finally distinguished himself by saving a soldier's life.

From Mytilini it's an easy 8 kilometers (5 miles) north to **⑫** **Pamfila's** tower mansions, once used by wealthy families as **⑬** summer homes, and then you come to **Pirgous Thermis,** with its 12th-century church, Panayia Tourloti. The village of **Thermi** nearby takes its name from the hot springs. A settlement existed here from before 3000 BC until Mycenaean times, centered on the spa's curative properties.

⓮ Mandamados, 37 kilometers (23 miles) north of Mytilini, is famous for its pottery, *koumari* urns that keep water cool even in scorching heat, and for its black icon of Archangel Michael in the 18th-century monastery, **Taxiarchos Michalis.** Visitors make a wish and press a coin to the archangel's forehead; if it sticks, the wish will be granted.

On the archangel's feast day—usually the third weekend after Easter—you will see an ancient, probably pagan custom. A bull and several sheep decorated with flowers are sacrificed in the monastery's courtyard. The faithful dip handkerchiefs in the blood, marking their foreheads to protect themselves from sickness. The next day everyone feasts on the meat, called *keskeri*. The same occurs at **Agia Paraskevi,** 15 kilometers (9 miles) southwest, where **horse races** are held after the distribution of the meat.

Five kilometers (3 miles) north of Mandamados, you'll come to a junction, where you should continue straight, turning left just **⓯** before Klio for the lovely port of **Skala Sikaminia.** Stratis Myrivilis used a composite of this town and Petra (*see below*) as the setting for his novel *The Mermaid Madonna.* If you've read it, you'll recognize the tiny chapel at the end of the jetty. Return to Sikaminia, and turn west.

⓰ Continue west to **Molyvos,** also known as Mithimna, a town you may dream about long after you leave. Come before high season and ascend to the Byzantine-Genoese **castle** for a hypnotic view down the tiers of red-tile roofs to the glittering sea. At dawn the sky begins to light up from behind the mountains of Asia Minor, knifing silver streaks through the placid sea as weary night fishermen come in. *No tel. Admission free. Open until sunset.* As you descend from the castle, the grapevine-sheltered lane passes weathered Turkish fountains and pastel houses weighed down by roses and geraniums, their backs turned defensively to the sea. On the waterfront, old men sit playing *tavli* (backgammon).

Although new hotels have been banned in the old town, Molyvos swells with tour groups in summer, and you may want **⓱** to stay overnight in **Petra,** 5 kilometers (3 miles) south on the creek of a large sandy bay. Atop a giant monolith (Petra means "rock" in Greek) is the 18th-century church Panayia Glikofiloussa (Virgin of Tenderness), reached by climbing 114 steps. The less ambitious may want to stroll the beach, visit Ayios Nikolaos church, with its 16th-century frescoes (off the square) or the intricately decorated Varelitzidaina mansion near the marketplace. *No tel. Admission free. Mon.–Sat. 9–1.*

Until recently the volcanic northwestern part of Lesbos was home to wild horses, believed to be the last link with the horse-breeding culture of the Troad, mentioned by Homer.

Four kilometers (2½ miles) after Antissa, the road forks right **⓲** for Sigri and passes the **monastery of Ayios Ioannis Theologos,** or Mon i Ipsilou, founded in 800 and rebuilt in the 12th century; **⓳** it has a small collection of 12th-century manuscripts. **Sigri,** 43 kilometers (26 miles) from Petra, is built around a lovely cove; at water's edge is a small Turkish castle in ruins, although its cannons are intact. Despite the apocryphal claim of a petrified forest—trees fossilized by volcanic ash—between Sigri and Eressos, it's not worth the search. If you're interested, take a look at the specimens in Sigri's square.

From Sigri travel southeast 15 kilometers (9 miles) past some
of the island's best beaches to **Eressos,** the birthplace of Sappho, and its neighbor, Skala Eressou. It is believed the poet
was born in the 7th century BC in ancient Eressos east of the
present village. Dubbed the Tenth Muse by Plato because of
her sensual lyric poetry and new poetic meter, she ran a school
for young women. Though she was married, with a daughter,
she earned the reputation of being a homosexual because her
surviving poetry is dedicated to her students. (The word "lesbi-
an" derives from Lesbos.) Sappho's works were burned, and
only fragments of her books survive. Despite its erotic reputation, Sapphic meter was in great favor in the medieval ages and
used in hymns, especially by Gregory the Great.

Skala Eressou has a wide sandy beach, castle ruins, and the
5th-century BC church, Ayios Andreas. The church has a mosaic floor and an archaeological museum housing local finds from
tombs in the ancient cemetery. *Harbor, tel. 0253/53332. Admission free. Open daily 8:30–3.*

From Eressos, return toward Mytilini on the main road via
Antissa. Three kilometers (2 miles) before Kalloni is the sleepy
15th-century **Limonas monastery,** complete with peacocks and
farmyard animals. A bishop has collected a jumble of plates,
doodads, and paintings in a sort of folk-art museum, but more
interesting is the treasury of Byzantine manuscripts. Women
are not allowed in the main church.

Continue east for about 20 kilometers (12 miles), and at the
junction 3 kilometers (2 miles) after Labou Mili turn right for
Agiassos village. It sits at the foot of Mt. Olympos, the island's
highest peak. (There are 19 mountains in the Mediterranean
named Olympos, almost all of them peaks sacred to the local
sky god, who eventually became associated with Zeus.) Despite its recent discovery by tourists, Agiassos remains a lovely
settlement with gray stone houses, cobblestone lanes, a medieval castle, and the church of Panayia Vrefokratousa. The latter was founded in the 12th century to house an icon believed to
be the work of St. Luke. On August 15 islanders flock here to
celebrate the Feast of the Assumption of the Virgin with dancing, drinking, and eating. On Clean Monday at the end of Carnival, costumed islanders take part in a custom known as *valia,*
an improvised exchange of satirical verse.

Plomari, 20 kilometers (12½ miles) south, set in a cliff face, is a
cheerful mix of flashy resort and quiet fishing village, known
for its potent ouzo. There's a lively night scene on the harbor,
where tourists gather after a long day at the beach. Southwest
of Agiassos lies **Vatera,** one of Lesbos's most beautiful beaches,
a long sandy strip lined with pine trees. From Agiassos return
to the main road and turn left; you'll come to Vatera after about
20 kilometers (12 miles). From there, it's about 53 kilometers
(33 miles) to Mytilini via Polichnitos, on the best road, and from
there you can fly back to Athens or catch a ferry to Chios.

Tour 3: Chios

*Numbers in the margin correspond to points of interest on the
Chios and Samos map.*

Apostrophe-shaped Chios, 48 kilometers (30 miles) long, with
its intact mastichochora (*see below*), eventful history, and im-

portant Byzantine monasteries, has a strong sense of place. It wasn't until the late 1980s that the first weekly charters from Northern Europe began; until then the island prospered solely from its export of mastic (a tree resin used in varnish and chewing gum) and its shipping dynasties. The island was home to the elite families that control Greece's private shipping empires: Livanos, Karas, Chandris; even Onassis came here from Smyrna. "Craggy Hios," as Homer called it, was an island of great natural beauty that has been decimated by severe forest fires, which left only the far north and the far south unscathed.

26 The main town, **Chios**, or Chora (which means "town"), is a busy commercial settlement on the east coast, oblivious to tourism. Its heart is the shambling bazaar district south and east of the main square (Platia Plastira). A few blocks away is the **old Turkish quarter** inside the *castro* (fort), built in the 9th century by the Byzantines. Under Turkish rule the Greeks lived outside the wall; the gate was closed daily at sundown. As you enter, you'll come to a courtyard with the 15th-century **Giustiani mansion.** In its airy rooms hang frescoes from Nea Moni and Panayia Krina church (*see below*). *Tel. 0271/22819. Admission free. Open Tues.–Sun. 9–3.*

In the fort's small square, Platia Frourio, look for the Turkish cemetery and the large marble tomb (with the fringed hat) of Kara Ali, chief of the Turkish flagship. Down the main street are elegant Ayios Georgios church (closed most of the time), with icons from Asia Minor; houses from the Genoese period; and in the north corner, the Turkish baths. In the tiny prison just inside the fortress, 75 leading Chiotes were jailed as hostages in 1822 before they were hanged by the Turks, part of the worst massacre committed during the War of Independence. The Turks, who conquered the Genoese in the 1500s, had been fond of the island for its mastic (which they chewed in the harems to sweeten their breath), and had allowed it to retain many privileges. But Chios, spurred by Samians who had fled to the island, joined the rest of Greece in rebellion. The revolt failed, and the Sultan retaliated: The Turks killed 30,000 Chiotes and enslaved 45,000, an event depicted by Delacroix in *The Massacres of Chios*. The painting shocked Western Europe and led indirectly to support for Greek independence.

A copy of the Delacroix hangs in the dusty post-Byzantine **museum** housed in the mosque off Platia Plastira. Note the *tugra* on the mosque, the swirling thumbprint of the Sultan that shows royal possession. Although the tugra is common in Istanbul, it is rarely seen elsewhere, and its presence indicated the favor Chios enjoyed under the Sultan. *Platia Plastira, tel. 0271/26866. Admission free. Open daily 10–3.*

The new **archaeological museum,** still with only one hall open to the public, should be completed soon. Its collection ranges from proto-Helladic pottery dug up in Emborio to a letter from Alexander the Great addressed to the Chiotes and dated 332 BC. *Michalon 10, tel. 0271/26664. Admission free until completed. Open Tues.–Sun. 8:30–3.*

Time Out   Savor the fragrant cinnamon-topped *rizogalo* (rice pudding) made every morning in the milk shop **To Kalamari.** It's on the corner of Vamva and Rodokanaki, off the waterfront. If you're

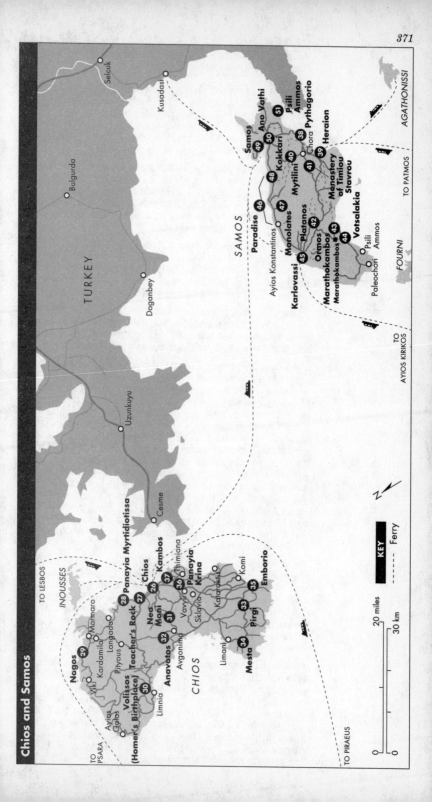

Chios and Samos

KEY

- - - - - Ferry

0 ____ 20 miles

0 ____ 30 km

TURKEY

Selçuk
Kuşadası
Bulgurda
Doğanbey
Uzunkuyu
Çeşme

CHIOS

TO PSARA
Ayiós Gálas
Víki
Marmáro
Kardámila
Langáda
Pityoús
Nagos 29
Limniá
**Volissós
(Homer's
Birthplace)
Teacher's Rock** 30
Avgónima
Anavatos 32
Nea Mani 31
27
Panayia Myrtidiotissa 28
Chios 26
Kambos 37
Vavýli
36 **Panayia Krina**
Thimianá
Sklaviá
Kalimásia
Komi
Pirgi 33
35 **Emborio**
Mesta 34
Limáni

TO LESBOS
INOUSSES

TO PIRAEUS

SAMOS

Ayios Konstantínos
Karlovassi 45
Paradise 46
Manolates 47
48
Kokkari 50
49 **Samos**
Ano Vathi
Psili Ammos 51
38 **Pythagorio**
Mytilini 40
41
Platanos
Monastery of Timiou Stavrou 42
Oranos
Marathokambos 43
Marathokambos
Votsalakia 44
Psili Ammos
Paleochóri

39 Chóra
Heraion

TO PATMOS
AGATHONISSI

FOURNI

TO AYIOS KIRIKOS

still not satisfied, pop next door for a half-dozen *loukoumades*, honey-dipped, nut-smothered fritters.

---

(27) Just above the port of Vrontados, 4 kilometers (2½ miles) north of Chios, is Daskalopetra, or **Teacher's Rock,** where Homer is said to have taught his pupils. Archaeologists believe it is actually part of an ancient altar. Legend has it that Homer was born on the island though Smyrna, Colophon, Salamis, Rhodes, Argos, and Athens also claim to be his birthplace.

(28) Continue north past the 19th-century monastery of **Panayia Myrtidiotissa** (Our Lady of the Myrtle), past the villages of Pantoukios; Langada (at Delphinion nearby, a 5th-century BC Athenian naval base was unearthed); Kardamila; and **Nagos** **(29)** harbor, where at the foot of a gorge choked with greenery a ruined temple of Poseidon was found.

(30) **Homer's birthplace** is thought to be about 29 kilometers (18 miles) southwest of Kardamila, at Volissos, an important northern village, which today is desolate, with only a few inhabitants. Its solid stone houses march up the hillside to the Genoese fort, where Byzantine nobles were once exiled.

(31) The island's most important monument is the 11th-century **Nea Moni,** a monastery 8 kilometers (5 miles) west of Chios. Emperor Constantine Monomachos VIII built it where three monks had found an icon of the Virgin in a myrtle bush.

The octagonal medieval church (*katholikon*) created by architects and painters from Constantinople exemplifies the artistic ideas prevailing during the 11th century in that city. Its distinctive three-part vaulted sanctuary has two narthexes, with no buttresses supporting the dome. This design, a single square space covered by a dome, closely connected with Constantinople, is rarely seen in Greece. The church's interior gleams with colored marble slabs and mosaics of Christ's life, austere yet sumptuous—with azure blue, ruby red, velvet green—and skillful applications of gold. The saints' expressiveness comes from their severe gaze, with heavy shadows under the eyes, and their vigorous poses. On the *iconostasis* hangs the icon—a small Virgin and Child facing left. Also inside the grounds are an ancient refectory, a vaulted cistern, and a large clock still keeping Byzantine time, with the sun rising and setting at 12.

Two kilometers (1¼ miles) from Nea Moni en route to Chios, the road turns southwest to Avgonima, from which there is a view of the west coast, and to the semi-abandoned medieval village of **Anavatos** to the north. In 1822, during the revolution, **(32)** 400 women and children threw themselves over the cliff here rather than surrender to the Turks. About 50 houses still stand in the heavily fortified town, where the only signs of life are the farmers who come to gather pistachios.

Return past Avgonima to the junction north of Nea Moni, and turn right (south) for Pirgi, one of the **mastichochora,** 30 kilometers (18 miles) away. Two dozen families named Columbus live here, who claim descent from Christopher Columbus, said to have been from Chios. The name Chios comes from the Phoenician word for mastic, the resin of the *pistacia lentisca*, evergreen shrubs that with few exceptions thrive only here. Every August incisions are made in the bark of the shrubs, the sap leaks out, permeating the air with a sweet smell, and in September it is harvested. This aromatic resin, which brought millions in revenue until the introduction of petroleum products, was used in varnishes, waxes, cosmetics, and in the somewhat addictive jelly beans that were a staple in the Ottoman harems.

③③ To enter **Pirgi** is to walk into a graphic designer's dream; many of the houses along the tiny arched streets are adorned with *xysta* (like Italian sgraffito), dizzying geometric patterns cut into the white plaster and outlined with gray paint. Especially lavish are the designs on houses near the main square, including the **Kimisis tis Theotokou church** (Dormition of the Virgin), built in 1694. Down an arcade off the square's northeast corner is the fresco-embellished 12th-century church, **Ayii Apostoli,** a replica of the earlier Nea Moni. The 17th-century frescoes that completely mask the interior, the work of a Cretan artist, have a distinct folk-art leaning. (Ask at the main square to find the current doorkeeper.)

③④ Eleven kilometers (8 miles) west of Pirgi is **Mesta,** the island's best-preserved medieval village, a labyrinth of twisting vaulted streets linking two-story stone-and-mortar houses supported by buttresses against earthquakes. The village sits inside a system of 3-foot-thick walls. One of the largest and wealthiest churches in Greece commands the main square, the 18th-century **Megas Taxarchis,** its vernacular baroque and rococo features combined in the late folk-art style of Chios.

③⑤ From Pirgi it's 8 kilometers (5 mi) southeast to the glittering black **volcanic beach near Emborio.** Known by locals as Mavra Liladia, the cove is formed by jutting volcanic cliffs; the water looks black from the dark smooth stones.

③⑥ On your return to Chios, near Varili, you'll see a road to the left marked to Sklavia. It takes you to the 12th-century **Panayia Krina** (Our Lady of the Source), where three layers of frescoes spanning six periods were discovered. The very earliest period is represented by portraits of the saints facing the entrance; most of the restored frescoes hang in the Giustiani mansion in Chios (*see above*).

③⑦ From Vavili, cross to the coastal road at **Thimiana,** where mastodon bones were found, and head north through the **Kambos** region. Here, behind forbidding walls adorned with coats of arms, aristocratic families built their estates—each a world of its own. The restored mansion of Philip Argentis, one of the first on the road into Kambos (left side) will give you an idea of the former grandeur of these houses. From Chios you may continue by ferry to Samos or travel back to Athens.

Tour 4: Samos

Once known as the Island of the Blessed, Samos possesses a felicitous landscape of lacy surf, mountain villages perched on ravines drowning in wildflowers—pink oleander, red poppy, purple sage—and significant ancient ruins. Its mountains, part of the great Asiatic spur that runs across Turkey, make for suprising twists in the landscape. For those who approach from the west, by boat from Athens, Mt. Kerkis seems to spin out of the sea, while in the distance Mt. Ambelos guards the terraced vineyards that produce the famous Samian wine. The island's ancient names attest to its sweet virtues: Homer called Samos *Hydrele*, the watery place, for its many clear springs, and it has been dubbed Anthemis for its flowers and *Pittousa* for its abundant pines. Although in the last decade Samos has become packed with charter tourists during July and August, it's large enough to allow you to escape the crowds easily.

During its heyday in the 6th century BC, the island contributed greatly to the ancient world. It was home to Aesop and to Aristarchos (the first in history to place the sun at the center of our universe), to the philosopher Epicurus and the mathematician Pythagoras, for whom the ancient capital (formerly Tigani, or "frying pan") was renamed. Remembered for the theorem $a^2 + b^2 = c^2$, Pythagoras also was the first to note the mathematical relations in music, and the beauty of proportions—ideas that brought near perfection to Classical architecture. Plutarch writes that Anthony and Cleopatra came to Samos "giving themselves over the feasting," that artists came from throughout the ancient world to entertain them, and kings vied to send the grandest gifts.

❸❽ Samos had been a democratic state, but in 535 BC **Pythagorio** fell to the tyrant Polycrates (540 BC–522 BC), who used his fleet of 100 ships to make profitable raids around the Aegean, until he was caught and crucified in 522 BC. His rule produced what Herodotus described as "three of the greatest building and engineering feats in the Greek world." The first is the **ancient mole** protecting the harbor on the southeast coast, on which the present harbor rests. The second is the **Efpalinion tunnel,** an underground aqueduct just north of town made with primitive tools and without measuring instruments. Efpalinion of Megaras, a hydraulics engineer, set two teams of slaves digging, one on each side of Mt. Kastri. Fifteen years later, they met in the middle with just a small difference in the elevation between the two halves. The tunnel is electrically lit, and though some spaces are tight and slippery, you may walk the first 1,000 feet. For information call the Pythagorio museum. The third achievement was the **Heraion** (*see below*), west of town, the largest temple ever built in Greece and one of the Seven Wonders of the Ancient World.

Little else remains from ancient Pythagorio except a few pieces of the wall and the ancient theater a few hundred yards above the tunnel. Today's village wraps around the harbor, its quiet streets filled with fragrant orange blossoms. At one corner sits a crumbling fortress built by Revolutionary hero Lycourgos Logothetis. That's his statue in the church courtyard next door. At night the villagers light votive candles in the church cemetery, a moving sight with the ghostly silhouette of the fortress and the moonlit sea in the background. The small **Pythagorio Museum** contains local finds, including headless statues, grave markers with epigrams to the dead, and portraits of Roman emperors. *Platia Pythagoras, tel. 0273/61400. Admission free. Open Apr.–Oct., Tues.–Sun. 8:30–3; hours may vary.*

❸❾ From Pythagorio, take the road west toward Chora, but bear left at the sign for the ruins of the **Temple of Heraion,** 6½ kilometers (4 miles) west. The early Samians worshipped Hera, believing she was born here near the stream Imbrassos and that there she also lay with Zeus. Several temples were built on the site, the last by Polycrates, who rebuilt the Heraion, enlarging it and lining it with two rows of columns, 133 in all, of which only one remains standing. At the semiannual celebrations to honor Hera, the faithful approached from the sea on the Sacred Way, which is still visible at the site's southeast corner. Nearby are replicas of a 6th-century BC sculpture depicting an aristocratic family, whose chiseled signature reads "Genelaos made me." The originals and the world's largest *kouros* (statue of a young man), also found here, are in the Samos archaeological museum (*see below*). The temple was damaged by fire in 525 BC and never completed, owing to Polycrates' untimely death.

40 From the island's former Turkish capital, the typical village of **Chora,** a short detour north on the Vathi road brings you to the village of **Mytilini** and its **paleontological museum,** which has local animal fossils dating back 15 million years. The prize exhibit, among the bones of ancient hippos, rhinos, and evolving three-toed horses, is a 13-million-year-old fossilized horse brain. *City hall, tel. 0273/51205. Admission free. Open Apr.– Oct., weekdays 8–3.*

41 The **monastery of Timiou Stavrou** (a few kilometers west of Chora) is worth a stop for a look at the icons, the carved wooden iconostasis, and the Bishops' Throne. On September 24, the monastery celebrates its feast day with a service followed by a *panegyre* (feast), with music, firecrackers, booths of coconut candy, plastic toys, and *loukoumades* (honey-soaked dumplings). The landscape still shows the charred signs of a 1989 fire that destroyed acres of pine forest.

The traditional village of **Pirgos** and its neighbor **Pandrossos,** on the side of Mt. Ambelos, are ideal for getting a glimpse of island life. And if you continue past Pandrossos, up over the mountain, within minutes you'll be in deep pine forest, where it occasionally gets misty even when the sun shines below. The network of dirt roads emerges on the other side of Mt. Ambelos, descending past **Vrondiani** monastery (1566) and the northern vineyards.

Time Out   Stop in the huge shaded courtyard of **Koutsi,** 5 kilometers (3 miles) after Pirgos, for the traditional snack of yogurt and fragrant Samian honey.

As you curve around the western side of the island, foreboding Mt. Kerkis hangs in the distance and the island's undeveloped west coast plummets below you. As you approach 11 kilometers (7 miles) west of Pirgos, watch for the junction to the right for **42** **Platanos,** another traditional village, where, except for "Greek nights" staged by travel agencies in summer, not much changes from year to year. In October Platanos gives a big bash when the new batch of homemade *tsipoura* is ready. The firewater flows freely, served with *mezes* (appetizers) and fruit soaked in alcohol, and people dance to the *rembetiko*.

Return to the road from Pirgos and travel north past Ayios Theodori for the junction of the road up to **Marathokambos.** The village stretches across the lower flanks of Mt. Kerkis, and on afternoons when the haze clears, the island of Patmos can be **43** seen on the horizon. The road descends south to **Ormos Marathokambos,** which still has a small caïque-building industry, and a bit farther west, to one of Samos' fine beaches, **44** **Votsalakia,** a long, pine-shaded strip of sand.

Return past Marothokambos to the main road, turn left, and go **45** 6 kilometers (4 miles) north through **Karlovassi.** The town seems rather grim until you take a closer look below the main square, where you see richly decorated churches and elaborate mansions, padlocked and slightly dilapidated, which hint of a time when Karlovassi was a center for the production of leather. Note the empty tanneries as you drive east along the coast.

Time Out | West of the town a pebble and sand beach, **Potami,** has shady pine trees, under which people camp, and interesting rock formations. Hidden in a reedy area halfway along the beach is a small white house where a local family serves lunch all afternoon. You can eat surrounded by greenery and watched over by the family donkey.

46 Shortly after **Ayios Konstantinos,** 12 kilometers (7½ miles) east of Karlovassi, begins the stretch known as **Paradise,** an area with constantly changing coastal views and lush foliage—from banana plants to oak trees. You'll cross through Platanakia, flanked by two large tavernas whose courtyards are shaded by plane trees. Walk up the road here a few hundred yards to Aidonia Park (Nightingale Park), where the bird's song is heard at sunrise and sunset. Farther east a winding road turns **47** off for **Manolates,** 5 kilometers (3 miles) up Mt. Ambelos through steep vineyards, with a beautiful view. Although Samian wine comes in white and rosé too, it is the dark sweet dessert wine about which Lord Byron wrote, "Raise high the bowl of Samian wine."

48 After the popular beaches of Avlakia, Tsabou, and Tsamadou, Paradise ends suitably in the fishing village of **Kokkari,** probably the most appealing place on the island. Until 10 years ago, there was nothing here except a few houses between two headlands, and though now there are several hotels, the town is still enchanting. Cross the spit to the eastern side of the headland and watch the moon rise over the lights of Vathi in the next bay.

49 After Kokkari you come to Malagari, where farmers bring their grapes to the winery every September, and 10 kilometers (6 miles) farther, at the head of the Vathi Bay, is **Samos,** the capital, also known as **Vathi.** In the morning at the harbor fishermen still untangle their nets to dry in the sun, and in the early afternoon everything shuts down. Tourism does not alter this centuries-old schedule. The stepped streets ascend from the shopping thoroughfare, which meanders from the port to the city park next to the **archaeological museum,** the town's most important sight. The museum's older wing has a collection of cast bronze griffin heads (the symbol of Samos), pottery, and gifts from ancient cities paying tribute. The new wing holds the impressive **kouros from Heraion.** It stands alone in the room, massive, with an inscrutable smile, the enigma of ancient Samos. It's so large (16½ feet tall) that the wing had to be built specifically to house it. *Platia Dimarchio, tel. 0273/ 27469. Admission: 500 dr. adults, 300 dr. students. Open Tues.–Sun. 8:30–3.*

50 If you walk past the museum uphill always veering right, you'll soon enter the quaint older village of **Ano Vathi,** where the pastel houses are jammed together, their balconies protruding into streets so narrow the water channel takes up most of the space. From here you have a view of the narrow gulf. To get to one of the best beaches on the island's east side, leave Samos on the road to Pythagorio, turn left at Mesokambos, and drive 6

⑤ kilometers (4 miles) east to sandy **Psili Ammos,** stopping first at pebbly **Mykali beach** for a stunning view of Turkey. From here you might fantasize about swimming the straits to Turkey and Mykali peak, less than 2 kilometers (1½ miles) across the sea.

Off the Beaten Track

Beach lovers can easily get from Karlovassi, by bus and on foot, to two delightful secluded coves: **Mikro Seitani** (pebble; about 30 minutes) and **Megalo Seitani** (sand; about 65 minutes). There are no stands there, and often no people, so bring your own picnic. From the port, walk or take the bus west to Potami beach, where the asphalt ends. After about 10 minutes you'll come to a dirt path that veers right. Ignore it. Turn off at the second path going left two minutes later, marked by a stone pile. After the stone hut, the trail winds through olive trees giving glimpses of the turquoise sea below. After another 15 minutes, another path bears left, but continue straight, and in less than five minutes you'll come upon the limpid cove of Mikro Seitani.

If you can manage to tear yourself away, continue to Megalo Seitani, along a path that has good views of Mt. Kerkis and in spring passes through masses of wildflowers. After about 55 minutes you'll see a path veering left; continue straight and you will reach Megalo Seitani in another 10 minutes.

Shopping

These are not really shopping islands, but local products you can't find in Athens make interesting gifts.

A rarely exported product of **Limnos** is the delicious wine; you might also look for the dried blue-black plums with their delicate aroma. **Lesbos** is famous for its chestnuts, its olive oil, and especially its ouzo. In Molyvos, the Athens School of Fine Arts occasionally holds sales of its paintings. Agiassos is known for its crafts and Mandamados for its koumari urns, which keep liquids cool. In **Chios** look for the ceramics of Armolia, the handwoven fabrics of Mesta, the ouzo, and the mastic products: ELMA chewing gum, *mastica* liqueur and *gliko koutaliou*, a sugary goo that's served on a spoon in water (a favorite with children). In Thimiana, 7 kilometers (4½ miles) south of Chios, the Women's Cooperative (tel. 0271/32000, open weekdays 9–9) sells traditional woven fabrics and rugs made from multicolored rags. Four kilometers (2½ miles) farther south is the village of Kallimasia, whose Popular Art Cooperative (tel. 0271/51–180, open Mon.–Sat. 9:30–12:30 and 3:30–6:30) has cloth dolls in Chian costumes. In Samos you can buy the famous sweet Samian wine, its famous honey, and its graceful ceramics painted with wildflowers. The most popular item is the "Pythagoras" cup, which leaks when it's more than half full. It was invented by Pythagoras to ensure his students didn't indulge too heavily during lessons.

Sports and Outdoor Activities

Participant Sports

Fishing In **Chios**, locals usually fish the bays of Kalamoti, Kardamila, and Limia; Chios harbor is good for spearfishing, as is the east coast near Kardamila. In **Lesbos** you can catch sea bream, horse mackerel, dorado, and blackfish everywhere. Most fishing in **Limnos** is in Plateos Bay and off Cape Moudros, In **Samos,** sea bream, dorado, red mullet, and blackfish are plentiful in Marathokambos and Samos bays.

Hunting Hunters in **Chios** should head for the hills near Pirgi for quail, turtledove, and partridge. In the hills of **Limnos,** local hunters go after partridge, hare, wild rabbit, and duck; there is a **hunting union** (tel. 0254/22062) whose members are occasionally around to answer questions. In **Lesbos** the small island of Ayios Georgios across from Petra offers duck, geese, quail, blackbirds, thrush, woodcock, partridge, and wild rabbit. **Samos** also has a **hunting union** (tel. 0273/27681); game here is mostly partridge, hare, thrush, and birds migrating to Africa.

Sailing Your charter agency will usually give basic details about where to find fuel and water. **Sun Yachting** (tel. 01/983–7312) in Athens specializes in charter rentals to Samos; you can pick up the boat in Piraeus or Pythagorio for one- and two-week rentals. In **Chios** you can moor in Kardamila, Limia, and Chios town; at the latter call 0271/27286 if you need fuel and 0271/27377 for water; repairs are available in the harbor. In **Limnos** both Myrina and Moudros have fuel, water, and repair services. You can moor at most large coastal villages in Lesbos for fuel and water, including Mytilini, Molyvos, Skala Sikaminias, Sigri, Plomari, and Skala Eressou. In **Samos,** Pythagorio, Karlovassi, and Samos town have fuel, water, and repair services.

Tennis Only a few of the better-class hotels have courts. If you're not a guest you might still persuade the management to let you play, but it's unlikely during high season. Hotels with courts in **Lesbos** (all near Molyvos) include **Sun Rise Bungalows** (tel. 0253/71713), **Alkeos** (tel. 0253/71002), **Aphrodite** (tel. 0253/71725), **Delfinia I Hotel and Bungalows** (tel. 0253/71373), and **Olive Press** (tel. 0273/71205). In **Limnos, Akti Myrina** (tel. 0254/22681) has courts, but they are indisputably for guests only. Near Pythagorio, on **Samos,** the **Doryssa Bay** (tel. 0273/61360), **Apollon** (tel. 0273/61683), and **Princessa** hotels (tel. 0273/61698) have courts.

Water Sports Most resort hotels provide water sports on their beaches. You can usually rent paddleboats and canoes on Romaiko Gialo beach in **Limnos**; paddleboats, canoes, and sailboarding equipment are available in **Lesbos** at Sigri, Vatera, and Skala Eressou. In **Samos** many beaches have Windsurfer rentals, including Heraion, Karlovassi, Mykali, Potokaki, Tsamadou, and Votsalakia.

Beaches

Many beaches are topless, unless they're part of the town's waterfront, but there is always a nonnude stretch where families congregate. Nude bathers should use discretion; in general, if you choose your spot carefully, you should have no problem with local people or the law.

Chios Emborio in the southeast has an unusual black-stone beach; in the southwest a string of secluded coves with good swimming runs between Elatas and Trachiliou bays, including a nudist beach with fine white pebbles about 2 kilometers (1¼ mi) north of Lithio. Near Chios town, Karfas beach fronts a shallow bay. In the north, try Marmaro and wooded Nagos.

Lesbos Some of the most spectacular beaches are sandy coves in the southwest, including a stretch from Skala Eressou (dark sand) to Sigri. In the southeast, there is a good sand/pebble beach at Ayios Isidoros near Plomari and a sandy beach in Gera bay just south of Skala Polihnitos. One of the southeast's most appealing beaches is the long, pine-rimmed sweep of Vatera.

Limnos Closest to town is "Swiss beach" at Akti Myrina, but there are better, quieter beaches south at Platis and Thanos all the way east to the almost mile-long stretch at Evgati near Kontias.

Samos Very good sand beaches can be found at Psili Ammos in the southeast and at the much less crowded, harder-to-reach Psili Ammos in the southwest. Along the north coast near Karlovassi is Potami with its picturesque rocks and pines, but here waves are much bigger. Closer to Kokkari on the north coast are the acclaimed coves of Tsamadou (nudist), Avlakia, and Tsabou, all just a few minutes from each other, and all to be avoided when the *meltemi* (northern winds) blow.

Dining and Lodging

Dining

Although the more touristy areas have succumbed to a certain mediocrity in their waterfront restaurants, you can still find delightful meals, especially in the villages. Unless noted, reservations are unnecessary, and casual dress is always acceptable. Be adventurous: go to the kitchen, point to what you want. The thing to order is fish, which except for smaller catch, is rather expensive. Remember that what restaurants often call lobster, *astakos*, is usually crayfish; and almost always, the shrimp is frozen. All other fish will be fresh, except for the dried cod used in *bakaliaro*. If you can find it, try *kakavia*, a fishermen's soup with small catch stewed with onions and tomatoes. In **Limnos**, specialties include *halvah*, with lemon squeezed over it to cut the sweetness. Limnos is also the place for octopus grilled over embers and sweet *trahanas*, wheat kernels boiled in milk and dried. Besides its mastic products, **Chios** is known for tangerines, eaten fresh or in *gliko koutaliou*, preserves in thick syrup. In **Lesbos**, try the *keskeri*, boiled meat with wheat, and Kalloni bay sardines, the fleshiest in the Mediterranean; eat them mashed with lemon and oil. Octopus simmered in wine, another island dish, goes perfectly with the famous island ouzo, most of it made in Plomari. A local dessert is the almond pudding called *baleze*. **Samos** is known for its wines, especially a sweet dessert-red called *moschato*.

Highly recommended restaurants in each price category are indicated by a star ★.

Category	Cost*
Very Expensive	over 6,000 dr.
Expensive	3,000 dr.–6,000 dr.
Moderate	1,800 dr.–3,000 dr.
Inexpensive	under 1,800 dr.

*per person, for 3-course meal, including appetizer, entrée, and dessert (usually fruit)

Lodging

With the exception of high season (August), you can always find accommodations. Most hotel rooms are very basic, with simple pine furniture, and little on the walls. These islands are still cheaper than the more popular Cyclades, but prices are starting to go up. Make sure to reserve early for the better category of hotel, especially in Pythagorio on Samos and Molyvo on Lesbos. Outside high season, you can usually bargain over the official prices and get away without paying for a compulsory breakfast. Hotels are not air-conditioned unless noted, and, even in those that are, you must sometimes insist that it be turned on. Islanders are extremely friendly hosts, and although they may get a little snappish now and then when the hordes descend in August, they still consider you a guest rather than a billfold.

Often, if you're discreet, you can camp on the beaches; make sure to ask permission if you see any houses nearby. Among the better official campgrounds is **Chios** at Ayios Isidoros (Chios, tel. 0271/74111, 0271/74112, or 0271/74113; closed Oct.–May), which has all the amenities and a beach site that looks across to Asia Minor. On Lesbos, **Dionyssos** (tel. 0253/61340; closed Oct.–Apr.) is at Vatera Beach, one of the island's best.

Unless noted otherwise, all hotels are open year-round. Highly recommended establishments are indicated by a star ★.

Category	Cost*
Very Expensive	over 20,000 dr.
Expensive	10,000 dr.–20,000 dr.
Moderate	6,000 dr.–10,000 dr.
Inexpensive	under 6,000 dr.

*Prices are official rate for double room with bath in high season, including tax and service and excluding breakfast. For those hotels in which half-board is compulsory, meals (one is breakfast) for 2 are included in price.

Chios

Dining **Bel Air.** With its black-lacquer furniture, stiff palm plants, piano and ubiquitous mirrors, the decor is a step up from most tavernas. The menu changes often: Look for *soupies me sevgola* (cuttlefish stuffed with mountain greens) and *soupa petropsaris* (rockfish soup). The schnitzel is filled with Edam and topped with onion-mushroom sauce. *Aegeou near Chandris Hotel, Chios town, tel. 0271/29947. MC, V. Moderate.*

★ **Hotzas.** This cozy taverna has a wood interior crowded with overhead barrels, brass implements, and family portraits. Mother and son cook succulent lamb with lemon sauce, and many vegetable dishes. Fish is available, although there's less choice in summer. The squid is always reliable, not tough or chewy, and is delicious eaten with the homemade retsina or ouzo. Avoid the snails, a disappointing garden variety boiled in red sauce. For dessert, order yogurt with homemade cherry or quince preserves. *Stef. Tsouris 74 and Kondili 3, Chios, tel. 0271/23117. No credit cards. Moderate.*

★ **O Moreas.** The owner spends hours picking herbs and greens on the mountains and the seashore (for example, a sort of seaweed for a salty taste atop salads). If you want to try the goat fricassee, you must order a day ahead, but otherwise you can take your pick of *kontosouvli xifias* (swordfish on the spit), *domatokeftedes* (fried tomato balls), *xirino krasato* (pork simmered in wine), or *melitzanes* (eggplants steeped in garlic). Sit outside for a view of the church, for which the owner has the key. *Mesta Sq., Mesta, tel. 0271/76400. No credit cards. Moderate.*

Limani Meston. Formerly the El Coral, this fish taverna has something for every budget, from inexpensive net fish to larger catch like sea bream and red mullet. Meats include homemade sausage, whole roasted piglets (order ahead), and lamb or beef on the spit. You can sit outside among the ivy and blossoms; where Mesta's charming harbor stretches before you, or on colder days, enjoy the fireplace with the locals. *Mesta harbor, 4 km (2 mi) from town, tel. 0271/76367, 0271/76365, or 0271/76365. No credit cards. Inexpensive.*

Lodging **Golden Sand.** This convenient hotel sits on the beach near Chios town, a few kilometers from the airport. Three boxy white buildings contain simple air-conditioned rooms with carved-wood furniture, shower or bath, and almost always a sea view. The hotel has some nice extras like a game room, a playground, and a huge buffet breakfast. On "Greek night" in summer, tour groups arrive for Greek music and dancing. *Beach Rd., Karfas, 82100, tel. 0271/32080, 0271/32081, or 0271/31010; fax 0271/31700. 108 rooms. Facilities: restaurant, bar, piano bar, playground, pool, gift shop, games room, beauty salon. AE, MC, V. Expensive.*

Chandris. As you pull into port you can't miss this shipowner's hotel; it looks like a giant apartment building and has a grand lobby, a dining room with a chandelier, and large plate glass windows. The air-conditioned rooms, in shades of blue and green, are quiet, and the service is excellent. *Prokymea, Chios, 82100, tel. 0271/25761 through 0271/25766. 156 rooms. Facilities: restaurant, bar, pool. AE, DC, MC, V. Moderate.*

Fedra. From the moment you enter this neoclassical house, painted the typical ocher with white gypsum around the windows and planted with jubilant flowers, you feel at home. This pension is an appealing, inexpensive alternative to the bigger hotels in town. All the rooms have baths and air-conditioning. *M. Livanou 13, Chios, 82100, tel. 0271/41129 or 0271/41130. 10 rooms. Facilities: café-bar. MC. Moderate.*

Kyma. Begun in 1917, this villa belonging to shipowner John Livanos was completed in 1922, the year the agreement for Chios's freedom from Turkey was signed in its living room. A modern cement addition only slightly mars the pension, with its stone facade and grillwork. Many of the architectural details remain—note the painted ceiling in the lobby. All rooms are air-conditioned, most have sea views, and several have whirlpool baths. The only problem: noise is from the street below. The breakfast is enough to make you bounce out of bed: yogurt, eggs, ham, fruit, and fresh Chios tangerine juice. *Chandris 1, Chios, 82100, tel. 0271/25552. 59 rooms. No credit cards. Moderate.*

★ **Traditional Settlements.** These medieval fortified houses, built into the maze of Mesta village, give a feel for life in a mastichochora. There are four two-story houses with rooms: The Argyroudi house has two rooms and a kitchenette under a vaulted baby-blue ceiling, decorated with vase-adorned alcoves and village furniture. The houses were built with small exterior doors and windows, but they face inward to a courtyard. Most rooms have private baths with showers. Mr. Pipilis makes all the arrangements; call him in advance. *Mesta, 82100, tel. 0271/76319. 8 rooms. No credit cards. Moderate.*

Lesbos

Dining
★ **Dagieles.** If you're not already enchanted with Agiassos village, you will be after stopping here for a coffee made on the *briki*, a special coffeepot that owner Stavritsa swears by. And you should try the dishes that entice the local police here throughout the winter: *kritharaki* (barley-shape pasta), *kokkinisto* (beef in red sauce), pork with oven-roasted potatoes, and *varkoules* ("little boats" of eggplant slices with minced meat). Fresh fish and grilled meat are also available. Mt. Olympos looms in the distance, and for a few short weeks in spring the air is laden with the scent of overhanging lilacs. *Agiassos near bus stop, tel. 0252/22241. No credit cards. Moderate.*

Dimitrakis. Mr. Dimitrakis's refrigerator looks like a mini fish market. On any given day he may have as many as 10 varieties. Locals call the restaurant the "little boat grill" because of its nautical decor. Try the simple grilled fish or the *bakaliaro* (fried cod with garlic sauce), and start your meal with *bourekakia* (ham-and-kasseri-cheese pie). With two cooks and seating for 200, the restaurant is hopping, and in the evening you can sit outside and eat dinner to the sound of rocking boats. *Dexios Limenarxios Rd., Fanari section of Mytilini, tel. 0251/ 23818. No credit cards. Moderate.*

★ **Gatos (To Pithari).** Gaze at Turkey, the castle, and the harbor from the veranda, or sit inside and watch the cooks chop and grind in the open kitchen. Besides the usual fresh fish, there are *stifado* (grilled meat) with garlic and onion pieces (better than the traditional whole onions because they soak up the flavor of the herbs). The beef fillet is tender, the lamb ribs nicely grilled. Breakfast is also served. *Main Rd., Molyvos, tel. 0253/ 71661. No credit cards. Closed Nov.–Mar. Moderate.*

Medusa. This new restaurant in a traditional stone house on the wharf offers some interesting specialties, including *ostraka mayirefta* (shellfish in red sauce), *moschari Medusa* (beef cooked in ceramic dishes), and *kalamarakia gemista* (squid stuffed with rice). As you sip your ouzo in front you might sample the grilled crayfish; the spinach, herb, or cheese pies; or *plagi* (oven-cooked beans called *gigantes*). The owners provide flawless service and quality at a low price. *Molyvos harbor, across from Ayios Georgios chapel, tel. 0253/71630. No credit cards. Closed Nov.–Apr. Moderate.*

Zourou. This fish restaurant, decorated with nets and dried lobsters, sea urchins, and shrimp, has been catering to local residents for 30 years. Try the bourekakia or the lemony *taramosalata* (fish-roe dip). Move on to the daily catch—grouper, crayfish, sea bream—and finish off with a big bowl of *kalamaki* (like vanilla ice cream with pieces of candied fruit). *Beach Rd., Vatera, tel. 0252/61259. No credit cards. Closed Nov.–Mar. Moderate.*

Asteria. Mr. Arapis has been overseeing this well-known taverna for more than 25 years, offering seven or eight mayirefta nightly and a complete grill selection, including thick, juicy beef patties and a spicy pork dish called *exohiko*. Among his specialties are eggplant with artichokes and *yiouvetsaki politiko* (beef cooked in a clay pot with *aromatika* [sweet spices]). In summer, customers sit outside on the harbor. *Kountourioti 56, Mytilini, tel. 0251/22689. No credit cards. Inexpensive.*

Dining and Lodging

Vatera Beach. Run by American Barbara Ballis and her Greek husband George, this low-key but well-designed hotel has all the makings of a higher-category lodging. Rooms in the four white-and-blue buildings have their own entrances, balconies, and a sea view; most have showers rather than baths. The Ballises stay here year-round, so small groups can arrange to visit in winter, when a fireplace and central heating make it a treat. Most of the food for the hotel's restaurant is raised or grown organically by Barbara: fruits, vegetables, pigs, even rabbits. *Vatera beach, 81300, tel. 0252/61212. 25 rooms. No credit cards. Closed Nov.–Apr. Moderate.*

Lodging

Aeolis. This cluster of beach bungalows offers all the comforts of a resort complex. From the raised pool area (preferable to the mediocre beach), guests have a view of the sea as well as Molyvos castle. The lounge has a marble fireplace, deep-seated sofas, and potted plants. Most of the bungalows have two or three beds, thick armchairs that fold out, and French doors onto a veranda. A hotel shuttle service runs up to town, as does the local bus. Half-board is mandatory, but since the rate includes buffet breakfast and another meal for two, it is still a good deal. *Outside Molyvos on rd. to Eftalou, 81108, tel. 0253/71772. 28 rooms. Facilities: restaurant, bar, snack bar, pool. MC, V. Closed Nov.–Mar. Expensive.*

Mytilana Village. Several buildings circling a pool comprise this hotel on a predominantly pebble beach in the Gulf of Yera. The rooms have "Swedish" blond-pine furniture, balconies, minibars, and bathtubs. The mandatory half-board is convenient, since most restaurants are a taxi drive away. The dining room has heavy wood chairs, a beamed ceiling, brick-outlined arches, and the same striped curtains you see everywhere. A local bus makes the round-trip into town once a day. *Ethnikis Odos, 6 km (4 mi) outside Mytilini toward Kalloni, 81107, tel.*

0251/20653, 0251/20654, or 0251/29655. 50 rooms. Facilities: restaurant, bar, pool. AE, DC, V. Closed Nov.–Mar. Expensive.

★ **Clara.** A superior hotel of its class, completed in 1991, Clara has a striking contemporary reception area in cool whites and gray. The bungalows all have spacious verandas with a view to the sea or the castle, and with their comfortable gray beds, steel blue covers, and pink curtains, are a cut above the usual. Guests can hop the shuttle bus to explore Petra, float in the large L-shape pool, or play a few sets of tennis. A buffet breakfast is served out on the terrace. *Avlaki, near Petra, 81109, tel. 0253/41522, 0253/41523, or 0253/41524, fax 0253/41535. 45 rooms. Facilities: restaurant, bar, pool, children's pool. AE, MC, V. Moderate.*

Rex. This delightful pension in one of the town's well-heeled neighborhoods is away from the noise of the port. The bougainvillea in front are so lavish that tourists often stop to photograph the entrance. The pension's mirrors and high ceilings lend the rooms a spacious feeling despite the dark carved furniture. Several rooms are available with private bath. *Katsakouli Kioski 3, Mytilini, 81100, tel. 0251/28523. 16 rooms. No credit cards. Moderate.*

Sea Horse. After you've had enough of the touristy ambience uptown, descend to this modest hotel overlooking the busy harbor. You'll feel you've stepped into a scene from *Never on Sunday.* Despite the traditional wood-and-stone exterior, the rooms are modern, half have showers, half have baths, all have a view across the harbor. Breakfast, served in a ground floor breakfast room, is Continental (à la carte items are available). *Molyvos harbor, 81108, tel. 0253/71320. 13 rooms. Facilities: cafeteria, bar. No credit cards. Moderate.*

★ **Villa 1900.** The renovated neoclassical house, in a fairly quiet location near the stadium, is a real treat, with stonework, a lush garden, and old-fashioned details like iron beds, family photographs, and, in a few rooms, ceilings painted with women and flowers. The best rooms are the three in the converted garret. Guests sit in the garden for breakfast, which includes eggs, and fruit juice from the hotel's trees. *Vostani 24, Mytilini, tel. 0251/23448, 01/806–5770, or 01/228–9379. 11 rooms. No credit cards. Moderate.*

Zaira. For an unusual setting, spend the night in this former olive mill, built in 1909. At the entrance to the main stone buildings stands the mill's smokestack, and a large red olive press graces the lounge. The traditional stonework is evident in the bar, in the restaurant with its beamed ceiling, and in walls of the guest rooms that line the courtyard. The rooms are air-conditioned, and the four suites have fireplaces. Just a few steps away is a small harbor, where a boat stops daily to take guests to the cove of Ayios Ermogenis. *Loutra, about 7 km (5 mi) outside Mytilini, tel. 0251/91004, 0251/91100, 0251/91101, or 0251/91102. 28 rooms. Facilities: restaurant, conference hall, gift shop. No credit cards. Closed Nov.–Mar. Moderate.*

Women's Agricultural Tourist Cooperative. You can immerse yourself in island life by rooming with a Greek family, or working in the fields through the cooperative. Women of the area (many speak rudimentary English) rent rooms (most with private baths, all with breakfast). They also run an excellent restaurant on the town square, with fish and meat dishes and *kotomakaronakia* (a local specialty of chicken and noodles baked in cream). *Office and restaurant on main sq., Petra,*

81109, tel. 0253/41238. 100 rooms. No credit cards. Inexpensive.

Limnos

Dining **Grigoris.** One of the newest tavernas, Grigoris already has won the hearts of locals for its fine food. There's a large variety of fish and excellent grilled meats, including hefty *xirines brizoles* (pork chops) and *biftekia* (beef patties). Try the *fava* (crushed yellow split peas in oil, garlic, and onion) and the *piperies gemistes* (stuffed peppers). For dessert, the shredded-wheat-and-honey confection called *kaidaifi* is sure to put you in a good mood. *Rixo Nera area of Myrina, on rd. to Akti Myrina, tel. 0254/24434. No credit cards. Moderate.*

Avra. Although the service may be slow (who's in a rush?), this large taverna on the harbor square serves substantial portions of mayirefta. Try the split roasted chicken basted with lemon-oregano sauce or the moussaka, *tsoutsoukakia* (sausage meatballs), or souvlakia. *The taverna sits across from Myrina port authority, tel. 0254/22523. No credit cards. Inexpensive.*

O Platanos. This family-style taverna sits in a square with two huge old plane trees planted 90 years ago. Because fish is expensive, the owner has a limited menu of traditional dishes: kokkinisto with okra, spinach, or peas; moussaka; pastitsio or *makaronada* (pasta); stifado; *xoriatiki* (large Greek salads); and *laxano dolmades* (grape leaves stuffed with cabbage and rice). The barrel wine is a hefty red from the village of Ayia Sofia. *Main rd. near bus sq., Myrina, tel. 0254/22070. No credit cards. Inexpensive.*

Lodging **Akti Myrina Bungalows.** This complex financed by Swiss inter-
★ ests, locally called Little Switzerland, is a destination in itself, dominating the scene from a fortified hill. The wood chalets are spacious, with individual air-conditioning, large baths, and ocean views; the rooms are done in quiet colors. You must book far in advance, as many guests are repeaters. The new fitness center has weights, aerobics classes, and a massage therapist on call. Bungalow No. 312's sunset view is one of the best. *Myrina, 81400, tel. 0254/22681 through 0254/22685 or 01/413–7907. 125 rooms. Facilities: 4 restaurants, game room, 2 pools, private beach, tennis courts, water sports. AE, DC, MC, V. Closed Nov.–Apr. Very Expensive.*

Afroditi. The owners run their hotel with cheerful efficiency, and it could easily belong to a higher category. Just a few yards from Swiss beach, the hotel is surrounded by geraniums, roses, petunias, and fruit trees. Besides the housekeeping apartments, there are five rooms on the roof. The spic-and-span rooms are brightly decorated with cane-and-bamboo furniture and have orthopedic mattresses. Guests can go for a spin on the speedboat or rent the hotel caïque. Prices for boat rental are negotiable. *Across from Ayios Pantelimon in Rixa Nera area, Myrina, 81400, tel. 0254/23489 or, in Athens, 01/964–1910. 25 rooms. Facilities: minibar, kitchen. AE, DC, MC, V. Closed Nov.–Mar. Moderate.*

Astron. A few notches below Akti Myrina, this is a good place for families who plan on a lengthier stay. Astron's larger housekeeping apartments can accommodate six. Although none of the rooms has an ocean view, the beach is close by. In early spring the rates are significantly lower; even in summer there's a discount for weekly and monthly stays. *Garofalidou 3,*

Myrina, 81400, tel. 0254/24392 or 0254/24393. 12 rooms. Facilities: café. V. Moderate.

Samos

Dining **Avgo tou Kokkora.** The name comes from the Greek tale of a woman who invited her son-in-law to dinner, promising such a variety of food that there'd even be an *avgo tou kokkora* (rooster's egg). Variety is the key here: Besides fresh fish, the seaside restaurant offers such unusual dishes as *kokkara krasata* (rooster in wine), *bastounia tou sef* (a fried ham-and-cheese appetizer), and *glosses tis petheras* (mother-in-law's tongue), made from beef tongue. There are the usual Greek foods, as well. There's a panorama of Kokkari Bay, and, best of all, Avgo tou Kokkora stays open until 3 AM. *Kokkari promenade, tel. 0273/92113. DC, MC, V. Moderate.*

Dionyssos. This new restaurant has a large menu with well-prepared, interesting dishes like swordfish or turkey on a skewer, lamb sautéed with olives, chicken cordon bleu with white sauce, and *parmezana* (chicken in Roquefort sauce). Forgo the usual Greek salad for salad Dionyssos, made with boiled potatoes, zucchini, onions, and tomatoes. Most people eat in the bamboo-shaded, terraced courtyard, but don't sit at the tables near the road or too close to the speakers piping in Greek music. *Rd. behind Karlovassi harbor, tel. 0273/34386. No credit cards. Closed Nov.–Mar. Moderate.*

Kariatides. Here you sit at water's edge, and no matter how crowded the place is the waiters can always squeeze in another table. The fresh-fish menu includes many kinds of sea bream and features the small but tasty *tsipouria* and the *kalamarakia tou chef* (squid in red sauce). House specialties also include a northern Greek dish of beef and pork mixed in lemon sauce, and *saganaki garides* (cheese and shrimp cooked in a ceramic pot). The wine list is long; for dessert there's *galaktobouriko* (creamy custard in pastry). *Kokkari promenade, tel. 0273/92276. No credit cards. Moderate.*

La Calma. Everybody at La Calma always seems to be having a good time. Maybe it's the setting, on a terrace over the water, or maybe it's the large selection, from the grilled fresh fish, to the traditional meat dishes such as kokkinisto, tender fillet, and roast chicken. For dessert, try the caramel custard or a glass of sweet Samian *moschato. Kefalopoulou 7, Vathi, tel. 0273/22654. No credit cards. Closed Nov.–Apr. Moderate.*

Lito. One of the better restaurants lining Pythagorio's esplanade, Lito has such interesting dishes as the addictive *kolokithakia gemista* (zucchini stuffed with feta and bacon). Besides the usual grilled meats, Lito has a mixed grill with beef patties, souvlakia, and liver; *biftekia à la Russe* (steak with an egg on top); and beef patties filled with Gouda and ham. Late risers can have breakfast all day. Look for the mustard-color awning and gray-and-blue chairs. *Pythagorio harbor, tel. 0273/61101. No credit cards. Closed Nov.–Mar. Moderate.*

The Steps. Turn left off the Samos waterfront, turn left between Dionyssos and Souda restaurants, climb the steps, and walk into a courtyard overhung with ivy and flowers, with candlelight, snow-white linen, and soft music. One of the chef's specialties is the mixed plate, which gives you a chance to try the souvlaki, lamb, village sausage, and a meatball. Lamb is roasted on a spit, sliced, and served with gravy. The Krissakis family also serve *exohiko* (roasted pork rump), swordfish grilled with lemon-oil sauce, and sole breaded like schnitzel. *Near Samos harbor, tel. 0273/28649. No credit cards. No lunch. Closed Nov.–Apr. Moderate.*

Dionyssos. When you tire of eating on Pythagorio's waterfront, where food is often overpriced and monotonous, take a taxi 7 kilometers (4¼ miles) to Mytilini for inexpensive well-cooked chops, *kotopoulo krasato* (chicken in wine), lemon chicken, and the seldom-seen chicken breast on a spit. The good appetizers go well with the chilled barrel retsina. Maybe then you'll be ready when a Gypsy vendor parks his van next to your table and pulls out some stereo speakers he's trying to sell. *Mytilini Sq., tel. 0273/51820. No credit cards. Inexpensive.*

★ **Gerania.** Despite the plastic mushrooms and plaster statues lining the entrance, the food here is wonderful. Appetizers are a forte: Among the best are *kapiritses* (bite-size bread fried in garlic and oil and sprinkled with oregano), *boxakia* (chicken livers wrapped in bacon), *rebithokeftedes* and *domatokeftedes* (fried garbanzo-bean and tomato dumplings, respectively). The meats include plump sausage, chops, and onion-laden burgers. For dessert, there are pastries and the Turkish *taou koxo* (made with chicken breast, milk, cream, and cinnamon, believe it or not). *5 km (3 mi) from Samos, in Kedros, tel. 0273/ 22941. MC, V. No lunch May–Sept.; no dinner Nov.–Mar. Closed weekdays Nov.–Mar. Inexpensive.*

Maritsa. This simple fish tavern, on a quiet, tree-lined side street, recently opened and quickly established a regular Pythagorio clientele. In the garden courtyard, you can try grilled tope, red mullet, octopus, and squid garnished with garlicky skordalia. The usual appetizers include a sharp tzatziki dip and a large xoriatiki salad, piled high with tomatoes, olives, and feta cheese. *Last st. on right off Logothetis as you descend to harbor, tel. 0273/61957. No credit cards. Inexpensive.*

Psarades. It's worth a detour to find this family-run tavern, where the men take their caïques out early, and good, inexpensive fish is served. About 100 yards east of Ayios Dimitrios you'll come to a sign for the taverna; turn left down the dirt road and continue to the end, to a terrace that looks over the sea, where kittens may nip at your heels and someone's baby is being scolded in the kitchen. There are pans and pans of fresh saddled bream and grouper, and you can also order *fassolada* (bean stew), *yiouvelakia* (rice-and-meat balls in white sauce), and pungent tzatziki and skordalia dips. You can sit here for hours, watching the waves and gazing at Turkey in the distance. *Ayios Dimitrios, 5 km (3 mi) outside Karlovassi, tel. 0273/32489. No credit cards. Inexpensive.*

Lodging **Doryssa Bay Hotel and Village.** If you require every comfort
★ imaginable, this is the place for you. The air-conditioned Doryssa has recently built a pseudo-village next door with pastel houses (containing housekeeping apartments), all different inside and out, a small church, a square, kafenio, and shops. The Doryssa has a tree-shaded beach where sometimes you hear nothing but German. Half-board is mandatory, but the food is much better than the usual hotel fare. (You can sample it by signing up for Greek night on Wednesday. There'll be Greek dancers and tables laden with seafood, meats, salads, and luscious desserts.) *Outside Pythagorio on main rd. to Chora, 83103, tel. 0273/61360. 300 rooms. Facilities: 3 restaurants, 2*

bars, pool, tennis court, water sports. AE, DC, MC, V. Closed
Nov.–Mar. *Very Expensive*.

Fito Bungalows Hotel. This place exudes peace and quiet: The
rooms are in a cluster of low-slung white buildings connected
by tree-shaded, rose-lined walkways and are tucked between
the sea and Glyfada lake. The rooms, which face the garden or
the sea, have fairly plain pine furniture and white walls, verandas, and air-conditioning. Buffet breakfast is served in the
main building, and there's a self-service restaurant with reliable Greek standards. The beach is shaded, and the water-
sports instructor from Doryssa Bay gives lessons here, too.
*Pythagorion, near Potokaki turnoff, 83103, tel. 0273/61582 or
0273/61896. 86 rooms. Facilities: restaurant, bar, beach bar,
pool, water sports, mud treatments. MC, V. Closed Nov.–Apr.
Moderate.*

Galaxy. Off the harbor in a very quiet neighborhood, this blos-
som-clad hotel is a cheerful respite from the waterfront's busy-
ness. If you step into the courtyard you see the pool
shimmering among greenery and hear guests laughing a-
round the bar. The simply furnished rooms all have balconies
overlooking the pool or the bay. *Aggagoi 1, Samos, 83100, tel.
0273/22265. 45 rooms. Facilities: bar, pool, roof garden. V.
Moderate.*

Olympia Beach/Olympic Village. At the bright-white Olympia
Beach hotel you're close enough to Kokkari to stroll into town
for a movie and far enough away to avoid the bustle. The immaculate rooms are spare, but all look out to sea and are decorated with flowered Samian ceramics. The same owners run the
nearby Olympia Village, whose apartments with a bedroom,
living room, two baths, and a kitchen are ideal for families. You
can walk to Tsamadou cove, favored for its shallow water, pine
trees, and secluded setting. *Beach rd., near Kokkari, 83100,
tel. 0273/92353. 12 rooms. Facilities: restaurant, bar. No credit
cards. Closed Nov.–Apr. Moderate.*

Paradise. Simple but elegant, the fairly new Hotel Paradise is
convenient to the bus station and within walking distance of the
harbor. Marble, dark wood, bird-of-paradise flower arrangements: The hotel is a cut above the rest. The owners have put in
a pool with a snack bar, and their many plants make the interior
resemble a hothouse. The rooms look out to sea or over the garden and the fields, so you're treated to evening birdsong!
*Kanari 21, Samos, 83100, tel. 0271/23911, 0271/23912, or 0271/
23913. 49 rooms. Facilities: snack bar, pool. MC, V. Closed
Nov.–Mar. Moderate.*

Samina Bay. Without a doubt the best hotel in Karlovassi, the
Samina Bay is convenient for those waiting to catch a ferry.
The hotel has spacious, air-conditioned guest rooms with white
lacquer furniture; the suites have bamboo furniture. Ask for a
room overlooking the pool—most of which also have a sea view.
A Mycenaean motif runs through the well-decorated reception
and bar area, and the extremely polite young staff is fluent in
several languages. Potami beach is a 15-minute walk. A breakfast buffet is served on the veranda, and you can usually arrange for other meals, too. *Main rd., near harbor, Karlovassi,
83200, tel. 0273/33900 or 0273/34004. 75 rooms. Facilities: restaurant, bar, sauna, playground. AE, DC, MC, V. Closed
Nov.–Mar. Moderate.*

Venus (Afroditi). Your first impression is of yellow flowers,
rose-red carpeting, and cool white marble—a modern interior
in an unremarkable building about 100 yards from the beach.

Mr. Kyriazi and his sons have renovated twice in 22 years. This year they're finishing a pool, sauna, and fitness center, and have begun a baby-sitting service. The reasonably priced rooms have wood ceilings, showers, and balconies that look out over vineyards. Breakfast is Continental or "American," which means yogurt, eggs, juice, cereal, and coffee. *In-town rd., Kokkari, 83100, tel. 0273/92230. 38 rooms. Facilities: pool, sauna, fitness center, beauty salon. AE, DC, MC, V. Closed Nov.–Apr. Moderate.*

Avli. For an inexpensive alternative, take a peek at this monastery-turned-pension. Your first impression will be of space and light as you walk into the large shaded courtyard, where guests spend evenings chatting over a drink, before they retire to the former nun's cells. Some of the rooms (all very basic) have private baths en suite (these are usually booked through tour agencies); most of the rest have their own numbered toilet cubicle close by. *Areos, 2 blocks from harbor, Samos, 83100, tel. 0273/22939. 20 rooms. No credit cards. Closed Oct.–May. Inexpensive.*

Galini. The new Galini is a good place to stay in Pythagorio without paying dearly for comfort. The large rooms (marble everywhere) face the town (three look out to sea), and have private safes, and every floor has a refrigerator. Because the hotel is reached by steps and no cars pass in front, it's very quiet (*galini* means tranquility). The friendly Kanata family serves breakfast in their garden. *Aesopos St., off Platia Dimarchion, 83103, tel. 0273/61167. 16 rooms. No credit cards. Inexpensive.*

Merope. Not much to look at, the Merope strives for high standards at reasonable rates. Each floor has a lounge; the simple rooms have the usual pine furniture, showers, and balconies, with fantastic views (ask for a room above the second floor). A local bus to Potami beach stops in front of the hotel; otherwise you can lounge by the pool or stroll down the street to see some of Karlovassi's fine old houses, some of them deserted. If you get hungry, the kitchen always has some well-prepared mayirefta on hand. *Main rd. in Pefkakia area, Karlovassi, 83200, tel. 0273/32650 or 0273/32651. 80 rooms. Facilities: bar, kitchen, pool. No credit cards. Closed Dec.–Mar. Inexpensive.*

The Arts and Nightlife

The Arts

Island municipalities often organize cultural events that range from philosophy conferences to evenings of folk music. **Chios** usually is host to the summer conference of the **International Society of Homeric Studies** (tel. 0271/24217). In summer on **Limnos,** the **Kechagiades folklore association** (call Myrina tourist office, tel. 0254/22200) presents island dances in costume, accompanied by the local version of a Cretan lyre. **Samos** sometimes hosts a **wine festival** (call Samos tourist office, tel. 0273/28530) in early fall with Panhellenic dances. The best-known celebration is the **Molyvos Theater Festival** (tickets, tel. 0253/71323; tourist office, tel. 0253/71347) held June–August in **Lesbos.** With the castle as backdrop, artists from all over Europe stage entertainment that ranges from a Dario Fo play to a Mikis Theodorakis concert.

Nightlife

Outdoor movie theaters may be disappearing in Athens, but they're still popular with islanders. Check the billboards in the town square for showings. Every summer brings a new wave of trendy bars and discos, usually clustered on the beach. They come and go, so ask what's new when you arrive. In **Chios, Karnaggio** (Leoforos Stenoseos, no tel.), a popular new bar with dancing, has opened outside town on the road to the airport; and in **Lesbos** the newest bar—packed on summer nights—is **To Museo** (The Museum, Vournazo 21, Mytilini, tel. 0251/42140), so called because it's ensconced in a neoclassical house with traditional furnishings. A classic bar in **Samos** that has endured because of its music, friendly owners, and splendid bay view, **No. 9** (Kefallopoulou 9, tel. 0273/22943), is in the bottom floor and courtyard of an old house on Samos Bay.

Festivals Perhaps more rewarding than discoing is joining in the island festivities called *panegyre,* which usually take place on a saint's day or patriotic holiday. In Thimiana, on **Chios,** on the last Sunday of Carnival (late February), islanders reenact the expulsion of the pirates in the **Festival of Mostras**; youths wave swords and dance the vigorous *talimi.* On Easter Saturday night the effigy of Judas is burned in Mesta, and in Pirgi on August 15 villagers perform local dances. On **Lesbos,** Agiassos is famous for its **Carnival** in February and for its August 15 procession joined by hundreds of islanders. In spring bull roasts and horse races take place in Mandamados (*see* Tour 2 in Exploring the Northern Islands, *above*), Ayia Paraskevi, and in Moria, where there's *keskeri* (meat with ground wheat) for everyone in town. One of **Limnos**'s biggest festivals takes place September 7 at Ayios Sozos monastery, with island dances and songs. In **Samos,** swimming races in Pythagorio commemorate the battle of Cavo Fonias on August 6, a day of celebration for the entire island. On September 7 and 8 at Vrontiani monastery, there's dancing in the square and a distribution to the faithful of meat boiled with ground wheat, to celebrate the holiday of the Panayia.

Greek Place-Names

Abram	Αμπράμι
Achaea	Αχαΐα
Acronauplia	Ακροναυπλία
Aegina, Aigina, Egina	Αίγινα
Aigaleo	Αιγάλεω
Aigion	Αίγιο
Akrotiri	Ακρωτήρι
Amfissa	Άμφισσα
Amphiareion	Αμφιαρείον
Anavatos	Ανάβατος
Andritsena, Andritsaina	Ανδρίτσαινα
Andros Town (Chora)	Άνδρος (Χώρα)
Ano Mera	Άνω Μερά
Anoyia	Ανώγεια
Antissa	Άντισσα
Apeiranthos, Apiranthos	Απείραθος
Apollonas	Απόλλωνας
Argolic Gulf, Argolikos Kolpos	Αργολικός Κόλπος
Argolid	Αργολίδα
Argos	Αργος
Arkadi Monastery	Μοναστίρι Αρκαδιού
Armolia	Αρμόλια
Arvanitis	Αρβανίτης
Askyphou plain	Οροπέδιο Ασκύφου
Aspropyrgos	Ασπρόπυργος
Avgonima, Avgonyma	Αυγώνυμα
Avlakia	Αυλάκια
Ayassos	Αγιάσος
Ayia Marina	Αγία Μαρίνα
Ayia Paraskevi	Αγία Παρασκευή
Ayia Roumeli	Αγία Ρουμέλη
Ayia Sofia	Αγιά Σοφία
Ayia Triada	Αγία Τριάδα
Ayia Varvara	Αγία Βαρβάρα
Ayii Deka	Άγιοι Δέκα
Ayii Theodori	Αγιοι Θεοδώροι
Ayioi Anargyroi	Αγιοι Ανάργυροι
Ayioi Pantes	Άγιοι Πάντες
Ayios Ioannis	Άγιος Ιωάννης
Ayios Nikolaos	Άγιος Νικόλαος
Ayios Titos	Άγιος Τίτος
Ayos Ermogenis	Αγιος Ερμογένης
Ayos Isidoros	Αγιος Ισίδωρος
Ayos Konstantinos	Άγιος Κωνσταντίνος
Ayos Pavlos	Άγιος Παύλος
Bassae	Βασσές
Batsi	Μπατσί
Bay of Korthion	Όρμος Κορθίου
Brauron	Βραυρώνα
Cabirion	Καβείριο
Cave of Psychro, Psikro	Ψυχρό
Chalki, Chalkio	Χαλκί, Χαλκείο
Cheimaros tower, Chimarou	Πύργος Χειμάρρου
Chios, Hios	Χίος
Chlemoutsi Castle, Hlemoutsi	Κάστρο Χλεμούτσι

Chora, Hora	Χώρα
Christos Elkomenos	Ελκόμενου Χριστού
Corfu	Κέρκυρα
Corinth, Korinthos	Κόρινθος
Cyclades	Κυκλάδες
Daskalopetra	Δασκαλοπέτρα
Dervenakia	Δερβενάκια
Diakofto	Διακοφτό
Didima	Δίδυμα
Dodecanese	Δωδεκάνησα
Drepano	Δρέπανο
Egina, Aegina, Aigina	Αίγινα
Ekali	Εκάλη
Elafonisi	Ελαφονήσι
Elefsina	Ελευσίνα
Eleusis	Ελεύσις
Elis	Ηλεία
Elounda	Ελούντα
Emborio	Εμπορειός
Engares	Εγγαρές
Epidauros, Epidavros	Επίδαυρος
Epiros, Epirus	Ήπειρος
Eressos	Ερεσός
Ermioni	Ερμιόνη
Evia, Euboia, Euboea	Εύβοια
Falasarna	Φαλάσαρνα
Filoti	Φιλότι
Flerio	Φλέριο
Fodhele, Fodele	Φόδελε
Fourni	Φούρνοι
Frangokastello	Φραγκοκάστελλο
Gaidouronisi	Γαϊδουρόνησι
Galanado	Γαλανάδο
Galatas	Γαλατάς
Gavrion	Γαύριο
Gefira, New Monemvassia	Γέφυρα, Νέα Μονεμβασιά
Georgioupolis, Yioryioupoli	Γεωργιούπολη
Geropotamos river	Γέρω Ποταμός
Glifa	Γλύφα
Glyfada	Γλυφάδα
Gortyna, Gortys	Γόρτηνα, Γόρτυς
Gournes	Γούρνες
Gournia	Γουρνιά
Grotta	Γρόττα, Γκρότα
Gulf of Yera	Κόλπος Γεράς
Hania, Chania	Χανιά
Hephaistia	Ηφαιστεία
Heraion, Ireon	Ηραίο
Heraklion, Iraklio	Ηράκλειο
Hora Sfakia	Χώρα Σφακίων
Hydra	Ύδρα
Hymettos	Υμηττός
Idean Cave, Ideo Andro	Ιδαίον Άντρον
Ierapetra	Ιεραπέτρα
Ikaria	Ικαρία
Iria	Ίρια
Isthmia	Ισθμία
Kaisariani	Καισαριανή
Kalamata	Καλαμάτα

Kalathas	Καλαθάς
Kalavrita	Καλάβρυτα
Kalloni	Καλλονή
Kaloritisa	Καλορίτισσα
Kamares Cave	Σπήλαιο Καμαρών
Kambia	Καμπιά
Kambos, Kampos	Κάμπος
Kaminia	Καμίνια
Kandia, Kantia	Κάντια
Kardamila, Kardamyla	Καρδάμυλα
Karlovassi	Καρλόβασι
Kastelli	Καστέλλι
Kastelli Kissamou	Καστέλλι Κισσάμου
Kastraki	Καστράκι
Kato Zakro	Κάτω Ζάκρος
Kavala	Καβάλα
Kavassilas	Καβάσιλας
Keratea	Κερατέα
Kiato	Κιάτο
Kithairon, Kitheron	Κιθαιρών
Knossos	Κνωσός
Kokkari	Κοκκάρι
Kommos	Κομμός
Komotini	Κομοτηνή
Korfes	Κορφές
Koronos	Κώρονας
Koropi	Κοροπί
Kosta	Κόστα
Koutsi	Κούτσι
Kranidi	Κρανίδι
Kritsa	Κριτσά
Kyllini, Kilini, Killene	Κυλλήνη
Labou Mili, Lampou Myli	Λάμπου Μύλοι
Laconia	Λακωνία
Lake Voulismeni	Λίμνι Βουλισμένη
Langada	Λαγκάδα
Larissa	Λάρισα
Lasithi, Lasithio	Λασίθι
Lato	Λάτω
Lechaion	Λεχαίον
Legrena	Λεγρενά
Lesbos	Λέσβος
Libyan Sea	Λιβυκόν Πελαγός
Ligourio	Λυγουριό
Limin Hersonissos, Chersonissos	Λίμην Χερσονήσου
Limnos, Lemnos	Λήμνος
Limonas monastery	Μονή Λιμώνας
Lissos	Λισσός
Livadi Valley	Λιβαδιά
Loutra Killinis	Λουτρά Κυλλήνης
Loutro	Λουτρό
Makriyialos, Makrigialos	Μακρύγιαλος
Makronissos	Μακρόνησος
Malagari	Μαλαγκάρι
Mallia, Malia	Μάλια
Mandamados, Mantamados	Μανταμάδος
Manolates	Μανολάτες
Marathokambos	Μαραθόκαμπος
Marathon	Μαραθώνας

Marina Village	Αγία Μαρίνα
Markopoulos	Μαρκόπουλο
Maroussi, Amaroussion	Μαρούσι, Αμαρούσιον
Matala	Μάταλα
Megali Vrissi	Μεγάλη Βρύση
Megara	Μέγαρα
Menites	Μένητες
Mesara	Μεσαρά
Mesogeion	Μεσογείων
Mesta	Μεστά
Methana	Μέθανα
Mikri Vigla	Μικρή Βίγλα
Miloi	Μύλοι
Mirabello Gulf, Kolpos Mirambellou	Κόλπος Μιραμπέλλου
Mires	Μοίρες
Mochlos, Mohlos	Μόχλος
Molyvos, Mithimna, Methimna	Μόλυβος, Μήθυμνα
Monemvassia, Monemvasia	Μονεμβασιά
Moni	Μονή
Moria	Μόρια
Moudras	Μούδρας
Mt. Helmos	Χελμός Όρος
Mt. Kynthos	Όρος Κύνθος
Mt. Lykaeon	Όρος Λύκαιον
Mt. Minthis	Όρος Μίνθη
Mt. Ornon	Όρος Ορνόν
Mt. Panahaiko, Panakhaikon	Όρος Παναχαϊκόν
Mt. Parnis, Parnitha	Ορος Πάρνης, Πάρνηθα
Mt. Profitis Ilias	Όρος Προφήτης Ιλίας
Mt. Taygettus, Taygettos	Όρος Ταΰγετος
Mt. Zas	Όρος Ζάς, Ζεύς
Mt. Ziria, Zíria, Mt. Killini	Ζήρια, Όρος Κυλλήνης
Mycenae, Mikine, Mikines	Μυκήνες
Myrina, Mirina, Kastro	Μύρινα, Κάστρο
Mystras	Μυστράς
Mytilinii	Μυτιλήνη
Nagos	Ναγός
Nauplion, Nafplio	Ναύπλιο
Naxos	Νάξος
Nea Epidauros	Νέα Επίδαυρος
Nea Makri	Νέα Μάκρη
Nea Moni	Νέα Μονή
Nemea	Νεμέα
Nida Plateau	Κάμπος Νίδας
Nimbros Gorge, Imbros Gorge	Φαράγγι Νίμπρου, Φαράγγι Ίμπρου
Olous	Ολούς
Olympia	Ολυμπία
Omalos Plain	Οροπέδιο Ομαλός
Ormos Marathokambos	Όρμος Μαραθόκαμπου
Paiania	Παιανία
Palaia Epidauros, Palea Epidaupus	Παλαιά Επίδαυρος
Palatia	Παλατία
Paleochora, Paleohora	Παλαιοχώρα
Paleokastro, Palekastro, Palaikastro	Παλαικάστρο
Paleopolis	Παλαιόπολη
Pallini	Παλλήνη
Pamfila	Πάμφιλα
Panagitsa	Παναγίτσα
Panagia Hrisafitissa	Παναγία Χρυσαφίτισσα

Pandrossos, Pandroson	Πάνδροσο
Pantanassa monastery	Μονή Παντάνασσας
Pantoukios	Παντουκιός
Paros	Πάρος
Pastra	Πάστρα
Pateras	Πατέρας
Patmos	Πάτμος
Patras, Patra	Πάτρα
Patroklou	Πάτροκλου
Paximadia	Παξιμάδια
Peloponnesos	Πελοπόννησος
Pendeli	Πεντέλη
Perama	Πέραμα
Perivleptos monastery	Μονή Περιβλέπτου
Perivoli	Μονή Περιβόλη
Petra	Πέτρα
Phaistos, Festos, Phaestos	Φαίστος
Phyle	Φυλή
Pikermi	Πικέρμι
Piraeus	Πειραιάς
Pirgos, Pyrgos	Πύργος
Pirgi Thermis	Πύργοι Θερμής
Pitsidia	Πιτσίδια
Plaka	Πλάκα
Platanos	Πλάτανος
Plataia	Πλαταιές
Platanakia	Πλατανάκια
Plati	Πλατύ
Plomari	Πλωμάρι
Polichnitos	Πολιχνίτος
Poliochni	Πολιόχνη
Poros	Πόρος
Portes	Πόρτες
Porto Heli, Porto Cheli, Portoheli	Πόρτο Χέλι
Potamia	Ποταμιά
Potamies, Potamos	Ποταμιές, Ποταμός
Pournias Bay	Κόλπος Πουρνιάς
Profitis Ilias	Προφήτης Ηλίας
Pseira	Ψείρα
Psili Ammos	Ψιλή Άμμος
Psiloritis, Ida, Idhi	Ψηλορείτης, Ίδη
Pyrgi	Πυργί
Pyrgos, Pirgos	Πύργος
Pythagorio	Πυθαγόρειο
Rafina	Ραφήνα
Repanidi	Ρεπανίδι
Rethymnon, Rethimno	Ρεθυμνό
Rhamnous	Ραμνούς
Rhodes	Ρόδος
Sacred Lake	Ιερή Λίμνη
Salamis, Salamina	Σαλαμίς, Σαλαμίνα
Salamis, straits of	Στενόν Σαλαμών
Samaria Gorge	Φαράγγι Σαμαριάς
Samos	Σάμος
Sangri	Σαγκρί
Sarakiniki Sarakina	Σαρακήνα
Saronic Gulf, Saronikos Kolpos	Σαρωνικός Κόλπος
Septsae, Spetses	Σπέτσες
Sigri	Σίγρι

Siteia, Sitia	Σητεία
Skala Eressou	Σκάλα Ερεσού
Sklavia	Σκλαβιά
Sklavokampos	Σκλαβοκάμπος
Souda Bay, O. Soudas	Ορμός Σούδας
Sougia, Souyia	Σούγια
Sounion	Σούνιο
Sparta	Σπαρτη
Spetses	Σπέτσες
Sphaka	Σφάκα
Spinalonga	Σπιναλόγκα
Stavros	Σταυρός
t'Apilarou castle	Κάστρο Απαλυρού
Tatoi	Τατόι
Thanos	Θάνος
Thessaloniki	Θεσσαλονίκη
Thimiana, Thymiana	Θυμιανά
Thorikos	Θορικό
Thripti	Θρυπτή
Timios Stavrou, Timiou Stavrou	Τίμιου Σταυρού
Tiryns, Tirinthos	Τίρυνς, Τίρυνθος
Tolo	Τολό
Toplou monastery	Μονή Τοπλού
Tragaia Valley	Τραγαία
Trahia	Τραχειά
Tripolis, Tripoli	Τρίπολη
Troezen	Τροιζήν
Tsabou	Τσαμπού
Tsamadou	Τσαμαδού
Tylissos	Τύλισος
Tzermiado	Τζερμιάδο
Vai	Βάι
Varia	Βαρειά
Varkiza	Βάρκιζα
Varybobi	Βαρυμπόμπη
Vatera	Βατερά
Vathi	Βαθύ
Vavili	Βαβίλοι
Virgin Odegetria Church	Παναγία Οδηγήτρια
Volissos	Βολισσός
Voni	Βόνη
Votsalakia	Βοτσαλάκια
Voula	Βούλα
Vouliagmeni	Βουλιαγμένη
Vouraikos Gorge	Φαράγγι Βουραϊκος
Vranas	Βρανάς
Vrisses	Βρύσες
Vrondiani monastery, Moni Yronda	Βρονδιανή or Μονή Βροντά
Vrontados	Βροντάδος
Xylokastro	Ξυλόκαστρο
Za Cave	Σπήλαιο Ζά or Ζεύς
Zagora	Ζαγορά
Zakhlorou	Ζαχλωρού
Zakro, Zakros	Ζακρος
Zoumberi	Ζούμπερι

Greek Vocabulary

The phonetic spelling used in English differs somewhat from the internationalized form of Greek place names. There are no long and short vowels in Greek; the pronunciation never changes. Note, also, that the accent is a stress mark, showing where the stress is placed in pronunciation.

Basics

Do you speak English?	Miláte angliká?
Yes, no	Málista *or* Né, óchi
Impossible	Adínato
Good morning, Good day	Kaliméra
Good evening, Good night	Kalispéra, Kaliníchta
Goodbye	Yá sas
Mister, Madam, Miss	Kírie, kiría, despiní
Please	Parakaló
Excuse me	Me sinchórite *or* signómi
How are you?	Ti kánete *or* pós íste
How do you do (Pleased to meet you)	Chéro polí
I don't understand.	Dén katalavéno.
To your health!	Giá sas!
Thank you	Efcharistó

Numbers

one	éna
two	dío
three	tría
four	téssera
five	pénde
six	éxi
seven	eptá
eight	októ
nine	enéa
ten	déka
twenty	íkossi
thirty	triánda
forty	saránda
fifty	penínda
sixty	exínda
seventy	evdomínda
eighty	ogdónda
ninety	enenínda
one hundred	ekató
two hundred	diakóssia
three hundred	triakóssia
one thousand	hília
two thousand	dió hiliádes
three thousand	trís hiliádes

Days of the Week

Monday	Deftéra
Tuesday	Tríti
Wednesday	Tetárti

Thursday	Pémpti
Friday	Paraskeví
Saturday	Sávato
Sunday	Kyriakí

Months

January	Ianouários
February	Fevrouários
March	Mátios
April	Aprílios
May	Maíos
June	Ióunios
July	Ióulios
August	Ávgoustos
September	Septémvrios
October	Októvrios
November	Noémvrios
December	Dekémvrios

Traveling

I am traveling by car . . . train . . . plane . . . boat.	Taxidévo mé aftokínito . . . me tréno . . . me aeropláno . . . me vapóri.
Taxi, to the station . . . harbor . . . airport	Taxí, stó stathmó . . . limáni . . . aerodrómio
Porter, take the luggage.	Akthofóre, pare aftá tá prámata.
Where is the filling station?	Pou íne tó vensinádiko?
When does the train leave for . . . ?	Tí óra thá fíyi to tréno ya . . . ?
Which is the train for . . . ?	Pío íne to tréno gía . . . ?
Which is the road to . . . ?	Piós íne o drómos giá . . . ?
A first-class ticket	Éna isitírio prótis táxis
No-smoking (compartment)	Apagorévete to kápnisna
Where is the toilet?	Póu íne í toaléta?
Ladies, men	Ginekón, andrón
Where? When?	Póu? Póte?
Sleeping car, dining car	Wagonlí, wagonrestorán
Compartment	Diamérisma
Entrance, exit	Íssodos, éxodos
Nothing to declare	Den écho típota na dilósso
I am coming for my vacation.	Érchome giá tis diakopés mou.
Nothing	Típota
Personal use	Prossopikí chríssi
How much?	Pósso?
I want to eat, to drink, to sleep.	Thélo na fáo, na pió, na kimithο΄.
Sunrise, sunset	Anatolí, díssi
Sun, moon	Ílios, fengári
Day, night	Méra, níchta
Morning, afternoon	Proí, mesiméri, *or* apóyevma
The weather is good, bad.	Ó kerós íne kalós, kakós.

On the Road

| Straight ahead | Kat efthían |
| To the right, to the left | Dexiá, aristerá |

Show me the way to . . . please.

Díxte mou to drómo . . .
   parakaló.

Where is . . . ? — Pou íne . . . ?
Crossroad — Diastávrosi
Danger — Kíndinos
Drive slowly! — Sigá!
Look out for the train (railroad crossing). — Prosséxte to tréno.

In Town

Will you lead me? take me?

Thélete na me odigíste?
   Me pérnete mazí sas?

Street, square — Drómos, platía
Where is the bank? — Pou íne i trápeza?
Far — Makriá
Police station — Astinomikó tmíma
Consulate (American, British) — Proxenío (Amerikániko, Anglikó)

Theater, cinema — Théatro, cinemá
At what time does the film start? — Tí óra archízi ee tenía?
Where is the travel office? — Pou íne to touristikó grafío?
Where are the tourist police? — Pou íne i touristikí astinomía?

Shopping

I would like to buy — Tha íthela na agorásso
Show me, please. — Díxte mou, parakaló.
May I look around? — Boró na ríxo miá matyá?
How much is it? — Pósso káni? (*or* kostízi)
It is too expensive. — Íne polí akrivó.
Have you any sandals? — Échete pédila?
Have you foreign newspapers? — Échete xénes efimerídes?
Show me that blouse, please. — Díxte mou aftí tí blouza.
Show me that bag. — Díxte mou aftí tí valítza.
Envelopes, writing paper — Fakélous, hartí íli
Roll of film — Film
Map of the city — Hárti tis póleos
Something handmade — Hiropíito
Wrap it up, please. — Tilíxeto, parakaló.
Cigarettes, matches, please. — Tsigára, spírta, parakaló.
Ham — Zambón
Sausage, salami — Loukániko, salámi
Sugar, salt, pepper — Záchari, aláti, pipéri
Grapes, cherries — Stafília, kerássia
Apple, pear, orange — Mílo, achládi, portokáli
Bread, butter — Psomí, voútiro
Peach, figs — Rodákino, síka

At the Hotel

A good hotel — Éna kaló xenodochío
Have you a room? — Échete domátio?
Where can I find a furnished room? — Pou boró na vró epiploméno domátio?

A single room, double room — Éna monóklino, éna díklino
With bathroom — Me bánio
How much is it per day? — Pósso kostízi tin iméra?
A room overlooking the sea — Éna domátio prós ti thálassa

For one day, for two days	Giá miá méra, giá dió méres
For a week	Giá miá evdomáda
My name is . . .	Onomázome . . .
My passport	Tó diavatirió mou
What is the number of my room?	Piós íne o arithmós tou domatíou mou?
The key, please.	To klidí, parakaló.
Breakfast, lunch, supper	Proinó, messimergianó, vradinó
The bill, please.	To logariasmó, parakaló.
I am leaving tomorrow.	Févgo (*or* anachoró) ávrio.

At the Restaurant

Waiter	Garsón
Where is the restaurant?	Pou íne to estiatório?
I would like to eat.	Tha íthela na fáo.
The menu, please.	To katálogo, parakaló.
Fixed-price menu	Menú
Soup	Soúpa
Bread	Psomí
Hors d'oeuvre	Mezédes, orektiká
Ham omelet	Omelétta zambón
Chicken	Kotópoulo
Roast pork	Psitó hirinó
Beef	Moschári
Potatoes (fried)	Patátes (tiganités)
Tomato salad	Domatosaláta
Vegetables	Lachaniká
Watermelon, melon	Karpoúzi, pepóni
Desserts, pastry	Gliká *or* pástes
Fruit, cheese, ice cream	Fróuta, tirí, pagotó
Fish, eggs	Psári, avgá
Serve me on the terrace.	Na mou servírete sti tarátza.
Where can I wash my hands?	Pou boró na plíno ta héria mou?
Red wine, white wine	Mávro krasí, áspro krasí
Unresinated wine	Krasí aretsínato
Beer, soda water, water, milk	Bíra, sóda, neró, gála
Greek (formerly Turkish) coffee	Ellenikó kafé
Coffee with milk, without sugar, medium, sweet	Kafé gallikó me, gála skéto, métrio, glikó

At the Bank, at the Post Office

Where is the bank? . . . post office?	Pou íne i trápeza? . . . to tachidromío?
I would like to cash a check.	Thélo ná isspráxo mía epitagí.
I would like to change some money.	Thelóna aláxo hrímata.
Stamps	Grammatóssima
By airmail	Aëroporikós
Postcard, letter	Kárta, grámma
Letterbox	Tachidromikó koutí
I would like to telephone.	Thélo na tilephonísso.

At the Garage

Garage, gas (petrol)	Garáz, venzíni
Oil	Ládi
Change the oil.	Aláksete to ládi.
Look at the tires.	Rixte mia matiá sta lástika.
Wash the car.	Plínete to aftokínito.
Breakdown	Vlávi
Tow the car.	Rimúlkiste tó aftokínito.
Spark plugs	Buzí
Brakes	Fréna
Gearbox	Kivótio tachíttion
Carburetor	Karbiratér
Headlight	Provoléfs
Starter	Míza
Axle	Áksonas
Shock absorber	Amortisér
Spare part	Antalaktikó

Index

Personal Itinerary

Departure *Date*

Time

Transportation

Arrival *Date* *Time*

Departure *Date* *Time*

Transportation

Accommodations

Arrival *Date* *Time*

Departure *Date* *Time*

Transportation

Accommodations

Arrival *Date* *Time*

Departure *Date* *Time*

Transportation

Accommodations

Personal Itinerary

Arrival *Date*   *Time*

Departure *Date*   *Time*

Transportation

Accommodations

Arrival *Date*   *Time*

Departure *Date*   *Time*

Transportation

Accommodations

Arrival *Date*   *Time*

Departure *Date*   *Time*

Transportation

Accommodations

Arrival *Date*   *Time*

Departure *Date*   *Time*

Transportation

Accommodations

Personal Itinerary

Arrival Date   Time

Departure Date   Time

Transportation

Accommodations

Arrival Date   Time

Departure Date   Time

Transportation

Accommodations

Arrival Date   Time

Departure Date   Time

Transportation

Accommodations

Arrival Date   Time

Departure Date   Time

Transportation

Accommodations

Personal Itinerary

Arrival *Date* *Time*

Departure *Date* *Time*

Transportation

Accommodations

Arrival *Date* *Time*

Departure *Date* *Time*

Transportation

Accommodations

Arrival *Date* *Time*

Departure *Date* *Time*

Transportation

Accommodations

Arrival *Date* *Time*

Departure *Date* *Time*

Transportation

Accommodations

Addresses

Name	*Name*
Address	*Address*
Telephone	*Telephone*
Name	*Name*
Address	*Address*
Telephone	*Telephone*
Name	*Name*
Address	*Address*
Telephone	*Telephone*
Name	*Name*
Address	*Address*
Telephone	*Telephone*
Name	*Name*
Address	*Address*
Telephone	*Telephone*
Name	*Name*
Address	*Address*
Telephone	*Telephone*
Name	*Name*
Address	*Address*
Telephone	*Telephone*
Name	*Name*
Address	*Address*
Telephone	*Telephone*

Addresses

Name

Address

Telephone

Name

Address

Telephone

Name

Address

Telephone

Name

Address

Telephone

Name

Address

Telephone

Name

Address

Telephone

Name

Address

Telephone

Name

Address

Telephone

Name

Address

Telephone

Name

Address

Telephone

Name

Address

Telephone

Name

Address

Telephone

Name

Address

Telephone

Name

Address

Telephone

Name

Address

Telephone

Name

Address

Telephone

Addresses

Name

Address

Telephone

Name

Address

Telephone

Name

Address

Telephone

Name

Address

Telephone

Name

Address

Telephone

Name

Address

Telephone

Name

Address

Telephone

Name

Address

Telephone

Name

Address

Telephone

Name

Address

Telephone

Name

Address

Telephone

Name

Address

Telephone

Name

Address

Telephone

Name

Address

Telephone

Name

Address

Telephone

Name

Address

Telephone

Fodor's Travel Guides

U.S. Guides

Alaska

Arizona

Boston

California

Cape Cod, Martha's Vineyard, Nantucket

The Carolinas & the Georgia Coast

Chicago

Disney World & the Orlando Area

Florida

Hawaii

Las Vegas, Reno, Tahoe

Los Angeles

Maine, Vermont, New Hampshire

Maui

Miami & the Keys

New England

New Orleans

New York City

Pacific North Coast

Philadelphia & the Pennsylvania Dutch Country

San Diego

San Francisco

Santa Fe, Taos, Albuquerque

Seattle & Vancouver

The South

The U.S. & British Virgin Islands

The Upper Great Lakes Region

USA

Vacations in New York State

Vacations on the Jersey Shore

Virginia & Maryland

Waikiki

Washington, D.C.

Foreign Guides

Acapulco, Ixtapa, Zihuatanejo

Australia & New Zealand

Austria

The Bahamas

Baja & Mexico's Pacific Coast Resorts

Barbados

Berlin

Bermuda

Brazil

Budapest

Budget Europe

Canada

Cancun, Cozumel, Yucatan Penisula

Caribbean

Central America

China

Costa Rica, Belize, Guatemala

Czechoslovakia

Eastern Europe

Egypt

Euro Disney

Europe

Europe's Great Cities

France

Germany

Great Britain

Greece

The Himalayan Countries

Hong Kong

India

Ireland

Israel

Italy

Italy's Great Cities

Japan

Kenya & Tanzania

Korea

London

Madrid & Barcelona

Mexico

Montreal & Quebec City

Morocco

The Netherlands Belgium & Luxembourg

New Zealand

Norway

Nova Scotia, Prince Edward Island & New Brunswick

Paris

Portugal

Rome

Russia & the Baltic Countries

Scandinavia

Scotland

Singapore

South America

Southeast Asia

South Pacific

Spain

Sweden

Switzerland

Thailand

Tokyo

Toronto

Turkey

Vienna & the Danube Valley

Yugoslavia

Special Series

Fodor's Affordables

Affordable Europe

Affordable France

Affordable Germany

Affordable Great
Britain

Affordable Italy

**Fodor's Bed &
Breakfast and
Country Inns Guides**

California

Mid-Atlantic Region

New England

The Pacific Northwest

The South

The West Coast

The Upper Great
Lakes Region

Canada's Great
Country Inns

Cottages, B&Bs and
Country Inns of
England and Wales

The Berkeley Guides

On the Loose in
California

On the Loose in
Eastern Europe

On the Loose in
Mexico

On the Loose in the
Pacific Northwest &
Alaska

**Fodor's Exploring
Guides**

Exploring California

Exploring Florida

Exploring France

Exploring Germany

Exploring Paris

Exploring Rome

Exploring Spain

Exploring Thailand

Fodor's Flashmaps

New York

Washington, D.C.

Fodor's Pocket Guides

Pocket Bahamas

Pocket Jamaica

Pocket London

Pocket New York
City

Pocket Paris

Pocket Puerto Rico

Pocket San Francisco

Pocket Washington,
D.C.

Fodor's Sports

Cycling

Hiking

Running

Sailing

The Insider's Guide
to the Best Canadian
Skiing

**Fodor's Three-In-Ones
(guidebook, language
cassette, and phrase
book)**

France

Germany

Italy

Mexico

Spain

**Fodor's
Special-Interest
Guides**

Cruises and Ports
of Call

Disney World & the
Orlando Area

Euro Disney

Healthy Escapes

London Companion

Skiing in the USA
& Canada

Sunday in New York

**Fodor's Touring
Guides**

Touring Europe

Touring USA:
Eastern Edition

Touring USA:
Western Edition

**Fodor's Vacation
Planners**

Great American
Vacations

National Parks of the
West

**The Wall Street
Journal Guides to
Business Travel**

Europe

International Cities

Pacific Rim

USA & Canada

WHEREVER YOU TRAVEL, *H*ELP IS NEVER FAR AWAY.

From planning your trip to providing travel assistance along the way, American Express® Travel Service Offices* are always there to help.

Greece

AGHIOS NIKOLAOS
Adamis Tours
Latousha
841-22-770

ATHENS
2 Hermou St., Syntagma Square
1-3-244-975

Athens Hilton Hotel
46 Vassilissis Sophias Ave.
1-722-0201

CORFU
Greek Skies Travel
20A Capodistriou St.
661-30883

CRETE
Adamis Tours
23, 25th August St., Heraklion
81-246-202

MYKONOS
Delia Travel
At the Quay
289-22322

PATRAS
Albatros Travel
48 Othonos Amalias Street
61-220-993

RHODES
Rhodes Tours
23 Ammochostou St.
241-21010

SALONICA
Doucas Tours
8 Venizelou St.
31-269-984

SANTORINI
X-Ray Kilo
Main Square
286-22624

SKIATHOS
Mare Nostrum Holidays
21 Papadiamanti St.
0427-21464